T0217127

Lecture Notes in Computer Science 1273

Edited by G. Goos, J. Hartmanis and J. van Leeuwen

Advisory Board: W. Brauer D. Gries J. Stoer

Springer

Berlin
Heidelberg
New York
Barcelona
Budapest
Hong Kong
London
Milan
Paris
Santa Clara
Singapore
Tokyo

Panos Antsaklis   Wolf Kohn
Anil Nerode   Shankar Sastry (Eds.)

Hybrid Systems IV

 Springer

Series Editors

Gerhard Goos, Karlsruhe University, Germany
Juris Hartmanis, Cornell University, NY, USA
Jan van Leeuwen, Utrecht University, The Netherlands

Volume Editors

Panos Antsaklis
Department of Electrical Engineering, The University of Notre Dame
Notre Dame, IN 46556, USA
E-mail: Panos.J.Antsaklis.1@nd.edu

Wolf Kohn
HyBrithms Corporation
11202 SE 8th Street, Bellevue, WA 98004-6420, USA
E-mail: wk@HyBrithms.com

Anil Nerode
Mathematical Sciences Institute, Cornell University
Ithaca, NY 14853, USA
E-mail: anil@math.cornell.edu

Shankar Sastry
Department of Electrical Engineering and Computer Science
University of California, Berkeley, CA 94720, USA
E-mail: sastry@eecs.berkeley.edu

Cataloging-in-Publication data applied for

Die Deutsche Bibliothek - CIP-Einheitsaufnahme

Hybrid systems. - Berlin ; Heidelberg ; New York ; Barcelona ;
Budapest ; Hong Kong ; London ; Milan ; Paris ; Santa Clara ;
Singapore ; Tokyo : Springer
  Literaturangaben
4. / Panos Antsaklis ... (ed.) 1997
(Lecture notes in computer science ; 1273)
ISBN 3-540-63358-8

CR Subject Classification (1991): C.1.m, C.3, D.2.1,F.3.1, F.1-2, J.2

ISSN 0302-9743
ISBN 3-540-63358-8 Springer-Verlag Berlin Heidelberg New York

© Springer-Verlag Berlin Heidelberg 1997
Printed in Germany

Typesetting: Camera-ready by author
SPIN 10547876   06/3142 – 5 4 3 2 1 0   Printed on acid-free paper

Preface

This volume consists of refereed papers related to the the Fourth International Conference on Hybrid Systems held in Ithaca, NY, on October 12–14, 1996. The previous meetings (both workshops and conferences) were held in Ithaca, NY, Lyngby, DK, and New Brunswick, NJ.

Hybrid systems research is devoted to modeling, design and validation of interacting systems of continuous processes (plants) and computer programs (control automata). Hybrid systems theory hopes to offer a logical, mathematical, and computational framework for understanding and designing complex heterogeneous systems. We hope that, in the future, hybrid systems will form a modeling and software tool environment for many areas, including distributed autonomous control, management, synchronization, discrete event systems, fuzzy control, rule-based systems, and real-time systems.

Current efforts in hybrid systems theory include the development of formal approaches for the specification and implementation of architectural, agent-based control, state estimation schema, and methodologies for the design of state identification and structural adaptivity and learning. Efforts in the application of hybrid systems methodologies are taking place in a wide spectrum of areas, including for instance systems for automated coding and compression, for air and land traffic control, for intelligent manufacturing, and for distributed interactive simulation. Hybrid systems is a burgeoning research area which is now featured in many international meetings in engineering and computer science.

This volume is the fourth in a series, the first three volumes of which are: Hybrid Systems I (R.L. Grossman, A. Nerode, A.P. Ravn, H. Rischel, Eds.), LNCS 736, 1993; Hybrid Systems II (P. Antsaklis, W. Kohn, A. Nerode, S. Sastry, Eds.), LNCS 999, 1995; and Hybrid Systems III (R. Alur, T.H. Henzinger, E. Sontag, Eds.), LNCS 1066, 1996.

No one volume can truly represent all of the current efforts in hybrid systems. This volume contains papers on models, formal verification, computer simulation, goal reachability, algorithms for extracting hybrid control programs, and application models for avionics, highway traffic control, and air traffic control. Here is a rough map.

Models:

- Desphande, Gollu, and Varaiya explain the SHIFT formalism for hybrid systems as developed for automated traffic control.

- Heymann, Lin, and Meyer introduce composite hybrid machines as a model for hybrid systems.

- Lemmon and Bett compare two different control strategies for safe supervision of hybrid systems. One is based on Fliess series and the other on model reference control.

- Nerode, Remmel, and Yakhnis describe variations on the notion of hybrid systems, such as continuous versus discrete sensing, in terms of a variety of hybrid games. They give a simple example of the extraction of finite state controllers from finite topologies approximating to a continuous state controller.

- Pappas and Sastry introduce a general notion of abstraction of continuous systems as a formalized tool for understanding how to model hybrid systems.

- Raisch and O'Young introduce a hierarchy of abstractions based on approximation accuracy for hybrid systems.

Verification:

- Branicky, Dolginova, and Lynch outline a toolbox for verifying that a hybrid system satisfies its specification, based on invariant state spaces.

Simulation:

- Branicky and Mattsson extend the simulation language Omola to cover Branicky's hybrid systems models.

Extraction of Control Programs:

- Brayman and Vagners show how to apply the Kohn-Nerode control extraction on manifolds algorithms to extract control programs for the example of the inverted pendulum.

- Knight, following the discrete event system tradition in which the plant is a finite automaton to be controlled to specification by another automaton, uses the Gurevich-Harrington method for solving automaton games to extract a finite state control automaton (if one exists) which forces the plant automaton to satisfy a specification in a temporal propositional logic without a fixed point operator.

- Stursberg, Kowalewski, Hoffman, and Preußig derive timed and linear automata from continuous models and give examples of verification in HyTech.

- Arehart and Wolovich show that for piecewise linear systems with adjustable parameters, hybrid switching between transfer matrices can eliminate discontinuities (bumps) in system trajectories using much lower order systems than when one enforces smooth variation of transfer matrices. (A virtue of hybrid control is that often computational and mathematical complexity of control programs can be reduced as compared to what is required to achieve the same goal with a smooth control program.)

Reachability of the Goal Set:

- Broucke and Varaiya investigate the decidability of the reachability of a goal for linear differential equations based hybrid automata and also the robustness of the reachability of a goal for non-linear differential equations based automata.

- Kourjanski and Variaya discuss a class of rectangular hybrid systems with a computable reachability set which is specified by a controllability condition.

- Kolen and Zhao give a computational analysis of the face reachability problem for a class of 3-dimensional dynamical systems defined by piecewise constant vector fields.

Application Models:

- **Avionics:** Cofer gives an informal hybrid systems overview of avionics automation and outlines tools he has developed for reliable implementations.

- **Freeway Traffic Control:** Kohn, Nerode, and Remmel develop a hybrid model for freeway traffic control based on the interaction between vehicle particles and void particles. The introduction of void particles allows one to model the entire traffic spectrum as a wave model. Their multiple agent hybrid control architecture for this problem has been implemented and the results of simulations are given.

- **Air Traffic Control:** Tomlin, Pappas, Lygeros, Godbole, and Sastry outline a decentralized hybrid control approach for air traffic management based on the on-board computation on the aircraft.

Acknowledgments: This volume consists of fully refereed papers on hybrid systems, submitted in response to an invitation issued at the Fourth International Hybrid Systems Conference held at the Mathematical Sciences Institute of Cornell University on October 12-14, 1996. We are indebted to W. Kone for handling the organization of the conference, to D. L. Drake for administrative support, and to Professor V.W. Marek of the University of Kentucky, whose help relieved the organizers of many worries. The very substantial graduate student and postdoctoral scholar attendance at the conference was made possible by travel support from the US Army Research Office and the Intelligent Systems program of National Science Foundation. The conference and volume preparation were sponsored by the Mathematical Sciences Institute of Cornell University and the DoD Multiple University Research Initiative, *Foundations of Intelligent Systems* (Principal Investigators: S. Sastry, UC Berkeley, Z. Manna, Stanford, and A. Nerode, Cornell).

June 1997

Panos Antsaklis, Notre Dame, IN
Wolf Kohn, Bellevue, WA
Anil Nerode, Ithaca, NY
Shankar Sastry, Berkeley, CA

Organizers:
P. Antsaklis
W. Kohn
A. Nerode
S. Sastry

Program Chair:
A. Nerode
Mathematical Sciences Institute
Cornell University
Ithaca, NY 14853 USA

Program Committee:
P. Antsaklis, U. of Notre Dame
M. Branicky, Case Western U.
P. Caines, McGill U.
L. Giles, NEC Research
R. Grossman,U. of Illinois, Chicago
T. Henzinger, Cornell U. and UC Berkeley
R. Jagadeesan, Loyola U.
S. Johnson, Williams C.
W. Kohn, HyBrithms Corp.
B. Krogh, Carnegie Mellon U.
R. Kurshan, ATT Research
M. Lemmon, U. of Notre Dame
O. Maler, VERIMAG
S. Narain, Bellcore
A. Nerode, Cornell U.
U. Ozguner, Ohio State U.
P. Ramadge, Princeton
J. Remmel, UCSD and HyBrithms Corp.
S. Sastry, UC Berkeley
B. Zeigler, U. of Arizona

Conference Secretary:
V.W. Marek, U. of Kentucky

Table of Contents

Bumpless Switching in Hybrid Systems 1
A.B. Arehart and W.A. Wolovich

A Toolbox for Proving and Maintaining Hybrid Specifications 18
M.S. Branicky, E. Dolginova, and N. Lynch

Simulation of Hybrid Systems 31
M.S. Branicky and S.E. Mattsson

Application of the Kohn-Nerode Control Law Extraction Procedure
to the Inverted Pendulum Problem 57
V. Brayman and J. Vagners

Decidability of Hybrid Systems with Linear and Nonlinear
Differential Inclusions 77
M. Broucke and P. Varaiya

Reliable implementation of Hybrid Control Systems for Advanced Avionics 93
D.D. Cofer

SHIFT: A Formalism and a Programming Language for Dynamic
Networks of Hybrid Automata 113
A. Deshpande, A. Göllü and P. Varaiya

Synthesis of Minimally Restrictive Legal Controllers for a
Class of Hybrid Systems 134
M. Heymann, F.Lin and G. Meyer

Control Theory, Modal Logic, and Games 160
J.F. Knight and B. Luense

Agent Based Velocity Control of Highway Systems 174
W.Kohn, A. Nerode and J.B. Remmel

A Computational Analysis of the Reachability Problem for a Class of
Hybrid Dynamical Systems 215
J.F. Kolen and F. Zhao

A Class of Rectangular Hybrid Systems with Computable Reach Set 228
M. Kourjanski and P. Varaiya

Safe Implementations of Supervisory Commands 235
M. Lemmon and C.J. Bett

Hybrid System Games: Extraction of Control Automata with
Small Topologies 248
A. Nerode, J.B. Remmel and A. Yakhnis

Hybrid Control Desgin for a Three Vehicle Scenario Demonstration
Using Overlapping Decompositions 294
O. Özgüner, C. Hatipoğlu, A. İftar and K. Redmill

Towards Continuous Abstractions of Dynamical and Control Systems 329
G.J. Pappas and S. Sastry

A Totally Ordered Set of Discrete Abstractions for a Given Hybrid or
Continuous System 342
J. Raisch and S. O'Young

Comparing Timed and Hybrid Automata as Approximations of Continuous
Systems 361
O. Stursberg, S. Kowalewski, I. Hoffmann, and J. Preußig

Hybrid Control Models of Next Generation Air Traffic Management 378
C. Tomlin, G. Pappas, J. Lygeros, D. Godbole, and S. Sastry

Author Index 405

Bumpless Switching in Hybrid Systems

Alan B. Arehart and William A. Wolovich

Laboratory for Engineering Man/Machine Systems
Brown University
Providence, RI 02912 USA

Abstract. This paper describes a way of designing a piecewise-linear system with discretely adjustable parameters (a hybrid linear system) in which we can switch the transfer matrix of the system without causing a discontinuity (a bump) in the system output. This is similar to the result that we could achieve by doing a bumpless transfer between multiple linear systems, but the order of a hybrid linear system will typically be much less than the combined order of the multiple systems that realize the same set of transfer matrices.

1 Introduction

A *hybrid system* is a system with interacting discrete and continuous components [8, 10]. Typically, a digital logic device (which may be called a mode changer, a tuner, a gain-scheduler, or a supervisor, depending on the application [9, 12]) will discretely switch various analog components into and out of use. Thus, the behavior of a hybrid system is that of one continuous system in one context, and the behavior switches discretely to that of other continuous systems in other contexts. We call the continuous system of each context a *regime* [10]. Examples of systems designed as hybrid systems are adaptive controllers, gain-scheduled controllers, and filters with parameters that can be tuned on-line.

We call a hybrid system, its output, and its switching *bumpless* if the output of the hybrid system remains a continuous function of time during all possible switches whenever its input is continuous [12]. Otherwise, we call the system, its output, and its switching *bumpy*. This paper describes how to achieve bumpless switching in two types of hybrid systems which have linear regimes.

The first type of hybrid system that we examine is a *multi-system* [12]. We illustrate its concept in Figure 1. In this architecture, there exist multiple linear subsystems, each with each with its own input $\hat{u}_i(t) \in R^m$, its own output $\hat{y}_i(t) \in R^p$, its own order $\hat{n}_i$, its own state $\hat{x}_i(t) \in R^{\hat{n}_i}$, and its own set of gain matrices $\{A_i, B_i, C_i, E_i\}$ $(i = 1, 2, \ldots, k)$. Represent the k subsystems in the state space as

$$
\begin{aligned}
\dot{\hat{x}}_i(t) &= \hat{A}_i \hat{x}_i(t) + \hat{B}_i \hat{u}_i(t), \\
\hat{y}_i(t) &= \hat{C}_i \hat{x}_i(t) + \hat{E}_i \hat{u}_i(t) \quad (i = 1, 2, \ldots, k).
\end{aligned}
\tag{1}
$$

An event-driven supervisor switches the main system input $u(t)$ and output $y(t)$ to connect with the appropriate subsystem input $\hat{u}_a(t)$ and output $\hat{y}_a(t)$

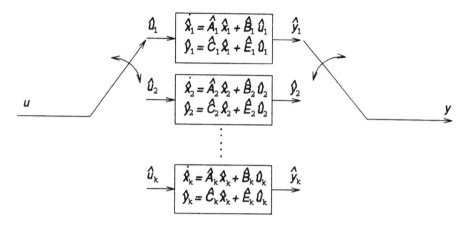

Fig. 1. A multi-system.

($a \in \{1, 2, \ldots, k\}$) at the appropriate time. We call a switch between subsystems in a multi-system a *transfer*. Note that only one subsystem, the *active* subsystem [6], is switched in at a time. The subsystems that are not switched in are *latent* subsystems [6]. By switching in the appropriate subsystem, a multi-system can realize any one of k frequency-dependent input/output relationships $y(s) = T_{yui}(s)u(s)$ ($i = 1, 2, \ldots, k$) for which the transfer matrices are

$$T_{yui}(s) = \hat{C}_i(sI - \hat{A}_i)^{-1}\hat{B}_i + \hat{E}_i \quad (i = 1, 2, \ldots, k). \tag{2}$$

The second type of hybrid system that we examine is a *hybrid linear system*. [14]. We illustrate its concept in Figure 2. Hybrid linear systems are also called *piecewise linear systems* [16] or *jump linear systems* [3, 10]. In this architecture, a supervisor adjusts the parameters of a single, piecewise-linear system. Thus, given k sets of appropriately-dimensioned gain matrices $\{A_i, B_i, C_i, E_i\}$, we can represent k regimes of a hybrid linear system in the state space as

$$\begin{aligned} \dot{x}(t) &= A_i x(t) + B_i u(t), \\ y(t) &= C_i x(t) + E_i u(t) \quad (i = 1, 2, \ldots, k). \end{aligned} \tag{3}$$

Note that, unlike the regimes of a multi-system, the regimes of a hybrid linear system share their input $u(t) \in R^m$, their output $y(t) \in R^p$, and their state $x(t) \in R^n$. By switching in the appropriate set of gain matrices, a hybrid linear system can realize any one of k relationships $y(s) = T_{yui}(s)u(s)$ ($i = 1, 2, \ldots, k$) for which the transfer matrices are

$$T_{yui}(s) = C_i(sI - A_i)^{-1}B_i + E_i \quad (i = 1, 2, \ldots, k).$$

Since the subsystems of a hybrid linear system share their state, the order of a hybrid linear system is often much lower than that of a multi-system which

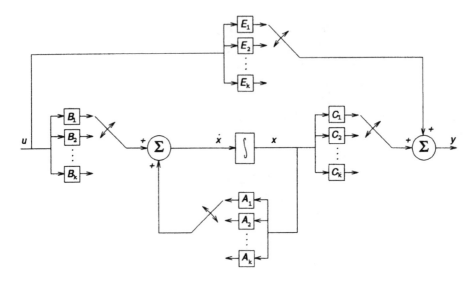

Fig. 2. A hybrid linear system.

realizes the same set of transfer matrices. While there are some situations, such as the on-line evaluation of alternate controllers [6], which require switching between multiple systems, we can generally reduce the complexity of a bumpless system if we can design it as a hybrid linear system instead of as a multi-system. After summarizing some established techniques for achieving bumpless transfers in a multi-system, this paper introduces a way to realize a set of switching transfer matrices as a bumpless hybrid linear system.

2 Bumpless Multi-Systems

This section summarizes two of the bumpless transfer techniques described by Graebe and Ahlén in [6].

2.1 Setting the State: SISO Case

For a multi-system implemented on a computer, one method of achieving bumpless transfer is to set the state of the switched-in subsystem at the switch time t_s to force the post-switch output $y(t_s^+)$ to equal the pre-switch output $y(t_s^-)$.

Example 1 (Filter Tuning). Suppose we use a multi-system filter with $k = 2$ single-input, single-output (SISO) subsystems of order $\hat{n}_1 = \hat{n}_2 = 1$ to process the signal $u(t) = \cos(\frac{\pi}{2}t)$. We switch the subsystems, given by (1), at time $t_s = 10$ to change the transfer function of the filter from

$$T_{yu1}(s) = \frac{4}{s+4} \quad \text{to} \quad T_{yu2}(s) = \frac{1}{s+1}. \tag{4}$$

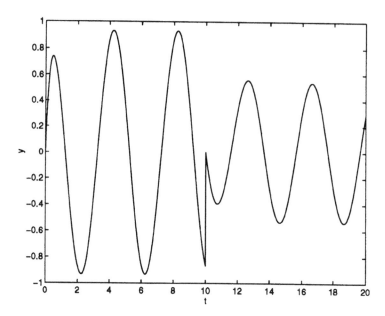

Fig. 3. There is a discontinuity in the output when we switch the filter transfer function without setting the state.

If the state of the second subsystem is $x_2(t_s^+) = 0$ just after the switch, then the bumpy output of Figure 3 will result. However, by observing the multi-system input $u(t_s^-)$ and output $y(t_s^-)$ just before the switch, we can compute that the state of the second subsystem should be set to

$$\hat{x}_2(t_s^+) = \frac{y(t_s^-) - \hat{E}_2 u(t_s^-)}{\hat{C}_2}$$

just after the switch to ensure continuity in the output. In this case, the bumpless output of Figure 4 would result.

2.2 Setting the State: MIMO Case

For the case of a multi-system with observable multi-input, multi-output (MIMO) subsystems given by (1), suppose that we would like to switch out subsystem $i \in \{1, 2, \ldots, k\}$ and switch in subsystem $j \in \{1, 2, \ldots, k\}$ $(j \neq i)$. If we can determine the first $(\hat{n}_i - 1)$ derivatives of the multi-system input and output just before the switch time t_s, then we can ensure not only that the output is continuous during a switch, but also that all of the $(\hat{n}_i - 1)$ output derivatives are continuous as well. Specifically, when switching out subsystem i, we would

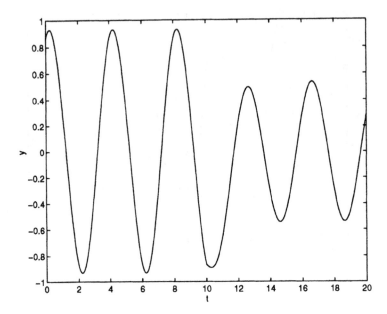

Fig. 4. The filter output is continuous if we set the state of the filter at the time of the switch to make the output just after the switch equal to the output just before the switch.

use the nonsingular observability matrix

$$
\mathcal{O}_i \triangleq \begin{bmatrix} \hat{C}_i \\ \hat{C}_i \hat{A}_i \\ \hat{C}_i \hat{A}_i^2 \\ \vdots \\ \hat{C}_i \hat{A}_i^{\hat{n}_i - 1} \end{bmatrix}
$$

and the lower triangular matrix

$$
\mathcal{M}_i \triangleq \begin{bmatrix} \hat{E}_i & 0 & 0 & \cdots & 0 & 0 \\ \hat{C}_i \hat{B}_i & \hat{E}_i & 0 & \cdots & 0 & 0 \\ \hat{C}_i \hat{A}_i \hat{B}_i & \hat{C}_i \hat{B}_i & \hat{E}_i & \cdots & 0 & 0 \\ \vdots & \vdots & \vdots & & \vdots & \vdots \\ \hat{C}_i \hat{A}_i^{\hat{n}_i - 2} \hat{B}_i & \hat{C}_i \hat{A}_i^{\hat{n}_i - 3} \hat{B}_i & \hat{C}_i \hat{A}_i^{\hat{n}_i - 4} \hat{B}_i & \cdots & \hat{C}_i \hat{B}_i & \hat{E}_i \end{bmatrix}
$$

to determine that the state of the switched-in subsystem j should be set to

$$\hat{x}_j(t_s^+) = \mathcal{O}_i^{-1} \begin{bmatrix} y(t_s^-) \\ \dot{y}(t_s^-) \\ \ddot{y}(t_s^-) \\ \vdots \\ \overset{(\hat{n}_i-1)}{y}(t_s^-) \end{bmatrix} - \mathcal{O}_i^{-1} \mathcal{M}_i \begin{bmatrix} u(t_s^-) \\ \dot{u}(t_s^-) \\ \ddot{u}(t_s^-) \\ \vdots \\ \overset{(\hat{n}_i-1)}{u}(t_s^-) \end{bmatrix}$$

at the time of a switch to ensure continuity in the output and its derivatives.

2.3 Tracking the Output of an Active Subsystem with the Output of a Latent Subsystem

We can use the following multi-system technique to bumplessly transfer control of a plant from an active (sub)controller to a latent (sub)controller. Say that an active controller C_a and a plant $\mathcal{P}$ are in the configuration of Figure 5, where $r(t)$ is the external reference, $\hat{u}_a(t)$ is the active control signal, and $y(t)$ is the plant output. Then by placing a latent controller C_l in the configuration of Figure 6, where C_t is a tracking controller, we force the output $\hat{u}_l(t)$ of C_l to track $\hat{u}_a(t)$. The error $e(t) = r(t) - y(t)$ acts as an input disturbance to the "plant" C_l.

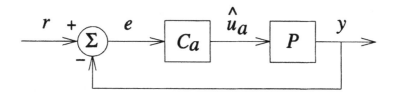

Fig. 5. The active controller C_a controls the plant $\mathcal{P}$.

We can make a bumpless transfer from C_a to C_l whenever $\hat{u}_l(t)$ is tracking $\hat{u}_a(t)$. To achieve the bumpless transfer, we switch the plant input from $\hat{u}_a(t)$ to $\hat{u}_l(t)$, and we remove the effect of the tracking loop on C_l by opening the loop at the tracking controller output $u_t(t)$. Thus C_l becomes the active controller C_a of Figure 5. Moreover, if we switch in a tracking loop for the former active controller, it will become a latent controller like the one in Figure 6. This makes it possible to do the bumpless transfers bidirectionally.

The tracking controller C_t is often chosen to be a diagonal matrix where each nonzero element is a high gain (a constant much greater than 1). Another obvious choice for C_t is a diagonal matrix where each nonzero element is a high gain integrator ($\frac{1}{s}$ multiplied by a constant much greater than 1).

Note that tracking is a more general bumpless transfer technique than setting the state because there are no restrictions on how the controller should be implemented. The controller does not have to be implemented on a computer, nor does not it have to be linear.

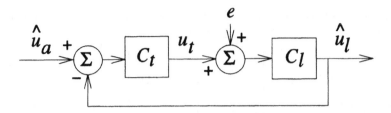

Fig. 6. The tracking controller $\mathcal{C}_t$ forces the output $\hat{u}_l(t)$ of the latent controller $\mathcal{C}_l$ to equal the output $\hat{u}_a(t)$ of the active controller $\mathcal{C}_a$. When $\hat{u}_l(t)$ is tracking $\hat{u}_a(t)$, we can bumplessly transfer control of the plant from $\mathcal{C}_a$ to $\mathcal{C}_l$. The error $e(t) = r(t) - y(t)$ between the active controller reference and the plant output acts as an input disturbance to the "plant" $\mathcal{C}_l$.

3 Bumpless Hybrid Linear Systems

The order of a multi-system with subsystems given by (1) is

$$\sum_{i=1}^{k} \hat{n}_i.$$

If tracking controllers with integrators are used for bumpless transfers between subsystems, the order of the multi-system will be even higher than this. Often a bumpless hybrid linear system of order no greater than

$$\max_{i \in \{1,2,\ldots,k\}} \hat{n}_i$$

can realize the same transfer matrices realized by such a multi-system.

As noted by Morse in [12], a hybrid linear system will be bumpless if all changes in its parameters occur before the state integrators. So, a hybrid linear system will be bumpless if, during all regime changes, only the gain matrices A_i and B_i switch values and C_i and E_i remain fixed (i.e., $C_i = C$ and $E_i = E$ for $i = 1, 2, \ldots, k$ and constant matrices C and E).

While a physically-realizable multi-system will typically have all of its gain matrices $\hat{E}_i$ equal to the zero matrix, a multi-system may not be designed such that all of its gain matrices $\hat{C}_i$ are equal to each other. However, if the subsystems of a multi-system are such that all k matrices $\hat{E}_i$ are identical to each other ($\hat{E}_i = E$) and all k matrices $\hat{C}_i$ have full rank p, then we can use the following procedure to design a bumpless hybrid linear system which realizes the same transfer matrices realized by the multi-system.

First, if the orders of the subsystems are not identical, let

$$n \stackrel{\Delta}{=} \max_{i=1,2,\ldots,k} \hat{n}_i \quad \text{and} \quad n_i \stackrel{\Delta}{=} n - \hat{n}_i \quad (i = 1, 2, \ldots, k).$$

Add n_i uncontrollable and unobservable modes to each subsystem by appropriately increasing the dimensions of $\hat{A}_i$, $\hat{B}_i$, and $\hat{C}_i$. In particular, add n_i columns of zeros to $\hat{C}_i$, add n_i rows of zeros to $\hat{B}_i$, and add a stable $(n_i \times n_i)$ lower right block to $\hat{A}_i$ to define C_i, B_i, and A_i. Then, the generally bumpy hybrid linear system with regimes

$$
\begin{aligned}
\dot{x}(t) &= A_i x(t) + B_i u(t), \\
y(t) &= C_i x(t) + E u(t) \quad (i = 1, 2, \ldots, k),
\end{aligned}
\tag{5}
$$

realizes the desired transfer matrices, given by (2), since

$$
\begin{aligned}
T_{yui}(s) &= C_i(sI - A_i)^{-1} B_i + E \\
&= \hat{C}_i(sI - \hat{A}_i)^{-1} \hat{B}_i + E \quad (i = 1, 2, \ldots, k).
\end{aligned}
\tag{6}
$$

Any transfer matrices that can be realized by a bumpy hybrid linear system with C_i of full rank and $E_i = E$ $(i = 1, 2, \ldots, k)$ can also be realized by a bumpless hybrid linear system. To see this, use a procedure, such as the one in Section 4, to non-uniquely determine k nonsingular $(n \times n)$ *switching conversion matrices* P_i and a $(p \times n)$ fixed matrix F such that

$$
C_i = F P_i \quad (i = 1, 2, \ldots, k).
\tag{7}
$$

Then the bumpless hybrid linear system with regimes

$$
\begin{aligned}
\dot{x}(t) &= P_i A_i P_i^{-1} x(t) + P_i B_i u(t), \\
y(t) &= F x(t) + E u(t) \quad (i = 1, 2, \ldots, k),
\end{aligned}
\tag{8}
$$

also realizes the transfer matrices given by (6) since

$$
\begin{aligned}
T_{yui}(s) &= F(sI - P_i A_i P_i^{-1})^{-1} P_i B_i + E \\
&= C_i(sI - A_i)^{-1} B_i + E \quad (i = 1, 2, \ldots, k).
\end{aligned}
$$

The regimes given by (8) are *equivalent* [18] to those given by (5).

Example 2 (Filter Tuning Revisited). Suppose we naively realized the filter transfer functions $T_{yu1}(s)$ and $T_{yu2}(s)$ in (4) with the scalar hybrid linear system regimes

$$
\begin{aligned}
\dot{x}(t) &= -4x(t) + u(t), \quad \text{and} \quad \dot{x}(t) = -x(t) + u(t), \\
y(t) &= 4x(t), \qquad\qquad\qquad\;\; y(t) = x(t).
\end{aligned}
$$

If we did not reset the state at the switch time $t_s = 10$, then a switch from the first regime to the second while processing $u(t) = \cos(\frac{\pi}{2}t)$ would cause a bump in the output as in Figure 3. However, if we realized the transfer functions by the equivalent regimes

$$
\begin{aligned}
\dot{x}(t) &= -4x(t) + 4u(t), \quad \text{and} \quad \dot{x}(t) = -x(t) + u(t), \\
y(t) &= x(t), \qquad\qquad\qquad\;\;\; y(t) = x(t),
\end{aligned}
$$

then a switch from the first regime to the second while processing $u(t)$ would occur bumplessly, as in Figure 4, without our having to reset the state.

4 Switching Conversion Matrices

For a given fixed matrix F, one way to determine a switching conversion matrix P_i that will make (7) hold is to first choose any p linearly independent columns of C_i and F, define the chosen columns as C_{pi} and F_p, and define the remaining columns as C_{ri} and F_r. Then determine permutation matrices P_{Ci} and P_F that can reorder the columns of C_i and F in the following manner:

$$C_i P_{Ci} = [\,C_{pi} \quad C_{ri}\,] \quad \text{and} \quad F P_F = [\,F_p \quad F_r\,].$$

Recall that a *permutation matrix* is a nonsingular matrix in which all the elements are 0, except for a single entry of 1 in each row and column.

If we let I be the identity matrix and define

$$M_i = \begin{bmatrix} F_p^{-1} C_{pi} & F_p^{-1}[C_{ri} - F_r] \\ 0 & I \end{bmatrix}, \tag{9}$$

then $C_i P_{Ci} = F P_F M_i$. Thus, (7) holds if

$$P_i = P_F M_i P_{Ci}^{-1}. \tag{10}$$

Note that if $F = [F_p \quad F_r] = [I \quad 0]$, then $P_F = I$. Moreover, if the first p columns of all $C_i = [C_{pi} \quad C_{ri}]$ are linearly independent, then $P_{Ci} = I$ as well. In such cases, (9) and (10) imply that

$$P_i = M_i = \begin{bmatrix} C_{pi} & C_{ri} \\ 0 & I \end{bmatrix}. \tag{11}$$

5 Bumpless Hybrid Linear Controllers

A hybrid linear controller is a hybrid linear system used for feedback control. This section describes one way to realize a bumpless, observer-based hybrid linear controller for a MIMO plant. The realization is efficient in that the order of the controller is no greater than that of the plant.

Consider a plant that can be modeled as a hybrid linear system with regimes defined by (3). If all of its regimes are stabilizable and detectable, then we can use an approach, such as the one in the Appendix or in [18], to determine gain matrices G_i and K_i $(i = 1, 2, \ldots, k)$ that will assign all of the controllable eigenvalues of $A_i + B_i G_i$ and all of the observable eigenvalues of $A_i + K_i C_i$ to the negative real half of the complex plane. Thus, we can stabilize the regimes of the plant with the corresponding regimes of an observer-based hybrid linear controller (Figure 7):

$$\dot{\tilde{x}}(t) = (A_i + K_i C_i)\tilde{x}(t) + (B_i + K_i E_i)u(t) - K_i y(t),$$
$$u(t) = G_i \tilde{x}(t) + r(t) \quad (i = 1, 2, \ldots, k), \tag{12}$$

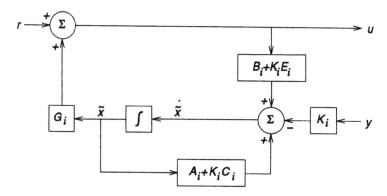

Fig. 7. Configuration of a regime for a generally bumpy hybrid linear controller.

where $r(t)$ is an external reference input and $\tilde{x}(t)$ is an estimate of $x(t)$. In the cases where the controller regime matched the plant regime, the closed-loop transfer matrices would be

$$T_{yri}(s) = (C_i + E_i G_i)(sI - A_i - B_i G_i)^{-1} B_i + E_i \quad (i = 1, 2, \ldots, k). \qquad (13)$$

A problem is that switching in a hybrid linear controller with gains determined using a standard approach will generally be bumpy.

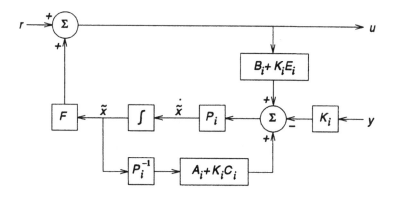

Fig. 8. Configuration of a regime for a bumpless hybrid linear controller.

However, if all of the matrices G_i are of full rank, we can non-uniquely determine k nonsingular $(n \times n)$ switching conversion matrices P_i and an $(m \times n)$ fixed matrix F such that $G_i = FP_i$ $(i = 1, 2, \ldots, k)$. Then we can stabilize the regimes of the plant with the regimes of an equivalent bumpless hybrid linear controller (Figure 8):

$$\dot{\tilde{x}}(t) = P_i(A_i + K_i C_i)P_i^{-1}\tilde{x}(t) + P_i(B_i + K_i E_i)u(t) - P_i K_i y(t),$$

$$u(t) = F\tilde{x}(t) + r(t) \quad (i = 1, 2, \ldots, k). \tag{14}$$

The closed-loop transfer matrices associated with this controller would be the same as those in (13).

Note that we can sometimes find a fixed controller that will stabilize a hybrid linear system and avoid using a hybrid linear controller altogether [2, 4].

6   Bumpless Switching Applications

The next two examples illustrate applications of bumpless switching to control problems.

Example 3 (Prevention of Input Saturation). In some cases, using a bumpless hybrid linear controller instead of a bumpy hybrid linear controller can prevent the plant input from saturating. Consider a plant modeled as a hybrid linear system with $k = 2$ regimes given by (3), with

$$A_1 = A_2 = \begin{bmatrix} 1 & 1 \\ 0 & 1 \end{bmatrix}, \quad B_1 = \begin{bmatrix} 0 & 0 \\ 0 & 1 \end{bmatrix}, \quad B_2 = C_1 = C_2 = \begin{bmatrix} 1 & 0 \\ 0 & 1 \end{bmatrix},$$

and $E_1 = E_2 = 0$ (the zero matrix). Suppose that a bumpy controller, with regimes given by (12), has the following observer gain matrices and feedback gain matrices:

$$K_1 = K_2 = \begin{bmatrix} -2 & 0 \\ 0 & -2 \end{bmatrix}, \quad G_1 = \begin{bmatrix} 1 & 0 \\ -4 & -4 \end{bmatrix}, \quad \text{and} \quad G_2 = \begin{bmatrix} -2 & 0 \\ 0 & -2 \end{bmatrix}.$$

Then, by letting $F = I$ and using (11), we see that the switching conversion matrices for a bumpless controller with equivalent regimes given by (14) are $P_1 = G_1$ and $P_2 = G_2$.

Figure 9 compares the plant input $u_2(t)$ for the plant controlled by the bumpy controller and the bumpless controller. To generate the trajectories, we applied a magnitude 1 step simultaneously to both of the reference inputs $r_1(t)$ and $r_2(t)$ at time $t = 0$, and then we switched the regimes of both the plant and the controller from regime 1 to regime 2 at $t = 10$. The advantage of a bumpless controller is clear in this case.

Example 4 (Input Surge Reduction). In some cases, using a bumpless hybrid linear controller can help prevent sudden switching-related surges or drops in the input. Consider a model, based on [5] and [13], for the longitudinal and vertical dynamics of a helicopter moving at different longitudinal airspeeds. The model is a hybrid linear system, with regimes as in (3), where

$$A_i = \begin{bmatrix} -0.0366 & 0.0271 & 0.0188 & -0.455 \\ 0.0482 & -1.0100 & 0.0024 & -4.020 \\ 0.1000 & \alpha_i & -0.7070 & \beta_i \\ 0 & 0 & 1 & 0 \end{bmatrix},$$

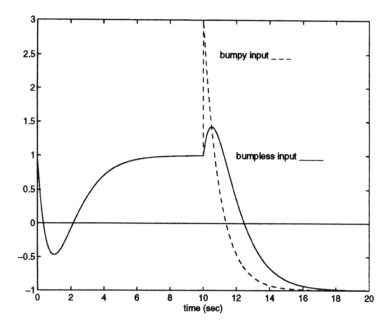

Fig. 9. In this case, by using a bumpless controller instead of a bumpy controller, we can avoid saturating the plant input.

$$
B_i = \begin{bmatrix} 0.422 & 0.176 \\ \gamma_i & -7.590 \\ -5.520 & 4.490 \\ 0 & 0 \end{bmatrix}, \quad C_i = \begin{bmatrix} 1 & 0 & 0 & 0 \\ 0 & 0 & 0 & 1 \end{bmatrix}, \quad \text{and } E_i = \begin{bmatrix} 0 & 0 \\ 0 & 0 \end{bmatrix},
$$

and where the values for the parameters $\{\alpha_i, \beta_i, \gamma_i\}$ for 5 airspeed ranges, which correspond to regimes, are

airspeed (knots)	regime i	α_i	β_i	γ_i
50–75	1	0.06635	0.1198	0.9775
75–100	2	0.2	0.5	1.9
100–125	3	0.285	0.9	2.73
125–150	4	0.3681	1.42	3.5446
150–175	5	0.5045	2.526	5.112

The state and control variables are

$$
\begin{bmatrix} x_1(t) \\ x_2(t) \\ x_3(t) \\ x_4(t) \end{bmatrix} = \begin{bmatrix} \text{vertical velocity of the helicopter} \\ \text{longitudinal velocity of the helicopter} \\ \text{pitch rate of the helicopter} \\ \text{pitch angle of the helicopter} \end{bmatrix}
$$

and
$$
\begin{bmatrix} u_1(t) \\ u_2(t) \end{bmatrix} = \begin{bmatrix} \text{collective pitch of the rotor blades} \\ \text{longitudinal cyclic pitch of the rotor blades} \end{bmatrix}.
$$

Note that $x_2(t)$ represents a deviation from trim condition rather than an absolute value.

Both the collective control and the cyclic control change the pitch angle of the rotor blades [15]. If we think of the spinning rotor as a disc, then the *collective control* changes the incidence of the blades evenly at all points on the disc. An increase in the collective pitch increases the rotor thrust and is generally used to increase the vertical velocity of the helicopter. The *cyclic control* changes the incidence of the blades in a periodic manner, so that blades passing through one part of the disc are feathered more than blades passing through other parts of the disc. A change in the cyclic pitch changes the line of action of the rotor thrust and is generally used to determine horizontal heading and speed. For analysis, we often decouple the components of the cyclic control that affect longitudinal and lateral velocity.

The helicopter model is an unstable system, and, without the addition of an automatic controller, a step function in either $u_1(t)$ or $u_2(t)$ will cause the helicopter to pitch at ever-increasing rates. For each of the helicopter regimes, we can design corresponding optimal hybrid linear controller regimes of the form (12) or (14). We can determine the feedback gain matrix G_i that minimizes the quadratic performance index

$$\int_0^\infty [x^T(t)x(t) + u^T(t)u(t)]dt, \tag{15}$$

and we can determine an observer gain matrix K_i by taking the transpose of the feedback gain matrix that minimizes (15) for the dual system

$$\dot{x}(t) = A_i^T x(t) + C_i^T u(t).$$

The superscript T denotes the transpose of a matrix.

For instance, the values of G_i and K_i for regime 4 and regime 5 are

$$G_4 = \begin{bmatrix} -0.9245 & 0.0171 & 0.9665 & 1.3876 \\ 0.0271 & 0.8448 & -0.1886 & -0.7148 \end{bmatrix},$$

$$G_5 = \begin{bmatrix} -0.9269 & -0.0538 & 0.9945 & 1.5210 \\ -0.0296 & 0.8518 & -0.0668 & -0.4734 \end{bmatrix},$$

$$K_4 = \begin{bmatrix} -1.0764 & 0.3322 \\ -0.9078 & 2.9441 \\ 0.0961 & -1.0749 \\ 0.3322 & -1.7434 \end{bmatrix}, \quad \text{and} \quad K_5 = \begin{bmatrix} -1.0798 & 0.4169 \\ -0.9512 & 3.6558 \\ 0.3207 & -2.1475 \\ 0.4169 & -2.2630 \end{bmatrix}.$$

Suppose that a few seconds after the helicopter has made a transition from regime 5 to regime 4, a gain-scheduler switches the hybrid linear controller from its regime 5 to its regime 4 in order to maintain optimal control. If the controller is bumpy, with regimes given by (12), then surges and drops will occur in the plant inputs at the time of the switch. However, by applying the approach in

Section 4, we can determine matrices

$$F = \begin{bmatrix} 1 & 0 & 0 & 0 \\ 0 & 1 & 0 & 0 \end{bmatrix}, \quad P_4 = \begin{bmatrix} -0.9245 & 0.0171 & 0.9665 & 1.3876 \\ 0.0271 & 0.8448 & -0.1886 & -0.7148 \\ 0 & 0 & 1 & 0 \\ 0 & 0 & 0 & 1 \end{bmatrix},$$

$$\text{and } P_5 = \begin{bmatrix} -0.9269 & -0.0538 & 0.9945 & 1.5210 \\ -0.0296 & 0.8518 & -0.0668 & -0.4734 \\ 0 & 0 & 1 & 0 \\ 0 & 0 & 0 & 1 \end{bmatrix}$$

such that the controller is bumpless, with regimes given by (14). This is illustrated in Figure 10, which we generated by applying a step input of magnitude 1 to both of the reference inputs at time $t = 0$ and then switching the controller from regime 5 to regime 4 at time $t = 10$.

7 A Note on the Simulations

In each example, we performed the simulations with SIMULINK [11]. We solved the differential equations in the simulation with a fifth order Runge-Kutta method, which used a fourth order method for step size control. The minimum and maximum step sizes were 10^{-9} and 10^{-1} seconds. We set the tolerance to 10^{-9} and all initial conditions to zero.

8 Conclusion

If a hybrid system is not carefully designed, discrete switching within the system can cause discontinuities, or bumps, in the system output. If the hybrid system is a controller, such surges can saturate the plant input or exert wear on plant components. Often, we can mitigate the effect of these surges by designing a bumpless hybrid system.

This paper discussed ways of achieving bumpless switching for two types of hybrid systems. After we reviewed established techniques for achieving bumpless transfers in a multi-system, we introduced a way of designing bumpless hybrid linear systems. The advantage of the hybrid linear system architecture is that its order is typically much less than that of a multi-system architecture.

Appendix

This appendix summarizes a recent approach [17] for determining a state feedback gain G that can arbitrarily position the poles of a multivariable system. By duality, we can also use this approach to determine an observer gain K that will arbitrarily set the eigenvalues of the observer.

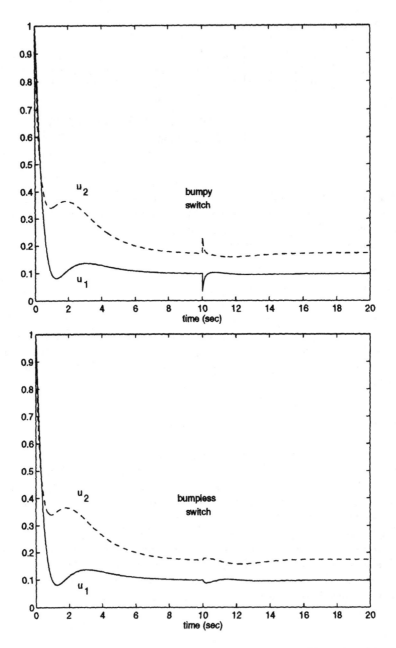

Fig. 10. At the time $(t = 10)$ of a switch, the inputs $u_1(t)$ and $u_2(t)$ of the system controlled by the bumpy controller drop and surge (top frame), while the inputs of the system controlled by the bumpless controller do not (bottom frame).

Consider any fixed, controllable, multi-input state-space system defined by the state matrix A and the input matrix $B = [\,b_1 \quad b_2 \quad \ldots \quad b_m\,]$ of full column rank $m < n$. Reorder the first n linearly independent columns of the controllability matrix

$$\mathcal{C} = [B \ AB \ \ldots \ A^{n-1}B],$$

to define the $(n \times n)$ nonsingular matrix

$$L = [b_1 \ Ab_1 \ldots A^{d_1-1}b_1 \ b_2 \ Ab_2 \ldots A^{d_2-1}b_2 \ \ldots A^{d_m-1}b_m],$$

the m controllability indices d_i, and the m integers $\sigma_k = \sum_1^k d_k$, so that $\sigma_1 = d_1$, $\sigma_2 = d_1 + d_2$, etc., with $\sigma_m = d_1 + d_2 + \ldots d_m = n$ [18].

If the m row vectors q_k are then defined as the σ_k rows of L^{-1}, it follows that

$$\hat{B}_m \triangleq \begin{bmatrix} q_1 A^{d_1-1}B \\ q_2 A^{d_2-1}B \\ \vdots \\ q_m A^{d_m-1}B \end{bmatrix}$$

will be a nonsingular, upper right triangular matrix, with all diagonal elements equal to 1, so that $|\hat{B}_m| = 1$.

If we choose m arbitrary stable monic polynomials $\delta_i(s)$, each of degree d_i, and define the *state feedback gain matrix*

$$G = -\hat{B}_m^{-1} \begin{bmatrix} q_1 \delta_1(A) \\ q_2 \delta_2(A) \\ \vdots \\ q_m \delta_m(A) \end{bmatrix},$$

it then follows that the n eigenvalues of $A + BG$ will correspond to the roots of $\delta(s) \triangleq \prod_1^m \delta_i(s)$.

Note that in the single-input ($m = 1$ and $B = b$) case, a single vector q would be defined as the last row of $\mathcal{C}^{-1}$. For any stable monic polynomial $\delta(s)$ of degree n, a choice of $g = -q\delta(A)$, which is known as Ackermann's formula [19], would then imply that the n eigenvalues of $A + bg$ will correspond to the roots of $\delta(s)$.

References

1. R. Alur, T. A. Henzinger, and E. D. Sontag (eds.), *Hybrid Systems III: Verification and Control*, Lecture Notes in Computer Science 1066, Springer, 1996.
2. A. B. Arehart and W. A. Wolovich, "A nonlinear programming procedure and a necessary condition for the simultaneous stabilization of 3 or more linear systems," in *Proceedings of the 34th IEEE Conference on Decision and Control*, pp. 2631–2632, Dec. 1995.
3. A. B. Arehart and W. A. Wolovich, "Bumpless switching controllers," in *Proceedings of the 35th IEEE Conference on Decision and Control*, pp. 1654–1655, Dec. 1996.

4. V. Blondel, *Simultaneous Stabilization of Linear Systems*. Springer, 1994.

5. Y.-K. Chin, *Theoretical and Computational Considerations for Finite Time Interval System Identification Without Initial State Estimation*. PhD thesis, Brown U., 1977.

6. S. F. Graebe and A. Ahlén, "Bumpless transfer," in *The Control Handbook*, W. S. Levine (ed.), pp. 381–388, CRC, Dec. 1995.

7. R. L Grossman, A. Nerode, A. P. Ravn, and H. Rischel (eds.), *Hybrid Systems*, Lecture Notes in Computer Science 736, Springer, 1993.

8. R. L. Grossman, A. Nerode, A. P. Ravn, and H. Rischel, "Introduction," in [7], pp. 1–3, Springer, 1993.

9. M. Lemmon, J. A. Stiver, P. J. Antsaklis, "Event identification and intelligent hybrid control," in [7], pp. 268–296, Springer, 1993.

10. M. Mariton, *Jump Linear Systems in Automatic Control*. Marcel Dekker, 1990.

11. MathWorks, *SIMULINK User's Guide*, 1992.

12. A. S. Morse, "Control using logic-based switching," in *Trends in Control*, A. Isidori (ed.), Springer, pp. 69-114, Sept. 1995.

13. K. S. Narenda and S. S. Tripathi, "Identification and optimization of aircraft dynamics," *Journal of Aircraft*, vol. 10, pp. 193–199, Apr. 1973.

14. H. S. Park, Y. S. Kim, W. H. Kwon, and S. J. Lee, "Model and stability of hybrid linear system," in [1], pp. 424–435, Springer, 1996.

15. J. Seddon, *Basic Helicopter Aerodynamics*, AIAA Education Series, 1990.

16. E. D. Sontag, "Interconnected automata and linear systems: a theoretical framework in discrete-time," in [1], pp. 436–448, Springer, 1996.

17. J. Wang and Y. Juang, "A new approach for computing the state feedback gains of multivariable systems," *IEEE Transactions on Automatic Control*, vol. 40, pp. 1823–1826, Oct. 1995.

18. W. A. Wolovich, *Linear Multivariable Systems*. Springer, 1974.

19. W. A. Wolovich, *Automatic Control Systems: Basic Analysis and Design*. Saunders, 1994.

A Toolbox for Proving and Maintaining Hybrid Specifications

Michael S. Branicky,* Ekaterina Dolginova,** and Nancy Lynch***

Dept. of Electrical Engineering and Computer Science
Massachusetts Institute of Technology
Cambridge, MA 02139-4307 USA

Abstract. Formal verification in computer science often takes a worst-case view towards performance and uses induction to prove specification invariants. In control theory, robust control takes a worst-case view towards performance; nominal performance proofs often use derivative information to prove invariance of specification sets. In this note, we explore a toolbox for proving (positive) invariance of state-space sets with respect to the actions of dynamical systems. The focus is on dynamical systems given by differential equations, building up to hybrid systems.

1 Introduction

We are interested in the formal verification of safety and performance properties of hybrid systems [1, 8, 17].

In computer science, there is large formal verification literature (e.g., [2, 5, 9, 11, 12, 16, 19]) of discrete-dynamic systems, such as automata. Usually, the proofs that verify safety and performance involve the search for certain formulas which are (proven to be) invariant over the actions of the system. This same style can be translated, almost brute force, into dealing with hybrid systems by including both continuous and discrete system actions [13, 14, 15]. Conceptually, the solution appears clear. However, in chasing these solutions one can often get stuck by thinking of the "traces" or solutions of differential equations (intermixed with discrete steps, of course) as the entities one is to verify.

Herein, we take a step back from this conceptual viewpoint and begin to look for the *mechanics* and *mechanisms* of proof necessary when discrete and continuous actions interact. Specifically, we want to look at tools that enable one to prove the positive invariance of sets with respect to the action of hybrid dynamical systems. This is merely the abstraction of many problems of verification: Is the system performing within safety/performance specifications (specs.)?

---

* During preparation: Post-doc, Lab. for Information and Decision Systems. Currently: Asst. Prof., Dept. of Electrical Eng. and Applied Physics, Case Western Reserve University, 10900 Euclid Avenue, Cleveland, OH 44106-7221. branicky@eeap.cwru.edu
** Undergraduate student, Lab. for Computer Science. katya@theory.lcs.mit.edu
*** Prof., Lab. for Computer Science. lynch@theory.lcs.mit.edu

Thus, we consider $S \subset \mathbf{R}^n$ (more generally, $S' \subset \mathbf{R}^n \times \mathbf{R}$) to be our (time-varying) specification set for a system Σ. The evolution of Σ is given by a dynamical system $\phi : \mathbf{R}^n \times \mathbf{R} \to 2^{\mathbf{R}^n}$ satisfying the following two properties:

- Initial Condition: $\phi(x, 0) = x$ for all x.
- Transitivity:

$$\phi(x, t_1 + t_2) \in \{x_2 \mid x_1 \in \phi(x, t_1), \ x_2 \in \phi(x_1, t_2)\}$$

The specifications are enforced by requiring the system Σ be such that S is (positively) invariant with respect to the dynamics ϕ, that is

$$\phi(S, t) \subset S, \text{ for all } t \geq 0. \tag{1}$$

The rest of this paper can be seen as making the above notion precise and giving tools for (a) verifying Equation (1), and (b) designing ϕ so that Equation (1) is verified, even in the presence of uncertainty.

When the dynamical system ϕ is a finite automaton, $t \in \mathbf{Z}$, and a spec. is usually given by a state formula whose invariance is verified via an induction proof. This induction is on the discrete actions available to the automata.

We want to develop similar tools in the case the dynamical systems are hybrid (viz., combining automata and differential equations). As a first step, we collect and develop tools here useful in proving invariance when the dynamical systems are given by differential equations. We want the invariance proofs to again be based on induction from local steps: *we want to use derivative information, not solve differential equations*. The reason is that the global information of an ODE solution is generally impossible to find.

The paper is organized as follows. In the next section we review existing theory in our context. Then we develop more directly applicable tools in Section 3. In Sections 4 and 5 we solve a toy example of platoon merge safety. We first formalize the problem with the computer science model of hybrid I/O automata [13] and then prove safety using our system theoretic tools. In this way, we explicitly demonstrate how our tools mesh with both computer science and control theory flavors of reasoning about hybrid systems.

2 The Basics

2.1 On Being Invariant

A formal treatment of positive invariant sets for differential equations appears in Bhatia and Szegö's fine book [4, pp. 306–322]. Their Corollary 3.4.22 (p. 316) follows some preliminaries.

We discuss the autonomous system

$$\dot{x} = g(x), \tag{2}$$

where $x \in \mathbf{R}^n$ and with solution denoted by ϕ. Throughout, we assume that for Equation (2), g is continuous on an open set $U \subset \mathbf{R}^n$.

Definition 1. A *curve* γ is a continuous function mapping some interval D_γ into $\mathbf{R}^n$. We always let D_γ represent the domain of the curve γ. If $\mathcal{F}$ is a family of curves, we say $\gamma^* \in \mathcal{F}$ is an *extension* of γ if $D_\gamma \subset D_{\gamma^*}$ and $\gamma = \gamma^*$ on D_γ. We say that γ is *maximal* in $\mathcal{F}$ if the only extension of γ is γ itself; that is maximal refers to the domain and *not* to the function values. For any curve γ, the notation $\gamma(\cdot; t, x)$ means that $t \in D_\gamma$ and $\gamma(t; t, x) = x$.

Definition 2. A set $S \subset U$ is called *positively (negatively) weakly invariant* for Equation (2) if for each $x \in S$ there exists a maximal solution $\phi(\cdot, x) = \phi$ such that $\phi(t, x) \in S$ for all $t \in [0, \sup D_\phi)$ (for all $t \in (\inf D_\phi, 0]$). A set $S \in U$ is called *positively (negatively) invariant* if for each $x \in S$ and each $\phi(\cdot, x)$, $\phi(t, x) \in S$ for all $t \in [0, \sup D_\phi)$ (for all $t \in (\inf D_\phi, 0]$). S is *(weakly) invariant* if it is both positively and negatively (weakly) invariant.

Definition 3. For $S \subset \mathbf{R}^n$, $x \in S$ and $v \in \mathbf{R}^n$, we say v is *subtangential* to S at x if
$$d(S, x + tv)/t \to 0 \text{ as } t \to 0^+.$$

Theorem 4. *The relatively closed set S is positively weakly invariant if and only if $g(x)$ is subtangential to S at x for all $x \in S$.*

Corollary 5. *If each solution $\phi(\cdot, x)$ of Equation (2) is uniquely determined by the initial condition x, then S is positively invariant if and only if $g(y)$ is subtangential to S for all $y \in S$.*

Statements for negative invariance hold replacing g by $-g$ above; invariance when both hold.

2.2 Fences that Hold Solutions

The following is summarized from [10]. Consider the first-order ODE
$$\dot{x} = f(t, x), \tag{3}$$
where $x \in \mathbf{R}$ and with solutions $x = u(t)$. A "fence" is some other function $x = \alpha(t)$ that channels the solutions in the direction of the vector field.

Definition 6. A continuous and continuously differentiable function $\alpha(t)$ is a *lower (resp. upper) fence* if
$$\dot{\alpha}(t) \leq f(t, \alpha(t)), \qquad [\text{resp. } f(t, \alpha(t)) \leq \dot{\alpha}(t)],$$

A fence is *strong* when the above inequalities are strict. A lower fence is *nonporous* if whenever $\alpha(t_0) \leq u(t_0)$, then $\alpha(t) \leq u(t)$ for all $t > t_0$; reversing the inequalities defines nonporous for upper fences.

Notes: (a) The definition of nonporous in [10] has the second inequality strict. We only require the given, weaker property. (b) Piecewise differentiable fences can be taken care of by checking that the required inequalities hold for both left and right derivatives.

Theorem 7. *A strong fence is nonporous.*

Theorem 8. *If f is Lipschitz with respect to x, then any fence is nonporous.*

3 Moving Forward

3.1 Multi-Dimensional Fences

The theory of fences discussed above is given only for one-dimensional state-spaces, i.e., $x \in \mathbf{R}$ in Equation (3) above. A similar theory exists for a class of ODEs in $\mathbf{R}^n$ known as *monotone systems* [18]. We outline a more general approach, motivated by the well-known concept of a Lyapunov function, below. The approach is distinct from Lyapunov functions in the usual sense, e.g., the function need not be positive definite.

The method starts by identifying with the specification set $S \subset \mathbf{R}^n$ a scalar function $s : \mathbf{R}^n \to \mathbf{R}$ such that

$$s(x) \text{ is } \begin{cases} > 0, \, x \in \text{int} S \\ = 0, \, x \in S \cap \partial S \\ < 0, \, x \notin S \end{cases} \tag{4}$$

Note that s is a generalized indicator function for the set S, viz. $S = \{x \mid s(x) \geq 0\}$. Thus, we may restrict our attention to showing the invariance of the nonnegative reals under the action of our dynamical system.

Suppose we wish to show that a specification region, given by $s(x) \geq 0$ is invariant over time. Thus, we want to show that $s(t) = s(x(t)) \geq 0$ for all $t > t_0$.

Theorem 9. *Suppose $\dot{s}(t)|_{s=0} \geq 0$. Then $s(t) \geq 0$ is invariant if either*

1. *There exists $\epsilon > 0$ such that $\dot{s}(t) > 0$ for all $s \in (-\epsilon, 0)$,*
2. *$\dot{s}(t)|_{s=0}$ is piecewise differentiable, and there exists $\epsilon > 0$ such that $\dot{s}(t) \geq 0$ for all $s \in (-\epsilon, 0)$,*
3. *$\dot{s}(t)|_{s=0}$ is Lipschitz.*

Proof. For parts (1) and (3), set $f(s, t) = \dot{s}(t)|_s$ and lower fence $\alpha(t) \equiv 0$. Apply Theorems 7 and 8. For part (2), use $\alpha(t) = s(t)$ as a fence for the constant function $f \equiv 0$.

3.2 Towards Robust Verification

We may address robustness issues by enforcing conditions such as

$$s(t) \geq \epsilon_1 > 0$$
$$\dot{s}(t)|_{\epsilon_1} \geq \epsilon_2 > 0$$

This provides the basis for "robust verification," in which a nominal system is provably verified by hand, and for which the effects of classes of perturbations (e.g., delay, sensor noise, unmodeled dynamics) can be provably ignored.

Below, we give three variations on a theme for using bounds on invariants in proving the correctness of perturbed systems given proofs for the nominal case and vice versa. Examples will be given in Section 5.2.

Bounding Invariants. Suppose there exists a function $s_L(t) \leq s(t)$, then to prove $s(t) \geq 0$ is invariant, it is sufficient to demonstrate $s_L(t) \geq 0$. Such a tactic is obviously useful in comparing systems; it might also be used if the derivative of $s(t)$ can not be computed but those of lower bound can be.

Bounding the Nominal Below. Suppose that in our perturbed system, we can only measure $\hat{s}(t)$, but that

$$s(t) \in [\hat{s}(t) - L, \ \hat{s}(t) + H],$$

where L, $H \in \mathbf{R}$. Suppose that we have verified a control law $u(s)$ such that $u(0)$ results in $\dot{s}(t) \geq 0$. Then, if we use $u(0)$ whenever $\hat{s}(t) - L \leq 0$, we obtain invariance of $s(t) \geq 0$ via an *implementation relation* (cf. [13]). **Note:** The constant L can be replaced with a function $L(t)$ with the same effect.

Bounding the Perturbed Above. Suppose that in our perturbed system, we can only measure $\hat{s}(t)$, but that

$$\hat{s}(t) \in [s(t) - l, \ s(t) + h],$$

where l, $h \in \mathbf{R}$. Suppose that we have a control law that maintains $s(t) \geq l$. Then, we have an existence proof that $\hat{s}$ can be kept above zero. However, such a control law might not be implementable only knowing $\hat{s}$. Again, l and h may be replaced by time-varying functions.

4 Platoon Merge Example–Setup

4.1 Introduction

In [7], a "robust merge platoon maneuver" is described and analyzed. There are four high-level specifications the system should meet:

1. Safety—the platoons are not supposed to collide at a relative speed greater than v_{allow}.
2. The merge should succeed, within a particular amount of time.
3. The merge is optimal, in that there is no other maneuver that could cause the merge to complete faster.
4. Passenger comfort, as measured by bounds on acceleration and jerk, is guaranteed.

Herein, *we only address the issue of safety.* We consider two platoons of vehicles, named 1 and 2, where platoon 1 precedes platoon 2 on a single track. Positions on the track are labeled with nonnegative reals, starting with 0 at a designated beginning point.

We assume the following constants:

- $v_{\text{allow}} \in \mathbf{R}^{\geq 0}$ is the value of the allowable (read also safe or acceptable) collision velocity,
- $a_{\min} \in \mathbf{R}^{\geq 0}$ is the absolute value of the maximum emergency deceleration.

The analysis in Appendix I of [7] is done in terms of vehicle velocities. Translating to vehicle positions, their analysis implies that safety is maintained (if $d = 0$) if

$$\Delta x(t) \geq \frac{v_2^2(t) - v_1^2(t) - v_{\text{allow}}^2}{2a_{\min}} \tag{5}$$

where

- x_1, x_2 are the positions of the lead and trailing platoons,
- $\Delta x = x_1 - x_2$, the difference in position of the lead and trailing platoons,
- $v_1 \equiv \dot{x}_1, v_2 \equiv \dot{x}_2$, are the velocities of the lead and trailing platoons.

In the remainder of this section we give a formal model of the platoon safety problem in terms of hybrid I/O automata [13]. In the next section, we prove invariance of Equation 5, in the presence of an abstract controller, using derivative information only.

4.2 Safety

Platoons. We model the system by a hybrid automaton that we call *Platoons*. Each platoon i has a position x_i and a velocity $\dot{x}_i$. The hybrid automaton *Platoons* has the following (non-e [13]) discrete actions:

Input: Internal:
    none   collide
Output:
    none

The variables are:

Input: Internal:
    none   none
Output:
    $\dot{x}_i \in \mathbf{R}^{\geq 0}$, $i \in \{1, 2\}$, initially arbitrary
    $x_i \in \mathbf{R}^{\geq 0}$, $i \in \{1, 2\}$; initially $x_2 = 0$ and x_1 is arbitrary
    collided, a Boolean, initially *false*

Thus, we assume that the velocities are nonnegative—the vehicles will never go backwards. Also, platoon 2 starts at the beginning position on the track.

collide
    Precondition:
        $x_1 = x_2$
        collided = *false*
    Effect:
        collided = *true*
        $\dot{x}_i$:= arbitrary value, $i \in \{1, 2\}$

We allow for fairly arbitrary behavior when cars collide: the velocities of both vehicles may change arbitrarily.

A trajectory of the hybrid system over the interval I (or I-trajectory [13]) w is included among the set of nontrivial trajectories exactly if:

1. *collided* is unchanged in w.
2. $\dot{x}_i$ is an integrable function in w, $i \in \{1, 2\}$.
3. For every $t \in I$, the following are true about $w(t)$:
   (a) $x_2 \leq x_1$.
   (b) The x_i values at t are obtained by integrals, working from $\dot{x}_i$.
4. For every $t \in I$ that is not the right endpoint of I, the following is true about $w(t)$: If $x_1 = x_2$ then *collided* = *true*.

Thus, we only consider executions in which the platoons do not bypass each other. The *collided* variable just keeps track of the first occurrence of a collision. This will be used in our statement of the correctness property below—we only want to assert what happens the first time a collision occurs.

Safety Condition. We consider the following safety condition on states of *Platoons*:

1. (Safety) If $x_1 = x_2$ and *collided* = *false*, then $\dot{x}_2 \leq \dot{x}_1 + v_{\text{allow}}$.

Note that this condition is formulated as an invariant assertion.

Let *Safe-Platoons* be the same as *Platoons* except that all the states are restricted to satisfy the safety condition. We will use *Safe-Platoons* as a correctness specification. It says that under all circumstances, the system guarantees that if the platoons ever collide, then the first time they do so, their relative velocity is no more than v_{allow}.

Implementation Structure. For implementations, we consider composed systems consisting of a piece modeling the real world, plus two pieces modeling controllers for the two cars. The real world model is like the *Platoons* automaton, except that the velocities of the two cars are normally controlled by acceleration variables set by two separate controllers. However, once a collision occurs, we uncouple the velocities from the controllers. This corresponds to allowing arbitrary behavior after the first collision.

Define *Controlled-Platoons* to be the same as *Platoons*, except for the following changes. *Controlled-Platoons* includes new input variables:

$\ddot{x}_i \in \mathbf{R}$, $i \in \{1, 2\}$, initially arbitrary

An I-trajectory w is included among the set of nontrivial trajectories of *Controlled-Platoons* exactly if:

1. w is a trajectory of *Platoons*.
2. If *collided* = *false* in w then $\dot{x}_i$ is obtained by integration from $\ddot{x}_i$, $i \in \{1, 2\}$.

Now we describe *Controller$_1$*. Its input and output variables are:

Input:

    $\dot{x}_i \in \mathbf{R}^{\geq 0}$, $i \in \{1, 2\}$

    $x_i \in \mathbf{R}^{\geq 0}$, $i \in \{1, 2\}$

    collided, a Boolean

Output:

    $\ddot{x}_1$

Controller$_1$ has no external actions.

    Controller$_1$ is an arbitrary hybrid automaton with the given interface, subject only to the following restrictions:

1. In any trajectory, $\ddot{x}_1$ is a bounded, piecewise continuous (and hence integrable) function.
2. In any state,
    (a) $\ddot{x}_1 \geq -a_{min}$.
    (b) If $\dot{x}_1 = 0$ then $\ddot{x}_1 \geq 0$. (It does not ask that the velocity go negative.)

    The interface of *Controller*$_2$ is analogous. Its input and output variables are:

Input:

    $\dot{x}_i \in \mathbf{R}^{\geq 0}$, $i \in \{1, 2\}$

    $x_i \in \mathbf{R}^{\geq 0}$, $i \in \{1, 2\}$

    collided, a Boolean

Output:

    $\ddot{x}_2$

Controller$_2$ has no external actions. *Controller*$_1$ is an arbitrary hybrid automaton with the given interface, subject only to restrictions on $\ddot{x}_2$ and $\dot{x}_2$ as for $\ddot{x}_1$ and $\dot{x}_1$, resp., in *Controller*$_1$ above.

The System. Compose *Controlled-Platoons*, *Controller*$_1$ and *Controller*$_2$ using hybrid automaton composition.

    We are supposed to design an instance of *Controller*$_2$ so that when it is composed in this way with arbitrary *Controller*$_1$, the resulting system satisfies the safety condition. We say that it *implements* the *Safe-Platoons* automaton, using a notion of implementation based on preserving hybrid traces. Here, the hybrid trace includes the output variables, which are the positions and velocities of both platoons plus the collided flag. That is enough to ensure that the safety condition of the spec. carries over to the implementation.

A Controller Implementation. We define a specific *Controller*$_2$, which we call C_2. We describe it very nondeterministically. The interface is already specified. C_2 has no discrete actions, and no internal variables.

    In any state of *Platoons*, define

$$safe\text{-}measure = x_1(t) - x_2(t) - \frac{(\dot{x}_2(t))^2 - (\dot{x}_1(t))^2 - (v_{allow})^2}{2a_{min}}$$

    This says that the distance between the two platoons is great enough to allow platoon 2 to slow down sufficiently before hitting platoon 1, even if platoon

1 decelerates at its fastest possible rate.[4] The initial value of $\ddot{x}_2$ is constrained as follows. In the initial state, if *safe-measure* ≤ 0, then $\ddot{x}_2 = -a_{min}$. (Otherwise, $\ddot{x}_2$ is arbitrary.) Therefore, if the position and velocity parameters are on the boundary of a certain "region", then $\ddot{x}_2$ is guaranteed to be the minimum possible—that is, platoon 2 is guaranteed to be decelerating as fast as possible.

C_2 is an arbitrary *Controller₂*, subject only to the following additional restriction on any *I*-trajectory w:

> If *collided* = *false* in $w(0)$ then for every $t \in I$, the following is true about $w(t)$: If *safe-measure* ≤ 0, then $\ddot{x}_2 = -a_{min}$.

The system we consider, called *Implemented-Platoons* is the composition of *Controlled-Platoons*, an arbitrary *Controller₁*, and C_2.

Correctness. We define a predicate S on states of *Implemented-Platoons*, as follows:

> Predicate S: If *collided* = *false* then *safe-measure* ≥ 0.

Note that C_2 is designed to guarantee explicitly that if S is ever violated, or even if it is in danger of being violated (because equality holds), platoon 2 is decelerating as fast as possible. We claim that this strategy is sufficient to guarantee that S is always true:

Lemma 10. *If S is true in the initial state of the system, then S is true in every reachable state.*

Proof. By induction on the number of steps in a hybrid execution. Initially, the claim is true by assumptions. The only (non-e) discrete steps are *collide* and internal steps of *Controller₁*.

1. *collide*
   The effect of the action ensures that *collided* = *true* in the post-state, which makes S true vacuously.
2. Internal step of *Controller₁*
   This does not affect any of the quantities involved in S.

Now we consider a trajectory w based on a closed interval $[0, t]$. Since a trajectory cannot change *collided*, and S is vacuously true if *collided* = *true*, we only need to consider the case where *collided* = *false* throughout w. We may

---

[4] It can be shown [6] that the region

$$\text{safe-measure} = \max\left\{ x_1 - x_2 - \frac{(\dot{x}_2)^2 - (\dot{x}_1)^2 - (v_{allow})^2}{2a_{min}}, \dot{x}_1 + v_{allow} - \dot{x}_2 \right\}$$

corresponds to the biggest possible safe region. The "relaxation" corresponding to the second argument of the max function says that the relative velocities of the two platoons are already close enough. Invariance has been proven using Theorem 9, part 2.

assume that S is true in $w(0)$. We must show that S is true in $w(t)$. By definition of S, we may assume that *safe-measure* ≥ 0 in state $w(0)$ and must show that this is true in state $w(t)$.

The remaining continuous action arguments are shown in the next section (see Remark 1), using only derivative information.

Lemma 11. *S implies the safety condition.*

Proof. If *collided* $=$ *true*, then S implies the safety condition vacuously. Hence, we must only deal with the case when *collided* $=$ *false*. This involves continuous variables and is shown in the next section (see Remark 2).

5 Platoon Merge Example–Analysis

In this section, we provide a system theoretic proof of the "correctness" of the "abstract controller" for platoon merge proposed in the previous section. Here, *correctness* means that safety is maintained; *abstract controller* means that the control law is specified by a list of (hopefully) minimal constraints. Any actual controller implementation that satisfies these constraints will maintain safety by inclusion. In other words, if we have proved the system correct when it is connected to an *arbitrary* set of behaviors (e.g., which satisfy some constraints or assumptions), then the system will behave correctly when any *particular* behavior within that set is actually connected. Note that this is simply the viewpoint of *worst-case analysis*.

Note: We must only finish the continuous parts missing from Lemmas 10 and 11. From those proofs, we may consider only the case where *collided* $=$ *false* in our continuous analysis below, which yields some simplifications in the resulting S and s.

5.1 The Nominal Case

Recall that the safety property that we wish to verify is

$$S: \qquad \text{If } \Delta x(t) = 0, \text{then } v_2(t) - v_1(t) \leq v_{\text{allow}}.$$

This says that if a collision occurs, it must be the case that the relative platoon velocity is less than the allowable collision velocity.

The following restrictions which were made on trajectories of *Implemented-Platoons* above are relevant in this section:

A_1: $\ddot{x}_i \geq -a_{\min}$, $i = 1, 2$.
A_2: $v_i \geq 0$, $i = 1, 2$.

We also use the following "safety invariant," which is a rewriting of Equation (5) above:

$$s(t) \equiv \Delta x(t) + \frac{v_1^2(t) - v_2^2(t) + v_{\text{allow}}^2}{2a_{\min}} \tag{6}$$

Remark 1. $s(t) \geq 0$ is invariant[5] if the following condition is met:

$$\mathcal{C}: \qquad \ddot{x}_2(t) = -a_{\min} \text{ when } s(t) = 0.$$

Proof. Dropping dependence on t, Equation (6) is equivalent to

$$s \equiv x_1 - x_2 + \frac{\dot{x}_1^2 - \dot{x}_2^2 + v_{\text{allow}}^2}{2a_{\min}},$$

so

$$\dot{s} = \dot{x}_1 - \dot{x}_2 + \frac{\dot{x}_1 \ddot{x}_1 - \dot{x}_2 \ddot{x}_2}{a_{\min}}.$$

But "control law" $\mathcal{C}$ says

$$\dot{s}|_{s \leq 0} = \dot{x}_1 - \dot{x}_2 + \frac{\dot{x}_1 \ddot{x}_1 + \dot{x}_2 a_{\min}}{a_{\min}},$$

$$\geq \dot{x}_1 - \dot{x}_2 + \frac{-\dot{x}_1 a_{\min} + \dot{x}_2 a_{\min}}{a_{\min}} \geq 0,$$

where the last inequality follows from $\mathcal{A}_1$. The conclusion then follows from Theorem 9, Part 2.

Note that the condition $\mathcal{C}$ represents the conditions of the abstract controller mentioned above. Any actual controller (implementation) that satisfies $\mathcal{C}$ will also maintain the invariant $s(t) \geq 0$. It remains to show that the invariant guarantees safety, i.e., it remains to show

Remark 2. $s(t) \geq 0$ implies $\mathcal{S}$.

Proof. First note that due to $\mathcal{A}_2$, $\mathcal{S}$ is automatically satisfied if $v_2 = 0$. Otherwise assume, for contradiction, that S is not met: $\Delta x = 0$ and

$$v_2 > v_{\text{allow}} + v_1.$$

Squaring both sides and again noting $\mathcal{A}_2$ yields the contradiction.

5.2 Perturbed Cases

In this section, we use the tools of Section 3.2 to easily prove safety under various relaxations from the nominal case, including (1) inbound delay, (2) outbound delay, and (3) sensor noise.

Below, we will use approximations of the form

$$\hat{s}(t) \equiv \hat{x}_1(t) - \hat{x}_2(t) + \frac{\hat{v}_1^2(t) - \hat{v}_2^2(t) + v_{\text{allow}}^2}{2a_{\min}}.$$

In this case (and dropping dependence on t)

$$s - \hat{s} \equiv e = (x_1 - \hat{x}_1) - (x_2 - \hat{x}_2) + \frac{(v_1^2 - \hat{v}_1^2) - (v_2^2 - \hat{v}_2^2)}{2a_{\min}}. \tag{7}$$

Note that if $\overline{e}(t) \geq e(t) \geq \underline{e}(t)$, then $s(t) \geq \hat{s}(t) + \underline{e}(t)$.

---

[5] Technically, $\{(x_1, x_2, v_1, v_2) \mid s(x_1, x_2, v_1, v_2) \geq 0\}$ is a positive invariant set.

Inbound Delay. This is the lag time in communicating sensor information from the first to second platoons. Hence, if the *inbound delay* is d then

$$\hat{x}_1(t) = x_1(t - d), \ \hat{v}_1(t) = v_1(t - d),$$
$$\hat{x}_2(t) = x_2(t), \qquad \hat{v}_2(t) = v_2(t - d),$$

in Equation 7 above. A simple calculation, taking into account $\mathcal{A}_{1,2}$, shows that $e(t) \geq \underline{e}(t)$ where

$$\underline{e}(t) \equiv v_1(t-d)\tilde{d} - a_{\min}\tilde{d}^2/2 + \frac{[(v_1(t-d) - a_{\min}\tilde{d})^2 - v_1^2(t-d)]}{2a_{\min}} = 0,$$

$\tilde{d} = \min\{d, v_1(t-d)/a_{\min}\}$, and the last equality follows after some algebra. So, by the arguments in Section 3.2, safety is maintained as long as full-braking is invoked for platoon 2 whenever $\hat{s}(t) \leq 0$.

Outbound Delay. In this case, the acceleration command for platoon 2 at time t, namely $\ddot{x}_2(t)$, is based on sensed readings at time $t - d$ if the *outbound delay* is d. Hence, we have Equation 7 *but with all variables at time $t + d$*. The situation is similar to inbound delay above in that one may compute bounds on $\hat{s}(t + d)$ versus $s(t + d)$ as a function of positions and velocities measured up to time t. For x_1, $\dot{x}_1$ this case is the same as above, and we can simply use

$$\hat{x}_1(t + d) = x_1(t), \qquad \hat{v}_1(t + d) = v_1(t).$$

This case is different than the previous one, though, in the sense that second platoon's controller may take into account the command it has sent over the past d time units in estimating its *own* position and velocity d units hence (assuming no collisions in between, of course). Summarizing, it uses

$$\hat{x}_2(t + d) = x_2(t) + v_2(t)d + \int_0^d (d - \sigma)\ddot{x}_2(t + \sigma)\, d\sigma,$$

$$\hat{v}_2(t + d) = v_2(t) + \int_0^d \ddot{x}_2(t + \sigma)\, d\sigma.$$

Invariance is maintained if we command full-braking at all times t (i.e., set $\ddot{x}_2(t) = -a_{\min}$ for all times t) such that $\hat{s}(t + d) \leq 0$.

Sensor Noise. Here, we measure $\hat{x}_i$ and $\hat{v}_i$. We assume (the same) uniform noise bound on the measurements of all variables, e.g., $|x_1(t) - \hat{x}_1(t)| \leq \delta$ and similarly for the other three measurements. Unequal bounds follow easily. Then, we have $e(t) \geq \underline{e}$ where

$$\underline{e} \equiv -\delta - \delta + \frac{v_1^2 - (v_1 + \delta)^2 - v_2^2 + (v_2 - m)^2}{2a_{\min}} = -2\delta - \frac{2v_1\delta + 2v_2 m + \delta^2 - m^2}{2a_{\min}},$$

where $m = \min(v_2, \delta)$.

Again, safety is maintained as long as full-braking is invoked for platoon 2 whenever $\hat{s}(t) + \underline{e} \leq 0$. If this is too conservative, a real application could get better estimates by considering intervals of measurements and the dynamic relationship of measured variables.

References

1. Panos Antsaklis *et al.*, editors. *Hybrid Systems II.* vol. 999, *Lecture Notes in Computer Science*. Springer, New York, 1995.
2. A. Benveniste and G. Berry, guest editors. *Proc. of the IEEE*, 79(9), 1991. Special Issue on The Synchronous Approach to Reactive and Real-Time Systems.
3. A. Benveniste and P. Le Guernic. Hybrid dynamical systems theory and the signal language. *IEEE Transactions on Automatic Control*, 35(5), 1990.
4. N. P. Bhatia and G. P. Szegö. *Dynamical Systems: Stability Theory and Applications*, vol. 35 of *Lecture Notes in Mathematics*. Springer, Berlin, 1967.
5. J. W. de Bakker *et al.*, editors. *Real-Time: Theory in Practice*, vol. 600 of *Lecture Notes in Computer Science*. Springer, New York, 1991.
6. E. Dolginova and N. Lynch. "Safety Verification for Automated Platoon Manuevers: A Case Study." In O. Maler, ed., *Hybrid and Real-Time Systems (HART '97)*, pp. 154–170, Springer, 1997.
7. J. Frankel *et al.* "Robust Platoon Maneuvers for AVHS," California PATH report, UCB, 1995. Preprint.
8. R. L. Grossman *et al.*, editors. *Hybrid Systems*, vol. 736 of *Lecture Notes in Computer Science*. Springer, New York, 1993. .
9. N. Halbwachs. *Synchronous Programming of Reactive Systems*. Kluwer Academic, Boston 1993.
10. J.H. Hubbard and B.H. West. *Differential Equations: A Dynamical Systems Approach*. Springer, New York, 1990.
11. M. Joseph, editor. *Formal Techniques in Real-Time and Fault-Tolerant Systems*, vol. 331 of *Lecture Notes in Computer Science*. Springer, New York, 1988.
12. N. Lynch. Distributed Algorithms. Morgan Kaufmann, San Francisco, 1996.
13. N. Lynch *et al.* Hybrid I/O Automata. In R. Alur, T. Henzinger, and E. Sontag, editors, *Hybrid Systems III*, pp. 496–510, Lecture Notes in Computer Science, vol. 1066, Springer, 1996.
14. O. Maler, Z. Manna, and A. Pnueli. From timed to hybrid systems. In de Bakker et al. [5], pp. 447–484.
15. Z. Manna and A. Pnueli. Verifying hybrid systems. In Grossman et al. [8], pp. 4–35.
16. Z. Manna and A. Pnueli. *The Temporal Logic of Reactive and Concurrent Systems*. Springer, New York, 1991.
17. A. Pnueli and J. Sifakis, guest editors. *Theoretical Computer Science*, 138(1), 1995. Special Issue on Hybrid Systems.
18. H.L. Smith. *Monotone Dynamical Systems: An Introduction to the Theory of Competitive and Cooperative Systems*. Mathematical Surveys and Monographs, Vol. 41. American Mathematical Society, Providence, RI, 1995.
19. Y.-J. Wei and P.E. Caines. Hierarchical COCOLOG for finite machines. In G. Cohen and J-P. Quadrat, editors, *Proc. 11th INRIA International Conference on the Analysis and Optimization of Systems*, vol. 199 of *Lecture Notes in Control and Information Sciences*, pp. 29–38, New York, 1994. Springer.
20. J. Lygeros, D. Godbole, S. Sastry. A verified hybrid control design for automated vehicles. Preprint.
21. A. Puri and P. Varaiya. Verification of hybrid systems using abstractions. Preprint.

Simulation of Hybrid Systems

Michael S. Branicky* and Sven Erik Mattsson**

Abstract. Hybrid systems—those composed of the interaction of discrete and continuous inputs, outputs, states, and dynamic equations—are an important class of models of complex, real-world phenomena. However, the simulation tools currently available seem to be (1) *ad hoc* retrofitting of existing packages, (2) hastily-built new languages, or (3) specialized software for particular subclasses (e.g., piecewise-constant dynamics). Our goal is to produce fast, high fidelity simulations of (networks of) a very broad class of hybrid systems in a user-friendly environment. In this paper, we first review expertise in the mathematical modeling of hybrid systems, viz. the hybrid dynamical systems of Branicky (HDS). Also, we discuss the object-oriented modeling and simulation of combined discrete/continuous systems using the Omola modeling language and Omsim simulation environment developed over the last eight years at Lund. Leveraging these, we are led to our main contribution: a general set of hybrid systems model classes which encompass HDS and hence several other models popularized in the literature that combine finite automata and discrete event systems with ordinary differential (ODEs) and differential algebraic equations (DAEs). These Omola model classes may be viewed as "templates" or "macros" for quick and easy entering of hybrid systems for subsequent analysis and numerically-sophisticated simulation using Omsim.

1 Introduction

Colloquially, a hybrid system has come to mean a system which is an amalgamation of continuous and discrete inputs, outputs, states, and dynamic equations. See Figure 1. Hybrid systems are those in which a melding of two worlds—the analog and the digital—exists, and they are intertwined to the extent that a "one-world" description is not desired, not tractable, or not possible. Such systems seem to naturally arise in a variety of applications due to autonomous or controlled phenomena.

In the autonomous case, the system evolution itself may fall naturally into A Finite number of different phases (a.k.a. modes or epochs), between which abrupt changes in continuous dynamics (switching) or continuous states (jumps or resets) occur. In the controlled case, a simple finite state machine may be used to regulate a physical process, such as may arise even in a simple thermostat.

* Dept. of Electrical Eng. and Applied Physics, Case Western Reserve U., 10900 Euclid Ave., Glennan 515B, Cleveland, OH 44106-7221 USA. branicky@eeap.cwru.edu
** Dept. of Automatic Control, Lund Institute of Technology, PO Box 118, S-221 00, Lund, SWEDEN. svenerik@control.lth.se

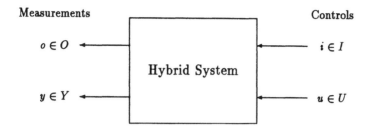

Fig. 1. Hybrid Control System.

In more complicated situations, a mixture of autonomous and controlled phenomena may be present. See Figure 1. Alternatively, a hybrid dichotomy may be invoked as a means of dealing with complexity through abstraction, e.g., using logic to switch among various continuous controllers (each with predictable behavior when used alone) in order to accomplish more global objectives, as in mode-switched aircraft. Of course, such abstractions may occur multiple times, leading to layered or hierarchical control schemes seen in robotics and communication networks.

We have already mentioned some real-world examples of hybrid systems. Application areas include power electronics (state-dependent circuit switching), motion control (disk drives, transmissions, stepper motors, position encoders), robotics (constrained robots, flexible manufacturing, interacting agents), intelligent transportation systems (automated highway systems, personal rapid transit), and aerospace (mode-switched flight, vehicle management systems, air traffic control). The reader may imagine more or consult the literature [8, 12, 3, 1].

Researchers in hybrid systems have been trying to build a theory for such systems in recent years. However, it is still a challenge to even accurately simulate them because of the sophistication needed to do mixed continuous/discrete simulation in a timely manner. Since these are important areas and examples, we begin here to develop a framework and a collection of computer tools to meet the hybrid systems simulation challenge.

Simulation is not a means unto itself, though, but a means to understanding. Backtrack a moment and consider a slightly more refined definition of a hybrid system which consists of a finite automaton or discrete-event system "supervising" the action of a collection of ODEs or DAEs by giving commands for when to switch between them, and how to update variables upon switching. See Figure 3. It is an instantiation of the digitally-regulated plant and two-layer control schemes mentioned above. However, it has been shown that even low-dimensional systems of this type possess rich behavioral possibilities, including the power of universal computation in as little as three dimensions [8]. Further, most engineering insight and tools have been developed for "one-world" scenarios.

Thus, with hybrid systems, we are also faced with low intuition and high complexity. In such a situation, we believe that simulation is an important tool

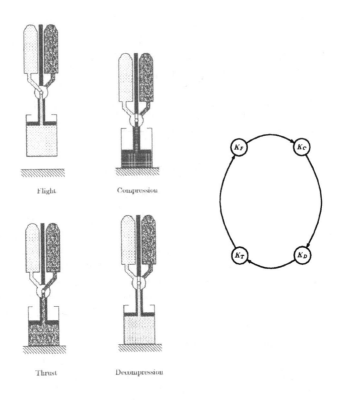

Fig. 2. Raibert's hopping robot: dynamic phases and controller.

to gaining intuition about, and a stepping stone to the automatic analysis of, hybrid systems. Further, we believe that many of the simulation tools currently available are lacking in some respect. Without classifying tools, they seem fall into one of the following three categories: (1) *ad hoc* retro-fitting of existing "one-world" packages, (2) hastily-built new languages, or (3) specialized software for particular subclasses (e.g., piecewise-constant dynamics). Therefore, it is the goal of this research to *produce fast, high fidelity simulations of (networks of) a very broad class of hybrid systems in a user-friendly environment.*

Our approach builds on a modeling language and simulation package, Omola and Omsim resp., designed from inception to handle mixed discrete/continuous simulation. Omola/Omsim uses a sophisticated mix of symbolic equation manipulation, solution approximation, zero-finding, and ODE/DAE solvers to accurately perform such mixed simulations. Omola/Omsim has been under research and development—and test through numerous projects, theses, and users—since 1989 in the CACE group in the Department of Automatic Control at Lund Institute of Technology. In this work, we have added a library of hybrid sys-

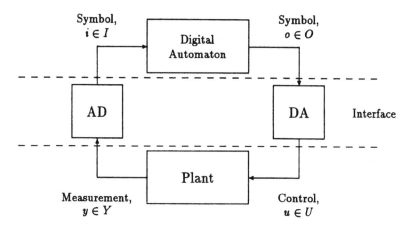

Fig. 3. Hybrid System.

tems *model classes*, which may be thought of as a set of templates or "macros," designed for the quick specification and simulation of a broad class of hybrid systems, viz. Branicky's hybrid dynamical systems (HDS). In previous work [8], HDS were shown explicitly to encompass various hybrid phenomena as well as six popular models of hybrid systems previously proposed in the literature [4, 6, 10, 13, 16, 17]. Given this, our macros may be used to easily simulate these systems as well. Indeed, we give explicit *model subclasses* suited to the purpose of simulating several interesting subclasses of hybrid systems, including those with autonomous switching [8], that due to Brockett [10], and a new one due to Artstein [5].

The paper is organized as follows. In the next section, we review HDS and present some examples used throughout. In Section 3, we discuss Omola and Omsim, introducing some of their philosophy, syntax, and capabilities. Section 4 presents our main contributions: two different instantiations of HDS model classes, as well as the model subclasses and examples mentioned above. Section 5 gives conclusions.

2 Hybrid Dynamical Systems

2.1 Background and Motivation

Hybrid systems involve both continuous-valued and discrete variables. Their evolution is given by equations of motion that generally depend on both. In turn these equations contain mixtures of logic, discrete-valued or *digital* dynamics, and continuous-variable or *analog* dynamics. The continuous dynamics of such systems may be continuous-time, discrete-time, or mixed (sampled-data), but is generally given by differential equations. The discrete-variable dynamics of hybrid systems is generally governed by a *digital automaton*, or input-output transition system with a countable number of states. The continuous and discrete dynamics interact at "event" or "trigger" times when the continuous state hits certain prescribed sets in the continuous state space. See Figure 3. *Hybrid control systems* are control systems that involve both continuous and discrete dynamics and continuous and discrete controls. The continuous dynamics of such a system is usually modeled by a controlled vector field or difference equation. Its hybrid nature is expressed by a dependence on some discrete phenomena, corresponding to discrete states, dynamics, and controls. The result is a system as in Figure 1.

In this paper, our focus is on the case of hybrid systems where the continuous dynamics is modeled by a differential equation[3]

$$\dot{x}(t) = \xi(t), \qquad t \geq 0. \tag{1}$$

Here, $x(t)$ is the *continuous component* of the state, taking values in some subset of a Euclidean space. $\xi(t)$ is a *controlled vector field* that generally depends on $x(t)$, the *continuous component* $u(t)$ of the control policy, and the aforementioned discrete phenomena. We have classified the discrete phenomena generally considered into four types [9]:

1. autonomous switching, where the vector field $\xi(\cdot)$ changes discontinuously when the state $x(\cdot)$ hits certain "boundaries";
2. autonomous impulses, where $x(\cdot)$ jumps discontinuously on hitting prescribed regions of the state space;
3. controlled switching, where $\xi(\cdot)$ changes abruptly in response to a control command; and
4. controlled impulses, where $x(\cdot)$ changes discontinuously in response to a control command.

Two examples that we will use throughout are

Example 1 (Hysteresis). Consider a system with hysteresis: $\dot{x} = H(x)$, where H is shown in Figure 4.

Note that this system is not just a differential equation whose right-hand side is piecewise continuous. There is "memory" in the system, which affects the vector field's value. Indeed, the system naturally has a finite automaton associated with the function H, as shown in Figure 5.

Example 2 (Planar Autonomous Switching).

$$\dot{x}(t) = M_{q(t)}x(t), \qquad x(t) \notin A_{q(t)}, \tag{2}$$
$$q(t^+) = \nu(x(t), q(t)), \qquad x(t) \in A_{q(t)} \tag{3}$$

where $q \in \{1, 2, \ldots, N\}$, $M_q \in R^{2 \times 2}$, and $A_q \subset \mathbf{R}^2$ for each q.

A particular instantiation is shown in Figure 6.

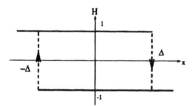

Fig. 4. Hysteresis Function.

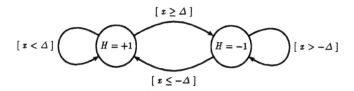

Fig. 5. Finite Automaton Associated with Hysteresis Function.

We also briefly describe two nice classes of hybrid systems from the literature. For pedagogic reasons, we have simplified the models by making them autonomous and changed notation.

Example 3 (Brockett's Model).

$$\dot{x} = f(x, p, z), \tag{4}$$
$$\dot{p} = r(x, p, z), \tag{5}$$
$$z\lceil p \rceil = \nu(x, p, z\lfloor p \rfloor). \tag{6}$$

where $x(t) \in X \subset \mathbf{R}^n$, $p(t) \in \mathbf{R}$, and the *rate equation* r is nonnegative for all arguments.

Brockett has mixed continuous and "symbolic" controls by the inclusion of the special *counter* variable p. The last equation means that z is updated whenever p passes through integer values.

Example 4 (Artstein's Model). Artstein's model consists of a finite number, N, of modules each of which executes its own dynamics, $\dot{x} = f_q(x)$ for a given time T_q. After timeout, execution switches to a different module depending on whether a test function, $\psi_q(x)$ is non-negative or not. In equations, one might write

$$[\dot{x}(t), \dot{\tau}(t)]^T = [f_{q(t)}(x(t)), 1]^T, \qquad 0 \leq \tau \leq T_{q(t)},$$
$$q(t^+) = \begin{cases} G_p(q(t)), & \psi_q(t)(x(t)) \geq 0, \\ G_n(q(t)), & \psi_q(t)(x(t)) < 0. \end{cases}, \tau = T_{q(t)},$$
$$\tau(t^+) = 0, \qquad \tau = T_{q(t)}.$$

where $x(t) \in X \subset \mathbf{R}^n$, and $q(t)$, $G_p(q(t))$, and $G_n(q(t)) \in \{1, 2, \ldots, N\}$.

---

[3] Please refer to [8] for background, references, and details.

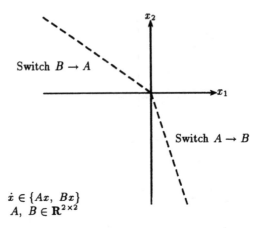

Fig. 6. Example planar switching rule; switches occur when state hits dotted lines.

2.2 A Mathematical Model

We now introduce a mathematical model of hybrid systems that is general enough to

- cover significant phenomena found in real-world examples and
- encompass other reasonable models,

but is specific enough

- to build on previous insight and results
- to be able to derive new theory.

We build on the much-studied notion of dynamical system. Briefly, a *dynamical system* [14] is a system

$$\Sigma = [X, \Gamma, \phi],$$

where X is an arbitrary topological space, the *state space* of Σ. The *transition semigroup* Γ is a topological semigroup with identity. The *extended transition map* $\phi : X \times \Gamma \to X$ is a continuous function satisfying the identity and semigroup properties [15]. We will also denote by dynamical system the system

$$\Sigma = [X, \Gamma, f],$$

where X and Γ are as above, but the *transition function* f is the *generator* of the extended transition function ϕ.

In this paper, we restrict our attention to the case where X is a subset of $\mathbf{R}^n$ for some $n \in \mathbf{N}$, $\Gamma = \mathbf{R}_+$, and the dynamics are given by vector fields: $\dot{x} = f(x)$.

Example 5. Recall a linear system, $\dot{x} = Ax$, has $\phi(x, t) = e^{At}x$.

Briefly, a hybrid dynamical system is an indexed collection of dynamical systems along with some map for "jumping" among them (switching dynamical system and/or resetting the state). This jumping occurs whenever the state satisfies certain conditions, given by its membership in a specified subset of the state space. Hence, the entire system can be thought of as a sequential patching together of dynamical systems with initial and final states, the jumps performing a reset to a (generally different) initial state of a (generally different) dynamical system whenever a final state is reached.

Formally, a *controlled hybrid dynamical system (CHDS)* is a system $H_c = [Q, \Sigma, \mathbf{A}, \mathbf{G}, \mathbf{C}, \mathbf{F}]$, with constituent parts as follows.

- $Q \subset \mathbf{N}$ is the set of *index* or *discrete states*.
- $\Sigma = \{\Sigma_q\}_{q \in Q}$ is the collection of controlled dynamical systems, where each

$$\Sigma_q = [X_q, \mathbf{R}_+, f_q, U_q, Y_q]$$

  is a controlled dynamical system. Here, the $X_q \subset \mathbf{R}^{d_q}$, $d_q \in \mathbf{N}$, are the *continuous state spaces* and the vector fields $f_q : X_q \times U_q \to \mathbf{R}^{d_q}$ represent the (controlled) *continuous dynamics*. $U_q \subset \mathbf{R}^{m_q}$ and $Y_q \subset \mathbf{R}^{p_q}$ are the *input* and *output spaces*, resp., with m_q, $p_q \in \mathbf{N}$.
- $\mathbf{A} = \{A_q\}_{q \in Q}$, $A_q \subset X_q$ for each $q \in Q$, is the collection of *autonomous jump sets*.
- $\mathbf{G} = \{G_q\}_{q \in Q}$, where $G_q : A_q \to S$ is the *autonomous jump transition map*, said to represent the *discrete dynamics*.
- $\mathbf{C} = \{C_q\}_{q \in Q}$, $C_q \subset X_q$, is the collection of *controlled jump sets*.
- $\mathbf{F} = \{F_q\}_{q \in Q}$, where $F_q : C_q \to 2^S$, is the collection of *controlled jump destination maps*.

Thus, $S = \bigcup_{q \in Q} X_q \times \{q\}$ is the *hybrid state space* of H_c. Roughly, the dynamics of H_c are as follows. The system is assumed to start in some hybrid state in $S \backslash A$, say $s_0 = (x_0, q_0)$. It evolves according to $f_{q_0}(\cdot, u)$ until the state enters—if ever—either A_{q_0} or C_{q_0} at the point $s_1^- = (x_1^-, q_0)$. If it enters A_{q_0}, then it *must* be transferred according to transition map $G_{q_0}(x_1^-)$. If it enters C_{q_0}, then we *may* choose to jump and, if so, we may choose the destination to be any point in $F_{q_0}(x_1^-)$. Either way, we arrive at a point $s_1 = (x_1, q_1)$ from which the process continues. See Figure 7.

The case where the sets U_q, $\mathbf{C}$, and $\mathbf{F}$ above are empty is simply a *hybrid dynamical system (HDS)*: $H = [Q, \Sigma, \mathbf{A}, \mathbf{G}]$. In equations, it might look as follows:

$$\dot{x}(t) = f(x(t), q(t)), \ x(t) \notin A_{q(t)}$$
$$\left.\begin{array}{l} q(t^+) = G_q(x(t), q(t)) \\ x(t^+) = G_x(x(t), q(t)) \end{array}\right\}, \ x(t) \in A_{q(t)}$$

Note: The case of GHDS with $|Q|$ finite is a coupling of finite automata and differential equations and includes several previously posed hybrid systems models [4, 6, 10, 13, 16, 17], systems with impulse effect [7], and hybrid automata [11]. For more details, refer to [8].

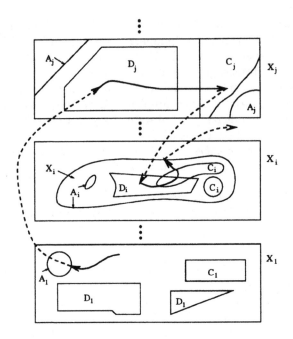

Fig. 7. Example dynamics of controlled hybrid dynamical system.

3 Omola and Omsim

3.1 Omola

Omola stands for "Object-oriented Modeling Language." It has been developed in the CACE group of the Dept. of Automatic Control at the Lund Institute of Technology. Development started in 1989. A recent, comprehensive description may be found in [2], which is the definitive reference for this summary.

Omola is a language for describing dynamic models. It is

- user-oriented, that is, it is intended that engineers specify models in Omola, not that computer scientists program them.
- high-level and textual.
- supports reuse, through an object-oriented philosophy.
- directly usable in simulation and analysis tools, e.g., Omsim.

Omola supports mixed continuous evolution and discrete events.

Omola has an object-oriented modeling philosophy. Models are to be perceived as *declarative*, encoding facts and relations. They are not thought of as procedures with inputs, outputs, and flow of information. Omola also supports acausal physical models. Thus,

$$
\begin{aligned}
R \times I &= V, \\
R &= V/I, \\
V/R &= I,
\end{aligned}
\tag{7}
$$

are all equally valid descriptions of a resistor.

Omola supports *modularity*. An Omola model encapsulates state and behavior much like an object in C++ encapsulates data and procedures.

Omola supports *abstract interfaces*, allowing one to use a model (as part of a bigger one) without knowing all details about its definition. However, there is no strict information hiding in Omola; access to all internal variables is always possible.

It is the view of Omola that *models are classes*. That is, *models are descriptions of a system type, not a representation of a particular system*. Going back to our resistor example, any one of the equations in (7) is a description of a system type, viz. **Resistor**. A particular resistor would be an instantiation of this model that must add the fact that, for example, $R = 2k\Omega$. Note that before a model can be simulated, all variables must be fully instantiated (this is checked automatically by Omsim).

Omola supports model *inheritance* as a mechanism for information sharing and reuse. We note that inherited attributes may be selectively over-ridden. Also, strictly speaking, Omola only supports single inheritance. However, a composite model may be composed of two parts, each of which inherits structure from other models. We call this *indirect inheritance* and will see an example below.

An inheritance diagram for an electric component library appears in Figure 8. There, **Class** and **Model** are basic Omola classes, which the user may think of as "empty slots." Omola has several predefined terminal classes, including **SimpleTerminal** for connecting *across* or *effort* variables like voltage; **ZeroSumTerminal** for *through* or *flow* variables like current; and **RecordTerminal** which consists of several terminals, in order to represent an aggregate of interaction variables.

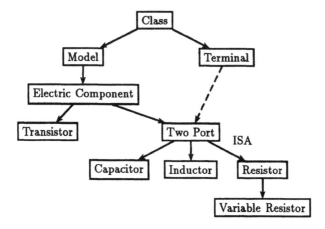

Fig. 8. Class hierarchy for electrical components.

Example 6 (Two Port). The `TwoPort` class in Figure 8 might include as subclasses two `RecordTerminal`'s, each composed of a `SimpleTerminal` (for V1 and V2) and a `ZeroSumTerminal` (for I1 and I2).

The former example uses the aforementioned mechanism of indirect inheritance since the `TwoPort` inherits both from the `ElectricComponent` class (as a subclass) and some `Terminal` classes (used as subcomponents), even though, strictly speaking, multiple inheritance has not been invoked.

Here is a simple fragment of Omola code for a resistor viewed as a two-port device (see Figure 8).

Omola 1 (Resistor Example)

```
Resistor ISA TwoPort WITH
  R ISA Parameter WITH
    default := 1.0;
  END;

  V1 - V2 = R * (I1 - I2);
  I1 = I2;
END;
```

Reserved words are in all capitals. Inheritance is accomplished through the `ISA` (and `ISAN`) command, refinements are given after `WITH`. The reader may guess from this that `Parameter` is an Omola base class consisting of a real value plus a default value. The symbol `:=` is used to denoted equality with causality specified, viz. the left-hand side is dependent on the right-hand side. The equality sign denotes an acausal relation. The relations should be self-explanatory.

3.2 Omsim

Omsim stands for "Omola Simulation" package. Again, our discussion is brief, with the reader directed to [2] for more details. Omsim

- provides a graphical model editor, used for input, visualization, and editing of models.
- compiles Omola to simulation code, performing consistency checks, sorting equations, determining causality, etc., and solving initialization problems.
- provides simulation tools, including plotters, access windows for changing parameters and initial conditions; output routines for exporting to files, printers, or Matlab; a variety of DAE and ODE solvers.
- may be controlled using "ocl" (Omsim Command Language) files instead of point-and-click menus for easy repetition of experiments or reuse of simulation environments.

Continuous Dynamics. Omsim can handle continuous-time dynamics given by general DAEs:

$$\dot{x} = f(x, y, t), \tag{8}$$
$$0 = g(x, y, t). \tag{9}$$

with the usual semantics from mathematics. It also allows $g = g(\dot{x}, x, t)$. Omsim does sophisticated pre-processing of models in compiling them into simulation code, including symbolic manipulation. Very roughly, the procedure is as follows.

1. Divide variables (into four classes of increasing complexity from constants, parameters, and discrete (defined below), to continuous-time varying).
2. Divide equations (according to the most complex of the four variable classes appearing therein).
3. Check consistency (are all variables defined, of correct type, etc.)
4. Sort equations into a block-lower triangular form. This includes determining causality (necessary not for modeling but for simulation!), eliminating derivatives, dividing blocks into the four classes, performing index reduction on any DAEs, determining which solver should be used (if not prescribed by the user), and outputting equations into a form required for the chosen DAE/ODE solver.

Discrete Events. Here, we discuss mostly Omola syntax for discrete events, postponing some semantics to the next section. Please see [2] for details. The fragment

```
x TYPE DISCRETE Real;
```

means that the value of x changes only at discrete times, i.e., $\dot{x} = 0$. Integers and booleans are automatically DISCRETEs.

Events, their conditions, and their side effects are specified using a template as follows:

```
<event name> ISAN Event WITH
  CONDITION := <logical expression>;
  <body of actions>
END;
```

Here, the logical expression can depend on a continuous variable, e.g., (y > 0), for y TYPE Real; a discrete variable, e.g., (i==1) for i TYPE Integer; or be edge-triggered, e.g., ^(y > 0). The latter condition is true only when y first becomes positive; it will not be true again until y becomes nonpositive and then positive again. The body of actions may, for example, reset variables based on other variables' or their own values. In the later case, the NEW operator is used to distinguish previous from new values of the variable. For example,

```
NEW(x) + x = 0;
```

will change the sign of x upon the event's firing. Events may also be scheduled to occur after some delay; scheduled events may be descheduled:

```
schedule(EventName, Delay);
deschedule(EventName);
```

Finally, event propagation can be specified with the following self-evident template:

```
WHEN <condition> [CAUSE <event list>]
  [DO <actions>] END;
```

The following is Omola code for the automaton of Figure 9.

Omola 2 (Finite State Automaton)

```
Server ISA Model WITH
  State TYPE DISCRETE (Passive, Active)    % textual names are allowed
  Start, Ready, Init ISAN Event;

transitions:
  WHEN State=='Passive AND Start DO        % they are referenced with '
    NEW(State) := 'Active;
  END;
  WHEN State=='Active AND Ready DO
    NEW(State) := 'Passive;
  END;

initialization:
  WHEN Init DO
    NEW(State) := 'Passive;
  END;
END;
```

The headings **transitions** and **initialization** are just that; they are arbitrary and do not affect the equations. Everything on a line after a % is a comment.

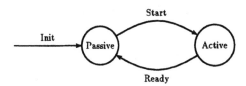

Fig. 9. Example finite state machine.

Detecting State-Dependent Events. We have mentioned that Omsim uses sophisticated techniques for dealing with mixed continuous/discrete events. The full discussion is quite involved and may be found in [2, pp. 200–208]. We try to give the reader a brief hint here. Those not interested in numerical details, however, may skip ahead to the next section.

First a word about ODE/DAE solvers. If there are no implicit equations, RKF45 is used, else an implicit Runge-Kutta scheme, Radau5, is used. For general DAEs, DASSL is used. DOPRI(4)5 is also available.

All boolean event conditions which refer to values of continuous variables are translated so that they occur on zero crossings, e.g., $x > xmax$ becomes $x - xmax$. Compound conditions are dealt with by introducing multiple event conditions.

Example 7. (**x>xmax**) **AND** (**y>ymax**) is not replaced by the non-differentiable **min(x-xmax,y-ymax)**. Instead, it is replaced by two event conditions.

We assume that purely discrete event conditions can be dealt with effectively (see [2] for details). However, continuous-time event conditions must be evaluated along with the continuous time solution. The root-finding program DASSRT is used in conjunction with DASSL to find the zero-crossings associated with these. An algorithm by Brankin et al., based on ALEVNT (herein, "A"), is used with Radau5. This algorithm is used with integration schemes that provide solutions between steps, so-called "dense output." This is done by returning a polynomial interpolation that is valid over the next interval. Algorithm A uses Sturm sequences to determine if a zero is present in the interval. If yes, Sturm sequences and bisection are used to locate the subinterval of the first root. Then, standard bisection and the secant algorithm are used to locate the root precisely. This will work well if the event functions are linear in the unknown variables. However, since Omsim allows nonlinear event functions, more must be done. Briefly, in general Omsim uses Algorithm A to approximately locate the event based on the approximate event function (evaluated using the approximated solution) and then iterates using bisection or secant based on the event function itself.

4 Simulating HDS

4.1 Two Approaches

We first discuss simulating hybrid dynamical systems (HDS) using Omsim, saving the more general case of Controlled HDS (CHDS) for later. There are two main approaches for representing HDS: distributed state and global state.

In the *distributed state* approach, one views the HDS as consisting of N different dynamic systems, each of which always exists and is either "active" (controlling the dynamics) or "inactive." Here, the state of the simulation is given by the concatenation of the states of each of the N systems, $[_1x, \ldots, _Nx]^T$ plus an integer, q, representing the currently active one. If the ith system is active, its dynamics is given by $_i\dot{x} = f_i(_ix)$, and it becomes inactive when $_ix$ hits A_i; if it is inactive, its state does not change (which is represented by setting its vector field to zero in that case), and it becomes active whenever $G(x, q) = (_i\xi, i)$. See Figure 10(a).

In the *global state* approach, we let $q(t)$ denote the active system and dynamically redefine the vector field to be given by $f_{q(t)}$, the test set by $A_{q(t)}$, and the transition map by $G_{q(t)}$. Here, we use one global continuous state, $x(t)$, which must be given a size equal to the largest dimension of the $_qx$. See Figure 10(b).

4.2 Distributed State HDS

We now build up a distributed state HDS model class, piece by piece,. We start with a dynamic system (DS) given by an ODE, represented in Omola 3.

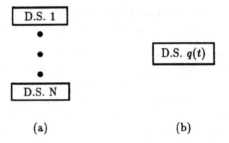

Fig. 10. Two approaches of storing state: (a) distributed, (b) global.

Omola 3 (DS class)

```
DS ISA Model WITH

parameters:
  d TYPE Integer;        % model order
  fx TYPE Column [d];

state:
  x TYPE Column [d];

behavior:
  x' = fx;
END;
```

The prime denotes derivation. Hence, this model simply says that the state has dimension **d** and the dynamics are given by a d-dimensional vector field **fx**. Hence, $\dot{x} = f(x)$, $x \in \mathbf{R}^d$.[4]

Now, we add the capability of switching the ODE between **Active** and **Inactive** modes. Recall that when in the inactive mode, the vector field is set to zero.

Omola 4 (Switched DS class)

```
SwitchedDS ISA DS WITH
variables:
  A TYPE Real;
  mode TYPE DISCRETE (Active, Inactive);
  Init, Restart ISAN EventInput;
  AutoJump ISAN EventOutput;
  f TYPE Column [d];

equations:
  fx = IF mode=='Inactive THEN 0.0 ELSE f;
```

---

[4] Columns, Rows, and Matrixs are only real-valued; indexing conventions are those widely used, viz. as in Matlab.

```
events:
  WHEN mode=='Active and A >= 0 CAUSE AutoJump DO
    NEW(mode) := 'Inactive;
  END;
  WHEN Restart DO
    NEW(mode) := 'Active;
  END;
END;
```

Note we have encoded $x \in A$ by a real value A's (whose functional form will be specified in instantiated models) being nonnegative.

What we would want now is to have a hybrid model that is a vector of SwitchedDS's, with size = N. For example,

Omola 5 (Distributed-State HS)

```
HybridSystem ISA Model WITH
  N, Q TYPE Integer;      % number of discrete states, active state
  Sigma TYPE SwitchedDS Column [N];
END;
```

Unfortunately, Omola does not currently support vectors of models—though this capability is being actively pursued. Of course, one can define templates—just once, then stored in a library—for each size of hybrid system. One can save some typing by doing this in an inductive manner using inheritance. However, below is an explicit example of a hybrid system with two discrete states.

Omola 6 (Two Distributed-State HS)

```
HybridSystem2 ISA Model WITH
  Q,d TYPE Integer;         % discrete state, cont. state's dim.
  x, Gx1, Gx2 TYPE Column[d]; % continuous states and resets

components:
  Q1, Q2 ISA SwitchedDS;

equations:
  x = IF Q==1 THEN Q1.x ELSE Q2.x;

  WHEN Q1.AutoJump CAUSE Q2.Restart DO
    new(Q2.x) := Gx1; END;
  WHEN Q2.AutoJump CAUSE Q1.Restart DO
    new(Q1.x) := Gx2; END;
END;
```

Of course, the case for higher N is a little more complicated, but we think the reader can figure out the general case readily.

We now give an Omola model of our hysteresis example using the above model classes.

Omola 7 (Hysteresis Example)

```
Mode1 ISA SwitchedDS WITH
  Delta ISA Parameter WITH default := 0.1; END;
  d = 1;
  f = 1;
  A = x-Delta;
END;

Mode2 ISA SwitchedDS WITH
  Delta ISA Parameter WITH default := 0.1; END;
  d = 1;
  f = -1;
  A = -x-Delta;
END;

Hysteresis ISA HybridSystem2 WITH
  d = 1;
  Q1 ISA Mode1;
  Q2 ISA Mode2;

  Gx1 := Q1.x;
  Gx2 := Q2.x;
END;
```

Each mode has dimension one, with dynamics given by either plus or minus one. Switching occurs from **Mode1** to **Mode2** whenever $x \geq \Delta$, which is equivalent to whenever $-x - \Delta \geq 0$. Here, we have specified Δ to be a parameter, **Delta**, with a default value of 0.1. In Omsim, we might look at simulation results with different values of the parameter, which could be changed using the aforementioned access windows. Finally, note that the reset maps are the identity since only the dynamics, and not the continuous state, is reset upon changing modes.

4.3 Global State HDS

Here is a global state model class of HDS. It parallels the equations of Section 2 closely enough that the reader should be able to follow the code, perhaps using the comments.

Omola 8 (Global State HS)

```
HDS ISA Model WITH

states:
  d TYPE Integer;          % max dim. of constituent state spaces
  x TYPE Column [d];       % continuous state
  N TYPE Integer;          % number of discrete states
  q TYPE DISCRETE Integer; % discrete state
```

```
continuous_dynamics:
  f TYPE Matrix [d,N];   % vector fields

  x' = f[1..d,q];

discrete_transitions:
  % autonomous switching functions
  Ajump TYPE Row [N];

  % autonomous switching map, discrete and continuous parts
  Gq TYPE Row [N];
  Gx TYPE Matrix [d, N];
  ModeChange ISAN Event;

  WHEN Ajump[q] >= 0 CAUSE ModeChange DO
    new(q) := Gq[q];
    new(x) := Gx[1..d,q];
  END;
END;
```

Note that we have added a ModeChange event. This was done for fun and could be used by Omsim to count events or change plotter colors (or execute some other actions) upon mode changes.

Now here is an Omola model of our hysteresis example using the HDS model classes.

Omola 9 (Hysteresis Example)

```
Hysteresis ISA HDS WITH
  Delta ISA Parameter WITH default := 0.1; END;
  N = 2;
  d = 1;
  f[1,1] = 1;
  f[1,2] = -1;
  Ajump[1] = x - Delta;
  Ajump[2] = -x - Delta;
  Gq[1] = 2;
  Gq[2] = 1;
  Gx[1,1] = x;
  Gx[1,2] = x;
END;
```

Again, note that the reset maps are the identity.

For the remainder of this paper, we will talk only of the global state model class HDS above and subclasses thereof.

4.4 Subclasses and Examples

In this section we show how several classes of hybrid systems models may be easily recovered as subclasses of the global state HDS above. An autonomous switched hybrid system is one where the continuous state does not change at autonomous jump times, that is, where the projection of the reset map G onto the continuous state is the identity: $G_x(x, q) = x$ for each discrete state q.

Omola 10 (Autonomous-switched HS)

```
AutoSwitch ISA HDS WITH
  Gx=x*ones(1,N);
END;
```

Here is a special case of an HDS, the model due to Zvi Artstein (see [5] and Example 4), which can naturally be represented as a subclass of HDS:

Omola 11 (Artstein's HS)

```
Artstein ISA HDS WITH
  dim TYPE Integer;
  T TYPE Row [N];

  d = dim + 1;

  f[d,1..N] = ones(1,N);

  Ajump = x[d]*ones(1,N) - T;

  Gx[1..d-1,1..N] = x[1..d-1]*ones(1,N);
  Gx[d,1..N] = zeros(1,N);
END;
```

Note that if the state has dimension dim, then the model has one more dimension, with x[d] representing the timer value τ in Example 4. The vector T denotes the vector of timeout values, $[T_1, \ldots, T_N]^T$. As expected, jumps occur whenever the timer, x[d] is greater than or equal to the timeout value. Note also that this variable is reset to zero—and the continuous state otherwise does not jump—upon timeout, no matter what the discrete state.

Brockett's model (see [10] and Example 3) may also be recovered as a subclass of the HDS model class:

Omola 12 (Brockett's HS)

```
Brockett ISA HDS WITH
  dim TYPE Integer;
  p, pfrac TYPE Real;          % p and its fractional part
  r TYPE Row [N];
  z TYPE DISCRETE Integer;

  d = dim + 2;

  p = x[d-1];
  pfrac = x[d];
  z = q;
```

```
f[d-1,1..N] = 0;
f[d,1..N] = r;

Ajump = x[d]*ones(1,N) - ones(1,N);

Gx[1..d-2,1..N] = x[1..d-2]*ones(1,N);
Gx[d-1,1..N] = (x[d-1]+1)*ones(1,N);
Gx[d,1..N] = zeros(1,N);
END;
```

Note that if the state has dimension **dim**, then the model has two more dimensions, with **x[d-1]**, **x[d]** now representing the counter, p, and its fractional part, resp. Note, however, that here jumps occur whenever the counter's fractional part, **x[d]**, is equal to one (and not at integer points); this is compensated for by resetting it to zero at jump times, yielding an equivalent description. Finally, note the portion of the continuous state corresponding to Brockett's original x, **x[1..d-2]** does not jump.

Below is a model class for switching among two linear systems in the plane. Note that it is autonomous switching, so that we can make it a subclass of **AutoSwitch**. Also note that the switching surfaces, given by the **Ajump** vector (inherited from **HDS** through **AutoSwitch**), are still unspecified.

Omola 13 (Switched Planar HDS)

```
Switcher ISA AutoSwitch WITH
  N=2;   d=2;
  A TYPE MATRIX [2, 2] := [1, -100; 10, 1];
  B TYPE MATRIX [2, 2] := [1, 10; -100, 1];

  f[1..2,1] = A*x;
  f[1..2,2] = B*x;

  Gq[1] = 2;
  Gq[2] = 1;
END;
```

Using the above template, we can now investigate the effect of different switching rules for the same underlying hybrid system. Here are two particular examples followed by a special model discussed below.

Omola 14 (Two Switching Systems)

```
SwitchQuadrant ISA Switcher WITH
  Ajump[1] = IF (x[1]>=0 AND x[2]<=0) THEN 1 ELSE -1;
  Ajump[2] = IF (x[1]<0 AND x[2]>=0) THEN 1 ELSE -1;
END;

SwitchStretch ISA Switcher WITH
  Ajump[1] = IF (x[1]>=0.75*-x[2] AND x[2]<=0) THEN 1 ELSE -1;
  Ajump[2] = IF (x[1]<=0 AND x[2]>=0.75*-x[1]) THEN 1 ELSE -1;
END;
```

Omola 15 (Augmented Switching System)

```
SwitchStretchPlus ISA SwitchStretch WITH
    Stop ISAN Event;
    xdum TYPE Real;
    WHEN ModeChange CAUSE Stop;
    xdum = 10;
END;
```

The last model above simply adds an event and a dummy variable to the SwitchStretch model. Stop is a special Omsim event which causes the simulation to halt at mode changes. Below is an example of ocl code used to simulate the model. We take advantage of the Stop event to count mode changes (allowing a maximum of 60) and the extra dummy variable to hack a color change in the plotter upon switching. Details are not important, but the interested reader may browse the comments. See Figure 11.

ocl 1 (Switching Example)

```
BEGIN
    Hybrid::SwitchStretchPlus m;   % create the model

    Simulator sim(m);              % make a simulator for it
    sim.display(10, 450);          % display the simulator
    sim.stoptime := 1;
    sim.outputstep:=0.005;

    Plotter Response(m);           % make a plotter
    Response.display(10, 150);
    Response.xrange(-3, 1);        % set the scales
    Response.yrange(-3, 1);
    Response.x(x[1]);              % define the variables to plot
    Response.y(x[2],xdum);         % define the variables to plot

    Plotter R(m);                  % make a plotter
    R.display(260, 150);
    R.xrange(0, 1);                % set the scales
    R.yrange(0.95, 2.1);
    R.y(q);                        % define the variables to plot

    m.q := 1;
    m.x := [0.3; 0.826];
    sim.start;

    for eventnum := [1:30] BEGIN   % simulate for 30 events
        Response.y(xdum,x[2]);     % change color on each event
        sim.continue;
        Response.y(x[2],xdum);     % do this by swapping variable order
        sim.continue;
    END;
END;
```

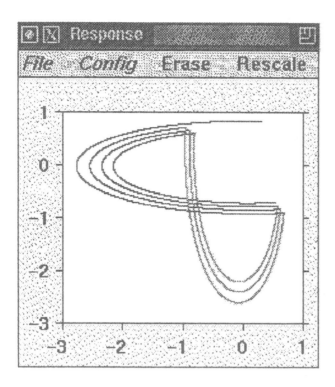

Fig. 11. Example planar switching system (screendump of Omsim plot window).

4.5 Adding Control

We hope the reader is seeing the power of Omola's object-oriented philosophy and the ease of reuse via subclasses by now. For completeness, though, we add controlled versions of DS's, HDS's, and Artstein's model. Then we give a model of Pait's two-state stabilizer for the simple harmonic oscillator (S.H.O.) (see Figure 12 and [5]).

A Controlled HDS (CHDS) is simply a subclass of HDS with inputs, outputs, and controlled switching added.

Omola 16 (CHDS)

```
CHDS ISA HDS WITH

inputs_outputs:
  m TYPE Integer;        % max dim. of constituent control spaces
  u TYPE Column [m];     % continuous control
  p TYPE Integer;        % max dim. of constituent output spaces
  y TYPE Column [p];     % continuous output
```

```
controlled_transitions:
  % controlled switching functions
  Cjump TYPE Row [N];

  % controlled switching map, discrete and continuous parts
  Fq TYPE Row [N];
  Fx TYPE Matrix [d, N];

  WHEN Cjump[q] >= 0 CAUSE ModeChange DO
    new(q) := Fq[q];
    new(x) := Fx[1..d,q];
  END;
END;
```

A controlled version of Artstein's HS is now a subclass of CHDS much as its autonomous version was one of HDS.

Omola 17 (Controlled Artstein)

```
CArtstein ISA CHDS WITH
  dim TYPE Integer;
  T TYPE Row [N];

  d = dim + 1;

  f[d,1..N] = ones(1,N);

  Ajump = x[d]*ones(1,N) - T;

  Gx[1..d-1,1..N] = x[1..d-1]*ones(1,N);
  Gx[d,1..N] = zeros(1,N);
END;
```

The above is a case where multiple inheritance would have been nice, that is, from both the CHDS and Artstein classes. Indeed, the reader may find it instructive to construct a CArtstein class as a subclass of Artstein, and then compare it with the above.

The code below instantiates the system in Figure 12. At this point, the reader should be able to understand it without comment. Note: do not confuse the S.H.O.'s velocity, y, with the Omola 18 variable y; the latter is a generic output measurement, which for the S.H.O. is the position, x a.k.a. x[1]. Note also, though, how easy it is to connect the two subcomponents in making Full2. Thus, using our macros, one can simulate interacting networks of controlled hybrid systems. Figure 13 shows the output of the Omsim simulation of the system shown in Figure 12 and specified in Omola 18. This time, we plotted a PostScript file generated by Omsim instead of a screendump. The two plot windows, from left to right, show the S.H.O.'s phase plane (with x[1] $\simeq x$ as the abcissa and x[2] $\simeq y$ as the ordinate) and the controller's discrete state (q $\simeq q \in \{1, 2\}$) versus time.

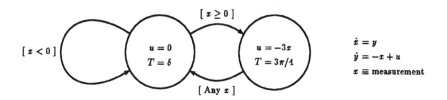

Fig. 12. Pait's two-state hybrid S.H.O. stabilizer and S.H.O. equations.

Omola 18 (S.H.O.)

```
SHO ISA CDS WITH
  d = 2;   m = 1;   p = 1;

  f[1] = x[2];
  f[2] = -x[1]+u[1];

  y[1]=x[1];
END;

SHOCont2 ISAN CArtstein WITH
  delta ISA Parameter WITH default := 0.1; END;

  N = 2;   dim = 0;   m = 1;   p = 1;

  y[1]=IF q==1 THEN 0 ELSE -3*u[1];

  Gq[1] = IF u[1] >=0 THEN 2 ELSE 1;
  Gq[2] = 1;

  Fq[1] = 1;
  Fq[2] = 1;

  Fx[1,1] = x;
  Fx[1,2] = x;

  Cjump[1] = -1;
  Cjump[2] = -1;

  T[1] = delta;
  T[2] = 2.3562;
END;

Full2 ISA Model WITH
  Plant ISA SHO WITH u[1]=Controller.y[1]; END;
  Controller ISA SHOCont2 WITH u[1]=Plant.y[1]; END;
END;
```

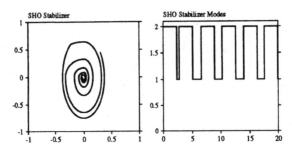

Fig. 13. Omsim simulation of Pait's SHO stabilizer (PostScript output).

5 Conclusions

Our goal is to produce fast, high fidelity simulations of (networks of) a very broad class of hybrid systems in a user-friendly environment. In this paper, we first reviewed a very broad class of hybrid systems: hybrid dynamical systems (HDS) [8]. We briefly discussed the object-oriented modeling and simulation tools for combined discrete/continuous systems: Omola and Omsim [2]. Leveraging these, we gave a general set of hybrid systems model classes which encompass HDS. HDS encompass several other hybrid systems models popularized in the literature; we made this explicit by representing them as subclasses of our HDS model class. These Omola model classes may be viewed as "templates" or "macros" for quick and easy entering of hybrid systems for subsequent analysis and numerically-sophisticated simulation using Omsim. They may be used to simulate networks of interacting dynamical and hybrid systems, a simple example of which was shown.

6 Acknowledgments

The first author did most of this work while visiting the Department of Automatic Control at the Lund Institute of Technology in May/June 1996. His thanks must go to Profs. Karl J. Astrom (Lund) and Sanjoy K. Mitter (MIT) for making the visit possible and to the lab members' hospitality and expertise for making it enjoyable and productive, resp. Omola/Omsim may be freely downloaded from Lund (http://www.control.lth.se/~cace/omsim.html).

56

References

1. R. Alur, T. A. Henzinger, and E. D. Sontag, editors. *Hybrid Systems III*, volume 1066 of *Lecture Notes in Computer Science*. Springer, New York, 1996.
2. M. Andersson. *Object-Oriented Modeling and Simulation of Hybrid Systems*. PhD thesis, Lund Institute of Technology, Dept. of Automatic Control, 1994.
3. P. Anstaklis, W. Kohn, A. Nerode, and S. Sastry, editors. *Hybrid Systems II*, volume 999 of *Lecture Notes in Computer Science*. Springer, New York, 1995.
4. P. J. Antsaklis, J. A. Stiver, and M. D. Lemmon. Hybrid system modeling and autonomous control systems. In Grossman et al. [12], pages 366–392.
5. Z. Artstein. Examples of stabilization with hybrid feedback. In [1] pages 173–185.
6. A. Back, J. Guckenheimer, and M. Myers. A dynamical simulation facility for hybrid systems. In Grossman et al. [12], pages 255–267.
7. D. D. Bainov and P. S. Simeonov. *Systems with Impulse Effect*. Ellis Horwood, Chichester, England, 1989.
8. M. S. Branicky. *Studies in Hybrid Systems: Modeling, Analysis, and Control*. ScD thesis, Massachusetts Institute of Technology, Dept. of Electrical Eng. and Comp. Science, June 1995.
9. M. S. Branicky, V. S. Borkar, and S. K. Mitter. A unified framework for hybrid control. In *Proc. IEEE Conf. Decision and Control*, pages 4228–4234, Lake Buena Vista, FL, Dec. 1994.
10. R. W. Brockett. Hybrid models for motion control systems. In H. L. Trentelman and J. C. Willems, editors, *Essays in Control: Perspectives in the Theory and its Applications*, pages 29–53. Birkhäuser, Boston, 1993.
11. A. Deshpande. *Control of Hybrid Systems*. PhD thesis, Univ. of California at Berkeley, 1994.
12. R. L. Grossman, A. Nerode, A. P. Ravn, and H. Rischel, editors. *Hybrid Systems*, volume 736 of *Lecture Notes in Computer Science*. Springer, New York, 1993.
13. A. Nerode and W. Kohn. Models for hybrid systems: Automata, topologies, stability. In Grossman et al. [12], pages 317–356.
14. K. S. Sibirsky. *Introduction to Topological Dynamics*. Noordhoff International Publishing, Leyden, The Netherlands, 1975. Translated by Leo F. Boron.
15. E. D. Sontag. *Mathematical Control Theory: Deterministic Finite Dimensional Systems*, volume 6 of *Texts in Applied Mathematics*. Springer, New York, 1990.
16. L. Tavernini. Differential automata and their discrete simulators. *Nonlinear Analysis, Theory, Methods, and Applications*, 11(6):665–683, 1987.
17. H. S. Witsenhausen. A class of hybrid-state continuous-time dynamic systems. *IEEE Trans. Automatic Control*, 11(2):161–167, 1966.

Application of the Kohn-Nerode Control Law Extraction Procedure to the Inverted Pendulum Problem

Vladimir Brayman*[1] and Juris Vagners[2]

[1] HyBrithms Corp. and
Department of Electrical Engineering
University of Washington, Seattle, WA
e-mail: vbrayman@hybrithms.com
[2] Department of Aeronautics and Astronautics
University of Washington, Seattle, WA
e-mail: vagners@aa.washington.edu

Abstract. The Kohn-Nerode control law extraction procedure offers an innovative way of formulating and solving a Hybrid System problem. The present paper is an attempt to show the main components of the method using the inverted pendulum as an example.

1 Introduction

The growing demand for control systems which are capable of controlling complex non-linear continuous plants with discrete intelligent (i.e. capable of handling heuristic knowledge about the system and its environment) controllers presents the need for a general theory for the analysis and synthesis of such systems. Hybrid Systems theory addresses these issues. In general, a hybrid system is a network of discrete logical devices (i.e. intelligent controllers) and continuous plants, where the controllers are capable of acquiring sensor information, modifying their databases (learning), and altering the design of control laws as a result of this learning to improve the behavior of the system. Examples of such systems include robotics, factory automation systems, air-traffic control and highway control systems, and database management systems.

Hybrid System methodology as it is developed in [Koh88a], [KN92], [KN93], [KNR95], and [KNRG94] is an attempt to answer these needs. It is implemented via an architecture called the Multiple Agent Hybrid Control Architecture (MAHCA) and is based on the notion of a hybrid system state. The latter incorporates evolution models using differential or difference equations, logic constraints, and geometric constraints. The set of hybrid states of a hybrid system can be construed as a differentiable manifold, which is called carrier manifold [KNRG94]. The Kohn-Nerode control law extraction procedure was introduced to extract digital programs (control automata) which yield approximations to optimal control polices. That is, the goal is to find a feedback control law $\gamma(x)$ for actuator control values which is a function

---

* Research supported by Dept. of Commerce Agreement 70-NANB5H1164.

of plant states x which produces a plant trajectory $x(t)$ minimizing the integral of a non-negative Lagrangian $L(x, \dot{x}, t)$ along the plant trajectory subject to constraints, logical requirements, and goals. It is well known from classical optimal control theory that there is no guarantee that there exists a real valued optimal control function $\gamma(x)$ for every control problem. However, often a relaxed, not necessarily physically implementable, solution [You80], [War72] exists when no real valued control function exists. The Kohn-Nerode control law extraction procedure produces a physically realizable control function $\gamma(x)$ such that the integral of Lagrangian over the trajectory determined by $\gamma(x)$ is within ϵ of the optimal value. The actual value of ϵ, determined by an end user, is a trade-off between performance and computational expenses. This approximation technique is suitable for a wide class of practical problems, where the ϵ-optimality is all that is required.

Differential geometry and Bellman's Dynamic Programming form a theoretical basis of the Kohn-Nerode control law extraction procedure. Differential geometry provides a powerful mathematical machinery. In fact, differential geometry and tensor calculus were the mathematical tools which allowed Einstein to formulate his general relativity theory [MP77]. Kohn, Nerode, and Remmel showed [KNR95] the connection between optimal control theory and differential geometry of Finsler manifolds. The homogeneity condition required for Finsler manifolds is too restrictive to apply to most mechanical systems. Thus they later relaxed this assumption and generalized the method to any pseudo-Riemannian manifold. The main idea is to reformulate the optimal control problem into one amenable to solution by the methods of differential geometry. A Hybrid System version of Bellman's dynamic programming methods (see [KNR96a]) can then be used to effectively compute solutions.

The objectives of the present paper are to give an introduction to certain key aspects of the Kohn-Nerode control law extraction procedure. In particular we will give a detailed account of the inverse variational method to construct the system Lagrangian and how to incorporate constraints into the system Lagrangian. We also give brief introductions to the Chattering Lemma and to Hybrid Dynamic Programming. For the present paper, we choose as an illustrative example of the nonlinear plant the inverted pendulum because it is a simple system but yet provides a significant number of features of many non-linear real-life control systems. However, the drawback of this example is that it is too simple to demonstrate the full power of the method.

The rest of this paper is organized as follows. Section 2 will be devoted to a general description of the Kohn-Nerode control law extraction procedure design approach. Then in the next sections, a more detailed description of the major components of the theory will be given. Section 3 will discuss the chattering phenomenon and its implication for the Kohn-Nerode control law extraction procedure. After that, in order to demonstrate the techniques, using an example, we will derive the model of the University of Washington Controls Laboratory linear track cart pendulum (LTCP) in the usual way. In section 5 we describe the system's evolution manifold. In section 6, the system's Lagrangian will be obtained from the LTCP model. Section 7 presents the implementation details. Some conclusions will be given at end.

2 Kohn-Nerode control law extraction procedure

In this section we will describe the Kohn-Nerode control law extraction procedure as a method for solving a non-linear optimal control problem, see [Koh88a], [KN92], [KN93], [KNR95], and [KNRG94]. First, we will formulate the Hybrid System control problem. Then the outline of the method will be given as a step-by-step procedure. We will discuss the most important steps of the procedure in more details in subsequent sections.

2.1 Problem formulation

A hybrid system is a control system consisting of a continuous plant subject to both disturbance and control, a digital controller, and analog-to-digital and digital-to-analog converters. The process of an interaction between the plant and the controller is viewed as follows. The controller reads digitized sensor data of the current state of the plant, computes the control for the next time interval, and imposes it on the plant. The plant obeying this control moves along the trajectory for this time interval until the next control law is issued, and cycle starts over again. It is assumed that

1. control remains the same during the time interval between two interactions,
2. time intervals are not necessarily equal.

Thus the optimal control problem for Hybrid Systems can be formulated in the following way.

Problem P *Given a model of a continuous plant, goal, performance specifications, and constraints, extract the digital control program as a function of the plant's states which will force the plant to move toward the goal along the optimal trajectory and meet the performance specifications.*

$$\min_{u} \quad J = \int_{t_o}^{t_f} L_c(x(t), u(t), t)dt \tag{1}$$

subject to

$$\dot{x}(t) = f_m(x(t), u(t), t), \quad a.e.t \in [t_o, t_f] \tag{2}$$

and constraints $\quad u(t) \in U, \quad x(t_o) \in E_o, \quad x(t_f) \in E_1.$

Remarks: We make the following assumptions.

1. The system trajectories $x(\cdot) : [t_o, t_f] \to M \subset \mathbf{R}^n$ (M is system's evolution manifold, see section 5) are Lipshitz continuous and have the derivative $\dot{x}(t)$ which exists a.e. $t \in [t_o, t_f]$. The control functions $u(\cdot) : [t_o, t_f] \to \mathbf{R}^m$ are measurable and bounded.
2. The sets E_o and E_1 in M are closed.
3. The functions f_m and L_c satisfy the Caratheodory conditions: they are continuous in (x, u) and measurable in t.

4. We assume that the optimal path is an ϵ-optimal chattering approximation [KNRG94] to a relaxed, not necessarily physically implementable solution [You80, War72].

2.2 Overview of the Kohn-Nerode control law extraction procedure

We will present the general overview of the Kohn-Nerode control law extraction procedure and then give a step-by-step algorithm for its construction. Starting from the description of a control problem, transform equation (2) into a vector field equation

$$\dot{x} = f_u(x) \tag{3}$$

where the vector field $f_u(x) = f_m(x, u)$ (where defined) and x is the vector, which incorporates the state vector, the cost function and all the constraints. We sometimes will drop the subscript of $f_u(x)$ and write simply $f(x)$. It is clear that there are uncountably many $f_u(x)$ and computing them is impractical. Instead, operator $f_u(x)$ can be approximated by the following procedure. Let TM be a vector bundle of M. Then a tangent space at a point x of M, $TM|_x$, is characterized in local coordinates by the basis $(v_1, \ldots, v_n) = (\frac{\partial}{\partial x_1}, \ldots, \frac{\partial}{\partial x_n})$. This means that we can write $f_u(x) = \sum_1^n \gamma_i v_i$. But the problem of finding an optimal combination of γ's is also difficult. Then we can use the Chattering Lemma (see section 3), which is fundamental for the Kohn-Nerode control law extraction procedure, and approximate the convex combination $\sum_1^n \gamma_i v_i$ with the chattering combination $CHC(v_i, \alpha_i)$ ($\sum_1^n \alpha_i = 1$, $\alpha_i \geq 0$). After that the chattering coefficients α_i ($i = 1, \ldots, n$) are computed. The control needed to move the system from the current point $x(t)$ to the next point $x(t + h)$ can then be recovered using the inverse differential map (actuator map).

step 1 Convert the original problem into the form suitable for the Kohn-Nerode control law extraction procedure.

step 2 Construct a evolution manifold for the system. The definition of the evolution manifold and the description of the process of its construction will be given in section 5.

step 3 Construct a non-negative Lagrangian on the evolution manifold such that the problem of minimizing this Lagrangian is equivalent to solving (2). This Lagrangian contains the information about the dynamics of the system as well as the optimality conditions. This Lagrangian must be convex in order to ensure the existence of the minimization problem. If it is not convex, a convexification procedure is applied [KNRG94].

step 4 Reformulate the problem from the step 1 as a Hybrid Dynamic Programming problem. Solve this problem using the methods of differential geometry. This includes computation of the fields of extremals of the original Lagrangian, parallel transport of the goal vector y_g along the geodesics to obtain the local goal, and computation of the chattering coefficients such that the linear combination of the fields of extremals with these coefficients approximates the local goal within the prescribed ϵ.

step 5 By using the actuator map, compute the control value u applied onto the plant for the next time interval.

step 6 Compute the coordinates of the next point. Check the constraint conditions. If the next point lies on the constraint manifold, introduce the constraints and compute new, "constraint" Lagrangian (see section 6.3). If the next point lies on the evolution manifold M (see section 5), use the same Lagrangian as in the previous time interval. If the next point lies on neither manifold, invoke an adapter (see [NK93]) to recompute the model.

The algorithm is shown in the Figure 1. In the figure, boxes represent the events in the computation and ovals represent automata which result in the events. Each automaton can be constructed from other automata. Figure 2 shows the construction of the inverse variational automaton.

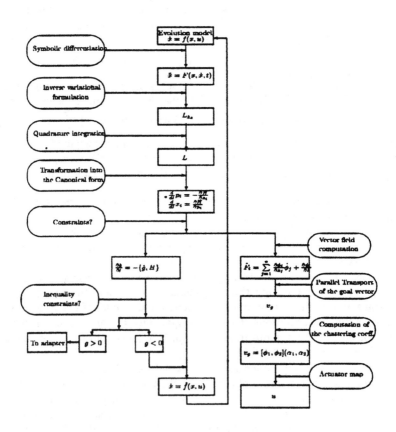

Fig. 1. Kohn-Nerode control law extraction procedure

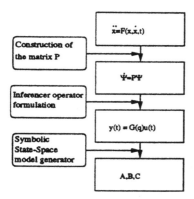

Fig. 2. Inverse Variational Automaton

3 Chattering

In this section, we will show that the chattering optimal control, which may not be physically realizable, can be approximated arbitrarily close by a physically realizable control. This leads to the Chattering Lemma, one of the fundamental results of the Kohn-Nerode control law extraction procedure.

Let $S = \{v_i, \quad i = 1, \ldots, n\}$ be a basis of the tangent space $TM|_x$ at the certain point x of the manifold M. A *Chattering Combination* of the elements of S is defined as follows:

$$v|_x(\tau) = \begin{cases} v_1, & \tau \in I_1 \\ v_2, & \tau \in I_2 \\ \vdots \\ v_n, & \tau \in I_n \end{cases}$$

where semi-open subintervals $I_i, \ (i = 1, \ldots, n)$ are defined as

$$I_i = \left[t + \sum_{k=0}^{i-1} \alpha_h^k h, t + \sum_{k=0}^{i} \alpha_h^k h \right), \quad (i = 1, \ldots, n),$$

where h is the control time interval and $\alpha_h^j, \ (\alpha_h^j \geq 0, \ \sum_j^n \alpha_h^j = 1)$ are *chattering coefficients*.

Theorem 1. Chattering Lemma ([KN97], see also [Ber74]) Let S be a basis defined above and let $\hat{S}$ be the set of all chattering combinations of S. Also let real $\varepsilon > 0$ be given. Then there exists a vector $\hat{v}_j \in \hat{S}$, defined for each tuple $\{\gamma_h^1, \ldots, \gamma_h^n\}$ $(\gamma_h^i \geq 0, \ \sum_i \gamma_h^i = 1)$, such that

$$\max_t \left| \int_0^t \left(\exp(\tau \hat{v}_j)x - \exp(\tau \sum \gamma_h^i v_i)x \right) d\tau \right| < \varepsilon \tag{4}$$

for all $\{\gamma_h^1, \ldots, \gamma_h^n\}$. Here $\exp(\tau \cdot)x$ denotes the flow on the manifold M.

From the Chattering Lemma, we conclude that every linear combination of the vectors of the basis S can be approximated by a chattering combination of these vectors with an arbitrary small error in the integral sense. This fact is useful for us because we can compute chattering coefficients and thus the chattering combination by means of the procedure described in the section 7.1.

4 The Dynamic Model of the Linear Track Cart Pendulum

We will start with the derivation of the model of the University of Washington Control Laboratory Linear Track Cart Pendulum setup using the results from [Sep94]. The Linear Track Cart Pendulum setup can be viewed as a system consisting of two parts: a cart with a simple pendulum and an electric motor with an amplifier. The cart has mass M and is moved along the horizontal track by the DC motor via the pulley-belt system. A single pendulum link with inertia J and mass m is attached to the cart. For convenience, we specify the position of the cart and the pendulum

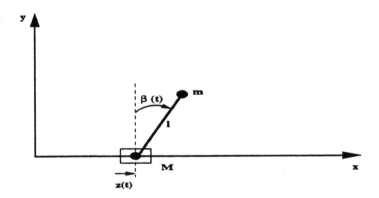

Fig. 3. Linear Track Cart Pendulum setup

at any time t by a pair of coordinates $(z(t), \beta(t))$ where $z(t)$ denotes the horizontal displacement and $\beta(t)$ denotes the angular displacement from the vertical in the clockwise direction. We let l denote the distance from the pendulum link base to its center of mass.

Then the model of the system is given by:

$$\begin{bmatrix} \ddot{z} \\ \ddot{\beta} \end{bmatrix} = \tag{5}$$

$$\begin{bmatrix} M+m+\frac{J_w}{r^2} & ml\cos\beta \\ ml\cos\beta & ml^2+J \end{bmatrix}^{-1} \left(\begin{bmatrix} ml\dot{\beta}^2\sin\beta - \left(c_1+\frac{D_w}{r^2}\right)\dot{z} \\ mgl\sin\beta - c_2\dot{\beta} \end{bmatrix} + \begin{bmatrix} \frac{Kk_i}{r} \\ 0 \end{bmatrix} u \right).$$

Numerical values for the constant coefficients in the equation above are given in the Appendix.

5 Evolution Manifold

In this section, we give the definition of an evolution manifold of a system. Then the evolution manifold of the linear track cart pendulum will be computed.

The evolution (differentiable) manifold of the system is its configuration space with constraints. The configuration space of the cart-pendulum system can be defined as a subset of $\mathbf{R}^3$: $\mathbf{R}^1 \times \mathbf{S}^1 \subset \mathbf{R}^1 \times \mathbf{R}^2$ which satisfies the equation

$$\sqrt{(x_c(t) - x_m(t))^2 + y_m(t)^2} = l. \tag{6}$$

That is, we assume that the cart at time t is at point $(x_c(t), 0)$ and the center of mass of the pendulum is at $(x_m(t), y_m(t))$. Thus

$$\begin{aligned} x_c(t) &= z(t) \\ x_m(t) &= z(t) + l\sin(\beta(t)) \\ y_m(t) &= l\cos(\beta(t)). \end{aligned} \tag{7}$$

We construct the evolution manifold of the system from its configuration space by imposing the constraints $-0.5 \leq x_c \leq 0.5$ and (6). The usual atlas in this case is

$$\varphi^{-1}(z,\beta) = (l\sin(\beta), z, l\cos(\beta)), \quad U_1 = \{-0.5 < z < 0.5, \quad 0 \leq \beta < 2\pi\}$$
$$\varphi^{-1}(z,\beta) = (l\sin(\beta), z, l\cos(\beta)), \quad U_2 = \{-0.5 < z < 0.5, \quad -\pi \leq \beta < \pi\}.$$

Figure (4) shows the embedding of the evolution manifold into $\mathbf{E}^3$. The corresponding mappings are given as follows

$$\begin{aligned} \mathbf{x}^+(u_1, u_2) &= (u_1, u_2, \sqrt{r^2 - u_1^2}), \quad -r < u_1 < r, -0.5 < u_2 < 0.5 \\ \mathbf{x}^-(u_1, u_2) &= (u_1, u_2, -\sqrt{r^2 - u_1^2}), \quad -r < u_1 < r, -0.5 < u_2 < 0.5 \\ \mathbf{y}^+(u_1, u_2) &= (\sqrt{r^2 - u_1^2}, u_2, u_1), \quad -r < u_1 < r, -0.5 < u_2 < 0.5 \\ \mathbf{y}^+(u_1, u_2) &= (-\sqrt{r^2 - u_1^2}, u_2, u_1), \quad -r < u_1 < r, -0.5 < u_2 < 0.5 \end{aligned} \tag{8}$$

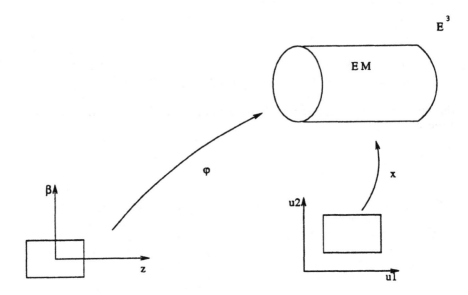

Fig. 4. Embedding the evolution manifold into $\mathbf{E}^3$

6 Constructing a Lagrangian

This section is devoted to the construction of a non-negative Lagrangian L on the evolution manifold of the system based on the method of [KNR96a]. This is a so called inverse variational problem. That is, given the differential equation describing the dynamics of a system, a cost function to minimize, and constraints, we construct a non-negative Lagrangian such that the extremals which minimize this Lagrangian are the solutions of the original differential equation, which obey the constraints. These extremals might or might not be physically realizable. We will then use approximation techniques to find physically realizable approximations.

6.1 Inverse variational problem

Introduce the feedback function $\gamma(x,t) = u$. Equation (2) becomes

$$\dot{x} = f(x(t), \gamma(x,t)) \tag{9}$$

Then take the derivative of both sides of this equation,

$$\ddot{x} = \frac{\partial f}{\partial x}\dot{x} + \frac{\partial f}{\partial u}\frac{\partial \gamma}{\partial x}\dot{x} + \frac{\partial f}{\partial u}\frac{\partial \gamma}{\partial t}. \tag{10}$$

This equation can be written as

$$\ddot{x} = F(x, \dot{x}, t) \tag{11}$$

with γ entering parametrically. Rewrite the Euler-Lagrange equation

$$\frac{d}{dt}L_{\dot{x}_i} - L_{x_i} = 0, i = 1, \ldots, n \tag{12}$$

as

$$\partial L_{\dot{x}} \begin{bmatrix} \dot{x} \\ \ddot{x} \\ 1 \end{bmatrix} - L_x = 0, \tag{13}$$

where $\partial L_{\dot{x}} = \left[(L_{\dot{x}_i x_j})\ (L_{\dot{x}_i \dot{x}_j})\ L_{\dot{x}_t} \right], i,j = 1, \ldots, n$.
Upon substituting for $\ddot{x}$ from the equation (2):

$$\partial L_{\dot{x}} \begin{bmatrix} \dot{x} \\ F \\ 1 \end{bmatrix} - L_x = 0, \tag{14}$$

and differentiating with respect to $\dot{x}$ of this equation one obtains

$$\left[\partial L_{\dot{x}_{i_1}}\ \partial L_{\dot{x}_{i_2}} \ldots \partial L_{\dot{x}_{i_n}} \right] \begin{bmatrix} \dot{x} \\ F \\ 1 \end{bmatrix} + \partial L_{\dot{x}} \begin{bmatrix} I \\ F_{\dot{x}} \\ 0 \end{bmatrix} - L_{x_{\dot{x}}} = 0. \tag{15}$$

where I is the identity matrix and $F_{\dot{x}} = \left[\frac{\partial F}{\partial \dot{x}_1}\ \frac{\partial F}{\partial \dot{x}_2} \ldots \frac{\partial F}{\partial \dot{x}_n} \right]$. With the assumption that L is in C^3 the following relations hold: $L_{\dot{x}_*} = L_{x_{\dot{x}}}$, $L_{\dot{x}_{*_*}} = L_{\dot{x}_{i_*}}$, and $L_{\dot{x}_{t_*}} = L_{\dot{x}_{*_t}}$. Thus the equation (15) can be rewritten as

$$\frac{d}{dt}L_{\dot{x}_*} + L_{\dot{x}_*} + L_{\dot{x}_*}F_{\dot{x}} - L_{x_*} = 0. \tag{16}$$

Take the transpose of (16) using the fact that $\left(\frac{d}{dt}L_{\dot{x}_*} \right)^T = \frac{d}{dt}L_{\dot{x}_*}$

$$\frac{d}{dt}L_{\dot{x}_*} + L_{x_*} + (F_{\dot{x}})^T L_{\dot{x}_*} - L_{\dot{x}_*} = 0. \tag{17}$$

Add (16) and (17) and divide by 2 to get the Lyapunov equation

$$-\frac{d}{dt}\Psi = \frac{1}{2}F_{\dot{x}}^T\Psi + \frac{1}{2}\Psi F_{\dot{x}} \tag{18}$$

where $\Psi(x, \dot{x}, t) = L_{\dot{x}_*}$. The solution of this equation will give the desired $L_{\dot{x}_*}$. Then L can be found by integration.

6.2 Solving the Lyapunov equation

Using the fact that Ψ is a symmetric matrix and applying the method introduced in [Bin70], we can rewrite the equation (18),

$$\begin{bmatrix} \dot{\Psi}_{11} \\ \dot{\Psi}_{12} \\ \dot{\Psi}_{22} \end{bmatrix} = \begin{bmatrix} -F_{\dot{x}11} & -F_{\dot{x}21} & 0 \\ -\frac{1}{2}F_{\dot{x}12} & -\frac{1}{2}(F_{\dot{x}11} + F_{\dot{x}22}) & -\frac{1}{2}F_{\dot{x}21} \\ 0 & -F_{\dot{x}12} & -F_{\dot{x}22} \end{bmatrix} \begin{bmatrix} \Psi_{11} \\ \Psi_{12} \\ \Psi_{22} \end{bmatrix}. \tag{19}$$

This equation can be solved for $\Psi = L_{\dot{x}_*}$ using the following technique.

Automaton as a differential equation solver Equation (19) can be rewritten in a more compact form

$$\dot{\Psi} = P\Psi \qquad (20)$$

where $\Psi(x, \dot{x}, t)$ is a vector and $P(x, \dot{x})$ is an (3×3) matrix. For each x, we can consider $\Psi = \Psi(t)$ and P to be a constant matrix. Define the shift operator to be $E_h(f(t)) = f(t+h) = f(t) + h\frac{d}{dt}f(t) + h^2\frac{d^2}{dt^2}f(t) + \ldots = \exp(h\frac{d}{dt})(f(t))$ for any rational function $f(t) \in C^\infty$. Then using the Taylor series expansion of Ψ with remainder, equation (20) can be written as follows,

$$\exp(hD)\Psi_i - \Psi_i = h(\sum_{j=1}^{n} P_{ij}\Psi_j + R_i(t)) \quad i = 1, \ldots, n, \qquad (21)$$

where $D = \frac{d}{dt}$ and $R_i(t)$ is the series remainder. $R_i(t)$ is defined such as to give the order of approximation to be less then the resolution of the sensors. Next define the operator $d = \frac{(\exp(hD)-1)}{h}$. It is easy to check that operator d is the derivation. Equation (21) can be rewritten as follows

$$d\Psi_i = \sum_{j=1}^{n} P_{ij}\Psi_j + R_i(t) \quad i = 1, \ldots, n, \qquad (22)$$

or in the matrix form

$$d\Psi = P\Psi + R(t) \qquad (23)$$

Then equation (20) becomes

$$\Psi = (dI - P)^{-1}R(t), \qquad (24)$$

where I is the identity matrix. The inverse matrix $(dI - P)^{-1}$ can be written as the ratio of two polynomials in d,

$$(dI - P)^{-1} = \frac{d^{n-1}I + d^{n-2}B_{n-2} + \ldots + dB_1 + B_0}{d^n + a_{n-1}d^{n-1} + \ldots + a_1d + a_0}. \qquad (25)$$

Then the matrices B_i and coefficients a_i can be computed using the Souriau-Frame-Faddeev algorithm [Ros70].

Next we will show how an automaton can be constructed by means of the symbolic state-space model generator [Che70] and [Koh88b].

Symbolic state-space model generator First, let's rewrite equation (24) as follows

$$y(t) = G(d)u(t) \qquad (26)$$

where $G_{ij}(d) = \frac{Q_{ij}(d)}{P_{ij}(d)}$, $i = 1, \ldots, l, j = 1, \ldots, m$ and the choice of the vectors $y(t)$ and $u(t)$ is obvious. Here d is a derivation. Let $D(d)$ be the least common denominator of all $G_{ij}(d)$ and let $r_j(t)$, $j = 1, \ldots, m$ be a set of decoupling variables which satisfy the relation

$$D(d)r_j(t) = u_j(t), \qquad (27)$$

$$j = 1, \ldots, m$$

Then from (26) and (27)

$$y_i(t) = \sum_{j=1}^{m} \frac{Q_{ij}(d)D(d)r_j(t)}{P_{ij}(d)} = \sum_{j=1}^{m} \hat{Q}_{ij}(d)r_j(t), \qquad (28)$$

$$i = 1,\ldots,l$$

Let the polynomials $D(d)$ and $\hat{Q}_{ij}(d)$ be in the following form $D(d) = \sum_{k=0}^{n} a_k d^k$, $a_n = 1$ and $\hat{Q}_{ij}(d) = \sum_{s=0}^{M_{ij}} (b_{ij})_s d^s$ for $i = 1,\ldots,l$ and $j = 1,\ldots,m$. For any $j = 1,\ldots,m$, let

$$x_{1j} = r_j(t)$$
$$x_{2j} = dr_j(t)$$
$$x_{3j} = d^2 r_j(t)$$
$$\vdots = \vdots$$
$$x_{nj} = d^{n-1} r_j(t)$$

Notice that from (27) $dx_{nj} = d^n r_j(t) = -a_{n-1}d^{n-1}r_j(t) - \cdots - a_0 r_j(t) + u_j(t)$. Thus we can write in the canonical controllable form

$$\begin{bmatrix} dx_{1j} \\ dx_{2j} \\ \vdots \\ dx_{nj} \end{bmatrix} = \begin{bmatrix} 0 & 1 & 0 & \cdots & 0 \\ 0 & 0 & 1 & \cdots & 0 \\ \vdots & \vdots & \vdots & \vdots & \vdots \\ -a_0 & -a_1 & \cdots\cdots & -a_{n-1} \end{bmatrix} \begin{bmatrix} x_{1j} \\ x_{2j} \\ \vdots \\ x_{nj} \end{bmatrix} + \begin{bmatrix} 0 \\ 0 \\ \vdots \\ 1 \end{bmatrix} u_j(t). \qquad (29)$$

And from (28)

$$y_i(t) = \begin{bmatrix} b_{i10} & b_{i11} & \ldots & b_{i1M_{i1}} & 0 & \ldots & 0 \end{bmatrix} x_1 + \cdots$$
$$+ \begin{bmatrix} b_{im0} & b_{im1} & \ldots & b_{imM_{im}} & 0 & \ldots & 0 \end{bmatrix} x_m =$$
$$\begin{bmatrix} C_{i1} & \ldots & C_{im} \end{bmatrix} \begin{bmatrix} x_1 \\ \vdots \\ x_m \end{bmatrix},$$

where the vectors x_j, $j = 1,\ldots,m$ are defined as it is transparent from (29). This shows how to find matrices A, B, and C such that

$$X(k+1) = AX(k) + Bu(k) \qquad (30)$$
$$y(k) = CX(k) \qquad (31)$$

The Maple procedures were developed using the computational method described in the previous section. The plot of the Lagrangian was obtained using these procedures.

6.3   Constraints introduction

First reformulate the problem in the canonical form. That is, find the canonical momenta p_i and the Hamiltonian H corresponding to the Lagrangian calculated in the previous step.

$$\frac{d}{dt}p_i = -\frac{\partial H}{\partial x_i}, \quad i = 1,..,n \tag{32}$$

$$\frac{d}{dt}x_i = \frac{\partial H}{\partial p_i}, \quad i = 1,..,n \tag{33}$$

where

$$p_i(x,\dot{x},t) = L_{\dot{x}_i}(x,\dot{x},t) \tag{34}$$

and

$$H = -L + \sum_{i}^{n} p_i \dot{x}_i, \tag{35}$$

for $i = 1...n$. Next introduce the state constraints. Let the state constraints be given as

$$g_i(x,\dot{x},t) = 0, \quad i = 1,\ldots,n. \tag{36}$$

If the Jacobian $\left(\frac{\partial p}{\partial \dot{x}}\right)$ is not equal to zero, then we can write

$$\hat{g}_i(x,p,t) = 0 \quad i = 1,\ldots,n. \tag{37}$$

It is clear that

$$\frac{d\hat{g}_i}{dt} = 0 \quad i = 1,\ldots,n, \tag{38}$$

and it follows that

$$\frac{d\hat{g}_i}{dt} = \frac{\partial \hat{g}_i}{\partial t} + \sum_j \frac{\partial \hat{g}_i}{\partial x_j}\frac{dx_j}{dt} + \sum_j \frac{\partial \hat{g}_i}{\partial p_j}\frac{dp_j}{dt} \tag{39}$$

$$= \frac{\partial \hat{g}_i}{\partial t} + \sum_j \frac{\partial \hat{g}_i}{\partial x_j}\frac{\partial H}{\partial p_j} - \sum_j \frac{\partial \hat{g}_i}{\partial p_j}\frac{\partial H}{\partial x_j} \tag{40}$$

$$= \frac{\partial \hat{g}_i}{\partial t} + \{\hat{g}_i, H\} = 0, \quad i,j = 1,\ldots,n, \tag{41}$$

where $\{\cdot,\cdot\}$ denotes the Poisson bracket [Olv93][page 390]. Equation (36) also implies that

$$\frac{\partial g}{\partial t} + \frac{\partial g}{\partial x}\dot{x} + \frac{\partial g}{\partial \dot{x}}\ddot{x} = 0. \tag{42}$$

We can rewrite this equation using (41)

$$\ddot{x} = \left(\frac{\partial g}{\partial \dot{x}}\right)^{-1}\left(-\{\hat{g}, H\} - \frac{\partial g}{\partial x}\dot{x}\right). \tag{43}$$

This also can be written as

$$\ddot{x} = \bar{F}(x,u). \tag{44}$$

Substitute $\bar{F}(x,u)$ into equation (13) and compute a new, "constraint", Lagrangian.

7 Solution of the minimization problem

This section describes the Hybrid Systems method for solving the problem of minimizing the Lagrangian obtained in the previous section. First we formulate the problem using the Dynamic Programming formalism. Then we solve this problem using differential geometry and the theory of chattering controls. The rest of this section is organized as follows. We give the general overview of Hybrid Dynamic Programming, see [KNR96b]. Then we will show how this method can be applied to the Linear Track Cart Pendulum problem.

7.1 Hybrid Dynamic Programming

Consider a variational problem

$$\min_{x(\cdot)\in M} \int_0^T L(x(t), \dot{x}(t), t)dt. \tag{45}$$

If $(N + 1)h = T$, then we can rewrite (45) as

$$\min_{x(\cdot)\in M} \sum_{n=0}^N \int_{nh}^{(n+1)h} L(x(t), \dot{x}(t), t)dt. \tag{46}$$

Define a counting variable Z_i (Z_i has real values and i runs over the integers)

$$Z_i = \sum_{n=0}^i \int_{nh}^{(n+1)h} L(x(t), \dot{x}(t), t)dt \tag{47}$$

so that

$$Z_{i+1} = Z_i + \int_{(i+1)h}^{(i+2)h} L(x(t), \dot{x}(t), t)dt. \tag{48}$$

If we replace the integral on the righthand side of (48) by its chattering approximation, we can define a new sequence of counting variables $\tilde{Z}_i$ by

$$\tilde{Z}_{i+1} = \tilde{Z}_i + \sum_{k=0}^s L(x((i+1)h), v_{i+1}^k, (i+1)h)\alpha_{i+1}^k h. \tag{49}$$

where s is the number of subintervals of h (see Section 3) and for each i

(a) v_i^k for $k = 0, \ldots, s$ is in the field of extremals of the original problem (45) at $x(ih)$ and

(b) α_i^k are nonnegative real numbers such that $\sum_{k=0}^s \alpha_i^k = 1$.

We can show that the original problem (45) which is to find $\min\limits_{x(\cdot)\in M} Z_N$ can be replaced by the relaxed problem which is to find

$$\inf_{\alpha_i^j} \tilde{Z}_N \tag{50}$$

where (from the Chattering Lemma)

$$\min_{x(\cdot)\in M} Z_N + O(h) \geq \inf_{\alpha_i^j} \tilde{Z}_N. \tag{51}$$

This formulation allows us to derive a dynamic programming equation for the relaxed problem. That is, define

$$V(\tilde{Z}_i, x, ih) = \inf_{\alpha_i^j} \tilde{Z}_i + \sum_{t=i+1}^{N} \sum_{k=0}^{s} L(x(th), v_t^k, th)\alpha_t^k h. \tag{52}$$

where $x = x(ih)$. Then by Bellman's Principle of Optimality,

$$V(\tilde{Z}, x, ih) = \inf_{\alpha_i^k} V(\tilde{Z}_{x,(i+1)h}, x((i+1)h), (i+1)h) \tag{53}$$

where

$$\tilde{Z}_{x,(i+1)h} = \tilde{Z} + \sum_{k=0}^{s} L(x(h), v_x^k(h), (i+1)h)\alpha_{i+1}^k h \tag{54}$$

and we have the boundary condition that

$$V(\tilde{Z}, x, N) = \tilde{Z}.$$

It then follows that (in the flat space)

$$V(\tilde{Z}, x, ih) = \tag{55}$$
$$\inf_{\alpha_i^k} \begin{bmatrix} V(\tilde{Z}, x, ih) + \\ \frac{\partial V}{\partial \tilde{Z}}(\tilde{Z}, x, ih) \cdot (\tilde{Z}_{x,(i+1)h} - \tilde{Z}) + \\ \frac{\partial V}{\partial x}(\tilde{Z}, x, ih) \cdot (x(h) - x) + \\ \frac{\partial V}{\partial t}(\tilde{Z}, x, ih) \cdot h + \\ O(h^2) \end{bmatrix}.$$

where

$$\tilde{Z}_{x,(i+1)h} - \tilde{Z} = \sum_{k=0}^{s} L(x(h), _x^k(h), (i+1)h)\alpha_{i+1}^k h \tag{56}$$

Simplifying (55) and dividing both sides by h, we obtain that

$$0 = \inf_{\alpha_i^k} \begin{bmatrix} \left(\frac{\partial V}{\partial \tilde{Z}}(\tilde{Z}, x, ih) \cdot \right. \\ \left. \left(\sum_{k=0}^{s} L(x(h), v_x^k(h), (i+1)h)\alpha_{i+1}^k\right)\right) \\ +\frac{\partial V}{\partial x}(\tilde{Z}, x, ih) \cdot \frac{(x(h)-x)}{h} + \\ \frac{\partial V}{\partial t}(\tilde{Z}, x, ih) + \\ \frac{O(h^2)}{h} \end{bmatrix}. \tag{57}$$

Note that in (57), the term $\frac{\partial V}{\partial t}(\tilde{Z}, x, ih)$ does not depend on the α_i^k's so that we have

$$-\frac{\partial V}{\partial t}(\tilde{Z}, x, ih) =$$

$$\inf_{\alpha_i^k} \begin{bmatrix} \left(\frac{\partial V}{\partial Z}(\tilde{Z}, x, ih) \cdot \\ \left(\sum_{k=0}^{s} L(x(h), v_x^k(h), (i+1)h)\alpha_{i+1}^k\right)\right) \\ +\frac{\partial V}{\partial \tilde{Z}}(\tilde{Z}, x, ih) \cdot \frac{(x(h)-x)}{h} + \\ \frac{O(h^2)}{h} \end{bmatrix}. \qquad (58)$$

Analyzing this equation, we note that the original problem is composed of two coupled minimization problems. The sum $\sum_{k=0}^{s} L(x(h), v_x^k(h), (i+1)h)\alpha_{i+1}^k$ can be viewed as the decision vector for the problem of minimizing $\tilde{Z}_N$ [Bel73]. At the same time there is a problem of finding the set of α_i^k's which minimizes this sum itself.

Equation (58) can be solved by means of differential geometry. The problem of minimizing $\tilde{Z}_N$ can be viewed as the problem of finding the parallel transport of the goal tangent vector along the geodesic to the point $x(t+h)$ [KNR95]. This global problem results in construction of a local goal. Then a minimizing set of chattering coefficients α_i^k, such that the linear combination of the primitive control actions with these coefficients approximates the local goal, can be found. This is a local problem. See figure (5).

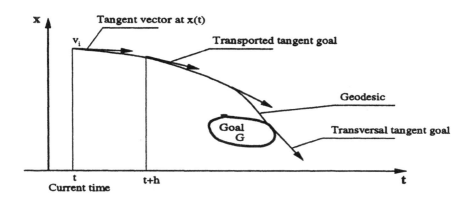

Fig. 5. Parallel Transport

Computing the geodesics The evolution manifold M in this problem is a subset of $\mathbf{R}^3$ where the trajectories of the system evolve. Figure (4) shows the embedding of the evolution manifold into $\mathbf{E}^3$.

The mappings are defined in the section 5. We will show how to find the geodesic for x^+ patch only. The geodesics for other patches will be the same by the uniqueness property of geodesics and due to the fact that patches overlap. A geodesic on a manifold is defined as the parametric curve $\alpha(t) = (\alpha_1(t), \alpha_2(t), \alpha_3(t))$ which solves the differential equation

$$\nabla_{\frac{d\alpha}{dt}} \frac{d\alpha}{dt} = 0 \tag{59}$$

Define $\eta(t) = \mathbf{x}^{-1} \circ \alpha(t)$. It follows that

$$\alpha(t) = \mathbf{x} \circ \eta(t). \tag{60}$$

In this case

$$
\begin{aligned}
T_\alpha &= \frac{d\alpha}{dt} \\
&= \partial(\mathbf{x} \circ \eta(t)) \\
&= \eta_1{}'(t)\mathbf{x}_{\mathbf{u}_1}(\alpha(t)) + \eta_2{}'(t)\mathbf{x}_{\mathbf{u}_1}(\alpha(t))
\end{aligned} \tag{61}
$$

where $\mathbf{x}_{\mathbf{u}_1}(\alpha(t)) = \frac{\partial \mathbf{x}}{\partial u_1}(\alpha(t))$ and $\mathbf{x}_{\mathbf{u}_2} = \frac{\partial \mathbf{x}}{\partial u_2}(\alpha(t))$ form basis of the tangent spaces at the points on M along $\alpha(t)$.

Equation (59) then becomes

$$\eta_k{}''(t) + \sum_{i,j=1}^{2} \Gamma_{ij}^{k} \eta_j{}'(t)\eta_i{}'(t) = 0, \quad k = 1..2. \tag{62}$$

where Γ_{ij}^{k} are the Christoffel symbols associated with the patch. Christoffel symbols are calculated using the formula (for a Riemannian manifold)

$$\Gamma_{ij}^{k} = \frac{1}{2} \sum_{k=1}^{2} g^{kl} \left(\frac{\partial g_{ik}}{\partial u_j} - \frac{\partial g_{ij}}{\partial u_k} + \frac{\partial g_{kj}}{\partial u_i} \right), \tag{63}$$

where $g_{ij} = < \frac{\partial \mathbf{x}}{\partial u_i}, \frac{\partial \mathbf{x}}{\partial u_j} >$, $i, j = 1, 2$ and the matrix (g^{kl}) is the inverse of (g_{ij}). Usually g_{ij} are called the coefficients of the Riemannian metric. The Christoffel symbols for the patches defined above are:

$$\boxed{\Gamma_{11}^{1} = \frac{u_1}{r^2 - u_1^2}} \tag{64}$$

and the rest of the Christoffel symbols equal to zero. Hence equation (62) becomes

$$\eta_1{}''(t) + \frac{\eta_1(t)}{r^2 - \eta_1^2(t)} \eta_1{}'(t)\eta_1{}'(t) = 0 \tag{65}$$

$$\eta_2{}''(t) = 0. \tag{66}$$

Upon solving this system for $\eta(t)$ one obtains

$$\eta(t) = (r\sin(ct + d), at + b), \tag{67}$$

where a, b, c, d are constants. Substituting (67) into equation (60) one obtains the equation of geodesics.

$$\boxed{\alpha(t) = (r\sin(ct + d), at + b, r\cos(ct + d))} \tag{68}$$

Computing the Chattering Coefficients Having found the vector of the local goal v_g and the fields of local extremals v_k^1, v_k^2, we want to find the coefficients α_k^1 and α_k^2 of the chattering combination of v_k^1 and v_k^2 such that this chattering combination approximates v_g. In this section, we will show how to compute chattering coefficients for the 2-dimensional case. By induction, this can be extended to n-dimensions.

Let $\Psi(t,x)$ be a smooth curve on manifold M parameterized by t and passing through the point $x \in M$ and defined by (see Figure 6):

$$\Psi(\varepsilon,x) = \exp(-\alpha_2\sqrt{\varepsilon}v_k^2)\exp(-\alpha_1\sqrt{\varepsilon}v_k^1)\exp(\alpha_2\sqrt{\varepsilon}v_k^2)\exp(\alpha_1\sqrt{\varepsilon}v_k^1). \qquad (69)$$

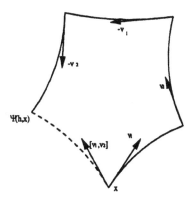

Fig. 6. Chattering approximation to the Lie bracket

Here x is the state of the system at time (kh). We also assume that $\Psi(0,x) = x$. Then using the results of the theorem 1.33 [Olv93], for sufficiently small $\varepsilon \geq 0$,

$$\begin{aligned}
\Psi(\varepsilon,x) = \Psi(0,x) &+ \alpha_k^1\alpha_k^2\{v_k^1(\eta(x)) - v_k^2(\zeta(x))\}\varepsilon \\
&+ \alpha_k^1\alpha_k^2\{\frac{1}{2}\alpha_k^1v_k^1(v_k^1(\eta(x))) - \frac{1}{2}\alpha_k^2v_k^2(v_k^1(\eta(x))) \\
&+ \alpha_k^2v_k^1(v_k^2(\eta(x))) - \alpha_k^1v_k^2(v_k^1(\zeta(x))) \\
&+ \frac{1}{2}\alpha_k^1v_k^1(v_k^2(\zeta(x))) - \alpha_k^2v_k^2(v_k^2(\zeta(x)))\}\varepsilon^{\frac{3}{2}} + O(\varepsilon^2),
\end{aligned} \qquad (70)$$

where $\zeta(x) = (\zeta_1(x), \zeta_2(x))$ and $\eta(x) = (\eta_1(x), \eta_2(x))$ are the coefficients of v_k^1 and v_k^2 respectively at x. We can write for the tangent vector v_t to this curve at x

$$v_t = \frac{\Psi(\varepsilon,x) - \Psi(0,x)}{\varepsilon} + O(\varepsilon^2) \qquad (71)$$

We want the tangent vector of the curve given by the equation (70) to coincide with the local goal. Thus we substitute v_g into (70) to get

$$v_g = \alpha_k^1 \alpha_k^2 [v_k^1, v_k^2]|_x + \alpha_k^1 \alpha_k^2 \{ \frac{1}{2} \alpha_k^1 v_k^1 (v_k^1(\eta(x)))$$
$$- \frac{1}{2} \alpha_k^2 v_k^2 (v_k^1(\eta(x))) + \alpha_k^2 v_k^1 (v_k^2(\eta(x)))$$
$$- \alpha_k^1 v_k^2 (v_k^1(\zeta(x))) + \frac{1}{2} \alpha_k^1 v_k^1 (v_k^2(\zeta(x))) \qquad (72)$$
$$- \alpha_k^2 v_k^2 (v_k^2(\zeta(x)))\}h + O(h^2),$$

where $[\,,\,]$ denotes the Lie bracket and $h = \sqrt{(\varepsilon)}$ is the step size defined such that the ϵ-optimality condition is satisfied. We can solve this algebraic equation to get chattering coefficients which give the chattering combination of the vectors v_k^1 and v_k^2 of the local basis of the tangent space at the current point x. This chattering combination approximates the local goal vector v_g.

8 Conclusions

In this work we introduced the major components of the Kohn-Nerode control law extraction procedure. It was shown how differential geometry and dynamic programming can be incorporated naturally by introducing the evolution manifold of the system for solving practical real-world problems, such as the inverted pendulum problem. Maple procedures for computing the inverse Lagrangian, introducing constraints and computing the chattering coefficients where developed and tested on the model of the University of Washington Controls Laboratory linear track cart pendulum. Currently the authors are working on the implementation of computing the local extremals and differential map in order to be able to run simulations. The results of this work will be reported in the future papers.

Acknowledgements Authors would like to acknowledge their sincere appreciation to the employees of HyBrithms Corp. Dr. Wolf Kohn, Dr. Jeff Remmel, and Dr. Anil Nerode for the invaluable discussions which gave rise to this work.

References

[Bel73]   Richard Bellman. *Methods of nonlinear analysis*. Academic Press, New York, 1973.

[Ber74]   L.D. Berkovitz. *Optimal Control Theory*. Springer-Verlag, New York, Heidelberg, Berlin, 1974.

[Bin70]   S. Bingulac. An alternate approach to expanding PA+A'P=-Q. *IEEE Trans. Automatic Control*, 15:135–136, 1970.

[Che70]   Chi-Tsong Chen. *Introduction to Linear System Theory*. Holt, Rinehart and Winston, Inc., New York, 1970.

[KN92]   W. Kohn and A. Nerode. An autonomous control theory: an overview. In *IEEE Symposium on Computer Aided Control System Design*, pages 204–210, Napa Valley, CA, March 1992.

[KN93]   W. Kohn and A. Nerode. Models for hybrid systems: automata, topologies, controllability and observability. *Hybrid Systems*, (736):317–356, 1993.

[KN97]   W. Kohn and A. Nerode. Quantum wave processor. Technical report, HyBrithms, 1997.

[KNR95]   W. Kohn, A. Nerode, and J. B. Remmel. Hybrid systems as finsler manifolds: Finite state control as approximation to connections. *Hybrid Systems II*, (999), 1995.

[KNR96a]   W. Kohn, A. Nerode, and J. B. Remmel. Continualization: A hybrid systems control technique for computing. In *Symposium on Control, Optimization and Supervision, CESA 96*, pages 517–521, Lille, France, 1996.

[KNR96b]   W. Kohn, A. Nerode, and J. B. Remmel. Feedback derivations: Near optimal controls for hybrid systems. In *Symposium on Control, Optimization and Supervision, CESA 96*, pages 507–511, Lille, France, 1996.

[KNRG94]   W. Kohn, A. Nerode, J. B. Remmel, and X. Ge. Multiple agent hybrid control: carrier manifolds and chattering approximations to optimal control. In *CDC94*, 1994.

[Koh88a]   W. Kohn. A declarative theory for rational controllers. In *Proc. 27th IEEE CDC*, pages 130–136, 1988.

[Koh88b]   W. Kohn. Symbolic generator of state space models. *Aerospace Simulation*, 19(2):299–307, 1988.

[MP77]   Richard S. Millman and George D. Parker. *Elements of Differential Geometry*. Prentice-Hall, Englewood Cliffs,NJ, 1977.

[NK93]   A. Nerode and W. Kohn. Multiple agent hybrid control architecture. In R. Grossman, A. Nerode, A. Ravn, and H. Rischel, editors, *Hybrid Systems*, number 736 in Lecture Notes in Computer Science, pages 297–316. Springer-Verlag, 1993.

[Olv93]   Peter J. Olver. *Applications of Lie Groups to Differential Equations*. Springer-Verlag, second edition, 1993.

[Ros70]   H.H. Rosenbrock. *State-space and Multivariable Theory*. John Wiley&Sons, N.Y, 1970.

[Sep94]   Kalev Sepp. Robust control of linear track cart-pendulum. Master's thesis, University of Washington, 1994.

[War72]   J. Warga. *Optimal Control of Differential and Functional Equations*. Academic Press, New York and London, 1972.

[You80]   L. C. Young. *Lectures on the Calculus Of Variations and Optimal Control Theory*. Chelsea Pub. Company, New York, N. Y., 1980.

Appendix A: System Parameters

Table 1. Numerical values of the Linear Track Cart Pendulum system parameters

Parameter	Symbol	Value	Unit
Mass of the cart	M	2.3	kg
Radius of the pulley	r	0.08	m
Distance from the pivot to the center of mass	l	0.1578	kg
Mass of the pendulum	m	0.324	kg
Inertia about the center of mass	J	0.008	$kg \cdot m^2$
Viscous friction coefficient between cart and track	c1	5	kg/s
Viscous friction coefficient at the pivot	c2	0.003	$kg \cdot m^2/rad \cdot s$
Motor and rotor inertia	J_m	0.00458	$kg \cdot m^2$
Motor constant	K	0.137	$V/(rad/sec)$
Current mode gain of the amplifier	k_i	1.2	A/V
Gravitational constant	g	9.807	m/s^2

Decidability of Hybrid Systems with Linear and Nonlinear Differential Inclusions

M. Broucke and P. Varaiya *

Department of Electrical Engineering and Computer Science
University of California, Berkeley CA 94720
mire, varaiya@eclair.eecs.berkeley.edu

1 Introduction

Hybrid systems are dynamic systems consisting of a two-level architecture in which the upper level is a finite automaton and the lower level is a continuous dynamical system. Models and architectures for hybrid systems have been proposed by a number of research groups [11, 12, 4, 13].

Applications for the hybrid modeling approach arise in control of systems that cannot easily be controlled through a single conventional control law, including switched systems; large scale systems and systems with multiple communicating control agents; systems with multiple control objectives; and systems modeling the interaction of (digital) computer processes and continuous plant dynamics. A critical area of investigation is analytical and algorithmic tools for the verification of qualitative properties of the trajectories of hybrid systems. The decidability problem is to determine for a given class of hybrid systems whether a property such as safety or fairness is verifiable by an algorithm that terminates in a finite number of steps.

Early results on decidability for hybrid systems were for restricted classes of models, beginning with the result in [2, 3] for timed automata that the reachability problem is PSPACE-hard. This result was extended to initialized multi-rate timed automata (where the value of a clock is initialized whenever the dynamics for that clock change) by a state transformation [4, 5]. [1] showed that hybrid automata with rectangular differential inclusions are equivalent to multi-rate automata. [15, 6] showed that a hybrid automaton with rectangular differential inclusions could more directly be transformed to a multi-rate automaton, so that the reachability problem is decidable. Kesten, et. al. [10] introduced a class of hybrid automata called integration graphs in which clocks that can change dynamics between locations are not tested within loops. It was shown that the reachability problem is decidable for the case of a single timer and the case of a single test involving integrators.

Undecidability results are built around transformations of classes of automata to an automaton that can replicate nondeterministic 2-counter machines. It is known that the halting problem for these systems in undecidable. For example, a two-rate timed system that is not initialized can model a nondeterministic 2-counter machine. The main results on undecidability are summarized in the paper [6].

* Supported by the California Department of Transportation through the California PATH program

A more detailed account of results on decidability and undecidability can be found in the review articles [15, 6, 8, 9].

In this paper we extend the decidability result of [1]. The techniques and results presented are close to those of [7]; here we focus on the problem of hybrid systems with inclusion dynamics. We consider the following class of hybrid systems. The continuous dynamics are governed by linear differential inclusions of the form $\dot{x} \in [L, U]x$ where L and U are diagonal $n \times n$ matrices. The clock values are compared to constants in the guards, and the assignments of clocks during a transition are to constant, possibly nondeterministic values. The second class we consider consists of hybrid automata with nonlinear differential inclusions where the ith clock component follows an inclusion of the form $\dot{x}_i \in [l_i, u_i]f_i(x_i)$.

Modeling the continuous dynamics using inclusions is well-based. The inclusion can be thought of as an abstraction of behaviors resulting from a continuous control system. If, for example, the control is a regulator it may not be necessary to model the continuous dynamics in detail in a verification of the combined discrete-continuous system: the behavior of the continuous system has been made predictable by control. The inclusion approach follows with the philosophy of hybrid modeling that allows for non-unique solutions from one initial condition. The loosening of precision in defining the behavior of the system is accomodated by the verification tools for non-deterministic finite automata.

The paper is organized as follows. We first review some terminology and definitions needed for the rest of the paper. The third section develops the main results for decidability of the reach set problem for hybrid systems with linear differential inclusions, robustness of the reach set calculation, and decidability of the reach set problem for hybrid systems with nonlinear differential inclusions.

2 Preliminaries

Notation $(\mathbf{R}^+)$ $\mathbf{R}$ is the set of (non-negative) reals and $(\mathbf{Z}^+)$ $\mathbf{Z}$ is the set of (non-negative) integers. For $x \in \mathbf{R}^n$, we write x_i for the ith component of x. $\bar{\sigma}$ refers to a finite sequence of events $\sigma(i) \in \Sigma$ where Σ is a set of events. $s \xrightarrow{\bar{\sigma}} t$ means there is an event sequence $\bar{\sigma}$ such that final state t can be reached from initial state s. If ψ is a set of transition relations, then we write ψ^* for the transitive closure of ψ. Also, denote $s \xrightarrow{\bar{\sigma}} t$ by $(s, \bar{\sigma}, t) \in \psi^*$. G^c refers to the complement of set G.

Finite automata A finite automaton is a system $A = (L, \Sigma, \psi, I)$ where L is a finite set of discrete locations, Σ is a finite set of events, $I \subseteq L$ is a set of initial locations, and $\psi \subset L \times \Sigma \times L$ is a set of transition relations. Associated with each transition between locations l and l' is an event $\sigma \in \Sigma$.

The semantics of automaton A are defined on sequences of events $\sigma \in \Sigma$. If Σ^* is the set of all finite sequences of events, then we say the *language* of a finite automata is the set of sequences over Σ accepted by A:

$$\mathcal{L}(A) = \{\bar{\sigma} \in \Sigma^* \mid (l, \bar{\sigma}, l') \in \psi^*\}.$$

A *run* of a finite automata A over a sequence $\bar{\sigma} \in \Sigma^*$ is a sequence of locations visited by the automaton as it reads $\bar{\sigma}$

$$l(1) \xrightarrow{\sigma(1)} l(2) \xrightarrow{\sigma(2)} l(3) \xrightarrow{\sigma(3)} \cdots l(m-1) \xrightarrow{\sigma(m-1)} l(m).$$

Timed automata A timed automaton is a system $T = (Q, \Sigma, \psi, I)$ where $Q = L \times \mathbf{R}^n$ and $\psi \subset L \times \Sigma \times L \times G \times J$. Associated with each location is a set of n clocks with valuations, $x \in \mathbf{R}^n$. The state of a timed automaton is $q = (l, x) \in Q$. $I \subseteq Q$ is a set of initial locations and clock valuations. The clocks record the elapsed time; that is, $\dot{x}_i = 1$. Clock values can be reset upon taking a transition whenever an enabling condition on that transition is satisfied. Thus, each edge of the automaton has an enabling condition or guard, $\delta \in G$, where G is the set of all enabling conditions. An edge can reset clock values by a reset condition or jump, $\lambda \in J$, where J is the set of all reset conditions. Edges are labeled $(q, \sigma, q', \delta, \lambda)$ where q and q' are the originating and final locations and clock valuations, respectively.

Enabling conditions are formulas generated by the grammar:

$$\delta := x_i \leq c_i | x_i \geq c_i | x_i < c_i | x_i > c_i | \delta_1 \wedge \delta_2 | \delta_1 \vee \delta_2 \text{ where } c \in \mathbf{Z}$$

The reset condition $\lambda \in J$ initializes components of x when a transition is taken. The reset $\lambda_i = [a_i, b_i]$ initializes x_i nondeterministically to a value between a_i and b_i, where $a_i, b_i \in \mathbf{Z}$. When a clock is not reset $\lambda_i = id$.

The semantics of a timed automaton T are defined on timed sequences of events. A *timed sequence* is a pair $(\overline{\sigma}, \overline{t})$ where $\overline{\sigma} \in \Sigma^*$ and $\overline{t} = t(1), t(2), \ldots$ is a time sequence that satisfies $t(k) \in \mathbf{R}^+$ and $t(k) < t(k+1)$. We say the *language* of a finite automata is the set of timed sequences over $\Sigma \times \mathbf{R}^+$ accepted by T:

$$\mathcal{L}(T) = \{(\overline{\sigma}, \overline{t}) \mid (q, \overline{\sigma}, q') \in \psi^*\} .$$

where we abuse notation and drop reference to the enabling condition and reset of transitions in ψ. A *run* of a timed automata T over a timed sequence $(\overline{\sigma}, \overline{t})$ is a sequence of states $\overline{q}$ visited by the automaton and if $q(k) = (l(k), x(k))$, there is an edge with event $\sigma(k)$ and enabling condition $\delta(k)$ which evaluates to true for clock values $x(k) = x(k-1) + t(k) - t(k-1)$. $x(k)$ are reset by $\lambda(k)$ at $t(k)$ after the transition is taken.

Decidability of timed automata was shown by Alur and Dill [2] by forming equivalence classes in the space of continuous clocks. The equivalence classes partition R^n into a finite number of regions. The enabling conditions can be defined for positive or negative values of the clocks, and the clocks can be reset to a positive or negative integer value. All the clocks have rate $+1$.

We review some relations on automata that will be useful in the sequel.

We say timed automata $T_1 = (Q_1, \Sigma_1, \psi_1, I_1)$ and $T_2 = (Q_2, \Sigma_2, \psi_2, I_2)$ are *isomorphic* if there exists a bijection $f : Q_1 \to Q_2$ such that for $\sigma_1 \in \Sigma_1$ there exists $\sigma_2 \in \Sigma_2$, such that (1) $f(I_1) = I_2$, and (2) for all states $q, q' \in Q_1$, $(q, \sigma_1, q') \in \psi_1$ iff $(f(q), \sigma_2, f(q')) \in \psi_2$.

Given timed automata $T_1 = (Q_1, \Sigma_1, \psi_1, I_1)$ and $T_2 = (Q_2, \Sigma_2, \psi_2, I_2)$, we say that T_2 *simulates* T_1 with relation $R \subset Q_1 \times Q_2$, if $(p, q) \in R$ and $p \xrightarrow{\sigma_1} p'$, with $\sigma_1 \in \Sigma_1$, imply that there exists $q' \in Q_2$ and $\sigma_2 \in \Sigma_2$ such that $q \xrightarrow{\sigma_2} q'$ and $(p', q') \in R$.

Given timed automata $T_1 = (Q_1, \Sigma_1, \psi_1, I_1)$ and $T_2 = (Q_2, \Sigma_2, \psi_2, I_2)$, we say $R \subset Q_1 \times Q_2$ is a *bisimulation* if T_2 simulates T_1 with R and T_1 simulates T_2 with $R^{-1} \in Q_2 \times Q_1$ where $R^{-1} = \{(q, p) | (p, q) \in R\}$.

For the sake of completeness, we state the following well-known result of [2].

Theorem 1 Let T be a timed automaton with n clocks. There exists a finite automaton U which is a bisimulation for T.

Finally, we define a class of initialized timed automata called PN (positive/negative) timed automata.

PN timed automata A PN timed automata is a system $T = (Q, \Sigma, D, \psi, I)$. $Q = L \times \mathbf{R}^n$, and L, $\mathbf{R}^n$, Σ, and I are the same as for timed automata. As before, associated with each edge is an event $\sigma \in \Sigma$, an enabling condition $\delta \in G$, and a reset condition $\lambda \in J$. What is new is a set $D \subset \mathbf{Z}^n$ of continuous state rates. A rate assignment $d \in D$ is associated with each location such that $\dot{x}_i = d_i$, where the components d_i take only one of three values $d_i = \{-1, 0, 1\}$. We require that $\lambda_i \neq id$ if d_i changes upon transitioning from one location to another; therefore, PN timed automata are initialized.

Lemma 2 Let $T = (Q, \Sigma, D, \psi, I)$ be a PN timed automaton. There exists a finite automaton U which is a bisimulation for T.

Proof PN timed automata are initialized multirate timed automata which are isomorphic to finite automata. [4, 5]. □

3 Hybrid systems

A hybrid automaton is a system $H = (Q, \Sigma, D, \psi, I)$, where $Q = L \times \mathbf{R}^n$, L is a finite set of discrete locations, Σ is a set of events, $\psi \subset L \times \Sigma \times L \times G \times J$ is the set of transition relations, and $I \subseteq Q$ is the set of initial locations. ψ labels edges of the automaton by $(l, \sigma, l', \delta, \lambda) \in \psi$. The edge is from location l to l', $\delta \in G$ is an enabling condition, and $\lambda \in J$ is a reset condition. The only change from PN timed automata is that D now defines a set of differential inclusions, with one inclusion associated with each component of the continuous state.

As before, enabling conditions are associated with the edges between discrete locations of the hybrid automaton and they are of the form:

$$\delta := x_i \leq c | x_i \geq c | x_i < c | x_i > c | \delta_1 \wedge \delta_2 | \delta_1 \vee \delta_2 \quad \text{where } c \in \mathbf{Z}$$

Likewise, reset conditions are defined on the edges between discrete states for some components of the continuous state. The reset is of the form $\lambda_i = [r_i, s_i]$ or $\lambda_i = id$ for $r_i, s_i \in \mathbf{Z}$. When λ_i is the identity relation, x_i is not reset. When $\lambda_i = [r_i, s_i]$, x_i is reset non-deterministically to a value between r_i and s_i.

We require $\lambda_i \neq id$ whenever the inclusion for x_i changes in a transition from l to l'.

The *reach set* of a hybrid automaton H, written $Reach_H(Q_0)$, $Q_0 \subseteq Q$, is the set of states that can be reached in any run starting from Q_0.

3.1 Hybrid automata with linear differential inclusions

Now we will extend our definition of hybrid automata to a class with a linear differential inclusion for the continuous state. We consider a hybrid automata $H =$

(Q, Σ, D, ψ, I) where, within each location l, the continuous dynamics satisfy an inclusion $\dot{x} \in [L, U]x \in D$. $L, U \in \mathbf{R}^{n \times n}$ are diagonal matrices so that the inclusion for x_i is

$$\dot{x}_i \in [l_i, u_i]x_i$$

and $u_i \geq l_i$.

The objective is to find a decidable simulation for this hybrid automaton. Several steps are needed to transform to a decidable class of automata. The trajectories generated by H form a "funnel" with a rectangular cross-section. The ith coordinate of the extremal trajectories have derivatives equal to the extreme values $l_i x_i$ or $u_i x_i$. These trajectories are made up of segments of increasing or decreasing exponentials.

The exponential segments may be initialized with a positive or negative reset value for each clock component. Referring to Figure 1, the essential features of the automaton that will be transformed for each location l are the reset conditions on transitions entering the location, the enabling conditions on the transitions leaving the location, and the inclusion in each location which will dictate how the reset and enabling conditions are modified.

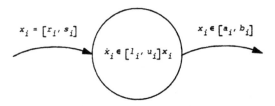

Fig. 1. Automata H: hybrid system with linear differential inclusions.

The steps of the transformation are:

1. Convert automaton H of Figure 1 to one with positive trajectories, automaton P of Figure 2.
2. Convert automaton P with positive trajectories and linear inclusions to one with an augmented continuous state space and linear differential equations, automaton A of Figure 4.
3. Convert automaton A to a PN timed automaton T.

Summary of transformation We consider each of the four steps above. We start with a hybrid automaton with linear differential inclusions.

Step 1 Within each location the trajectories of each component is either positive or negative, accordingly as its initial value is positive or negative. If necessary, we use a change of variables $x_i \to -x_i$ to make the initial condition positive. We need to keep track of this change of variables, and that is done by adding a "discrete" state (equivalently, by splitting the location into several locations). Call the new automaton P.

Step 2 In each location, the continuous state of P satisfies an inclusion of the form:

$$\dot{x}_i \in [l_i, u_i]x_i.$$

Convert P to an automaton L with $2n$ states. To state x_i of P is associated a pair of states y_{2i-1}, y_{2i} of L which satisfy the linear differential equations

$$\dot{y}_{2i-1} = l_i y_{2i-1}, \quad \dot{y}_{2i} = u_i y_{2i}.$$

The reach set of P is a rectangle whose $2n$ vertices are given by the reach set of L.

Step 3 Convert L to a PN automaton T as follows. Within each location, each component y_j of a trajectory of L is an exponential. With an appropriate choice of α_j in the nonlinear change of variables, $\alpha_j \ln y_j \to z_j$, the z_j trajectories have a constant slope of -1, 0 or 1. This is a PN automaton T, except that the guards in T need no longer be rational because of the nonlinear transformation.

Step 4 Change the guards of H so that the guards of T become rational. This can be done with arbitrarily small changes. Call the resulting hybrid automaton H'. Using Theorem 7 it follows that H' is a simulation of H.

Automaton P The first step is to convert all negative valued components of x to positive values; in other words, if any reset condition sets a component of x to a negative value, we will transform it to a positive value. We define two variables $h_i = sgn(x_i)$ and $w_i = |x_i|$ so that $x_i = h_i w_i$ and construct an automaton P shown in Figure 2. It consists of the same discrete locations and transitions as the original automaton but has continuous states $w_i \geq 0$ and includes an additional discrete state variable $h \in \mathbf{Z}^n$ that records the sign of the continuous components of the original automaton, so that the new discrete state is $l' = (l, h)$. Thus, if the original automaton has m discrete states, the new automaton has $m3^n$ discrete states. Automaton P has only positive valued exponential trajectories.

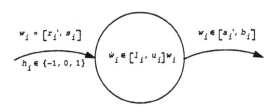

Fig. 2. Automaton P: hybrid system with linear differential inclusions and positive-valued trajectories.

The variable h is assigned upon entering a discrete location by recording the sign of the trajectory in the original automaton after a reset occurs. For a reset of the form $x_i := [r_i, s_i]$ with $r_i, s_i > 0$, $h_i = 1$. If $r_i, s_i < 0$, then $h_i = -1$. If there is no reset on x_i then $h_i = id$. Finally, if $r_i < 0$ and $s_i > 0$ for any component of x, the transition can be split into three transitions. The first transition includes all negative resets $x_i := [r_i, s_i]$, $r_i, s_i < 0$ and for any reset with $r_i < 0$ and $s_i > 0$, a new reset $x_i := [r_i, 0)$. The second transition includes for any reset with $r_i < 0$ and $s_i > 0$, a new reset $x_i := 0$. The third transition consists of all resets $x_i := [r_i, s_i]$, $r_i, s_i > 0$ and for any reset with $r_i < 0$ and $s_i > 0$, a new reset $x_i := (0, s_i]$. Thus, for all i, the first transition assigns $h_i = -1$, the second assigns $h_i = 0$, and the

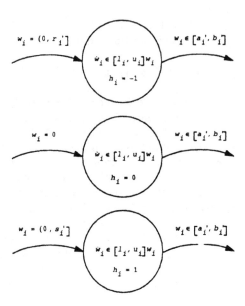

Fig. 3. Automata P: hybrid system with linear differential inclusions.

third assigns $h_i = 1$. This case is shown in Figure 3. If there is no reset for x_i, then $h_i = id$ in each of the three transitions.

Enabling conditions of P are of the form $w_i \in [a'_i, b'_i]$ where $a'_i = a_i$ if $h_i = 0$ or $h_i = 1$, and $a'_i = -a_i$ if $h_i = -1$. A similar transformation applies to b'_i.

Lemma 4 Automaton H and automaton P are isomorphic.

Proof Automaton H and automaton P have identical discrete locations and transitions, and the tranformation of the continuous states is described by the bijection $x_i = h_i w_i$. The transformation of the resets and enabling conditions is explained above. □

A consequence of Lemma 4 is that if the bijection from automaton H to automaton P is f then $Reach_P(f(Q_0)) = f(Reach_H(Q_0))$.

Automaton A In the second step we consider the automaton P with positive trajectories and follow the approach of [6] where an automaton with differential inclusions is converted to an automaton with differential equations. Thus, we form a new automaton A with an augmented state space in $\mathbf{R}^{2n}$ such that corresponding to each component x_i there are two components, y_{2i-1} and y_{2i} in automaton A, with dynamics:

$$\dot{y}_{2i-1} = l_i y_{2i-1}$$
$$\dot{y}_{2i} = u_i y_{2i} .$$

See Figure 4. y_{2i-1} and y_{2i} satisfy $y_{2i-1} \leq x_i \leq y_{2i}$. Further, the reach sets are related as follows. When automaton P reaches (l, w), automaton A reaches $\{l\} \times [y_1, y_2] \times ... \times [y_{2n-1}, y_{2n}]$.

The reset condition $w_i := [r'_i, s'_i]$ is transformed to $y_{2i-1} := r'_i$ and $y_{2i} := s'_i$. To obtain the new enabling conditions for automaton A, consider an enabling condition

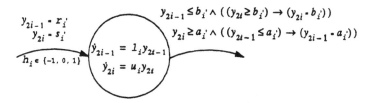

Fig. 4. Automaton A: hybrid system with linear clock rates.

of the form $a_i' \leq w_i \leq b_i'$. If w_i of automaton P satisfies $w_i \geq a_i'$, then in automaton A, $y_{2i} \geq a_i'$. When the transition is taken and $y_{2i-1} \leq a_i'$, it is necessary to reset the lower trajectory y_{2i-1} to a_i'. Thus, the enabling condition $w_i \geq a_i'$ becomes

$$(y_{2i} \geq a_i' \wedge ((y_{2i-1} \leq a_i') \longrightarrow (y_{2i-1} := a_i')) \tag{1}$$

Similarly, if $w_i \leq b_i'$, then $y_{2i-1} \leq b_i'$ and if $y_{2i} \geq b_i'$, it must be reset to b_i', so the enabling condition becomes

$$(y_{2i-1} \leq b_i' \wedge ((y_{2i} \geq b_i') \longrightarrow (y_{2i} := b_i')). \tag{2}$$

The next theorem will show that there is a simulation relation between automaton A and automaton P and this relation will allow us to relate the reach sets of the two types of automata.

First we need a definition and a fact. If H is a hybrid automaton, then the reverse system is H^{-1} where if $(l, \sigma, l', \delta, \lambda) \in \psi_H$ then $(l', \sigma, l, \delta, \lambda) \in \psi_{H^{-1}}$ and $D_{-H} = -D_H$, that is all rates are reversed.

Fact 4 If A and B are automata, and B simulates A with simulation relation $S \subset Q_A \times Q_B$ and A^{-1} simulates B^{-1} with S^{-1}, and $Q_0 \subset Q_B$, then $Reach_A(S^{-1}(Q_0)) = S^{-1}(Reach_B(Q_0))$.

The next theorem gives the required relation between automaton A and automaton P, whose proof is found in [16].

Theorem 5 Let $P = (Q, \Sigma, D, \psi, I)$ be a hybrid automaton with linear differential inclusions $\dot{w} \in [L, U]w \in D$ where $L, U \in \mathbf{R}^{n \times n}$ are diagonal matrices and $w_i(t) \geq 0 \ \forall t$. There exists an automaton A with linear dynamics that simulates P with relation S^{-1} and P^{-1} simulates A^{-1} with relation S. The simulation relation is $S \subset (L, \mathbf{R}^n) \times (L, \mathbf{R}^{2n})$

$$S = \{((l, y), (l, w)) \mid y_{2i-1} \leq w_i \leq y_{2i}\} .$$

Automaton T The last step of our procedure is to apply a transformation to the variables y of A to obtain a PN timed automaton T. Consider the upper trajectory formed by y_{2i}. Define a new state variable $z_{2i} = y_{2i} + v_{2i}$ and pick the feedback v_{2i} to satisfy $\dot{v}_{2i} = -u_i y_{2i} + d_i$. Then,

$$\dot{z}_{2i} = \dot{y}_{2i} + \dot{v}_{2i} = d_i .$$

In the z state space the linear dynamics have been transformed to constant rates: $\dot{z}_{2i-1} = c_i$ and $\dot{z}_{2i} = d_i$ and we may pick $c_i, d_i \in \mathbf{R}$, $c_i \leq d_i$. If we apply this technique to all continuous state components, we obtain a new automaton T with constant rate dynamics.

Note that the transformation from y to z variables can be achieved equivalently by the bijection:

$$z_{2i-1} = \begin{cases} \frac{c_i}{l_i} \ln y_{2i-1} & \text{if } l_i \neq 0 \\ y_{2i-1} & \text{if } l_i = 0 \end{cases} \tag{3}$$

$$z_{2i} = \begin{cases} \frac{d_i}{u_i} \ln y_{2i} & \text{if } u_i \neq 0 \\ y_{2i} & \text{if } u_i = 0 \end{cases} \tag{4}$$

Next we must transform the enabling conditions to the z coordinates. Consider $y_{2i} \geq a_i'$. Let $y_{2i}^o > 0$ be the initial condition for y_{2i} in a location l. Suppose first that $a_i' > 0$. If $u_i > 0$ we can find a time when y_{2i} first reaches a_i' after which the enabling condition is satisfied, i.e., $t \geq \frac{1}{u_i} \ln \frac{a_i'}{y_{2i}^o}$. At that time the upper component z_{2i} will have reached

$$z_{2i} = d_i t + z_{2i}^o = \frac{d_i}{u_i} \ln |a_i'| - \frac{d_i}{u_i} \ln |y_{2i}^o| + z_{2i}^o \ . \tag{5}$$

To eliminate the dependence on initial conditions, pick $z_{2i}^o = \frac{d_i}{u_i} \ln |y_{2i}^o|$. If we pick $d_i > 0$, then the enabling condition becomes $z_{2i} \geq \frac{d_i}{u_i} \ln |a_i'|$.

If $u_i < 0$ then we are interested in the first time that y_{2i} no longer satisfies $y_{2i} \geq a_i'$. This translates to the condition $t \leq \frac{1}{u_i} \ln \frac{a_i'}{y_{2i}^o}$. Note that if $a_i' > y_{2i}^o$ the condition is never satisfied, as expected. Now if we pick initial conditions as before and select $d_i < 0$ the enabling condition is the same as before: $z_{2i} \geq \frac{d_i}{u_i} \ln |a_i'|$.

The third case, when $a_i' > 0$ and $u_i = 0$ corresponds to the transformation $z_{2i} = y_{2i}$; thus the enabling condition becomes $z_{2i} \geq a_i'$. When $a_i' \leq 0$ the enabling condition is always satisfied because y_{2i} is positive-valued, so the enabling condition is *true*.

Finally, we must consider what happens when $y_{2i}^o = 0$. This case arises whenever a transition is taken that sets $h_i = 0$ and $y_{2i} \geq a_i'$ is either always true or always false. We transform the enabling condition by setting $u_i = 0$, which implies $z_{2i} = y_{2i}$; thus, $z_{2i} \geq a_i'$ is the transformed enabling condition.

We can now pick values for the rate d_i following the choices that simplified the enabling conditions in the preceding discussion:

$$d_i = \begin{cases} 1 & u_i > 0 \\ -1 & u_i < 0 \\ 0 & h_i u_i = 0 \end{cases}$$

This selection of rates is almost in the form of a PN timed automaton, except that the rates cannot be assigned a priori because of the dependence on h_i. To remove this dependence, recall that we have partitioned the transitions so that they assign h_i uniquely. Consider transitions with the label $h_i = 0$. We can create a new discrete location l^o which has as input transitions, those transitions of location l, with $h_i = 0$ and with the same output transitions of l. Also, we redefine $u_i = 0$ in location l^o since this does not change the dynamics. With this modification of the automaton, we may assign rates for d_i:

$$d_i = \begin{cases} 1 & u_i > 0 \\ -1 & u_i < 0 \\ 0 & u_i = 0 \end{cases} \tag{6}$$

To summarize, the transformation of enabling condition expressions $y_{2i} \geq a'_i$ is:

$$
\begin{array}{ll}
(a'_i > 0) \wedge (u_i \neq 0) & \longrightarrow (z_{2i} \geq \frac{d_i}{u_i} \ln |a'_i|) \\
(a'_i > 0) \wedge (u_i = 0) & \longrightarrow (z_{2i} \geq a'_i) \\
(a'_i \leq 0) & \longrightarrow (true) \, .
\end{array} \tag{7}
$$

After repeating the above procedure for enabling condition expressions $y_{2i-1} \leq b_i$ for the lower component, the transformed expression is:

$$
\begin{array}{ll}
(b'_i > 0) \wedge (l_i \neq 0) & \longrightarrow (z_{2i-1} \leq \frac{c_i}{l_i} \ln |b'_i|) \\
(l_i = 0) & \longrightarrow (z_{2i} \leq b'_i) \, .
\end{array} \tag{8}
$$

where we do not include the case of $(b'_i \leq 0)$ because it always evaluates to *false*. The rate for z_{2i-1} is selected by:

$$c_i = \begin{cases} 1 & l_i > 0 \\ -1 & l_i < 0 \\ 0 & l_i = 0 \end{cases} \tag{9}$$

after creating new locations l^o with input transitions that set $h_i = 0$ and then setting $l_i = 0$ in l^o.

The resets are transformed according to the bijection from y to z. $y_{2i-1} := r'_i$ becomes

$$
\begin{array}{ll}
z_{2i-1} := \frac{c_i}{l_i} \ln r'_i & \text{if } r'_i > 0 \\
z_{2i-1} := r'_i & \text{if } r'_i = 0 \text{ or } l_i = 0
\end{array} \tag{10}
$$

Similarly, for resets $y_{2i} := s'_i$,

$$
\begin{array}{ll}
z_{2i} := \frac{d_i}{u_i} \ln s'_i & \text{if } s'_i > 0 \\
z_{2i} := s'_i & \text{if } s'_i = 0 \text{ or } u_i = 0
\end{array} \tag{11}
$$

Theorem 6 Automaton A and automaton T are isomorphic.

Proof We construct a bijection from locations and transitions of A to locations and transitions of T: either the locations are identical, or locations in A with $h_i = 0$ can be mapped to a location in T uniquely. The continuous states are related by the bijection of Equation 3. The enabling conditions are related by Equations 7 and 8, and the reset conditions are related by Equations 10 and 11. $\qquad \square$

A consequence of Theorem 6 is that we can relate the reach sets of the two automata; namely, if the bijection from automaton A to automaton T is f then $Reach_T(f(Q_0)) = f(Reach_A(Q_0))$.

Theorem 7 Let $H = (Q, \Sigma, D, \psi, I)$ be a linear hybrid automaton with differential inclusions $\dot{x} \in [L, U]x \in D$ where $L, U \in \mathbf{R}^{n \times n}$ are diagonal matrices. There exists a decidable hybrid automaton $H' = (Q, \Sigma, D, \psi', I)$ with Q, Σ, D, and I the same as in H. The enabling conditions δ' of H' can be made arbitrarily close to δ.

Proof The proof relies on invoking the steps of the transformation just described. First, Lemma 4 says we can calculate $Reach_H$ from $Reach_P$. Theorem 5 says we can calculate $Reach_P$ from $Reach_A$. Finally, Theorem 6 says we can calculate $Reach_A$ from $Reach_T$. We want to show that by a perturbation of the enabling conditions of H, P will be a PN timed automaton, and we showed in Lemma 2 that we can obtain a finite computation of $Reach_T$; that is, reachability of T, a PN timed automaton, is decidable.

To construct the adjusted enabling conditions of H', partition the real line in intervals of length $\frac{1}{q}$, $q \in \mathbf{Z}_+$. Considering Equations 7 and 8, we require that the expressions on the right-hand sides are rational, so we can find the smallest $\beta_i \in \mathbf{Z}$ and largest $\alpha_i \in \mathbf{Z}$ such that

$$\frac{\alpha_i}{q} \leq \frac{d_i}{u_i} \ln |a_i'|; \quad \frac{c_i}{l_i} \ln |b_i'| \leq \frac{\beta_i}{q} \ .$$

We define

$$a_i'' = \exp(\frac{\alpha_i u_i}{q d_i})$$

$$b_i'' = \exp(\frac{\beta_i l_i}{q c_i}) \ .$$

Then given any $\epsilon > 0$

$$|a_i''|[1 + o(\epsilon)] \geq |a_i'| \geq |a_i''|$$
$$|b_i''|[1 - o(\epsilon)] \leq |b_i'| \leq |b_i''|$$

This follows by picking $q = \max\{\frac{u_i}{d_i \epsilon}, \frac{l_i}{c_i \epsilon}\}$ and noting that

$$\frac{\alpha_i + 1}{q} \geq \frac{d_i}{u_i} \ln |a_i'| \geq \frac{\alpha_i}{q}$$

$$\implies |a_i''| \exp(\frac{u_i}{d_i q}) \geq |a_i'| \geq |a_i''|$$

$$\implies |a_i''|[1 + o(\epsilon)] \geq |a_i'| \geq |a_i''| \ .$$

The same argument applies for b_i''. Thus, if we use a_i'' and b_i'' in Equations 7 and 8 for automaton H', then after transformation to automaton T, the enabling conditions are defined on rationals and the result follows. □

Lemma 8 The set of decidable hybrid automata with linear differential inclusions is dense.

Proof Follows from the fact that the rationals are dense. □

3.2 Robustness

Theorem 7 constructs a modified automaton whose reach set is an approximation of the original automaton's reach set. The modified automaton is an over-approximation in that it has more permissive enabling conditions and thus will allow more trajectories than the original automaton H.

It is interesting to ask what is the robustness of the reach set calculation to perturbations of the enabling conditions. To make progress on this question, it is helpful to characterize the form of the reach set. Let $S_{[0,t]}(x^0)$ be the set of trajectories ϕ on the interval $[0,t]$ starting from x^0, and let $R(x^0,t)$ be the reach set for a time transition starting from the continuous state x^0. That is, $R(x^0,t) = \{\phi \mid \phi \in S_{[0,t]}(x^0)\}$. Each component ϕ_i satisfies

$$x_i^0 \exp(l_i t) \le \phi_i(t) \le x_i^0 \exp(u_i t)$$

where $\phi_i(0) = x_i^0$, so we can write

$$R(x^0,t) = \{F(t)x^0 \mid \exp(l_i t) \le F_i(t) \le \exp(u_i t)\},$$

where $F(t)$ is a diagonal $n \times n$ matrix with diagonal elements $F_i(t)$.

Now consider hybrid trajectories. Define the set of hybrid trajectories on an interval $[0,t]$ to be $H_{[0,t]}(x^0)$. As before, $Reach(x^0,t)$ is the set of states that can be reached from the initial state $q^0 = l^0 \times x^0$. We write $\pi \in H_{[0,t]}$ a hybrid trajectory as

$$\pi : (l^0, \phi^0, I^0), ..., (l^m, \phi^m, I^m)$$

where $I^i = [t_i, t_{i+1}]$ is the time interval of the ith phase, $\tau_i = t_{i+1} - t_i$ is the duration, and $\phi^i : I^i \to R^n$, $\phi^i \in S_{[t_i, t_{i+1}]}(x^i)$.

The kth phase (l^k, ϕ^k, I^k) of a hybrid trajectory consists of three components:
1) initial condition: ϕ^{k-1},
2) time transition: $R(\phi^{k-1}, \tau_k)$,
3) enabling condition and reset, forming the graph $E_k : G_k \times \lambda_k$, where G_k is the enabling condition and λ_k is the reset. λ_k can be represented in general form as the map $\lambda_k(x) = A_k x + B_k$ where A_k is an $n \times n$ matrix and $B_k \subset R^n$ is convex. We can write the kth phase in the form of a discrete update of the continuous states:

$$\begin{aligned} \phi^k &= A_k[R(\phi^{k-1}, \tau_k) \cap G_k] + B_k \\ &= \Phi^k(\phi^{k-1}, \tau_k). \end{aligned} \tag{12}$$

where $R(\phi^{k-1}, \tau_k) = F(\tau_k)\phi^{k-1}$, as defined above. Thus, the reach set at time t is:

$$\begin{aligned} Reach(x^0,t) &= \bigcup_{\sum_{k=1}^m \tau_k = t} \Phi^m(...\Phi^2(\Phi^1(x^0, \tau_1), \tau_2), ...\tau_m) \\ &= \bigcup_{\sum_{k=1}^m \tau_k = t} (\phi^m \circ ... \circ \phi^1)(x^0) \end{aligned}$$

where we take the union over hybrid trajectories on $[0,t]$.

Now the approximate reach set is obtained by small perturbations of the enabling regions G_k. The outer reach set approximation is obtained from Equation (12) be replacing G_k by $G_k^\epsilon = G_k + B_\epsilon$, where B_ϵ is an ϵ-ball, and it is denoted by $Reach^\epsilon(x^0,t)$. The main result for the outer reach set approximation is that under certain conditions, as ϵ goes to zero, the outer reach set approximation will approach the original reach set. The necessary conditions and result are summarized in the following theorem, whose proof can be found in [14].

Theorem 9 Assume that the enabling regions are closed, the initial region X^0 is compact, and there are at most a finite number of steps over a finite time interval.

Then the outer reach set approximation approaches the original reach set; that is, as $\epsilon \to 0$,

$$\bigcap_{\epsilon > 0} Reach^\epsilon(X^0, t) = Reach(X^0, t).$$

We consider next the inner reach set approximation which is obtained from Equation (12) by replacing G_k by $G_{k\delta} = \{x \mid d(x, G_k^c) > \delta\}$. The inner reach set approximation is denoted $Reach_\delta(X^0, t)$. It is clear that $\cup_{\delta > 0} Reach_\delta(X^0, t) \subset Reach(X^0, t)$. If $x \in Reach(X^0, t)$ it can be shown that every neighborhood of x contains a point of $\cup_{\delta > 0} Reach_\delta(X^0, t)$ so x is a limit point. Therefore, $x \in cl(\cup_{\delta > 0} Reach_\delta(X^0, t))$. The main result for the inner reach set approximation is the following [14].

Theorem 10 Assume that the enabling regions are closed, the initial region X^0 is compact, and there are at most a finite number of steps over a finite time interval. Then the inner reach set approximation will approach the interior of the original reach set; that is

$$cl(\bigcup_{\delta > 0} Reach_\delta(X^0, t)) = Reach(X^0, t).$$

3.3 Hybrid automata with nonlinear differential inclusions

We consider nonlinear hybrid automata in which the ith state component x_i follows an inclusion of the form $\dot{x}_i \in [l_i, u_i] f_i(x_i)$, with $l_i \leq u_i$, $l_i, u_i \in \mathbf{R}$, and

$$f_i(x_i) := 1 \mid x_i \mid f_i(x_i)$$

where $f_i(x_i)$ is continuous.

We will use a transformation technique analogous to the linear case to show that reachability for this class of nonlinear hybrid automata is decidable.

First, we will consider the ith clock component of location l of automaton H. We assume $f_i(x_i)$ has a finite number of zeros, so that we can identify a finite number of regions of f_i, labeled ρ_{ik}, ordered from left to right, and corresponding to the positive, negative, and zero-valued segments of f_i. Each ρ_{ik} identifies a range of values of x_i, i.e. $\rho_{ik} = [\alpha_{ik}, \beta_{ik}]$, $\alpha_{ik}, \beta_{ik} \in \mathbf{R}$. ρ_{ik} can be closed such as $\rho_{ik} = [-1, -1]$ or open, such as $\rho_{ik} = (-1, 0)$. We also identify the sign of each region: $h_{ik} = \{sgn(f_i(x_i)) \mid x_i \in \rho_{ik}\}$.

The procedure, as before, is to convert automaton H with inclusions to automaton P with clock components labeled by the regions defined above. Then convert automaton P to automaton A with linear differential equations. Finally, convert automaton A to PN timed automaton T.

We first construct automaton P. Suppose there are n clocks and each f_i has k_i regions. For each location l of automaton H, we create $\Pi_{i=1}^n k_i$ locations in automaton P. Define $h = [h_1 \ldots h_n]'$ with $h_i = sgn(f_i(x_i))$ Observe that in the linear case we kept track of the sign of the trajectory which could not change without a reset, because of the linear dynamics. Here we record invariant regions ρ_{ik} of the components of the trajectories and the clock components only change regions through a reset.

Any edge from location l' to l of H must have an edge from l' to each of the $\Pi_{i=1}^{n} k_i$ locations of P. Correspondingly, each reset $x_i := [r_i, s_i]$ is split into $\sigma = k_i$ resets:

$$x_i := [r_i^1, s_i^1], [r_i^1, s_i^1] \subseteq h_{i1}$$

$$\vdots$$

$$x_i := [r_i^\sigma, s_i^\sigma], [r_i^\sigma, s_i^\sigma] \subseteq h_{i\sigma}$$

The edges are now labeled with the modified resets. That is, if the resets corresponding to one of the new edges are $x_i := [r_i^j, s_i^j]$, $i = 1, \ldots n$, then $h_i = sgn(f_i(x_i))$ with $x_i \in \rho_{ij}$. Thus, we have ensured that within the new location, the invariant regions encoded in ρ are fixed. Automaton P, in summary, has an augmented set of locations, modified resets $x_i := [r_i', s_i']$ for each edge, a vector h associated with each location, inclusions $\dot{x}_i \in [l_i, u_i] f_i(x_i)$, and the same enabling conditions $x_i \in [a_i, b_i]$ as for automaton H.

The second step is to transform the nonlinear inclusions to nonlinear differential equations. The resulting automaton A has differential equations

$$\dot{y}_{2i-1} = l_i f(y_{2i-1})$$
$$\dot{y}_{2i} = u_i f(y_{2i})$$

The reset condition $x_i := [r_i', s_i']$ is transformed to $y_{2i-1} := r_i'$ and $y_{2i} := s_i'$, as before. The enabling conditions are given in Equations (1) and (2) with $a_i' = a_i$ and $b_i' = b_i$.

The last step is to transform automaton A to automaton T with linear dynamics. We consider first the upper trajectory of component i, formed by y_{2i}. As before, define a new state variable $z_{2i} = y_{2i} + v_{2i}$ and pick the feedback v_{2i} to satisfy $\dot{v}_{2i} = -u_i f(y_{si}) + d_i$. Then $\dot{z}_{2i} = d_i$.

Consider the transformation of the enabling condition $y_{2i} \geq a_i$. Here we make use of the fact that the location records the invariant region of each clock component and retains the sign of the derivative in the vector h. The transformed enabling condition has three cases. Case (a) is

$$\text{if}(y_{2i} \in \rho_{ik} \wedge a_i \in \rho_{ij}, j < k) \rightarrow (\text{true})$$

in which y_{2i} stays in a region whose values are larger than a_i. Case (b) is

$$\text{if}(y_{2i} \in \rho_{ik} \wedge a_i \in \rho_{ij}, j > k) \rightarrow (\text{false})$$

in which y_{2i} stays in a region whose values are smaller than a_i. The last case is when $y_{2i} \in \rho_{ik}$ and $a_i \in \rho_{ik}$. In this case, there are three subcases. First, if $h_{ik} u_i > 0$ the ith clock has positive derivative. Define the indefinite integral

$$F(w) = \int \frac{dw}{u_i f_i(w)}.$$

Then, $y_{2i} = a_i$ when $t = F(a_i) - F(y_{2i}^0)$. Then

$$z_{2i}(t) = d_i t + z_{2i}^0$$
$$= d_i(F(a_i) - F(y_{2i}^0)) + z_{2i}^0.$$

We pick $z_{2i}^0 = d_i F(y_{2i}^0)$ to cancel initial conditions. Then we obtain the transformed enabling condition

$$z_{2i} \geq F(a_i)$$

where we choose $d_i = 1$. The transformed reset condition for this case is $z_{2i} := F(r_i)$.

The second subcase is when $h_{ik} u_i < 0$ and the ith clock has negative derivative. One can check that the correct transformed enabling condition is $z_{2i} \geq -F(a_i)$ and the transformed reset condition is $z_{2i} := -F(r_i)$. Finally, the last subcase is when $\dot{y}_{2i} = 0$ and the enabling condition and reset condition are unchanged.

The transformation for the lower trajectory y_{2i-1} follows in a similar manner as above.

The steps outlined above lead to the follow result.

Theorem 11 Let $H = (Q, \Sigma, D, \psi, I)$ be a nonlinear hybrid automaton with differential inclusions $\dot{x}_i \in [l_i, u_i] f_i(x_i)$ with $l_i \leq u_i$, $l_i, u_i \in \mathbf{R}$ and $f : \mathbf{R}^n \to \mathbf{R}^n$. There exists a decidable hybrid automaton $H' = (Q, \Sigma, D, \psi', I)$ with Q, Σ, D, and I the same as in H. The enabling conditions δ' of H' can be made arbitrarily close to δ.

Acknowledgements The authors are grateful to Anuj Puri and Tom Henzinger for their helpful suggestions on this problem.

References

1. A. Puri and P. Varaiya. Decidability of hybrid systems with rectangular differential inclusions. In D.L. Dill, ed., *Computer-Aided Verification*, LNCS 818, pp. 95-104, Springer-Verlag, 1994.
2. R. Alur and D. L. Dill. Automata for modeling real-time systems. In *"Proc. 17th ICALP: Automata, Languages and Programming*, LNCS 443, Springer-Verlag, 1990.
3. R. Alur, D. L. Dill. A theory of timed automata. *Theoretical Computer Science*, no. 126, pp. 183-235, 1994.
4. R. Alur, C. Courcoubetis, T. A. Henzinger, and P. H. Ho. Hybrid Automaton: An algorithmic approach to the specification and verification of hybrid systems. In R. L. Grossman, A. Nerode, A. P. Ravn, and H. Rischel, eds., *Hybrid Systems I*, LNCS 736, pp. 209-229, Springer-Verlag, 1993.
5. R. Alur, C. Courcoubetis, N. Halbwachs, T. Henzinger, P. Ho, X. Nicollin, A. Olivero, J. Sifakis, and S. Yovine. The algorithmic analysis of hybrid systems. *Theoretical Computer Science*, no. 138, pp. 3-34, 1995.
6. T. Henzinger, P. Kopke, A. Puri, and P. Varaiya. What's decidable about hybrid automata? In *Proc. 27th Annual Symp. Theory of Computing Science*, pp. 373-382, ACM Press, 1995.
7. T. Henzinger and P. Ho. Algorithmic analysis of nonlinear hybrid systems. In P. Wolper, ed., *Computer Aided Verification*, LNCS 939, pp. 225-238, Springer-Verlag, 1995.
8. T. Henzinger. Hybrid automata with finite bisimulations. In *"Proc. 22nd ICALP: Automata, Languages and Programming*, LNCS 944, pp. 324-335, Springer-Verlag, 1995.
9. T. Henzinger. The theory of hybrid automata. In *Proc. 11th IEEE Symposium on Logic in Computer Science*, pp. 278-292, New Brunswick, NJ, 1996.
10. Y. Kesten, A. Pnueli, J. Sifakis, and S. Yovine. Integration graphs: a class of decidable hybrid systems. In R. L. Grossman, A. Nerode, A. P. Ravn, and H. Rischel, eds., *Hybrid Systems I*, LNCS 736, pp. 179-208, Springer-Verlag, 1993.

11. A. Nerode and W. Kohn. Multiple agent hybrid control architecture. In R. L. Grossman, A. Nerode, A. P. Ravn, and H. Rischel, eds., *Hybrid Systems I*, LNCS 736, pp. 297-316, Springer-Verlag, 1993.
12. A. Nerode and W. Kohn. Models for hybrid systems: automata, topologies, controllability, observability. In R. L. Grossman, A. Nerode, A. P. Ravn, and H. Rischel, eds., *Hybrid Systems I*, LNCS 736, pp. 317-356, Springer-Verlag, 1993.
13. X. Nicollin, A. Olivero, J. Sifakis, and S. Yovine. An approach to the description and analysis of hybrid systems. In R. L. Grossman, A. Nerode, A. P. Ravn, and H. Rischel, eds., *Hybrid Systems I*, LNCS 736, pp. 149-178, Springer-Verlag, 1993.
14. A. Puri, M. Broucke, and P. Varaiya. On the trajectories of hybrid systems. Presented at *Int. Conf. Hybrid Systems*, Cornell University, Ithaca, NY, October 1996.
15. A. Puri, and P. Varaiya. Decidable hybrid systems. *Mathematical and Computer Modeling*, vol. 23, no. 11-12, pp. 191-202, June 1996.
16. A. Puri. Theory of hybrid systems and discrete event systems. University of California, Berkeley, 1995.

Reliable Implementation of Hybrid Control Systems for Advanced Avionics *

Honeywell Technology Center, Minneapolis, MN 55418

Abstract. The avionics systems of modern aircraft must manage a complex array of continuous and discrete dynamics that govern aircraft operations. Producing the software that implements such systems and provably satisfies stringent safety requirements is a difficult problem. Expanded cockpit automation, addition of data links to bring more information into the cockpit, and planned upgrades to the air traffic management system will increase the system complexity and the magnitude of this problem. This paper describes avionics automation from a hybrid systems perspective and presents initial results of our research in providing methods for reliable implementation of these systems.

1   Introduction

The avionics suite of a modern aircraft may be decomposed into five concurrent functions shown in Figure 1: flightplanning, navigation, guidance, control, and stability augmentation [12]. The flightplanning function computes a sequence of route segments (flightplan) that define a four dimensional trajectory from the origin to the destination. The flightplan takes into consideration factors such as air traffic control (ATC) instructions, weather, airspace restrictions, and cost/time objectives. The navigation function determines the four dimensional position of the aircraft. The position is computed by integrating information from air data sensors, inertial sensors, radio data, and GPS. The guidance function compares the actual aircraft position with the flightplan and determines actions required to correctly track the flightplan. It generates a set of targets for aircraft parameters such as heading, altitude, and speed, and the required control mode. Control modes specify what method should be used to control these aircraft parameters. The control function instantaneously adjust pitch, roll, yaw, and thrust of the aircraft to track the guidance targets. The stability augmentation function converts the control function commands into elevator, rudder, trim, and throttle settings using feedback control and knowledge of the aircraft dynamics.

Any or all of these functions may be automated. In manual operation the pilots fly the aircraft using the yoke, throttle, and rudder pedals, with the assistance of the stability augmentation function. In automated control, pilots enter targets and control modes via the mode control panel. In the latest aircraft,

---

* This work was supported in part by NASA contract NAS 2-14291

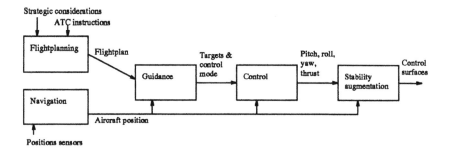

Fig. 1. Functions found in modern avionics systems.

flightplanning, guidance, and control may all be automated. In this configuration pilots provide strategic information such as ATC clearances, mission requirements, and weather information and are assisted in the construction and optimization of a flightplan using a database of flight legs and waypoints.

We make the following observations regarding modern avionics systems:

– Modern avionics no longer perform only closed-loop control and display functions. They are deeply embedded in the operation of the aircraft.
– They are *hybrid* systems since they perform not only continuous transformations of input and output data but include complex decision logic that monitors the aircraft state and determines which transformations should be executed in the current scenario. It has been estimated that 80 % of the specification of modern avionics systems is dedicated to describing the reactive decision-making logic.
– Since these systems carry out high-level functions such as flightplanning and guidance that were formerly delegated to the flight crew, their correct operation is imperative for the safety of the passengers and crew.

Avionics systems are therefore good examples of large, real-world hybrid control systems. The reliable implementation of these systems presents unique challenges to researchers and engineers.

2 Problem description and objectives

Figure 2 illustrates a simplified vertical guidance function in which the method used to control aircraft altitude varies with the current flight phase. In this function, the aircraft thrust can be controlled to maintain a constant speed or to track a given altitude command. Similarly, the elevator angle can be controlled to maintain a constant angle of attack or to track altitude. An operational procedure or mode specifies which control law should be used to compute each of these outputs. The procedure to be invoked is determined by the current operational scenario of the aircraft. The current scenario is computed based on the

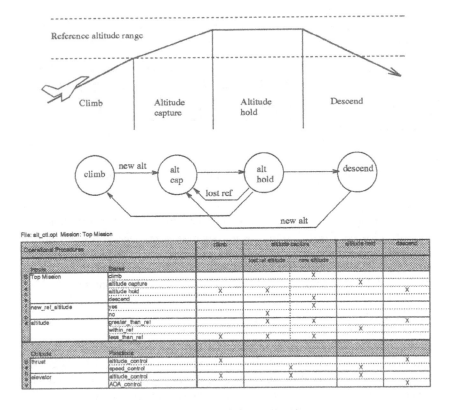

Fig. 2. Vertical guidance function.

current altitude, the presence or absence of a new reference altitude command, and the last operational procedure invoked.

Future aircraft automation systems will have to cope with a larger and larger number of operational modes governing the execution of more complex transformation functions. Already, conventional aircraft autopilots support multiple modes such as maintaining a constant rate of descent or flight path tracking. Digital data links will soon be added to aircraft to create a distributed computer network for air traffic management with airborne and ground-based elements, and automation modes will expand to include new procedures and optimizations.

One plan being investigated and, in part, actually implemented by the FAA for the next generation air traffic management system is known as *free flight*. Free flight will allow individual airlines and aircraft maximal freedom in selecting their own routes between regions of more tightly controlled airspace surrounding terminals. Some of the objectives of the plan are to reduce flight times, operating costs, and congestion.

As a result of free flight, there will be additional operating modes associated with the transition of aircraft from unstructured airspace to structured airspace, with associated changes in roles for the air and ground systems when the transitions occur. There will also be conflict resolution modes to maintain safe separation between multiple aircraft approaching each other from various directions [9], [10]. In addition, ATC will occasionally enact airspace and airport reconfigurations in response to events such as unscheduled service needs, weather circumstances, or accidents.

The specification, verification, and implementation of the complex software for hybrid control systems such as aircraft avionics is a significant challenge for systems and software engineers. As an example, consider the Traffic-alert Collision Avoidance System (TCAS II) used in aircraft today. This system provides aircraft with warnings and simple instructions (ascend/descend) to prevent possible collisions with other aircraft. Such a system is a precursor of the much more sophisticated system required by a free flight implementation. However, even the current TCAS is estimated to have over 10^{40} states and poses a serious verification problem [3].

Because of the critical functions performed by these systems, they must provide high assurance of reliable operation. In general terms, this means that there must be no surprises during system operation. This is of special concern in light of recent incidents and accidents involving aircraft with highly automated cockpits. Investigations have revealed that pilots are at times confused about what the automation is doing and may be surprised by unexpected mode transitions [6]. In some cases, this points to a need for improved training and human-centered engineering practices. In others, the response of the automation to all possible scenarios must be better understood and perhaps modified.

The current practice in designing avionics systems (and in many other complex systems) is document based and largely manual. Design decisions are artificially staged and grouped together into documents characterizing the phase of development. Traceability tools are used to link the chain of design decisions that lead to implementation of a product. Every specification requirement must be met by some line(s) of code in the final implementation and, conversely, every line of code must correspond to a specification requirement

Honeywell is developing a strategy called *model-based development* for the specification, analysis, and implementation of large operationally embedded systems. Our approach is to fix the architecture for a class of systems (a product family) we intend to build. The architecture establishes invariant features of the product family and provides a standard structure into which specific components may be integrated. The chosen architecture for a particular class of systems is driven by both theoretical constraints and software producibility issues.

Once the product architecture is fixed, techniques for specification, analysis, simulation, and synthesis can be developed. These techniques are automated and integrated in a unified framework with the necessary software tools, thus fixing the development process. The result is a manufacturing discipline for that product family.

The *operational procedure* methodology we discuss here addresses the production of hybrid control systems and is illustrated in Figure 3. The methodology is based on a formal specification language, called operational procedure tables

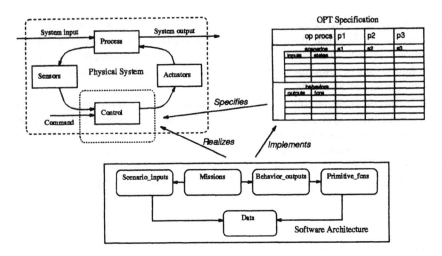

Fig. 3. Controller, specification, and implementation.

(OPT), that permits a simple intuitive expression of the requirements amenable to both mathematical analysis and automatic translation into required software artifacts such as code, documentation, and test plans.

3 Operational procedure methodology

The key principle of the operational procedure methodology is to model both the stimulus and response characteristics of a system, but to keep these two aspects of the model separate and to provide a link between them [7]. A tabular syntax was chosen for the specification language because of its familiarity to systems engineers. Other syntaxes (such as a state- transition graphical language like Statecharts [2] or RSML [8]) are easily added and may be appropriate for some applications.

3.1 Overview of the model

An operational procedure specification defines the mission or operational objectives of a system. It is expressed as a table (see the OPT in Figure 2) with the following sections:

- Operational procedures - system modes and the associated tasks required to achieve the mission objectives during a particular phase of operations.
- Scenario inputs and states - conditioned system input data used as basis for mode selection.
- Scenario definitions - situations in which a particular operational procedure is to be invoked.

- Behavior definitions - set of transformations to be performed when the associated operational procedure is invoked.
- Behavior outputs and functions - functions or algorithms that produce system outputs.

A realistic table with a single behavior output is shown in Figure 4. The top portion of the table defines the stimulus characteristics of the system. It specifies the mapping from the current input state of the system to the operational procedure that should be invoked.

System inputs must first be transformed into a set of logical scenario inputs. System input data may be continuous or discrete-valued and may be produced by physical environment sensors, pilot commands, or other software processes. A scenario input returns one of a finite number of scenario input states, computed from the current system input data. Each scenario input has an associated input function that retrieves the required system input data and computes the correct scenario input state value. For example, a continuous input such as altitude may be mapped to a set of ranges.

The input state is used to compute the current scenario, which identifies the operational and environmental situation in which the system is functioning at any given time. A scenario is defined by the enumeration of a specific combination of scenario input states and appears as a column in an OPT. The tabular format represents a logical predicate in conjunctive normal form that specifies a region in the input state space where a particular scenario is active. In Figure 2 the scenario "lost ref altitude" of the "altitude capture" procedure is selected when

(Top Mission = altitude hold) AND
(new_ref_altitude = no) AND
((altitude = greater_than_ref) OR (altitude = less_than_ref)).

Operational procedures define groups of scenarios with identical behaviors. An operational procedure maps its set of scenarios into a single behavior. Whenever a particular scenario becomes active as a result of a change in the input state, the system transitions to the specified operational procedure and executes the corresponding behavior.

In a finite state machine representation of an OPT the operational procedures correspond to states and the scenarios correspond to state transitions. The actual input state conditions under which a transition will occur are specified by the scenario definitions. The current operational procedure may or may not be part of the input state used for scenario selection. If it is, a normal (partially connected) finite state machine results. If not, the system behaves as a fully-connected state machine and the operational procedures merely partition the input state space.

The bottom portion of the table defines the response characteristics of the system. It specifies the mapping from operational procedures to the system output transformations to be executed. Each operational procedure a behavior has associated with it. A behavior defines a collection of transformations to be performed together.

File: vsc.opt Mission: Vertical Steering Command

Operational Procedures		Set Vertical Steering Command to Zero							Synchronize Vertical Steering Command With Existing VSCommand	Track Path With Tight Command Control Law		Track Path With Tight (Lightly Damped Control Law	
Inputs	**States**	Altitude Out of Range	Altitude Rate Out of Range	Alt Arspeed Out of Range	Extreme Altitude Error Baseline Close Tracking Path	Extreme Altitude Error Close Hysteresis Tracking Path	Extreme Altitude Error Hysteresis Close Tracking the Path	Crew Request to Track Path	Start Tracking Path	Easy Tracking with Hard Extend Hysteresis
Altitude Error (he)	> 50 ft	> 50 ft			> 50 ft	> 50 ft	> 50 ft			between 30 ft
	between 30 ft and 50 ft	between 30 ft			between 30 ft	between 30 ft			within +/- 30 ft	within +/- 30 ft
	within +/- 30 ft				within +/- 30 ft	within +/- 30 ft		within +/- 30 ft	within +/- 30 ft	between - 30 ft
	between - 30 ft and -50 ft	between - 30 ft			between - 30 ft	between - 30 ft				
	< - 50 ft	< - 50 ft			< - 50 ft	< - 50 ft	< - 50 ft			
Altitude Error Rate (he dot)	> 4.0 ft/sec	> 4.0 ft/sec			> 4.0 ft/sec	> 4.0 ft/sec	> 4.0 ft/sec			between 2.5
	between 2.5 ft/sec and 4.0 ft/sec	between 2.5			between 2.5				within +/- 2.5	within +/- 2.5
	within +/- 2.5 ft sec				within +/- 2.5	within +/- 2.5		within +/- 2.5	within +/- 2.5	between -2.5
	between -2.5 ft/sec and -4.0 ft/sec	between -2.5			between -2.5	between -2.5				
	< - 4.0 ft/sec	< -4.0 ft/sec			< - 4.0 ft/sec	< - 4.0 ft/sec	< - 4.0 ft/sec			
TAS	Within Range (200 to 700)			not Within	Within Range (	Within Range (	Within Range (	Within Range (	Within Range (	Within Range (
	not Within Range									
Groundspeed	Within Range				Within Range	Within Range	Within Range	Within Range	Within Range	Within Range
	not Within Range									
Mode Engagement Request	Accepted								Accepted	
	Sent but Not Accepted							Sent but Not		
	Not Sent									
Vertical Steering Command	Set Vertical Steering Command to Zero	Set Vertical	Set Vertical		Synchronize	Synchronize	Synchronize	Set Vertical	Synchronize	Track Path With
	Synchronize Vertical Steering Command With				Track Path With	Track Path With	Track Path With			
	Track Path With Tight (Lightly Damped) Control			Track Path With						
			Set Vertical Steering Command to Zero					Synchronize Vertical Steering Command In Current Vertical Steering Command	Track Path With Tight (Lightly Damped) Control Law	
Outputs	**Relations**									
Vertical Steering Command	Set to Zero			Set to Zero				Initialize to		
	Initialize to Current VSCommand									
	Compute VSCommand								Compute VSCommand	

Fig. 4. Operational procedure table.

A behavior output defines a data output of the system or an object manipulated by the system. Behavior output functions define a finite set of transfer functions and algorithms that may be applied to each of the behavior outputs. A behavior definition identifies the functions that are to be applied to each behavior output when the corresponding operational procedure is active. Only one behavior output function can be selected for a behavior output for a given operational procedure.

Considerable flexibility is provided in the definition of functions used to compute input states and behavior outputs. In the simplest case, these functions may be enumerations, directly mapping a discrete system input variable to one of the scenario input states, or turning a binary- valued behavior output on or off.

In other instances, the desired output function may be a complex control law for flight path tracking. Our integrated suite of design tools includes a variety of graphical programming languages appropriate to different engineering disciplines that can be used to specify such functions. The code generated automatically by these tools or other hand-coded functions can be inserted into the operational procedure framework.

An important feature for managing complexity is the provision for hierarchical organization of operational procedures for both inputs and outputs. A behavior output function may be defined to be another OPT, or *sub-mission*. When this function is invoked by an operational procedure in the parent table, it causes the sub-mission table to be executed. The sub-mission has its own operational procedures, which are selected based on the sub-mission scenario input state. The scenario inputs of the sub-mission may or may not overlap those of the parent table. The behavior of the sub-mission may specify the execution of primitive functions or may invoke sub- missions of its own. A simple mission and one of its sub-missions is shown in Figure 5. There is no limit on the depth of the hierarchy, although there is a tradeoff in human understanding of the specification between individual table size and hierarchical complexity.

File: Invert1 Mission: Top Mission

Operational Procedures		Normal	Inverted
Inputs	States		
invert_mode	true		X
	false	X	
Outputs	Functions		
Output	M:normal	X	
	M:inverted		X

Sub-Mission: inverted

Operational Procedures		op1	op2
Inputs	States		
input	on	X	
	off		X
Outputs	Functions		
Output	on		X
	off	X	

Fig. 5. Mission with one of its sub-missions.

Similarly, scenario input functions may be defined as OPTs called *interpretation missions*. In this case the behavior portion of the interpretation mission table consists of a single enumerated output that corresponds to one of the input states in the parent table.

3.2 Semantics

An OPT must specify the system response to all of the input conditions it may encounter during a mission. The system response is updated whenever the table is evaluated. Figure 6 illustrates the activities performed in the evaluation of a single operational procedure table. At the start of an evaluation cycle, the scenario inputs are read from the data package (which provides the interface with system I/O parameters) to determine the current input state. The decision logic defined by the table is evaluated to determine which scenario is satisfied by the input state. The corresponding operational procedure is then invoked. The behavior associated with the operational procedure defines which functions should be executed for each behavior output. Each of these functions is executed, reading input data and writing output data to/from the data package.

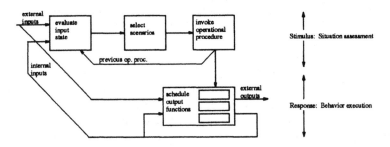

Fig. 6. Execution semantics and data flow.

An OPT may be thought of as a finite state machine (FSM) with guard conditions on its transitions and output behaviors defined on states (therefore, a Moore machine). The basic FSM definition is extended to describe the state selection logic and continuous output behaviors associated with each state. The OPT FSM is driven not by events, but by the state of its inputs at each time the specification is evaluated. Evaluation is normally performed periodically, at which time the inputs are sampled and evaluated to compute the next machine state and produce the specified output behavior.

3.3 Notation

Formally, the model is denoted by the 8-tuple $(U, Y, S, P, p_0, \sigma, \pi, \beta)$. Figure 7 illustrates the components of the model.

U – *Scenario input space.* There are m inputs, each ranging over an enumerated set of input values. The current input state u is a vector belonging to U, defined as

$$U = U_1 \times \ldots U_m$$

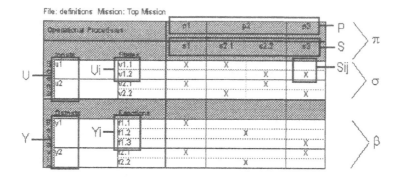

Fig. 7. Operational procedure table.

$$|\,U_i\,| = m_i$$
$$U_i = \{v_{i1}, \ldots v_{im_i}\}$$

Inputs are assigned one of the enumerated input state values by input functions. An input function may access a continuous variable and assign a state based on the range the variable lies in, or it may access existing enumerated variables in the system.

Y – Behavior output space. There are q outputs, each taking values from an enumerated set of behavior output functions. Thus,

$$Y = Y_1 \times \ldots Y_q$$
$$|\,Y_i\,| = q_i$$
$$Y_i = \{f_{i1}, \ldots f_{iq_i}\}$$

A behavior output function may be a primitive function or a sub-mission. A primitive function specifies a value to be assigned to the output or a function to be executed that will assign a value to the output. A sub-mission specifies another table that must be evaluated to assign a value to the output.

S – Scenarios. There are r scenarios that represent a grouping of possible input states, denoted by

$$S = \{s_1, \ldots s_r\}.$$

Each scenario defines a specific situation or configuration of the environment to which the system must react by producing a specified behavior. We desire that the scenarios completely partition the input space U so that every possible input state belongs to one and only one scenario.

P – Operational procedures. There are n operational procedures, corresponding to states in a FSM. The set of operational procedures is denoted by

$$P = \{p_1, \ldots p_n\}.$$

Operational procedures define groups of scenarios with identical behaviors. An operational procedure maps its set of scenarios into a single behavior. Whenever a particular scenario becomes active as a result of a change in the input state, the system transitions to a new operational procedure and executes the corresponding behavior.

p_0 – *Initial operational procedure.* This is one of the defined operational procedures $p_0 \in P$ and becomes the initial value of the state variable p upon system startup.

σ – *Scenario selection function.* Defines the mapping of input states to scenarios.

$$\sigma : U \to S$$

The scenario selection function associates a scenario with the current input state based on the evaluation of a set of logical predicates defined over the input space. Each scenario s_i has an associated predicate c_i in conjunctive normal form (CNF) that is defined by the entries in the scenario definition columns of the table. The scenario selection function is evaluated as

$$\sigma(u) = s_i \Leftrightarrow c_i \text{ is true}$$

For σ to be a function and not merely a relation, exactly one c_i must be true for any $u \in U$.

A predicate c defined on U is said to be *satisfiable* if there exists some $u \in U$ for which c is true. For c an arbitrary predicate on U, we will interpret $s(c)$ to mean

$$\sigma(c) = \{\sigma(u) \mid u \in U \text{ satisfying } c\}.$$

If σ is a function then $\sigma(c_i)$ will be a singleton for all $s_i \in S$. For scenario s_i, the predicate c_i is defined by a collection of sets

$$s_{ij} \subseteq U_j, j \in \{1 \ldots m\},$$

one for each input. These sets define the valid values for each input for that scenario. Therefore, c_i is defined by

$$c_i = \bigwedge_{j=1\ldots m} (u_j \in s_{ij})$$
$$= \bigwedge_{j=1\ldots m} (\bigvee_{v \in s_{ij}} (u_j = v))$$

which is a predicate over U in CNF.

π – *Operational procedure partition function.* Each scenario, when selected, activates a single operational procedure as defined by this function.

$$\pi : S \to P$$

The function π is an onto function so every operational procedure has at least one scenario mapped to it and every scenario belongs to exactly one operational procedure. The equivalence classes induced by π partition S into sets of scenarios that invoke the same operational procedure.

$$[s_i] = \{s \in S \mid \pi(s) = \pi(s_i)\}$$

β – *Behavior selection function.* This function defines which behavior output function is selected for each of the q outputs when a given operational procedure is invoked.

$$\beta : P \to Y$$

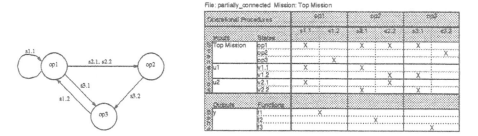

Fig. 8. State-transition representation of a OPT specification.

In the discrete portion of an OPT (Figure 8), the operational procedures correspond to states and the scenarios correspond to state transitions. The actual input conditions under which a state transition will occur are specified by the scenario definitions. For example, scenario s2.1 specifies that a transition to operational procedure op2 will occur if the previous operational procedure ("Top Mission") was op1 *and* input u1 = v1.1 *and* input u2 = v2.2.

OPTs may be used to specify either combinatorial or sequential logic for scenario selection depending on whether the previous operational procedure is included in the input state used for scenario selection. If scenario selection is independent of the previous operational procedure the system behaves as a combinatorial function and the operational procedures merely partition the input space. However, if the previous operational procedure is included in the input state, it is convenient to redefine the scenario selection function as

$$\sigma : P \times U \to S$$

and define the *decision function*

$$\delta : P \times U \to P$$
$$\delta = \pi \circ \sigma.$$

In the example above, the previous operation procedure is used as an input. Thus we have

$$\delta(\text{op1}, (\text{v1.1}, \text{v2.2})) = \text{op2}.$$

3.4 Specification analysis

For an OPT specification to be well-behaved, the table must describe a function from the input space U to the output space Y. This means that

1. The specification defines no more than one output for any $u \in U$. Thus, s is a function rather than a relation. This condition is called *consistency*.
2. The specification defines an output for every $u \in U$. Thus, s is a total function, defined over the entire input space. This condition is called *completeness* [4], [5].

If σ is verified to be complete and consistent, and therefore a function, then $\beta \circ \pi \circ \sigma$ mapping U to Y is also a function.

For σ to be complete, the disjunction of the scenario selection conditions c_i over all scenarios in S must be a tautology. Thus

$$\bigvee_{i=1...r} c_i = \text{true}.$$

For σ to be consistent, the scenario selection conditions must be pairwise disjoint. Thus

$$\forall s_i, s_k \in S, i \neq k[c_i \wedge c_k = \text{false}].$$

Since

$$
\begin{aligned}
c_i \wedge c_k \quad &\text{is satisfiable} \\
&\Leftrightarrow \exists u \in U[(\bigwedge_{j=0...m} (u_j \in s_{ij})) \wedge (\bigwedge_{j=0...m} (u_j \in s_{kj}))] \\
&\Leftrightarrow \exists u \in U[\bigwedge_{j=0...m} (u_j \in s_{ij}) \wedge (u_j \in s_{kj})] \\
&\Leftrightarrow \bigwedge_{j=0...m} (s_{ij} \cap s_{kj} \neq \emptyset)
\end{aligned}
$$

we may restate the condition for consistency in terms of the table entries s_{ij} as

$$\forall s_i, s_k \in S, \exists j \in \{0...m\}[s_{ij} \cap s_{kj} = \emptyset].$$

In many specifications it may be acceptable for some scenarios to overlap as long as they belong to the same equivalence class. We call such a specification *weakly consistent*, formally defined as

$$\forall s_i, s_k \in S[(c_i \wedge c_k \text{ satisfiable}) \Rightarrow (\pi(s_i) = \pi(s_k))]$$

If the weak consistency condition holds, then even though σ is a relation the resulting decision function δ maps each input to a unique operational procedure. For any input u, let

$$\sigma(u) = \{s_i \in S \mid u \text{ satisfies } c_i\}.$$

Then weak consistency implies that

$$\forall s_i \in \sigma(u)[\pi(s_i) = p]$$

and therefore $\pi(\sigma(u)) = p$. Hence $\beta \circ \pi \circ \sigma$ is also a function, as desired.

Of the two properties discussed above, consistency is the simpler property to verify. Consistency of a table can be checked in $O(r^2 m)$ operations. However, verifying completeness of a table may, in the worst case, require examination of the entire input space U, which is exponential in m. Fortunately, this is seldom necessary for real specifications, although completeness checking is always the more computationally intensive task.

The approach used in our methodology is to construct a decision diagram from the scenario definitions. A decision diagram is an acyclic graph that models a decision function. By this we mean a function that selects one of a finite number of outcomes based on a finite number of finite-valued inputs. In [1], decision diagrams are defined for binary inputs, and methods for optimally reducing the size of the diagrams are given.

Each node in a decision diagram corresponds to a decision input (Figure 9). Outgoing arcs are labeled with the different input state values and the outcomes that are valid when that input state is observed. In our implementation the terminal nodes are the active operational procedures for any input condition. Each input state in U must specify a path through the diagram leading to one of the operational procedures.

A decision diagram is built up from the scenarios in an OPT. For the first scenario, the diagram consists of a single path. As each new scenario is added, a branch is added at an input node if the input takes a different state value in that scenario.

Completeness and consistency are checked from a decision diagram by examining the arc labels. In a complete specification, every input state will appear on some outgoing arc of each input node. A consistent specification will have no overlapping scenario labels on the outgoing arcs of the final input nodes.

For very large tables, construction and checking of the decision diagram for a completeness check can be unacceptably slow. It may be acceptable for a final check of a large table to run for several hours overnight. However, the ability to quickly check a table during its design and add or modify scenarios based on the

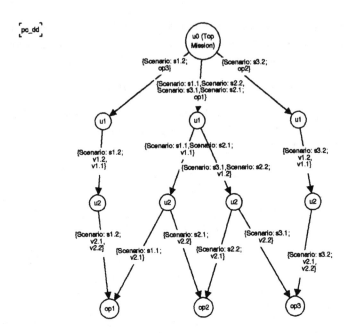

Fig. 9. Decision diagram for the OPT in Figure 8.

results is almost a necessity. Some alternatives to speed up the analysis during table design should be provided.

In the current software tool, the findings of the analysis are reported in the query editor. For a consistency check this is a set of scenario patterns, each of which was found to match more than one scenario. Running a query on each of these patterns identifies the overlapping scenarios so that they can be fixed. For a completeness check, all scenario patterns not found in the table are returned. To fix the table, each of these patterns must be added as a new scenario of either a new or an existing operational procedure. For a new table of any significant size, hundreds (or even thousands) of patterns may be returned.

One simple way to speed up the analysis would be to set a user-definable cap on the number of patterns to be returned. The entire decision diagram must still be constructed, but only a portion of it will be searched in identifying the first n incomplete scenario patterns. Once the first set of discrepancies have been repaired, the next set can be supplied. This sort of incremental approach to table design is useful because the correction of one incompleteness (or inconsistency) often resolves others.

A better way to reduce analysis time is to construct and analyze the decision diagram incrementally. This can be done by fixing the value of one or more inputs and only constructing the corresponding portion of the decision diagram. The resulting subdiagram can be checked for completeness and consistency, revealing defects in the specification. We call such a check a limited scope correctness check. If this process is repeated for every possible value of the chosen input(s) then the entire specification is correct.

To justify the use of limited scope correctness checking we require the following definition and theorem.

Definition. Given a mission M with m inputs, the *input-restricted mission* $M \mid_{u_i = v_{ij}}$ is defined by

$$M \mid_{u_i = v_{ij}} = (U', Y, S', P', \sigma', \pi', \beta)$$

where

$$U' = U \setminus u_i$$
$$S' = \{s_k \in S \mid v_{ij} \in s_{kj}\}$$
$$\sigma' : U' \to S' : \sigma'(u) = s_k \Leftrightarrow \bigwedge_{j \neq i} (u_j \in s_{kj})$$
$$\pi' = \text{the restriction of } \pi \text{ to } S'$$

The following theorem provides a recursive definition of completeness and consistency.

Theorem. *A mission M with m inputs is complete and consistent if:*
Case $m = 1$: For all $v_{1j} \in U_1$ there exists exactly one s_k such that $v_{1j} \in s_{kj}$.
Case $m > 1$: For an arbitrary input i

1. *For all $v_{ij} \in U_i$ there exists some scenario s_k with $v_{kj} \in s_{kj}$.*
2. *For all $v_{ij} \in U_i$, $M \mid_{u_i = v_{ij}}$ is complete and consistent.*

Proof.
Case $m = 1$: Identical to definition.
Case $m > 1$:
    M is complete since for any $u \in U$ we have $\sigma'(u') = s_k$ for some $s_k \in S'$ and $u_i \in s_{ki}$ for all $s_k \in S'$. Thus $s_k \in \sigma(u)$ and $\sigma(u) \neq \emptyset$.
    M is consistent since if $\mid S' \mid = 1$ then $\sigma(u)$ is uniquely defined by the s_k such that $u_i \in s_{ki}$. If $\mid S' \mid > 1$ then $\sigma(u)$ is uniquely defined by the $s_k \in S'$ such that $\sigma'(u') = s_k$. $\square$

A limited scope correctness check such as this could be implemented using something like the existing query editor. The value for one or more inputs could be specified in the scenario pattern and all matching scenarios identified. Then completeness and consistency checks could be run on the table formed by the matching scenarios restricted to the unspecified inputs.

Consider the table in Figure 8. If we first fix input u1 = v1.1, then $S' = \{s1.1, s1.2, s2.1, s3.2\}$ as shown in Figure 10. $M \mid_{u1 = v1.1}$ is complete and consistent because each combination of the remaining inputs "Top Mission" and u2 is represented in S' exactly once. Similarly, fixing u1 = v1.2 gives $S' = \{s1.2, s2.2, s3.1, s3.2\}$ and $M \mid_{u1 = v1.2}$ is also complete and consistent. Thus the entire table is complete and consistent.

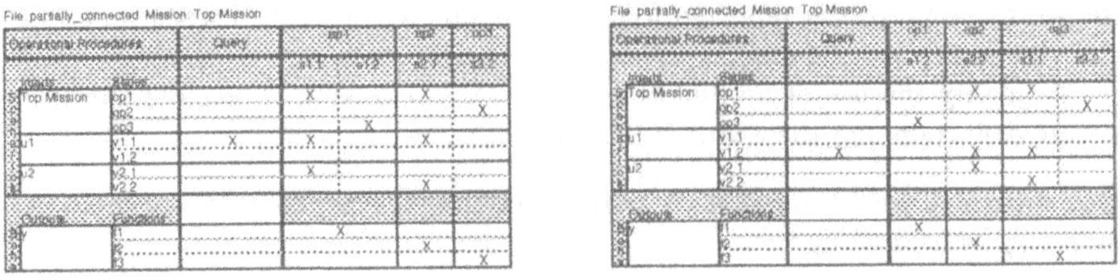

Fig. 10. Limited scope correctness check on input u1.

3.5 The HOPTs software tool

Honeywell has produced a prototype software tool to specify, analyze, and implement operational procedure tables. The HOPTs (Hierarchy of Operational Procedure Tables) tool was created using DoME (Domain Modeling Environment). DoME is the result of work jointly funded by Honeywell and DARPA and provides an infrastructure of Smalltalk classes and methods for rapid prototyping of graphical modeling tools.

In a traditional software development process, the verification of completeness and consistency of the specification can be extremely time-consuming and is prone to errors. The HOPTs tool automates this analysis and provides mechanisms for resolving errors and omissions uncovered in the specification. In addition, a general purpose query tool is provided for identifying and grouping scenario definitions that satisfy user-specified criteria.

Once the specification has been created and verified to be complete and consistent, the code implementing it can be automatically generated. Other artifacts, such as System Requirements Documents and test plans, can be automatically generated as well.

A mission specified by an OPT hierarchy is a single schedulable task in the avionics system of which it is a part. The operating system executive issues periodic calls to this task. During each iteration the input state is computed, the currently applicable scenario is selected, and the required output functions are identified, ordered, and executed.

A variety of user-selectable options are provided for implementing the scenario selection logic. The methods provided include a simple if-then-else structure, a Boolean sieve algorithm, and creation and reduction of a finite decision diagram for the decision logic. Each implementation provides different advantages in terms of execution time, stability, and size that may be needed depending on the limitations of the hardware platform.

3.6 Distinctive features

There are a number of features that distinguish the operational procedure model, and HOPTs as a tool, from other requirements specification methods.

1. Design for synchronous execution.

   Other specification languages that we are aware of are geared toward event-triggered execution semantics. The most direct implementation of a system specified in this way would be an interrupt-driven implementation. Operational procedure models are designed to implement synchronous, input-driven systems. The system only changes state when one of its inputs changes. These inputs are sampled periodically and used to select the current operational procedure, which specifies the functions to be executed during the current cycle.

   Synchronous systems provide advantages in terms of reliability, predictability, and schedulability to satisfy resource constraints in the system. In addition, continuous-variable feedback control laws typically rely on fixed periodic data sampling and execution. It makes sense to design these systems using a specification language designed for describing synchronous systems.

2. Specification of hybrid systems.

   The ability to specify hybrid systems is an explicit part of the model. The discrete-event component of a hybrid system is modeled in the stimulus portion of a mission. The current operational procedure may be identified as the mission state. Transitions between procedures are triggered by the scenario selection logic in response to changes in the system input The continuous-variable component of a system is modeled in the response portion of a mission. The behavior to be executed while an operational procedure is active consists of a set of output functions. This ability to specify outputs driven by different continuous-valued functions in response different mission scenarios is a key feature of the model.

3. State semantics.

   The "states" of a mission are its operational procedures. These are intentionally called operational procedures rather than states to emphasize a difference in meaning. An operational procedure corresponds to a phase of a mission during which the system must perform a specified behavior. It may be modeled as a state in a FSM, but its primary purpose is not to represent the logical state of an automaton as in many other models.

4. Hierarchical organization.

   Complex missions may be decomposed by specifying behavior output functions as sub-missions. Hierarchical organization aids scalability and human comprehension.

5. Model-based development.

   A single model is the basis for system specification, analysis, and artifact generation. A single tool is used to perform these activities.

4 Experience with the model

The HOPTs tool and operational procedure methodology are being used in the NASA High Speed Research program to specify the vertical flightpath management function for the High Speed Civil Transport cockpit [11]. This function provides the altitude target, speed target, vertical speed target, and pitch/thrust control mode outputs required by the rest of the automation to maintain the aircraft's vertical flight plan.

The specification consists of 19 hierarchical tables that define a total of 118 different operational procedures. These operational procedures represent the set of tasks required to achieve the origin–destination mission of a commercial air transport in the vertical and longitudinal axes. The scenarios that invoke the operational procedures represent all the possible combination of states of inputs that affect the mission and include airspace regulations, Air Traffic Control clearances, airline policies, and the operational limits of the aircraft. Special procedures to handle abnormal operation associated with an engine-out condition are also included.

Once in the OPT format, the correctness analysis and software artifact generation were accomplished automatically. The result was a complete and consistent specification, and a System Requirements Document and Ada code implementing the specification.

5 Ongoing work and future plans

We have presented some initial results from our research into the specification, analysis, and implementation of operationally embedded hybrid systems. The focus of this work is the reliable implementation of advanced avionics for future aircraft. The operational procedure methodology provides for the simple and intuitive expression of system requirements in a framework amenable to both mathematical analysis and automatic translation into required software artifacts such as code, documentation, and test plans. The key to the methodology is the structure provided by fixing an appropriate architecture for this class of system.

Our ongoing work will address other capabilities necessary to make this a practical tool for developing large hybrid systems. We are incorporating mechanisms to support the reuse of specification components and multi-user capabilities. Analysis techniques need to be extended to cover additional safety properties and to include the continuous dynamics. For example, it would be useful to identify impossible input conditions, such as those resulting from mutually exclusive input states or precluded by virtue of the output computations in the current operational procedure.

6 References

1. S. B. Akers, "Binary Decision Diagrams," *IEEE Trans. on Computers*, Vol. C-27, No. 6, pp. 509–516, June 1978.
2. D. Harel, "Statecharts: A visual formalism for complex systems," *Science of Computer Programming*, Vol. 8, pp. 231-274, 1987.
3. M. P.E. Heimdahl, *Static Analysis of State-Based Requirements: Analysis for Completeness and Consistency*, PhD thesis, University of California, Irvine, 1994.

4. M. P.E. Heimdahl, N. G. Leveson, "Completeness and consistency analysis of state-based requirements," In *Proceedings of the 17th Int'l Conf. on Software Engineering*, April 1995.

5. C. L. Heitmeyer, B. L. Labaw, D. Kiskis, "Consistency checking of SCR- style requirements specifications," In *Proceedings of the Int'l Symposium on Requirements Engineering*, March 1995.

6. D. Hughes, M. A. Dornheim, "Accidents direct focus on cockpit automation," *Aviation Week and Space Technology*, Jan. 30, 1995.

7. T. King, Jon Krueger, J. Ward, B. Hughes, M. Michaels, L. Sherry, *Generating software from a hierarchy of operational procedure tables*, Honeywell Technology Center technical report SST-R94-009, 1994.

8. N. G. Leveson, M. P.E. Heimdahl, H. Hildreth, J. D. Reese, "Requirements specification for process-control systems," *IEEE Trans. on Software Engineering*, vol. 20, no. 9, Sept. 1994.

9. G. J. Pappas, C. Tomlin, S. Sastry, "Conflict resolution for multi-agent hybrid systems," In *Proceedings of the 35th IEEE Conf. on Decision and Control*, December 1996.

10. S. Sastry, G. Meyer, C. Tomlin, J. Lygeros, D. Godbole, G. Pappas, "Hybrid control in air traffic management systems," In *Proceedings of the 34th IEEE Conf. on Decision and Control*, December 1995.

11. L. Sherry, P. Polson, M. Feary, C. S. Hynes, "Design of an Intentional Vertical Flightpath Management Function for the HSCT Cooperative Cockpit," Honeywell Air Transport Systems publication C69-5370-002 under NASA Langley Research Center contract NAS1-20219, October 1995 *(NASA contractor report number pending)*.

12. L. Sherry, D. Youssefi, C. S. Hynes, "A formalism for the specification of operationally embedded reactive avionic systems," Honeywell publication C69- 5370-001 under NASA Langley Research Center contract NAS1-20219, October 1995 *(NASA contractor report number pending)*.

SHIFT: A Formalism and a Programming Language for Dynamic Networks of Hybrid Automata

Akash Deshpande, Aleks Göllü and Pravin Varaiya
{akash,gollu,varaiya}@eecs.berkeley.edu

Department of Electrical Engineering and Computer Sciences
and
California PATH
University of California at Berkeley, Berkeley, CA 94720

Abstract. SHIFT is a programming language for the specification and simulation of dynamic networks of hybrid automata. Such systems consist of components which can be created, interconnected and destroyed as the system evolves. Components exhibit hybrid behavior, consisting of continuous-time phases separated by discrete-event transitions. Components may evolve independently, or they may interact through their inputs, outputs and exported events. The interaction network itself may evolve.

SHIFT is being used in real-life applications such as automated highway systems, coordinated autonomous submarines, air traffic management, and material handling systems. We believe that the SHIFT model offers the proper level of abstraction for describing these and other similar applications whose operation cannot be captured easily by conventional models.

We have implemented a compiler and a run-time system for SHIFT. The compiler translates a SHIFT program into a C program, which, when run, simulates the design specified in the SHIFT source program. More information about SHIFT can be found at the URL
http://www.path.berkeley.edu/shift.

1 Introduction

SHIFT is a programming language for describing and simulating dynamic networks of hybrid automata. Such systems consist of components which can be created, interconnected and destroyed as the system evolves. Components exhibit hybrid behavior, consisting of continuous-time phases separated by discrete-event transitions. Components may evolve independently, or they may interact through their inputs, outputs and exported events. The interaction network itself may evolve.

The SHIFT model was motivated by our need for tools that support dynamically reconfigurable hybrid systems [13]. Our primary application was the specification and analysis of different designs for automatic control of vehicles and highway systems [30, 9]. We needed to capture the behavior of vehicles, sensors, actuators, communication devices and controllers in a structured and modular specification [5, 6]. Models for these components were to be provided by different groups of experts and then integrated in different ways for comparative analysis. From our previous experience in modeling [18, 11], analysis [26, 4, 15] and implementation [8, 12, 14], we adopted the hybrid systems approach for modeling the system components. Since spatial relationships between vehicles change as they move, our application displayed a dynamically changing network of interactions between system components.

We investigated several system description frameworks [24, 16, 17, 10, 19, 22, 29, 32] and some of their real-time extensions, but found none that suited our needs sufficiently well. Most support only static configurations of system components and mainly provide discrete event behavior description with limited real-time extensions. However, we needed to describe models with switched differential equations (such as a vehicle with automatic gear shift) and coordinated behaviors (such as communicating controllers). Standard simulation tools such as Matlab or MatrixX, while suitable for numerical integration of fixed sets of differential equations, are difficult to use in applications with rapidly changing sets of differential equations (due to component creation and deletion), complex stopping conditions (such as existential queries on the state of the world), and complex program logic (such as synchronous compositions of state machines).

Recent extensions to the DEVS [32] formalism have introduced notions of dynamic reconfiguration [1, 25]. However, the DEVS formalism is primarily aimed at discrete event simulation and the extensions for continuous evolution laws are limited. Furthermore, these approaches are not suitable for large scale system development since they do not provide a formal modeling language. Model specification in DEVS is done with C++ or SmallTalk classes that implement the mathematical model. Other characteristics of these approaches are discussed in [2].

The hybrid systems approach [3] satisfied our needs for component modeling but not for modeling dynamically reconfigurable interactions between components. The Omola/Omsim [23] language has a very similar approach to hybrid system modeling as SHIFT. Both systems provide a modeling language with simulation semantics; both support discrete event and continuous time behavior representation; both have the necessary constructs for hierarchical modeling and specification reuse. However, Omola is designed to represent statically interconnected objects and does not provide the means of querying the components in the world with existential quantifiers. In SHIFT, these queries are used to express and evaluate the evolution of the interconnections among components as the world evolves.

Most general-purpose programming languages support dynamic reconfigurability. But the abstraction facilities in general-purpose programming languages such as C or C++ would not allow us to write simple, concise descriptions of our designs. SHIFT was designed to remedy this situation by providing both high-level system abstractions and the flexibility of programming languages.

The goal of SHIFT is to be easy to learn and use. We strived to keep the language design simple and small. SHIFT has only one number type (corresponding to the C **double** type), no functions (although it can use external functions written in C) and it has no memory management primitives, relying on garbage collection in its implementation. In spite of its simplicity, SHIFT programs are surprisingly powerful yet compact. This is because of the high-level system abstractions provided by SHIFT, including differential equations, state transitions and synchronous compositions, all within the framework of dynamic networks of hybrid automata.

Whereas the initial application that led to the development of SHIFT was modeling and simulation of vehicles and highways, the SHIFT language has since also been used in coordinated autonomous submarines [28], air traffic control systems [20], and material handling systems.

In section 2, we describe a simplified version of the SHIFT model. We discuss the models of a type, a component and the world and give the formal semantics of the model. In section 3, we describe the main features of the SHIFT language—states, inputs, outputs, differential equations and algebraic definitions, discrete states and state transitions—and provide two examples illustrating these features. In section 4, we describe the run-time environment for simulating SHIFT programs; in particular, we discuss how the mathematical model and its semantics describe the SHIFT programming language.

2 The SHIFT Model

The model presented in this section is austere and simplified.

In the SHIFT model, the *world* W consists of a set of hybrid *components* $h_1, \ldots, h_w$:

$$W = \{h_1, \ldots, h_w\}.$$

Each component h is in a particular *configuration* C_h, and collectively these determine the configuration of the world:

$$C_W = (C_{h_1}, \ldots, C_{h_w}).$$

The world evolves in a sequence of phases. During each phase, time flows while the configuration of the world remains fixed. In the transition between phases, time stops and the set of components in the world and their configurations are allowed to change. Each component has both continuous-time dynamics and discrete-event dynamics which depend on the configuration of the world. Components obey continuous-time dynamics within each phase and discrete-event dynamics in phase transitions.

The SHIFT mathematical model is class based [31]. The components are organized into *types* that describe the prototypical behavior of a component. We say that a component is an instantiation of its type. Type descriptors are an implicit and static part of the world. A given world may contain many definitions

$W_H = \{H_1, \ldots, H_k\}$. The subset of the world that consists of components of type H_i is denoted by $W{:}H_i{}^1$.

In a class based model one has to distinguish a variable's *name* from its *value*. Below when we refer to a variable x in the context of a type, we refer to the variable's name and when we refer to a variable x in the context of a component, we refer to its value.

Another important concept in a class based model is that of a *component id*. We assume that each component in the world has a unique identifier.

2.1 Type Description

In this section, we describe a simplified SHIFT model for the description of a type. In addition to what we describe here, the type description mechanism in the SHIFT language (See Section 3) provides several programming conveniences such as distinguishing input, output, and state variables in a type.

In this simplified model, a type is the tuple

$$H = (q \in Q,\ Q \text{ finite,} \text{---the discrete state variable,}$$

$$x = (x_1, \ldots, x_n), \text{---the continuous state variables,}$$

$$C = C_{M_0} \cup (M_1\ C_1, \ldots, M_m\ C_m), \text{---the configuration state variables}$$

$$L = \{l_1, \ldots, l_p\}, \text{---the event labels}$$

$$F = \{F_q \mid q \in Q\} \text{---the flows, and}$$

$$T\text{---the transition prototypes.})$$

To be accurate, the discrete states of H should be referred to as Q_H, and similarly for the other elements in the type description. We drop the subscript where it is obvious from context.

The continuous state variables of a type are given by x with each $x_i \in \mathbf{R}^2$. The continuous evolution laws for these variables are given by F as described below.

C_{M_0} is a tuple $(M_{0_1}\ C_{0_1}, \ldots, M_{0_p}\ C_{0_p})$ where $M_{0_i} \in W_H$ and $C_{0_i} \in W{:}M_{0_i}$ and p is a constant. In essence, C_{0_i} is a reference to another component of type $M_{0_i}{}^3$. We define $C_0 = \{C_{0_1}, \ldots, C_{0_p}\}$.

For $i = 1, \ldots, m$, $M_i \in W_H$ and $C_i \subset W{:}M_i$. In a component, C_i may have a different number of elements in different phases. C_i, $i = 1, \ldots, m$ can be thought of as a set-valued reference to other components in the world.

The event labels L in a type are values.

---

[1] The mathematical model does not represent inheritance which is part of the SHIFT language. In the mathematical model, $W{:}H_i$ are disjoint, in the language $W{:}H_i$ are partially ordered with respect to subset inclusion.

[2] Recall that in a type a continuous state variable x_i is a name and in a component it takes on a value in $\mathbf{R}$.

[3] In a type, C_{0_i} is a name; in a component it takes on a value in $W{:}M_{0_i}$. Note that M_{0_i} and p are values in a type.

Each type is a prototypical hybrid automaton A_H with Q as its discrete states. In each discrete state $q \in Q$ the flow of each continuous variable x_i is defined either by F_q as a differential equation or by G_q as an algebraic definition. These definitions, respectively, take the form

$$\dot{x}_i = F_{i,q}(x, x_{C_0}) \text{ or}$$
$$x_i = G_{i,q}(x, x_{C_0}).$$

Here, x_{C_0} denotes the vector obtained by listing the continuous variables of all elements of C_0. We require that there be no cyclic dependencies between algebraically defined variables.

T is a finite set of tuples of the form

$$\delta = (q, q', E, g, a)$$

where $q, q' \in Q$ are respectively the *from* and *to* states of δ, E is a set of event labels, g is a guard predicate, and a is an action that alters the state of the world. The guard predicate takes one of two forms:

1. $g(x, x_{C_0})$ or
2. $\exists c \in C_i \; g(x, x_c, x_{C_0})$, $1 \le i \le m$.

In the second form, multiple quantifiers are permitted (with obvious modifications of the form), and the quantifiers may be negated. The quantified variables may be used in the action a[4]. Informally, for δ to be taken, the guard must evaluate to true.

Each event label in E takes one of four forms:

1. l, with $l \in L$;
2. $c : l$, with $c \in C_0$ and l an event label in the type of c;
3. $\exists c \in C_i \; c : l$, with $1 \le i \le m$ and l an event label in the type of c (the quantified variable may be used in the action a); and
4. $\forall c \in C_i \; c : l$, with $1 \le i \le m$ and l an event label in the type of c.

The event labels place synchronization constraints on the world. Informally, a transition with the label $c : l$ can be taken if and only if c takes a transition with the label l. The constraint extends naturally to labels with quantified variables.

In SHIFT, an "internal" transition, that is a transition which does not synchronize with others, is specified by leaving E empty. As a mathematical convenience, we assume that such internal transitions are labeled ϵ.

The action a is a map from x, x_{C_0} and any quantified variables in the guard or event labels to (x, C). It has the direct effect of resetting the continuous state and the configuration of the component. The action may also create new components and initialize them. In SHIFT, actions may also reset the inputs of components in C_0.

---

[4] It may not always be meaningful to use a quantified variable in an action. For example, in a guard of the form $\nexists c \in C_1 \; g(\ldots)$, c carries no meaningful information that can be used in the action.

2.2 Component Description

A component h of type H assigns, at each time, values to its state variables (q, x, C). Associated to h is a hybrid automaton A_h derived from the prototypical automaton A_H using the values of C. The discrete states of A_h are the same as the discrete states of A_H—i.e., Q.

The transitions of A_h, denoted T_h, are obtained by transforming the transition prototypes of A_H into an equivalent set of transitions. The transformation rules are given here for the purpose of explaining the model—they are not actually used in the implementation of the SHIFT run-time system.

- A transition prototype with a guard of the form $\exists c \in C \; g(x_h, x_c, x_{C_0})$ yields $|C|$ transitions, one for each component $c \in C$, with guards $g(x_h, x_c, x_{C_0})$.
- An event label l in the transition prototype is replaced by the event label $h : l$ in the transition.
- An event label $c : l$ in the transition prototype is retained without change in the transition.
- A transition prototype with an event label in the form $\exists c \in C \; c : l$ yields $|C|$ transitions, one for each $c \in C$, with event label $c : l$.
- A transition prototype with an event label of the form $\forall c \in C \; c : l$ yields one transition with $|C|$ event labels, one for each $c \in C$, labeled $c : l$.

A transition prototype with multiple existential quantifiers in the guards or event labels yields one transition for each element in the cross product of the domains of those variables.

Finally, we assume that T_h contains a trivial self-looping transition
$(q, q, \emptyset, True, I)$
for each $q \in Q$, where I is the identity function. Such a transition is not actually specified in SHIFT; we introduce it as a mathematical convenience.

Let $events(A_h)$ be the set of all events appearing on the transitions of A_h:

$$events(A_h) = \cup_{t \in T_h} E_t.$$

2.3 World Description

Now we describe the hybrid automaton A_W associated to the world. The set of discrete states of A_W is the cross product $Q_W = Q_{h_1} \times \cdots \times Q_{h_w}$. Similarly, the set of continuous states of A_W is the cross product of the sets of continuous states of the components in W. The dynamics of the continuous state variables are governed by the flows defined in the component automata. The transitions T_W of A_W are tuples $\Delta = (\delta_1, \ldots, \delta_w)$ with each $\delta_i \in T_{h_i}$. Let

$$events(\Delta) = \cup_i E_{\delta_i}.$$

T_W satisfies the following condition: $\Delta \in T_W$ if and only if

1. $events(\Delta) \neq \emptyset$—i.e., not all transitions are trivial,

2. $events(\delta_i) = events(\Delta) \cap events(A_{h_i})$ for each i—i.e., events taken by each component are exactly the events taken by the world that are of interest to that component, and

3. $\not\exists \Delta' \in T_W$ such that $events(\Delta')$ is a strict subset of $events(\Delta)$—i.e., Δ is minimal.

The guard associated to $\Delta \in T_W$ is the conjunction of the guards of the component transitions in Δ:

$$g_\Delta = \wedge_i g_{\delta_i}.$$

The action associated to Δ is the parallel execution of the actions of the component transitions in Δ—i.e., each map a_{δ_i} is evaluated using the state of the world just before the transition.

Our model performs synchronous composition of multiple automata. Our choice of this definition of world transitions rested on a tradeoff between ease of use and efficiency of implementation. An alternative would be to describe pair-wise cause-effect relationships between the transitions of different components [13, 21]. Programs written using the synchronous composition approach can be exponentially smaller than those written using cause-effect relationships. However, the algorithm for determining world transitions in the synchronous composition approach is exponentially more complex than the corresponding algorithm for the cause-effect synchronization approach. Thus, we preferred ease of use over efficiency of implementation. Cause-effect synchronizations can also be described in SHIFT using symbol-valued input-output connections.

Example of SHIFT Synchronization Rules

In a component, the value of an event label of the form $c : l \in E$ is given by a component id $c \in W$ and an event label $l \in L$ from the type definition, e.g. (H1 2):11. For simplicity, in our example below we substitute simpler values for event labels as indicated in Figure 1.

Fig. 1. Simplifying Event Labels

Consider a world with three components C1, C2, and C3, each with three discrete states. Consider three different states of the world, A, B, and C. The discrete state of each component in each of these world states is highlighted. In Figure 2, we have omitted the trivial transitions, assume they are all denoted by t_{s_i} where s_i is the discrete state, otherwise transitions are denoted by t_{s_i,s_j} where s_i and s_j are the from and to states respectively.

In the world state A, the only possible collective transition is $(t_{s1}, t_{s4}, t_{s7,s8})$. In the world state B, the possible collective transitions are $(t_{s2}, t_{s5}, t_{s7,s8})$ and

3 The SHIFT Language

In this section we describe the main features of the SHIFT language and relate them to the model in section 2. We introduce the SHIFT syntax with simple examples and give a complete program in Section 3.1. The complete SHIFT syntax is given in the SHIFT reference manual [27]. Larger size examples can be found at the SHIFT home page.

SHIFT provides two native data types—number and symbol, and it provides mechanisms for defining additional types. Variables of type number have piecewise constant or piecewise continuous real-valued time traces. The latter variables are declared to be of type continuous number. Variables of type symbol have piecewise constant symbol-valued time traces.

SHIFT provides three mechanisms for defining additional types: set, array and type. A variable of type set(T), where T is a native or user-defined type, contains a set of elements of type T. A variable of type array(T) contains a one-dimensional array of elements of type T.

A component prototype is defined by the SHIFT type declaration. This is similar to the C struct declaration. The equivalent of C structure members are the inputs, outputs, and states of a SHIFT type. These correspond to the continuous state variables x and the configuration variables C in the model. Thus one can write:

```
type Car {
    input continuous number throttle;
    output continuous number position, velocity, acceleration;
    state continuous number fuel_level;
        Car car_in_front;
        Controller controller;
    ...
}
```

Dividing the continuous state from the model into inputs, outputs, and state in the language allows for more structured programming. SHIFT defines the manners in which variables of each kind may be used. For instance, state variables are not visible outside the component, and the input variables of a component may only be defined by another component.

A component type declaration also specifies the component's continuous and discrete behavior. This is done through additional syntactic constructs or *clauses*, each starting with a meaningful keyword.

Groups of common equations can be given a name through the flow clause. The special flow name default defines the default behavior of a set of variables in all states. In the example, the cruising state redefines velocity, which becomes algebraically defined (as a constant in this case) instead of differentially defined (as the integral of the acceleration).

The discrete clause defines the possible values for q (the component's discrete state variable) and associates a set of differential equations and algebraic definitions to each discrete state. For instance:

```
type Car {
    ...
    flow default {
        position' = velocity;
        velocity' = acceleration;
    }

    discrete
        accelerating { acceleration = 3; },
        cruising { velocity = 30; },
        braking { acceleration = -5; };
    ...
}
```

Transitions between states are defined in the **transition** clause, as in the following example.

```
type Car {
    ...
    transition
        accelerating -> cruising {}
            when velocity >= 30,
        cruising -> braking {}
            when position(car_in_front) - position < 5;
    ...
}
```

The example uses the state variable **car_in_front** containing a reference to another **Car**, whose relative position is used in deciding when to apply brakes.

Transitions are labeled by a (possibly empty) set of event labels. These labels allow transitions to synchronize with each other. Suppose that we wish the car to brake when a roadside controller signals an emergency. This can be specified with the transition

```
cruising -> braking   controller:emergency
```

The definition of the **Controller** type must include an exported event, **emergency**, and at least one transition that triggers it.

```
type Controller {
    ...
    export emergency;
```

transition
    normal -> panic_mode { emergency }
    when *some critical condition*;
  . . .

}

Some other clauses provided by SHIFT are do, setup, global and function. The do clause associates actions to transitions. The setup clause defines the component's initializations, input-output connections and externally defined event synchronizations. The global clause defines global variables and the function clause declares external functions written in C or other programming languages.

SHIFT types may be organized in an inheritance hierarchy. A subtype is required to conform to its supertype's interface by declaring a superset of inputs, outputs and exported events.

The following examples illustrate the main features of SHIFT.

3.1 The Particle Example

In this example, a particle source creates particles at the rate of one per second and places them at the beginning of a 1000m track. The speed of the particles is initialized from the speed posted by the track monitor. The particles travel down the track and exit when they reach the end, notifying the track monitor of their exit. The track monitor updates its posted speed based on the exit speeds of particles. At externally provided time intervals, the monitor commands all particles between 500m and 1000m to raise their speeds by 10%. Figure 3 illustrates this example.

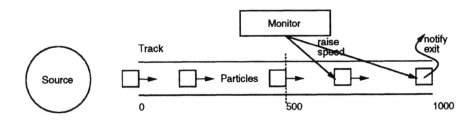

Fig. 3. Particles-Source-Monitor

The Particle Type

The prototypical behavior of particles is shown in Figure 4. Each particle has a continuously varying position along the track, given by the real-valued state variable x. Each particle has a real-valued piecewise constant output variable speed. The default flow of the particle is given by the equation

$$\dot{x} = speed.$$

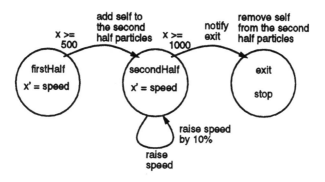

Fig. 4. Particle

The particle has three discrete states, firstHalf, secondHalf and exit, indicating that the particle is in firstHalf when $x < 500$, in secondHalf when $500 \leq x < 1000$ and in exit when $x \geq 1000$. This behavior is not automatic but must be programmed. The particle's flow in the exit state is stop, a SHIFT keyword, which assigns the rate 0 to all continuously changing variables. A "stopped" component that is unreachable and unable to participate in any world transition is, in effect, deleted from the world.

The particle exports two events, raiseSpeed and notifyExit, which may be used for synchronization by other components in the system.

The particle transitions from firstHalf to secondHalf on an internal event when $x >= 500$. As a part of this transition, it adds itself to the globally defined set secondHalfParticles. The particle loops in secondHalf on the event raiseSpeed, raising its speed by 10%. The particle transitions from secondHalf to exit on the event notifyExit when $x >= 1000$, removing itself from the set secondHalfParticles.

The SHIFT description of the particle type is given below.

```
type Particle
{
    discrete
        firstHalf,
        secondHalf,
        exit stop;
    state continuous number x;
    output number speed;
    export raiseSpeed, notifyExit;
    flow default { x' = speed };
    transition
        firstHalf -> secondHalf {}
            when x >= 500
            do {secondHalfParticles := secondHalfParticles + {self};};
```

```
    secondHalf -> secondHalf {raiseSpeed}
        do { speed := 1.1*speed; };
    secondHalf -> exit notifyExit
        when x >= 1000
        do {secondHalfParticles := secondHalfParticles - {self};};
}
```

The Source Type

The prototypical behavior of a source is shown in Figure 5. It has a contin-

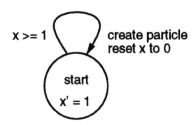

Fig. 5. Source

uously varying real-valued state variable x that measures the elapsed time from the last transition. It has a state variable **monitor** of type **Monitor**, which is a link to the track monitor.

The source has one discrete state **start** in which the flow specification is

$$\dot{x} = 1.$$

The source loops in **start** on an internal event when $x >= 1$, creating a new particle whose speed is initialized from the monitor's output, and resetting the timer x to 0. The SHIFT description of the source type is given below.

```
type Source
{
    state continuous number x;
          Monitor monitor;
    discrete start { x' = 1 };
    transition
        start -> start {}
            when x >= 1
            do {
                create(Particle, speed := speed(monitor));
                x := 0;
            };
}
```

The Monitor Type

The prototypical behavior of a monitor is shown in Figure 6. It has a con-

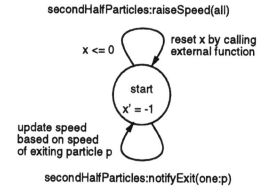

Fig. 6. Monitor

tinuously varying real-valued state variable x that counts down the time to the next **raiseSpeed** broadcast. It has a real-valued output **speed**.

The monitor has one discrete state, **start**, in which the flow is $\dot{x} = -1$. It loops in **start** synchronously on the event **notifyExit** with exactly one particle in the set **secondHalfParticles**, and it updates its **speed** output to be the average of its old speed and the speed of the exiting particle. It loops in **start** synchronously with exactly all particles in the set **secondHalfParticles** on the event **raiseSpeed** when $x \leq 0$, and it resets x to the next broadcast time using an externally defined function **nextBroadcastTime()**. The SHIFT description of the monitor type is given below.

```
type Monitor
{
    output number speed;
    state continuous number x;
    discrete start { x' = -1 }
    transition
        start -> start {secondHalfParticles:notifyExit(one:p)}
            do { speed := 0.5*(speed + speed(p)); };
        start -> start {secondHalfParticles:raiseSpeed(all)}
            when x <= 0
            do { x := nextBroadcastTime(); };
}
```

External Function Declaration

The externally defined function **nextBroadcastTime()** is declared within the SHIFT program as follows.

```
function nextBroadcastTime() -> number;
```

Global Variables

The program has three global variables: monitor, initialized to a component of type Monitor, source, initialized to a component of type Source and secondHalfParticles, a set of particles, initialized to the empty set. The SHIFT description of these global variables is given below.

```
global Monitor monitor
        := create(Monitor, speed := 100,
            x := nextBroadcastTime());
global Source source := create(Source, monitor := monitor);
global set(Particle) secondHalfParticles := {};
```

A SHIFT program begins execution by initializing global variables. The components created as part of this initialization begin exercising their dynamical behavior as soon as all global variables are initialized. In this example, the source would create the first particle after one time unit, and the monitor would execute raiseSpeed when the initially specified next broadcast time elapses.

4 The SHIFT Run-time Environment

A SHIFT program is executed by alternating between the "continuous" and "discrete" steps. In the continuous step, all differentially defined variables are integrated simultaneously using the fourth-order Runge-Kutta numerical integration algorithm. Since all continuous variables are integrated simultaneously, SHIFT yields more accurate results than simulators that perform component-wise integration using piecewise constant approximations of interacting components.

During the continuous step, the state of the world is examined periodically for enabled world transitions using the synchronization algorithm described in [7]. When an enabled transition is found, the discrete step is executed by "taking" the transition. The run-time system takes transitions as soon as they are enabled. The SHIFT language and semantics permit but do not require the as-soon-as semantics in the implementation, and programs written with such an assumption may not work correctly under other implementations of SHIFT.

There are three ways of interacting with a SHIFT program: through a command line interface, the graphical user interface *TkShift*, and the C application program interface. SHIFT program output can be obtained for on-line and off-line analysis and animation.

The particle example results in the following sequence of transitions in the Monitor and in Particle 0. Note that the simulation step size is 0.05 seconds and the nextBroadcastTime is 5 seconds. Sample SHIFT output is shown below.

```
...
{Time 5.05} {CollectiveTransition 5 (Monitor 0)}
```

```
{Monitor 0 {Transition start -> start}
    {local}
    {external {raiseSpeed all {}}}
    {speed 100.000000} {x 5.050000} }
...
{Time 6} {CollectiveTransition 7 (Particle 0)}
    {Particle 0 {Transition firstHalf -> secondHalf}
        {local}
        {external}
        {speed 100.000000} {x 500.000000} }
...
{Time 10.1} {CollectiveTransition 16 (Particle 3) (Particle 1)
        (Particle 0) (Particle 2) (Particle 4) (Monitor 0)}
    {Monitor 0 {Transition start -> start}
        {local}
        {external {raiseSpeed all {(Particle 4), (Particle 2),
            (Particle 0), (Particle 1), (Particle 3)}}}
        {speed 100.000000} {x 5.050000} }
    {Particle 0 {Transition secondHalf -> secondHalf}
        {local raiseSpeed}
        {external}
        {speed 100.000000} {x 910.000000} }
...
{Time 10.95} {CollectiveTransition 17 (Monitor 0) (Particle 0)}
    {Monitor 0 {Transition start -> start}
        {local}
        {external {notifyExit one (Particle 0)}}
        {speed 100.000000} {x 0.850000} }
    {Particle 0 {Transition secondHalf -> exit}
        {local notifyExit}
        {external}
        {speed 110.000000} {x 1003.500000} }
...
```

A graph, obtained from TkShift, of the **speed** variable of the **Monitor** over time is given in Figure 7.

4.1   Connecting the Mathematical Model and the Language

In this section we use the particle example to describe how the mathematical model relates to the SHIFT programming language.

As we stated earlier the mathematical model is austere and simplified and does not represent facilities for structured programming. In the mathematical model state, input, and output variables are all represented by x. In the mathematical model the global variables are assumed to be members of a type with one component that is created during the intialization of the world $A_W(0)$. Below we assume **secondHalfParticles** is a configuration state variable in the **Monitor** .

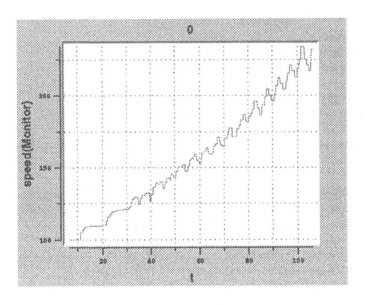

Fig. 7. Graph of speed vs time in Monitor

With these simplifications, the mathematical model representation of the **Particle** type is given as follows:

$Particle =$
$\quad Q = \{firstHalf, secondHalf, exit\}$
$\quad x = x, speed$
$\quad C = \{\{\}, \; ()\}$
$\quad L = \{raiseSpeed, notifyExit\}$
$\quad F = \{ \; F_{x,firstHalf} = speed, \; F_{x,secondHalf} = speed, \; F_{x,exit} = 0,$
$\quad\quad\quad F_{speed,firstHalf} = 0, \; F_{speed,secondHalf} = 0, \; F_{speed,exit} = 0 \; \}$
$\quad T = \{ \; (\; firstHalf, \; secondHalf, \; \{\}, \; (x >= 500), \; \textbf{omitted} \;)$
$\quad\quad\quad (\; secondHalf, \; secondHalf, \; \{raiseSpeed\}, \; (),$
$\quad\quad\quad\quad (speed := 1.1 * speed) \;)$
$\quad\quad\quad (\; secondHalf, \; exit \; \{notifyExit\}, \; (x >= 1000), \; \textbf{omitted} \;) \; \}$

The mathematical model representation of the **Monitor** type is given as follows:

$Monitor =$
   $Q = \{start\}$
   $x = x, speed$
   $C = \{\{\}, (Particle\ secondHalfParticles)\}$
   $L = \{\}$
   $F = \{\ f'_{x,start} = -1,\ f'_{speed,start} = 0\ \}$
   $T = \{\ (\ start,\ start,\ \{\exists c \in secondHalfParticles\ c : notifyExit\},\ (),$
              $(speed := 0.5 * (speed + speed(c)))\ )$
       $(\ start,\ start,\ \{\forall c \in secondHalfParticles\ c : raiseSpeed\},$
              $(x < 0),\ (x := nextBroadCastTime)\ )$

Next consider a world state with three **Particle** components, with respective **x** position 300, 700 and 900 and speeds 120. The mathematical representation of the component **Particle 2** would be as follows:

$Particle\ 2 =$
   $q = \{secondHalf\}$
   $x = 700, 120$
   $C = \{\{\}, ()\}$
   $L = \{raiseSpeed, notifyExit\}$
   $F_q = \{\ f'_x = 120,\ f'_{speed} = 0\ \}$
   $T = \{$
      $(\ firstHalf,\ secondHalf,\ \{\},\ (False),\ omitted\ )$
      $(\ secondHalf,\ secondHalf,\ \{Particle2 : raiseSpeed\},\ (),$
          $(speed := 1.1 * speed)\ )$
      $(\ secondHalf,\ exit,\ \{Particle2 : notifyExit\},\ (False),\ omitted\ )\}$

Assuming an **x** value of 2 and a **speed** value of 130, the mathematical representation of the component **Monitor 1** would be as follows:

$Monitor\ 1 =$
   $q = \{start\}$
   $x = 2, 130$
   $C = \{\{\}, (Particle2, Particle3)\}$
   $L = \{\}$
   $F = \{\ f'_x = -1,\ f'_{speed} = 0\ \}$
   $T = \{$
      $(\ start,\ start,\ \{Particle2 : notifyExit\},\ (),$
          $(speed := 0.5 * (speed + speed(Particle2)))\ )$
      $(\ start,\ start,\ \{Particle3 : notifyExit\},\ (),$
          $(speed := 0.5 * (speed + speed(Particle3)))\ )$
      $(\ start,\ start,\ \{Particle2 : raiseSpeed, Particle3 : raiseSpeed\},$
          $(False),\ (x := nextBroadCastTime)\ )$

In both examples transition prototypes in the types are used to evaluate the transitions of the components based on the configuration state variables. In Particle 2 the event label *notifyExit* in the type is transformed into *Particle2 : notifyExit*. In Monitor 1 the first transition in the type is transformed into two transitions, whereas the second transition in the type is transformed into a transition with two event labels. At another world state if the configuration state variable secondHalfParticles changes its value, the transitions in Monitor 1 are transformed accordingly.

5 Conclusion

We described the SHIFT formalism and programming language for dynamic networks of hybrid automata. We presented the SHIFT models of a type, a component and the world and gave the formal semantics of the model. We described the main features of SHIFT, such as states, inputs, outputs, differential equations and algebraic definitions, discrete states and state transitions, and illustrated them using examples. We described the run-time environment for simulating SHIFT programs and gave the algorithm for determining synchronized transitions.

We have implemented a compiler which translates a SHIFT program into a C program. The generated C program is compiled linked with run-time SHIFT libraries to obtain an executable. The executable program, when run, simulates the design specified in the SHIFT source program.

SHIFT is being used as a system description, integration and simulation environment in the Automated Highway Systems project of the National AHS Consortium. At Porto University, it is used for describing and simulating coordinated submarine maneuvers for ocean weather profiling. Other SHIFT projects include air traffic management systems and material handling systems. The class based modeling environment of SHIFT and its ability to dynamically reconfigure the synchronization requirements among components have greatly simplified problem specification in these systems.

Acknowledgements

The authors thank Marco Antoniotti, Datta Godbole, Michael Kourjanski, Luigi Semenzato, Raja Sengupta, Joseph Sifakis, Joao Sousa, D. Swaroop, Daniel Wiesman and Sergio Yovine for stimulating discussions and valuable comments, insights and contributions. This project was funded by the California PATH program of the University of California at Berkeley and by the National Automated Highway Systems Consortium.

References

1. F. Barros. Dynamic Structure Discrete Event Specification Formalism. In *Transactions for the Society for Computer Simulation*. No 1, pp. 35-46 1996.

2. F. Barros. Dynamic Structure discrete event systems: A comparison of methodologies and environments. In *Proc. SPIE's Aerosense '97* in Orlando Florida.

3. R. Alur, C. Courcoubetis, T. Henzinger, and P. Ho. Hybrid Automata: An Algorithmic Approach to the Specification and Verification of Hybrid Systems. In *Hybrid Systems*, LNCS 736, Springer-Verlag, 1993, pp. 209-229.

4. A. Deshpande and P. Varaiya. Viable Control of Hybrid Systems. In *Hybrid Systems II*, LNCS 999, Springer-Verlag. 1995.

5. A. Deshpande, D. Godbole, A. Göllü, L. Semenzato, R. Sengupta, D. Swaroop and P. Varaiya. *Automated Highway System Tool Interface Format*. California PATH Technical Report (draft). 24 January 1996.

6. A. Deshpande, D. Godbole, A. Göllü, P. Varaiya. "Design and Evaluation Tools for Automated Highway Systems." In *DIMACS* 1995 and in *Hybrid Systems III*, LNCS, Springer-Verlag, 1996.

7. A. Deshpande, A. Göllü, L. Semenzato. "The SHIFT Programming Language and Run-time System for Dynamic Networks of Hybrid Automata". To appear in Proceedings of IEEE.

8. F. Eskafi, Delnaz Khorramabadi, and P. Varaiya, An Automatic Highway System Simulator. In *Transpn. Res.-C* Vol. 3, No. 1, pp. 1-17, 1995.

9. F. Eskafi, A. Göllü. "Simulation Needs for Automated Highway Planning". To appear in *Transactions of Society of Computer Simulation*.

10. *Estelle – A Formal Description Technique Based on Extended State Transition Model.* ISO9074, 1988

11. D. Godbole, J. Lygeros, E. Singh, A. Deshpande and E. Lindsey. Design and Verification of Communication Protocols for Degraded Modes of Operation of AHS. In *Conference on Decision and Control*. 1995.

12. A. Göllü. Object Management Systems. *PhD Thesis*, UC Berkeley 1995.

13. A. Göllü, P. Varaiya. "Dynamic Networks of Hybrid Automata", *Fifth Annual Conference on AI, Simulation, and Planning in High Autonomy Systems*, pp. 244-251, Gainesville, Florida. 1994.

14. A. Göllü, P. Varaiya. "SmartAHS: A Simulation Framework for Automated Vehicles and Highway Systems". To appear in *International Journal of Mathematical and Computer Modeling*.

15. J. Haddon, D. Godbole, A. Deshpande and J. Lygeros. Verification of Hybrid Systems: Monotonicity in the AHS Control System. In *DIMACS*. 1995.

16. C.A.R. Hoare. *Communicating Sequential Processes*, Prentice/Hall International, 1985

17. G.P. Hong and T.G. Kim. The DEVS Formalism: A Framework for Logical Analysis and Performance. In *Fifth Annual Conference on AI, Simulation, and Planning in High Autonomy Systems*, pp. 170-278, Gainesville, Florida. 1994.

18. A. Hsu, F. Eskafi, S. Sachs, P. Varaiya. Protocol Design for an Automated Highway System. In *Discrete Event Dynamic Systems: Theory and Applications 2*, (1993): 183-206.

19. Kemal Inan and Pravin Varaiya. Finitely Recursive Process Models for Discrete Event Systems. In *IEEE Trans. Auto. Control*, vol. AC-33, no. 7, pp. 626-639, July 1988.

20. Tak-Kuen Juhn Koo, Yi Ma, George J. Pappas and Claire Tomlin. "SmartATMS: A Simulator for Air Traffic Management Systems" Submitted to Winter Simulation Conference 1997.

21. R. Kurshan. *Computer-Aided Verification of Coordinating Processes: The Automata-Theoretic Approach*. Princeton University Press, 1994.

22. *LOTOS – A Formal Description Technique Based on the Temporal Ordering of Observational Behavior.* ISO8807, 1XS989

23. S.E. Mattsson and M. Anderson. The Ideas Behind Omola. In *Proc. IEEE Symposium on Computer Aided Control System Design, CADCS '92.* Napa, CA, March 17-19 1992.

24. R.Milner. *A Calculus of Communicating Systems,* Springer-Verlag, 1980

25. H. Praehofer, F. Auernig, adn G. Resinger. "An Environment for DEVS-based multiformalisms simulation in Common Lisp/CLOS", *Discrete Event Dynamic Systems: Theory and Application,* 3(2):119-149, 1993.

26. A. Puri and P. Varaiya. Driving safely in smart cars. In *American Control Conference,* pp. 3597-3599, 1995.

27. L. Semenzato, A. Deshpande and A. Göllü. *Shift Reference Manual.* California PATH Technical Report (draft). 28 June 1996.

28. Joao Sousa and Aleks Göllü. "A Simulation Environment of the Coordinated Operation of Multiple Autonomous Underwater Vehicles" Submitted to Winter Simulation Conference 1997.

29. Specification and Description Language SDL. *International Telecommunications Union-T Rec.Z.100* 1988.

30. P. Varaiya. Smart cars on smart roads: problems of control. In *IEEE Trans. Automatic Control,* vol. 38, No. 2, 1993.

31. Peter Wegner. "Concepts and Paradigms of Object-Oriented Programming", *ACM SIGPLAN OOPS Messenger,* 1(1), Aug 1990.

32. Bernard Zeigler. *Multifaceted modeling and discrete event simulation.* Academic Press, London, Orlando, 1984.

Synthesis of Minimally Restrictive Legal Controllers for a Class of Hybrid Systems[1]

Michael Heymann[2], Feng Lin[3] and George Meyer[4]

Abstract. In this paper, we study the control of *Composite Hybrid Machines* (CHMs) subject to safety specifications. CHMs are a fairly general class of hybrid systems modeled in modular fashion as the concurrent operation of *Elementary Hybrid Machines* (EHMs). The formalism has a well-defined synchronous-composition operation that permits the introduction of the controller as a component of the system. The task of a legal controller is to ensure that the system never exits a set of specified legal configurations. Among the legal controllers, we are particularly interested in designing a minimally-restrictive (or minimally-interventive) one, which interferes in the system's operation only when constraint violation is otherwise inevitable. Thus, when composed to operate concurrently with another legal controller, our controller will never interfere with the operation of the other. Therefore, a minimally-restrictive controller provides maximum flexibility in embedding additional controllers designed for other control objectives to operate concurrently, while eliminating the need to re-investigate or re-verify the legality of the composite controller. We describe in detail an algorithm for controller synthesis and examine through several examples questions associated with algorithm termination and controller existence.

1 Introduction

Various definitions have been proposed in the literature to capture the intuitive idea that hybrid systems are dynamic systems in which discrete and continuous behaviors coexist and interact [3] [4] [7] [8] [19] [22]. Broadly speaking, they are systems in which changes occur both in response to events that take place discretely, asynchronously and sometimes nondeterministically, and in response to dynamics that represents (causal) evolution as described by differential or difference equations of time. Thus, most physical systems that can be represented by formal behavior models are hybrid in nature.

[1] This research is supported in part by the National Science Foundation under grant ECS-9315344 and NASA under grant NAG2-1043 and in part by the Technion Fund for Promotion of Research.

The work by the first author was completed while he was a Senior NRC Research Associate at NASA Ames Research Center, Moffett Field, CA 94035.

[2] Department of Computer Science, Technion, Israel Institute of Technology, Haifa 32000, Israel, e-mail: heymann@cs.technion.ac.il.

[3] Department of Electrical and Computer Engineering, Wayne State University, Detroit, MI 48202, e-mail: flin@ece.eng.wayne.edu.

[4] NASA Ames Research Center, Moffett Field, CA 94035, e-mail: meyer@tarski.arc.nasa.gov.

In recent years there has been a rapidly growing interest in the computer-science community in modeling, analysis, formal specification and verification of hybrid systems (see, e.g. [4] [24]). This interest evolved progressively from logical systems, through "logically-timed" temporal systems [2] to real-time systems modeled as timed automata [20] and, most recently, to a restricted class of hybrid systems called *hybrid automata* [3] [19]. Thus, the computer-science viewpoint of hybrid systems can be characterized as one of discrete programs embedded in an "analog" environment.

In parallel, there has been growing interest in hybrid systems in the control-theory community, where traditionally systems have been viewed as "purely" dynamic systems that are modeled by differential or difference equations [5] [7] [8]. More recently, control of purely discrete systems, modeled as discrete-event systems, also received attention in the literature [25] [26] [16]. The growing realization that neither the purely discrete nor the purely continuous frameworks are adequate for describing many physical systems, has been an increasing driving force to focus attention on hybrid systems. Contrary to the computer-science viewpoint that focuses interest in hybrid systems on issues of analysis and verification [21] [23], the control-theory viewpoint is to focus its interest on issues of design.

Typical hybrid systems interact with the environment both by sharing signals (i.e., by transmission of input/output data), and by event synchronization (through which the system is reconfigured and its structure modified). Control of hybrid systems can therefore be achieved by employing both interaction mechanisms simultaneously. Yet, while this flexibility adds significantly to the potential control capabilities, it clearly makes the problem of design much more difficult. Indeed, in view of the obvious complexity of hybrid control, even the question of what are tractable and achievable design objectives, is far from easy to resolve [10].

In the present paper we examine the control problem for a class of hybrid systems called *composite hybrid machines* (CHMs). These constitute hybrid systems consist of the concurrent operation of *elementary hybrid machines* (EHMs) using a well-defined synchronous composition formalism that allows both signal sharing and event synchronization. A controller can then be coupled with the plant by means of synchronous composition.

The goal of a legal controller considered in the present paper, is to ensure the safety of the system in the sense that it will never violate its legal specification given by a set of (illegal) configurations that must be avoided. In other words, a *legal* controller must prevent the system from ever entering the illegal configurations. Among all legal controllers, we are interested in minimally restrictive ones.

A legal controller is minimally restrictive if, when composed to operate concurrently with any other legal controller, it will remain inactive except at the boundary of legal region where controller inaction would lead to inevitable safety violation, therefore, can be composed to operate concurrently with any other controller that may be designed to achieve other requirements such as liveness specifications or optimality. There is no need to re-investigate or re-verify legality of the composite controller.

We confine our attention to a special class of CHMs where system dynamics is *rate-limited* and legal guards are conjunctions or disjunctions of atomic formulas in the dynamic variables (of the type $S < C$, $S > C$, $S \leq C$, or $S \geq C$). We present an algorithm for synthesis of the minimally restrictive legal controller.

2   Design Philosophy

Intuitively, a controller for legal behavior of a hybrid system is minimally restrictive if it never takes action unless constraint violation becomes imminent. When the latter happens, the controller is expected do no more than prevent the system from becoming "illegal". This is a familiar setting in the discrete-event control literature since, there, the role of the controller has traditionally been viewed as that of a *supervisor* that can only intervene in the system's activity by event disablement [25] [26]. Thus, a minimally restrictive supervisor of a discrete-event system is one that disables events only whenever their enablement would permit the system to violate the specification.

It is not difficult to see that a natural candidate for a "template" of a minimally restrictive supervisor is a system whose range of possible behaviors coincides with the set of behaviors permitted by the specification. The concurrent execution of the controlled system and such a supervisor, in the sense that events are permitted to occur in the controlled system whenever they are possible in the controller template, would then constrain the system to satisfy the specification exactly. We shall then say that we have employed the specification as a candidate implementation. If all the events that are possible in the system but not permitted by the candidate supervisor can actually be disabled, we say that the specification is *implementable* or (when the specification is given as a legal language) *controllable* [25]. Generally, a specification may not be implementable because not all the events can be disabled.

The standard approach to supervisory controller synthesis can then be interpreted as an iterative procedure where, starting with the specification as a candidate implementation, at each stage of the iteration the specification is tightened so as to exclude behaviors that cannot be prevented from becoming illegal by instantaneous disablement of events [12] [13]. The *sub-specification* thus obtained, is then used as a new candidate implementation. When the procedure converges in a finite number of steps (a fact guaranteed in case the system is a finite automaton and the specification a regular language), the result is either an empty specification (meaning that a legal supervisor does not exist) or a minimally restrictive implementable sub-specification.

In the present paper we shall employ the same design philosophy for the synthesis of minimally restrictive controllers of hybrid systems. However, due to the addition of continuous dynamics and dynamic transitions caused by continuous dynamics, the synthesis problem for hybrid systems becomes much more complex. In particular, it is often necessary to "split" configurations into legal and illegal sub-configurations by considering some weakest preconditions, safe-exit conditions, and preemptive conditions that depend explicitly on continuous dynamics.

3 Comparison with Other Work

As state before, the basic approach employed in our synthesis method is standard in the supervisory control theory of discrete-event systems, where a similar (least) fixed-point algorithm is usually employed (see, e.g., some of our own work on discrete-event systems [11] [12] [13] [14] [16] [17] [18] [9]). Needless to say, however, that there are significant differences between this work and that of supervisory control.

Our hybrid-machine formalism, while similar in spirit to the well-known hybrid automata model, (see, for example, [3]), differs from the latter in some subtle (but important) detail. Most importantly, we insist that vertices (and hence configurations) be always *completely guarded*, thereby insuring that CHMs are always well-defined (and every run is physically realizable). This prevents the possibility of ill-defined behaviors (that are possible in hybrid automata and are frequently referred to as the "prevention of time from progressing"). Furthermore, our model provides an explicit mechanism for interaction between EHMs by introducing input/output events and shared variables. Such an explicit mechanism is critical to controller specification and design as proposed in this paper.

Finally, there are other recent works on control synthesis; in particular, the works reported in [6] [20] where attention is confined to timed automata, and where a similar fixed-point approach to control-synthesis is proposed. There are, however, significant differences between our work and the latter. First, we extend our attention to hybrid machines rather than confine it to timed automata. This allows, for example, dynamics of bounded-rate without resetting rather than constant rate with resetting. Our model also allows dynamic transitions in addition to event transitions. Secondly, contrary to that of [6] [20], our plant is autonomous in the sense that it can run by itself without the intervention of a controller. Because of this property, our control is "supervisory". It gives the plant freedom to do what it wants as long as there is no safety violation. Finally, and most importantly, we develop an explicit synthesis algorithm for design of a minimally restrictive controller, while in [6] [20] the fixed-point algorithm is only abstractly outlined (in the discrete-event control spirit) but no explicit algorithm is given.

Another noteworthy difference between the control problem for timed automata and hybrid automata is the decidability issue. While in the timed automata case the control synthesis problem is always decidable (a fact proved in [20]), this is not the case in hybrid automata (see [10]) and in fact our synthesis algorithm may not terminate as is demonstrated in a simple example in Section 6.

4   Hybrid Machines

We first introduce a modeling formalism for a class of hybrid systems which we call *hybrid machines* and which are a special case of *hierarchical hybrid machines* to be discussed elsewhere. We begin by an informal example.

4.1   Illustrative example

Figure 1 describes schematically a hybrid system that consists of a water-tank with water supplied by a pump and with outflow controlled by a two-position valve.

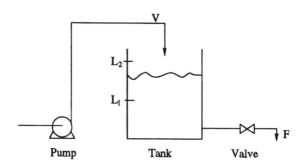

Fig. 1. Water Tank System

The system is described graphically in Figure 2 as a *composite hybrid machine* (CHM) that consists of three *elementary hybrid machines* (EHMs) running in parallel:

$$PUMP\|TANK\|VALVE.$$

The EHM **Tank** has three *vertices* <high>, <normal> and <low>, representing the tank's "high" , "normal" and "low" levels , respectively. The dynamic behavior of the tank's water level L is described by the equations $\dot{x} = V - F, L = x$, where x is the (internal) state of the vertex, and V and F are the rates of water inflow and outflow, respectively. In this example, the (continuous) dynamic equations are same at all three vertices. In general, however, they may be different. The quantities V and F constitute *input-signals* to the EHM **Tank** and *output-signals* of the EHMs **Pump** and **Valve**, respectively. **Tank** may reside at a given vertex provided the vertex invariant [.] is true. Thus, it may reside at the vertex <normal> so long as the invariant $[L_1 \leq L \wedge L \leq L_2]$ is satisfied, and similarly for the other vertex invariants. The transitions between the three vertices are *dynamic* in the sense that they are triggered, respectively, by the guards $[L > L_2]$, $[L \leq L_2]$, $[L \geq L_1]$ and $[L < L_1]$ becoming true. The self-loop dynamic transition of the vertex <normal> labeled

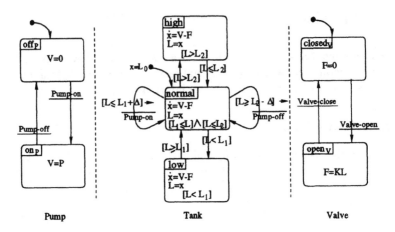

Fig. 2. Water Tank System CHM

by $[L{\leq}L_1 + \Delta]{\rightarrow}\overline{pump - on}$ is guarded by the predicate $[L{\leq}L_1 + \Delta]$ (where $\Delta > 0$ is some small constant), and upon occurrence triggers the *output-event* $\overline{pump - on}$. (Throughout, underlined event labels denote input-events and overlined event labels denote output-events.) Similarly, the other self-loop transition of the vertex <normal> is guarded by $[L{\geq}L_2 - \Delta]$ and triggers the output-event $\overline{pump - off}$. The EHM **Tank** is initialized at the vertex <normal> with initial water level L_0 (that lies between the lower bound L_1 and the upper bound L_2).

The EHM **Pump** has two vertices: $<$ off$_P$ $>$ and $<$ on$_P$ $>$. At the vertex $<$ off$_P$ $>$, the pump is off, reflected by the vertex output $V = 0$. Similarly, at the vertex $<$ on$_P$ $>$, the pump is running and the vertex output V is the pump's (constant) flow rate P. The transitions between the two vertices are labeled by the *input-event* labels $\underline{pump - on}$ and $\underline{pump - off}$. These transitions are triggered by and take place concurrently and synchronously with the output-events $\overline{pump - on}$ and $\overline{pump - off}$, respectively.

Finally, the EHM **Valve** can be at either of the vertices $<$ open$_V$ $>$ or $<$ closed$_V$ $>$. Transition between the two vertices are labeled by input-events $\underline{valve - open}$ and $\underline{valve - closed}$, respectively. These transition labels do not appear as output-events in any of the other parallel EHMs but can be received from the (unmodeled) environment. When **Valve** is closed, the rate of outflow is $F = 0$ and when it is open, the rate is proportional to the water level in the tank $F = KL$.

Notice that in general there are two mechanisms for communication between parallel EHMs: (1) Input/output-event synchronization; by which transitions are synchronized. Transitions labeled by input-events can take place only in synchrony with a corresponding output-event that is being transmitted either by a parallel EHM or by the environment. (However, an output-event can be triggered without participation of any input-event, if no corresponding input-event is feasible.) (2) Signal sharing; by which outputs (output signals) of a vertex are available as vertex inputs to any other parallel EHM.

4.2 Elementary hybrid machines

With the above illustrative example in mind, we can now formally define hybrid machines as follows. An elementary hybrid machine is denoted by

$$EHM = (Q, \Sigma, D, I, E, (q_0, x_0)).$$

The elements of EHM are as follows.

- Q is a finite set of vertices.
- Σ is a finite set of event labels. An event is an input event, denoted by $\underline{\sigma}$ (underline), if it is received by the EHM from its environment; and an output event, denoted by $\overline{\sigma}$ (overline), if it is generated by the EHM and transmitted to the environment.
- $D = \{d_q = (x_q, y_q, u_q, f_q, h_q) : q \in Q\}$ is the dynamics of the EHM, where d_q, the dynamics at the vertex q, is given by:

$$\dot{x}_q = f_q(x_q, u_q),$$
$$y_q = h_q(x_q, u_q),$$

with x_q, u_q, and y_q, respectively, the state, input, and output variables of appropriate dimensions. f_q is a Lipschitz continuous function and h_q a continuous function. (A vertex need not have dynamics associated with it, that is $d_q = \emptyset$, in which case we say that the vertex is *static*.)
- $I = \{I_q : q \in Q\}$ is a set of invariants. I_q represents conditions under which the EHM is permitted to reside at q. A formal definition of I_q will be given in the next subsection.
- $E = \{(q, G \wedge \underline{\sigma} \to \overline{\sigma'}, q', x_{q'}^0) : q, q' \in Q\}$ is a set of edges (transition-paths), where q is the exiting vertex, q' the entering vertex, $\underline{\sigma}$ the input-event, $\overline{\sigma'}$ the output-event, G the guard to be formally defined in the next subsection, and $x_{q'}^0$ the initialization value for $x_{q'}$ upon entry to q'.
  $(q, G \wedge \underline{\sigma} \to \overline{\sigma'}, q', x_{q'}^0)$ is interpreted as follows: If G is true and the event $\underline{\sigma}$ is received as an input, then the transition to q' takes place with the assignment of the initial condition $x_{q'}(t_0) = x_{q'}^0$ (here t_0 denotes the time at which the vertex q' is entered). The output-event $\overline{\sigma'}$ is transmitted at the same time. If $\overline{\sigma'}$ is absent, then no output-event is transmitted. If $x_{q'}^0$ is absent, then the initial condition is inherited from x_q (assuming x_q and $x_{q'}$ represent the same physical object and hence are of the same dimension). If $\underline{\sigma}$ is absent, then the transition takes place immediately upon G become true. (Such a transition is called a dynamic transition and is sometimes abbreviated as (q, G, q') when $\overline{\sigma'}$ and $x_{q'}^0$ are absent or understood.) If G is absent, the guard is always true and the transition will be triggered by the input-event $\underline{\sigma}$. (Such a transition is called an event transition and sometimes abbreviated as $(q, \underline{\sigma}, q')$ when $\overline{\sigma'}$ and $x_{q'}^0$ are absent or understood.)
- (q_0, x_0) denote the initialization condition: q_0 is the initial vertex and $x_{q_0}(t_0) = x_0$.

For the EHM to be well-defined, we require that all vertices be *completely guarded*. That is, every invariant violation (possible under the dynamics) implies that some guard associated with a dynamic transition becomes true. (It is, in principle, permitted that more than one guard become true at the same instant. In such a case the transition that will actually take place is resolved nondeterministically.) Note that we do not require the converse to be true. That is, a transition can be triggered even if the invariant is not violated. We further require that, upon entry to a vertex q', the invariant $I_{q'}$ be true. It is however possible that, upon entry to q', one of the guards at q' is already true. In such a case, the EHM will immediately exit q' and go to a vertex specified by (one of) the true guards. Such a transition is considered instantaneous. Naturally, we only allow finite chains of such instantaneous transitions to be possible, otherwise we say that the EHM is *divergent*. That is, for the EHM to be *nondivergent*, the guards must be such that no sequence of instantaneous transitions can form a loop.

In this paper we will study a restricted class of hybrid machines called *bounded-rate* hybrid machines, characterized by the following assumption.

Assumption 1 The dynamics described by f_q and h_q has the following properties: (1) $h_q(x_q, u_q)$ is a linear function; and (2) $f_q(x_q, u_q)$ is bounded by a lower limit k_q^L and an upper limit k_q^U, that is, $f_q(x_q, u_q) \in [k_q^L, k_q^U]$.

An execution of the EHM is a sequence

$$q_0 \xrightarrow{e_1, t_1} q_1 \xrightarrow{e_2, t_2} q_2 \xrightarrow{e_3, t_3} \dots$$

where e_i is the ith transition and t_i is the time when the ith transition takes place. For each execution, we define its trajectory, path and trace as follows.

- The trajectory of the execution is the sequence of the vector time functions of the state variables:

$$x_{q_0}, x_{q_1}, x_{q_2}, \dots$$

where $x_{q_i} = \{x_{q_i}(t) : t \in [t_i, t_{i+1})\}$.
- The path of the execution is the sequence of the vertices.
- The input trace of the execution is the sequence of the input-events.
- The output trace of the execution is the sequence of the output-events.

Remark. It is easily seen that discrete-event systems and continuous-variable systems are special cases of the hybrid systems as described above. Indeed, we notice that if there is no dynamics in an EHM (and hence no D and I), then

$$EHM = (Q, \Sigma, E, q_0)$$

where edges E are labeled only by events: a typical discrete-event system. Similarly, if there is no event and only one vertex in an EHM (and hence no need to introduce Q, Σ, I and E), then

$$EHM = (D, x_0) = (x, y, u, f, h, x_0),$$

which is a typical continuous-variable system.

4.3 Composite hybrid machine

A composite hybrid machine consists of several elementary hybrid machines running in parallel:

$$CHM = EHM^1 \| EHM^2 \| ... \| EHM^n.$$

Interaction between EHMs is achieved by means of signal transmission (shared variables) and input/output-event synchronization (message passing) as described below.

Shared variables consist of output signals from all EHMs as well as signals received from the environment. They are shared by all EHMs in the sense that they are accessible to all EHMs. A shared variable S_i can be the output of at most one EHM. If the EHM of the output variable does not update the variable, its value will remain unchanged. The set of shared variables defines a signal space $S = [S_1, S_2, ..., S_m]$.

Transitions are synchronized by an input/output synchronization formalism. That is, if an output-event $\bar{\sigma}$ is either generated by one of the EHMs or received from the environment, then all EHMs for which σ is an active transition label (i.e., σ is defined at the current vertex with a true guard) will execute σ (and its associated transition) concurrently with the occurrence of $\bar{\sigma}$. An output-event can be generated by at most one EHM. Notice that input-events do not synchronize among themselves. Notice further that this formalism is a special case of the prioritized synchronous composition formalism [11], where each event is in the priority set of at most one parallel component.

By introducing the shared variables S, we can now define invariants and guards formally as boolean combinations of inequalities of the form (called *atomic formulas*)

$$S_i \geq C_i \quad \text{or} \quad S_i \leq C_i,$$

where S_i is a shared variable and C_i is a real constant.

Remark. For consistency of the computations, we should mainly deal with closed invariants as well as closed guards (that is, the sets in which the invariants or guards are true are closed). Since the complement of a closed set is not closed, we should distinguish, for $S_i \geq C_i$, its strict negation $S_i < C_i$ and its negation $S_i \leq C_i$. To ensure the closedness, we will maily consider negation (unless otherwise stated) and, with some abuse of notation, write $\neg(S_i \geq C_i) = (S_i \leq C_i)$. Thus, it is possible that a boolean expression and its negation are both true at a point or on a hyperplane. If this matters, as in the case that several guards become true simultaneously, we will introduce suitable prioritization, as will be discussed below.

To describe the behavior of

$$CHM = EHM^1 \| EHM^2 \| ... \| EHM^n,$$

we define a *configuration* of the CHM to be

$$q = < q^1_{i_1}, q^2_{i_2}, ..., q^n_{i_n} > \in Q^1 \times Q^2 \times ... \times Q^n$$

where Q^j is the set of vertices of EHM^j (components of the EHMs are superscripted).

When all the elements of q are specified, we call q a *full* configuration. When only some of the elements of q are specified, we call q a *partial* configuration and we mean that an unspecified element can be any possible vertex of the respective EHM. For example, $< , q^2_{i_2}, ..., q^n_{i_n} >$ is interpreted as the set

$$< , q^2_{i_2}, ..., q^n_{i_n} > = \{ < q^1_{i_1}, q^2_{i_2}, ..., q^n_{i_n} > : q^1_{i_1} \in Q^1 \}$$

of full configurations. Thus, a partial configuration is a compact description of a set of (full) configurations.

A transition

$$< q^1_{i_1}, q^2_{i_2}, ..., q^n_{i_n} > \xrightarrow{l} < q^1_{i'_1}, q^2_{i'_2}, ..., q^n_{i'_n} >$$

of a CHM is a triple, where $q = < q^1_{i_1}, q^2_{i_2}, ..., q^n_{i_n} >$ is the source configuration, $q' = < q^1_{i'_1}, q^2_{i'_2}, ..., q^n_{i'_n} >$ the target configuration, and l the label that triggers the transition. l can be either an event or a guard (becoming true). Thus, if $l = \underline{\sigma}$ is an event (generated by the environment), then either $q^j_{i'_j} = q^j_{i_j}$ if $\underline{\sigma}$ is not active at $q^j_{i_j}$, or $q^j_{i'_j}$ is such that $(q^j_{i_j}, \underline{\sigma} \to \overline{\sigma'}, q^j_{i'_j}, x^0_{q^j_{i'_j}})$ is a transition in E^j. On the other hand, if $l = G$ is a guard, then there must exists a transition $(q^m_{i_m}, G \to \overline{\sigma'}, q^m_{i'_m}, x^0_{q^m_{i'_m}})$ in some EHM^m and for $j \neq m$, either $q^j_{i'_j} = q^j_{i_j}$ if $\underline{\sigma'}$ is not defined at $q^j_{i_j}$, or $q^j_{i'_j}$ is such that $(q^j_{i_j}, \underline{\sigma'} \to \overline{\sigma''}, q^j_{i'_j}, x^0_{q^j_{i'_j}})$ is a transition in E^j.

For brevity we shall sometimes denote the transition simply by (q, l, q'). Note that for simplicity, we do not specify the output events and initial conditions, since they are defined in the EHMs.

The transitions are assumed to occur instantaneously and concurrent vertex changes in parallel components are assumed to occur exactly at the same instant (even when constituting a logically triggered finite chain of transitions).

Remark. Based on the above definition, a CHM can be viewed as the same object as an EHM:

$$CHM = (Q, \Sigma, D, I, E, (q_0, x_0))$$

where

$$Q = Q^1 \times Q^2 \times ... \times Q^n,$$
$$\Sigma = \Sigma^1 \cup \Sigma^2 \cup ... \cup \Sigma^n,$$
$$D = \{ (x_q, y_q, u_q, f_q, h_q) : q = < q^1_{i_1}, q^2_{i_2}, ..., q^n_{i_n} > \in Q^1 \times Q^2 \times ... \times Q^n \}$$

combines all the dynamics of $q^j_{i_j}, j = 1, 2, ..., n,$

$$I = \{I_{q_{i_1}^1} \wedge I_{q_{i_2}^2} \wedge ... \wedge I_{q_{i_n}^n} :< q_{i_1}^1, q_{i_2}^2, ..., q_{i_n}^n >\in Q^1 \times Q^2 \times ... \times Q^n\},$$

E is defined as above, and

$$(q_0, x_0) = (< q_0^1, q_0^2, ..., q_0^n >, (x_0^1, x_0^2, ..., x_0^n)).$$

Therefore, we can define an execution of a CHM in the same way as that of an EHM.

Recall that our model also allows guarded event transitions of the form

$$q \xrightarrow{G \wedge \sigma} q'.$$

However, since for the transition to take place the guard must be true when the event is triggered, a guarded event transition can be decomposed into

$$q_1 \underset{\xleftarrow{\neg G}}{\overset{G}{\rightarrow}} q_2 \xrightarrow{\sigma} q',$$

where q has been partitioned into q_1 and q_2, with $I_{q_1} = I_q \wedge \neg G$ and $I_{q_2} = I_q \wedge G$. It follows that a guarded event transition can be treated as a combination of a dynamic and an event transition.

Thus, transitions in CHMs can be classified into two types: (1) dynamic transitions, that are labeled by guards only, and (2) event transitions, that are labeled by events.

5   Control

5.1   Specifications

As stated in the previous section, a CHM can interact with its environment in two ways: (1) by signal transmission (shared variables), and (2) by input/output-event synchronization. Formally, a *Controller* of a CHM is a hybrid machine C that runs in parallel with the CHM. The resultant system

$$CHM \| C$$

is called the *controlled* or *closed-loop* system. The objective of control is to force the controlled system to satisfy a prescribed set of behavioral specifications.

For conventional (continuous) dynamical systems, control specification might consist of the requirement of stability, robustness, disturbance rejection, optimality and the like. For discrete-event systems, specifications of required behavior are typically given as *safety* specifications, where a prescribed set of unwanted behaviors or configurations is to be avoided, or *liveness* specifications, where a prescribed set of termination conditions is to be met, or both.

For general hybrid systems, specifications can, in principle, be of a very complex nature incorporating both dynamic requirements and the logical (discrete) aspects.

In the present paper we consider only safety specifications given as a set of *illegal* configurations

$$Q_b = \{q = <q_{i_1}^1, q_{i_2}^2, ..., q_{i_n}^n > \in Q^1 \times Q^2 \times ... \times Q^n : q \text{ is illegal}\}$$

that the system is not permitted to visit.

Our goal is to synthesize a controller that guarantees satisfaction of the above stated configuration-based safety requirement. A controller that achieves the specification is then said to be *legal*.

In this paper, we shall consider only restricted interaction between the controller and the CHM by permitting the controller to communicate with the CHM only through input/output-event synchronization. Thus, we make the following assumption.

Assumption 2 C can only control the CHM by means of input/output-event synchronization. That is, C can only control event transitions in the CHM.

Thus, the controller is assumed not to generate any (dynamic) output signals that may affect the CHM.

We shall assume further that C can control all the event transitions in the CHM. That is, all the (externally triggered) event transitions are available to the controller. This leads to no essential loss of generality because, when some of the events are *uncontrollable*, we can use the methods developed in supervisory control of discrete-event systems [25] [26] to deal with uncontrollable event transitions. We shall elaborate on this issue elsewhere.

A legal controller C is said to be *less restrictive* than another legal controller C' if every execution permitted by C' is also permitted by C (a formal definition will be given in the next subsection). A legal controller is said to be *minimally restrictive* if it is less restrictive than any legal controller.

With a slight modification of the formalism that we shall present in the next subsection, two or more controllers can be combined by parallel composition to form a composite controller. An important characteristic of a minimally restrictive controller is the fact that when it is combined with any other controller (legal or not), that is possibly designed for satisfying some other specifications, such as liveness or optimality, the combined controller is guaranteed to be safe (i.e., legal). Hence, no further verification of safety will be needed. Furthermore, the minimally restrictive controller will intervene with the action of the other controller only minimally; that is, when it is absolutely necessary to do so in order to guarantee the safety of the system.

5.2 Control synthesis

As stated, our control objective is to ensure that the system CHM never enter the set of illegal configurations Q_b. Such entry can occur either via an event transition or via a dynamic transition. Since all event transitions are at the disposal of the controller, prevention of entry to the illegal set via event transitions is a trivial matter (they simply must not be triggered). Therefore, in our control synthesis we shall focus our attention on dynamic transitions. Intuitively, the minimally restrictive legal controller must take action, by forcing the CHM from the current configuration to some other legal configuration, just in time (but as late as possible) to prevent a dynamic transition from leading the system to an illegal configuration. Clearly, entry to a configuration which is legal but at which an inescapable (unpreventable) dynamic transition to an illegal configuration is possible, must itself be deemed technically illegal and avoided by the controller. Thus the controller synthesis algorithm that we present below, will iterate through the (still) legal configurations and examine whether it is possible to prevent a dynamic transition from leading to an illegal configuration. In doing so, it will frequently be necessary to "split" configurations by partitioning their invariants into their *legal* and *illegal* parts.

In order to do this, we will need to consider first the time at which a predicate will become true. We begin by considering an atomic formula

$$P = (S_i \geq C_i).$$

Suppose that at a given instant t at which $S_i(t) = S_i$, P is false; that is, $S_i \leq C_i$ (or actually $S_i < C_i$). Then the interval of time that will elapse before P can become true is bounded by the minimum value

$$T_{min}(true(P)) = \begin{cases} (C_i - S_i)/r_i^U & \text{if } r_i^U > 0 \\ \infty & \text{otherwise,} \end{cases}$$

and the maximum value

$$T_{max}(true(P)) = \begin{cases} (C_i - S_i)/r_i^L & \text{if } r_i^L > 0 \\ \infty & \text{otherwise,} \end{cases}$$

where, r_i^L and r_i^U are the lower and upper bounds of $\dot{S}$, respectively (recall that, by our assumption, the shared variables S_i are rate-bounded; that is, $\dot{S}_i \in [r_i^L, r_i^U]$).

If, at the instant t, P is true, then clearly $T_{min}(true(P)) = T_{max}(true(P)) = 0$. Similarly, if P is given by

$$P = (S_i \leq C_i),$$

then if, at the instant t, P is true, $T_{min}(true(P)) = T_{max}(true(P)) = 0$, and otherwise, the minimum interval is

$$T_{min}(true(P)) = \begin{cases} (C_i - S_i)/r_i^L & \text{if } r_i^L < 0 \\ \infty & \text{otherwise,} \end{cases}$$

and the maximum interval is

$$T_{max}(true(P)) = \begin{cases} (C_i - S_i)/r_i^U & \text{if } r_i^U < 0 \\ \infty & \text{otherwise.} \end{cases}$$

For conjunction of two predicates, $P = P_1 \wedge P_2$, it is clear that

$$T_{min}(true(P)) = max\{T_{min}(true(P_1)), T_{min}(true(P_2))\}$$

$$T_{max}(true(P)) = max\{T_{max}(true(P_1)), T_{max}(true(P_2))\},$$

and for disjunction of two predicates, $P = P_1 \vee P_2$

$$T_{min}(true(P)) = min\{T_{min}(true(P_1)), T_{min}(true(P_2))\}$$

$$T_{max}(true(P)) = min\{T_{max}(true(P_1)), T_{max}(true(P_2))\}.$$

Also, if a predicate is always false: $P = false$, then

$$T_{min}(true(P)) = T_{max}(true(P)) = \infty.$$

To streamline the ensuing analysis, we shall assume that the invariants of all legal configurations are expressed in conjunctive normal form

$$I = (I_{11}\vee...\vee I_{1l_1})\wedge...\wedge(I_{m1}\vee...\vee I_{ml_m}),$$

where $I_{ij}=(S_{ij} \geq C_{ij})$, $I_{ij}=(S_{ij} \leq C_{ij})$. Similarly, all the guards are in conjunctive normal form

$$G = (G_{11}\vee...\vee G_{1l_1})\wedge...\wedge(G_{m1}\vee...\vee G_{ml_m}).$$

When competing guards become true simultaneously, we shall give priority to a legal guard (i.e., one that leads to a legal configuration) over an illegal one, and we shall resolve nondeterministically between competing legal guards.

Without loss of generality, we shall assume that the invariant is violated if and only if one or more of the guards is true - recall the difference between negation and strict negation as discussed in the previous remark. (Otherwise, we can conjoin with the invariant the negation of the guards.)

The role of the least restrictive controller is to force event transitions (to other legal configurations) at "the boundary of the legal region". To specify the forcing condition formally, we need to introduce, for a predicate P, $critical(P)$ that captures the fact that P is about to be violated. Thus, for $P = (S_i \leq C_i)$, we define

$$critical(P) = \begin{cases} (S_i \geq C_i) & \text{if } r_i^U > 0 \\ false & \text{otherwise,} \end{cases}$$

Similarly, for $P = (S_i \geq C_i)$,

$$critical(P) = \begin{cases} (S_i \leq C_i) & \text{if } r_i^L < 0 \\ false & \text{otherwise.} \end{cases}$$

For conjunction of two predicates $P = P_1 \wedge P_2$,

$$critical(P) = critical(P_1) \vee critical(P_2).$$

and for disjunction of two predicates $P = P_1 \vee P_2$,

$$critical(P) = critical(P_1) \wedge critical(P_2).$$

For the CHM to move from one configuration q to another configuration q', the invariant $I_{q'}$ must be satisfied upon entry to q'. (Notice that if q' is the legal subconfiguration of a configuration whose invariant has been split to a legal part and an illegal part, satisfaction of the invariant $I_{q'}$ is not automatically satisfied.) Thus, let us define $wp(q, l, q')$ to be the weakest precondition under which the transition (q, l, q') will not violate the invariant $I_{q'}$ upon entry to q'. Since some of the shared variables that appear in $I_{q'}$ are possibly (re-)initialized upon entering q', the condition $wp(q, \underline{\sigma}, q')$ can be computed from $I_{q'}$ by substituting into $I_{q'}$ the appropriate initial (entry) values of all the shared variables that are also output variables of q'. That is, if y_j is the jth output variable of q' and $S_i = y_j$ is a shared variable that appears in $I_{q'}$, then the value of S_i must be set to

$$S_i = h_j(x_{q'}^0, u_{q'}).$$

With these preliminaries, we can now discuss our synthesis algorithm. Let us consider a legal configuration q. As discussed earlier, we assume that transitions leaving q are either dynamic transitions or event transitions, and can lead to either legal or illegal configurations. Therefore, we classify the transitions into four types:

1. Legal event transitions that lead to legal configurations:

$$ET_g(q, Q_b) = \{(q, \underline{\sigma}, q') : q \xrightarrow{\sigma} q' \wedge q' \notin Q_b\}.$$

2. Illegal event transitions that lead to illegal configurations:

$$ET_b(q, Q_b) = \{(q, \underline{\sigma}, q') : q \xrightarrow{\sigma} q' \wedge q' \in Q_b\}.$$

3. Legal dynamic transitions that lead to legal configurations:

$$DT_g(q, Q_b) = \{(q, G, q') : q \xrightarrow{G} q' \wedge q' \notin Q_b\}.$$

4. Illegal dynamic transitions that lead to illegal configurations:

$$DT_b(q, Q_b) = \{(q, G, q') : q \xrightarrow{G} q' \wedge q' \in Q_b\}.$$

Since transitions in $ET_b(q, Q_b)$ can be prevented by simply not being triggered, we need not discuss them further. If $DT_b(q, Q_b) = \emptyset$, then no dynamic transition from q leads to an illegal configuration and hence there is no need to split q. Otherwise, if $DT_b(q, Q_b) \neq \emptyset$, we may need to split q as discussed below. Let us consider the different cases.

Case 1. $DT_g(q, Q_b) = \emptyset$

Since $DT_g(q, Q_b) = \emptyset$, the only way to prevent transitions in $DT_b(q, Q_b)$ from taking place, is for the controller to trigger an event transition $(q, \underline{\sigma}, q') \in ET_g(q, Q_b)$, provided this set is nonempty, thereby forcing the CHM from q to q'.

To find under what condition we can count on such a $(q, \underline{\sigma}, q')$ to take the CHM to another legal state q', we define the following *safe-exit condition*

$$sc(q, \underline{\sigma}, q') = (T_{max}(true(wp(q, \underline{\sigma}, q'))) \leq T_{min}(false(I_q))),$$

where

$T_{max}(true(wp(q, \underline{\sigma}, q')))$ is the latest time $wp(q, \underline{\sigma}, q')$ will be true, and
$T_{min}(false(I_q))$ is the earliest time I_q will become false.

Therefore, $sc(q, \underline{\sigma}, q')$ is true if $wp(q, \underline{\sigma}, q')$ is guaranteed to be satisfied before I_q is violated. Under this condition, the CHM can always be forced to safely exit q. Notice that $wp(q, \underline{\sigma}, q') \Rightarrow sc(q, \underline{\sigma}, q')$, that is, we can always safely exit to q' when $wp(q, \underline{\sigma}, q')$ is satisfied.

If $I_q \not\Rightarrow sc(q, \underline{\sigma}, q')$, then we will split the configuration q into two sub-configurations q_1 and q_2 by partitioning the invariant I_q (and associating with each of the sub-configurations the corresponding invariant) as

$$I_{q_1} = I_q \wedge sc(q, \underline{\sigma}, q')$$
$$I_{q_2} = I_q \wedge \neg sc(q, \underline{\sigma}, q').$$

Clearly, the dynamics of q_1 and q_2 and the transitions leaving and entering these configurations are the same as for q, except that the transition $(q_2, \underline{\sigma}, q')$ is not permitted or is impossible (because of the invariant violation). Also the transition from q_1 to q_2 is dynamic with the guard $\neg sc(q, \underline{\sigma}, q')$ (strict negation), and from q_2 to q_1 with guard $sc(q, \underline{\sigma}, q')$.

Clearly, q_1 is legal in the sense that from it the transition to the legal configuration q' can be forced, while q_2 is not legal. From q_1, the dynamic transitions in $DT_b(q_1, Q_b)$ and the dynamic transition $(q_1, \neg sc(q, \underline{\sigma}, q'), q_2)$ are illegal and must not be permitted. To prevent these transitions from taking place in a minimally restrictive manner, $\underline{\sigma}$ must be forced just before any one of them can actually take place. In other words, $\underline{\sigma}$ must be forced just before I_{q_1} becomes false.

The condition under which the transition $(q, \underline{\sigma}, q')$ will be forced is then

$$critical(I_{q_1}) = critical(I_q \wedge sc(q, \underline{\sigma}, q')).$$

If there are more than one legal event transition in $ET_g(q, Q_b)$, then we will split q into q_1 and q_2 as follows.

$$I_{q_1} = I_q \wedge (\vee_{(q, \underline{\sigma}, q') \in ET_g(q, Q_b)} sc(q, \underline{\sigma}, q'))$$
$$I_{q_2} = I_q \wedge \neg(\vee_{(q, \underline{\sigma}, q') \in ET_g(q, Q_b)} sc(q, \underline{\sigma}, q')).$$

The condition under which a legal event transition $(q, \underline{\sigma}, q')$ needs to be forced is given by

$$critical(I_{q_1}) \wedge wp(q, \underline{\sigma}, q').$$

Case 2. $ET_g(q, Q_b) = \emptyset$

Since $ET_g(q, Q_b) = \emptyset$, the transitions in $DT_b(q, Q_b)$ will be prevented from taking place, only if they are either preempted by some dynamic transitions in $DT_g(b, Q_b)$ or will never take place due to the dynamics at q.

Note that because of configuration splitting, the target configuration of a dynamic transition guarded by a guard G, may depend on the dynamic condition at the source configuration at the instant when G becomes true. Thus, if the configuration q' is split into q_1' and q_2', then we may have either $(q, G, q_1') \in$

$DT_g(q, Q_b)$ or $(q, G, q'_2) \in DT_b(q, Q_b)$ depending on the dynamic conditions. To deal with such cases effectively, it will be convenient to modify (q, G, q') by the following equivalent dynamic transition

$$(q, G \wedge wp(q, G, q'), q').$$

Clearly, the dynamic transition $(q, G, q') \in DT_b(q, Q_b)$ will be preempted by another dynamic transition, provided I_q, the invariant of q, becomes false before $G \wedge wp(q, G, q')$ becomes true. The earliest time $G \wedge wp(q, G, q')$ will become true is $T_{min}(G \wedge wp(q, G, q'))$ and the latest time I_q will become false is given by $T_{max}(false(I_q)) = T_{max}(true(\neg I_q))$. Therefore, to ensure that the transition (q, G, q') will not take place, it must be required that the following *preemptive condition*

$$pc(q, G, q') = (T_{min}(true(G \wedge wp(q, G, q'))) > T_{max}(false(I_q)))$$

be satisfied[5]. Therefore, we will split the configuration q into two sub-configurations q_1 and q_2, by partitioning the invariant I_q as

$$I_{q_1} = I_q \wedge pc(q, G, q')$$
$$I_{q_2} = I_q \wedge \neg pc(q, G, q').$$

As in Case 1, the dynamics of q_1 and q_2 and the transitions leaving and entering these configurations are the same as for q, except that the transition (q_1, G, q') is now impossible.

If there are more than one illegal dynamic transition at q, then we will split q into q_1 and q_2 as follows.

$$I_{q_1} = I_q \wedge (\wedge_{(q,G,q') \in DT_b(q,Q_b)} pc(q, G, q'))$$
$$I_{q_2} = I_q \wedge \neg(\wedge_{(q,G,q') \in DT_b(q,Q_b)} pc(q, G, q')).$$

General case.

That is, we require neither $ET_g(q, Q_b) = \emptyset$ nor $DT_g(q, Q_b) = \emptyset$. In this general case, we can either rely on legal dynamic transitions to preempt the illegal dynamic transitions, or if this does not happen, force some legal event transitions. Therefore, we shall split q into q_1 and q_2 as follows.[6]

$$I_{q_1} = I_q \wedge ((\wedge_{(q,G,q') \in DT_b(q,Q_b)} pc(q, G, q')) \vee (\vee_{(q,\underline{\sigma},q') \in ET_g(q,Q_b)} sc(q, \underline{\sigma}, q')))$$
$$I_{q_2} = I_q \wedge (\neg(\wedge_{(q,G,q') \in DT_b(q,Q_b)} pc(q, G, q')) \wedge \neg(\vee_{(q,\underline{\sigma},q') \in ET_g(q,Q_b)} sc(q, \underline{\sigma}, q'))).$$

---

[5] We take the convention that if $T_{min}(true(G \wedge wp(q, G, q'))) = \infty$, then $pc(q, G, q') = true$ even if $T_{max}(false(I_q)) = \infty$.

[6] If $(q, G, q') \in DT_b(q, Q_b)$ cannot be prevented from occurring, then we must consider q as illegal. In that case $I_{q_1} = false$ and $I_{q_2} = I_q$.

The condition under which a legal event transition $(q, \underline{\sigma}, q')$ needs to be forced is now given by[7]

$$critical(I_{q_1}) \wedge wp(q, \underline{\sigma}, q') \wedge (\neg(\wedge_{(q,G,q') \in DT_b(q,Q_b)} pc(q, G, q'))).$$

Notice that if we adopt the convention that

$$\wedge_{(q,G,q') \in DT_b(q,Q_b)} pc(q, G, q') = true \quad if \; DT_b(q, Q_b) = \emptyset$$
$$\vee_{(q,\underline{\sigma},q') \in ET_g(q,Q_b)} sc(q, \underline{\sigma}, q') = false \quad if \; ET_g(q, Q_b) = \emptyset,$$

then this general case covers both Case 1 and Case 2.

From the above discussions, we can now formally describe our synthesis algorithm.

Algorithm 1 *(Control Synthesis)*
Input

- The model of the system

$$CHM = (Q, \Sigma, D, I, E, (q_0, x_0)).$$

- The set of illegal configurations $Q_b \subseteq Q$.

Output

- The controller

$$C = (Q^c, \Sigma^c, D^c, I^c, E^c, (q_0^c, x_0^c)).$$

Initialization

1. Set of bad configurations

$$BC := Q_b;$$

2. Set of pending configurations

$$PC := Q - Q_b;$$

3. New set of pending configurations

$$NPC := \emptyset;$$

4. For each $q \in PC$ set its *configuration origin* as

$$CO(q) = q;$$

Iteration

---

[7] There is a possible complication if the newly defined guards form an instantaneous configuration-cluster (formed by simultaneously true guards) that may force an unbounded instantaneous sequence of consecutive transitions. If this occurs, further analysis will be required.

5. For all $q \in PC$ do

$$I_{q_1} := I_q \wedge ((\wedge_{(q,G,q') \in DT_b(q,BC)} pc(q,G,q'))$$
$$\vee (\vee_{(q,\underline{\sigma},q') \in ET_g(q,BC)} sc(q,\underline{\sigma},q')));$$
$$I_{q_2} := I_q \wedge (\neg(\wedge_{(q,G,q') \in DT_b(q,BC)} pc(q,G,q'))$$
$$\wedge \neg(\vee_{(q,\underline{\sigma},q') \in ET_g(q,BC)} sc(q,\underline{\sigma},q')));.$$

If $I_{q_1} \neq false$, then

$$NPC := NPC \cup \{q_1\};$$
$$CO(q_1) := CO(q);$$

If $I_{q_2} \neq false$, then

$$BC := BC \cup \{q_2\};$$

6. If $PC = NPC$, go to 8.
7. Set

$$PC := NPC;$$
$$NPC := \emptyset;$$

Go to 5;

Construction of C

8. Define vertices, events and dynamics:

$$Q^c := PC;$$
$$\Sigma^c := \Sigma \cup \{\tilde{\sigma} : \sigma \in \Sigma\};$$
$$D^c := \emptyset;$$

9. Define transitions:

$$E^c := \{(q, critical(I_q) \wedge wp(q,\underline{\sigma},q')$$
$$\wedge (\neg(\wedge_{(q,G,q'') \in DT_b(q,BC)} pc(q,G,q''))) \to \overline{\sigma}, q') :$$
$$q, q' \in Q^c \wedge (CO(q), \underline{\sigma}, CO(q')) \in E\};$$
$$E^c := E^c \cup \{(q, wp(q,\underline{\sigma},q') \wedge \tilde{\underline{\sigma}} \to \overline{\sigma}, q') :$$
$$q, q' \in Q^c \wedge (CO(q), \underline{\sigma}, CO(q')) \in E\};$$

10. End.

Therefore, the controller C has no dynamics. Its vertices are copies of the legal configurations of CHM that survive after the partition. Its events include the output-events $\overline{\sigma}$ and the input-events $\tilde{\sigma}$ from the environment or other controllers. Its transitions are of two types: (1) dynamic transitions that are triggered when the CHM is about to become potentially illegal; and (2) guarded event transitions that are triggered by input-events.

Another controller D can be embedded into C as follows. First, all the output-events $\overline{\sigma}$ in D are replaced by $\widetilde{\overline{\sigma}}$ to obtain $\widetilde{D}$. Then the embedded control system is given by

$$CHM||C||\widetilde{D}.$$

We can now prove the following

Theorem 1. If Algorithm 1 terminates in a finite number of steps and if there is no instantaneous configuration-cluster (that may force an unbounded instantaneous sequence of consecutive transitions), then the controller synthesized is a minimally restrictive legal controller in the following sense.

1. For any controller D, an execution in $CHM||C||\widetilde{D}$ will never visit illegal configurations Q_b.
2. For any legal controller D, an execution is possible in $CHM||D$ if and only if its corresponding execution is possible in $CHM||C||\widetilde{D}$.

Proof

Since Algorithm 1 terminates in a finite number of steps and no sequence of instantaneous transitions form a loop, the controller is well defined. In particular, time progresses as execution continues and during any finite interval of time only a finite number of transitions take place.

To prove part 1, it is sufficient to show that an execution in $CHM||C||\widetilde{D}$ will only visit configurations in

$$Q^c \subseteq Q - Q_b.$$

If this is not the case, then there exists an execution

$$q_0 \xrightarrow{e_1,t_1} q_1 \longrightarrow ... \longrightarrow q_{n-1} \xrightarrow{e_n,t_n} q_n$$

such that $q_0, q_1, ..., q_{n-1} \in Q^c$ but $q_n \notin Q^c$.

Let us consider the transition from q_{n-1} to q_n. It cannot be an event transition because such illegal event transitions are not permitted by C. If it is a dynamic transition, then since it is not preempted at q_{n-1}, it implies that $q_{n-1} \notin Q^c$, a contradiction.

To prove part 2, let us assume that

$$q_0 \xrightarrow{e_1,t_1} q_1 \longrightarrow ... \longrightarrow q_{n-1} \xrightarrow{e_n,t_n} q_n$$

is a possible execution of $CHM||D$ but the last transition from q_{n-1} to q_n is impossible in $CHM||C||\widetilde{D}$, that is, $q_n \notin Q^c$. Then by our construction of q_n, there exists a continuation of the execution in $CHM||D$

$$q_n \xrightarrow{e_{n+1},t_{n+1}} q_{n+1} \longrightarrow ... \xrightarrow{e_{n+m},t_{n+m}} q_{n+m}$$

that will lead to an illegal configuration $q_{n+m} \in Q_b$. This execution cannot be prevented by D, a contradiction to the hypothesis that D is legal.

On the other hand, if

$$q_0 \xrightarrow{e_1,t_1} q_1 \longrightarrow ... \longrightarrow q_{n-1} \xrightarrow{e_n,t_n} q_n$$

is a possible execution of $CHM||C||\tilde{D}$ but the last transition from q_{n-1} to q_n is impossible in $CHM||D$, then this last transition must be triggered by a dynamic transition in C when the following guard becomes true:

$$G_c = critical(I_{q_{n-1}}) \wedge wp(q_{n-1}, \underline{\sigma}, q_n)$$
$$\wedge(\neg(\wedge_{(q_{n-1},G,q')\in DT_b(q_{n-1},BC)}pc(q_{n-1}, G, q'))).$$

Since the transition (q_{n-1}, G_c, q_n) does not take place in $CHM||D$, by our construction of G_c, the next transition

$$q_{n-1} \xrightarrow{e'_n,t'_n} q'_n$$

could lead to $q'_n \notin Q^c$. By the same argument as above, we conclude that D is illegal, a contradiction. ∎

Examples will be given in the next section to illustrate the algorithm.

6 Discussion and Examples

Our algorithm works for most examples we encounted in practice. An example to show how our algorithm solves a steam boiler control problem [1] has been given in [15].

There are, however, situations in which our algorithm does not resolve the controller design problem. In the first type of situations, the algorithm terminates finitely, but the closed loop system includes instantaneous configuration-cluster and possibly inescapable instantaneous unbounded sequences of transitions. In this case, a minimally restrictive legal controller may or may not exist as is shown in Examples 1 and 2 below, and further analysis beyond the algorithm is necessary. In the second type of situations, the algorithm does not terminate as shown in Example 3.

Example 1. In this example, we will see that although the algorithm terminates, it does so with instantaneous loops (a special case of instantaneous configuration-cluster), and the controller obtained is not legal (since a legal controller does not exist).

Consider the hybrid system shown in Figure 3. It models a two-tank system, where both tanks are leaking with rate 2. A pump with rate 3 can be switched between the two tanks (event σ_1 and σ_2). The system starts with both tanks non-empty ($x_1(0) > 0, x_2(0) > 0$). The system becomes illegal when one of the tanks becomes empty, which is represented by illegal configuration c that has no dynamics and true invariant. Since $2 + 2 > 3$, no legal controller exists that can prevent the system from becoming illegal eventually. However, as we will show below, the algorithm terminates.

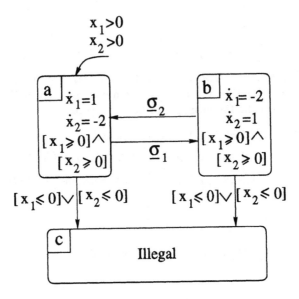

Fig. 3. CHM of Example 1

Initialization

$$BC = \{c\},$$
$$PC = \{a, b\},$$
$$I_a = I_b = [x_2 \geq 0] \wedge [x_1 \geq 0].$$

1st Iteration

$$pc(a, [x_1 \leq 0] \vee [x_2 \leq 0], c) = false,$$
$$sc(a, \underline{\sigma_1}, b) = I_a.$$

Therefore,

$$I_{a_1} = I_1 \wedge (pc(a, [x_1 \leq 0] \vee [x_2 \leq 0], c) \vee sc(a, \underline{\sigma_1}, b)) = I_a.$$

Similarly,

$$I_{b_1} = I_b.$$

Since there is no change to I_a and I_b, the algorithm terminates after just one step.

The controller C generated by the algorithm is shown in Figure 4. The guard G_1 trigging the event transition $\overline{\sigma_1}$ is calculated as follows.

$$critical(I_a) = [x_1 \leq 0] \vee [x_2 \leq 0],$$
$$wp(a, \underline{\sigma_1}, b) = [x_1 \geq 0] \wedge [x_2 \geq 0],$$
$$G_1 = critical(I_a) \wedge wp(a, \underline{\sigma_1}, b).$$

Similarly, G_2 can be calculated, which is the same as G_1. Clearly, the controller in Figure 4 is not a legal controller and, in fact, a minimally restrictive legal controller does not exist. This however does not contradict Theorem 1 because there exists an instantaneous loop in C that occurs when $x_1 = x_2 = 0$.

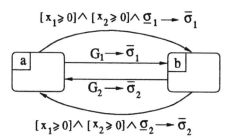

Fig. 4. Controller of Example 1

Example 2. Although the controller designed by the algorithm is not guaranteed to be legal when there exist instantaneous loops, such instantaneous loops do not necessarily invalidate the resulting controller. This can be shown by changing the pumping rate from 3 to 5. This change will not affect the synthesis procedure and the resulting controller is the same. Under this rate, however, the controller is legal and minimally restrictive.

Example 3. This example shows that our algorithm may not terminate. In this example there exists no minimally restrictive legal controller.

Let us modify Example 1 by assuming that there is a one second delay in switching the pump. That is, it takes one second for the switching command to be actually executed. The modified two-tank system is shown in Figure 5. As in Example 1, no legal controller exists because $2 + 2 > 3$.

Table 1 illustrates the computation of the algorithm and shows that the algorithm does not terminate.

Example 4. Consider the same system as in Example 3, but change the pumping rate from 3 to 5. Under this rate, the algorithm terminates and generates the following legal and minimally restrictive controller: Switching the pump to tank i when $x_i = 2, i = 1, 2$.

Examples 3 and 4 show that whether the algorithm terminates may depend on the (continuous) dynamics of the system.

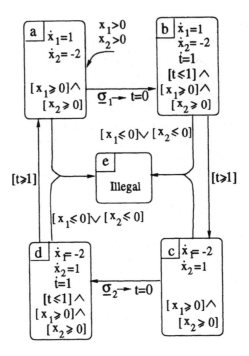

Fig. 5. CHM of Example 3

	a	b	c	d
initial	$[x_1 \geq 0] \wedge [x_2 \geq 0]$	$[x_1 \geq 0] \wedge [x_2 \geq 0] \wedge$ $[t < 1]$	$[x_1 \geq 0] \wedge [x_2 \geq 0]$	$[x_1 \geq 0] \wedge [x_2 \geq 0] \wedge$ $[t < 1]$
1st	$[x_1 \geq 0] \wedge [x_2 \geq 0]$	$[x_1 \geq 0] \wedge [x_2 > 2-2t] \wedge$ $[t < 1]$	$[x_1 \geq 0] \wedge [x_2 \geq 0]$	$[x_1 > 2-2t] \wedge [x_2 \geq 0] \wedge$ $[t < 1]$
2nd	$[x_1 \geq 0] \wedge [x_2 > 2]$	$[x_1 \geq 0] \wedge [x_2 > 2-2t] \wedge$ $[t < 1]$	$[x_1 > 2] \wedge [x_2 \geq 0]$	$[x_1 > 2-2t] \wedge [x_2 \geq 0] \wedge$ $[t < 1]$
3rd	$[x_1 \geq 0] \wedge [x_2 > 2]$	$[x_1 > t+1] \wedge [x_2 > 2-2t]$ $\wedge [t < 1]$	$[x_1 > 2] \wedge [x_2 \geq 0]$	$[x_1 > 2-2t] \wedge [x_2 > t+1]$ $\wedge [t < 1]$
4th	$[x_1 > 1] \wedge [x_2 > 2]$	$[x_1 > t+1] \wedge [x_2 > 2-2t]$ $\wedge [t < 1]$	$[x_1 > 2] \wedge [x_2 > 1]$	$[x_1 > 2-2t] \wedge [x_2 > t+1]$ $\wedge [t < 1]$
...	...	...	...	...

Table 1. Controller synthesis of Example 3

References

1. J.-R. Abrial, 1995. Steam-boiler control specification problem. *Dagstuhl Meeting: Method for Semantics and Specification.*
2. R. Alur and D. Dill, 1990. Automata for modeling real-time systems. *Proc. of the 17th International Colloquium on Automata, Languages and Programming*, pp. 322-336.
3. R. Alur, C. Courcoubetis, T. A. Henzinger, and P.-H. Ho, 1993. Hybrid automata: an algorithmic approach to the specification and verification of hybrid systems. *Hybrid Systems, Lecture Notes in Computer Science, 736*, Springer-Verlag, pp. 209-229.
4. R. Alur, C. Courcoubetis, N. Halbwachs, T. A. Henzinger, P.-H. Ho, X. Nicollin, A. Olivero, J. Sifakis, and S. Yovine, 1995. The algorithmic analysis of hybrid systems. *Theoretical Computer Science, 138*, pp. 3-34.
5. P.J. Antsaklis, J.A. Stiver, and M. Lemmon, 1993. Hybrid system modeling and autonomous control systems. *Hybrid Systems, Lecture Notes in Computer Science, 736*, Springer-Verlag, pp. 366-392.
6. E. Azarin, O. Maler, and A. Pnueli, 1995. Symbolic Controller Synthesis for Discrete and Timed Systems, *Hybrid Systems II, Lecture Notes in Computer Science, 999*, Springer Verlag, pp. 1-20.
7. M. S. Branicky, 1995. Universal computation and other capabilities of hybrid and continuous dynamical systems. *Theoretical Computer Science, 138*, pp. 67-100.
8. R. W. Brockett, 1993. Hybrid models for motion control systems. In H.L. Trentelman and J.C.Willems (Eds.), *Essays in Control: Perspectives in the theory and its applications*, pp. 29-53, Birkhauser, Boston.
9. S. L. Chung, S. Lafortune and F. Lin, 1992. Limited lookahead policies in supervisory control of discrete event systems. *IEEE Transactions on Automatic Control, 37(12)*, pp. 1921-1935.
10. T. Henzinger, P. Kopke, A. Puri and P. Varaiya, 1995. What's decidable about hybrid automata, *Proc. of the 27th Annual ACM Symposium on the Theory of Computing.*
11. M. Heymann 1990. Concurrency and discrete event control, *IEEE Control Systems Magazine, Vol. 10, No.4*, pp 103-112.
12. M. Heymann and F. Lin, 1994. On-line control of partially observed discrete event systems. *Discrete Event Dynamic Systems: Theory and Applications, 4(3)*, pp. 221-236.
13. M. Heymann and F. Lin, 1996. Discrete event control of nondeterministic systems. control of nondeterministic systems, *CIS Report 9601*, Technion, Israel.
14. M. Heymann and F. Lin, 1996. Nonblocking supervisory control of nondeterministic systems, *CIS Report 9620*, Technion, Israel.
15. M. Heymann, F. Lin and G. Meyer, 1997. Control Synthesis for a Class of Hybrid Systems Subject to Configuration Based Safety Constraints. in O. Maler (Ed.), "Hybrid and Real-Time Systems", Proceedings of HART97, *Lecture Notes in Computer Science 1201* pp. 376-390, Springer Verlag.
16. F. Lin and W. M. Wonham, 1988. On observability of discrete event systems. *Information Sciences, 44(3)*, pp. 173-198.
17. F. Lin and W. M. Wonham, 1990. Decentralized control and coordination of discrete event systems with partial observation. *IEEE Transactions on Automatic Control, 35(12)*, pp. 1330-1337.

18. F. Lin and W. M. Wonham, 1994. Supervisory control of timed discrete event systems under partial observation, *IEEE Transactions on Automatic Control, 40(3)*, pp. 558-562.

19. O. Maler, Z. Manna and A. Pnueli, 1991. From timed to hybrid systems. In *Real Time: Theory in Practice*, Lecture Notes in Computer Science 600, pp. 447-484. Springer-Verlag.

20. O. Maler, A. Pnueli and J. Sifakis, 1995. On the synthesis of discrete controllers for timed systems, Lecture Notes in Computer Science 900, pp. 229-242. Springer-Verlag.

21. Z. Manna and A. Pnueli, 1993. Verifying hybrid systems. *Hybrid Systems, Lecture Notes in Computer Science, 736*, Springer-Verlag, pp. 4-35.

22. A. Nerode and W. Kohn, 1993. Models for hybrid systems: automata, topologies, controllability, observability. *Hybrid Systems, Lecture Notes in Computer Science, 736*, Springer-Verlag, pp. 317-356.

23. X. Nicollin, A. Olivero, J. Sifakis, and S. Yovine, 1993. Am approach to the description and analysis of hybrid systems. *Hybrid Systems, Lecture Notes in Computer Science, 736*, Springer-Verlag, pp. 149-178.

24. X. Nicollin, J. Sifakis, and S. Yovine, 1991. From ATP to timed graphs and hybrid systems. In *Real Time: Theory in Practice*, Lecture Notes in Computer Science 600, Springer-Verlag, pp. 549-572.

25. R. J. Ramadge and W. M. Wonham, 1987. Supervisory control of a class of discrete event processes. *SIAM J. Control and Optimization, 25(1)*, pp. 206-230.

26. P. J. Ramadge and W. M. Wonham, 1989. The control of discrete event systems. *Proceedings of IEEE, 77(1)*, pp. 81-98.

Control Theory, Modal Logic, and Games*

Julia. F. Knight[1] and Brian Luense[2]

[1] University of Notre Dame
[2] University of Chicago

Abstract: We consider a class of discrete systems, with specifications stated in
a certain modal temporal language (chosen for simplicity). We show that if the
regulator can in some way guarantee satisfaction of a specification, then it can
do so acting as a deterministic finite automaton, and we can effectively find an
appropriate automaton, or determine that there is none. Our result is not really
new. It (and similar results for more expressive languages) can be obtained easily
from a result of Landweber and Büchi on "regular" games, together with the fact
that our language gives rise to games of this sort (see the excellent surveys [T]
and [E]). We use a result of Gurevich and Harrington [G-H] to show the existence
of appropriate automata. The actual construction is explicit. The set of states is
determined through elementary considerations of which partial records might be
useful to the regulator.

§0. Introduction

We consider a system made of a plant and a regulator. There is a finite set P
of *observable plant states* which serve as outputs from the plant and inputs to the
regulator, and there is a finite set R of *regulator settings* which serve as outputs
from the regulator and inputs to the plant. Time is measured in discrete steps. A
run of the system is an infinite sequence $\pi = p_0 r_0 p_1 r_1 p_2 r_2...$, where $p_n \in P$ and
$r_n \in R$.

We suppose that there is a fixed initial plant state p_0. In addition, we may
suppose that p_{n+1} is limited to a subset of P determined by p_n and r_{n+1}. Similarly,
we may suppose that r_0 is limited to a fixed subset of R, and r_{n+1} is limited to a
subset of R determined by r_n and p_{n+1}. We think of these restrictions as imposed
by the hardware. For example, it may be impossible for the water level in a tank to
go from full to empty without passing through some intermediate state. Similarly,
it may not be permissible to turn on a burner under the tank unless the water is
observed to reach a certain level.

The conditions above limit the plant and regulator to the moves of a pair of
non-deterministic finite automata. This setting has been studied extensively. There
is a body of literature describing the class of all runs of such a system (see [D-R]).
The following problems are natural from the point of view of control theory. They
were also stated by Church [C], presumably for their mathematical interest.

---

* The authors are grateful to Jenny Davoren, Yuri Gurevich, Michael Lemmon, and Anil
Nerode.

1. Decide, for a given specification, whether the regulator can move in such a way as to guarantee satisfaction.

2. Find a strategy for the regulator, assuming that there is one.

3. Make the strategy practical, if possible.

We state specifications in a modal temporal language, with propositional variables p, for $p \in P$, the usual logical connectives, and modal operators O (next time), ◊ (some time), and □ (always). We chose this language because it is relatively simple, and it allows us to state some interesting specifications. Control theorists such as Wonham and his collaborators [O], [T-W] have used various modal temporal languages in stating specifications for discrete systems. Computer scientists such as Manna and Pnueli [M-P], or Vardi and Wolper [V-W] have analyzed their relative expressive power, etc. (see [E]).

We think in terms of games. Let T be a tree consisting of finite sequences, with no terminal nodes. Then $[T]$ denotes the set of all paths through T. If $W \subseteq [T]$, then $G(T, W)$ denotes a game in which two players alternate moves to produce a path $\pi \in [T]$. The first player (i.e., the one who moves first) wins if $\pi \notin W$, and the second player wins if $\pi \in W$. A strategy for either player is a function f, defined on all $\sigma \in T$ of appropriate length, giving a possible next move. A winning strategy for a given player is one which guarantees a win for that player. The game is determined if one of the players has a winning strategy.

In the context of our system, let T consist of the finite partial runs $p_0 r_0 p_1 r_1 p_2 r_2 \ldots$, so $[T]$ is the set of all runs. For a given specification φ, let W_φ be the set of runs satisfying φ. Then $G(T, W_\varphi)$ is a game in which the regulator wins just in case the specification is satisfied. By a deep result of Martin [M] (Borel determinacy), such games are determined. However, Martin's result does not say that we can decide who has a winning strategy. It does not say that we can find a strategy. It does not guarantee that there is a strategy which is at all practical–in principal, each move may depend on the full history of play.

We show that there is an effective procedure which, for any specification φ, either finds a deterministic finite automaton providing a winning strategy for the regulator in the game $G(T, W_\varphi)$, or says that the plant has a winning strategy–so there is no strategy of any kind for the regulator. We consider automata of the form $M = (P, S, s_0, \tau)$, where S is a finite set (S is the set of states), $s_0 \in S$ (s_0 is the initial state), and $\tau : S \times P \to S$ (τ is the transition function). Let $\mathcal{M}(S)$ be the set of these automata in which S is the set of states. Using $M \in \mathcal{M}(S)$, together with an output function $i : S \to R$ we obtain runs of the form $\pi = p_0 i(s_0) p_1 i(s_1) p_2 i(s_2) \ldots$, where $s_{n+1} = \tau(s_n, p_n)$. (If there are restrictions on the initial and next regulator settings, these are reflected in restrictions on s_0 and τ.)

As we indicated, what we are doing is not really new. It is well-known that specifications in our language, and in more expressive languages, give rise to "regular" games (see [E]). By results of Büchi and Landweber [La], [B-L], for any regular game, some player has a strategy acting as a deterministic finite automaton, we can decide the winner, and we can find the automaton. There is a clever proof of this result due to Rabin [R₂], see [T, p. 175]. While the construction of the automaton is effective, it may require some effort to trace.

We make use of a result of Gurevich and Harrington [G-H]. Given specification φ, we determine a natural set S and an output function $i : S \to R$ such that if the regulator has a winning strategy in $G(T, W_\varphi)$, then it has a strategy given by some $M \in \mathcal{M}(S)$, together with i. There are only finitely many $M \in \mathcal{M}(S)$, and the problem of deciding whether a given M serves is not difficult.

In §1, we describe the language for specifications. In §2, we describe results on determinacy and "forgetful" determinacy of games. In §3 and §4, we give the proof of the main result. In §5, we indicate what our results say about the expressive power of the language.

§1. Language for specifications

The language we use is as in [K-P]. The symbols are:

(1) propositional variables p, for $p \in P$,

(2) logical connectives &, ¬ (we introduce →, etc., as abbreviations),

(3) modal operators O, ◊, and □,

(4) parentheses (,).

The class of formulas of the language is defined in the natural way. Here are some sample formulas.

(1) ◊p, saying that plant state p will be reached some time,

(2) □(p → ◊q), saying that every time the plant enters state p, it will again enter state q,

(3) □(p → (O q∨ OOq)), saying that every time the plant enters state p, it will enter state q within the next two steps.

(4) ◊(p & O□ (¬p & ◊(q & O□ ¬q))), saying that there is a last appearance of plant state p, and, some time later, a last appearance of state q.

For a sequence $\pi = p_0 r_0 p_1 r_1 p_2 r_2 ...$, π^s denotes the tail formed by removing the first $2s$ terms from π. We define what it means for a sequence π (normally a tail of some element of $[T]$) to satisfy a formula φ. We use the notation $\pi \models \varphi$ for this.

(1) for $p \in P, \pi \models p$ iff π begins with p,

(2) $\pi \models (\varphi \,\&\, \psi)$ iff $\pi \models \varphi$ and $\pi \models \psi$,

(3) $\pi \models \neg\varphi$ iff $\pi \not\models \varphi$,

(4) $\pi \models O\varphi$ iff $\pi^1 \models \varphi$,

(5) $\pi \models \Diamond\varphi$ iff there exists s such that $\pi^s \models \varphi$,

(6) $\pi \models \Box\varphi$ iff for all s, $\pi^s \models \varphi$.

Remark: The modal operators $\Diamond$ and $\Box$ resemble quantifiers in some respects. However, there is no "prenex normal form"–in general, we cannot bring the modal operators to the front. There is a notion of rank which, at least in some situations, substitutes for quantifier complexity.

The rank of φ, denoted by rank(φ), is defined as follows:

(1) for $p \in P$, rank(p) $= 0$,

(2) rank($\varphi \,\&\, \psi$) $= \sup\{\text{rank}(\varphi), \text{rank}(\psi)\}$,

(3) rank($\neg\varphi$) $= \text{rank}(\varphi)$,

(4) rank($O\varphi$) $= \text{rank}(\Diamond\varphi) = \text{rank}(\Box\varphi) = \text{rank}(\varphi) + 1$.

We define a family of equivalence relations $\sim_n$. Suppose π and π^* are infinite sequences (tails of runs). Let $\pi \sim_0 *$ iff π and π^* begin with the same $p \in P$. Let $\pi \sim_{n+1} \pi^*$ iff for all s there exists t such that $\pi^s \sim_n \pi^{*t}$, and vice versa.

Proposition 1.1. For all n, and all sequences π and π^* (tails of runs), the following are equivalent:

(1) $\pi \sim_n \pi^*$

(2) for all formulas φ of rank at most n, $\pi \models \varphi$ iff $\pi^* \models \varphi$.

The proof is an easy induction.

§2. Determinacy and forgetful determinacy

In this section, we first indicate what the result of Martin [M] says in our setting. This is for background only. We then state the result of Gurevich and Harrington [G-H] which we shall use.

There is a topology on $[T]$ with basic open neighborhoods $N_\sigma = \{\pi \in [T] : \pi \supseteq \sigma\}$, for $\sigma \in T$. The Borel subsets of $[T]$ are the members of the least class $\mathbb{B}$ which contains the basic open neighborhoods and is closed under countable unions and complements. The game $G(T, W)$ is said to be <u>Borel</u> just in case W is Borel.

Proposition 2.1. For all formulas φ and all $s \in \omega$, $\{\pi \in [T] : \pi^s \models \varphi\}$ is Borel. In particular, for all φ, $W_\varphi = \{\pi \in [T] : \pi \models \varphi\}$ is Borel.

Proof: The proof is by induction on φ. If φ is p, where $p \in P$, then $\{\pi \in [T] : \pi^s \models \varphi\}$ is open since it is the union of finitely many basic open neighborhoods. The clauses for the logical connectives are trivial–any Boolean combination of Borel sets is Borel. For the modal operators, note that $\{\pi \in [T] : \pi^s \models O\varphi\} = \{\pi \in [T] : \pi^{s+1} \models \varphi\}$, $\{\pi \in [T] : \pi^s \models \Diamond\varphi\} = \bigcup_{r \geq s} \{\pi \in [T] : \pi^r \models \varphi\}$, and $\{\pi \in [T] : \pi^s \models \Box\varphi\} = \bigcap_{r \geq s} \{\pi \in [T] : \pi^r \models \varphi\}$. From this it is clear that if the statement holds for φ, then it holds for $O\varphi$, $\Diamond\varphi$, and $\Box\varphi$.

From Martin's result [M] and Proposition 2.1, we obtain the following.

<u>Theorem 2.2</u>. For each formula φ, $G(T, W_\varphi)$ is determined.

As we remarked in §0, the strategy in Theorem 2.2 may be such that each move depends on the whole history of play. Gurevich and Harrington [G-H] proved a result which gives much nicer strategies, at least in certain settings. Rabin [R] proved a very powerful decidability result in logic. Rabin's original proof was extremely complicated, and the result of Gurevich and Harrington was designed to simplify the most difficult sections. There are other simplifications, due to McNaughton [Mc], Muller and Schupp [M-S], and others.

To state the result of Gurevich and Harrington, we need some notation. For $C \subseteq [T]$, Inf(C) denotes the set of sequences π (tails of runs) with infinitely many initial segments in C.

<u>Theorem 2.3</u> (Forgetful Determinacy). Let $C_1, ..., C_r$ be disjoint subsets of T. Let E be an equivalence relation on T such that if $\sigma E \sigma^*$, then

(a) the lengths of σ and σ^* are both odd or both even,

(b) for any finite sequence ν,

(i) $\sigma\nu \in T \Leftrightarrow \sigma^*\nu \in T$,

(ii) for $i = 1, ..., r, \sigma\nu \in C_i \Leftrightarrow \sigma^*\nu \in C_i$.

If W is a Boolean combination of the sets Inf(C_i), then one of the players has a deterministic strategy f such that for any $\sigma, \sigma^* \in dom(f)$, if $\sigma \in \sigma^*$, then $f(\sigma) = f(\sigma^*)$.

Remark: In our setting, (b)(i) will be implied by the condition that the last plant state and regulator setting in σ and σ^* agree. This is where we use the assumption that our plant and regulator are only limited to the moves of a pair of non-deterministic finite automata.

§3. Determining an appropriate set of states

In this section, we describe the states for our automata.

Theorem 3.1. For each n, we can find a finite set S and a function $i : S \to R$ such that for all formulas φ of rank n, if there is a strategy guaranteeing satisfaction of φ, then there is one provided by some $M \in \mathcal{M}(S)$ together with the output function i.

The proof of Theorem 3.1 will require some work, and we need a definition. Let σ be a finite initial segment of one of our tails of runs. The n-record of σ, denoted by $\rho(n, \sigma)$, is defined below. The reader who is familiar with [G-H] will recognize n-records as generalized "latest appearance records."

If length$(\sigma) < 2n + 1$, then $\rho(n, \sigma)$ is defined trivially to be the sequence of plant states in σ. Suppose length$(\sigma) \geq 2n + 1$. Let $\rho(0, \sigma)$ consist of just the initial plant state in σ. Let $\rho(n + 1, \sigma)$ be the finite sequence with $\rho(n, \sigma)$ and $\rho(n, \sigma^1)$ as the first two terms, followed by the distinct values of $\rho(n, \sigma^k)$, for all k such that $2k + 2n + 1 \leq$ length(σ), arranged in order of latest appearance (i.e., in order of the greatest k such that the n-record appears as $\rho(n, \sigma^k)$).

Example If $\sigma = p r_0 p' r_1 p'' r_2 p' r_3 p r_4 p'$, then $\rho(1, \sigma) = (p, p', p'', p, p')$.

Remark: $\rho(n, \sigma)$ can be computed just from the sequence of plant states in σ.

In Theorem 3.1, the set S will consist of the pairs (ρ, r), where ρ is a possible n-record and $r \in R$. We define $i : S \to R$ in the obvious way, letting $i(\rho, r) = r$. We must show that for a formula φ of rank n, if the regulator has a winning strategy for $G(T, W_\varphi)$, then there is one provided by some $M \in \mathcal{M}(S)$, with the output function i. The case where $n = 0$ is trivial. For a formula φ of rank 0, W_φ is either $[T]$ or ϕ. The formula is satisfied, or not, regardless of the strategy of the regulator. For $n > 0$, we use Forgetful Determinacy to obtain $M \in \mathcal{M}(S)$.

We define an equivalence relation E on T, letting $\sigma E \sigma^* \Leftrightarrow$ the following hold:

(i) the lengths of σ and σ^* are both odd or both even,

(ii) the last regulator outputs in σ and σ^* match,

(iii) $\rho(n, \sigma) = \rho(n, \sigma^*)$ (this implies that the last plant states match).

Remark: For each n, there are only finitely many distinct possible n-records.

For each possible n-record ρ, let $C_\rho = \{\sigma \in T : \rho(n, \sigma) = \rho\}$.

We must check that E and the family of C_ρ 's satisfy the conditions of Theorem 2.3. Suppose $\sigma E \sigma^*$. Since the last plant states and regulator outputs match, for any finite sequence ν, $\sigma\nu \in T \Leftrightarrow \sigma^*\nu \in T$, by the remark after Theorem 2.3. Showing that $\sigma\nu \in C_\rho \Leftrightarrow \sigma^*\nu \in C_\rho$ requires some simple lemmas.

Lemma 3.3. From $\rho(n, \sigma)$, we can determine the initial $(n + 1)$-tuple of plant states in σ.

Proof: For $n = 0$, the statement is trivial. Supposing the statement for n, consider $\rho(n + 1, \sigma)$ (where σ has length $\geq 2n + 3$). The first two terms of $\rho(n, \sigma)$ yield the initial $(n + 1)$-tuples of plant states in σ and σ^1. Combining these, we have the initial $(n + 2)$-tuple of plant states in σ.

Lemma 3.4. If $n > 0$, then from $\rho(n, \sigma)$, we can determine the final n-tuple of plant states in σ.

Proof: Let $\text{end}(n, \sigma)$ consist of the last $2n - 1$ terms of σ. While $\rho(n, \sigma)$ does not yield $\text{end}(n, \sigma)$, we have $\rho(n - 1, \text{end}(\sigma))$ as the last term of $\rho(n, \sigma)$. By Lemma 3.3, we can determine the n-tuple of plant states in $\text{end}(\sigma)$.

Lemma 3.5. If $\sigma r p \in T$, then $\rho(n, \sigma r) = \rho(n, \sigma)$, and we can determine $\rho(n, \sigma r p)$ from $\rho(n, \sigma)$ and p.

Proof: For $n = 0$, this is trivial. Supposing the statement for n, we prove it for $n + 1$. Say $\rho(n + 1, \sigma) = (\rho_0, \rho_1, \rho_2, ..., \rho_t)$, where each ρ_i is the n-record for some end segment of σ. Let ρ_i^* be the n-record for the corresponding n-segment of σ^*. From ρ_t, we can determine the final n-tuple of plant states in σ. Then we have the final $(n + 1)$-tuple of plant states in σ^*. By the remark before Lemma 3.2, this is enough to give us $\rho^* = \rho(n, \text{end}(\sigma^*))$. Now, $\rho(n + 1, \sigma^*)$ is obtained from $(\rho_0^*, \rho_1^*, ..., \rho_t^*, \rho^*)$ by dropping all but the last occurrence of any n-record, after the first two terms.

Using Lemma 3.5, we can show that if $\sigma E \sigma^*$ and $\sigma\nu, \sigma^*\nu \in T$, then $\sigma\nu E \sigma^*\nu$, by an easy induction on the length of ν. We have established that E and the C_ρ's satisfy the conditions of Theorem 2.3. We must show that for any formula φ of rank n, W_φ is a Boolean combination of the sets $\text{Inf}(C_\rho)$. This is equivalent to showing that for any run π, the set of n-records which occur infinitely in π determines the $\sim_n$-class of π. That is our goal in the next few lemmas.

Lemma 3.6. If $m > n$, then from the set of m-records which occur infinitely often in π, we can determine the set of n-records which occur infinitely often in π.

Proof: It is enough to show that the n-records which occur infinitely often in π are the first terms of $(n + 1)$-records which occur infinitely often in π. For any $(n + 1)$-record which occurs infinitely often, the first term is obviously an n-record which occurs infinitely often. Let $\pi|k$ be the initial segment of π of length $2k+1$, having $k+1$ plant states. Suppose ρ is an n-record which occurs infinitely often, say $\rho = \rho(n, \pi|k)$ for all k in the infinite set K. Since there are only finitely many possibilities for $\rho(n+1, \pi|k)$, for $k \in K$, there is an infinite subset K' on which $\rho(n+1, \pi|k)$ is the same.

<u>Lemma 3.7</u>. From the set of n-records which occur infinitely often in π, we can determine the k-tuples of successive plant states which appear infinitely often, for all $k \leq n$.

Proof: For $n = 0$, the statement is trivial. For $n = 1$, the statement is also clear, since the plant states which appear infinitely often are the ones which are <u>last</u> in some infinitely occurring 1-record. Supposing the statement for n, we prove it for $n+1$. The infinitely occurring n-records are the ones which are last in some infinitely occurring $(n+1)$-record. The $(n+1)$-tuples which appear infinitely in π are the initial $(n+1)$-tuples of these n-records, determined as in Lemma 3.6.

For infinite sequences π, we define a kind of limiting n-record, in which the order of latest appearance is ignored. Let $Rec(0, \pi)$ be the first plant state in π, and let $Rec(n+1, \pi) = (Rec(n, \pi), Rec(n, \pi^1), \{Rec(n, \pi^s) : s \leq 0\})$.

<u>Lemma 3.8</u>. For infinite sequences π and π^* (tails of runs):

$$Rec(n, \pi) = Rec(n, \pi^*) \Leftrightarrow \pi \sim_n \pi^*.$$

The proof is an easy induction on n.

<u>Lemma 3.9</u> (Main Lemma). For an infinite sequence π (a tail of a run), the n-records which occur infinitely in π determine $Rec(n, \pi)$. Hence, they determine the $\sim_n$-class of π.

Proof: Let $I(k, \pi)$ be the set of k-tuples which appear infinitely often in π. By Lemma 3.7, from the set of n-records which occur infinitely in π, we can determine $I(k, \pi)$, for all $k \leq n$.

<u>Claim</u>: From the sets $I(k, \pi)$ and any one infinitely occurring n-record, we can recover $Rec(n, \pi)$.

We illustrate the idea for small values of n. If $n = 0$, then for all $s \geq 0$, $\rho(0, \pi|s)$ consists of the initial plant state, and so does $Rec(0, \pi)$. Suppose $n = 1$, and take s such that $\pi|s$ includes the initial pair of plant states and the final appearance of any single plant state which appears but is not in $I(1, \pi)$. We alter $\rho(1, \pi|s)$, leaving the initial pair, but dropping any later terms which are in $I(1, \pi)$. We may record the information in a tree with two ordered levels. At level 0, we have the initial pair. Its successors, at level 1, are the single plant states, in the order listed. This tree, which we call $B(1, \pi)$, is independent of s. It includes the following information about bounded behavior in π: the initial pair of plant states, and the plant states which appear in π but are not in $I(1, \pi)$, in order of last appearance. From $B(1, \pi)$ and $I(1, \pi)$, we can recover $Rec(1, \pi)$.

Suppose $n = 2$, and take s such that $\pi | s$ includes the initial triple, the final appearance of any plant state which appears but is not in $I(1, \pi)$, and the final appearance of any pair which appears but is not in $I(2, \pi)$. Say $\rho(2, \pi | s) = (\rho_0, \rho_1, \rho_2, ..., \rho_k)$, where each ρ_i is a 1-record. We alter $\rho(2, \pi | s)$, keeping the first two terms, but dropping any later ρ_i in which the first pair is in $I(2, \pi)$ and the single plant states are all in $I(1, \pi)$. We then alter the 1-records ρ_i, keeping the first two terms, but dropping any later terms which are in $I(1, \pi)$. We may record the information in a tree with three ordered levels. At level 0, we have the initial triple. Its successors, at level 1, are the initial pairs from those ρ_i which were not dropped, in order. For each such ρ_i, the successors of the initial pair, at level 3, are the single plant states which were not dropped.

This tree, which we call $B(2, \pi)$, is independent of s. It includes the following information about bounded behavior in π: the initial triple, the single plant states which appear only finitely often, in order of last appearance, the pairs which appear in the intervals before and between the last appearances of singles, in order of last appearance, and the pairs which appear only finitely often after the last appearance of the last single, also in order of last appearance. From $B(2, \pi)$, together with $I(2, \pi)$ and $I(1, \pi)$, we can recover $Rec(2, \pi)$.

For arbitrary n, take s such that $\pi | s$ includes the initial $(n + 1)$-tuple and all final appearances of k-tuples for $k \leq n$. From $\rho(n, \pi | s)$, we can determine the initial $(n + 1)$-tuple of plant states, the initial n-tuple of each $(n - 1)$-record, the initial $(n - 1)$-tuple of each $(n - 2)$-record listed for any $(n - 1)$-record, etc. We arrange these tuples in a finite tree with ordered levels. On top, at level 0, we put the initial $(n + 1)$-tuple. Below that, at level 1, are the n-tuples corresponding to the $(n - 1)$-records listed in the n-record, in the same order (first, second, and then the whole set in order of latest appearance). At level 2, below the n-tuple of a particular $(n - 1)$-record are the $(n - 1)$-tuples corresponding to the $(n - 2)$-records listed in the $(n - 1)$-record, again in the same order, etc.

The tree that we have described depends on our choice of s, displaying the latest appearances of various <u>infinitely</u> appearing k-tuples. Now, at level 1, we keep the first two n-tuples, but drop the later n-tuples which are in $I(n, \pi)$ and whose subtrees consist entirely of k-tuples in $I(k, \pi)$, for $k \leq n$. For each $(m + 1)$-tuple which we are keeping, we keep the first two successors, but drop the later successors which are in $I(m, \pi)$ and whose subtrees consist entirely of k-tuples in $I(k, \pi)$ for $k \leq m$. The resulting tree, which we call $B(n, \pi)$, is independent of s, as above.

Let T_1 be the set of 1-level trees consisting of a single element of $I(1, \pi)$. Let T_2 be the set of 2-level trees consisting of a pair (p_1, p_2) from $I(2, \pi)$ on top, and below that, p_1, p_2, followed by all elements of $I(1, \pi)$. In general, for $1 \leq k \leq n$, let T_k be the set of k-level trees consisting of a k-tuple $(p_1, ..., p_k)$ from $I(k, \pi)$ on top, and below that, first the $(k-1)$-level trees corresponding to $(p_1, ..., p_k - 1)$ and $(p_2, ..., p_k - 2)$, and then all trees in T_{k-1}.

For $1 \leq k \leq n$, below each $(k+1)$-tuple in $B(n, \pi)$ (at level $n - k$), we attach all of the trees from T_k. We do this in such a way that the new successors of a given $(k+1)$-tuple–the top nodes in the trees from T_k–come after those successors which were present in $B(n, \pi)$. We denote the fattened tree by $U(n, \pi)$. While $B(n, \pi)$ gave the information about bounded behavior in π, $U(n, \pi)$ includes the information about unbounded behavior.

From $U(n, \pi)$, we can recover $Rec(n, \pi)$. Each k-tuple in $U(n, \pi)$, with the subtree below it, corresponds to $Rec(k-1, \pi^m)$ for some $m \geq 0$. We do not know m, of course, but if a given $(k+1)$-tuple corresponds to $Rec(k, \pi^m)$ then the successors are k-tuples, arranged in some order so that the first (with its subtree) corresponds to $Rec(k-1, \pi^m)$, the second corresponds to $Rec(k-1, \pi^{m+1})$, and the ones after that correspond to the distinct values of $Rec(k-1, \pi^{m+s})$.

This is all that we shall say about the proof of Lemma 3.9.

Remark: Given a formula φ of rank n and the set of n-records which appear infinitely in π, we can determine whether $\pi \models \varphi$.

The remark is easily established, by induction on n.

We are ready to complete the proof of Theorem 3.1. Suppose φ is a formula of rank n. By Lemma 3.9, W_φ is a Boolean combination of the sets $Inf(C_\rho)$, where ρ is an n-record. We are in a position to apply Theorem 2.3. We conclude that in the game $G(T, W_\varphi)$, one of the players has a winning strategy f such that for any pair of E-equivalent nodes σ, σ^* on which it is the given player's turn, $f(\sigma) = f(\sigma^*)$. Suppose f is a strategy for the regulator. We show that f can be implemented by some $M \in \mathcal{M}(S)$, with output function i.

For σ of odd length, the E-class of σr is determined by $\rho(n, \sigma)$ and r. By Lemma 3.5, $\rho(n, \sigma r p)$ is determined by $\rho(n, \sigma)$ and p, so the E-class of $\sigma r p$ is determined by $\rho(n, \sigma), r$, and p. In M, the initial state is (ρ_0, r_0), where $\rho_0 = \rho(n, p_0)$ and $r_0 = f(p_0)$. Then we have a well-defined transition function τ such that if $\sigma r p \in T, \rho, \rho(n, \sigma r p) = \rho'$, and $f(\sigma r p) = r'$, then $\tau((\rho, r), p) = (\rho', r')$. We let M have this transition function. We let the initial state be (ρ, r), where $\rho = \rho(n, p_0), r = f(p_0)$. This completes the proof.

§4 Main result

Our aim is to prove the following.

Theorem 4.1. For any formula φ, we can either find a deterministic finite automaton guaranteeing satisfaction of φ, or know that the plant can guarantee satisfaction of $\neg\varphi$.

By Theorem 3.1, given a specification φ, we can find a finite set S and $i : S \to R$ such that either the regulator can guarantee φ acting as some $M \in \mathcal{M}(S)$ with output function i, or else the plant can guarantee $\neg\varphi$. To complete the proof of Theorem 4.1, we need the following.

Theorem 4.2 Given a finite set S, a function $i : S \to R$, and a formula φ, we can either find $M \in \mathcal{M}(S)$ which, together with i, guarantees satisfaction of φ, or else say for sure that there is no such M.

We offer a choice of arguments for Theorem 4.2.

I. We can reduce Theorem 4.2 to the following result, for the setting in which the regulator is a deterministic finite automaton with just R as the set of states.

Theorem 4.3. Given a formula φ , we can either find $M \in \mathcal{M}(R)$ guaranteeing satisfaction of φ, or else say for sure that there is no such M. (Moreover, the procedure is uniform in φ and our description of T.)

There is an elementary proof of Theorem 4.3 in [K-P]. To derive Theorem 4.2 from Theorem 4.3, we define a new tree T^*, made up of those finite sequences $p_0 s_0 p_1 s_1 p_2 s_2 \ldots$, with $s_n \in S$, such that the corresponding sequence

$$p_0 i(s_0) p_1 i(s_1) p_2 i(s_2)\ldots$$

is in T. For each $\pi^* \in [T^*]$, there exists $\pi \in [T]$ with exactly the same odd terms as π^*, and since our definition of satisfaction depends only on these terms, we have $\pi^* \models \varphi \Leftrightarrow \pi \models \varphi$. Let $W_\varphi^* = \{\pi^* \in [T^*] : \pi^* \models \varphi\}$.

Now, replacing T by T^*, we are in a position to apply Theorem 4.3. For any formula φ, we can either find $M \in \mathcal{M}(S)$ which, with i as the output function, guarantees satisfaction of φ, or else say for sure that there is no such M. Suppose that we find $M \in \mathcal{M}(S)$. Let f be the corresponding winning strategy for the regulator in $G(T^*, W\varphi^*)$. Then $i \circ f$ is a winning strategy for the regulator in $G(T, W_\varphi)$.

II. We sketch a direct proof of Theorem 4.2. Since $\mathcal{M}(S)$ is finite, it is enough to give a procedure for deciding whether a given $M \in \mathcal{M}(S)$, with i, guarantees satisfaction of φ. With M as the regulator, the system has a fixed initial state pair (p_0, s_0), and for any given state pair (p, s), there is a fixed finite set of next possible state pairs (p', s'). Thus, the system, with the given M, the M-system, forms a non-deterministic finite automaton.

Claim: We can determine for which sets α, there is a run π of the M-system in which α is the set of state pairs which occur infinitely often.

Proof of claim: We can determine whether the M-system can pass (in finitely many steps) from the initial state pair to a pair in α. We can also determine whether, given two pairs $(p, s), (p', s')$ in α, whether the M-system can pass from (p, s) to (p', s') so that all intermediate state pairs are in α. (For this, it may be helpful to use a state diagram.)

Suppose φ has rank n. Given the set of state pairs which occur infinitely often in a run π, we can determine the set of n-records which appear infinitely often in π, we can determine the set of n-records which appear infinitely often in π. Then by the remark after Lemma 3.9, we can determine whether $\pi \models \varphi$. Thus, by checking all finite subsets α of S, we can determine whether φ is true in all runs of the M-system.

§5. Expressive power of the language (normal form)

Our language has formulas of arbitrarily high rank. It is easy to see that the equivalence relations $\sim_n$ partition $[T]$ into strictly smaller classes as n increases. However, the $\sim_n$ classes, and the sets W_φ, all lie at a low level in the Borel hierarchy. They are Boolean combinations of the sets $Inf(C_\rho)$, which are G_δ.

The analysis in §3 indicates exactly what the formulas of a given rank can say, providing a kind of "normal" form. We say that φ is <u>complete rank n</u> if the set of runs satisfying φ forms a single $\sim_n$-class.

Theorem 5.1.

(a) Each $\sim_n$-class is characterized by a complete rank n formula.

(b) For any formula φ of rank n, there is a formula φ^*, satisfied in exactly the same runs as φ, where φ^* is a finite disjunction of complete rank n formulas (still of rank n).

Proof: (a) For any run π, there is a natural formula describing $Rec(n, \pi)$. For example, if $\pi = p_0 r_0 p_1 r_1 p_2 r_2...$ and P_1, P_2, respectively, consist of those $p \in P$ which do, and do not occur in π, we take the complete rank 1 formula

$$p_0 \ \& \ Op_1 \ \& \ (\bigwedge_{p \in P_1} \Diamond p) \ \& \ (\bigwedge_{p \in P_2} \Box \neg p).$$

(b) The set of runs satisfying φ is a finite union of $\sim_n$-classes, and φ^* is the disjunction of the corresponding complete rank n formulas.

As we indicated earlier, we chose our language for its simplicity. There are many other modal temporal languages, and their features and relative strength have been analyzed extensively. We refer the reader to [E] and [E-J].

References

[B] Büchi, J. R., "On a decision method in restricted second order arithmetic," in *Proc. Internat. Congr. on Logic, Methodology, and Philosophy of Science*, ed. by Nagel et al., Stanford Univ. Press, 1960, pp. 1-11.

[B-L] Büchi, J. R. and L. H. Landweber, "Solving sequential conditions by finite-state strategies," *Trans. Amer. Math. Soc.*, vol. 138(1969), pp. 295-311.

[C] Church, A., "Logic, arithmetic, and automata," in *Proc. Internat. Congress Math.*, 1963, pp. 23-35.

[D-R] Diekert and Rozenberg, *The Book of Traces*.

[E] Emerson, E.A., "Temporal and modal logic," in *Handbook of Theoretical Computer Science, vol. B: Formal Models and Semantics*, ed. by van Leeuwen, 1990, Elsevier, pp. 997-1072.

[E-J] Emerson, E. A., and C. S. Jutla, "Tree automata, mu-calculus, and determinacy," *Proc. of the 1991 IEEE Symp. on Foundations of Computer Science*, pp. 368-377.

[G-H] Gurevich, Yu., and L. Harrington, "Automata, trees, and games," *Proc., 14th A.C.M. Symposium on the Theory of Computing*, San Francisco. 1982.

[K-P] Knight and Passino, "Decidability for a temporal logic used in discrete event system analysis," *International J. of Control*, vol. 52(1990), pp. 1489-1506.

[La] Landweber, L. H., "Decision problems for ω-automata," *Math. Systems Theory*, vol. 3(1969), pp. 376-384.

[Lu] Luense, Senior Honors Thesis, University of Notre Dame, 1995.

[M-P] Manna, Z., and A. Pnueli, "Verification of concurrent programs: the temporal framework," in *The Correctness Problem in Computer Science*, ed. by R. S. Boyer and J. S. Moore, Academic Press, 1982, pp. 215-273.

[M] Martin, D., "Borel determinacy," *Ann. Math.*, vol. 102(1975), pp. 363-371.

[Mc] McNaughton, R., "Testing and generating infinite sequences by a finite automaton, *Inform. and Control*, vol. 9(1966), pp. 521-530.

[M-S] Muller, D. and Schupp, "Alternating automata on infinite trees," *Theoret, Comput. Sci.*, vol. 54(1987), pp. 267-276.

[O] Ostroff, J. S., *Real-Time Computer Control of Discrete Systems Modeled by Extended State Machines: a Temporal Logic Approach*, Ph.D. dissertation, Department of Electrical Engineering, University of Toronto, 1987.

[R₁] Rabin, M., "Decidability of second order theories and automata on infinite trees," *Trans. of the Amer. Soc.*, vol. 141(1969), pp. 1-35.

[R₂] Rabin, M., *Automata on Infinite Objects and Church's Problem*, Ameri. Math. Soc., Providence, 1972.

[T-W] Thistle, J. G., and W. M. Wonham, "Control problems in a temporal logic framework, *International J. of Control*, vol. 44(1985), pp. 943-976.

[T] Thomas, W., "Automata on infinite objects," in *Handbook of Theoretical Computer Science, vol. B: Formal Models and Semantics*, ed. by van Leeuwen, 1990, Elsevier, pp. 135-191.

Agent Based Velocity Control of Highway Systems

Wolf Kohn*[1] and Anil Nerode**[2] and Jeffrey B. Remmel***[3]

[1] HyBrithms Corp.[†]
11201 S.E. 8th Street, Bldg. J, Suite 140
Bellevue, Washington
e-mail: wk@hybrithms.com
[2] Mathematical Sciences Institute
Cornell University, Ithaca, NY 14853
e-mail: anil@math.cornell.edu
[3] HyBrithms Corp. and
Department of Mathematics
University of California at San Diego San Diego, CA 92093
e-mail; jremmel@ucsd.edu

Abstract. In this paper we present a hybrid systems approach to freeway traffic control. We introduce a model of traffic which includes both vehicles and voids, where a void is a unit of space greater than the normal following distance between vehicles. The introduction of voids allows us to successfully model traffic flow via a wave model. We discuss the fundamentals of the Multiple Agent Hybrid Control Architecture which was used to implement our control of freeway traffic and the results of a simulation of our control. The main conclusion of our simulation is that one can significantly increase traffic throughput by controlling only 5-9% of the vehicles.

1 Introduction

This paper presents an architecture for the real-time feedback control of hybrid systems through a communication network composed of multiple decision makers herein refereed to as agents. The paper discusses some recent results from the theory of Hybrid systems, developed by the authors, related to the behavior of the architecture and illustrates them with a simple highway control system. This application was selected because it shares many elements of commonality with many other areas of application such as distributed control, sensor fusion, manufacturing shop-floor control and hybrid routing in communication networks; and yet it requires relatively modest modeling efforts.

Our architecture implements formal real-time intelligent controllers with learning capabilities. This architecture, termed the Multiple-Agent Hybrid Control Architecture (MAHCA), [21, 22], provides a knowledge-based, formal implementation

* Research supported by Dept. of Commerce Agreement 70-NANB5H1164.
** Research supported by ARO under the MURI program "Integrated Approach to Intelligent Systems", grant no. DAAHO4-96-1-0341.
*** Research supported by Dept. of Commerce Agreement 70-NANB5H1164.
† HyBrithms Corp was formerly know as Sagent Corporation

framework for deducing on-line feedback control and reactive strategies for processes involving multiple agents. The architecture includes capabilities for structural adaptation as a function of predictable and unpredictable events in the processes under control. This characteristic is necessary for satisfying performance requirements in the unavoidable presence of sensory and knowledge uncertainty.

We will illustrate the functional and operational characteristics of MAHCA in terms of a two-agent controller version whose goals are to maximize traffic throughput in a freeway network and to provide a dynamic route planning for selected cars through the network with minimum average time. The highway example was chosen because it explicitly exhibits some the basic properties of hybrid systems in a clear fashion. In addition we were able to demonstrate a property of these systems which is unique. That is, one can achieve a significant increase in throughput by controlling a relatively small number of vehicles. This result is a consequence of the implicit inter-vehicle constraints that limit the degrees of freedom for control in the freeway to a small percentage of the total vehicle by vehicle aggregated degrees of freedom. This implies that a platooning effect is achieved spontaneously by controlling the velocity of about 9-14% of the cars in the freeway network.

The organization of this paper is as follows. In section 2, we shall provide an overview of our freeway network model. In section 3, we shall descibe the generic variational model of MAHCA agent. In section 4, we shall give an overview of the architecture of MAHCA agent and how it carries out its computations. Finally in section 5, we will discuss the results of a simulation of our highway control. In particular, at the end of the paper, we will provide a series of charts which give the results of controlling 5%, 8%, and 9% of the vehicles.

2 Freeway Network Model and Control

The freeway network model we will use in our illustration of MAHCA is composed of two elements the Network Geometry and the Network Dynamics. We discus these elements in the next two subsections.

The substance in a traffic flow is, of course, vehicles. However, in addition to modeling the flow of vehicles, the model also includes the flow of voids, where a void is a unit of space greater than the normal following distance between vehicles. As vehicles (referred to generically as "cars" in what follows) travel from a source $(x = 0)$ to the destination $(x = L)$, the voids travel in the reverse direction, i.e. starting at $x = L$.

The introduction of voids eliminates a major problem with wave models. That is, such models are only valid for high uniform densities. Modeling the voids and their interaction with cars permits the generation of more realistic density distributions. When the voids are also modeled, the sparse density of vehicles become high densities of voids, allowing for model validity at low vehicle densities. This representation is patterned after the model of propagation of electrons and holes in semiconductor junctions.

For incorporating driver behavior and policies we use a Toda lattice representation vehicle interaction for each policy and generate the composite wave model via a formal aggregation procedure similar to the one proposed in [44].

A freeway segment is treated a single pipe with a capacity density corresponding to an average lane car velocity of 50 miles/hr for the number of lanes considered. Individual lanes are not modeled. Accidents are represented as reductions in the capacity of the segment.

2.1 Network Geometry

The network geometry is represented by a segment directed graph (SDG). An SDG is a structure composed of two types of sets: an edge set (E) and a node set (N). The set of edges (E), represent unidirectional freeways. Each edge (freeway) is modeled as a composite of one or more segments. The set of nodes (N) is composed of three, not necessarily disjoint, subsets: sources (S), interior nodes (I) and destination nodes (D). A source node represents a point at which cars enter the network, a destination node is a point at which cars leave the network and an interior node a point at which cars flow from one or more freeway segments to other freeway segments These concepts are illustrated in Figure 1.

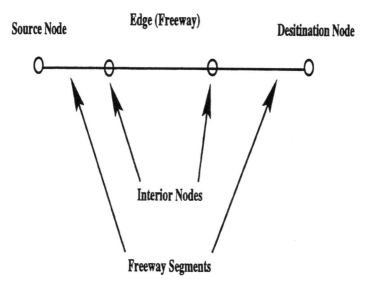

Fig. 1. Geometry of the Model

From the geometric point of view, an edge is a connected straight line with a direction, indicated by an arrow at its destination point, containing two or more nodes. An edge is composed of one or more segments where a segment is a line in between two nodes. A two-way freeway is represented by two edges with opposite directions. Thus, independently of the actual map characteristics of a freeway segment, in our model a freeway segment is represented by a straight line which we assume has the same length as the freeway segment it represents. This simplifying assumption does not cause inaccuracies because we model the constraints due to the geography and other constraints on traffic flow with a capacity function that we will describe in the next subsection.

Figure 2 shows the geometric model of the freeway system of the greater Houston area. This network was used to exercise our 2-agent implementation of MAHCA. Some of the simulation results will be presented in section 5.

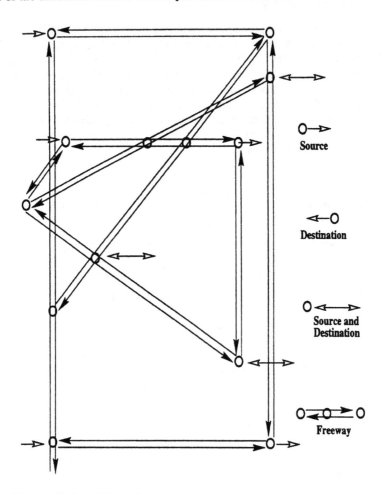

Fig. 2. Houston Highway Network

2.2 Freeway Network Dynamics

For the purpose of representing traffic flow dynamics, we view the freeway segments as pipes with variable cross-section carrying a composite fluid of two types of interacting particles, "car" and "void" particles. The void particles represent statistical averages of inter-car distances. In each segment, cars flow in the direction of the segment edge while voids flows in the opposite direction.

The central principle behind our dynamics model of freeway networks is that the number of cars and voids flowing through a freeway segment are conserved quantities. This principle is an extension of the one proposed [16] and [24] and is now widely used in analysis of freeway control [25].

Rather than introduce the principle in its more general form, we will motivate it informally from a simple particle model of single lane freeway segments. This exercise is important because many aspects of freeway dynamics [24], such as driver behavior, are easily stated in terms of particle models.

The general idea behind particle models in a single lane freeway segment is the following. We set up a coordinate system with origin at the beginning node of the segment (we assume that a freeway segment inherits the direction of its edge). We assume that there are on the average M cars and $M - 1$ voids in the segment and that the speed at which the n-th car and the n-th void move, at time t are functions of the positions of the $(n - 1)$-th and $(n + 1)$-th cars and the $(n - 1)$-th void in the lane. In symbols,

$$\dot{x}_n(t + \delta) = f(s_{n-1}(t), x_{n-1}(t), x_{n+1}(t)) \tag{1}$$
$$\dot{s}_n(t + \delta) = -g(s_{n-1}(t), x_{n-1}(t), x_{n+1}(t)) \tag{2}$$

where $x_k(t)$ and $s_l(t)$ are respectively the position of the k-th car and l-th void in the segment at time t and f and g are functions that capture driver behavior, car characteristics and geographic and environmental constraints. For the n-th car and n-th void ($n = 1, ..., M$) in the segment, the functions f and g map the positions of neighboring cars and voids at time t to the speeds of the n-th car and n-th void at time $t + \delta$ where δ is a positive real number modeling average driver reaction time.

For the purposes of characterizing highway segment velocity control and car routing through the network, the model above is not satisfactory. We need a model that gives a global view of the dynamics. With this goal in mind we have transformed the particle model above into a wave model [25]. In a wave model, the cars, the voids and their interactions, in each freeway segment, are expressed by a set of coupled partial differential equations expressing conservation of mass (of cars and voids) and velocity of cars and voids. These equations are given in (3) - (5) and (6) and (7) below.

$$\frac{\partial \rho^c}{\partial t} + \frac{\partial Q^c}{\partial x} + k_1(C^c - \rho^c)\rho^v - k_2(C^v - \rho^v) = 0 \tag{3}$$
with
$$Q^c = Q_0^c(\rho^c) - d\frac{\partial \rho^c}{\partial x}$$

$$\frac{\partial \rho^v}{\partial t} + \frac{\partial Q^v}{\partial x} + k_1(C^v - \rho^v)\rho^c - k_2(C^c - \rho^c) = 0 \tag{4}$$
with
$$Q^v = Q_0^v(\rho^v) - d_1\frac{\partial \rho^v}{\partial x}$$

In (3) and (4), t is time, x is the freeway space variable, ρ^j, for $j = c$ or v, are the densities of the car and void particles (cars/mile, and voids /mile), Q^j, for $j = c$ or v, are the flows of cars and voids (cars /sec and voids/sec) respectively. The capacity of the freeway segment at each point is given by the functions C^j, for $j = c$ or v, in cars/sec and voids/sec respectively. The coefficients k_1 and k_2 are empirical coefficients expressing the transference from voids to cars and cars to voids respectively. Finally, d and d_1 are aggregated empirical diffusion coefficients expressing driver behavior dependencies on the neighboring cars and voids. In (3) and (4), the functions Q_0^j, $j = c$ for cars or $j = v$ for voids, are called the free flows (for cars and voids respectively and measuring the number of cars and voids per second), and are given by

$$Q_0^j(\rho^j) = \frac{\sum_{i=1}^{n_j} a_i^j(\rho^j)^i}{\sum_{i=1}^{n_j} b_i^j(\rho^j)^i} \text{ with } j = c \text{ or } j = v \tag{5}$$

where a_i^j and b_i^j are empirical coefficients. In particular for, Greenber's law of traffic flow for freeway segments under heavy load [24], (5) is the Padé approximant to the natural logarithmic function.

Equations (6) to (8) express the wave velocity dynamics v^j, for $j = c$ or v, of cars and voids along a freeway segment. In (6), k_3 and V^u represent the control fields in each segment. V^u is the recommended wave velocity and k_3 is the percentage of cars that are controlled. Since the dynamics of an individual car is constrained by its neighbors the controller does not have to control all the cars on the segment to achieve the desired *goal* which is to *maximize throughput* for the freeway network.

$$\frac{\partial v^c}{\partial t} + v^c \frac{\partial v^c}{\partial x} = -\frac{1}{\delta}\left(v^c - k_3 V^u + d\frac{\frac{\partial \rho^c}{\partial x}}{\rho^c}\right) \tag{6}$$

$$\frac{\partial v^v}{\partial t} + v^v \frac{\partial v^v}{\partial x} = \frac{1}{\delta}\left(v^v - v^c + d_1\frac{\frac{\partial \rho^v}{\partial x}}{\rho^v}\right) \tag{7}$$

The equations in (8), express the boundary conditions for each freeway segment. The right-hand side of the first equation expresses the gradient of the density of cars and voids being pumped into the segment. The right-hand side of the second equation in (8) expresses the density of particles leaving the segment.

$$\frac{\partial \rho^j}{\partial x}(t, 0) = \rho^j(t) \; j = v \text{ or } c \tag{8}$$
with
$$\rho^j(t, 1) = e^j(t)$$

The exchange between voids and cars is given by

$$\frac{\partial \rho^c}{\partial t} + \frac{\partial \rho^v}{\partial t} + \frac{\partial Q_0^c}{\partial x} + \frac{\partial Q^v}{\partial x} = 0. \tag{9}$$

This equation forms the rule which guarantees the conservation of the total number of "units" (cars and voids) in the freeway system.

The model outlined above, characterizes the dynamics of freeway segments and hence the freeway network. This model constitutes the specific (problem dependent) equational knowledge required to control the freeway network using MAHCA. The next subsection formulates the highway velocity control problem as a multiple agent, knowledge-based control problem.

2.3   Control Problem

The overall goal of the control system is to maximize throughput for the freeway network by controlling the velocity V^u and the percentage of controlled cars k_3, referred to as the control actions, in each segment. We associate with each segment i a control agent A_i which generates the control actions for the corresponding segment as a function of sensory data, goal data, current status data and information from the other agents via a communication network herein referred to as the *Control Network*. A formal model of the control network and its dynamics is given in section 3.

3   Control Network

3.1   A MAHCA Agent's Model

In general, a hybrid system has a hybrid state, the simultaneous dynamical state of all plants and digital control devices. Properly construed, the hybrid states will form a differentiable manifold which we call the *carrier manifold* of the system. To incorporate the digital states as certain coordinates of points of the carrier manifold, we "continualize" the digital states. That is, we view the digital states as finite, real-valued, piecewise-constant functions of continuous time and then we take smooth approximations to them. This also allows us to consider logical and differential or variational constraints on the same footing, each restricting the points allowed on the carrier manifold. In fact, all logical or discontinuous features can be continualized without practical side-effects. This is physically correct since for any semiconductor chip used in an analog device, the zeros and ones are really just abbreviations for sensor readings of the continuous state of the chip. Every constraint of the system, digital or continuous, is incorporated into the definition of what points are on the carrier manifold. Lagrange constraints are regarded as part of the definition of the manifold as well, being restrictions on what points are on the manifold.

More specifically, let A_i, $i = 1, \ldots, N(t)$ denote the agents active at the current time t. In our model, t takes values on the real line. At each time t, the status of each agent in the network is given by a point in a locally differentiable manifold M [24]. The Behavior function B_i of an active agent A_i is given by a continuous function,

$$B_i : M \times T \to R^+ \tag{10}$$

where T is the real line (time space) and R^+ is the positive real line. M is contained in the Cartesian Product

$$M \subseteq G \times S \times X \times A \tag{11}$$

where G is the spaces of goals, S is the space of sensory data, X is the space of controller states and A is the space of control actions. In the freeway network, X is the space of current distributions of car and void densities and velocities in its segments, S is the space of measurements of car and void densities along the segment (one sensor each third of a mile), A is the space spanned by the velocity and percentage fields, and G is the set of car and void densities that maximizes throughput.

From an agent's point of view, the dynamics of the control network is characterized by certain trajectories on the manifold M. These trajectories characterize the flow of information through the network and its status. Specifically, we need to define two items:

(i) a set of generators for the behavior functions at time t,

$$\{B_i(p, t) : i = 1, \ldots N, p \in M\} \tag{12}$$

and

(ii) the control actions issued by the agents.

We will see shortly that these actions are implemented as infinitesimal transformations defined in M. The general structure of the behavior function in (12) for an agent A_i at time t is given in (13) below:

$$B_i(p, t) = F_i(U_i, B, \alpha_i)(p, t) \tag{13}$$

where F_i is a smooth function, B is the vector of behavior functions, C_i^u is the behavior modification function for the i-th agent, and α_i is the command action issued by the i-th agent. We will devote the rest of this subsection to characterizing this model.

We start with a discussion of the main characteristics of the manifold M. In general a manifold M is a topological space (with topology Θ) composed of three items:

(a) A set of points of the form of (11).

(b) A countable family of open subsets of M, U_i such that

$$\bigcup_i U_i = M.$$

(c) A family of smooth homeomorphisms, $\{\phi_i : \phi_i : U_i \to V_i\}$, where for each j, V_j is an open set in R^k. The sets U_i are referred to in the literature as coordinate neighborhoods or charts. For each chart U_j the corresponding function ϕ_j is referred to as its coordinate chart.

The coordinate chart functions satisfy the following additional condition:

Given any charts U_i and U_j such that $U_i \cap U_j \neq \emptyset$, the function $\phi_i \circ \phi_j^{-1} : \phi_j(U_i \cap U_j) \to \phi_i(U_i \cap U_j)$ is smooth.

In the literature, one usually finds an additional property, which is the Hausdorff property in the definition of manifolds [25]. Since this property does not hold in our application we will not discuss it.

Now we proceed to customize the generic definition of the manifold to our application. We start with the topology Θ associated with M. We note that the points of M have a definite structure, see (11), whose structure is characterized by the interval of values in the space G of goals, the space S of sensory data, the space X of controller states and the space A of control actions. The number of these parameters equals k. The knowledge about these parameters is incorporated into the model by defining a finite topology Ω on R^k [5].

The open sets in Ω are constructed from the clauses encoding what we know about the parameters. The topology Θ of M is defined in terms of Ω as follows. For each open set W in Ω such that $W \subseteq V_j \subseteq R^k$, we require that the set $\phi_j^{-1}(W)$ be in Θ. The sets constructed in this way form a basis for Θ so that a set $U \subseteq M$ is open if and only if for each $p \in U$, there is j and an open set $W \in \Omega$ such that $W \subseteq V_j$ and $p \in \phi_j^{-1}(W)$.

To characterize the actions commanded by a MAHCA agent we need to introduce the concept of derivations on M. Let F_p be the space of real valued smooth functions f defined in a neighborhood a point p in M. Let f and g be functions in F_p. A *derivation* v of F_p is a map

$$v : F_p \to F_p$$

that satisfies the following two properties.

$$v(f + g)(p) = (v(f) + v(g))(p) \qquad \text{(Linearity)} \qquad (14)$$
$$v(f \cdot g)(p) = (v(f) \cdot g + f \cdot v(g))(p) \qquad (\text{ Leibniz Rule}) \qquad (15)$$

Derivations define vector fields on M and a class of associated curves called integral curves [26]. Suppose that C is a smooth curve on M parameterized by $\psi : I \to M$ where I a subinterval of R. In local coordinates, $p = (p^1, ..., p^k)$, C is given by k smooth functions $\psi(t) = (\psi^1(t), \dots, \psi^k(t))$ whose derivative with respect to t is denoted by $\dot{\psi}(t) = (\dot{\psi}^1(t), \dots, \dot{\psi}^k(t))$. We introduce an equivalence relation on curves in M as the basis of the definition of tangent vectors at a point in M [14]. Two curves $\psi_1(t)$ and $\psi_2(t)$ passing through a point p are said to be equivalent at p (notation: $\psi_1(t) \sim \psi_2(t)$), if there exists $\tau_1, \tau_2 \in I$ such that

$$\psi_1(\tau_1) = \psi_2(\tau_2) = p \qquad (16)$$
$$\dot{\psi}_1(\tau_1) = \dot{\psi}_2(\tau_2). \qquad (17)$$

Clearly, $\sim$ defines an equivalence relation on the class of curves in M passing through p. Let $[\psi]$ be the equivalence class containing ψ. A *tangent vector* to $[\psi]$ is a derivation, $v|_p$, such that in local coordinates $(p^1, \dots, p^k)$, it satisfies the condition that given any smooth function $f : M \to R$,

$$v|_p(f)(p) = \sum_{j=0}^{k} \psi^j(t) \frac{\partial f(p)}{\partial p^j} \qquad (18)$$

where $p = \psi(t)$. The set of tangent vectors associated with all the equivalence classes at p defines a vector space called the *tangent vector space* at p, denoted by TM_p. The set of tangent spaces associated with points in M can be "glued" together to form a manifold called the *tangent bundle* which is denoted by TM,

$$TM = \bigcup_{p \in m} TM_p.$$

For our purposes, it is important to specify explicitly how this gluing is implemented. This will be explained below after we introduce the concept of a vector field and discuss its relevance in the model.

A *vector field* on M is an assignment of a derivation $v|_p$ to each point p of M which varies smoothly from point to point. That is, if $p = (p^1, ..., p^k)$ are local coordinates, then we can always write $v|_p$ in the form

$$v|_p = \sum_j \lambda^j(p) \frac{\partial}{\partial p^j} \tag{19}$$

Then v is a vector field if the coordinate functions λ_i are smooth.

Comparing (18) and (19) we see that if ψ is a parameterized curve in M whose tangent vector at any point coincides with the value of v at a point $p = \psi(t)$, then in the local coordinates $p = (\psi^1(t), \dots, \psi^k(t))$, we must have

$$\dot{\psi}^j(t) = \lambda^j(p) \text{ for } j = 1, \dots, k. \tag{20}$$

In our application, each command issued by the MAHCA agent is implemented as a vector field in M. Each agent constructs its command field as a combination of 'primitive' predefined vector fields. Since the chosen topology for M, Θ, is not metrizable, we cannot guarantee a unique solution to (20) in the classical sense for a given initial condition. However, they have solutions in a class of continuous trajectories in M called *relaxed curves* [33]. In this class, the solutions to (20) are unique. We discuss the basic characteristics of relaxed curves as they apply to our process control formulation and implementation in Section 4. Next, we describe some of their properties as they relate to our plant model and control process. For this objective, we need to introduce the concept of flows in M.

If v is a vector field, any parameterized curve passing through a point p in M is called an *integral curve associated with* v if in local coordinates (5) holds. An integral curve associated with a field v, denoted by $\Psi(t, p)$ is termed the flow generated by v if it satisfies the following properties:

$$\Psi(t, \Psi(\tau, p)) = \Psi(t + \tau, p) \text{ (semigroup property)} \tag{21}$$
$$\Psi(0, p) = p \text{ (initial condition)}$$
$$\text{and}$$
$$\frac{d}{dt}\Psi(t, p) = v \,|_{\Psi(t,p)} \text{ (flow generation)}$$

Now we are ready to customize these concepts for our model. Let $\Delta > 0$ be the width of the current decision interval, $[t, t + \Delta)$. Let $C_i^u(p, t)$ be the unsatisfied demand at the beginning of the interval. Agent A_i has a set of primitive actions:

$$\{v_{i,j} : j = 1, \dots, n_i \text{ where } v_{i,j}|_p \in TM_p \text{ for each } p \in m\}. \tag{22}$$

During the interval $[t, t + \Delta)$, agent A_i schedules one or more of these actions to produce a flow which will bring the system closer to the goal. In particular, A_i determines the fraction $\alpha_{i,j}(p, t)$ of Δ that action $v_{i,j}$ must be executed as a function of the external perturbation functions $S_{r,i}(t, p)$ and the vector of the behavior functions of the agents in the network $B(p, t) = (B_1(p, t), \dots, B_{N(t)})$. Figure 3 conceptually

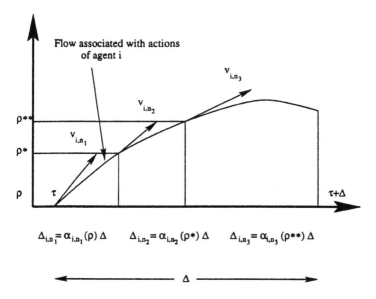

Fig. 3. Conceptual illustration of agent action schedule

illustrates a schedule of actions involving three primitives. We will use this example as means for describing the derivation of our model. The general case is similar.

The flow Ψ_i associated with the schedule of Figure 3 can be computed from the flows associated with each of the actions:

$$\Psi_i(\tau, p) = \begin{cases} \Psi_{v_{i,n_1}}(\tau, p) \text{ if } t \leq \tau \leq t + \Delta_{i,n_1} \\ \Psi_{v_{i,n_2}}(\tau, \Psi_{v_{i,n_1}}(\tau, p)) \text{ if } t + \Delta_{i,n_1} \leq \tau \leq t + \Delta_{i,n_1} + \Delta_{i,n_2} \\ \Psi_{v_{i,n_3}}(\tau, \Psi_{v_{i,n_2}}(\tau, \Psi_{v_{i,n_1}}(\tau, p))) \\ \qquad \text{if } t + \Delta_{i,n_1} + \Delta_{i,n_2} \leq \tau \leq t + \Delta_{i,n_1} + \Delta_{i,n_2} + \Delta_{i,n_3} \end{cases} \tag{23}$$

where $\Delta = \Delta_{i,n_1} + \Delta_{i,n_2} + \Delta_{i,n_3}$ and $\alpha_{i,n_1} + \alpha_{i,n_2} + \alpha_{i,n_3} = 1$. We note that the flow Ψ_i given by (23) characterizes the evolution of the process as viewed by agent A_i. The vector field $v_i|_p$ associated with the flow Ψ_i is obtained by differentiation and the third identity in (21). This vector field applied at p is proportional to

$$[v_{i,n_1}, [v_{i,n_2}, v_{i,n_3}]] \tag{24}$$

where $[.,.]$ is the Lie bracket due to the parallelogram law, see [42]. The Lie bracket is defined as follows. Let v and w, be derivations on M and let $f : M \to R$ be any real valued smooth function. The Lie bracket of v and w is the derivation defined by

$$[v, w](f) = v(w(f)) - w(v(f)),$$

see [10].

Thus the composite action $v_i|_p$ generated by the i-th agent to control the process is a composition of the form of (24). Moreover from a version of the Chattering lemma and duality [18], we can show that this action can be expressed as a linear combination of the primitive actions available to the agent as follows.

$$[v_{i,n_1},[v_{i,n_2},v_{i,n_3}]] = \sum_j \gamma_j^i(\alpha)v_{i,j} \tag{25}$$

$$\sum_j \gamma_j^i(\alpha) = 1$$

where the coefficients γ_j^i determined by the fraction of time that each primitive action $v_{i,j}$ is used by agent i.

The effect of the field defined by the composite action $v_i|_p$ on any smooth function (equivalent function class) is computed by expanding the right hand side of (23) in a Lie-Taylor series [10]. In particular, we can express the change in the behavior modification functions C_i^u due to the flow over the interval Δ in terms of $v_i|_p$. The evolution of the modified behavior function C_i^u over the interval starting at point p is given by

$$C_i^u(t+\Delta,p'') = C_i^u(t,\Psi_i(t+\Delta,p)) \tag{26}$$

Expanding the right hand side of (26) in a Lie-Taylor series around (t,p), we obtain,

$$C_i^u(t+\Delta,p'') = \sum_j \frac{\left(v_i|_p(C_i^u(p,t))\right)^j \Delta^j}{j!}$$

where

$$\left(v_i|_p(\cdot)\right)^j = v_i|_p\left(\left(v_i|_p(\cdot)\right)^{j-1}\right) \tag{27}$$

and

$$\left(v_i|_p\right)^0(f) = f \text{ for all } f.$$

In general, the series in the right hand side of (27) will have countable many non-zero terms. In our case, since the topology of M is finite due to the fact that it is generated by finitely many logic clauses, this series will have only finitely many non-zero terms. Intuitively, this is so because in computing powers of derivations (i.e., limits of differences), we need only to distinguish among different neighboring points. In our formulation of the topology of M, this can only be imposed by the information in the clauses of the agent's Knowledge Base. Since each agent's Knowledge Base has only finitely many clauses, there is a term in the expansion of the series in which the power of the derivation goes to zero because we cannot distinguish between two points which cannot be separated by open sets in the finite topology. This is important because it allows the series in the right-hand side to be effectively generated by a locally finite automaton. We will expand on the construction of this automaton in the next section when we discuss the inference procedure carried out by each agent.

We note that given the set of primitive actions available to each agent, the composite action is determined by the vector of fraction functions α_j . We will see in the next section that this vector is inferred by each agent from the proof of existence of solutions of an optimization problem.

Now we can write the specific nature of the model formulated in expression (13). At time t and at point $p \in M$ the behavior modification function of agent i is given by :

$$C_i^u(p, t) = C_i^u(p, t^-) + S_{r,i}(p, t) + \sum_k Q_{i,k} B_k(p, t^-) \qquad (28)$$

where t^- is the end point of the previous update interval, $S_{r,i}$ is the external perturbation function to agent i, and $Q_{i,k}$ is a multiplier determining how much of the current behavior modification requirements of agent A_k is allocated to agent A_i. This allocation is determined from the characteristics of the process both agents are controlling and from the process description encoded in the agent's knowledge base. The actual request for service from agent k to agent i is thus the term, $Q_{i,k} B_k(p, t^-)$. The information sent to agent i by agent k is the behavior modification function $B_k(p, t^-)$ at the end of the previous interval. Finally the point $p \in M$ carries the current status of the process monitored by the agents appearing in (28). Agent k thus contributes to Agent i's new control only if $Q_{i,k} \neq 0$.

This concludes our description of the model. For space considerations, some details have been left out. In particular those related to the strategy for activation and deactivation of agents. These will be discussed in a future paper.

4   The Multiple Agent Hybrid Control Architecture

In this section, we describe the main operational and functional characteristics of our intelligent controller. As we mentioned in the introduction, this controller is implemented as a distributed system composed of agents and a communication network. We referred to the latter as the control network in the previous section. The architecture realizing this system, called the Multiple-Agent Hybrid Control Architecture (MAHCA), operates as an on-line distributed theorem prover. At any update time, each active agent generates actions as side effects of proving an existentially quantified subtheorem (lemma) which encodes the desired behavior of the logic communications network as viewed by the agent. The conjunction of lemmas at each instant of time, encodes the desired behavior of the entire network.

Each agent of MAHCA consists of five modules: a Planner, a Dynamic Knowledge Base, a Deductive Inferencer, an Adapter and a Knowledge Decoder. We briefly overview the functionality of an agent in terms of its modules.

The *Knowledge Base* stores the requirements of operations or processes controlled by the agent. It also encodes system constraints, inter-agent protocols and constraints, sensory data, operational and logic principles and a set of primitive inference operations defined in the domain of equational terms.

The *Planner* generates a statement representing the desired behavior of the system as an existentially quantified logic expression herein referred to as the Behavior Statement.

The *Inferencer* determines whether this statement is a theorem in the theory currently active in the Knowledge Base. If the behavior statement logically follows from the current status of the knowledge base, the inferencer generates, as a side effect of proving this behavior statement to be true, the current control action schedule. If the behavior statement does not logically follow from the current status of the knowledge base, that is, the desired behavior is not realizable, the inferencer transmits the failed terms to the *Adapter* module for replacement or modification.

Finally, the *Knowledge Decoder* translates data from the other agents and incorporates them into the Knowledge Base of the agent.

In each agent of MAHCA, the behavior statement is the formulation of a relaxed variational optimization problem whose successful resolution produces an action schedule of the form of (24). Each agent operates as a real-time theorem prover in the domain of relaxed variational theory [39]. A customized version of this theory, enriched with elements of differential geometry, equational logic and automata theory provides a general representation for the dynamics, constraints, requirements and logic of the control network . We devote the rest of this section to the discussion of the main elements of this theory in the context of the operational features of MACHA.

The architecture is composed of two items: The Control Agent, and the control network. These items are illustrated in Figures 4 and 5 respectively. We will discuss them in the remaining of this section.

4.1 Architectural Elements of a control agent:

We will discuss next the functionality of the five modules of a control agent. These are: the Knowledge Base, the Planner, the Inferencer, the Knowledge Decoder and the Adapter.

4.1.1. Knowledge Base: The Knowledge Base consists of a set of equational first order logic clauses with second order extensions. The syntax of clauses is similar to the ones in the Prolog language. Each clause is of the form

$$Head \leftarrow Body \tag{29}$$

where *Head* is a functional form, $p(x_1, ... x_n)$, taking values in the binary set $[true, false]$ and $x_1, x_2, \ldots, x_n$ are variables or parameters in the domain M of the MAHCA network. The symbol $\leftarrow$ stands for logical implication. The variables appearing in the clause head are assumed to be universally quantified. The *Body* of a clause is a conjunction of one or more logical terms

$$e_1 \wedge e_2 \wedge \ldots \wedge e_n \tag{30}$$

where $\wedge$ is the logical 'and'. Each term in (30) is a relational form. A relational form is one of the following: an equational form, an inequational form, a covering form, or a clause head. The logical value of each of these forms is either true or false. A relational form e_i is true precisely at the set of tuples of values S_i of the domain taken by the variables where the relational form is satisfied and is false for the complement of that set. Thus for $e_i = e_i(x_1, \ldots, x_n)$, S_i is the possibly empty subset of M^n

$$S_i = \{(x_1, \ldots, x_n) \in M^n : e_i(x_1, \ldots, x_n) = true\}$$

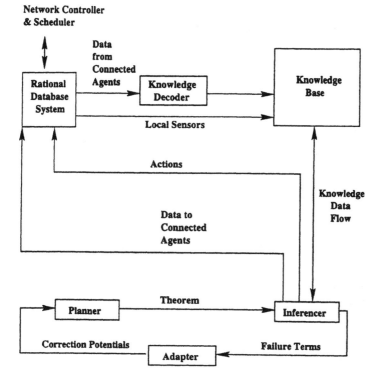

Fig. 4. Control Agent

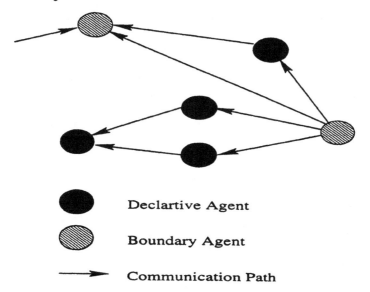

Fig. 5. Network of Cooperating Control Agents

so that

$$e_i(x_1, \ldots, x_n) = false \text{ if } (x_1, \ldots, x_n) \in M^n/S_i.$$

The generic structure of a relational form is given in Table 1.

Form	Structure	Meaning
equational	$w(x_1, \ldots, x_n) = v(x_1, \ldots, x_n)$	equal
inequational	$w(x_1, \ldots, x_n) \neq v(x_1, \ldots, x_n)$	not equal
covering	$w(x_1, \ldots, x_n) < v(x_1, \ldots, x_n)$	partial order
clause head	$q(x_1, \ldots, x_n)$	recursion,chaining

Table 1. Structure of the Relational Form

In Table 1, w and v are polynomic forms with respect to a finite set of operations whose definitional and property axioms are included in the Knowledge Base. A polynomic form v is an object of the form $v(x_1, \ldots, x_n) = \sum_{\omega \in \Omega}(v, \omega) \cdot \omega$ where Ω^* is the free monoid generated by the variable symbols $\{x_1, \ldots, x_n\}$ under juxtaposition. The term (v, ω) is called the coefficient of v at ω. The coefficients of a polynomic form v take values in the domain of definition of the clauses. The domain in which the variables in a clause head take values is the manifold M described in section 2. The logical interpretation of (29) and (30) is that the *Head* is true if the conjunction of the terms of *Body* are jointly true for instances of the variables in the clause head. M is contained in the Cartesian product :

$$M \subseteq G \times S \times X \times A \tag{31}$$

where G is the space of goals, S is the space of sensory data, X is the space of controller states and A is the space of control actions. These were described in section 2. G, S, X, and A are manifolds themselves whose topological structure are defined by the specification clauses in the Knowledge Base, see Figure 6. These clauses, which are application dependent, encode the requirements on the closed-loop behavior of the model of the agent. In fact the closed loop behavior, which we will define later in this section in terms of a variational formulation, is characterized by continuous curves with values in M. This continuity condition is central because it is equivalent to requiring the system to look for actions that make the closed loop behavior satisfy the requirements of the plant model.

The denotational semantics of each clause in the knowledge base is one of the following:

1. a conservation principle,
2. an invariance principle, or
3. a constraint principle.

Conservation principles are one or more clauses about the balance of a particular process in the dynamics of the system or the computational resources. For instance, equation (28) encoded as a clause expresses the conservation of demand in the logic communications network

$$conservation\_of\_unsatisfied\_demand(p,t,[Q_{i,k}],S_{r,i},[B_k],\Delta,C_i^u(t,p)) \leftarrow$$

$$C_i^u(t+2\Delta,p'')=\sum_j \frac{\left(v_i|_p(C_i^u(t+\Delta,p'))\right)\Delta^j}{j!} \wedge$$

/* encoding of equation (13) */

$$C_i^u(t+\Delta,p')=C_i^u(t,p)+S_{r,i}(t,p)+\sum_k Q_{i,k}B_k(t,p,\dot{p}) \wedge \qquad (32)$$

/* encoding of equation (15) */

$$process\_evolution(p,t,p'') \wedge \text{ /* encoding of equation (13) */}$$

$$consevation\_of\_unsatisfied\_demand(p'',t+\Delta,[Q_{i,k}],S_{r,i},[B_k],\Delta,C_i^u(t+2\Delta,p''))$$

In (32), the first equational term relates the segment car density for agent i at the current time to the density in the past and the net current density of the other agents connected to agent i. The last term of the rule implements the recursion.

As another example, consider the following clause representing conservation of computational resources:

$$comp(Load,Process,Op\_count,Limit) \leftarrow process(process\_count)$$
$$\wedge \ process\_count \cdot Load_1 - Op\_count < Load$$
$$\wedge \ Load_1 < Limit$$
$$\wedge \ comp(Load_1,Process,Op\_count,Limit).$$

where $Load$ corresponds to the current computational burden, measured in VIPS (Variable Instantiations Per Second), $Process$ is a clause considered for execution, and Op_count is the current number of terms in process.

Conservation principles always involve recursion whose scope is not necessarily a single clause, as in the example above, but with chaining throughout several clauses.

Invariance principles are one or more clauses establishing constants of the evolution of agent's behavior modification functions in a general sense. These principles include stationarity, which plays a pivotal role in the formulation of the theorems proved by the architecture, and geodesics. The necessary conditions for maximizing throughput in the freeway network constitute an example of this type of principle. The importance of invariance principles lies in the reference they provide for the direction of unexpected events.

Constraint principles are clauses representing engineering limits to actuators or sensors and, most importantly, behavior policies. The clauses defining the capacity function in each segment are examples of these type of principles. Another example in this application is given by the clauses that define the lifting strategy for embedding discrete varying trajectories into M (interpolation rules).

The clause database is organized in a nested hierarchical structure illustrated in Figure 6. The bottom of this hierarchy contains the equations that characterize the algebraic structure defining the terms of relational forms, i.e an algebraic variety [45].

At the next level of the hierarchy, three types of clauses are stored: Generic Control Specifications, System Representation and Goal Class Representation.

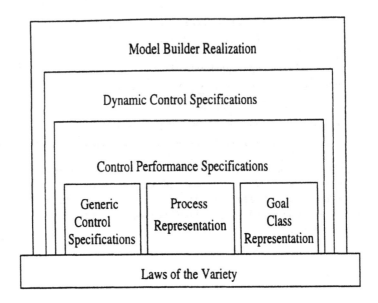

Fig. 6. Knowledge Base Organization

The *Generic Control Specifications* are clauses expressing general desired behavior of the system. They include statements about stability, complexity and robustness that are generic to the class of declarative rational controllers. These specifications are written by constructing clauses that combine laws of the kind which use the Horn clause format described earlier. Examples of these types of clausse are the one that specifies the range of the parameters in the traffic model for which the system is stable.

The *Process Representation* is given by clauses characterizing the dynamic behavior and structure of the plant, which includes sensors and actuators. These clauses are written as conservation principles for the dynamic behavior and as invariance principles for the structure. As in the case of Generic Control Specifications, they are constructed by combining a variety of laws in the equational Horn clause format. An example of this type of clause are the density and velocity equations of the freeway segments given in section 2 encoded in Horn clause format.

The *Goal Class Representation* contains clauses characterizing sets of desirable operation points in the domain (points in the manifold M). These clauses are expressed as soft constraints; that is, constraints that can be violated for finite intervals of time. They express the ultimate purpose of the controller but not its behavior over time.

The next level of the hierarchy involves the *Control Performance Specifications*. These are typically problem dependent criteria and constraints. They are written in equational Horn clause format. They include generic constraints such as speed and time of response, and qualitative properties of state trajectories [39].

Dynamic Control Specifications are equational Horn clauses whose bodies are modified as a function of the sensor and goal commands.

Finally, *Model Builder Realization* clauses constitute a recipe for building a procedural model (an automaton,) for generating variable instantiation (unification), and for theorem proving.

4.1.2. The Planner:

The function of the theorem Planner, which is domain-specific, is to generate, for each update interval, a symbolic statement of the desired behavior of the system, as viewed, say by agent j, throughout the interval. The theorem statement that it generates has the following form.

Given a set of primitive actions there exists a control schedule $v_i|_p$ of the form (25) and a fraction function differential $d\alpha(\cdot)$ (Figure 3) in the control interval $[t, t + \Delta)$ such that $d\alpha(\cdot)$ minimizes the functional

$$\int_t^{t+\Delta} L_i\big(\Psi_i(\tau, p), v_i|_p(G(_i(\tau, p)))\big)\, d\alpha(p, d\tau) \tag{33}$$

subject to the following constraints:

$$g_i(S_i, \Psi_i(t + \Delta, p)) = G_i(t, X_i)$$
$$\text{(local goal for the interval)},$$
$$\sum_m Q_{i,m}(p, t) L_m(p, t) = V_i(p, t) \tag{34}$$
$$\text{(inter-agent constraint, see (28))}$$
$$\text{and}$$
$$\int_t^{t+\Delta} d\alpha(p, d\tau) = 1$$

In (33), L_i is the *Local Relaxed Lagrangian* of the system as viewed by Agent i for the current interval of control $[t, t + \Delta)$. This function, which maps the Cartesian product of the state and control spaces into the real line with the topology defined by the clauses in the knowledge base, captures the dynamics, constraints and requirements of the system as viewed by agent i. The relaxed Lagrangian function L_i is a continuous projection in the topology defined by the knowledge base (see [36]) in the coordinates of the i-th agent of the global Lagrangian function L that characterizes the system as a whole.

In (34), p represents the state of the process under control as viewed by the agent and G_i is the parallel transport operator bringing the goal to the current interval, see [27]. The operator G_i is constructed by lifting to the manifold the composite flow (see equation (23)). We note that the composite flow and the action schedule are determined once the fraction function is known and that this function is the result of the optimization (33), (34). In particular, the action schedule is constructed as a linear combination of primitive actions, see equation (25).

The term $d\alpha(\cdot)$ in (33) is a Radon probability measure [40] on the set of primitive control actions or derivations that the agent can execute for the interval $[t, t + \Delta)$. It measures, for the interval, the percentage of time to be spent in each of the primitive

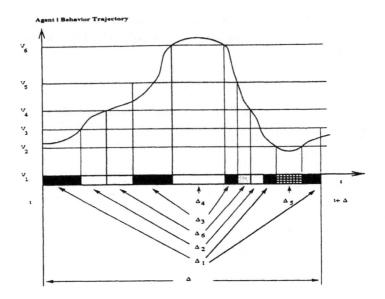

Fig. 7. Illustration of optimization

derivations. The central function of the control agent is to determine this mixture of actions for each control interval. This function is carried out by each agent by inferring from the current status of the knowledge base whether a solution of the optimization problem stated by the current theorem exists, and, if so, to generate corresponding actions and state updates. Figure 7 illustrates the relations between the primitive actions and the fraction of Δ they are active in the interval $[t, t + \Delta)$.

The expressions in (34) constitute the constraints imposed in the relaxed optimization problem solved by the agent. The first one is the local goal constraint expressing the general value of the state at the end of the current interval. The second represents the constraints imposed on the agent by the other agents in the network. Finally, the third one indicates that is a probability measure. Under relaxation and with the appropriate selection of the domain, see [21], the optimization problem stated in (33) and (34) is a convex optimization problem. This is important because it guarantees that if a solution exists, it is unique up to probability, and also, it guarantees the computational effectiveness of the inference method that the agent uses for proving the theorem.

The construction of the theorem statement given by (33) and (34) is the central task carried out in the Planner. It characterizes the desired behavior of the process as viewed by the agent in the current interval so that its requirements are satisfied and the system "moves" towards its goal in an optimal manner.

4.1.3. Adapter:

The function under the integral in (33) includes a term, referred to as the "catch-all" potential, which is not associated with any clause in the Knowledge Base. Its function is to measure unmodeled dynamic events. This monitoring function is carried out by the Adapter which implements a generic commutator principle similar to the Lie bracket discussed in section 3.1, see (24). Under this principle, if the value of the catch-all potential is empty, the current theorem statement adequately models the status of the system. On the other hand, if the theorem fails, meaning that there is a mismatch between the current statement of the theorem and system status, the catch-all potential carries the equational terms of the theorem that caused the failure. These terms are negated and conjuncted together by the Inferencer according to the commutation principle (which is itself defined by equational clauses in the Knowledge Base) and stored in the Knowledge Base as an adaptation dynamic clause. The Adapter then generates a potential symbol, which is characterized by the adaptation clause and corresponding tuning constraints. This potential is added to criterion for the theorem characterizing the interval.

The new potential symbol and tuning constraints are sent to the Planner which generates a modified local Lagrangian for the agent and goal constraint. The new theorem, thus constructed, represents adapted behavior of the system. This is the essence of reactive structural adaptation in the our model

At this point, we pause in our description to address the issue of robustness. To a large extent, the adapter mechanism of each controller agent provides the system with a generic and computationally effective means to recover from failures or unpredictable events. Theorem failures are symptoms of mismatches between what the agent thinks the system looks like and what it really looks like. The adaptation clause incorporates knowledge into the agent's Knowledge Base which represents a recovery strategy. The Inferencer, discussed next, effects this strategy as part of its normal operation.

4.1.4. Inferencer:

The Inferencer is an on-line equational theorem prover. The class of theorems it can prove are represented by statements of the form of (33) and (34), expressed by an existentially quantified conjunction of equational terms of the form:

$$\exists Z \big(W_1(Z,p) \; rel_i \; V_1(Z,p) \wedge \ldots \wedge W_n(Z,p) \; rel_i \; V_n(Z,p) \big) \qquad (35)$$

where Z is a tuple of variables each taking values in the domain D, p is a list of parameters in D, and $\{W_i, V_i\}$ are polynomial terms in the semiring polynomial algebra:

$$\tilde{D}\langle \Omega \rangle \qquad (36)$$

where $\tilde{D} = (D, \langle +, \cdot, 1, 0 \rangle)$ a semiring algebra with additive unit 0 and multiplicative unit 1. In (35), rel_i, $i = 1, \ldots, n$ are binary relations on the polynomial algebra. Each rel_i can be either an equality relation ($=$), inequality relation ($\neq$), or a partial order relation ($<$). In a given theorem, more than one partial order relation may appear. In each theorem, at least one of the terms is a partial order relation that defines a complete lattice on the algebra that corresponds to the optimization problem. This lattice has a minimum element if the optimization problem has a minimum. Given a theorem statement of the form of (35) and a knowledge base of equational clauses, the Inferencer determines whether the statement logically follows from the clauses in the Knowledge Base, and if so, as a side effect of the proof, generates a non-empty subset of tuples with entries in M giving values to Z. These entries determine the agent's actions. Thus, a side effect is instantiation of the agent's decision variables. In (36), Ω is a set of primitive unary operations, $\{v_i\}$, the infinitesimal primitive fields defined in section 3. Each v_i maps the semiring algebra, whose members are power series involving the composition of operators from Z to itself

$$v_i : \tilde{D}\langle\langle Z \rangle\rangle \rightarrow \tilde{D}\langle\langle Z \rangle\rangle. \qquad (37)$$

These operators are characterized by axioms in the Knowledge Base and are process dependent. In formal logic, the implemented inference principle can be stated as follows: Let Σ be the set of clauses in the Knowledge Base. Let $\Rightarrow$ represent implication. Proving the theorem means to show that it logically follows from Σ, i.e.

$$\Sigma \Rightarrow theorem. \qquad (38)$$

The proof is accomplished by sequences of applications of the following inference axioms:

(i) equality axioms
(ii) inequality axioms
(iii) partial order axioms
(iv) compatibility axioms
(v) convergence axioms
(vi) knowledge base axioms
(vii) limit axioms

The specifics of these inference axioms can be found in [13] where it is shown that each of the inference principles can be expressed as an operator on the Cartesian product

$$\tilde{D}\langle\langle W \rangle\rangle \times \tilde{D}\langle\langle W \rangle\rangle. \qquad (39)$$

Each inference operator transforms a relational term into another relational term. The inferencer applies sequences of inference operators on the equational terms of the theorem until these terms are reduced to either a set of ground equations of the form of (40) or it determines that no such ground form exists.

$$Z_i = \alpha_i, \alpha_i \in D \qquad (40)$$

The mechanism by which the inferencer carries out the procedure described above is by building a procedure for variable goal instantiation which in our case is a locally finite automaton. We refer to this automaton as the Proof Automaton. This important feature is unique to our approach. The proof procedure is customized to the particular theorem statement and Knowledge Base instance it is currently handling. The structure of the proof automaton generated by the Inferencer is illustrated in Figure 8.

In Figure 8, the initial state represents the equations associated with the theorem. In general, each state corresponds to a derived equational form of the theorem

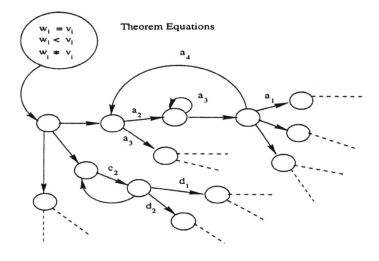

Theorem Equations

Inference Rules: a_i , b_i , c_i , d_i , e_i

Fig. 8. Conceptual Structure of the Proof Automaton

through the application of a chain of inference operators to the initial state that is represented by the path,

$$S_0 \xrightarrow{inf_1} S_1 \xrightarrow{inf_2} \ldots \xrightarrow{inf_k} S_k.$$

Each edge in the automaton corresponds to one of the possible inferences. A state is terminal if its equational form is a tautology, or it corresponds to a canonical form whose solution form is stored in the Knowledge Base. In traversing the automaton state graph, values or expressions are assigned to the variables. In a terminal state, the equational terms are all ground states (see (40)). If the automaton contains at least one path starting in the initial state and ending in a terminal state, then the theorem is true with respect to the given Knowledge Base and the resulting variable instantiation is a valid one. If this is not the case, the theorem is false. The function of the complete partial order term present in the conjunction of each theorem provable by the inferencer is to provide a guide for constructing the proof automaton. This is done by transforming the equational terms of the theorem into a canonical fixed point equation, called the Kleene-Schutzenberger Equation (KSE) [13], which constitutes a blueprint for the construction of the proof automaton. This fixed point coincides with the solution of the optimization problem formulated in (33) (34), when it has a solution. The general form of KSE is

$$Z = E(p) \cdot Z + T(p) \tag{41}$$

In (41), E is a square matrix, with each entry a rational form constructed from the basis of inference operators described above, and T is a vector of equational forms from the Knowledge Base. Each non-empty entry, $E_{i,j}$, in E corresponds to the edge in the proof automaton connecting states i and j. The binary operator ".·" between $E(p)$ and Z represents the "apply inference to" operator. Terminal states are determined by the non-empty terms of T. The p terms are custom parameter values in the inference operator terms in $E(\cdot)$.

A summary of the procedure executed by the inferencer is presented in Figure 9.

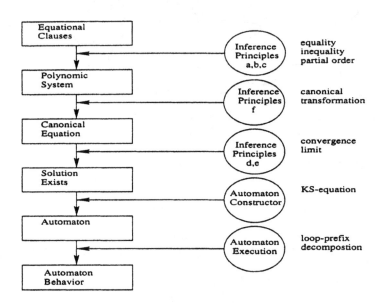

Fig. 9. Summary of Inferencer Procedure

We note that the construction of the automaton is carried out from the canonical equation and not by a non-deterministic application of the inference rules. This approach reduces the computational complexity of the canonical equation (low polynomic) and is far better than applying the inference rules directly (exponential).

The automaton is simulated to generate instances of the state, action and evaluation variables using an automaton decomposition procedure [41] which requires $nlog_2n$ time, where n is the number of states of the automaton. This "divide and conquer" procedure implements the recursive decomposition of the automaton into a cascade of parallel unitary (one initial and one terminal state) automata. Each of the resulting automata on this decomposition is executed independently of the others. The behavior of the resulting network of automata is identical with the behavior obtained from the original automaton, but with feasible time complexity.

The Inferencer for each control agent fulfills two functions, (i) to generate a proof for the system behavior theorem of each agent generated by the Planner (equations (33) and (34)) and (ii) to function as the central element in the Knowledge Decoder. We now describe its function for proving the behavior theorem. Later, we will overview its function as part of the Knowledge Decoder. To show how the Inferencer is used to prove the Planner theorem, (33), (34), first, we show how this theorem is transformed into a pattern of the form of (35). Since (33), (34) formulates a convex optimization problem, a necessary and sufficient condition for optimality is provided by the following dynamic programming formulation.

$$V_i(Y, \tau) = inf_{\alpha_i} \int_\tau L_i(\Psi_i(\tau, Y), v_i|_p(G_i(\tau, p))) d\alpha(p, d\tau) \qquad (42)$$

$$\frac{\partial V_i}{\partial \tau} = inf_{\alpha_i} H(Y, \frac{\partial V_i}{\partial \tau}, \alpha_i)$$

$$\text{where } Y(t) = p \text{ and } \tau \in [t, t + \Delta)$$

In (42), the function V_i, called the optimal cost-to-go function, characterizes minimality starting from any arbitrary point inside the current interval. The second equation is the corresponding Hamilton-Jacobi-Bellman equation for the problem stated in (33) and (34) where H is the Hamiltonian of the relaxed problem. This formulation provides the formal coupling between deductive theorem proving and optimal control theory. The inferencer allows the real-time optimal solution of the formal control problem resulting in intelligent distributed real-time control of the multiple-agent system. The central idea for inferring a solution to (42) is to expand the cost-to-go function $V(.,.)$ in a rational power series V in the algebra

$$\tilde{D}\langle\langle(Y, \tau)\rangle\rangle. \qquad (43)$$

Replacing V for V_j in the second equation in (42) gives two items: a set of polynomic equations for the coefficients of V and a partial order expression for representing the optimality. Because of convexity and rationality of V, the number of equations to characterize the coefficients of V is finite. The resulting string of conjunctions of coefficient equations and the optimality partial order expression are in the form of (35). A detailed algorithmic approach to solving (42) which we call hybrid dynamic programming can be found in [28]

In summary, for each agent, the inferencer operates according to the following procedure.

Step 1: Load current theorem (33), (34).
Step 2: Transform theorem to equational form (35) via (42).
Step 3: Execute proof according to figure 9.

If the theorem logically follows from the Knowledge Base (i.e., it is true), the inferencer procedure will terminate on step 3 with actions. If the theorem does not logically follow from the Knowledge Base, the Adapter is activated, and the theorem is modified by the Planner according to the strategy outlined above. This mechanism is the essence of reactivity in the agent. Because of relaxation and convexity, this mechanism ensures that the controllable set of the domain is strictly larger than the mechanism without this correction strategy.

4.1.5 Knowledge Decoder:

The function of the Knowledge Decoder is to translate knowledge data from the network into the agent's Knowledge Base by updating the inter-agent specification clauses. These clauses characterize the second constraint in (42). Specifically, they express the constraints imposed by the rest of the network on each agent. They also characterize the global-to-local transformations (see [23]). Finally, they provide the rules for building generalized multipliers for incorporating the inter-agent constraints into a complete unconstrained criterion, which is then used to build the cost-to-go function in the first expression in (42). A generalized multiplier is an operator that transforms a constraint into a potential term. This potential is then incorporated into the original Lagrangian of the agent which now accounts explicitly for the constraint.

The Knowledge Decoder has a built-in inferencer used to infer the structure of the multiplier and transformations by a procedure similar to the one described for (14). Specifically, the multiplier and transformations are expanded in a rational power series in the algebra defined in (43). Then the necessary conditions for duality are used to determine the conjunctions of equational forms and a partial order expression needed to construct a theorem of the form of (42) whose proof generates a multiplier for adjoining the constraint to the Lagrangian of the agent as another potential.

The conjunction of equational forms for each global-to-local transformation is constructed by applying the following invariant imbedding principle:

> For each agent, the actions at given time t in the current interval, as computed according to (42), are the same actions computed at t when the formulation is expanded to include the previous, current, and next intervals.

By transitivity and convexity of the criterion, the principle can be analytically extended to the entire horizon. The invariant imbedding equation has the same structure as the dynamic programming equation given in (42), but with the global criterion and global Hamiltonians instead of the corresponding local ones.

The local-to-global transformations are obtained by inverting the global-to-local transformations which, in turn, are obtained by expressing the invariant embedding equation as an equational theorem of the form of (35). These inverses exist because of convexity of the relaxed Lagrangian and the rationality of the power series.

It is important at this point to interpret the functionality of the Knowledge Decoder of each agent in terms of what it does. The multiplier described above has the effect of aggregating the rest of the system and the other agents into an equivalent companion system and companion agent, respectively, as viewed by the current agent. This is illustrated in Figure 10.

The aggregation model (Figure 10) describes how each agent perceives the rest of the network. This unique feature allows us to characterize the scalability of the architecture in a unique manner. Namely in order to determine computational complexity of an application, we have only to consider the agent with the highest complexity (i.e., the local agent with the most complex criterion) and its companion.

4.2 Architectural Elements of a Declarative Control Network

The inter-agent communication network's main function is to transfer inter-agent constraints among agents according to a protocol written in equational Horn clause language. These constraints include application dependent data and, most importantly, inter-agent synchronization. The inter-agent synchronization strategy is very simple. An agent is synchronous with respect to the network if its inter-agent constraint multiplier is continuous with respect to the current instance of its active

System

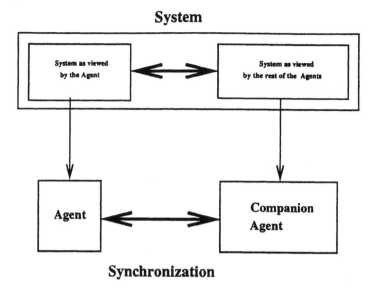

Synchronization

Fig. 10. The Companion Agent

knowledge. Since the equational Horn clause format allows for the effective test of continuity (which is implicitly carried out by the inferencer in the Knowledge Decoder), a failure in the Knowledge Decoder theorem results in a corrective action toward re-establishing continuity with respect to the topology defined by the current instance of the Knowledge Base [20].

The specification of the geometry of the network, as a function of time, is dictated primarily by global observability. By global observability, we mean the closure of the knowledge of the system as whole relative to the scope the systems reactivity. One of the central tasks in any application is to provide knowledge in the equational clause format to characterize global observability for the hybrid system.

4.3 Summary the MAHCA Architecture

Our formulation gives a precise statement of a hybrid control problem in terms of a multiple agent hybrid declarative control. Our approach characterizes the problem via a knowledge base of equational rules that describes the dynamics, constraints and requirements of plant.

For the traffic control application, the Behavior statement or ATC statement is represented as a Lagrangian of the form

$$min_\alpha \int_\Omega L(\rho^c, v^c, \rho^v, v^v, \frac{\partial \rho^c}{\partial x}, \frac{\partial v^c}{\partial x}, \frac{\partial \rho^v}{\partial x}, \frac{\partial v^v}{\partial x}, \frac{\partial \rho^c}{\partial t}, \frac{\partial v^c}{\partial t}, \frac{\partial \rho^v}{\partial t}, \frac{\partial v^v}{\partial t}, t, x)d\alpha \quad (44)$$

where $\Omega = \{\langle x, t \rangle : 0 \leq t \leq \infty, 0 \leq x \leq 2.8\}$

The Goal is maximize the average throughput, given as:

$$max\left(lim_{T\to\infty}\int_0^T\int_0^L Q(\rho^c, v^c, \rho^v, v^v, V^u)dxdt.\right) \tag{45}$$

The sensor data is given by

$$\begin{array}{cc} \rho^c(\tau, x_i) & v^c(\tau, x_i) \\ \rho^v(\tau, x_i) & v^v(\tau, x_i) \end{array}$$

where $i = 1, 2, \ldots, 9$ to represent sensor inputs at one-third mile intervals and $\tau = 1, 2, \ldots$ seconds.

Finally, the actions for the traffic control consist solely of the commanded velocity vector V^u.

We have developed a canonical representation of interacting networks of controllers. Given a connectivity graph with N nodes (controllers) and the corresponding agent's knowledge bases, a network of 2N agents can be constructed with the same input-output characteristics, so that each agent interacts only with another (equivalent) companion agent, whose knowledge base is an abstraction of the knowledge in the network. Thus, in general, the multiple-agent controller for any network configuration is reduced to a set of agent pairs.

One agent of the agent pair maintains coordination with other agent pairs across the network. We call that agent of the pair which represents network information the Thevenin Agent, after the author of a similar theorem in electrical network theory. The proof carried out by the Thevennin Agent generates, as a side effect, coordination rules that define what and how often to communicate with other agents. These rules also define what the controller needs from the network to maintain intelligent control of its physical plant.

Our approach develops a canonical way to prove the theorem characterizing the desired behavior for each agent by constructing and executing on-line a finite state machine called the "proof automaton." The inference process is represented as a recursive variational problem in which the criterion is an integral of a function called the Generalized Lagrangian. The Generalized Lagrangian maps the Cartesian product of equational rules and inference principles to the real line, thus effectively providing a hill-climbing heuristic for the inference strategy of the theorem prover (see section 3). In MAHCA the inference steps play a role analogous to action signals in conventional control while the vector fields on the carrier manifold M constitute generators of feedback laws (section 2).

5 Simulation

5.1 Simulation Parameters and Operation

The simulation parameters and constants for the demonstration runs were

T Length of simulation run = 20 minutes, with data snapshots of 20 second intervals (fixed).

k_3 Percentage of cars complying with commanded velocity varied from 5% to 9%. This rule was not rigid. The simulation runs demonstrated adaption of this rule (to a lower value) when the system began drifting to an instable condition.

δ Average response time = 1.5 seconds (variable).

C^c Car capacity coefficient, determined for a 4 lane freeway.

Those parameters marked "variable" were subject to adaptation by the architecture in response to explicit or inferred changes in the environment.

Accidents were introduced at a random point (after a 100 second "priming" period) at a random location between freeway position $x = 1.38$ and $x = 1.43$. At this point C^c was reduced by one-half.

The simulation uses a standard 4-th order Runga-Kutta Integration scheme for time and 2-nd order Adam-Bashworth integration for space.

The simulation produces loop sensor values as inputs for the control functions. Sensors appear in pairs (120 ft apart) at one-third mile intervals and provide velocity and density data for vehicles and voids. The simulation simulates ideal sensors, free of bad data and able to detect voids.

The simulation was implemented in Prolog using the same set of equations as those encoded into the Knowledge Base. Although the equations are the same, the simulation is completely different operational entity and only interacts with the MAHCA control agents by providing them with sensor inputs and accepting their control actions.

Execution of the simulation is performed by a single top-level prolog rule.

$$
\begin{aligned}
traffic\_demo(Inputs, Outputs) : - \\
simulation\_on\_off(Stop), \\
simulation(Inputs, Sensor\_out, Action\_in, Outputs), \\
controller\_on\_off(Bool), \\
record(Actions\_in, Sensors\_out, Inputs, Outputs), \\
repeat.
\end{aligned}
\tag{46}
$$

In this rule, *traffic_demo* is the main rule. The *Inputs* parameter is expected to contain the operational parameters (such as maximum running time). The *Outputs* parameter will become instantiated with the status of the simuluation.

The *simulation_on_off* rule provides a mechanism for setting *Stop* to true to shut down the simulation.

In *Simulation*, the *Inputs* and *Action_in* parameters are used as inputs to compute the next set of *Sensor_out* values and a new set of simulation *Outputs* (used for recording purposes only).

Like *simulation_on_off*, *contoller_on_off* is a mechanism for setting *Bool* to *True* to invoke the controller or *False* to turn it off. During the initial 100 second priming period, *Bool* will be *False*.

The *controller* rule invokes the inferencing process to compute a new set of *Action_in* values for the simulator from the set of *Sensor_out* values.

Finally, *record* will report, to the terminal and/or to the data files, the values from the action lists, sensor outputs, and other simulation and controller inputs and outputs. The data was recorded every 60 seconds, starting with $t = 160$, the end of the first control period following the initial 100 second priming.

5.2 Discussion

The control will compute and broadcast travel speeds for each segment of the freeway. When followed by individuals, the throughput of the whole system will increase. Compliance on the part of drivers assumes adoption of the philosophy that adherence to less than intuitive speeds is in their best interest.

The control can also be used to determine and transmit navigational instructions throughout a network of freeway corridors, accomplished by tracking the wave propagations over the segments and guiding a percentage of the vehicles to maximize throughput of the system as opposed to minimizing travel for individual cars.

In the abstraction of individual vehicles into a continuous wave model, some information is lost. Since the freeway segment is regarded as one unit, with a width parameter representing the number of lanes, knowledge of any particular lane is not tracked. Incidences, real, such as stalled vehicles, or imaginary, such as "rubber necking", are modeled as a reduction in the width of the segment. Individual vehicles are simply contributing particles to the wave, so exact speed and location of any one vehicle is not known.

This model can easily be extended to perform other duties for an intelligent highway system. For example, detection of incidents can be accomplished by inspecting shock waves which result for such discontinuities. From the characteristic of the shock wave, the nature of the incident can be determined, e.g. a slow moving truck or speeding emergency vehicle. This capability is theoretically possible and has been demonstrated in a simulation, but it is very difficult to validate with empirical data. By comparing inconsistencies between the observed and expected density and velocity values in the waves as they propagate along the freeway corridor, errant sensor data can be eliminated. For traffic signal processing, red lights can be viewed as a total restriction of the highway and green lights as an instantaneous removal of the restriction which is naturally coordinated with signal changes for yellow lights and cross traffic. The modeling of voids becomes especially important in these cases.

The reactive capability of the execution strategy of the architecture is exploited to provide two major functions. Appearance of shock waves in the solution triggers reactivity to decompose the wave generator into continuous and shock components to reflect changed conditions. Over the longer term, the reactivity can be used to fine tune the equations to account for subtle changes in the nature of the vehicles, such as average length, and driver policies, such as speeds and following distances.

5.3 Preliminary Analysis

This section gives a brief preliminary analysis of the results of simulations that were run by Brian Coles of Intermetrics. The referenced charts appear at the end of the paper. There are three sets of charts, one with 5 % of controlled cars, one with 8 % of controlled cars, and one with 9 % of controlled cars. (With this last set, the 9 % represents the initial percentage of controlled cars. Over time, this was lowered by the Inferencer.) In each set there are three graphs showing the densities and velocities of cars and voids, taken at $t = 160$, $t = 700$, and $t = 1300$, the end of the simulation run. The last two graphs in each set show the differences in velocity and density values over intervals equal to about $1/4$ of the simulation run. For all of these graphs, the horizontal units are miles along the corridor. Velocities are measured in miles/hour and densities are measured in cars (or voids) per mile.

Along the portion of the freeway corridor before the accident, the density wave initially has a high amplitude, but as the velocity control of the cars begins to take effect, the amplitude of the wave diminishes. Charts 1-3, 6-8, and 11-13 show this phenomena for samples of freeway dynamics at different times and for different percentages of control.

After the accident along the freeway, control is not needed because vehicle densities never approach the saturation limit. Vehicles are free to travel as fast as they want, within legal limits, of course.

For 9% control, versus no control, the throughput increases 28%. Less than 5% control yields unstable behavior and is not effective in eliminating grid-lock. As the percentage of controlled cars increases between 5% and 9%, the grid-lock is monotonically reduced, compare charts 3 and 13. At 9% control, the grid-lock is successfully cleared. Between 9% and 14%, the gridlock is successfully cleared, but throughput is reduced. In an effort to achieve the goal of maximizing throughput, the controller reduces the percentage of control vehicles. Above 14% control, the system experiences performance degradation due to overdeterminism.

The interaction between void and car density dynamics shown in charts 4, 5, 9, 10, 14, and 15 demonstrates many density distributions that are possible, but can not be generated by representing the dynamics as car densities alone.

The wave segments generated in the controller allow for easy decomposition between continuous and shock elements, see for example charts 1 and 6. This capability alone allows the control to infer accidents and recompute the control law accordingly. We observed a one-to-one correlation (as expected) between theorem failures and the appearance of the shock component.

In the accident region, the four variables show peaks, see charts 2, 7, 12. These peaks, however, do not appear at the same freeway locations. There are phase shifts which are due to the asymetry between the car and void particles. The void velocities has a phase shift over car velocities, see charts 4, 5, 9, 10, 14 and 15. This phase shift is expoited by the controller to schedule the commanded velocity profile to meet the goal of maximizing throughput. The effects of the dynamics due to an incident are detected earliest in the void density dynamics.

Void and car densities together appear to satisfy the additive conservation law, as to be expected from models for binary population dynamics (void and car particles).

The flow of velocity and density waves qualitatively agrees with emperical observation.

Our runs show that traffic congestion latency decreases significantly as the percentage of controlled cars increases. After incident removal with no control, the car density goes to nominal after 32 minutes. With 9% control the car density goes to nominal after only 12 minutes. This difference is directly due to the scheduling of velocities before the accident. That is, the command velocity distribution before the accident under control is lower than the velocity distribution with no control

References

1. Alur, R., Henzinger, T.A., and Sontag, E.D., eds., *Hybrid Systems III*, Lecture Notes in Computer Science vol. 1066, Springer-Verlag, (1996).

2. Antsaklis, P., Kohn, W., Nerode, A, and Sastry, S. eds., *Hybrid Systems II*, Lecture Notes in Computer Science vol. 999, Springer-Verlag, (1995).

3. Crossley, J.N., Remmel, J.B., Shore, R.A. and Sweedler, M.E., *Logical Methods* Birkhauser, (1993).

4. Dodhiawala, R.T., V. Jagoenathan and L.S. Baum, "Erasmus System Design: Performance Issues" Proceedings of Workshop on Blackboard Systems Implementation Issues, AAAI, Seattle, WA., July 1987.

5. Garcia, H.E. and A. Ray "Nonlinear Reinforcement Schemes for Learning Automata" Proceedings of the 29th IEEE CDC Conference, Vol. 4, pp 2204- 2207, Honolulu, HA, Dec. 5-7, 1990.

6. Ge, X., Kohn, W., Nerode, A. and Remmel, J.B., "Algorithms for Chattering Approximations to Relaxed Optimal Control. MSI Tech. Report 95-1, Cornell University. (1995)

7. Ge, X., Kohn, W., Nerode, A. and Remmel, J.B.,"Hybrid Systems: Chattering Approximations to Relaxed Control," *Hybrid Systems III*, (R. Alur, T.A. Henzinger, E.D. Sontag, eds.) Lecture Notes in Computer Science **1066**, Springer, (1996), 76-100.

8. Gelfand, I.M. and Fomin, S.V., *Calculus of Variations*, Prentice Hall, 1963.

9. Grossman, R.L., Nerode, A., Ravn, A. and Rischel, H. eds., *Hybrid Systems*, Lecture Notes in Computer Science 736, Springer-Verlag, (1993).

10. Kohn, W., "A Declarative Theory for Rational Controllers" Proceedings of the 27th IEEE CDC, Vol. 1, pp 131-136, Dec. 7-9, 1988, Austin, TX.

11. Kohn, W., "Application of Declarative Hierarchical Methodology for the Flight Telerobotic Servicer" Boeing Document G-6630-061, Final Report of NASA- Ames research service request 2072, Job Order T1988, Jan. 15, 1988.

12. Kohn, W., "Rational Algebras; a Constructive Approach" IR&D BE-499, Technical Document D-905-10107-2, July 7, 1989.

13. Kohn, W., "The Rational Tree Machine: Technical Description & Mathematical Foundations" IR&D BE-499, Technical Document D-905-10107-1, July 7, 1989.

14. Kohn, W., "Declarative Hierarchical Controllers" Proceedings of the Workshop on Software Tools for Distributed Intelligent Control Systems, pp 141-163, Pacifica, CA, July 17-19, 1990.

15. Kohn, W., "Declarative Multiplexed Rational Controllers" Proceedings of the 5th IEEE International Symposium on Intelligent Control, pp 794-803, Philadelphia, PA, Sept. 5, 1990.

16. Kohn, W., "Declarative Control Architecture" CACM Aug 1991,Vol34, No8.

17. Kohn, W., "Advanced Architectures and Methods for Knowledge-Based Planning and Declarative Control" IR&D BCS-021, ISMIS'91, Oct. 1991.

18. Kohn W., "Multiple Agent Inference in Equational Domains Via Infinitesimal Operators" Proc. Application Specific Symbolic Techniques in High Performance Computing Environment". The Fields Institute, Oct 17-20 1993.

19. Kohn W., "Multiple Agent Hybrid Control" Proc of the NASA-ARO Workshop on formal Models for Intelligent Control, MIT,sept 30- Oct2, 1193.

20. Kohn, W. and Murphy, A., "Multiple Agent Reactive Shop Floor Control" ISMIS'91, Oct. 1991.

21. Kohn, W. and Nerode, A., "Multiple Agent Declarative Control Architecture" Proc. of the workshop on Hybrid Systems, Lygby, Denmark, Oct 19-21, 1992.

22. Kohn, W. and Nerode, A., "Multiple Agent Hybrid Control Architecture" In [9], (1993), 297-316.

23. Kohn W., and Nerode, A., "Multiple-Agent Hybrid Systems" Proc. IEEE CDC 1992, vol 4, pp 2956-2972.

24. Kohn, W. and Nerode, A., "An Autonomous Systems Control Theory: An Overview" Proc. IEEE CACSD'92, March 17-19, Napa, Ca.,pp 200- 220.

25. Kohn W,, and Nerode A. "Models For Hybrid Systems: Automata, Topologies, Controllability, Observability" In [9], (1993) 317-356.

26. Kohn W. and Nerode, A., "Multiple Agent Autonomous Control-A Hybrid Systems Architecture" In [3], (1993) 593-623.

27. Kohn, W., Nerode, A. and Remmel, J.B., " Hybrid Systems as Finsler Manifolds: Finite State Control as Approximation to Connections", In [2], (1995), 294-321.

28. Kohn, W., Nerode, A. and Remmel, J.B., "Feedback Derivations: Near Optimal Controls for Hybrid Systems", Proceedings of CESA'96 IMACS Multiconference, Vol 2. 517-521.

29. Kohn, W., Nerode, A. and Remmel, J.B., "Continualization: A Hybrid Systems Control Technique for Computing", Proceedings of CESA'96 IMACS Multiconference, Vol 2. 507-511.

30. Kohn, W. and Remmel, J.B., "Digital to Hybrid Program Transformations", Proceedings of the 1996 IEEE International Symposium on Intelligent Control, 342-347.

31. Kohn, W., and Remmel, J.B., "Implementing Sensor Fusion Using a Cost Based Approach", to appear in the Proceedings of ACC'97.

32. Kohn,W., Remmel, J.B., and Nerode, A. Scalable Data and Sensor Fusion via Multiple-Agent Hybrid Systems, submitted to IEEE Transactions on Automatic Control.

33. Kohn, W. and T. Skillman, "Hierarchical Control Systems for Autonomous Space Robots" Proceedings of AIAA Conference in Guidance, Navigation and Control, Vol. 1, pp 382-390, Minneapolis, MN, Aug. 15-18, 1988.

34. Kowalski, R., *Logic for Problem Solving*, North Holland, NY, 1979.

35. Kuich, W. and Salomaa, A., *Semirings, Automata, Languages*, Springer Verlag, NY., 1985.

36. Lloyd, J.W. *Foundations of Logic Programming* second extended edition, Springer Verlag, NY, 1987.

37. Liu, J.W.S., "Real-Time Responsiveness in Distributed Operating Systems and Databases" proceedings of the Workshop on Software Tools for Distributed Intelligent Control Systems, Pacifica, CA., July 17-19, 1990, pp 185-192.

38. Nii, P.H., "Blackboard Systems: The Blackboard Model of Problem Solving and the Evolution of Blackboard Architectures" the AI Magazine, Vol. 7, No. 2, Summer 1986, pp 38-53.

39. Padawitz, P., '*Computing in Horn Clause Theories*, Springer Verlag, NY, 1988.

40. Robinson, J.A., '*Logic: Form and Function*, North Holland, NY, 1979.

41. Skillman, T. and Kohn, W., et.al., "Class of Hierarchical Controllers and their Blackboard Implementations" Journal of Guidance Control & Dynamics, Vol. 13, N1, pp 176-182, Jan.-Feb., 1990.

42. Warner, F.W., *Foundations of Differential Manifolds and Lie Groups*, Scott-Foresman, Glenview, Ill.

43. Warga, K., '*Optimal Control of Differential and Functional Equations*, Academic Press, NY., 1977.

44. Witham, M., *Wave Dynamics: Theory and Application*, McGraw Hill, (1976).

45. Young, L.C., '*Optimal Control Theory*, Chelsea Publishing Co., NY, 1980.

5% Control, t=160

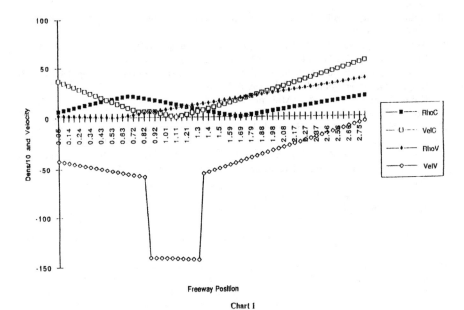

Chart 1

5% Control, t=700

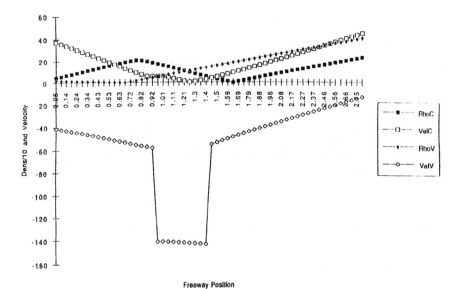

Chart 2

5% Control, t=1300

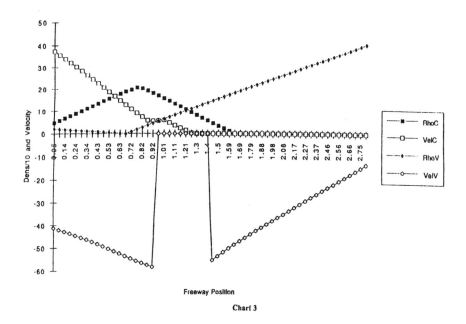

Chart 3

5% Control, Delta VelC

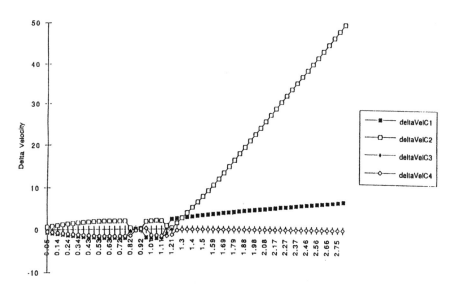

Chart 4

5% Control, Delta RhoC

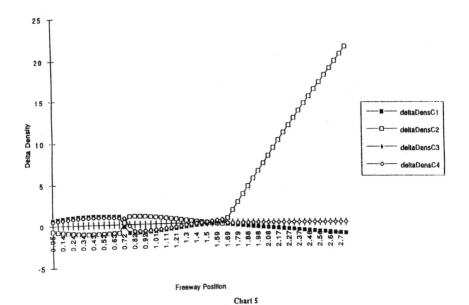

Chart 5

8% Control, I=160

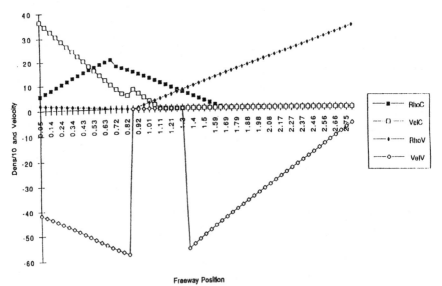

Chart 6

8% Control, l=700

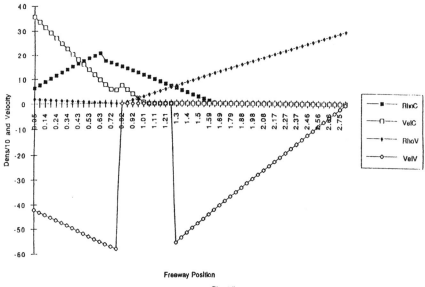

Freeway Position

Chart 7

8% Control, l=1300

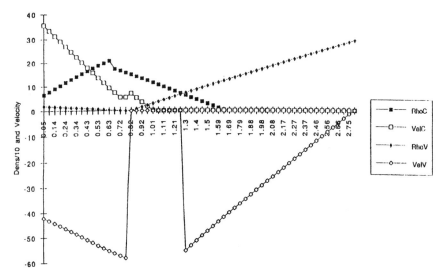

Freeway Position

Chart 8

8% Control Delta VelC

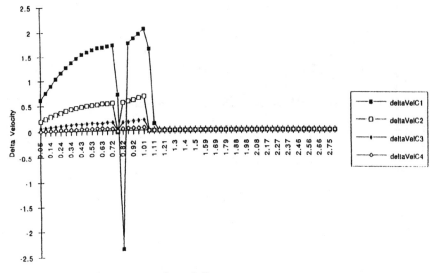

Chart 9

8% Control, Delta RhoC

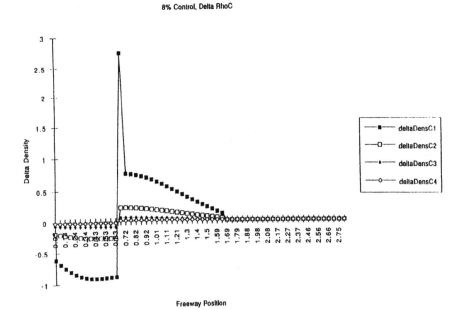

Chart 10

212

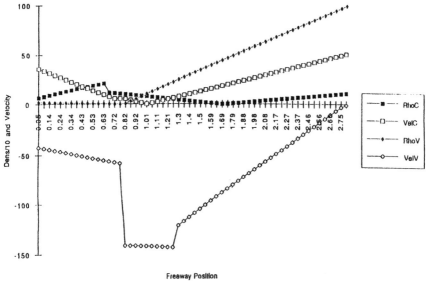

Chart 11

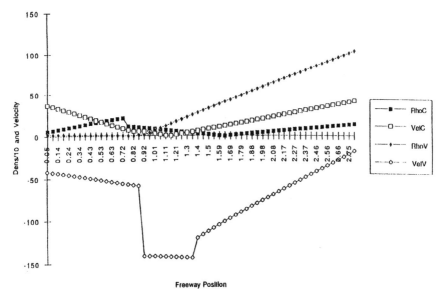

Chart 12

9% Control, t=1300

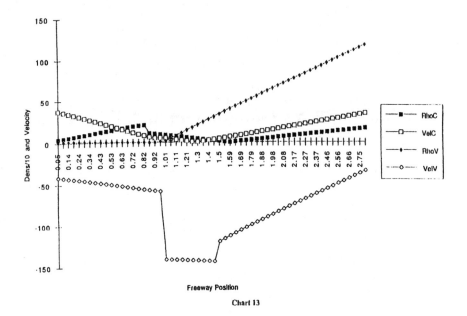

Chart 13

9% Control Delta VelC

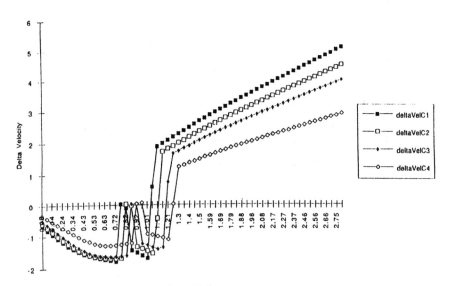

Chart 14

9% Control, Delta RhoC

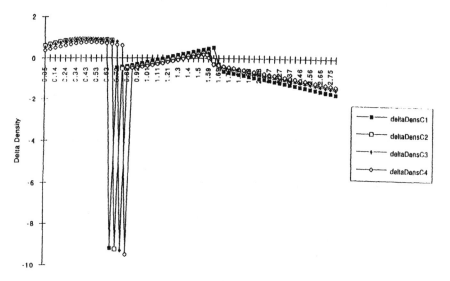

Freeway Position

Chart 15

A Computational Analysis of the Reachability Problem for a Class of Hybrid Dynamical Systems*

John F. Kolen[1] and Feng Zhao[2]

[1] Department of Computer Science, The University of West Florida, 11000 University Parkway, Pensacola FL 32514, USA. Email: jkolen@ai.uwf.edu
[2] Department of Computer and Information Science, The Ohio State University, Columbus OH 43210, USA. Email: fz@cis.ohio-state.edu

Abstract. Hybrid systems possess continuous dynamics defined within regions of state spaces and discrete transitions among the regions. Many practical control verification and synthesis tasks can be reduced to reachability problems for these systems that decide if a particular state-space region is reachable from an initial operating region.

In this paper, we present a computational analysis of the face reachability problem for a class of three-dimensional dynamical systems whose state spaces are defined by piecewise constant vector fields and whose trajectories never return to a state-space region once they exit the region. These systems represent a restricted class of control systems whose dynamics results from a juxtaposition of piecewise parameterized vector fields. We had previously developed a computational algorithm for synthesizing the desired dynamics of a system in phase space by piecing together vector fields geometrically. We demonstrate in this paper that the reachability problem for this class of systems is decidable while the computation is provably intractable (i.e., PSPACE-hard). We prove the intractability via a reduction of satisfiability of quantified boolean formulas to this reachability problem. This result sheds light on the computational complexity of phase-space based control synthesis methods and extends the work of Asarin, Maler, and Pnueli [2] that proves computational undecidability for three-dimensional constant-derivative systems.

1 Introduction

Understanding the reachability property of a complex dynamical system is one of the most important objectives of control design and analysis. Many practical systems are nonlinear and operate in multiple state-space regions where dynamics varies significantly from one region to another. For example, electro-mechanical systems such as switching power regulators often go through a sequence of discrete transitions induced by switching control signals. These systems possess both continuous dynamics within each region of a state space and discrete transitions among the regions. Although the control law within a region is often

---

* An early version of this paper appeared as [10]

simple, the overall system can exhibit extremely complex dynamical behaviors. Dynamical systems of this type are called hybrid systems [3, 5, 6, 12].

This paper and several others define the dynamics of systems in terms of a polyhedral partition of state space and a linear flow defined within each polytope. The resulting system dynamics is locally linear, yet globally nonlinear. Hybrid systems of this type represent a class of control systems that schedule control gains for different operating regimes. Many control verification and synthesis tasks can be reduced to the reachability problem that decides if a particular state-space region can be reached from an initial region and if so, find a practical algorithm for synthesizing a control path. In Zhao [16, 17] and Bradley and Zhao [4], we have developed algorithms for synthesizing the desired dynamics for a system in phase space; the algorithms form a graph representing transitions of parameterized phase-space vector-field flows and search out the graph for optimal control paths. Stiver, Antsaklis, and Lemmon [15] presented a similar approach called the invariant based control synthesis that projects target regions in state space. Hence, it is important to characterize the computational properties of these reachability algorithms and if they are intractable, identify classes of hybrid systems for which these algorithms are practical.

Maler and Pnueli [11] examined a class of hybrid systems known as two-dimensional multi-linear systems. They found that many reachability question (point, region, and face) can be decided in a finite amount of time. Their proof exploits the fact that no flow lines in two dimensions can intersect. Asarin, Maler, and Pnueli [2] restricted the multi-linear system to dynamical systems having piecewise-constant derivatives. In short, their descriptive vocabulary excludes systems with state-space regions containing rotational and non-parallel flows. The 2D reachability question remains decidable under this restriction. They were able to prove, however, the undecidability of 3D reachability by constructing a two-stack automaton using the primitives available to piecewise-constant derivative dynamical systems. Two of the three state dimensions encode the stack state of the automaton, while different regions of state space embody the control state.

Alur and Dill [1] proved that the reachability problem for timed automata, a class of finite automata with real-valued clock variables, is PSPACE-complete. Henzinger et al. [7] and Puri and Varaiya [13] presented the decidability result for a class of hybrid systems called rectangular automata that generalize the timed-automata to multirate systems with rectangular constraints. Informally, the rectangular automata are hybrid systems whose continuous components are constrained by rectangular state-space envelops. Henzinger et al. have developed a PSPACE reachability algorithm for the class of reinitialized rectangular automata. Similarly, Kesten et al. [9] obtained a decidability result on the so-called integration graphs, a class of hybrid systems with restricted clocks.

In this paper, we investigate the reachability problem for a class of three-dimensional dynamical systems, the so-called visit-once piecewise constant derivative (VOPCD) systems. This class of systems differ from rectangular systems studied in Henzinger et al. [7] or Puri and Varaiya [13] in that VOPCD systems permit a more general polyhedral partition of state spaces. While we initially prove that the reachability question for the VOPCD systems is decidable, our main focus is the complexity analysis of the reachability computation. We will show that the reachability problem is PSPACE-hard and hence the intractability. The VOPCD systems, defined more precisely in the next section, are a class of transition dynamical systems with no recurrent behaviors, i.e., the systems will not return to a state-space region after an exit. They represent a restricted class of hybrid systems which can be synthesized by methods such as Zhao [17] or Stiver, Antsaklis, and Lemmon [15] and are interesting from a practical point of view. A computational complexity analysis of these systems could shed light on the identification of classes of hybrid systems for which state-space algorithms are practical and domain-specific constraints that make these systems tractable.

2 Definitions

We define a dynamical system and a piecewise constant derivative system following the definitions of Asarin, et al. [2].

Definition 1 Dynamical System. An (autonomous) dynamical system is $H = (X, f)$ where X is the state-space and f is a partial function from X to X such that $\dfrac{d^+x}{dt} = f(x)$ is the differential equation governing the evolution of x. A trajectory of H starting at some $x_0 \in X$ is $\zeta : T \to X$ such that $\zeta()$ is a solution of the equation with initial condition $x = x_0$ and for every t, $f(\zeta(t))$ is defined and is equal to the right derivative of $\zeta(t)$.

Definition 2 PCD system. A piecewise constant derivative (PCD) system is a dynamical system $H = (X, f)$ where f is a (possibly partial) function from X to X such that the range of f is a finite set of vectors $C \subset X$, and for every $c \in C$, $f^{-1}(c)$ is a finite union of convex polyhedral sets.

We then define the class of systems discussed in this paper as:

Definition 3 VOPCD system. A visit-once PCD system is a PCD system $H = (X, f)$ where f is composed of a set of convex regions P such that for all initial conditions x_0 and time segments $[r, s] \subseteq \Re^+$ if $q \in (r, s)$ then $\phi(\zeta(r)) = \phi(\zeta(s))$ if and only if $\phi(\zeta(r)) = \phi(\zeta(q))$. The function $\phi : X \to P$ identifies the region associated with a position in state space.

For simplicity of presentation, we assume that the system may be degenerate, i.e., there may exist vector fields parallel to the face of its region. In the constructions below, these faces will play no computational role. Constants appearing in the specification of the VOPCD systems discussed in this paper are assumed rational.

By definition, the trajectories of a VOPCD system never revisit the same region. This is an important restriction of the PCD system. Eliminating cyclic flows undermines the dual push-down automata construction described by Asarin et al. [2]. In fact, point, face, and region reachability are decidable in the context of VOPCD. Consider face reachability (point and region reachability follow similar arguments). First, guess a sequence of faces, $\{b_0, b_1, \ldots, b_n\}$, between the initial, b_0, and the final face, b_n. A simple procedure can validate this sequence: Let a_0 be the set of points on the initial face b_0. If b_0 does not share a convex polytope with face b_1 then the sequence is invalid. Otherwise, project a_0 onto b_1 using f to create a_1. If a_1 is empty, reject the sequence. Repeat this process ($a_i \to a_{i+1}$) until a set of points is projected onto the final face. The algorithm accepts if that final face contains any points ($a_n \neq \emptyset$). The number of faces, combined with the visit once constraint, produces a finite collection of possibilities that can be exhaustively examined.

While this algorithm is computable for all dimensions, does a faster, more efficient algorithm exist? Unfortunately, for three dimensions and higher, reachability in VOPCDs is intractable. To prove this assertion we will rely upon the following set of definitions.

Definition 4 3SAT. Let B be a finite set of boolean variables. Let c_i be a clause over B such that $|c_i| = 3$. Does there exist a set of assignments to B such that $\wedge_{i=1}^{n} c_i$ is true?

Definition 5 QBF. Let F be a well-formed quantified Boolean formula $F = (Q_1 b_1)(Q_2 b_2) \ldots (Q_n b_n) E$ where E is a Boolean expression involving the variables $b_1, b_2, \ldots, b_n$ and each Q_i is either $\exists$ or $\forall$. Is F true?

Definition 6 3D-VOPCD-REACH. Given a deterministic 3D VOPCD system and two faces f_s and f_e of its polyhedra, is f_e reachable from f_s?

First, we will prove that 3SAT reduces to 3D-VOPCD-REACH. By adding another building block, we can extend this reduction to QBF. Therefore, 3D-VOPCD-REACH is PSPACE hard. Since the decidability algorithm described above is within PSPACE, we conclude that 3D-VOPCD-REACH is PSPACE-complete.

3 The Building Blocks

The proof of 3SAT $\Rightarrow$ 3D-VOPCD-REACH involves the construction of a deterministic 3D VOPCD system that will search for satisfying variable assignments for a given 3SAT instance. Rather than testing a single variable assignment at a time, the apparatus will test sets of variable assignments in parallel. We represent a variable assignment within the digit encoding of a single number. This allows us to represent a set of variable assignments as set of numbers. For instance, the open interval $(0, 1)$ can represent the set of all possible variable assignments. We will construct several building blocks for manipulating these assignment sets. Each of the building blocks will act like a computational filter, stripping away unwanted (unsatisfactory) variable assignments. For instance, there will be a variable testing block that checks the truth value of a boolean variable. These blocks will be combined to check clause satisfaction (is one of the conjunctive clause terms true?). By cascading clause satisfaction, one can compute satisfactory variable assignments for CNF expressions. Even quantified boolean formulas can be tested by introducing quantifier filters and nondeterminism.

3.1 Variable assignment

A variable assignment can be represented by a single rational number. Let b_i be zero if the ith boolean variable is false and one otherwise. The assignment, a, is simply

$$\sum_{i=1}^{n} \frac{2b_i + 1}{5^i}$$

This Cantor-like representation is preferred over a simple binary representation since it eliminates ambiguities. Consider a binary encoding (0=false, 1=true) such as $0.0111\ldots$ and $0.1000\ldots$. While they are the same number, they do not represent the same assignment. To avoid this problem entirely, we will use the digits 1 and 3 (base 5) to encode the computational state of our system. If we run across $0.1333\ldots$ it can not be confused with $0.3111\ldots$ [14]. Thus, determining the variable assignments specified by some value, a, will require a finite amount of computational resources. This representation is also insensitive to noise. If twelve variables are assigned truth values, this representation requires finite resolution. Lower order terms (e.g., $5^{-i}b_i$ where $i > 12$) do not affect the assignment of variable values. Thus, the entire set of possible truth value assignments can be conveniently encoded as the open set $(0, 1)$, and $(0.2, 0.4)$ represents the assignment of true to b_1. Note that for $i > 1$ the regions associated with being true (or false) are not connected. In fact, the number of regions grows exponentially with i.

3.2 Variable assignment testing

Before building clauses, we need to explain how we will test the assignment of a particular variable. One of the limitations of the 2D multi-linear system that Maler and Pnueli [11] took advantage of was the inability of two flows to converge and become a single flow (Figure 1). Since the apparatus will combine the outputs of several filters to produce a single flow, another dimension is added to the variable assignment. This extra dimension also serves as a temporary storage of a finite amount of information. For simplicity, assume that for the assignment (x, y), x carries the assignment while y serves as the temporary store.

First, consider the case of testing the b_1 variable. Let (x, y) be an assignment set. Those assignments where b_1 is true will be found in the range $(0.6, 0.8) \times (0, 1)$. Likewise, the false assignments will be found in $(0.2, 0.4) \times (0, 1)$. A filter which splits these two flows is given in Figure 2. The concave block region not involved with information processing properties of the block (the white areas of

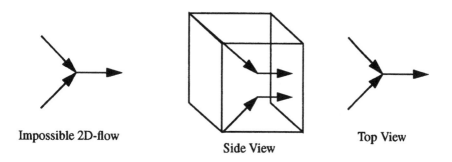

Fig. 1. Impossible flow in 2D system, but possible in projection of 3D system.

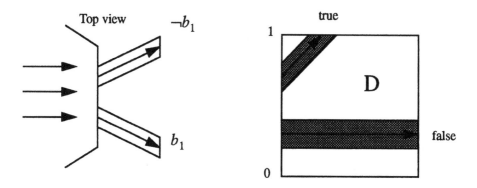

Fig. 2. Testing the first variable: Divert flows prefixed by the variable assignment.

the D box in Figure 2) may be decomposed into a collection of convex regions exhibiting arbitrary flows without affecting the results described below.

While we could further subdivide the regions produced by this filter, such a choice would produce an exponential number of filters due to the topology of the variable assignment representation space. We generalize this mechanism to the other variables via two packing/unpacking functions $ShiftL$ and $ShiftR$. The $ShiftL$ function will take the high order variable assignment and "push" it into the temporary storage dimension, while $ShiftR$ will "pop" the top most assignment in the temporary area back to the primary area. Formally,

$$ShiftL(x,y) = (5x - \lfloor 5x \rfloor, \frac{y}{5} + \frac{\lfloor 5x \rfloor}{5})$$

while $ShiftR(x,y)$ is identical to $ShiftL(y,x)$ after exchanging the arguments.[3]

---

[3] $ShiftR(x,y)^T = \begin{bmatrix} 0 & 1 \\ 1 & 0 \end{bmatrix} ShiftL(y,x)^T$, assuming row vectors.

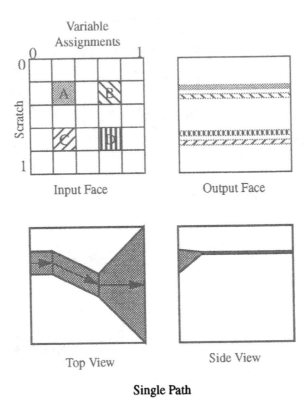

Single Path

Fig. 3. The *ShiftL* box.

Note that these functions are over 2D spaces. They will be implemented as flows from one polytope face to another face. For instance, in Figure 2, the D box will divert the true assignments of b_1 to the left, while the false assignments will continue undiverted. A box similar to D can be constructed for *ShiftL*. While the function is not a VOPCD mapping, it can be decomposed into a collection of VOPCD mappings by examining the effects of *ShiftL* on various input regions. For instance, the region corresponding to top most variable false and last shifted variable false is $(0.2, 0.4) \times (0.2, 0.4)$; see face A in Figure 3. This region on the input face is mapped to $(0, 1) \times (0.24, 0.28)$. The path that implements this mapping consists of three successive convex polytopes, as shown in Figure 3. The appendix at the end of the paper shows that a VOPCD flow mapping one face of a 3D convex polytope to another face can be constructed from a sequence of primitive VOPCD flows over a triangulation of the polytope.

From now on, the *ShiftL* box will be referred to as the L box. The R box that implements *ShiftR* function is identical to the L box, except that the B and C inputs are swapped.

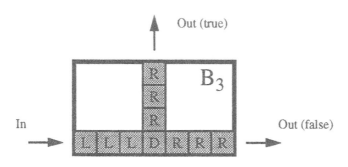

Fig. 4. The B_3 box for splitting sets of assignments depending upon the value of b_3.

Now we are ready to construct a box that will split a set of variable assignments based upon the assignment of a single variable. Let b_i be the variable we are interested in. The B_i box has four parts. First, the variable must be exposed. Exposure of the ith variable requires $i - 1$ iterations of $ShiftL$. We can implement this by chaining $i - 1$ L boxes. Next, the stream is split into the "true" flow and "false" flow with the D box. Finally, the variable assignments of the earlier variables must be reconstituted by two chains of $i - 1$ R boxes. The resulting B_3 box for testing the assignment of b_3 appears in Figure 4. In the event of testing a variable for a value of false, a $\neg B_i$ box can be constructed from that of B_i by swapping the out flow directions in box D.

4 Clause Construction

Each clause c_i in a 3SAT instance is the disjunction of three boolean variables. Thus, a clause is satisfied if at least one of the variables is true. Each clause will have its own processing box. These boxes divert satisficing assignments in one direction and unsatisfying assignments in another direction. We can use B boxes to test for the individual variables. The disjunction requires a special construction. Recall that sets of variable assignments are represented by an open unit square and that only the x-coordinate contains assignment information. The y-dimension is used as a scratch pad. Up to this point, each box has maintained this constraint for all of their output ports. In order to perform the disjunction, we will merely map the incoming unit squares into another unit square while preserving the x-dimension and contracting the y-dimension. From the top, this would appear as multiple flows converging, but only one flow exiting (see Figure 5). We call such a box that tests if a clause is satisfactory the C box.

5 SAT Instance Construction

The last step of the construction is to link C boxes for each clause in the SAT instance — satisficing output of the ith clause is connected to the input of the $i + 1^{th}$ clause.

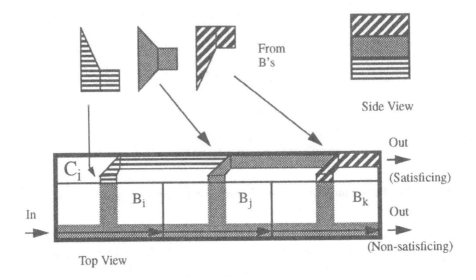

Fig. 5. The clause box for clause i $(b_i \wedge b_j \wedge b_k)$.

Theorem 7. *3D-VOPCD-REACH is NP-HARD.*

Proof. Let x be a n clause instance of 3SAT. Construct a 3D VOPCD system as described above using x as the specification. The construction involves $O(n)$ regions specified by rational numbers of fixed precision. If the *out* port of the C_n is reachable from the *in* port of C_1, then x is satisfiable.

While we can recruit 3D-VOPCD-REACH to help solve any NP problem, it is unclear that the reachability problem itself can be computed in nondeterministic polynomial time. The decidability algorithm described earlier in this paper might serve as a candidate algorithm to make the reachability problem NP-complete. The difficulty of this approach will be apparent in the next section.

6 Constructing Quantifiers

In order to prove that 3D-VOPCD-REACH is PSPACE-hard, we will use quantified boolean formulas (QBF). Recall that QBFs contain boolean clauses and quantifiers. Without loss of generality, we restrict our QBFs to contain only 3CNF clauses. This allows us to use the construction method described above in the 3SAT proof. Another set of filters implement the logical quantifiers. These filters (see Figure 6) restrict the inflowing variable assignment sets. Initially, the *exist* ($\exists$) and *for all* ($\forall$) filters will be chained and separated with *ShiftL* components. The *ShiftL* boxes expose the quantified variables. After the last quantifier

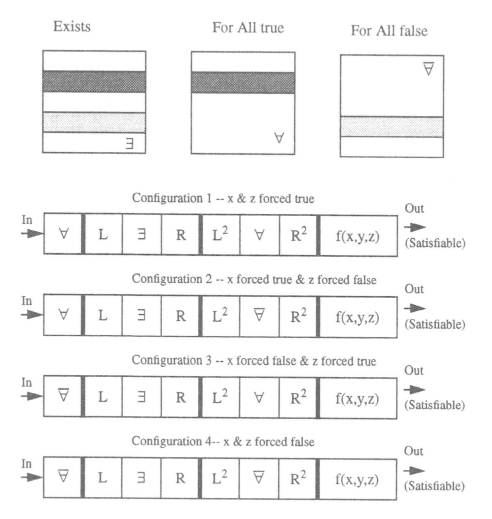

Fig. 6. The *Exists* and *For All* filters. The example is $(\forall x \exists y \forall z) f(x, y, z)$. If the *out* face is unreachable from the *in* face in any of the four constructions, then the expression is unsatisfiable. R^2 indicates the composition of two R blocks. Dark vertical lines separate groups of blocks that implement an individual quantifier (e.g. $R^2 \forall L^2$ implements $\forall z$.

is specified, the sequence of *ShiftR* boxes will return variable assignments from the temporary dimension.

Since 3SAT is a special case of QBF in that only existential quantifiers are used (there exists a set of variable assignments that satisfy this boolean expression), the behavior of the 3SAT construction should not be any different from the corresponding QBF construction where the existential quantifiers are explicitly included. This equivalence is due to the fact that a filter implementing $\exists x$

does not impede any useful trajectories. Universal quantifiers are slightly more complex. In order to interpret the effects of these quantifiers we need to ask two questions: is the expression satisfiable when the variable is true, and is the expression satisfiable when the variable is false. For example, $(\forall x \exists y) f(x, y)$ is equivalent to $((\exists y) f(true, y)) \land ((\exists y) f(false, y))$. This latter expression can be evaluated for satisfiability via two VOPCD constructions: one in which $x = true$ and the other maintains $x = false$. The satisfiability of the original expression is determined by the satisfiability of both constructions. Figure 6 provides an example with two universally quantified variables. Note that the number of possible configurations increases exponentially with the number of universally quantified variables. Fortunately, we can use polynomial-time nondeterminism to find a counterexample configuration to demonstrate the unsatisfiability of the original expression. As the expression is translated into a VOPCD, the particular version (true or false) of a $\forall$ filter is nondeterministically chosen. The output will be connected to the input of the clause set apparatus. As before, the algorithm tests for reachability from the input of the first quantifier box to the output of the clause set box. If one of the choices creates an unreachable condition, then the QBF instance is unsatisfiable.

Theorem 8. *3D-VOPCD-REACH is PSPACE-complete.*

Proof. Guess a quantifier construction and verify (in non-deterministic polynomial time) that the *in* and *out* faces are unreachable. Thus, 3D-VOPCD-REACH is coNPSPACE hard. The algorithm used in the proof of decidability is in PSPACE. Since PSPACE=NPSPACE=coNPSPACE, the theorem is true.

7 Summary

We have presented a complexity analysis for a restricted class of hybrid systems, known as 3D VOPCD systems, that have piecewise-constant derivatives and no recurrent region visits. We demonstrated the decidability of face reachability and then proved that this computation is PSPACE-complete. The proof relies on a geometric construction of a VOPCD system that searches for satisfying variable assignments for a given 3SAT instance, and additional reductions for QBF.

This investigation is motivated by our work on computational phase-space synthesis of global control laws for nonlinear systems [17, 18]. We have formulated the control synthesis problem as search in a stack of phase spaces parameterized by control actions, using a geometric partition of trajectories called flow pipes. We are interested in characterizing the computational complexity of this search. While this paper addressed the intractability of reachability for a class of multi-region systems, many questions remain unanswered. For instance, if we relax the visit-once condition, what additional constraints from practical control systems would make the reachability problem decidable and even computationally tractable?

8 Acknowledgments

This work is supported in part by ONR Young Investigator Award N00014-97-1-0599, NSF Young Investigator Award CCR-9457802, NSF grant CCR-9308639, Alfred P. Sloan Foundation Research Fellowship, and a grant from Xerox Palo Alto Research Center.

References

1. Alur, R., Dill, D.L.: A theory of timed automata. *Theoretical Computer Science* **126**. (1994) 183–235.
2. Asarin, E., Maler, 0., Pnueli, A.: Reachability analysis of dynamical systems having piecewise-constant derivatives. *Theoretical Computer Science* **138**. (1995) 35–65.
3. Back, A., Guckenheimer, J., Myers, M.: A dynamical simulation facility for hybrid systems. In *Hybrid Systems, Lecture Notes In Computer Science* **736**. (1993) Springer.
4. Bradley, E., Zhao, F.: Phase-Space Control System Design. *IEEE Control Systems* **12(2)**. (1993) 39–47.
5. Branicky, M.: Universal computation and other capabilities of hybrid and continuous dynamical systems. *Theoretical Computer Science* **138**. (1995) 67–100.
6. Brockett, R.W.: Hybrid models for motion control systems. In Trentelman et al. (eds.), *Essays in Control: Perspectives in the Theory and its Applications*. (1993) Birkhauser.
7. Henzinger, T.A., Kopke, P.W., Puri, A., Varaiya, P.: What's decidable about hybrid automata? In *Proceedings of the 27th Annual Symposium on Theory of Computing*. (1995) 373–382. ACM Press.
8. Henzinger, T.A., Ho, P.H., Wong-Toi, H.: Algorithmic analysis of nonlinear hybrid systems. Technical Report. (1996) EECS, UC Berkeley.
9. Kesten, Y., Pnueli, A., Sifakis, J., Yovine, S.: Integration graphs: a class of decidable hybrid systems. In R.L. Grossman, A. Nerode, A.P. Ravn, and H. Rischel (eds.), *Hybrid Systems. Lecture Notes in Computer Science* **736**. (1993) 179–208. Springer-Verlag.
10. Kolen, J.F., Zhao, F.: The intractability of face reachability in 3D visit-once piecewise-constant derivative systems. Technical report OSU-CISRC-1/96-TR06. (1996) Computer and Information Science, Ohio State University.
11. Maler, 0., Pnueli, A.: Reachability Analysis of Planar Multi-linear Systems. In C. Courcoubetis (ed.), *Proceedings of the 5th Workshop on Computer-Aided Verification. Lecture Notes in Computer Science* **697**. (1993) 194–209. Springer-Verlag.
12. Nerode, A., Kohn, W.: Models for hybrid systems: automata, topologies, controllability, observability. In *Hybrid Systems, Lecture Notes In Computer Science* **736**. (1993) Springer-Verlag.
13. Puri, A., Varaiya, P.: Decidability of hybrid systems with rectangular differential inclusions. In D.L. Dill (ed.), *CAV94: Computer-aided verification, Lecture Notes in Computer Science* **818**. (1994) 95–104, Springer-Verlag.
14. Siegleman, H. T., Sontag, E. D.: On the computational power of neural networks. *Journal of Computer and System Sciences* **50**. (1995) 132–150.
15. Stiver, J.A., Antsaklis, P.J., Lemmon, M.D.: An invariant based approach to the design of hybrid control systems containing clocks. In *Hybrid Systems III, Lecture Notes in Computer Science* **1066**. (1995) 464–474.

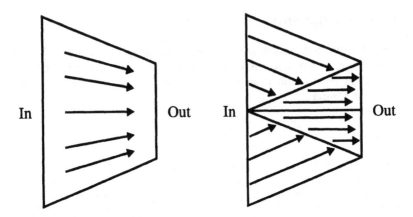

Fig. 7. Construct a VOPCD flow that maps from an edge of a convex polygon to another edge. A 3D VOPCD flow for a convex polytope can be likewise constructed.

16. Zhao, F.: Computational dynamics: modeling and visualizing trajectory flows in phase space. *Annals of Mathematics and Artificial Intelligence* **8**. (1993) 3–4.
17. Zhao, F.: Intelligent simulation in designing complex dynamical control systems. In Tzafestas and Verbruggen (eds.), *Artificial Intelligence in Industrial Decision Making, Control, and Automation.* (1995) 127-158. Kluwer.
18. Zhao, F., Loh, S., May, J.: Phase-Space Nonlinear Control Toolbox: the Maglev experience. Technical report OSU-CISRC-4/97-TR24. (1997) Computer and Information Science, Ohio State University.

Appendix

A Construction of VOPCD flow within a convex polytope.

We show that a VOPCD flow for a convex polytope can be constructed from simpler VOPCD flows on a polyhedral partition of the polytope. Consider a 2D convex polygon shown in Figure 7. To construct a VOPCD flow from the edge labeled "in" to the edge labeled "out", we first partition the polygon into a collection of triangles. Next, we find a sequence of adjacent triangles that connect the "in" face to the "out" face. For each triangle in the sequence, a VOPCD flow that maps one face to another is the flow parallel to the 3rd face of the triangle. The desired VOPCD flow from "in" to "out" is the concatenation of the VOPCD flows of the triangles in the sequence. See Figure 7.

For a 3D convex polytope, we can likewise triangulate the polytope and form the VOPCD flow from VOPCD flows of the tetrahedra. A VOPCD flow from one face to another face of a tetrahedron is the flow parallel to the other two faces of the tetrahedron.

A Class of Rectangular Hybrid Systems with Computable Reach Set*

Mikhail Kourjanski and Pravin Varaiya

michaelk@eecs.berkeley.edu and varaiya@eecs.berkeley.edu
Department of Electrical Engineering and Computer Science
University of California, Berkeley CA 94720

Abstract. A class of rectangular hybrid systems is presented whose reach set is computable. The class is specified in terms of a controllability condition. That condition can be verified.

1 Introduction

Rectangular hybrid systems are a natural generalization of multi-rate timed automata. These systems have been studied for purposes of verification, control, and as approximations of more general hybrid systems [1, 2, 3, 4, 5].

Since properties of safety, liveness and control of a hybrid system can often be recast as properties of its reach set, it is useful to know whether the reach set is (finitely) computable. Unlike timed automata, the reach set of a rectangular system is not always computable.

The most important class of rectangular systems with computable reach set are the "initialized" systems. These are systems in which a continuous state variable is re-initialized following a discrete transition whenever that transition leads to a change in the dynamics of that continuous variable. It is easy to check if a rectangular system is initialized.

The reach set of a rectangular system is computable if the reach set stops increasing or saturates after a finite number of discrete transitions. Whether a system's reach set saturates is, unfortunately, not decidable. A controllability condition that guarantees reach set saturation for general hybrid systems was given in [6], but that condition, too, is not decidable. Our main result is that when specialized to rectangular systems that condition is decidable.

We also present a rectangular system whose reach set has a fractal boundary. This system does not meet the controllability condition.

---

* Research supported by NSF Grant ECS9417370 and ARO Contract DAAH04-94-G-0026.

2 Reach set of rectangular system

The definition of a rectangular system is the same as in the papers cited above. However, the notation follows that introduced in [7]. A rectangular hybrid system H has a continuous state that evolves in $\mathbb{R}^N$ and a finite number of discrete states indexed $i = 1, ..., K$. To the discrete state i there corresponds a triple of the form $[Z_i, R_i^S, U_i]$. Z_i is a compact rectangle of $\mathbb{R}^N$; R_i^S is a point-to-set "linear" map of the form $R_i^S(x) = A_i x + R_i$ where A_i is a diagonal matrix and R_i is a compact rectangle of $\mathbb{R}^N$; U_i is also a compact rectangle of $\mathbb{R}^N$ representing the differential inclusion

$$\dot{x} \in U_i. \tag{1}$$

A discrete transition into state i can be taken any time the continuous state is in the enabling zone Z_i. The continuous state is then reset according to the map R_i^S and the state subsequently evolves according to (1). Thus the system is non-deterministic: there is choice of the switching point within Z_i, the reset state within R_i^S and the velocity within U_i. We assume that

$$Z_i \cap Z_j = \emptyset, \ R_i^S(Z_i) \cap R_j^S(Z_j) = \emptyset \ i \neq j. \tag{2}$$

A *path* is any finite or infinite sequence of enabling zones $Z_1, Z_2, ...$ The path is *feasible* provided there exists a sequence of states $x(1), x(2), ...$ such that

$$x(i+1) = A_i x(i) + u(i)t_i + r(i), \ i = 1, 2, ... \tag{3}$$

for some

$$x(i) \in Z_i, \ u(i) \in U_i, \ r(i) \in R_i, \ t_i \geq 0. \tag{4}$$

A sequence $x(1), x(2), ...$ that satisfies (3,4) is called a *trajectory* (in that path).

The feasibility of a particular finite path Z_i, $i = 1, ..., M$, is equivalent to the existence of a solution to the corresponding linear program (3, 4). We want to know if there is *any* finite trajectory which reaches a particular target enabling zone (or a target state). That reachability question is not decidable.

3 Viability and computable reach sets

The natural way of answering the reachability question is to build a tree of feasible paths leading to the target. By checking if the target is reachable for each level of the tree being built we will find a solution in a finite number of steps provided the target is reachable. However we won't be able to determine if the target is in fact unreachable, because if there are trajectories with infinitely many transitions and the target is unreachable we have no criterion to stop incrementing and evaluating the tree. But if we know at some point that the reach set has saturated, i.e., stopped increasing, then we can *trim* the tree and get a decidable reachability problem. In order to do this we need more facts about reachability and controllability.

Definition The hybrid system H is called *viable* if there exists a trajectory with infinitely many discrete transitions. This trajectory and its path are also called viable.

Because of condition (2) a viable trajectory has a positive lower bound on the time spent in every discrete state.

A sufficient condition for a system to be viable is that it has a periodic orbit. Suppose $Z_1, ..., Z_M = Z_1$ is a path. Then H has a periodic orbit in that path if there exists a solution to the system (3)–(4) with $x(M) = x(1)$.

We know from [7] that a particular path with $Z_M = Z_1$ can be evaluated for a periodic orbit using linear programming techniques. We don't know how to characterize a viable system which has no periodic orbit. (An example of such a system is given in section 7.)

4 Controllability condition and extended system

Definition Transition $(Z_i \to Z_j)$ is *fully controllable* if $\forall x \in Z_i$, $\forall y \in Z_j$

$$y = A_i x + u(i)t_i + r(i) \tag{5}$$

for some $u(i) \in U_i$, $t_i \geq 0$ and $r(i) \in R(i)$.

We denote a fully controllable transition as $[Z_i \to Z_j]_{ctrl}$.

In order to proceed further we choose a fixed-valued parameter $\varepsilon > 0$.

Definition We create an ε-extended system $\tilde{H}$ by extending for each discrete state the allowable reset addition (4):

$$\tilde{R}_i = R_i + B_\varepsilon,$$

where B_ε is an ε-cube: $-\varepsilon \leq x_i \leq \varepsilon$.

Definition A subsystem H_s is called *strongly nonviable* (w.r.t. chosen $\varepsilon > 0$) if it contains no viable path, and for each feasible path within the subsystem H_s the same path in $\tilde{H}_s$ contains no periodic orbit.

5 The Alternative and computable reach set

We propose the following Alternative:

Definition A system H satisfies *the Alternative* if each subsystem of H is either *strongly nonviable* or *contains a fully controllable transition*.

Theorem 1 If H satisfies the Alternative then its reach set is computable.

Proof. Consider the tree of all feasible paths in H. We will show that each infinite path in this tree can be terminated at a finite point beyond which the reach set does not increase along that path. Indeed, by the Alternative, an infinite path will contain infinitely many occurrences of the same fully controllable transition $[Z_i \rightarrow Z_j]_{ctrl}$. But since every point in Z_j can be reached from every point in Z_i, it follows that no new states are reached after the second occurrence of this transition, hence this path can be terminated at this point. If we trim the tree in this manner, every path will terminate. It follows using the same argument as in the proof of [6, Theorem 5] that the resulting tree is finite. The reach set along this finite tree is evidently computable.

6 Decidability of compliance

We now show that membership in the class of systems satisfying the Alternative is decidable.

Theorem 2 It is decidable whether the system H satisfies the Alternative.

Proof. Given $\varepsilon > 0$, there is $M < \infty$ such that in every feasible path in H of length at least M there is a trajectory $x^*(1), x^*(2), \ldots$ such that two points $x^*(i)$ and $x^*(j)$ along the trajectory are in the same enabling zone and $x^*(i) - x^*(j) \in B_\varepsilon$. Hence in $\tilde{H}$, this trajectory could be modified so that $x^*(i) = x^*(j)$ to yield a periodic orbit. If H has no fully controllable transition along this path, it does not satisfy the Alternative. That is, H satisfies the Alternative if (1) in every non-viable path of length less than M, $\tilde{H}$ has no closed orbit and (2) along every feasible path of length M, H has a fully controllable transition.

7 Example

In this section we present an example of a rectangular hybrid system with a viable trajectory without periodic orbits.

The system has nine discrete states and its continuous state evolves in $\mathbb{R}^3$.

```
DIMENSION 3
STATE  1
  EZONE(x1: 7..10;  x2: 5.5..9;  x3: 0.0) DYNAMICS(u1: -6; u2: 6; u3: 4)
STATE  2
  EZONE(x1: 0;  x2: 11..19; x3: 1..9) DYNAMICS(u1: 4; u2: 6; u3: 2)
STATE  3
  EZONE(x1: 50..65;  x2: 100; x3: 30..39) DYNAMICS(u1: -2; u2: -4; u3: 4)
STATE  4
  EZONE(x1: 30..39;  x2: 50..59; x3: 80) DYNAMICS(u1: 2; u2: 2; u3: 3)

STATE  5_1
  EZONE(x1: 40;  x2: 53..60.82; x3: 80..99)
  DYNAMICS(u1: -23; u2: -12; u3: -40)
STATE  5_2
```

```
EZONE(x1: 40; x2: 60.859..68; x3: 80..99)
DYNAMICS(u1: -23; u2: -12; u3: -40)
STATE 5_3
 EZONE(x1: 40.033; x2: 53..68; x3: 80..90.59)
 DYNAMICS(u1: -23; u2: -12; u3: -40)
STATE 5_4
 EZONE(x1: 40.033; x2: 53..68; x3: 90.672..99)
 DYNAMICS(u1: -23; u2: -12; u3: -40)

STATE 6
 EZONE(x1: 16..25; x2: 50; x3: 50..63) DYNAMICS(u1: -9; u2: -36; u3: -46)
```

Enabling zones are 2-dimensional rectangles in $\mathbb{R}^3$. Dynamics are fixed (the U_i are singletons), and there are no resets. Following [7] we know that the rotation angle in this system is not commensurable with π.

Fig.1,2 show an evolution of the segment $[(8,7),(8,8)]$ through the system. An arbitrary small segment will eventually break into two pieces while evolving through the system. A discontinuity brought in by nonintersecting zones $\{Z_{5_i}\}_{i=1,\ldots,4}$ creates bounded separation.

Fig.3 shows a phase portrait of the system in the enabling zone of STATE 1. There are two fractal attractors in the system; for each starting point the trajectory converges to a set of small ellipsoids in a finite time (fragment of the phase portrait is shown in Fig.4).

An object of interest is the discontinuous boundary of attraction (fragment shown in Fig.5). It does not have a periodic orbit because the rotation angle is incommensurable with π. At the same time it is a viable trajectory, highly unstable towards any perturbation. This hybrid system does not satisfy the Alternative.

8 Conclusion

A new class of rectangular hybrid systems with decidable reachability is presented. We have shown that a certain level of control is sufficient to make the reachability decidable. Further development in this direction may be possible by means of investigating the dependencies between viability and reachability, which brings in the question of control synthesis.

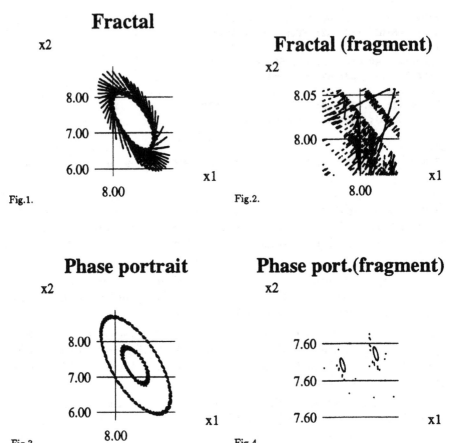

Fractal

x2

8.00

7.00

6.00

8.00

x1

Fig.1.

Fractal (fragment)

x2

8.05

8.00

8.00

x1

Fig.2.

Phase portrait

x2

8.00

7.00

6.00

8.00

x1

Fig.3.

Phase port.(fragment)

x2

7.60

7.60

7.60

x1

Fig.4.

Boundary of attraction

x2

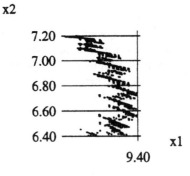

7.20

7.00

6.80

6.60

6.40

9.40

x1

Fig.5.

References

1. R. Alur, L. Fix and T.A. Henzinger. A Determinizable Class of Timed Automata. *Proc. 6th Workshop Computer-Aided Verification 1994*, LNCS 818, Springer-Verlag, 1994. pp. 1-13.

2. A. Olivero, J. Sifakis and S. Yovine. Using Abstractions for the Verification of Linear Hybrid Systems. *Proc. 6th Workshop Computer-Aided Verification 1994*, LNCS 818, Springer-Verlag, 1994. pp. 81-94.

3. A. Puri and P. Varaiya. Decidability of Hybrid Systems with Rectangular Differential Inclusions. *Proc. 6th Workshop Computer-Aided Verification 1994*, LNCS 818, Springer-Verlag, 1994. pp. 95-104.

4. T.A. Henzinger, P. Kopka, A. Puri and P. Varaiya. What's decidable about hybrid automata?. *STOCS*, 1995.

5. A. Puri, V. Borkar and P. Varaiya. ϵ-approximation of differential inclusions. *Hybrid Systems III: verification and control*, LNCS 1066, Springer-Verlag, 1996.

6. A. Deshpande and P. Varaiya. Viable Control of Hybrid Systems. *Hybrid Systems II*, Springer-Verlag, 1995. pp. 128-147.

7. M. Kourjanski and P. Varaiya. Stability of Hybrid Systems. *Hybrid Systems III: verification and control*, LNCS 1066, Springer-Verlag, 1996. pp. 413-423.

Safe Implementations of Supervisory Commands

Michael Lemmon and Christopher J. Bett*

Department of Electrical Engineering
University of Notre Dame
Notre Dame, IN 46556

Abstract. This paper compares two different types of control strategies used to safely implement supervisory commands of hybrid dynamical systems. Both approaches considered in this paper switch between members of a family of control agents to ensure that constraints on the plant state are not violated at any time. The first approach is motivated by a hybrid system architecture outlined in [7] and uses a Fliess functional series of the plant's output to form a system of linear inequalities characterizing safe control inputs. Control signals are determined by solving a sequence of linear programs. The second approach is a model reference control approach to hybrid systems introduced in [8] and uses a known safe dynamical reference model to characterize the desired plant behavior. The controller is determined by representing the resulting error dynamics as a linear parameter varying system and applying linear robust control techniques to enforce a bounded amplitude performance level. The fundamental results underlying each of the methods are derived; both approaches are compared with regard to their complexity, performance, and sensitivity to modeling uncertainty. A numerical example is included for illustration.

1 Introduction

This paper considers the high level supervision of continuous time dynamical control systems evolving over a state set which is dense in $\Re^n$. It is assumed that a supervisory command is characterized by a set of guard conditions and a goal condition. These guard and goal conditions are inequality conditions on the plant's state. A control system is used to implement the supervisory command. This controller is said to be "safe" when the controlled plant's state trajectory triggers the goal condition in finite time without triggering any of the guard conditions. This paper compares two different types of controllers used to safely implement supervisory commands.

Both approaches considered in this paper switch between members of a family of control agents to ensure the guard conditions are not triggered. The first approach is motivated by a hybrid system architecture outlined in [7]. This approach uses a Fliess functional series of the plant's output to form a system of linear inequalities characterizing safe control inputs. In this method, control signals can be determined by solving a sequence of linear programs (LP). The second approach is a model reference control approach to hybrid systems introduced in [8]. In this approach, the controlled plant follows a reference model which is known to be safe. The error dynamics of this system are represented as a linear parameter varying (LPV) system whose controllers enforce a bounded amplitude performance level. This paper formally derives the fundamental results behind both of these methods and compares both approaches with regard to their complexity, performance, and sensitivity to modeling uncertainty.

A formal definition of "safe" controllers is given in section 2. The remainder of the paper discusses the two methods for characterizing safe controllers which were outlined above. The first method will be referred to as the LP-method since it solves a sequence of linear programs to determine safe control signals. The LP-method is discussed in section 3. The fundamental result in section 3 is a set of inequality constraints characterizing locally safe piecewise constant control signals. The second method is referred to as the MRC-method since it uses a model reference control (MRC) approach to formulate the controller synthesis problem. The MRC method is discussed in section 4. The fundamental results in this section are sufficient conditions characterizing controllers ensuring bounded-amplitude performance for the switched control system. Section 5 compares both methods and draws some general conclusions about their relative strengths and weaknesses.

* The authors gratefully acknowledge the partial financial support of the Army Research Office (DAAH04-95-1-0600, DAAH04-96-1-0134).

2 Safe Supervisory Controllers

Hybrid dynamical systems arise when the time and/or the state space have mixed continuous and discrete natures. Such systems frequently arise when computers are used to control continuous state systems. In recent years, specific attention has been focused on hybrid systems in which a discrete-event system is used to supervise the behavior of plants whose state spaces are dense in $\Re^n$. In this class of hybrid control systems, commands are issued by a discrete-event system to direct the behavior of the plant. These commands are high-level directives to the plant which require that the supervised plant satisfy logical conditions on the plant's state. The simplest set of conditions are inequality conditions on the plant's state.

Assume that the plant's dynamics are generated by the differential equation

$$\dot{x} = f(x, u) \tag{1}$$

where $x \in \Re^n$ is the state, $u \in \Re^m$ is the control input, and $f : \Re^n \times \Re^m \to \Re^n$ is a Lipschitz continuous mapping. A *supervisory directive* to this system is characterized by a set of functionals, $h_j : \Re^n \to \Re$ for $j = 0, \ldots, N$, that separate the state space. The functionals, h_j, are said to *separate* the state space if and only if for all $x, y \in \Re^n$ such that $h_j(x) > 0$ and $h_j(y) < 0$, there exists $0 < \lambda < 1$ such that $h_j(\lambda x + (1 - \lambda)y) = 0$. The functional, h_0, is said to be the *goal trigger* and the other functionals, h_j for $j = 1, \ldots, N$, are called the *guard triggers*. Consider a state feedback controller,

$$u = k(x) \tag{2}$$

Such a controller is said to be *safe* if and only if there exist finite times T_1 and T_2 ($T_1 < T_2$) such that

- $h_j(x(t)) < 0$ for all $t_0 \le t < T_2$ ($j = 1, \ldots, N$),
- $h_0(x(t)) < 0$ for all $t_0 \le t < T_1$,
- and $h_0(x(t)) > 0$ for all $T_1 < t < T_2$.

Essentially, these conditions state that the goal condition is triggered in finite time without any of the guard triggers being violated. Assume that we have a monotone increasing function $r(t)$ such that $r(0) = h_0(x(0))$ and $r(T_1) = 0$. We can use this "reference" function to rewrite the preceding list of conditions as a set of inequality constraints such that the guard triggers ($j = 1, \ldots, N$) satisfy $h_j(x(t)) < 0$ and the goal trigger satisfies $h_0(x(t)) - r(t) > 0$ for all $t \in [0, T_2]$.

3 LP-Method

The LP-method is motivated by a hybrid system architecture outlined in [7]. This method characterizes safe control signals as a set of linear inequality constraints. The LP-method assumes that the plant's differential equation has the form

$$\dot{x} = f_0(x) + \sum_{i=1}^{m} f_i(x)u_i(t) \tag{3}$$

where $f_i : \Re^n \to \Re^n$ are analytic functions forming a nonsingular distribution of vector fields in $\Re^n$. It is also assumed that the set of trigger functions $\{h_j\}_{j=1}^{N}$ is analytic.

Assume that the trigger functions, $h_j(x(t))$, are known at time, t. Under appropriate conditions, it is possible to represent the trigger functions at time $t + \delta$ as a Fliess functional series. To formally state these results, some notational conventions need to be introduced. Let $f : \Re^n \to \Re^n$ be a vector of analytic functions, $f' = \begin{bmatrix} f_1 & f_2 \cdots f_n \end{bmatrix}$ where $f_i : \Re^n \to \Re^n$ ($i = 1, \ldots, n$). The Lie derivative of an analytic function $h : \Re^n \to \Re$ with respect to vector field f is

$$L_f h(x) = \sum_{i=1}^{n} \frac{\partial h}{\partial x_i} f_i(x) \tag{4}$$

Let $i \in \{1, \ldots, m\}$ be an *index* and let $i_1, \ldots, i_k$ be a sequence of indices of length k called a *multi-index*. The set of all multi-indices will be denoted as I^*. Associated with the multi-index $i_1, \ldots, i_k$ is the iterated integral,

$$E_{i_k,\ldots,i_1}(t) = \int_0^t d\xi_{i_k} \cdots \xi_{i_1} \tag{5}$$

where for $i = 1, \ldots, m$,

$$\xi_i(t) = \int_0^t u_i(\tau) d\tau \tag{6}$$

$$\int_0^t d\xi_{i_k} \cdots d\xi_{i_1} = \int_0^t d\xi_{i_k}(\tau) \int_0^\tau d\xi_{i_{k-1}} \cdots d\xi_{i_1} \tag{7}$$

The following theorem which is proven in [6] will be used in our following development.

Proposition 1. *[6] Consider the system given by equations 3. If there exist $K > 0$ and $M > 0$ such that*

$$\left| L_{f_{i_1}} \cdots L_{f_{i_k}} h_j(x(t)) \right| \leq K k! M^k \tag{8}$$

for all k, j, and all multi-indices in I^*, then there exists a real $\Delta > 0$ such that for all $\delta \in [0, \Delta]$ and piecewise continuous control functions $u_i(t)$ defined over $[t, t + \Delta]$ subject to the constraint

$$\max_{\delta \in [0,\Delta]} |u_i(t + \delta)| < 1 \tag{9}$$

then the series

$$h_j(x(t)) + \sum_{k=1}^\infty \sum_{I^*} L_{f_{i_1}} \cdots L_{f_{i_k}} h_j(x(t)) \int_0^\delta d\xi_{i_k} \cdots d\xi_{i_1} \tag{10}$$

is uniformly and absolutely convergent to $h_j(x(t + \delta))$.

If we can find a control signal, u, so that the safety conditions are satisfied over $[t, t + \delta]$, for all t then we say the control is locally safe. The Fliess series is a formal series over the control symbols, u_i. It provides a means of expressing the values of the trigger functions, h_j, over a finite interval, $[t, t + \delta]$. It therefore makes sense to use the Fliess series in characterizing control inputs, u_i, ensuring local safety of the control system. The following proposition provides just such a characterization.

Proposition 2. *Consider the system given by equation 3 and let $r(t)$ be a known reference trigger such that $\dot{r}(t) = R > 0$ and $r(0) = h_0(x(0))$. Assume that proposition 1 holds and that $x(0)$ is safe. If there exist $\gamma > 0$, $\gamma_1 > 0$, and $\Delta > 0$ such that the constant vector $u^* \in \Re^m$ satisfies*

$$-\gamma < h_j(x(0)) + \sum_{i=1}^m [L_{f_i} h_j(x(0))] u_i^* \Delta \quad (j = 1, \ldots, N) \tag{11}$$

and

$$|u_i^*| \leq 1 \quad i = 1, \ldots, m \tag{12}$$

and

$$R - \gamma_1 < \sum_{i=1}^m [L_{f_i} h_0(x(0))] u_i^* \tag{13}$$

then the constant control $u(t) = u^*$ generates a safe state trajectory in $[0, \Delta)$.

Proof: Assuming that proposition 1 holds, then there exists $K > 0$ and $M > 0$ such that the growth constraint 8 is satisfied. Given inequality 12, we know that the Fliess series is uniformly convergent in an interval, $[0, \Delta]$, and that for any $\delta \in [0, \Delta]$, we can expand $h_j(x(\delta))$ as

$$h_j(x(\delta)) = h_j(x(0)) + \sum_{k=1}^\infty \sum_{i_1,\ldots,i_k} L_{f_{i_1}} \cdots L_{f_{i_k}} h_j(t) E_{i_1,\ldots,i_k}(\delta) \tag{14}$$

Assuming a constant u^* over this interval, we see that

$$h_j(x(\delta)) = h_j(x(0)) + \sum_{i=1}^{m} L_{f_{i_1}} \cdots L_{f_{i_k}} h_j(x(0)) u_{i_1}^* \cdots u_{i_k}^* \frac{\delta^k}{k!}$$

$$= h_j(x(0)) + \sum_{i=1}^{m} L_{f_i} h_j(x(0)) u_i^* \delta + o_j(\delta) \tag{15}$$

The tail term is

$$o_j(\delta) = \sum_{k=2}^{\infty} \sum_{i_1,\ldots,i_k} L_{f_{i_1}} \cdots L_{f_{i_k}} h_j(x(0)) u_{i_1}^* \cdots u_{i_k}^* \frac{\delta^k}{k!} \tag{16}$$

The magnitude of the tail is bounded as

$$|o_j(\delta)| \leq K(Mm\delta)^2 \left(\frac{1}{1 - Mm\delta} \right) \tag{17}$$

for $\delta < 1/Mm$.

We now take $\Delta = \rho/Mm$ where $\rho < 1$, then

$$|o_j(\delta)| \leq K \frac{\rho^2}{1 - \rho} = \gamma \tag{18}$$

We take the right-hand side of this inequality to be the γ of our theorem and immediately conclude that inequality 15 can be written as

$$h_j(\delta) \leq h_j(x(0)) + \sum_{i=1}^{m} L_{f_i} h_j(x(0)) u_i^* \Delta + \gamma \tag{19}$$

For $j = 1, \ldots, N$, this implies that the state is safe at time Δ. It is also safe at time zero. Since our bound is linear this must also hold for all δ between 0 and Δ. So for all time in $[0, \Delta)$, the desired inequality constraints ensure the guard triggers are not violated.

We now turn to the terminating trigger, $h_0(x(t))$. In this case, we require that $h_0(x(t)) > r(\delta)$ for all $\delta \in [0, \Delta]$. By assumption, $h_0(x(0)) \geq r(0)$ and we know by that $r(\delta) = r(0) + R\delta$. To ensure our other constraint is satisfied, we require

$$r(0) + R\delta < h_0(x(0)) + \sum_{i=1}^{m} L_{f_i} h_0(x(0)) u_i^* \delta + K(Mm\delta)^2 \left(\frac{1}{1 - Mm\delta} \right) \tag{20}$$

Assuming that $r(0) = h_0(x(0))$, we see that the condition reduces to

$$R < \sum_{i=1}^{m} L_{f_i} h_0(x(0)) u_i^* + KMm \frac{\rho}{1 - \rho} \tag{21}$$

We treat this last quantity as γ_1, and our result follows. □

Proposition 2 characterizes the *set* of locally safe control signals. In practice, a specific control signal will need to be chosen from this set. This selection is made with respect to an assumed cost functional, $J(u)$. The "optimal" locally safe control is determined by finding the control signal that minimizes this given cost subject to the local safety conditions represented by the inequality constraints in proposition 2. A particularly simple choice for the cost is a linear function of u. If we restrict $0 < u_i < 1$ for all $i = 1, \ldots, m$, then our cost functional becomes

$$J(u) = w'u = \sum_{i=1}^{m} w_i u_i \tag{22}$$

where w is an m-vector of positive weights. The control signal minimizing this cost is obtained by solving the following linear programming problem

$$\begin{aligned}
\text{minimize:} \quad & w'u \\
\text{with respect to:} \quad & u \\
\text{subject to:} \quad & A(t)u < b \\
& 0 < u_i < 1
\end{aligned} \tag{23}$$

where

$$A(t) = \begin{bmatrix} L_{f_1}h_0 & L_{f_2}h_0 & \cdots & L_{f_m}h_0 \\ L_{f_1}h_1 & L_{f_2}h_1 & \cdots & L_{f_m}h_1 \\ \cdot & \cdot & \cdots & \cdot \\ L_{f_1}h_p & L_{f_2}h_p & \cdots & L_{f_m}h_p \end{bmatrix} \tag{24}$$

and

$$b = \begin{bmatrix} R - \gamma_1 \\ -\gamma \\ \cdot \\ -\gamma \end{bmatrix} \tag{25}$$

Note that the constraint matrix $A(t)$ is a function of time.

The preceding discussion solved an LP problem to find a constant control, u^*, for a time $t \in [0, T)$ which was locally safe. A safe control trajectory, $u^*(t)$, for all $t \in [0, T)$, can be determined by solving a sequence of linear programs at the time instants $t_0 + n\Delta$, where n is the set of positive integers and Δ is given by the growth constants in proposition 2. The constraint matrices $A(t)$ are obtained from our knowledge of the distribution, $\{f_0, f_1, \ldots, f_n\}$ as well as the current state vector. This essentially means that an LP problem must be solved at the sampling instant $t_0 + n\Delta$ to determine the piecewise constant control u^* that is used over the interval $[t_0 + n\Delta, t_0 + (n+1)\Delta]$. Provided these constraint matrices do not change too quickly, we can expect such an on-line approach to control-signal generation to ensure the safety of the commanded transition.

Example: A simple example of this approach is used to illustrate the approach. The following example has been modified from [5] to yield a plant which is affine in the control. The modified plant equations are

$$\dot{x}_1 = -x_1 + u_1 \tag{26}$$
$$\dot{x}_2 = -x_2 + (1 + x_1^2)u_2 \tag{27}$$

We can rewrite this as a linear combination of vector fields,

$$\begin{bmatrix} \dot{x}_1 \\ \dot{x}_2 \end{bmatrix} = \begin{bmatrix} -x_1 \\ -x_2 \end{bmatrix} + \begin{bmatrix} 1 \\ 0 \end{bmatrix} u_1 + \begin{bmatrix} -1 \\ 0 \end{bmatrix} u_2 + \begin{bmatrix} 0 \\ 1 + x_1^2 \end{bmatrix} u_3 + \begin{bmatrix} 0 \\ -(1 + x_2)^2 \end{bmatrix} u_4 \tag{28}$$

The control objective is to move the plant from an initial state near the operating point $(0, 0)$ to a point near $(2.5, 2)$.

The guard triggers are

$$h_1(x) = x_2 - 1.25x_1 + .5 \tag{29}$$
$$h_2(x) = -x_2 + 1.25x_1 + .5 \tag{30}$$

with a goal trigger,

$$h_0(x, t) = x_1(0) - Rt \tag{31}$$

where R is the desired rate at which we want to achieve the desired goal set. These regions are illustrated in figure 1.

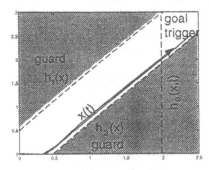

Fig. 1. Guard and goal triggers for example.

A simple Matlab script was written to simulate this system. Figure 1 illustrates the state trajectory that was generated by this approach. In this case, the LP-problems determining safe controls were computed at a rate $\Delta = .1$. The weighting vector w was chosen to be a vector of ones. As can be seen, the selected controls basically select one control strategy that drives the system in the direction of the h_2 guard trigger. Once within a distance γ of that guard trigger, the control strategy changes to a chattering policy which drives the system state along the boundary until the terminal condition is satisfied. The chattering nature of the control policy is seen in figure 2.

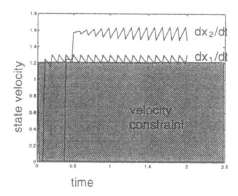

Fig. 2. Chattering control policy

This example illustrates some fundamental characteristics of the LP-approach to safe controller generation. In the first place, this is an on-line procedure which requires the solution of an LP problem at each sampling instant. The computation of the control requires significant information about the underlying vector fields generating the system's dynamics. Finally, this approach tends to produce a chattering control strategy, as shown in figure 2.

4 MRC-Method

A model reference control (MRC) approach for implementing safe controllers was introduced in [8]. In this approach, the plant is forced to follow a reference trajectory, $x_m(t)$, which is known to be safe with a worst case tracking error of γ. Provided there exists a time T such that $h_0(x_m(T)) > \gamma$ and for all $0 < t < T$ and $j = 1, \ldots, N$ that $h_j(x_m(t)) > -\gamma$, the plant trajectory, $x_p(t)$, is guaranteed to be safe.

In this framework, synthesis of safe switched controllers is accomplished by examining the error between the plant and reference trajectories. Suppose that the plant state dynamics are generated by

$$\dot{x}_p = f_p(x_p, u) \tag{32}$$

and let the reference trajectory be generated by

$$\dot{x}_m = f_m(x_m) \tag{33}$$

Defining the state error signal, $x = x_m - x_p$, yields the differential equation

$$\dot{x} = f(x_m, x, u) = f_m(x_m) - f_p(x_p, u) \tag{34}$$

The control input is generated by a controller $u = k(x_m, x)$ which is dependent on the reference model state and the reference error.

One control strategy is to choose a collection of setpoints along the reference trajectory, $x_m(t)$, and design linear control agents at each of the setpoints using the plant model obtained from linearizing about the corresponding setpoint. This is the basic idea behind the switched linear control agent approach introduced in [8]. Note that each of the control agents designed using this approach are designed for local performance near each of the setpoints; performance of the switched system will be difficult to guarantee, in general. Thus, the linear control agents should demonstrate robustness to the nonlinearities in the system lost in the linearization. One way of incorporating this robustness requirement into the design is to use linear parameter varying (LPV) plant models at each of the setpoints.

An LPV model of the error dynamics may be obtained by rewriting the dynamics of equation 34 as

$$\dot{x} = A(\theta)x + B_u(\theta)u + B_w(\theta)w \tag{35}$$
$$z = Cx + Du \tag{36}$$

where $w = 1$ is introduced as a fictitious disturbance. The s-dimensional parameter vector, θ, is a function $S(x_m, x, u)$. The vector θ is assumed to vary continuously over a compact subset $\tilde{\Theta} \subset \Re^s$; this assumption is denoted $\theta \in \mathcal{F}_{\tilde{\Theta}}$. For each of the local plant models, θ is assumed to vary continuously over a compact subset $\Theta \subseteq \tilde{\Theta}$ for a time interval $[\tau_s, \tau_f]$; this assumption is denoted $\theta \in \mathcal{F}_\Theta[\tau_s, \tau_f]$. This notation distinguishes a *parameter variation* over Θ from a point in Θ which will be denoted $\theta \in \Theta$. The vector z will be called the *objective signal* and is chosen (via C and D) to reflect not only the the trigger constraints, but also control energy constraints. The entire LPV system will be denoted as $\Sigma(\tilde{\Theta}, A, B, C, D)$ where $B = [B_u \; B_w]$.

Let $\mathcal{T}_i = [t_i, t_{i+1})$ denote the time interval over which the ith setpoint controller issued. Note that if each individual setpoint controller satisfies the performance requirement,

$$\sup_{t \in \mathcal{T}_i} \|z(t)\| < \gamma \tag{37}$$

then local safety of the control directive will be preserved. Local setpoint controllers are therefore obtained by solving what is called a finite horizon $\mathcal{L}_1$, or *bounded-amplitude*, optimal control problem for LPV systems.

There are, unfortunately, relatively few results for the solution of $\mathcal{L}_1$ optimal control problems. In [4], it was shown that optimal solutions to this problem are irrational or infinite dimensional, even for rational and finite-dimensional plants. For deterministic linear time-invariant systems [9] an approach to $\mathcal{L}_1$ optimal control synthesized a sub-optimal controller minimizing an upper bound on the bounded-amplitude gain by solving a set of linear matrix inequalities. To use this prior work in our synthesis problems, however, existing synthesis methods must be extended to LPV systems. The following theorem provides a characterization of systems whose $\mathcal{L}_1$ gains are bounded.

Note: The remainder of the paper will use the following notation: the infinite-horizon ∞-norm of a signal $x(t)$ is defined as $\|x(t)\|_\infty := \sup_t \|x(t)\|$ where $\| \cdot \|$ is the Euclidean norm. $\mathcal{L}_\infty^n$ is the space of n-dimensional vector signals with finite ∞-norm; $B\mathcal{L}_\infty^n$ is the space of n-dimensional vector signals with ∞-norm bounded by 1. For a constants $\tau < T$, finite-horizon ∞-norm of a signal $x(t)$ defined on the interval $[\tau, T]$ is $\|x(t)\|_{\infty, [\tau, T]} := \sup_{t \in [\tau, T]} \|x(t)\|$. $\mathcal{L}_\infty^n[\tau, T]$ and $B\mathcal{L}_\infty^n[\tau, T]$ are defined in an analogous manner. Recall that $\theta \in \mathcal{F}_\Theta[\tau, T]$ is an s-dimensional signal $\theta(t)$ which takes values on a compact subset $\Theta \subset \Re^s$ for $t \in [\tau, T]$. This implies that $\theta \in \mathcal{L}_\infty^s[\tau, T]$

Proposition 3.
Given constants $r > 0$, $\gamma > 0$ and $T > 0$ and the LPV system $\Sigma(\tilde{\Theta}, A, B, C, D)$ with $u = 0$. Let Θ be a compact subset of $\tilde{\Theta}$ and suppose there exists $\alpha > 0$ and $\beta \geq 0$ and a positive definite matrix $P \in \Re^{n \times n}$ satisfying

$$P \geq \frac{r}{\gamma^2}C'C \tag{38}$$

and

$$A'(\theta)P + PA(\theta) + \left(2\beta + \frac{\alpha}{r}\right)P + \frac{1}{\alpha}PB_w(\theta)B_w(\theta)'P \leq 0 \tag{39}$$

for all $\theta \in \Theta$. If $\theta \in \mathcal{F}_\Theta[0, T]$ and $w \in B\mathcal{L}_\infty^{n_w}[0, T]$, then

- *if $x'(0)Px(0) \leq r$ then $x'(t)Px(t) \leq r$ and $z'(t)z(t) \leq \gamma^2$ for all $t \in [0,T]$*
- *if $\beta > 0$ and $x'(0)Px(0) = r_0 > r$, then $x'(t)Px(t) \leq r$ for all $t \in [t_d, T]$ where*

$$t_d := -\frac{1}{2\beta} \log\left(\frac{r}{r_0}\right) \tag{40}$$

(assuming $t_d \leq T$).

Proof: Let $r > 0$, $\gamma > 0$ and $T > 0$ and assume there are constants $\alpha > 0$ and $\beta \geq 0$ and a positive definite matrix P so that the conditions of the theorem are satisfied. For any $\theta \in \Theta$,

$$\frac{1}{\alpha}PB(\theta)B'(\theta)P \geq 0 \tag{41}$$

If equation 39 holds for all $\theta \in \Theta$, then

$$A'(\theta)P + PA(\theta) + \left(\frac{\alpha}{r} + 2\beta\right)P \leq -\frac{1}{\alpha}PB(\theta)B'(\theta)P \leq 0 \tag{42}$$

Using Schur complements, this inequality is true if and only if

$$\begin{bmatrix} A'(\theta)P + P(\theta) + \rho P & PB(\theta) \\ B'(\theta)P & -\alpha I \end{bmatrix} \leq 0 \tag{43}$$

where $\rho = 2\beta + \alpha/r$. This inequality is true if and only if

$$\begin{bmatrix} \xi \\ \nu \end{bmatrix}' \begin{bmatrix} A'(\theta)P + PA(\theta) + \rho P & PB(\theta) \\ B'(\theta)P & -\alpha I \end{bmatrix} \begin{bmatrix} \xi \\ \nu \end{bmatrix} \leq 0 \tag{44}$$

for all $\xi \in \Re^n$ and $\nu \in \Re^{n_w}$. Expanding, it is apparent that

$$\xi'[A'(\theta)P + PA(\theta) + 2\beta P]\xi + \nu'B'(\theta)P\xi + \xi'PB(\theta)\nu - \frac{\alpha}{r}[\xi'P\xi - r] + \alpha[1 - \nu'\nu] \leq 0 \tag{45}$$

This last equation implies that

$$\xi'[A'(\theta)P + PA(\theta)]\xi + \nu'B'(\theta)P\xi + \xi'PB(\theta)\nu \leq -2\beta\xi'P\xi \leq 0 \tag{46}$$

for all ξ and ν such that $\xi'P\xi \geq r$ and $\nu'\nu \leq 1$.

Now consider a function, $V : \Re^n \to \Re$, such that $V(\xi) = \xi'P\xi$. Along trajectories of the LPV system with $u = 0$, the time derivative of $V(x(t))$ is

$$\frac{dV}{dt}(x(t)) = x'(t)[A'(\theta(t))P + PA(\theta(t))]x(t) + w'(t)B'(\theta(t))Px(t) + x'(t)PB(\theta(t))w(t) \tag{47}$$

and from equation 46, it is immediately evident that

$$\frac{dV}{dt}(x(t)) \leq -2\beta V(x(t)) \leq 0 \tag{48}$$

for any $x(t)$ and $w(t)$ such that $x'(t)Px(t) \geq r$ and $w'(t)w(t) \leq 1$ with $t \in [0,T]$.

Assume, for some $w \in B\mathcal{L}_\infty^{n_w}[0,T]$, that there is a trajectory with initial state $x(0)$ satisfying $V(x(0)) = x'(0)Px(0) \leq r$ and $V(x(T)) > r$. Since $V(x(t))$ is differentiable in t, the mean value theorem may be used to imply the existence of a time $\tau \in [0,T]$ such that $V(x(\tau)) \geq r$ and $\dot{V}(x(\tau)) > 0$. This is a contradiction of equation 48, so one must conclude that $x'(t)Px(t) \leq r$, hence $z'(t)z(t) \leq \gamma^2$, for all $t \in [0,T]$.

If $V(x(0)) > r$, then the differential inequality implies that

$$V(x(t) \leq V(x(0)) - \int_0^t 2\beta V(x(\tau))d\tau \tag{49}$$

and the Bellman-Gronwall inequality may be used to conclude that

$$V(x(t)) \leq V(x(0))e^{-2\beta t} \tag{50}$$

Now suppose that $V(x(0)) = r_0 > r$, $\beta > 0$ and let t_d be the *dwell time* given in equation 40. If $t_d \leq T$, then

$$V(x(t)) \leq r_0 e^{-2\beta t_d} = r \tag{51}$$

for all $t \in [t_d, T]$. $\qquad\qquad\qquad\qquad\qquad\qquad\qquad\qquad\qquad\qquad\qquad\qquad\qquad\qquad\square$

Proposition 3 characterizes a class of uncontrolled ($u = 0$) LPV systems where $\|z\|_{\infty,[0,T]} \leq \gamma$ and where the parameter variation is confined to the set Θ. The next result helps characterize a class of controlled LPV systems using linear state feedback, $u = Kx$.

Proposition 4.
Given $\gamma > 0$ and an LPV system $\Sigma(\tilde{\Theta}, A, B, C, D)$ with state space realization

$$\begin{bmatrix} \dot{x}(t) \\ z(t) \end{bmatrix} = \left[\begin{array}{c|cc} A(\theta) & B_u(\theta) & B_w(\theta) \\ \hline C & 0 & D \end{array} \right] \begin{bmatrix} x \\ u \\ w \end{bmatrix} \tag{52}$$

Let $\Theta \subseteq \tilde{\Theta}$ be a compact subset and consider a state feedback control law $u = Kx$ where $K \in \Re^{n_u \times n}$. Define $\tilde{A}(\theta) = A(\theta) + B_u(\theta)K$. Then, there exist constants $\alpha_1 \geq \alpha_2 > 0$, a positive definite matrix $P \in \Re^{n \times n}$ and a controller K satisfying

$$P \geq \frac{1}{\gamma^2}(C + DK)'(C + DK) \tag{53}$$

and

$$\tilde{A}(\theta)P + P\tilde{A}(\theta) + \alpha_1 P + \frac{1}{\alpha_2}PB_w(\theta)B_w(\theta)'P \leq 0 \tag{54}$$

for all $\theta \in \Theta$ if and only if there exists a positive definite matrix $Q \in \Re^{n \times n}$ and a matrix $V \in \Re^{n_u \times n}$ such that for all $\theta \in \Theta$

$$\begin{bmatrix} Q & QC' + V'D' \\ CQ + DV & \gamma^2 I \end{bmatrix} \geq 0 \tag{55}$$

and

$$QA'(\theta) + A(\theta)Q + \alpha_1 Q + \frac{1}{\alpha_2}B_w(\theta)B_1'(\theta) + B_u(\theta)V + V'B_u'(\theta) \leq 0 \tag{56}$$

Proof: Assume that there exists a positive definite matrix Q and a matrix V such that

$$\begin{bmatrix} Q & QC' + V'D' \\ CQ + DV & \gamma^2 I \end{bmatrix} \geq 0 \tag{57}$$

Using Schur complements, this holds if and only if

$$Q - \frac{1}{\gamma^2}(QC' + V'D')(CQ + DV) \geq 0 \tag{58}$$

If we let $P = Q^{-1}$ and $K = VQ^{-1}$, then this holds if and only if

$$P \geq \frac{1}{\gamma^2}(C + DK)'(C + DK) \tag{59}$$

which establishes the first condition in the proposition.

Now assume that there also exist constants $\alpha_1 \geq \alpha_2 > 0$ such that

$$\tilde{A}(\theta)P + P\tilde{A}(\theta) + \alpha_1 P + \frac{1}{\alpha_2}PB_w(\theta)B_w(\theta)'P \leq 0$$

for all $\theta \in \Theta$. Substituting $P = Q^{-1}$ and $K = VQ^{-1}$ as above,

$$[A(\theta) + B_u(\theta)K]'P + P[A(\theta) + B_u(\theta)K] + \alpha_1 P + \frac{1}{\alpha_2}PB_w(\theta)B_w'(\theta)P \tag{60}$$

$$= Q^{-1} \left[QA'(\theta) + A(\theta)Q + \alpha_1 Q + \frac{1}{\alpha_2} B_u(\theta)B'_u(\theta) + B_w(\theta)V + V'B'_w(\theta) \right] Q^{-1} \tag{61}$$

Since $Q^{-1} > 0$, the conclusion of the theorem immediately follows. □

The following remarks summarize the importance of propositions 3 and 4.

- Under the assumptions of proposition 3 and 4, it should be apparent that if the inequalities 55 and 56 hold, then under control $u = Kx$, the objective function $z = (C + DK)x$ will have a finite horizon sup-norm less than γ provided that the parameter variation is bounded according to $\theta \in \mathcal{F}_\Theta[0, T]$.
- From the proof of proposition 4 it should be apparent that the matrices Q and V satisfying inequalities 55 and 56 parameterize a set of locally safe controllers. In particular, for any such Q and V, the controller is $K = VQ^{-1}$.
- The importance of inequalities 55 and 56 is that these can be used to form matrix inequalities which are *linear* in Q and V. These inequalities need only be satisfied *pointwise* over Θ without regard to parameter variation rate, as long as the parameter variation is bounded according to $\theta \in \mathcal{F}_\Theta[0, T]$.
- Note that the θ dependence of inequality 56 limits its usefulness: verifying the condition for all $\theta \in \Theta$ may be unreasonable or infeasible. In certain cases, however, the computational burden can be significantly reduced. For instance, if $A(\theta)$, $B_u(\theta)$ and $B_w(\theta)$ can be written as linear fractional transformations in θ, and if the parameter set Θ is a polytope, then it is possible to express inequality 56 as a matrix inequality which is independent of θ and linear in the variables Q and V. Derivation of such LMIs is a straightforward application of the results in [3]; a detailed proof is beyond the scope of this paper but can be found in [2].

The results in proposition 3 are extremely important in determining whether or not a given set of linear setpoint controllers will safely execute a supervisory directive. Let $\mathcal{T}_i$ be the time interval when the ith setpoint controller is used. This controller is characterized by the matrices P_i, the radius r_i, and constants, α_i and β_i. The results in this proposition state that the controlled system will be locally safe if the error satisfies $x'(t_i)P_i x(t_i) \leq r_i^2$. To ensure that the plant behavior is safe under the next $(i + 1\text{st})$ setpoint controller, one must ensure that $x'(t_{i+1})P_{i+1}x(t_{i+1}) \leq r_{i+1}^2$. The problem here is that the second condition is not guaranteed if the switch occurs too quickly. This is where the second part of proposition 3 has something to add. Specifically, if the state at time t_i starts outside of the invariant set for the $i + 1$st setpoint controller, then there is a minimum time called the dwell time, after which the state is guaranteed of being within the required distance. In particular, let $r_i P_{i+1} \leq r_{i+1} P_i$ and assume that P_i and P_{i+1} both satisfy the conditions for setpoint controllers in proposition 3. It is readily apparent that if $t_{i+1} - t_i \geq t_d$, where

$$t_d = -\frac{1}{2\beta_i} \log \frac{r_{i+1}}{r_i}, \tag{62}$$

then

$$\|z\|_{\infty,[t_i, t_{i+2}]} \leq \gamma \tag{63}$$

The satisfaction of the inequality constraints, of course, also requires that $\theta(t)$ lie in Θ_1 for $t_i \leq t < t_{i+1}$ (i.e. $\theta \in \mathcal{F}_{\Theta_1}[t_i, t_{i+1}]$) and in Θ_2 for $t_{i+1} \leq t \leq t_{i+2}$. Satisfaction of this parameter variation condition is non-trivial to verify.

The preceding discussion has outlined how the conditions determined in proposition 3 can be used to ensure safe behavior between the switch of two different setpoint controllers. These conditions are summarized in the following proposition.

Proposition 5 LPV Switching Lemma.
Given LPV systems $\Sigma(\tilde{\Theta}, A_1, B_1, C_1, D_1)$, and $\Sigma(\tilde{\Theta}, A_2, B_2, C_2, D_2)$ with associated controllers K_1 and K_2, let the ith controller $(i = 1, 2)$ be characterized by matrix P_i, and constants, r_i, α_i, and β_i so that the conditions of propositions 3 and 4 are satisfied for compact parameter sets $\Theta_i \subseteq \tilde{\Theta}$. Assume that controller K_1 is used over time interval $t \in [t_0, t_s)$ and that controller K_2 is used for time interval $t \in [t_s, T]$ for any $T > t_s$. If $r_1 P_2 \leq r_2 P_1$ and the switch time t_s satisfies

$$t_s - t_0 \geq -\frac{1}{2\beta_1} \log \frac{r_2}{r_1}, \tag{64}$$

and if $\theta \in \{\mathcal{F}_{\Theta_1}[t_0, t_s], \mathcal{F}_{\Theta_2}[t_s, T]\}$ then $\|z\|_{\infty,[0,T]} \leq \gamma$.

The LPV switching lemma suggests a means of testing to see whether or not a given collection of linear setpoint controllers will generate a safe trajectory. Essentially, this involves verifying the dwell-time condition for all possible switching times and verifying the conditions on the parameter variation. The required dwell-times may be computed from the synthesis LMIs and the coupling condition $r_1 P_2 \leq r_2 P_1$. Switching times and parameter variation bounds are more difficult to verify, but in many cases, a *nominal parameter trajectory*, $S(x_m(t), 0, 0)$, may be used to estimate these quantities off-line [1]. These estimates may then be compared to the dwell-time results as a sufficient condition for safeness.

Example: As an illustration of some of the important aspects of the MRC-approach, the methods described above were applied to the process control example described in section 3. The reference model

$$\begin{aligned} \dot{x}_{m1} &= x_{m1} - 1.63 - x_{m1}/(1 + 0.5\sin 10(x_{m1} - 1.63)) \\ \dot{x}_{m2} &= 1 \end{aligned} \tag{65}$$

is specified to move the plant from an initial state near the operating point $(x_{p1}, x_{p2}) = (2.5, 2)$ to a point near $(x_{p1}, x_{p2}) = (1, 3)$ in 1 second. The performance weights for the objective function were chosen as $C = I$ and $D = 0.1I$; the desired bound on the objective function was $\gamma = 0.5$.

The LPV error system is derived as

$$\begin{aligned} \dot{x} &= A(\theta)x + B_u(\theta)u + B_w(\theta)w \\ z &= Cx + Du \end{aligned} \tag{66}$$

with

$$A(\theta) = \begin{bmatrix} -1 & 0 \\ 0 & -1 \end{bmatrix}, \quad B_w(\theta) = \begin{bmatrix} \theta_1 - 1.63 \\ \theta_2 + 1 \end{bmatrix} \quad \text{and} \quad B_u(\theta) = \begin{bmatrix} -1 & 0 \\ 0 & -\theta_3 - 1 \end{bmatrix}, \tag{67}$$

and parameter mapping

$$\begin{bmatrix} \theta_1 \\ \theta_2 \\ \theta_3 \end{bmatrix} = S(x_m, x, u) = \begin{bmatrix} 2x_{m1} - x_{m1}/(1 + 0.5\sin 10(x_{m1} - 1.63)) \\ x_{m2} + (2x_{m1}x_1 - x_1^2)u_2 \\ x_{m1}^2 \end{bmatrix}. \tag{68}$$

Linear state feedback control agents, $u = Kx$, were designed by choosing setpoints, $\theta^{nom} = S(x_m^{nom}, 0, 0)$ and solving the appropriate synthesis LMIs for parameter sets

$$\Theta := \left\{ \theta \,\middle|\, \sup_{i=1,\ldots,s} |\theta_i - \theta_i^{nom}| \leq \vartheta \right\}$$

for a design parameter $\vartheta > 0$. Switching control was achieved by switching a new feedback controller into the loop whenever the parameter variation evolved onto the boundary of the current agent's parameter set. The new control agent was chosen to minimize a distance measure in the parameter space.

A Matlab program was written to solve the appropriate synthesis LMIs, as indicated above, and simulate the closed loop system. Simulations were performed for various values of ϑ, resulting in experiments requiring varying numbers of models. The resulting trajectory for nine models is depicted in figure 3a. Figure 3a also depicts the reference trajectory and forbidden (shaded) regions of the state space. Note that the resulting trajectory is safe and nonchattering. Similar results were observed for different numbers of models. Figure 3b depicts the resulting trend observed for increasing numbers of models. Note the monotonic improvement in performance with increasing numbers of models. The average $\|\theta_{err}\|$ represents a mismatch between the reference model dynamics and the multiple agent controlled system; the result in the figure indicates that an increase in the number of agents (via a reduction in ϑ) results in improved dynamical model matching. The other performance curves are self-explanatory.

As with the previous example of the LP-approach, this example depicts some of the fundamental characteristics of the MRC-approach. The approach is an off-line procedure which requires the solution of LMI problems. In the present form, the computation of the control requires explicit

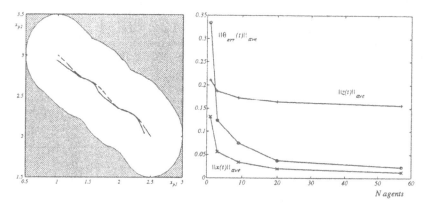

Fig. 3. Simulation Results: *(a)* reference trajectory (dashed) and controlled plant state (solid) with forbidden regions (shaded). *(b)* Average performance versus number of agents

knowledge of the plant dynamics and direct measurement of the plant state. However, because the approach is based primarily on Lyapunov and structured uncertainty methods for robust control design, the approach should be extendable to uncertain systems. The computational burden is large, but it is off-line and the payoff is a nonchattering control which satisfies amplitude constraints.

5 Conclusions

This paper has compared two methods for safe implementation of supervisory commands in hybrid dynamical control systems, called the LP method and the MRC method. Both methods appear to be able to guarantee the bounded amplitude performance requirements dictated by the hybrid design problem, assuming knowledge of the plant dynamics. The LP method produces a chattering control policy versus the nonchattering control policy generated by the MRC method. Both methods require that the plant dynamics do not vary too rapidly.

While both methods require explicit knowledge of the plant dynamics, the MRC method appears to be more amenable to incorporation of modeling uncertainty and disturbances into the design, yielding robust control policies. Furthermore, the designs may be accomplished using the same tools as for the nominal case since the design tools are linear robust design techniques. The LP method may offer such advantages, but they are not apparent.

In the area of numerical complexity, the LP method requires the solution of simple linear programming problems which, of course, can be solved quickly and efficiently. This advantage is offset, somewhat, by the fact that the linear programs must be solved on-line and often. On the other hand, the MRC method requires the solution of a series of larger convex optimization problems. However, while this requires a more computationally intensive effort, the procedure is performed off-line and must only be performed once.

References

1. C.J. Bett and M.D. Lemmon. Bounded amplitude control using multiple linear agents. Technical Report ISIS-97-004, Department of Electrical Engineering, University of Notre Dame, Notre Dame, IN, 1997.
2. C.J. Bett and M.D. Lemmon. Finite horizon bounded amplitude control of linear parameter varying systems. Technical Report ISIS-97-002, Department of Electrical Engineering, University of Notre Dame, Notre Dame, IN, 1997. Submitted for publication in *Automatica*. Short version to appear 1997 Automatic Control Conference.

3. Stephen Boyd, Laurent El Gaoui, Eric Feron, and Venkataramanan Balakrishnan. *Linear Matrix Inequalities in System and Control Theory*. Society for Industrial and Applied Mathematics, 1994.

4. M.A. Dahleh and J.B. Pearson. L^1-optimal compensators for continuous-time systems. *IEEE Transactions on Automatic Control*, 32(10):889–895, October 1987.

5. Akash Deshpande and Pravin Varaiya. Viable control of hybrid systems. In Panos Antsaklis, Wolf Kohn, Anil Nerode, and Shankar Sastry, editors, *Hybrid Systems II*, pages 128–147. Springer-Verlag, 1995. Lecture Notes in Computer Science, Volume 999.

6. A. Isidori. *Nonlinear Control Systems*. Springer-Verlag, 2nd edition, 1989.

7. W. Kohn and A. Nerode. Multiple agent autonomous hybrid control systems. In Grossman, Nerode, Ravn, and Rischel, editors, *Hybrid Systems*, pages 297–316. Springer-Verlag, 1993. Lecture Notes in Computer Science, Volume 736.

8. M. Lemmon and C. Bett. Robust hybrid control system design. In *Proceedings of the 1996 IFAC World Congress*, volume J, pages 395–400, San Francisco, CA, June 1996.

9. K. Nagpal, J. Abedor, and K. Poolla. An LMI approach to peak-to-peak gain minimization: filtering and control. In *Proceedings of the American Control Conference*, pages 742–746, Baltimore, Maryland, June 1994.

Hybrid System Games: Extraction of Control Automata with Small Topologies

Anil Nerode[*1] and Jeffrey B. Remmel[**2] and Alexander Yakhnis[***]

[1] Mathematical Sciences Institute
Cornell University, Ithaca, NY 14853
e-mail: anil@math.cornell.edu
HyBrithms Corp.
[2] HyBrithms Corp.[†]
11201 S.E. 8th Street, Bldg. J, Suite 140
Bellevue, Washington and
Department of Mathematics
University of California at San Diego San Diego, CA 92093
e-mail; jremmel@ucsd.edu
[3] Mathematical Sciences Institute
Cornell University, Ithaca, NY 14853
e-mail: ayakh@math.cornell.edu

1 Introduction

Hybrid control is the control of continuous plants by sequential automata. This usually means frequent changes in the continuous conventional control law applied to the plant, changes based on sensor measurements of the trajectory. This typically yields plant trajectories without smooth tangents at the discrete times when the control law ordered by the control program changes. How and when to make these control law changes is the business of the sequential automaton. The question is then how should we model this and how can we find control sequential automata to meet a prescribed performance specification.

We propose a game framework for analyzing, extracting and verifying digital control programs for continuous plants by regarding such programs as finite state winning strategies in associated games. We call such interacting systems of digital control programs and continuous plants "hybrid systems" and model them as networks of interacting concurrent digital programs or automata, following [36], [37]. This extends to hybrid systems the paradigm introduced by A. Nerode, A. Yakhnis, and V. Yakhnis [38] for analyzing concurrent digital programs meeting program specifications as winning finite state strategies in

* Research supported by ARO under the MURI program "Integrated Approach to Intelligent Systems", grant no. DAAHO4-96-1-0341.
** Research supported by Dept. of Commerce Agreement 70-NANB5H1164.
*** supported by DARPA- US ARMY AMCCOM (Picatinny Arsenal, N. J.) contract DAAA21-92-C-0013 to ORA Corp.
† HyBrithms Corp was formerly known as Sagent Corporation

associated two person games. This hybrid game formulation is intended to facilitate the transfer of recent tools from logic, concurrency, and dynamical systems to extraction and verification of digital control programs for continuous systems. Hybrid Games also facilitate infusion into hybrid systems theory of many ideas from the traditional differential game approach to control.

The Basic Model

We now introduce our basic model for Hybrid Control which is essentially the same as the model discussed in [24]. A finite control automaton is an automaton with finite input and output alphabets and a finite number of internal states. Its input letters are fired by measurements of plant state. Its output letters are control signals, that is mode switches, for the plant controller. Our basic model for a simple hybrid system consists of the following.

1. A finite control automaton, which is usually thought of as some sort of logical device or program which makes inferences based on current information about the plant state to deduce when to change control laws for the plant. See Kohn-Nerode [24], [25].

2. A continuous plant controller obeying the control law currently supplied by the finite control automaton.

3. A continuous plant being controlled. We include in the plant the physical plant controller (actuator), but not the finite control automaton feeding control orders (mode switches) to the physical plant controller.

4. An analog-to-digital or, equivalently, a signal to symbol, converter supplying to the finite control automaton as input digitized sensor data sampled from the plant.

5. A digital-to-analog or, equivalently, a symbol to signal converter converting symbolic control orders output by the control automaton into a control function of time regulating the parameters of the physical plant controller.

These elements are pictured in Figure 1.

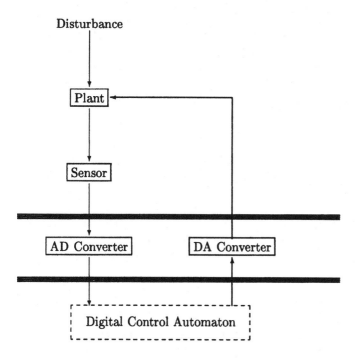

ANALOG WORLD

Disturbance

Plant

Sensor

AD Converter   DA Converter

Digital Control Automaton

DIGITAL WORLD
Figure 1.

We summarize the essential features of hybrid systems model of [24]. We think of the sequential control automaton as completing "work cycles" in successive intervals Δt_k of time. During the interval Δt_k, a control law u_k which is imposed by the sequential control automaton at the end of the previous interval is active in controlling the system. Also the sequential control automaton is subject during Δt_k to an input v_k to the system. During the first phase of Δt_k, the sequential control automaton is accumulating a sensor data history s about the system through the analog-to-digital converter. The sequential control automaton starts interval Δt_k in a certain initial state, uses s to compute a new control law u_{k+1} and a new automaton state and, at the end of Δt_k, it outputs u_{k+1} through the digital-to-analog converter to the plant controller for use in the next interval Δt_{k+1}. Then all processes start over for Δt_{k+1}. We envisage the input as encoding all the partial information available to the control automaton about the state of the plant. A hybrid control run thus will be a possibly infinite sequence

$$u_0, v_0, u_1, v_1, \ldots.$$

We shall see that it is very natural to view such a hybrid control run as play of a game between two players, Plant and Control. That is, Control and Plant alternate moves in a game in which Control moves by listing full information about control law u_k for Plant's use, and then Plant moves by listing the partial information v_k about the plant state for Control's use. The range of values of u_k and v_k and the relationship between u_k and v_k is dependent on the particular application. Then, in the spirit of [38], we can view a successful sequential control automaton as implementing a winning strategy for Control. That is, in any play in which Control follows the winning strategy and Plant plays according to the rules of the game, i.e. follows its differential equations, the plant trajectories will meet the desired performance specification.

Performance Specifications

Our performance specifications are usually open sets of trajectories. Quoting an example of Kohn, the Boeing 737 was to be designed so that if a cup of coffee is no more than 3/4 full anywhere in the aircraft, it never spills during maneuvers. This is not a conventional optimality requirement. It is a "perform sufficiently well" criterion which we call an ϵ-performance criterion or, alternately, an ϵ-optimality condition. For example, such a criterion might require that we produce a trajectory whose costs is within a user defined ϵ of the minimum cost trajectory.

Outline of Paper

In sections 2 and 3, we present game models for extraction, analysis, and verification of control strategies for simple hybrid systems. All games will be between two players, Plant and Control. The objective of any game is for Control to force Plant to obey its performance specification. In the game model presented in section 2, measurements of Plant state are made at discrete times (discrete sensing) and changes in the control order to the plant are also made at discrete times (discrete mode switching). Such games are an adaptation to hybrid systems of the games of A. Nerode, A. Yakhnis, and V. Yakhnis [38]. The latter were introduced to extract, analyze, and verify digital concurrent programs.

In Section 3, we introduce "continuous sensing games" to model plants characterized by continuous dynamics, such as a system of ordinary differential equations, with a controller which continuously senses the plant state. We assume that the controller is allowed to reset the parameters of the plant dynamics at a sequence of discrete times only. Such controllers allow us to model directly analog sensors which continuously sense the plant state and which output exact real number control parameters to the physical plant controller at discrete times. In most cases, we will assume that the values output by the controller are purely digital, one of a finite number of control order, to be implemented by a digital to analog converter. Even in such cases, such a controller must be regarded as non-digital if the input values allowed are exact real numbers, even if there are only a finite number of internal states and a finite number of output control orders (mode switches). Our methodology is to start by extracting a continuously sensing, discretely acting, feedback control function which meets the performance specification. The discrete sensing games of Section 3 can then be thought of as subgames of continuous sensing games in which the information sensed between discrete sampling times is ignored.

Thus continuous sensing games are a second class of games between two players, Plant and Control. After each control order is sent by Control to the plant, Plant displays a segment of a plant trajectory y which begins when control order is given, with initial condition the plant state at that time, and which ends when the next control order is issued. We can think of this segment as a contiguous block of Plant moves, one at each time in that interval. In this picture the Plant move at a time $\tau > t$ in the interval is just the plant state $y(\tau)$. In the same picture, a Control move occurs at the same instant τ and is either *no action* or a control order. We call the latter moves essential Control moves. We assume that essential Control moves occur only at a discrete sequence of times. Each such time is the end of a block of Plant moves. According to this picture, in a continuous sensing game, Plant plays continuously, Control has continuous knowledge of Plant moves, and Control makes essential moves only once in a while.

The motivation for introducing continuous sensing games is that they help us extract strategies for a digital controller which will meet performance specifications. The idea is that it often easier to find a (non-digital) continuous state strategy for Control in a continuous sensing game which forces the plant to meet performance specifications. We then extract a finite state strategy for a finite state digital controller doing approximately the same thing by approximating to the continuous strategy for the non-digital controller using the Kohn-Nerode method of extracting finite control automata from finite open covers.

In Section 4, we discuss performance specifications and the Kohn-Nerode method cover method ([24], appendix 2). It works as follows. Suppose we are given a controller which meet an open specification. Then the Kohn-Nerode method takes an open finite cover of that controller within the open specification and interprets it as:

1. A finite automaton with a finite input alphabet and a finite state alphabet.

2. A digital to analog converter.

3. An analog to digital converter.

4. A control automaton for the plant.

When considered as a hybrid system, the plant plus the automaton derived from the cover forces the plant to obey the open performance specification. We carry out this process for a simple model of a water pump used to maintain a certain range of values of the water in a water tank. That is, we shall explicitly construct a strategy for Control in a continuous sensing game which models this system and then show how we can easily approximate such a strategy to construct a strategy for Control in a corresponding discrete sensing game. Finally we shall show how this enables us to design a digital control automaton for the hybrid system which meets the performance specifications as well as how to construct the Kohn-Nerode small topologies for the hybrid system which will verify the controllability-observability of the system in the sense of [24].

2 Games with Discrete Sensing and Discrete Mode Switching

In this section, we provide a game setting for the specification, extraction, and verification of digital control programs for hybrid systems. Extracting a control program for a continuous plant which forces the plant to obey a performance specification is identified with extracting a winning finite state strategy in an associated game. The performance specification itself is identified with a set of acceptable plant state trajectories. The games introduced in this section and the next section, each have two players, Control and Plant. In our games, we represent the effect on plant state of unknown disturbances and uncertain measurements by allowing multiple legal moves for Plant. For example, one source of multiple possible moves for Plant is that, with a given initial condition, each disturbance over a time interval $[t, t + \Delta]$ can yield a different plant state trajectory over that interval and hence a different final plant state at the end of the time interval. Another source of multiple Plant moves is measurement errors. We assume Control sends perfect information to the physical plant controller, namely a suitable control law for the next interval of time. However Plant sends imperfect information to the Control program, namely sensory measurements of plant state with error. Thus our games are games with perfect information on the control law transmitted by Control to Plant, but with imperfect information on Plant state transmitted to Control by Plant.

Our game approach is different from traditional methods of extracting control in the presence of disturbances or measurement uncertainties. For example, one traditional control engineering approach is to start instead with a deterministic plant model which does not incorporate either disturbances or measurement uncertainties, to proceed to extract a suitable control program for the deterministic model, and afterwards to determine the effect of small changes in measurements and parameters on observability, controllability, and stability of the hybrid system. Another approach is to model the Plant by stochastic differential equations in the first place, and to look for stochastic control programs with optimal control features. A third approach is to use a two person differential game between Control and Plant or between Control and Disturbance. This usually entails extracting continuous control strategies which change control values continuously, based on continuous measurements of plant state. To extract such a continuously sensing continuously controlling strategy using differential games usually requires elaborate mathematical apparatus when it is possible at all. Our games approach differs from all three. Control strategies are not derived directly from a deterministic model. The model does not involve stochastic processes. It is a game approach, but not the usual differential games approach. In our games, one player, Plant, is constrained to follow a differential or difference equation guided by controls and subject to disturbances. The change is that, in our games, measurements of Plant state are communicated to Control only at discrete prescribed times, while a change in the control function imposed by Control on the Plant can be imposed instantaneously. The changes imposed by Control on the plant are event-driven based on the current state of the control automaton and the current measurement of plant state. Restricting Control in this way is natural if Control is to be a digital program, since a digital program changes its state based on a discrete sequence of successive input symbols representing plant measurements. Even if Control is not restricted to a digital program with finite alphabets and states, the discrete sensing, discrete mode switching control strategies turn out to be useful as intermediate idealized programs to extract before refining them to finite state strategies which give controllable-observable behavior.

The system model underlying our game is the hybrid systems model of Kohn-Nerode, [24] and [25], to which the reader is referred. The games approach stems from the Nerode-Yakhnis-Yakhnis [38] formulation of extracting concurrent programs as solving an appropriate game. The hybrid systems games were first announced in Nerode-Yakhnis [36],[37].

Control automata which sense plant state at discrete times but exercise control over the plant continuously, with only occasional mode switching, operate in the following way. Their input alphabets, internal states, and output alphabets can be any finite or infinite nonempty set. They can be regarded as nondeterministic automata operating in continuous time. They change their input alphabet letter and internal state instantaneously at a discrete sequence of time instants only, being in the previous automaton state in a non-empty open interval preceding each such moment. These are the moments when sense data about the plant are communicated to the control automaton. Only at these times does the control automaton instantaneously change its output letter, called a control order. This output letter is to be interpreted in applications as a control order to the plant physical controller to change the control law used in that physical controller. For instance, in Kohn-Nerode extraction procedure [26, 15], this issued control order is a chattering control implemented via a finite sequence of "primitive" control actions, each specifying a physical controller parameter to be used for some period. Such a control order is a finite sequence of infinitesimal generators of flows. Each flow is to be followed in the prescribed order for a prescribed relative duration of the interval of time over which this control order persists.

In summary, control orders, or mode switches, are issued by the control automaton on an event driven basis based on past sense measurements of plant state. Although we allow the set of control automaton states to be infinite, in all our examples the automaton will be finite state, while the input alphabet representing possible sense measurements will be infinite.

Next we describe the underlying assumptions on the plant model and the control automaton for our basic discrete sensing game.

We assume as a physical realizability requirement that the discrete times at which the the control automaton issues control orders, $t_0 < t_1 < t_2 < t_3 < ....$, have a positive lower bound for the differences $t_{i+1} - t_i$. This usually called the Zeno requirement. We call these sequences admissible time sequences. In this section, we shall assume that for all i, $t_{i+1} - t_i = T$ is a fixed positive constant T. In a later section, this simplification is dropped.

Plant model

Our basic assumption of the plant model are the following.

1. We assume the plant is modeled by an ordinary vector differential equation

$$\dot{y}(t) = f(t, y(t), u(t), d(t)),$$

   where $y(t)$ is the plant state, $u(t)$ is a control function, and $d(t)$ is disturbance function.

2. The time t will range over the real interval $[0, \infty)$. Plant state trajectories $y(t)$, control functions of time $u(t)$, and disturbance functions of time $d(t)$ will be defined on $[0, \infty)$.

3. The function $y = y(t)$, which we call the plant state trajectory, takes values in X, the set of plant states. There will be a class S of admissible plant state trajectories.

4. The function $u = u(t)$ takes its values in a set U of admissible control values. There will a class C of admissible control functions.

5. The function $d = d(t)$ takes its values in a set D of admissible disturbance values. There will be a class $\mathcal{D}$ of admissible disturbance functions of time.

6. The sets of admissible plant states, control values, and disturbance values are assumed to be subsets of fixed finite dimensional Euclidean spaces.

Here is the kind of problem we want to solve. Suppose that a subset V of the plant states is specified, which we call the *viability set*. Suppose that a subset of the viability set V is given, which we call the *goal set* G. We want to extract a control strategy which satisfy the following conditions.

1. Starts the plant at time t_0 in a prescribed plant state y_0 in the viability set V.

2. Ensures that at all subsequent times t, the plant state $y = y(t)$ is also in the viability set V.

3. Ensures, as a winning condition for the game, that the plant state enters the goal set G by a designated time. (Alternative winning condition might that the plant state eventually enters the goal set G or the plant state must enter G in a certain time interval (t_{f_1}, t_{f_2}).)

All the control automaton can do at time t is to define the control law for the next interval to be incorporated into the control function of time. But the control automaton has no influence over the disturbance function of time $d = d(t)$ encountered. Thus the control automaton must select the next control law in such a way as to keep the plant state in the viability set V and lead to the goal, at a designated time or eventually, as required, no matter what admissible disturbance function is encountered.

All the information the control automaton has available to decide what new control to impose is its own automaton state plus the current sensor measurements of plant state.

In summary, the problem is to construct a control automaton which, given both its current state and measurement of plant state at the end of the current interval, changes to a new state and outputs new control law to be used for the next interval such that if the plant state starts at time t_0 in the viability set V, with a prescribed initial control, the plant state trajectories stay entirely within V and either enters the goal set G by a prescribed time or alternately eventually enters the goal set G.

Admissible Control Functions

Assume that the set of admissible control functions C is a set of functions which contains a set of functions C_0 from $[0, 1]$ to U. If $a < b$, and c is a control law from C_0, then the corresponding control law on $[a, b]$ is defined as the function $c((t-a)/(b-a))$. Our minimal assumption on the set of admissible control laws C is the following.

Suppose that u maps $[0, \infty)$ into U and there exists a sequence of times $t_0 < t_1 < t_2 < t_3 < ....$ such that for every n, there is a function c in C_0 for which c corresponds to u restricted to $[t_n, t_{n+1})$. Then u is in C.

We also assume a similar relation between the set D_0 of admissible disturbances mapping $[0, 1]$ to V, and the set of admissible disturbance functions D of time mapping $[0, \infty)$ to D. We do not specify exactly the closure conditions on C or on D. In some contexts, C is the set of all continuous functions, D is the set of all measurable functions, etc.

Uniqueness of Plant State Trajectories

We assume that each admissible control function and disturbance function gives rise to a unique plant state trajectory. That is, suppose the classes C, D and the plant function f are given. We shall assume that our plant model satisfies the following condition.

Given an admissible control function u, an admissible disturbance function d, an admissible plant state y_0, a time t_0, there exists a unique admissible plant trajectory function $y = y(t)$ with domain $[t_0, \infty)$ such that $y(t_0) = y_0$ and for all $t \geq t_0$, y satisfies

$$\dot{y}(t) = f(t, y(t), u(t), d(t)).$$

Bounded Measurement Error

We assume that if y is a plant state and m is its measurement, then there exists an $e > 0$ such that $|y - m| \leq e$.

We are now in position to define the legal positions of the a discrete sensing game. Assume that we are given a fixed admissible time sequence $t_i = t_0 + i\Delta t$.

Game Positions

Each (legal) position in the game will be a sequences of moves

$$m_0, c_0, m_1, c_1, ..., m_n, c_n$$

alternating between the players, with Plant moving first. Plant makes even numbered moves. Control makes odd numbered moves. Here is the simultaneous inductive definition of the notion of (legal) positions of the game, and of the trajectory associated with a position.

1. Suppose that p is the opening (null) position. Plant may choose as a move any admissible Plant state m_0. We call any admissible state x such that $|x - m_0| < e$ a trajectory associated with that position. That is, we interpret each such x as a possible measurement of true Plant state m_0 at time t_0, and also as a degenerate trajectory starting and ending at t_0.

2. Suppose that p is a position p of odd length. Control may choose as move any admissible control law c from C. The trajectories associated with position pc are the same as the trajectories associated with p.

3. Suppose that $p = p'c$ is a non-null position of even length with c its last move made at time t_i. Inductively, suppose we have already defined the set of all plant trajectories associated with p'. Then Plant may choose as move at position p any m such there exists a trajectory associated with p whose end state z has $|z - m| < e$. Inductively, we define the trajectories associated with the position p, m as those trajectories extending at least one trajectory associated with p to a trajectory defined also on $[t_i, t_{i+1}]$ which solves on that interval the same differential equation, using the control function of time on that interval associated with c and using some disturbance function of time on that interval associated with an admissible disturbance. Thus for any n, if Control makes move c at time t_n, then the control function of time applied to the Plant in $[t_n, t_{n+1}]$ is $c(t - t_n)/(t_{n+1} - t_n))$. If d is in D_0, the corresponding disturbance function of time on the time interval $[t_n, t_{n+1}]$ is $d((t - t_n)/(t_{n+1} - t_n))$. Due to our trajectory field assumption, on $[t_n, t_{n+1}]$, there is a unique plant trajectory $y = y_{x,c,d,t_n}$ determined by the plant state $x(t_n)$ on the trajectory $x(t)$ associated with p, together with the control law c from C_0 and the disturbance d from D_0 and the differential equation.

$$\dot{y}(t) = f(t, y(t), u(t), d(t)).$$

For any x (in a Euclidean space) define $Ball(x, e) = \{y \in E^n : |x - y| \leq e\}$. For any subset Y the space, define $Ball(Y, e) = \cup_{x \in Y} Ball(x, e)$ The plant moves m can then be described as

$$\{z \in Ball(PlantStates, e) \mid (\exists v \in D)(|y_{x,c,v,t_i}(t_{i+1}) - z| \leq e\}.$$

We define the set of finite plays of the game to be the set of legal positions described above. An infinite play is an infinite sequence, each finite initial segment of which is a finite play. Trajectories associated with infinite plays are similarly defined.

There are alternate definitions of "winning the game", depending on what control problem has to be modeled. For example, given the basic control problem of trying to bring the plant from some initial point x in the viability set V to a point in the the goal set, G, the appropriate notion of "winning the game" is as follows.

Winning a Play

We say that Control wins play μ, or alternately that μ is a winning play for Control, if

1. μ is a finite play.

2. For the last Plant move m of μ, $Ball(m, e)$ is a subset of the goal set G.

3. All states traversed along all plant trajectories associated with μ are in the viability set V.

We note that there are other natural notions of winning plays depending on the control problem to be solved. For example, we might define Control as winning a play if all associated plant trajectories stay in an ϵ neighborhood of a fixed curve in plant state space. For example if $\phi(t)$ is optimal plant trajectory with respect to some Lagrangian L, then we might take the viability set V for this example as the set of pairs (x, t) such that x is a plant state and t is a time and $|x - \phi(t)| \leq \epsilon$. Our games can easily be modified to deal with a variety of control problems.

A *strategy* for Control is a map F from the set of positions of the game of odd length into C_0. The idea here is that, given a play $m_0, c_0, m_1, c_1, ..., m_n$, the function $F(m_0, c_0, m_1, c_1, ..., m_n) = c_n$ determines the next move of Control. We say that a play $P = m_0, c_0, m_1, c_1, ..., m_n, c_n$ is generated by the strategy F, or that p is play in which Control follows F, if for all i, $c_i = F(m_0, c_0, m_1, c_1, ..., m_i)$. Strategies for Plant can be defined in a similar manner.

The notion of which strategies are winning for Control depends on the definition of what it means for Control to win the game. In the remainder of this section a strategy F for Control is a *winning strategy* if, whenever Control follows F, Control will **eventually** reach a winning position, no matter what initial position m_0 in the viability set V is chosen by the Plant to start the game and no matter what the subsequent moves of Plant are.

An *automaton strategy* for Control is an automaton with the following properties.

1. The set of automaton states S is any non-empty set.

2. The automaton input alphabet is $Ball(V, e)$ where V is the viability set.

3. The automaton output alphabet is C_0.

4. The automaton transition table $M(s, m)$ and its output function $H(s, m)$ are such that the output is produced simultaneously with the automaton shifting to its new state $r \in M(s, m)$.

We call such an automaton a control automaton.

We say that a Control automaton strategy generates a play

$$\mu = m_0, c_0, m_1, c_1, ..., m_n ..., c_n.$$

if

1. $c_0 = H(s_0, m_0)$ and the next control automaton state is $s_1 = M(s_0, m_0)$ where s_0 is the initial state of the automaton.

2. At time $t_k = t_0 + kT$ in a position with last Control move c_k and last Plant move m_k, the next control automaton state is $s_{k+1} = M(s_k, m_k)$ and the next control law is $c_{k+1} = H(s_k, m_k)$.

We say that an automaton strategy for Control, or equivalently control automaton, is *winning* for Control if whenever Control generates plays following the control automaton as described above, then Control will reach a winning position, no matter what initial move m_0 in the viability set V is chosen by the Plant to start the game, and no matter what the subsequent moves of Plant are.

Finite Input-Output Alphabet Games

Real digital controllers are finite state machines with finite input and output alphabets. We adapt our definitions for using such controllers as Control strategies. First let V' be a finite subset of $Ball(V, e)$ such that

$$(\forall\, y \in V)(\exists y' \in V')\; (|y - y'| \leq \delta).$$

Then if we we replace V by V' in all the definitions above and we assume that the set of controls C_0 is finite, then we have defined a subclass of games which we call finite alphabet discrete sampling games. For these games the control automata are always finite automata.

We end this section by giving an explicit example of how a problem that has been studied in the literature can be expressed in game language.

Railroad Problem: This is a variation of a problem considered by Schneider and Marzullo [32]. Here the plant is a train whose plant state space consists of pairs (y, ζ) where y is a position on a line and ζ is the train velocity at that position. Thus the plant space is a subset of a 2- dimensional Euclidean space. The plant dynamics are given by

$$\begin{cases} \dot{y} = \zeta \\ \dot{\zeta} = u + v \end{cases}$$

where u is a control parameter and v is the train engine acceleration. Sensors can measure the train position and velocity with known error bounds. We assume that there is a common bound e on uncertainty in position and velocity. There is a viability set V based on a partition of the track into contiguous blocks. For each block, there are regulations requiring that certain minimum and maximum velocity bounds be respected when the train is on that block. That is, suppose there are $n \geq 1$ blocks, and each block is defined by its beginning position and its length (b_i, ln_i), $0 \leq i \leq n - 1$. The corresponding velocity bounds are (min_i, max_i). Thus

$$V = \{(y, \zeta) \mid b_i \leq y \leq b_i + ln_i \Rightarrow \zeta \in [min_i, max_i], 0 \leq i \leq n - 1\}.$$

The velocity is assumed to be in a fixed direction along a straight railroad line. Hence all positions of the train are in that direction from the initial position 0. The goal set is defined by a distance $D > 0$ from the origin where

$$D \leq \sum_{0 \leq i \leq n-1} ln_i.$$

That is,

$$G = Ball((D, e) \times \{0\}.$$

The problem is to guide the train to stop within the interval $[D - e, D + e]$ while satisfying the blocks constraints along the way.

3 Continuous Sensing, Discrete Mode Switching

In this section, we define a second class of games which we call continuous sensing games. Throughout this section, we keep the same set of assumptions on the plant model and continue that same notation as used in section 2. Our basic underlying model is a hybrid system in which the plant state is sensed continuously, but new control orders (mode switches) are issued at discrete times. We illustrate this idea with the following simple example.

Water Level Monitor

Our water level monitor is a generalization of an example analyzed in [1]. The plant consists of a water pump and a water tank. The controller issues control orders to turn on or turn off to the pump. The plant state is the pair consisting of the water level $y \geq 0$ and the state of the pump $pmp \in \{on, off\}$, telling whether the pump is on or off. The state of the pump determines the dynamics of the water level. We assume that the water level y satisfies

$$\dot{y} = \begin{cases} f_1(y) \text{ if the pump is on} \\ f_2(y) \text{ if the pump is off} \end{cases} \tag{1}$$

where f_1 and f_2 are continuous functions such that

$0 < a' < f_1(y) \leq a$, for all y and

$0 > -b' > f_2(y) \geq -b$, for all y.

Moreover, we shall assume that there are constants L_1 and L_2 such that for all x and y, $|f_i(x) - f_i(y)| \leq L_i|x - y|$ for $i = 1, 2$.

Thus the states of the plant can naturally be partitioned into two disjoint classes; one class where the pump is on and the other class where the pump is off. The controller has two control actions $\{pon, poff\}$ which cause transitions between the two classes of plant states. We assume that the transitions take time up to $d > 0$, the delay, to complete. That is, until a transition has been completed, the pump is regarded as being in its preceding state and the corresponding equation for the water level dynamics applies.

Our controller has only two states: $\{son, soff\}$. The action of the controller is the following. If the controller receives a measurement y of the current water level when the controller is in state son, then it checks whether the condition $y \geq g$ holds where $g > 0$ is a given constant. If the condition holds, then the controller outputs a order $poff$ to cause the pump to be turned off and the controller shifts to the state $soff$ instantaneously. Otherwise, the controller remains in its state son and outputs no order to the pump. If the controller is in the state $soff$ and receives a measurement y, then it checks whether the condition $y \leq h$ holds where $h > 0$ is another constant. If the condition $y \leq h$ holds, then the controller outputs the order pon to cause the pump to be turned on and instantaneously shifts to the state son. Otherwise, the controller remains in the state $soff$ and outputs no order to the pump.

We note that while the controller instantaneously shifts to a new state, the pump does not instantaneously change its corresponding state, so the controller may lose the natural correspondence between its state and the state of the pump. Note also that the controller is not digital, since it is expected to act at the exact instant when the water level satisfies the conditions causing the controller to shift states and the water level is measured continuously.

The controller and the plant interact forever. We wish to find those values of (g, h) which will guarantee that the water level is maintained forever between two constants $0 < u < v$. That is, we want to design our controller to pick (g, h), so that at all times t, $u \leq y(t) \leq v$.

Formally, a plant state is a pair $(y(t), z(t))$, where $y(t)$ is the water level, $z(t) = 1$ if the pump is on at time t, and $z(t) = 0$ if the pump is off at time t. The control parameter takes on only two values, 0 and 1, where 0 indicates that the pump has been told to turn off and 1 indicates that the pump has been told to turn off. There is no disturbance. The space of control laws is the set of piecewise constant functions with values in $U = \{0, 1\}$. The dynamics of the plant has a form given by (1). The conditions on the f_i which ensure that the systems always has unique fully extendable trajectories for any given initial condition, given at the end of the section, are satisfied.

This ends temporarily our discussion of the the water tank example. We go on to the definition of a general class of games which will describe examples like this one.

Next we present two equivalent game models for continuous sensing games.

Game Model I

We begin with a plant given by an ordinary differential equation with control and disturbance. We consider the set of plant trajectories that begin at a time t_0 at a points x_0 and satisfy the plant dynamics described at the previous section for some admissible set of control functions C and some admissible set of disturbance functions D. We write $TRAJ$ for the set of all functions $Y(t) : [t_0, \infty) \to X$ such that there exists a control function $u \in C$ and a disturbance function $v \in D$ such that

1. $Y(t_0) = x_0 \in X$ and

2. $\dot{Y}(t) = f(t, Y(t), u(t), d(t))$ for all $t \geq t_0$.

We are assuming that there is a unique $Y \in TRAJ$ corresponding to any choice of t_0, $Y(t_0)$, $u(t)$, and $d(t)$.

Here is the game. There are two players: Plant and Control. Plant moves are taken from X but their choice is governed by certain members of $TRAJ$. Control moves are taken from the set $(C \cup \{no\ action\}) \times [0, \infty)$. Suppose the game starts at time t^*. The exchange of moves between Plant and Control results in a function of time

$$\mu(t) = \langle y(t), z(t) \rangle$$

where $y(t) \in X$ and $z(t) \in (C \cup \{no\ action\}) \times \{t\}$. A value of such function at time t is a pair of the last plant state $y(t)$ observed and the corresponding Control move which we regard here as occurring instantaneously. To determine its next move $z(t)$, Control may utilize all values of $y(\tau)$ at all times τ up to and including t. We call such a function μ a play, if the following is true. There is a strictly increasing sequence of times $\{t_k : k \geq 0, t_0 = t^*\}$ such that for every $k \geq 0$, $z(t_k) \in C \times \{t_k\}$ and for every $t \in (t_k, t_{k+1})$, $z(t) = (no\ action, t)$ and $y(t) = Y_k(t)$, where $Y_k(.)$ is a member of $TRAJ$ determined by $t_k, x_0 = y(t_k)$, the control law in $z(t_k)$, and some admissible disturbance $d(t) \in D$. That is, if $z(t_k) = (u_k(.), t_k)$, then $Y_k(t)$ satisfies that $Y_k(t_k) = y(t_k)$ and $\dot{Y}_k(t) = f(t, Y_k(t), u_k(t), (t))$ for all $t_k \leq t$ for some admissible disturbance function $d(t)$. We call the moves of Control at the times t_k for $k \geq 0$ *essential Control moves* and the moves at the time $t \notin \{t_k : k \geq 0\}$, i.e. where $z(t) = (no\ action, t)$, *inessential Control moves*. If the sequence $\{t_k : k \geq 0, t_0 = t^*\}$ is finite with the last index being n, we put $t_{n+1} = \infty$ and the above definition of a play applies.

Definition 1. Call a sequence $\{t_k : k \geq 0\}$ **realizable** if

$$inf\{(t_0 - t^*), (t_{k+1} - t_k) : k \geq 0\} > 0.$$

Call a play of the game, **realizable** if the sequence of instances of essential Control moves in it is realizable. We will consider that the plays which are not realizable are lost by Control.

Game model II

Next we will describe the plays in our continuous sensing game in a slightly different but equivalent way in order to bring out the resemblance with those games in which moves alternate in discrete time. Only the essential control moves will be displayed in plays. Assume that, at the start of the game the time is t^*, the plant state is $x^* \in X$, and the initial control law is $u^*(t)$. We define a block to be a contiguous segment of a play over a right-open interval of time where the corresponding Control moves are inessential except for the leftmost Control move. A block may be infinite if there is no essential Control move after it. In presenting a block, we suppress the inessential Control moves in it and we specify the moves of Plant by giving the element $Y \in TRAJ$ that determines its moves in the segment. We remove the Control move from the leftmost pair of moves in the block and place it in front of the block not regarding it as a part of the block. A play of the game is thus represented as a sequence of blocks alternating with a sequence of essential Control moves. Finite sequences of this sort are called the positions of the game. A play is a sequence of positions such that each next position extends the preceding one. We will describe all admissible positions by means of induction on the length of positions. We will simultaneously define by induction a segment of the plant trajectory corresponding to a position in the game. Thus we will define, by induction on n, the positions p_n, the plant trajectory segment γ_n corresponding to the position p_n, and the right ends $t(n)$ of the domains of γ_n.

(1) $n = 1$.
Then we let $p_1 = \langle u^\star(.), t^\star \rangle$. The corresponding segment γ_1 of the plant trajectory is a single point $(t^\star, x^\star)$, i.e. $\gamma_1(t^\star) = x^\star$. We denote the right end of the time interval of γ_1 as $t(1) = t^\star$.

Next suppose that the positions p_{n-1} corresponding to $n - 1$ successive admissible moves are defined along with the corresponding plant trajectory γ_{n-1} which is defined over the interval $[t^\star, t(n - 1)]$.

(2) $n = 2 \cdot k + 2$.
Suppose $p_{n-1} = \langle u^\star(.), t^\star \rangle \cdot B_0 \cdot z_0 \cdot ... \cdot B_{k-1} \cdot z_{k-1}$. Then the next admissible block B_k of Plant moves is specified by any member $Y_k : [t(n - 1), \infty) \to X$ of $TRAJ$ such that $Y_k(t(n - 1)) = \gamma_{n-1}(t(n - 1))$ and satisfies

$$\dot{Y}_k(t) = f(t, Y_k(t), u_{k-1}(t), d(t)) \text{ for all } t \geq t(n - 1)$$

where $u_{k-1}(.)$ is the control law $u_{k-1}(.)$ that occurs in the last Control move z_{k-1} and $d(.) \in \mathcal{D}$. The plant trajectory corresponding to the p_n is the function $\gamma_n : [t^\star, \infty) \to X$ defined by

$$\gamma_n(t) = \begin{cases} \gamma_{n-1}(t) & \text{if } t \in [t^\star, t(n - 1)] \\ Y_k(t) & \text{if } t > t(n - 1). \end{cases}$$

(3) $n = 2 \cdot k + 3$.
Suppose $p_{n-1} = \langle u^\star(.), t^\star \rangle \cdot B_0 \cdot z_0 \cdot ... \cdot B_{k-1} \cdot z_{k-1} \cdot B_k$. Then a position of length n extending p_{n-1} is of the form, $p_n = p_{n-1} \cdot z_k$ where z_k is any Control move of form $\langle u_k(.), t_k \rangle$ such that $t_k > t_{k-1}$ and $z_{k-1} = \langle u_{k-1}, t_{k-1} \rangle$. We then put $t(n) = t_k$ and γ_n equal to γ_{n-1} restricted to the interval $[t^\star, t(n)]$.

An infinite sequence of positions, linearly ordered by extension, defines an infinite play. All finite sequences of the form

$$\langle u^\star(.), t^\star \rangle \cdot B_0 \cdot z_0 \cdot ... \cdot B_{k-1} \cdot z_{k-1} \cdot B_k$$

are plays too. Plays which are not realizable in the sense of definition 5.1 are regarded as lost by Control.

It is easy to see that there is a natural bijection between the plays of Game Model I and the plays of Game Model II.

Remark   For convenience of notation, we will suppress the symbols for blocks B_k of Plant moves and use instead the plant trajectory Y_k which specifies the block. We also suppress the first move in the plays described inductively above because we regard it as fixing the game. That is, the initial move simply corresponds to giving initial settings of the plant, including initial control parameter values. Thus we will denote a play by a sequence of the form

$$Y_0, z_0, Y_1, z_1, ..., Y_k, z_k, ...$$

According to our definition, each of the trajectories $Y_i : [t_{i-1}, \infty) \to X$ is infinite. (Here we make the convention that $t_{-1} = t^*$). Of course, in the case when there is another essential control move after time t_{i-1}, we only use the finite trajectory segment, $y_i = Y_i$ restricted to $[t_{i-1}, t_i]$, to determine the final plant trajectory. Thus an even more compact notation for a play is a sequence of the form

$$y_0, z_0, y_1, z_1, ..., y_k, z_k, ...$$

We note, however, that this last notation could be misleading since it makes it appear that the time of the next essential move of Control is part of the previous move of Plant. A move of Plant does not force the timing of the next essential Control, this is forced by Control's strategy.

A winning condition for Control is a set of realizable plays whose corresponding plant trajectories γ satisfy the performance specification imposed on the hybrid system. For example, in the water level game, the performance specification is that for all t, $u \leq y(t) \leq v$.

We are interested in existence of winning strategies for Control in such a game. Intuitively, a strategy is any kind of systematic behavior of Control in a game which determines its next move on the basis of the knowledge of the previous moves of the players in a play. A winning strategy is a behavior that is

1. defined for all positions which are reached while using such a behavior and

2. all plays generated by such a behavior are winning for Control.

Following Büchi, we consider a description of such a behavior by means of an automaton whose input alphabet is the set of the opponent's moves X, and whose output alphabet is $(C \cup \{no\ action\}) \times [0, \infty)$. We do not require at this point that either of the alphabets be finite, and we do not require that the automaton set of states be finite.

Such an automaton is to be capable of continuously reading its input. At the end of this section, we give a formal definition of a continuous input-discrete output automaton and describe sufficient conditions for such an automaton to generate exclusively realizable plays.

Modeling Delays   We can model a delay in resetting the next control law to be imposed on the plant. Such a delay may depend on the current control and on the next control law. We assume that the two laws determine an upper bound d for the reset time interval. We model this in the game rules for Plant. If Control makes a move $(u_k(.), t_k)$, we view this as an order to reset the current control law to $u_k(.)$. The actually time τ_k at which we change to the new control law will be some $\tau_k \in [t_k, t_k + d]$. The Plant moves which form the next block will be of the form

$$Y_k(t) = \begin{cases} Y_{k-1}(t) & \text{for } t_k \leq t \leq \tau_k \\ Z_k(t) & \text{for } t \geq \tau_k \end{cases}$$

where Z_k mapping $[\tau_k, \infty)$ into the plant states is the unique trajectory determined by the initial condition $Z_k(\tau_k) = Y_{k-1}(\tau_k)$, the control law $u_k(.)$, and an admissible disturbance function $d(.)$. All the rest is as in the preceding definition of the game, except that it is the reset times, rather than the time Control moves, which determine the plant trajectory corresponding to a play. The realizability of a play is determined by the sequence of reset times, so we must assume that for any k, $t_{k+1} - t_k$ exceeds the positive lower bound d.

3.1 Uniqueness and Extendability of Plant Trajectories

Next we discuss sufficient conditions for the plant trajectory corresponding to a play to be unique and continuous. For an example of such a condition, consider the Caratheodory conditions ([12]) to be imposed on the plant model f modified to allow control and disturbance parameters.

Caratheodory Conditions

We consider plants modeled by the vector ordinary differential equation

$$\dot{y} = f(t, y, u, d)$$

where $t \in [t_0, \infty)$, $x \in X$, $u \in U$, $d \in D$, and which satisfy the following conditions.

CC 1: For every u and for almost all t, the function $f(t, x, u, d)$ is continuous in (x, d).

CC 2: For every u and every x, the function f is measurable in (t, d).

CC 3: For every u, there is function $m(.)$ over $[t_0, \infty)$, which is Lebesgue integrable over every finite interval of its domain and such that $|f(t, x, u, d)| \leq m(t)$ in $[t_0, \infty)$ for every x and d.

Theorem 2. *Suppose that the admissible control laws are piecewise constant over time, that disturbances are measurable functions over time, and that the plant dynamics f satisfy Caratheodory conditions CC 1-CC 3. Suppose also that*

1. *The plant state space X coincides with the Euclidean space containing it.*

2. *For every $u \in U$, there is a function $L(.)$ over $[t_0, \infty)$, which is Lebesgue integrable over every finite interval of its domain, and such that $|f(t, x, u, d) - f(t, y, u, d)| \leq L(t) \cdot |x - y|$ for every x, y and d, and*

3. *For every u, there is a constant a such that $|f(t, x, u, d)| \leq a \cdot (1 + |x|)$ for all t, x and d.*

Then to every realizable play in the continuous sensing game described above, there corresponds a unique absolutely continuous plant trajectory defined over $[t^*, \infty)$, where t^* is the time the play begins.

Proof. We show by induction on k the uniqueness and absolute continuity of the plant trajectory γ corresponding to a segment of a play up to time t_k and defined over the interval $[t^*, t_k]$. It is sufficient to do the inductive step. Assume that the statement is true for k.

(A) If there is no essential control move after t_k, consider

$$\dot{y}(t) = f(t, y(t), u_k, d(t))$$

for $t \geq t_k$. Here $d(.)$ is a measurable disturbance that occurs in the plant for $t \geq t_k$, u_k is the value of the constant control function which is part of the essential Control move at t_k. We have to show existence, uniqueness of an absolute continuous function satisfying the differential equation for $t \geq t_k$ and beginning from the point $\gamma(t_k)$. This would yield an absolutely continuous extension of the plant trajectory realizing the trajectory corresponding to a play. By assumption (1), we may assume that $\gamma(t_k) \in X$. We have to check only that $F(t, y) = f(t, y, u_k, d(t))$ satisfies the standard Caratheodory conditions, a uniqueness of a solution condition, and an extendability condition. The standard Caratheodory conditions CC 1-CC 3 are obtained from **CC 1**- **CC 3** by omitting control and disturbance parameters. We will check them for F.

Original Caratheodory condition CC 1: According to **CC 1**, there is a set E of the measure 0 of times such that for any t not in E, $f(t, y, u_k, d)$ is continuous in (y, d). Fix such a t. Then $f(t, y, u_k, d(t))$ is continuous in y. That is, $F(t, y)$ is continuous in y for all t not in E. This verifies the original condition CC 1.

Original CC 2: We need only show that for every y, $F(t, y)$ is measurable in t. By **CC 2**, $f(t, y, u_k, d)$ is measurable in (t, d) for every y. Since $d(.)$ is measurable and the composition of measurable functions is measurable, it follows that $f(t, y, u_k, d(t))$ is measurable in t for every y. This is the desired conclusion for F.

Original CC 3: The adapted **CC 3** gives the function $m(.)$ for f depending on u. So we take the m corresponding to u_k and it provides the desired bound for F.

From the standard Caratheodory conditions for F, it follows that there exist solutions of the equation $\dot{y}(t) = F(t, y(t))$ for every $t^{**} \geq t^*$, $x^{**} \in X$ in some interval $[t^{**}, t^{**} + p]$ where $p > 0$ and $y(t^{**}) = x^{**}$, see [12], page 4.

The uniqueness of F easily follows from assumption (2). That is, choose the function $L(.)$ according to (2) which corresponds to u_k. Then

$$|F(t, x) - F(t, y)| = |f(t, x, u_k, d(t)) - f(t, y, u_k, d(t))| \leq L(t) \cdot |x - y|.$$

It then follows that there is a *unique* trajectory of F passing through every point (t^{**}, x^{**}), see [12], page 5.

Finally we consider the extension of solutions of $\dot{y} = F(t, y)$. Since the standard Caratheodory conditions are satisfied by F, according to [12], page 7, every solution can be extended on both sides of an initial condition to the boundary of any closed and bounded domain of F. By condition (3), choose a to correspond u_k. Then $|F(t, y)| \leq a \cdot (1 + |y|)$. From estimates based on this condition, it follows that the states of any trajectory over a finite closed interval of time lie in a finite ball B whose radius depends only on size of the interval. Using (1), we may choose for any $t > t^*$, the domain for F to be $[t^*, t] \times B$. This is a closed and bounded domain. From the quoted theorem, it follows that a solution can be extended on the whole of $[t^*, t]$.

This completes the demonstration of existence of the unique absolutely continuous plant trajectory satisfying $\dot{y}(t) = f(t, y(t), u_k, d(t))$ for all $t \geq t_k$.

(B) There is an essential Control move at $t_{k+1} > t_k$. For a construction of a plant trajectory up to t_{k+1} corresponding to a play, we have to show that there is the unique absolutely continuous plant trajectory satisfying $\dot{y}(t) = f(t, y(t), u_k, d(t))$ for all $t \in [t_k, t_{k+1}]$. In this case, the proof is similar to the proof used for case (A). $\qquad\qquad\qquad\qquad\qquad\qquad\qquad\qquad\qquad\qquad\qquad\square$

We note that the conclusions of the theorem hold, in particular, for f independent of time and if for all control values u, f is continuous in (x, d) and satisfies conditions (1)-(3) of the theorem.

3.2 Continuous Input-Discrete Output Automata.

Next we want to consider the analogues of an automaton winning strategy for continuous sensing games. For this purpose, we introduce continuous input-discrete output automata to represent strategies for Control in continuous sensing games.

We adopt the following definition of the behavior of an ordinary automaton in continuous time. First we define the notion of an automaton run on an input word as a function of continuous time. Recall the ordinary definition of a run for a finite state automaton. Let $x = x_0 x_1 \ldots x_n$ be an input word. Then a run $r = r(0), r(1), \ldots$ is the sequence of the automaton states satisfying

$r(0) = s_{in}$ and

$r(k + 1) = M(r(k), x_k)$ for all $k \geq 0$

where s_{in} is the automaton initial state and M is its transition table.

Definition 3. Suppose $0 \leq t_0 < t_1 < \ldots < t_n$ is an increasing sequence of times at which the letters of an input word $x = x_0 x_1 \ldots x_n$ are read. A function $r : [0, \infty) \to S$ is a **run of the automaton in continuous time** if

$$r(t) = \begin{cases} s_{in} & \text{if } t \in [0, t_0] \\ M(r(t_k), x_k) & \text{if } n > k \geq 0 \wedge t \in (t_k, t_{k+1}] \\ M(r(t_n), x_n) & \text{if } t \in (t_n, \infty) \end{cases}$$

Definition 3 says that system trajectories, viewed in the automaton state space, are functions of time that are piecewise constant, continuous from the left at all times.

Continuously Reading Automata

We now introduce a definition of the input-output automata used to model controllers capable of continuously reading input that may continuously change. We adopt the view that transitions are instantaneous and that state transitions are continuous from the left for automaton runs which correspond to a continuous stream of input in time. We also restrict attention to the output of the automaton at a discrete sequence of times.

Definition 4. A continuous-input discrete-output automaton consists of
1. A nonempty set of states S,
2. A nonempty input alphabet I,
3. An output alphabet $J \cup \{no\ action\}$ where $J \cap \{no\ action\} = \emptyset$,
4. A transition table $M : S \times I \to S$,
5. An output function $H : S \times I \to J \cup \{no\ action\}$,
6. An initial state s_{in}.

For example, the controller described previously for water level translates into the following continuous input-discrete output automaton. Its set of states is $S = \{son, soff\}$, the initial state is $s_{in} = son$, the input alphabet is $I = \{y : y \geq 0, y \in R\}$, and the alphabet of essential outputs is $J = \{pon, poff\}$. Here R is the set of reals. The transition table and the output function are defined as follows:

$$M(son, y) = \begin{cases} soff & \text{if } y \geq g \\ son & \text{if } y < g \end{cases}$$

$$M(soff, y) = \begin{cases} son & \text{if } y \leq h \\ soff & \text{if } y > h \end{cases}$$

$$H(son, y) = \begin{cases} soff & \text{if } y \geq g \\ no\ action & \text{if } y < g \end{cases}$$

$$H(soff, y) = \begin{cases} son & \text{if } y \leq h \\ no\ action & \text{if } y > h \end{cases}$$

Definition 5. Let $TIME = [t^*, \infty)$, $r(0) = s_{in}$. Suppose that $x(.)$ maps $TIME$ into I. A run of a continuous-input discrete-output automaton corresponding to the input stream $x(.)$ is a function $r : TIME \to S$ such that for every $t \in TIME$, there is a duration $\tau > 0$ such that $r(t') = M(s, x(t))$ for every $t' \in (t, t+\tau]$. The output function of a continuous-input discrete-output automaton corresponding to the input stream $x(.)$ and a run r is the function $h : TIME \to J \cup \{no\ action\}$ defined by $h(t) = H(r(t), x(t))$.

Given a run r of a continuous-input discrete-output automaton A corresponding to an input stream $x(.)$, we define the set of *switching times* of r, $SW(r)$, to be the set of all $t \in TIME$, such that $M(r(t), x(t)) \neq r(t)$.

The difference between our continuous input-discrete output automaton and a standard Mealy machine is that we allow the input to be an arbitrary function of continuous time rather than a piecewise constant function of time which reflects input at discrete instants only. We call the subset J of the automaton output alphabet, the alphabet of *essential outputs*.

The definition of run for a continuous-input discrete-output automaton gives rise to piecewise constant and continuous from the left state space functions which represent the transitions. One of the reasons we adopt this definition is to avoid the difficulties associated with the following automaton. Let $S = \{0,1\}$, $s_{in} = 0$, $I = [5, 10]$, $t_0 = 1$, and the automaton transition function be given by

$$M(0, 5) = 1$$
$$M(1, x) = 0 \text{ for } x > 5.$$

Suppose the input function is $x(t) = 5 \cdot t$. Then a transition should occur at $t = t_0$. However if such a transition does occur, then at *any* later instant $t_1 > t_0$ where the new state is $s = 1$ another transition from the state $s = 1$ back to the state $s = 0$ must occur. So at some $t_2 > t_1$, the automaton is again in state $s = 0$. This would imply that such transition times occur arbitrarily close to t_0. But this is inconsistent with our intuition of an automaton transition while continuously reading the input because there is no finite interval of the form $(t_0, t_0 + \tau]$ during which the automaton is in a fixed state.

Definition 6. Assume that the automaton input alphabet I is a subset of a Euclidean space. Call the sets $G_s = \{i : M(s, i) \neq s\}$ the switching sets. We say that a continuous input-discrete output automaton A has **separated switching sets** if for every s, and s', the Euclidean distance between the sets G_s and $G_{s'}$ is positive, i.e. $\rho(G_s, G_{s'}) > 0$. Here $\rho(G_s, G_{s'}) = \inf\{\rho(x, x') : x \in G_s, x' \in G_{s'}\}$ where $\rho(x, x')$ is the usual Euclidean distance function.

Theorem 7. *Consider a continuous input automaton with the following properties.*

(a) Its set of states is finite.

(b) Its input alphabet is a subset of a Euclidean space E.

(c) Its switching sets of inputs are separated.

(d) Its switching sets of inputs are closed in the subset topology of E.

Then for every input function $x(.)$ which is continuous over $TIME = [t^*, \infty)$, there is a unique run of the automaton over $x(.)$. Moreover, the set $SW(r)$ of switching times during the run is discrete with no limit points in $TIME$.

Proof. Clearly, if $G_{s_{in}}$ does not intersect the range of $x(.)$, then $r(t) = s_{in}$ for all $t \in TIME$. In this case, SW is empty and clearly the conclusions of the theorem are satisfied. Suppose $G_{s_{in}}$ does intersect the range of $x(.)$. Then $x^{-1}(G_{s_{in}}) \neq \emptyset$. This set is also closed, since by assumption $x(.)$ is continuous and $G_{s_{in}}$ is closed.

Hence, there is the least time t_0 such that $t_0 \in x^{-1}(G_{s_{in}})$. This is the first switching time. We include t_0 in SW. We associate the state $s_0 = s_{in}$ with t_0.

Next suppose we have constructed an increasing sequence of switching times $t_0, \ldots, t_k$ and the sequence of the corresponding states up to $s_0, \ldots, s_k$ at these switching times. Consider $s_{k+1} = M(s_k, x(t_k))$. Then either $x^{-1}(G_{s_{k+1}}) \cap (t_k, \infty) = \emptyset$, in which case $r(t) = s_{k+1}$ for all $t > t_k$, or $x^{-1}(G_{s_{k+1}}) \cap (t_k, \infty) \neq \emptyset$. If $x^{-1}(G_{s_{k+1}}) \cap (t_k, \infty) \neq \emptyset$, then the set $x^{-1}(G_{s_{k+1}}) \cap [t_k, \infty)$ is closed. Moreover t_k cannot be a limit point of $x^{-1}(G_{s_{k+1}}) \cap [t_k, \infty)$. That is, if t_k were such a limit point, there would be a sequence of points t'_j in $x^{-1}(G_{s_{k+1}})$ converging to t_k. But then, because of the continuity of $x(.)$, it must be that $x(t_k)$ is a limit point of a sequence $x(t'_j)$ of points from $G_{s_{k+1}}$. This would contradict the separateness of $G_{s_{k+1}}$ from the switching set G_{s_k} containing $x(t_k)$. Then we let t_{k+1} be the least element of $x^{-1}(G_{s_{k+1}}) \cap [t_k, \infty)$.

Thus by induction, we can define two sequences $\{t_k\}$ and $\{s_k\}$ such that for all k,

$$t_{k+1} \in x^{-1}(G_{s_{k+1}}) \cap (t_k, \infty)$$

and

$$s_{k+1} = M(s_k, x(t_k)).$$

Let SW be the set of elements in the first sequence. We claim that SW has no finite limit points in $TIME$. Indeed suppose the sequence t_k converges to $t^{**} > 0$. Since the set of states S is finite, there is a strictly positive number $\alpha = min\{\rho(G_s, G_{s'}) : s \neq s', s, s' \in S\}$. Choose $\varepsilon < \alpha/2$. By continuity of x, there exists an $\delta > 0$ such that $|t - t^{**}| < \delta$ implies $|x(t) - x(t^{**})| < \varepsilon$. Consider k_0 such that for every $k > k_0$, $|t_{k+1} - t_k| < \delta$. Then for all such k

$$|x(t_{k+1}) - x(t_k)| < 2 \cdot \varepsilon = \alpha$$

However for all k, $x(t_k) \in G_{s_k}$ and by the separateness of the switching sets, it follows that

$$|x(t_{k+1}) - x(t_k)| > \alpha.$$

This is a contradiction and hence the set $SW(r)$ has no finite limit points.

Since no transitions are possible at times between switching times, we have, besides the constant run mentioned above, two more types of runs depending on whether the set of switching times SW is finite or infinite. If SW is finite with last switching time t_n, then set

$$r(t) = \begin{cases} s_{in} & \text{if } t = t_0 \\ M(r(t_k), x(t_k)) & \text{if } n > k > 0 \wedge t \in (t_k, t_{k+1}] \\ M(r(t_n), x(t_n)) & \text{if } t \in (t_k, \infty). \end{cases}$$

If SW is infinite, then set

$$r(t) = \begin{cases} s_{in} & \text{if } t = t_0 \\ M(r(t_k), x(t_k)) & \text{if } k \geq 0 \wedge t \in (t_k, t_{k+1}] \end{cases}$$

The uniqueness of runs follows by induction on the switching times.

□

Next, we single out a property of a continuous-input discrete-output automaton which has been proved in the previous proposition, but can be established with a slightly weaker assumption. We will use this fact later in this section.

Proposition 8. *Suppose that the premises of Theorem 7 hold, but the requirement that the set of the automaton states be finite is omitted. Then at any state at which the automaton is continuously reading a continuous function $x : TIME \to I$, either the automaton remains in this state forever or there is a finite time $t > 0$ at which a transition to a different automaton state takes place.*

Definition 9. A run r of a continuous-input discrete-output automaton is **realizable** if

(a) Both transitions to new states and essential outputs, occur only at discrete times $DT = \{t_0 < t_1, < \ldots\}$. That is, $M(r(t), x(t)) = r(t)$ and $H(r(t), x(t)) = no\ action$ for t not in DT and $r(t_k) \neq r(t_{k+1})$ and $H(r(t_k), x(t_k)) \in J$ for $k \geq 0$.

(b) $r(t) = M(r(t_k), x(t_k))$ for every $k \geq 0$, $t \in (t_k, t_{k+1}]$.

(c) $inf(\{(t_{k+1} - t_k) : k \geq 0\}) > 0$.

If the sequence DT is finite and n is the last index k occurring in it, define $t_{n+1} = \infty$. Then (a)-(c) of the definition apply to the interval (t_n, t_{n+1}).

For example, the continuous input-discrete output automaton representing the controller for the water pump given above satisfies the premises of the Proposition 7. Therefore it has runs over continuous water level trajectories $y(.)$. Moreover, the proposition tells us that these runs are realizable.

Conditions (a) and (b) given in the definition of a realizable run reflect our intuition of automaton transitions as described above. The definition synchronizes transitions to new states with essential outputs. For automata with separated switching sets which satisfy the other conditions of Theorem 7, once this synchronization is present, every run is automatically realizable.

Condition (c) prevents the set of transition times DT from having finite limit points. We call (c) a realizability condition. The definition of realizable run here has the same motivation as that of realizable time sequence in [24] and of "bounded from below" sampling intervals for a controller in [36].

By taking $I = X \times [0, \infty)$, we can make the automaton transition table and the output function depend explicitly on time, $M(s, x, t); H(s, x, t)$. We can then ensure that the conditions (a)-(c) are satisfied for all runs of the automaton over any input function $x(.)$ by choosing a discrete set $DT = \{t_0 < t_1 < \ldots\}$ satisfying (c), defining $M(s, x, t) = A(s, x)$ and $H(s, x, t) = B(s, x)$ for $t \in DT$, and defining $M(s, x, t) = s$ and $H(s, x, t) = no\ action$ for $t \notin DT$, where A and B are transition tables which are not dependent on time.

3.3 Automata as Strategies

Next we explain how we can use a continuous-input discrete-output automaton as a strategy for Control in our continuous sensing games. First choose an input alphabet $I = X$ and an alphabet of essential outputs $J = C \times [0, \infty)$. Control uses the continuous-input discrete-output automaton in the following way. Suppose t is the current time and $t_k < t$ is the last time the automaton output was an essential Control move. If $y(t)$ is the current input, the automaton stays in its current state s or shifts into another state according to its transition function $M(s, y(t))$ and outputs the respective Control move according to its output function $H(s, y(t))$. If at time t, there is a shift to another state, then the next essential Control move occurs at t and $t_{k+1} = t$. However the sequence of automaton states resulting may not form a run, much less a realizable run, in the course of reading an input. We call the automaton a *realizable strategy* for Control if whenever Control uses the automaton as its strategy, then the resulting play produces a realizable run.

Since the set of plant states is usually a subset of a Euclidean space, it is natural to consider automata with closed and separated switching sets as strategies for Control. However even if Control use this type of automaton, it will not always produce plays whose realizability can not be established by appealing to Theorem 7. The reason is that the automaton output affects the future input and may result in the automaton input not being a continuous function of time, so that Theorem 7 does not apply. Such an automaton is given below.

Control strategies need not produce realizable runs

Consider the plant with a scalar control and disturbance:

$\dot{y} = d$, for $u = 0$

$\dot{y} = -d$, for $u = 1$

$d \in Z$, $d > 0$

$y(0) = 0$, and initially the control parameter is set to 0.

Consider the following automaton represented strategy for the player Control:

$S = \{0, 1\}$

$s_{in} = 0$

$I = \{y : y \in R\}$

$J = \{u := 0, u := 1\}$. (Here we think of the essential control moves as orders to set the control parameter to the indicated values.)

Let $\alpha > \beta > 0$ be given and let the transition table be defined by:

$$M(0, y) = \begin{cases} 1 \text{ if } y \geq \alpha \\ 0 \text{ if } y < \alpha \end{cases}$$

$$M(1, y) = \begin{cases} 0 \text{ if } y \leq \beta \\ 1 \text{ if } y < \beta \end{cases}$$

Here we assume The output function is defined by

$$H(0,y) = \begin{cases} u := 1 & \text{if } y \geq \alpha \\ no\ action & \text{if } y < \alpha \end{cases}$$

$$H(1,y) = \begin{cases} u := 0 & \text{if } y \geq \beta \\ no\ action & \text{if } y < \beta \end{cases}$$

It is easy to see that there are exactly two switching sets, namely, $G_0 = (\alpha, \infty)$ and $G_1 = (-\infty, \beta)$. Thus since $\beta < \alpha$, these are separated switching sets. If this strategy always produced realizable runs, then the corresponding plant trajectories would be continuous. But we exhibit a plant trajectory from a game which uses the automaton as a Control strategy and which produces a discontinuous plant trajectory. Assume that the disturbance is initially $d = 1$ at time $t = 0$, and that the disturbance doubles after each automaton state switch. We will get the first switch at time α, the second will occur $(\alpha - \beta)/2$ seconds later, the third will occur $(\alpha - \beta)/2^2$ after the second, and so on. The switch times t_k are the sums of the first k terms of this series. That is, they are $t_k = \sum_{i=0}^{k-1} \frac{\alpha - \beta}{2^i}$. this sequence has a finite limit point 2α. Hence there are times arbitrary close to 2α from the left where the plant state is $y = \alpha$ and the plant state $y = \beta$. Thus the plant trajectory is not continuous at $t = 2\alpha$.

Plants with Realizable Control Strategies

Next we define a class of plants together with a class of input-output automata which are guaranteed to produce realizable strategies for Control.

Suppose the plant is modeled by a system of differential equations of the form

$$\dot{x} = f(x, u, d), u \in U, d \in D, x \in X,$$

where u is a control parameter and d is disturbance parameter. Assume that $U \subseteq E^m$, $D \subseteq E^k$, and that $X \subset E^n$. We allow an additional source of nondeterminism in the plant of the following sort. For each pair of parameters (u, u'), there is a delay in resetting u to u', bounded by distance $\rho(u, u')$. Let t^* and x^* be the initial conditions for the plant. Assume that we have only piecewise constant control functions, so that we can identify control parameter value u with the constant control function $u(t) = u$ for all $t \geq t'$, where t' is a resetting time of a previous control parameter value to u.

Consider the following strategy A for Control in the continuous sensing game in which the plant state x is being sensed by Control. Let A be a continuous-input discrete-output automaton such that:

1. Its state space S is finite.

2. Its input alphabet is $I = X$.

3. Its alphabet of essential control moves is $J = U \times [0, \infty)$.

4. Its transition table M satisfies the condition of separateness of switching sets.

5. The switching set for the initial state contains the initial plant state $x^* \in G_{s_{in}}$.

6. The automaton output function $H(s, x)$ produces an essential output only when x is in the switching set G_s, otherwise $H(s, x) = $ *no action*.

In particular, $H(s_{in}, x^*) = (u, t^*)$ for some $u \in U$ so that the first output to be produced by the automaton is an essential move.

Theorem 10. *Suppose that the plant is modeled by*

$$\dot{y} = f(t, y, u, d)$$

as described above. Suppose that f satisfies the Caratheodory conditions **CC 1,** **CC 2,** *and* **CC 3,** *where we assume that there is a fixed function $m(.)$ for f, independent of the value u of the control parameter for condition CC3. Assume that the automaton A described above has closed separated switching sets. Then for every play μ consistent with Control following the strategy A, the resulting automaton state function is a realizable run of A.*

Proof. We show first that the use of A by the player Control results in the production of runs of A. By the conditions in the paragraph preceding the theorem, the first control move according to A is essential. The control laws here are constant functions. Suppose there are no more essential control moves. Since the control laws here are constant functions, an essential move creates continuous plant trajectories because of the three Caratheodory conditions satisfied by the plant model. It then follows by Theorem 10 that the corresponding run is realizable.

Now suppose a finite number of essential control moves were made from the beginning of the play. Consider a time t^{**} at which the last essential control move was made. That is, if s^* is the state of A at time t^{**}, then the automaton input x^{**} at time t^{**} is in the switching set G_{s^*}. We may assume that the interaction of the automaton A and the plant has produced the plant trajectory γ up to time t^{**} and $\gamma(t^{**}) = x^{**}$. In other words $\gamma(t^{**}) \in G_{s^*}$. We wish to show that there is a positive $\tau > 0$ such that there is no essential automaton outputs and transitions to new states in the interval $(t^{**}, t^{**}+\tau)$. It is easy to see that, even with the finite delay corresponding to resetting the control according to $\langle u, t^{**}\rangle = H(s^*, x^{**})$, the input to the automaton is a continuous plant trajectory because the function f satisfies the Caratheodory conditions **CC 1,** **CC 2,** and **CC 3.** It follows from Proposition 4.3 that there are two alternatives. The first alternative is that the automaton stays forever in this state. This produces a valid realizable run and play with t^{**} being the last essential Control move. The second alternative is that there is $\tau > 0$ such that the next essential move occurs at $t^{**}+\tau$. this means that there are no essential outputs or transitions to new states in $(t^{**}, t^{**} + \tau)$, since these occur at the same time according to the definition of A, and the transitions to new states do not occur in this alternative for such an interval.

It follows that when Control uses A in the game, the set of times at which essential moves are made is a discrete set. We let $DT(\mu)$ denote this set for the play μ. Next fix a play μ and consider an initial sequence $\{t_k : k \geq 0\}$ of $DT = DT(\mu)$ that begins with the time of the first essential control move. Clearly, every finite initial segment of this sequence determines a position in the game for which there is a corresponding continuous plant trajectory. Suppose that q is a limit point of this sequence. Due to assumption CC 3, we get the following estimate for any plant trajectory γ:

$$|\gamma(t') - \gamma(t)| \leq \int_t^{t'} m(t)dt.$$

Since the integral is absolutely continuous, it follows that the

$$lim_{k\to\infty}|\gamma(t_{k+1}) - \gamma(t_k)| = 0.$$

By the argument above, it follows that for every k, $\gamma(t_k) \in G_{s_k}$, where s_k is the automaton state at which the transition occurs at the switch time t_k. Moreover, the sets $G_{s_{k+1}}$ and G_{s_k} are distinct since the states s_{k+1} and s_k are distinct. The fact that the above limit is 0 and the fact that there are only a finite number of switching sets would imply that for some pair of states s and s', the distance between G_s and $G_{s'}$ is 0. But this contradicts our assumption that there is nonzero distance between the switching sets. Thus the sequence $\{t_k\}$ has no finite limit points. Since the set of switching instants DT is the set of times of essential Control moves and this set has no finite limit points, the corresponding play is realizable. $\qquad\qquad\qquad\qquad\qquad\qquad\qquad\qquad\qquad\qquad\qquad\qquad\qquad\quad$ $\Box$

We note that for the water level monitor problem describe above, the bound function for the Caratheodory condition $CC\ 3^\star$ is $m(t) = max\{a, b\} \cdot t$. Thus the plays produced by the suggested automaton controller are all realizable.

4 From Continuous to Discrete Sensing Games

In this section we fully analyze the water pump example. We start by explicitly constructing a continuous-input discrete-output automaton $A(g, h)$ for a pair of parameters $g > h$ as described in the previous section. By Theorem 10, we know that if Control uses $A(g, h)$ for its strategy in the continuous sensing game for the water level monitor, then it will always produce realizable runs for $A(g, h)$. We shall show that for any desired water levels, $u < v$, we can pick (g, h) in such a way that if Control uses the automata $A(g, h)$ for its strategy in the continuous sensing game, then Control will win in the sense that we will guarantee that at all times t, the water level $y(t)$ will satisfy $u \leq y(t) \leq v$ assuming that $u \leq y(0) \leq v$. Then we shall show how we can use the continuous-input discrete-output automaton $A(g, h)$ to design a finite automaton which will control the plant, that is, the water tank plus pump, to meet the desired performance specification. Finally, we shall show that we can explicitly extract Kohn-Nerode small topologies which will verify the controllability and observability of our discrete control strategy.

The (g,h)-Automaton $A(g,h)$

With any pair (g,h) of positive numbers with $g > h$ we associate a (g,h)-automaton $A(g,h)$ with continuous input alphabet and a three letter output alphabet. (This is essentially the same automaton that was described in the previous section.)

1. The input alphabet consists of the numbers in interval M of possible water levels y.

2. The two automaton states are $son, soff$.

3. The three letter output alphabet is $pon, poff, no\ action$.

The transition table and output function of this automaton are defined as follows.

$$M(son, y) = \begin{cases} soff \text{ if } y \geq g \\ son \ \ \text{ if } y < g \end{cases}$$

$$M(soff, y) = \begin{cases} son \ \ \text{ if } y \leq h \\ soff \text{ if } y > h \end{cases}$$

$$H(son, y) = \begin{cases} soff \ \ \ \ \ \text{ if } y \geq g \\ no\ action \text{ if } y < g \end{cases}$$

$$H(soff, y) = \begin{cases} son \ \ \ \ \ \ \ \text{ if } y \leq h \\ no\ action \text{ if } y > h \end{cases}$$

The the switching sets for $A(g,h)$ are $G_{son} = [g, \infty)$ and $G_{soff} = (-\infty, h]$. We can thus guarantee that $A(g,h)$ has separated switching sets if we impose the requirement that $g > h$.

Theorem 11. *If parameters g and h in the continuous sensing game for the water level monitor with maximum delay d satisfy the conditions:*

$$\begin{array}{lll} (1)\ g > h, & (2)\ g + a \cdot d \leq v, & (3)\ h - b \cdot d \geq u, \\ (4)\ h - b \cdot d \leq y(0) < g, & (5)\ \frac{g-h}{a} > d, & (6)\ \frac{g-h}{b} > d, \end{array} \tag{2}$$

then the strategy $A(g,h)$ is a winning strategy for the player Control in any game where the initial state of Control is son and the initial state of the pump is pon.

Proof Suppose $\mu = Y_0, z_0, Y_1, z_1, \ldots$ is a play consistent with A. We have to show two things. First we must show that the strategy induced by $A(g,h)$ is applicable at every position of Control in this play. That is, we must show that if Control using this strategy, then he never gets stuck in the sense that he is unable to make a move according to the strategy. This is the perpetual property [48], [38]. Second we must show that $A(g,h)$ induces a winning strategy for Control, i.e. that the water level trajectory $y(.)$ corresponding to any play consistent with the game initial condition and the strategy $A(g,h)$ has the property that for all times $t \geq 0$, $u \leq y(t) \leq v$. We show both properties by induction on the length of a position in the play.

The initial position of the play is $p = \langle pon, 0 \rangle$ and the initial trajectory of the plant is just $\langle 0, y(0) \rangle$. That is, the initial control sent to the plant is that the pump should be on. Now since $y(0)$ satisfies $v \leq h - b \cdot d \leq y(0) \leq g < v$, we see that the initial trajectory is within acceptable bounds.

Consider the first block of plant moves which is specified by its corresponding trajectory Y_0. By our assumptions, we have that for all t,

$$0 < a' \leq \dot{Y}_0(t) \leq a.$$

Thus Y_0 will be a strictly increasing function so that there will be some time $t_1 > 0$ such that $Y_0(t_1) = g$. It is easy to see that $t_1 \leq (g - y(0))/a'$

Thus at time t_1, Control issues the order that the pump should be turned off and switches to state $soff$. Thus $z_0 = \langle poff, t_1 \rangle$.

Now consider the next block of plant moves which is specified by its corresponding trajectory Y_1. Because of the delay in switching from the pump being on to the pump being off after the control order to turn the pump off has been issued, there is some $0 \leq \tau_1 \leq d$ such that the pump remains on between time t_1 and time $t_1 + \tau_1$ and then the pump turns off. Thus the corresponding trajectory Y_1 satisfies

$$0 < a' \leq \dot{Y}_1(t) \leq a \quad \text{if } t_1 \leq t \leq t_1 + \tau_1$$
$$0 > -b' \geq \dot{Y}_1(t) \geq -b \quad \text{if } t > t_1 + \tau_1$$

It is then easy to see that the trajectory Y_1 must reach its maximum at time $t = t_1 + \tau_1$ and that this maximum value is bounded by $g + a\tau_1 \leq g + ad \leq v$. After time $t_1 + \tau_1$, Y_1 is strictly decreasing so that there must be some time $t_2 > t_1$ such that $Y_1(t_2) = h$. It is easy to see that $d < \frac{g-h}{b} \leq t_2 - t_1 \leq \frac{g+ad-h}{b'}$. Since $t_2 - t_1 > d$ it follows that the state the pump will be $soff$ at time t_2. Thus at time t_2, Control issues a order that the pump be turned on and switches to state son. Thus $z_1 = \langle pon, t_2 \rangle$. It then easily follows that the values of the trajectory Y_1 between times $t = t_1$ and $t = t_2$ takes on its maximum value at time $t_1 + \tau_1$ and its minimum value at time t_2 where $Y_1(t_2) = h$. Thus the values of $Y_1(t)$ lie between h and $g + ad$ and hence meets our performance specifications.

Now consider the next block of plant moves which is specified by its corresponding trajectory Y_2. Again, because of the delay in switching from the pump being off to the pump being on after the control order to turn the pump on has been issued, there is some $0 \leq \tau_2 \leq d$ such that the pump remains off between time t_2 and time $t_2 + \tau_2$ and then the pump turns on. Thus the corresponding trajectory Y_2 satisfies

$$0 > -b' \geq \dot{Y}_2(t) \geq -b \quad \text{if } t_2 \leq t \leq t_2 + \tau_2$$
$$0 < a' \leq \dot{Y}_2(t) \leq a \quad \text{if } t > t_2 + \tau_2$$

It is then easy to see that the trajectory Y_2 must reach its minimum at time $t = t_2 + \tau_2$ and that this minimum value is bounded below by $h - a\tau_2 \geq h - bd \geq u$. After time $t_2 + \tau_2$, Y_2 is strictly increasing so that there must be some time $t_3 > t_2$ such that $Y_2(t_3) = g$. It is easy to see that $d < \frac{g-h}{a} \leq t_3 - t_2 \leq \frac{g-h+bd}{a'}$. Since

$t_3 - t_2 > d$ it follows that the state the pump will be *son* at time t_3. At time t_3, Control issues a order that the pump be turned off and switches to state *soff*. Thus $z_2 = \langle poff, t_3 \rangle$. It then easily follows that the values of the trajectory Y_2 between times $t = t_2$ and $t = t_3$ takes on its minimum value at time $t_2 + \tau_2$ and its maximum value at time t_3 where $Y_2(t_3) = g$. Thus the values of $Y_2(t)$ lie between $h - bd$ and g and hence meet our performance specifications.

Thus the behavior of the system between the position ending in z_1 and the position ending in z_3 meets the performance specification and the requirement that Control can follow the strategy determined by $A(g, h)$. Note that at time t_1, the water level is g and the pump is on and at time t_3 the water and the pump is on. It is then straightforward to prove by induction that at time t_{2n+1} the water level will be g and the pump will be on and that exactly the same analysis will apply to the behavior of the system between the position ending in z_{2n+1} and the position ending in z_{2n+3}. Hence it follows that the strategy for Control induced by $A(g, h)$ is a winning strategy for Control as claimed. $\square$

It should be clear that in the statement of Theorem 11 we can replace the assumption that the pump is initially on and $u \leq y(0) < g$ by the assumption that the pump is initially off and $h < y(0) \leq g + a \cdot d$ and the conclusion of the Proposition will continue to hold.

4.1 The (g, h)−Automata for Discrete Sampling and Measurement Errors

We now modify our continuous sensing game for the water level monitor in two ways. First we shall assume that Control, instead of continuously sensing the plant state, senses the plants state only at discrete times $t_0 < t_1 < t_2 < \ldots$, where there is some positive $\Delta > 0$ such that $t_{k+1} - t_k \geq \Delta$ for all $k \geq 0$.

Second, we shall assume that Control is not able to exactly measure the plant state, but only that Control can measure the plant state within some error e. Our goal is to specify a continuous-input discrete-ouput automaton strategy for Control in such a game and the sequence of sampling times $t_0 < t_1 < t_2 < \ldots$ so that if Control measures the plants state at the times $t_0 < t_1 < t_2 < \ldots$ with an error of no more than e and follows the strategy induced by the continuous-input discrete-ouput automaton, then Control will ensure that the plant meets the performance specifications.

In this case, we shall assume that $t_0 = 0$ and that $t_k = k\Delta$ for all $k > 0$ so that we are sampling every Δ seconds, where $\Delta > d$ and d is the maximum delay that can occur between the time at which Control issues a order to the pump to turn off or on and the time the pump actually achieves the state required by the order. Moreover, we shall continue to use the automaton $A(g, h)$ for the strategy for Control. Thus the behavior of the system is the following:

A. Suppose that the automaton is in state *son* and receives as input measurement m. Then, instantaneously,

1. if $m \geq g$, then the automaton outputs *poff* and also shifts its state to *soff*, and

2. if $m < g$, then the automaton remains in state *pon*, and outputs *no action*.

B. Suppose that the automaton is in state *soff* and and receives input measurement m. Then, instantaneously,

1. if $m \leq h$, then the automaton outputs *pon* and shifts to state *son*, and

2. if $y > h$, then the automaton remains in state *soff* and outputs *no action*.

Thus our problem is find Δ and the parameter g and h to ensure that the water level $y(t)$ stays within the desired bounds, i.e. that for all t, $u \leq y(t) \leq v$. First of all, since we pick $\Delta > d$, we will be guaranteed that the plant and automaton states correspond to each other at the end of each sampling interval. That is, if initially the plant state and the initial state of $A(g, h)$ are such that if the initial state of $A(g, h)$ is *soff*, then the pump is off and if initial state of $A(g, h)$ is *son*, then the pump is on, then at some time before the end of each sampling interval the state of $A(g, h)$ the pump will correspond to each other.

It is then quite easy to derive the necessary conditions on the parameters g and h to guarantee that the control automaton $A(g, h)$ provides a winning strategy for Control in our modified game. That is, all we do have to do is analyze the plant trajectories for given input measurement and states of $A(g, h)$. We consider the following cases.

Case 1 Suppose that the plants state is *son* and at time t_k, Control receives a measurement $m_k < g$. Now by assumption, if the actual water level at time t_k is $y(t_k)$, then

$$m_k - e \leq y(t_k) \leq m_k + e.$$

Assume also that the pump is on at time t_k so that in this case the automaton remains in state *son* and issues the order *no action* and the pump remains on for the next Δ seconds. Then since the plant trajectory $y(.)$ between t_k and $t_{k+1} = t_k + \Delta$ must satisfy

$$0 < a' \leq \dot{y}(t) \leq a,$$

it is easy to see that $y(t)$ is a strictly increasing function in this interval and that

$$y(t_{k+1}) \leq y(t_k) + a\Delta \leq m_k + a\Delta + e \leq g + a\Delta + e.$$

Now if we find that the measurement received at time t_{k+1}, m_{k+1}, is still less than g, then of course the automaton will continue to be in state *son* and issue the order *no action* so that the pump will remain on, the plant trajectory $y(.)$ between t_{k+1} and t_{k+2} will be strictly increasing, and $y(t_{k+2}) \leq g + a\Delta + e$. We will continue on this way until we find the least $l > k$ such that the measurement received at time t_l will be greater than or equal to g. By our analysis, the actual plant state $y(t_l)$ will bounded by $g + a\Delta + e$. At that point, the automaton will issue the order for the pump to be turned off and switch to state *soff*. What happens to the trajectory $y(t)$ between times t_l and $t_{l+1} = t_l + \Delta$? It is easy to see that our analysis of Theorem 11 now applies. That is, there will be some $\tau_l \leq d < \Delta$ such that the trajectory satisfies

$$0 < a' \leq \dot{y}(t) \leq a \quad \text{if } t_l \leq t \leq t_l + \tau_l$$
$$0 > -b' \geq \dot{y}(t) \geq -b \quad \text{if } t_l + \tau_l < t \leq t_{l+1}.$$

It is then easy to see that the trajectory $y(t)$ in the interval $[t_l, t_{l+1}]$ must reach its maximum at time $t = t_l + \tau_l$ and that this maximum value is bounded by $y(t_l) + a\tau_1 \leq y(t_l) + ad \leq g + a\Delta + e + ad$. Then after time $t_l + \tau_l$, $y(t)$ is strictly decreasing. It is now easy to see that if we pick g so that

$$g + ad + a\Delta + e \leq v,$$

then we will ensure that following the $A(g, h)$ strategy will ensure that the water level never becomes greater than v. There is also a lower bound which is imposed on g which comes from the fact that the minimum value of $y(t)$ in the interval $[t_l, t_{l+1}]$ must be greater than or equal to u. Since we are assuming that $m_l \geq g$, we know that $y(t_l) \geq g - e$. If we assume that there is no delay in turning the pump off, then $y(t)$ could be strictly decreasing in the interval. It is then easy to see that in such a situation, $y(t_{l+1})$ could be as small as $g - e - b\Delta$. Moreover it could be that $g - e - b\Delta - e \leq h$ so that $m_{l+1} \leq h$. In that situation, the pump will be off and our controller would tell the pump to turn on. However there could be a maximum delay of time d before the pump turns on and the the water level once again starts to increase. Thus there could be a further drop of $-bd$ in the water level during this delay so that the water level could become as small as $g - e - b\Delta - bd$. Thus we must also assume that $g - bd - b\Delta - e \geq u$ or equivalently that $u - bd + b\Delta + e \leq g$. In case 2, we will deal with the case when $m_{l+1} > h$.

Case 2. Suppose that the plants state is $soff$ and at time t_k, Control receives a measurement $m_k > h$. Again the actual water level $y(t_k)$ satisfies

$$m_k - e \leq y(t_k) \leq m_k + e.$$

Assume also that the pump is off at time t_k so that in this case the automaton remains in state $soff$ and issues the order no $action$ and the pump remains off for the next Δ seconds. Then since the plant trajectory $y(.)$ between t_k and $t_{k+1} = t_k + \Delta$ must satisfy

$$0 > -b' \geq \dot{y}(t) \geq -b,$$

it is easy to see that $y(t)$ is a strictly decreasing function in this interval and that

$$y(t_{k+1}) \geq y(t_k) - b\Delta \geq m_k - b\Delta - e \geq h - b\Delta - e.$$

Now if we find that the measurement received at time t_{k+1}, m_{k+1}, is still greater than h, then of course the automaton will continue to be in state $soff$ and issue the order no $action$ so that the pump will remain off, the plant trajectory $y(.)$

between t_{k+1} and t_{k+2} will be strictly decreasing, and $y(t_{k+2}) \geq h - b\Delta - e$. We will continue on this way until we find the least $l > k$ such that the measurement received at time t_l will be less than or equal to h. By our analysis, the actual plant state $y(t_l)$ will bounded below by $h - b\Delta - e$. At that point, the automaton will issue the order for the pump to be turned on and switch to state *son*. Again use our analysis of Theorem 11 to analyze what happens to the trajectory $y(t)$ between times t_l and $t_{l+1} = t_l + \Delta$. That is, there will be some $\tau_l \leq d < \Delta$ such that the trajectory satisfies

$$0 > -b' \geq \dot{y}(t) \geq -b \quad \text{if } t_l \leq t \leq t_l + \tau_l$$
$$0 < a' \leq \dot{y}(t) \leq a \quad \text{if } t_l + \tau_l < t \leq t_{l+1}.$$

It is then easy to see that the trajectory $y(t)$ in the interval $[t_l, t_{l+1}]$ must reach its minimum at time $t = t_l + \tau_l$ and that this minimum value is bounded below by $y(t_l) - b\tau_l \geq y(t_l) - bd \geq h - b\Delta - e - bd$. Then after time $t_l + \tau_l$, $y(t)$ is strictly increasing. It is now easy to see that if we pick h so that

$$h - bd - b\Delta - e \geq u,$$

then we will ensure that following the $A(g, h)$ strategy will ensure that the water level never becomes less than u. There is also upper bound which is imposed on h which comes from the fact that the maximum value of $y(t)$ in the interval $[t_l, t_{l+1}]$ must be less than or equal to v. Since we are assuming that $m_l \leq h$, we know that $y(t_l) \leq h + e$. If we assume that there is no delay in turning the pump on, then $y(t)$ could be strictly increasing in the interval. It is then easy to see that in such a situation, $y(t_{l+1})$ could be as large as $h + e + ba\Delta$. Note that the case when $m_{l+1} < g$ was handled in Case 1. However it could be that $h + e + a\Delta + e \geq g$ so that $m_{l+1} \geq g$. In that situation, the pump will be on and our controller would tell the pump to turn off. However there could be a maximum delay of time d before the pump turns off and the the water level once again starts to decrease. Thus there could be a further rise of ad in the water level during this delay so that the water level could become as large as $h + e + a\Delta + ad$. Thus we must also assume that $h + ad + a\Delta + e \leq v$ or equivalently that $h \leq v - ad - a\Delta - e$.

Below is the proposition asserting the conditions for correctness of the $A(g, h)$ control automaton.

Theorem 12. *Suppose in the discrete sampling game for the water level monitor, we have a maximum delay of d for switching plant states, we are given a finite sampling time $\Delta > d > 0$ and a measurement error bound $e \geq 0$. Choose the numbers $h < g$ so that*

$$u + bd + b\Delta + e \leq g, h \leq v - ad - a\Delta - e.$$

Suppose that the initial water level is between $h + e$ and $v - a \cdot d$ and the pump is on or the initial water level is between $u + b \cdot d$ and $g - e$ and the pump is off. Suppose that initially the pump and the control automaton are both in the "on" *state or both in the "off" state. With the A(g, h)-controller introduced above, the water level satisfies the performance specification that $u \leq y(t) \leq v$ at all times $t \geq 0$.*

Proof By using the analysis of Case 1 and Case 2 above, one can easily prove by induction k that if Control follows the $A(g, h)$ strategy in our modified game, then in each interval $[t_k, t_{k+1}]$, the trajectory of the plant $y(t)$ will always satisfy that $u \leq y(t) \leq v$. We leave the details to the reader. □

We note that the inequalities on g and h in Theorem 12 automatically impose the following upper bound on the size of the sampling interval Δ:

$$\Delta \leq \frac{v - u + d(a + b) - 2e}{a + b}.$$

4.2 Topological Finite Automata from Open Covers

In appendix II of [24], there is a general method which, given a hybrid system whose performance specification is autonomous, extracts a finite automaton which which can be used to guarantee that the hybrid system will meet its performance specifications as well as to extract small topologies which guarantee the stability of the system. Our goal in this section is to follow appendix II of [24] and construct a finite open cover yielding a finite control automaton and small topologies for our water level monitor example which guarantee that the water level always stay within specified bounds. Here, when we say that the performance specification is autonomous, we mean the following. We assume that the plant is modeled by a differential equation

$$\dot{y} = f(y, u, d)$$

where u is a control parameter and d is a disturbance parameter. Then in each interval of time $\Delta = [t_0, t_1]$ and any given plant state y that lies within a certain set of acceptable values, we want to find a control law $u(.)$ such that if we use the control law $u(t)$ to determine the plant trajectory, then for any acceptable disturbance $d(t)$, our plant trajectory should meet the required performance specification. That is, any function $y(t)$ such that $y(t_0) = y$ and $\dot{y}(t) = f(y(t), u(t), d(t))$ for all $t \in \Delta$ must meet our performance specification. We assume that our choice of suitable control functions $u(t)$ for any interval Δ depends only on the plant state x and the internal state of the controller but not on the time t which is the start of the interval. In this situation, the problem of meeting performance specification is equivalent to determining a set Q of "acceptable "pairs $(x, u(t))$ of plants states and control functions. That is, each pair represents a plant trajectory which begins at the plant state of the pair and is guided by the control law of the pair which satisfies the our performance specifications over the sampling interval Δ. Note that in this situation, the control law $u(t)$ is a function of time over the sampling interval that takes values in the range of values of the control parameter.

For example, the range of the control parameter for the water pump-tank system is the set of orders for the pump or equivalently the set of states of the pump $\{1 = \text{'}pon\text{'}, 0 = \text{'}poff\text{'}\}$ and every control law is a constant function over the sampling interval with the range being the pump states. In what follows, we adapt the definition of the set of pairs Q to reflect the presence of possible delays in switching the pump states. Thus for the water tank and pump example, we let Q consist of the pairs such that for any admissible delay in switching to a new pump state as directed by Control in the sampling interval Δ, the the water level which correspond to the plant trajectory stays within our required bounds.

In the general setting for autonomous performance specification, the first stage of finding a control automaton in the small topologies satisfying the specification is to find a control function.

Definition 13. A **feedback control function** H is a map that assigns to each pair of a plant state x reached at the end of a sampling interval Δ and the current control law u used in Δ, a control law u' such that the corresponding plant trajectory over the next sampling interval Δ' satisfies the performance specification over that interval.

A useful model to keep in mind is to think of the control $u(t)$ as being determined by a physical controller. Thus the automaton communicates with the physical controller by setting the state of the physical controller s_u which has the effect of imposing the control $u(t)$ for the next sampling interval. In such a situation, we can identify the control laws with the states of the physical controller. For example, in the case of the water pump and tank example where the control functions are piecewise constant, we may represent u its value which is either pon or $poff$. For the rest of this section, we shall use this model so that instead of talking about the current control law of the sampling interval, we will talk about the current state of the physical controller, etc.

Definition 14. The automaton $A(H)$ associated with a control function H is defined as follows.

1. Its set of states is the set of states of the physical controller K. (In the more general language, K would be the set of possible control laws which occur in pairs in Q.)

2. Its input alphabet is the set of plant states $U = PS$.

3. Its output function $H(u, k)$ is the feedback control function.

4. Its transition table $M(u, k)$ models the switching of control laws output by the controller, i.e. $M(u, k) = H(u, k)$ for all $u \in U$ and $k \in K$.

Next we want to isolate some properties of the automaton $A(H)$ or equivalently the feedback control function H which will guarantee that we can perpetually apply our control strategy.

Definition 15. Say that the automaton $A(H)$ associated with a feedback control function H is **correct with respect a performance specification and a region** $B \subseteq PS \times K$ if the following holds. For any pair $a = (y, k) \in B$ and for any admissible disturbance $d(t)$, any trajectory beginning from y and guided by the control corresponding to k during the delay for switching to new state of the physical controller $H(y, k)$ and by the control $H(y, k)$ after the delay satisfies the performance specifications and ends up in B at the end of the sampling interval. Here "ends up in B" means that if y_1 is plant state corresponding the trajectory at the end of the sampling interval, then $(y_1, H(y, k)) \in B$.

Definition 16. Suppose that there is a region B in the domain of the feedback control function H such that for any pair $(y, k) \in B$ and for any admissible disturbance $d(t)$, any trajectory beginning from y and guided by the control corresponding to k during the delay for switching to new state of the physical controller $H(y, k)$ and by the control control $H(y, k)$ after the delay satisfies the performance specifications and ends up in B at the end of the sampling interval. Then we call such a control function a **guiding feedback control function** relative to B.

The definitions above can easily be extended to apply to the case when the control function is set-valued as introduced in appendix II of [24]. The idea of a set-valued feedback control function is that one computes a set of controls or in our case a set of physical controller states from a pair consisting of a plant state and a physical controller state and then selects from that set one control or physical controller state which will be used to determine the plant trajectory in the next sampling interval Δ. The set of control functions or physical controller states that we compute should be such that for every control function or physical controller state that could have been chosen from the set and every admissible disturbance, the corresponding plant trajectory always satisfies the performance specifications.

Set-valued feedback control functions arise naturally in our context. Consider a map H from the pairs (m, k) ((measurement, physical controller state)) into the set of states of the physical controller. If we take the measurements as inputs to the control automaton and identify the map H with the control automaton output function, we of course have an ordinary function as opposed to a set-valued one. However suppose that we assume that a measurement can be any value that approximates a plant state within some error bound. That is, we view a measurement as a set-valued function over plant states from which an nondeterministic choice of an element from a set is made. For example, suppose that the map above is $H(m, k)$, where m is a measurement, and k is a physical controller state. Then the corresponding set-valued feedback control function is $G(y, k) = \{H(m, k) : |m - y| \le e\}$. Here $e > 0$ is the measurement error bound.

In appendix II [24], the graph of G is assumed closed. But our G is not closed. So we take the closure of the graph of G and consider a corresponding set-valued function G' whose graph is that closure. So our control function will be G'. The topologies that are used in the construction of G' are the natural

Hausdorff topologies on the plant state space and on the space of states of the physical controller following [24]. The fact that the topological spaces are Hausdorff means that if the state space K of the physical controller is finite, then the K must have the discrete topology since the only Haussdorff topology on a finite set is the discrete topology.

It is also important for applying the methodology of appendix II that the domain of the feedback control function be a subset of the set Q. This is true of the graph of G but not necessarily for the closure of G because the domain of the closure of G may include boundary points of Q which are not in Q. In the case we consider, the closure of G will in fact lie entirely in Q.

Now let us go back to our water level monitor example. Let $K = \{pon, poff\}$ be the range of control values or equivalently the states of the pump. Let the variable k range over the set K. Here, the map $H(m, k)$ is defined by

$$H(pon, y) = \begin{cases} poff \text{ if } y \geq g \\ pon \quad \text{otherwise} \end{cases}$$

$$H(poff, y) = \begin{cases} pon \quad \text{if } y \leq h \\ poff \text{ otherwise} \end{cases}$$

A water level y is taken from the set $[u, v]$, which carries the natural Euclidean topology. There is only one Hausdorff topology on the set K, the discrete topology.

To construct the function G note that for each control automaton state the function H is continuous except at one point in the range of y. The point of discontinuity for H is either g or h at respective automaton states on, off. It follows that if y is separated from, say, g, by more than the error bound e, then the function has a singleton set as a value. One can see that at points $g - e, g + e, h - e, h + e$, the value of G is still a singleton. At points near to g, h by less than e, the value of G is K since H has a different value to the right of g than to the left of g. Thus

$$G(pon, y) = \begin{cases} \{pon\} \text{ if } y < g - e \\ K \qquad \text{if } g - e \leq y < g + e \\ \{poff\} \text{ if } y \geq g + e \end{cases}$$

$$G(poff, y) = \begin{cases} \{pon\} \quad \text{if } y \leq h - e \\ K \qquad \text{if } h - e < y \leq h + e \\ \{poff\} \text{ if } y > h + e \end{cases}$$

Now consider the closure G' of the graph of G. Here we use the same letter for the set-valued function and for its graph. Here is the resulting closure.

$$G'(pon, y) = \begin{cases} \{pon\} \quad \text{if } y < g - e \\ K \qquad \text{if } g - e \leq y \leq g + e \\ \{poff\} \text{ if } y > g + e \end{cases}$$

$$G'(poff, y) = \begin{cases} \{pon\} & \text{if } y < h - e \\ K & \text{if } h - e \le y \le h + e \\ \{poff\} & \text{if } y > h + e \end{cases}$$

Note that the definition of the function G also makes sense for exact measurements ($e = 0$), but in that case the corresponding function G' is multi-valued only at the points of discontinuity $(g, on), (h, off)$ of H. This nondeterminacy makes clear the arbitrary nature of the choice of a strict or non strict inequality in the definition of H. That is, we obtain four functions which are variants of H, differing from H only in having non-strict inequalities in the definition. All give rise to the same G'.

We distinguish between three slightly different automata, Aut_1, Aut_2, and Aut_3, which depend on our pair of parameters g and h. For all three automaton, the set of states is $\{pon, poff\}$, the input alphabet is the set of water levels and the output alphabet the same as the set of states. Thus we need only define their output functions $H_i(y, k)$ and their transition tables $M_i(y, k)$. For the automaton $Aut_1(g, h)$, the output function $H_1(y, k)$ and the transition table $M_1(y, k)$ are both equal to the function $H(y, k)$ defined above. If we think of this automaton as a strategy for Control in the discrete sampling game with error measurements, then Aut_1 gives essentially the same strategy as the automaton $A(g, h)$ described in the previous section. The only difference between the two automaton is when in the state pon when $y \le g$, $Aut_1(g, h)$ outputs pon while $A(g, h)$ outputs $no\ action$. However we regard both of these instructions to a pump which is on to be the same, i.e. they both keep the pump on. Similarly when in the state $poff$ when $y \ge h$, $Aut_1(g, h)$ outputs $poff$ while $A(g, h)$ outputs $no\ action$. Again we regard both of these instructions to a pump which is off to be the same, i.e. they both keep the pump off. Thus by Proposition 12 Aut_1 is a winning strategy for Control in the discrete sampling game with error measurements. Now as observed above, if we think about the action of the strategy as a function of plant states instead of on measurements where we assume that the absolute value of the difference between the measurement and the actual plant state is no more than e, then the transition table and the output function are nondeterministic and are give by the function G defined above. Thus we define a second automaton $Aut_2(g, h)$ whose transition table and output function are given by G, i.e. for all (y, k), $M_2(y, k) = H_2(y, k) = G(y, k)$. Of course Aut_2 is a nondeterministic automaton and the output function is set valued. We shall assume that the automaton operates as follows. If Aut_2 is in state s and is reading input y and goes to state s' at its next step so that $s' \in M_2(s, y)$, then the output of the automaton in that circumstance is also s'. That is, our definitions ensure that for the pair (s, y), the possible new states and the possible outputs come from the same set since $M_2(s, y) = H_2(s, y)$. We are thus making the additional assumption that such choices are coordinated for any (s, y). In this way, we can use Aut_2 as a strategy for Control since our assumption will ensure that the internal state of the automaton Aut_1 and the state of pump are always coordinated at the end of sampling intervals if they start out coordinated. If we think of Aut_2 as a strategy for Control in the discrete sampling game without errors in measurements, i.e. in the discrete sampling game where the error bound $e = 0$, then this strategy for Control will produce exactly the same set of runs with respect to plant states as the strategy Aut_1 produces in the discrete sampling game with error measurements. Hence Aut_2 is a winning strategy for control in the discrete sampling games without error measurements. Finally we consider yet another nondeterministic automaton Aut_3 whose transition table and output function are given by G' instead of G. Again we assume that Aut_3 operates so that if Aut_3 is in state s and is reading input y and goes to state $s' \in M_3(s, y)$ at its next step, then the output of the automaton in that circumstance is also s'.

Remark

The differences between the control strategy Aut_1 in our discrete sampling game with errors in measurements bounded by e and the control strategy Aut_2 in our discrete sampling game without error measurements can be explained in terms whether we consider the analog to digital converter as part of the plant or whether we want to consider the analog to digital converter as part of the digital controller. That is, if we consider the analog to digital converter as part of the plant, then it is natural to assume that the digital controller receives only plant measurements and this situation is most naturally modeled as a discrete sampling game with errors in measurements where the control automaton is deterministic. However, if we consider the analog to digital converter as part of the digital controller, then the most natural way to model this situation is that we have a discrete sampling game without errors in measurements and that the control automaton behaves in a nondeterministic manner as described by Aut_2. Thus our choice of using Aut_1 in a discrete sampling game with errors in measurements or of using Aut_2 in a discrete sampling game without errors in measurements comes down to the choice of where in Figure 1 we wish to place the analog to digital converter, i.e on the digital side or on the analog side.

Our next proposition states that Aut_3 is also a winning strategy for Control in the discrete sampling games without error measurements.

Theorem 17. *Suppose in the discrete sampling game without errors in measurements for the water level monitor, we use finite sampling intervals of size Δ and that the maximum delay d for switching to new plant state is such that $\Delta > d > 0$. In addition assume $e \geq 0$ and that g and h satisfy*

1. $g \leq v - a \cdot d - a \cdot \Delta - e$;

2. $g - e \geq h + e$;

3. $h \geq u + b \cdot d + b \cdot \Delta + e$.

Suppose that the initial water level is between $h + e$ and $v - a \cdot d$ and the pump is on, or the initial water level is between $u + b \cdot d$ and $g - e$ and the pump is off. Suppose that initially the pump and any of the two control automata, Aut2 or Aut3, are both in the on state or both in the off state. Then Aut_2 and Aut_3 are winning strategies for Control in such discrete sampling games without errors in measurements for the water level monitor.

Proof The proof of Theorem 12 that $Aut1$ is a winning strategy for Control in discrete sampling games with errors in measurement bounded by e can be is easily adapted to prove that that either Aut_2 or $Aut3$ is a winning strategy for Control in the discrete sampling games without errors in measurement. The proof is by induction on the length of positions as before. We leave the details to the reader. □

The content of Theorem 17 can be restated as the following property of the feedback control function G'. Suppose the water level y is between $h + e$ and $v - a \cdot d$ and the pump is on or y is between $u + b \cdot d$ and $g - e$ and the pump is off. Suppose that the next control law is chosen from the set $G'(y, k)$, where k is the state of the pump as specified above at the beginning of the sampling interval Δ. Then the water level lies in the interval $[u, v]$ over the next sampling interval. Thus G' can indeed be used as a feedback control function for the water level and pump states in the region

$$A = [h + e, v - a \cdot d] \times \{on\} \cup [u + b \cdot d, g - e] \times \{off\}.$$

Moreover, the water level and the state of the pump at the end of the sampling interval satisfy the same assumptions that are satisfied by this data at the beginning of the sampling interval. That is, the trajectories that have begun in A will end in A at the end of a sampling interval if they are guided by a control law determined by the set-valued control function. According to our earlier definition, the feedback control function G' restricted to A is a guiding feedback control function.

Constructing Open Covers

We now consider an open cover of the graph of G' restricted to the region A. Our goal is to construct a finite automaton with small topologies approximating G'. We presented A above as a disjoint union of two open and closed (clopen) sets. Correspondingly, the graph of G' is a disjoint union of clopen sets. It is sufficient to cover each of the clopen sets independently. Choose $\epsilon > 0$ so small that the sets below are subsets of the graph of G'. To visualize the regions below more clearly, recall that we have the following the inequalities:

$$h - e \leq g - e \leq g + e \leq v - a \cdot d \text{ and}$$

$$u + b \cdot d \leq h - e \leq h + e \leq g - e.$$

Here is the open cover for the first clopen set:

$$V_1 = [h + e, g - e + \epsilon) \times \{on\} \times \{on\},$$
$$V_2 = (g - e - \epsilon, g + e + \epsilon) \times \{on\} \times K,$$
$$V_3 \ (g + e - \epsilon, v - a \cdot d] \times \{on\} \times \{off\}.$$

Similarly here is an open cover for the second clopen set:

$$V_4 = [u + b \cdot d, h - e + \epsilon) \times \{off\} \times \{on\},$$
$$V_5 = (h - e - \epsilon, h + e + \epsilon) \times \{off\} \times K,$$
$$V_6 = (h + e - \epsilon, g + e] \times \{off\} \times \{off\}.$$

Let $U_1, U_2, U_3, U_4, U_5, U_6$ be the leftmost components of $V_1, V_2, V_3, V_4, V_5, V_6$ respectively. The input alphabet of the small topologies automaton will consist of the two disjoint lists. Namely the join irreducibles of the lattice under inclusion generated by U_1, U_2 and U_3 which consist of

$$U_1, U_2, U_3, U_1 \cap U_2, U_2 \cap U_3$$

and the set of join irreducibles of the lattice under inclusion generated by U_4, U_5 and U_6 which consists of

$$U_4, U_5, U_6, U_4 \cap U_5, U_5 \cap U_6.$$

In the notation of [24], the sets $V_i, i = 1, \ldots, 6$, correspond to an open cover of the graph of G' restricted to A. The sets of the cover are of the form $V_i = A_i \times B_i$, with $1 \le i \le 6$ where

$A_i = U_i \times \{on\}\ 1 \le i \le 3,$
$B_1 = \{on\},\ B_2 = K,\ B_3 = \{off\};$ and
$A_i = U_i \times \{off\},\ 3 \le i \le 6,$
$B_4 = \{on\},\ B_5 = K,\ B_6 = \{off\}.$

The finite automaton in the small topologies described in [24] assigns to each join-irreducible in the lattice generated by the open sets A_i, a set of control laws. That is, we attach to every non-empty join irreducible A_i' in the lattice generated by the A_i's, an open set

$$O(A_i') = \cup_{z \in \Gamma_i} B_z,$$

where $\Gamma_i = \{z \mid A_i' \subseteq A_z\}$.

In our case it is easy to check that we obtain the following assignments of $O(A_i')$ for the join-irreducibles A_i':

1. the sets $U_i \times \{on\}$, $1 \le i \le 3$ are mapped respectively to $\{on\}, K, \{off\}$.

2. the sets $U_i \times \{off\}$, $3 \le i \le 6$ are mapped respectively to $\{on\}, K, \{off\}$.

3. each of the following four join irreducibles, $(U_1 \cap U_2) \times \{on\}), (U_2 \cap U_3) \times on\}$, $(U_4 \cap U_5) \times \{off\}, (U_5 \cap U_6) \times \{off\}$, is mapped to K.

Let $H(u, k)$ be any set-valued function which is consistent with the above assignments where u ranges over the set U of join irreducibles in the lattices generated by U_1, U_2, U_3 and by U_4, U_5, U_6. Formally, the finite automaton in the small topologies corresponding to the above data is the following:

1. The set of states $S = K$.

2. The input alphabet is the set U.

3. The output alphabet $V = K$.

4. The nondeterministic output function is based on the set-valued function H described in the assignments above.

5. The transition table $M : U \times K \to K$ is defined by $M(u, k) = H(u, k)$.

The automaton can be used for control as follows. Let y be a water level and k be the automaton current state.

1. The analog to digital converter transforms y into the least join-irreducible u that contains y.

2. The automaton maps u nondeterministically into a pump state $k' \in H(u, k)$, and outputs k' to the plant.

This automaton is parameterized by the ϵ entering the definitions of U_i'. Are there values of ϵ which guarantee that water level trajectories arising from the automaton satisfy the control requirements? While considering this question we may ask whether the automaton output function is related to a suitable feedback control function. Should it happen to be a guiding feedback control function for some region of Q, then the control automaton would satisfy the control requirements if it began its operation in that region.

Consider the following "feedback control function": $f(y, k) = H(u, k)$, where u is the least join-irreducible that contains y. It is then easy to see that:

When $k = on$:

$$f(y, k) = \begin{cases} K & \text{if } y \in (g - e - \epsilon, g + e + \epsilon) \\ on & \text{if } y \in [h - e, g - e - \epsilon] \\ off & \text{if } y \in [g + e + \epsilon, v - a \cdot d] \end{cases}$$

When $k = off$,

$$f(y, k) = \begin{cases} K & \text{if } y \in (h - e - \epsilon, h + e + \epsilon) \\ on & \text{if } y \in [u + b \cdot d, h - e - \epsilon] \\ off & \text{if } y \in [h + e + \epsilon, g + e] \end{cases}$$

We have three objects now: the finite automaton in the small topologies, the corresponding function f, and the control automaton associated with f. It is easy to see that each of the three objects have the same set of water level trajectories over the region A generated by the object. It follows that if f is a guiding feedback control function over A, then the finite automaton with small topologies is correct.

We can conclude that f is a guiding feedback control function from the following general fact and Theorem 17.

Proposition 18. *Suppose $A \subseteq PS \times K$ and f, F are two set-valued functions over A with values subsets of K. Suppose that the graph of f is a subset of the graph of F and F is a guiding feedback control function. Then so is f.*

Proof It is clear that all the plant trajectories generated by f constitute a subset of those generated by F. The conclusion desired is immediate. $\square$

Consider F, which is determined by g, h and $e' = e + \epsilon$. Assume that the premises of Theorem 17 are satisfied by this data for some $\epsilon_0 > 0$. It follows from

Theorem 17 that F is a guiding control function. It follows from the proposition above that so is f for any $\epsilon \leq \epsilon_0$.

Remark The control automaton $Aut1$ described above is a formal representation of the controller from [1]. That paper does not mention using a sampling interval $\Delta > 0$. We can interpret this as meaning that water level is measured and tested continuously. Continuous measurement and testing in the presence of pump delay can cause the above control automaton and the controller from [1] to produce an infinite number of outputs in a finite interval of time, a physical impossibility. Consider a time t at which the automaton outputs a request to change the pump state. Suppose that just prior to that time the pump was "on" and the state of the automaton was *son*. Suppose that the pump delay is $d > 0$. Since the water level continues to increase during the delay, and the automaton continuously samples the input, the automaton senses the condition $y \geq g$ at all times in the interval $(t, t + d)$. Thus the automaton will produce an essential output at each time in that interval. Our assumption that we sample (measure, sense) after each interval of length $\Delta > d > 0$ eliminates this source of unrealizable behavior. Sampling at times separated by a positive bound $\Delta > 0$ cannot be dispensed in modeling a plant with delays.

Later papers will investigate open covers and the corresponding finite automata with small topologies for a variety of control problems.

References

1. R. Alur, C. Courcoubetis, T. Henzinger, Pei-Hsin Ho, Hybrid Automata: An Algorithmic Approach to the Specification and verification of hybrid Systems, Workshop on Hybrid Systems, Denmark, October 1992.

2. P. Antsaklis, W. Kohn, A. Nerode, and S. Sastry, eds., *Hybrid Systems II*, Lecture Notes in Computer Science vol. 999, Springer-Verlag, (1995).

3. K.R. Apt and E-R. Olderog, *Verification of Sequential and Concurrent Programs*, Springer-Verlag, 1991.

4. J. P. Aubin, *Differential Inclusions, Set Valued Maps, and Viability*, Springer-Verlag, 1984.

5. J. P. Aubin, *Set Valued Analysis*, Birkhauser, 1990.

6. J. P. Aubin, *Viability Theory*, Birkhauser, 1991.

7. J-P.Aubin and I. Ekeland, *Applied Nonlinear Analysis*, Wiley-Interscience, 1984.

8. L.D. Berkovitz, Thirty Years of Differential Games, in Emilio O. Roxin (editor), *Modern Optimal Control*, Marcel Dekker, Inc., 1989.

9. Robert S. Boyer, Milton W. Green, J. Strother Moore, The Use of a Formal Simulator to Verify a Simple Real Time Control Program,Technical Report No. ICSCA-CMP-29, Software Systems Science, National Science Foundation, Washington, D.C. 20550, July, 1982. DTIC Selected Sept. 16 1983.

10. J. R. Büchi, *The Collected Works of J. Richard Büchi* (S. MacLane,. Siefkes, eds.), Springer-Verlag, 1990. 1990.

11. K. M. Chandy and J. Misra, *An Introduction to Parallel Program Design*, Addison-Wesley, 1988.

12. A. F. Filippov, *Differential Equations with Discontinuous Right Hand Side*, Kluwer Academic Publishers, 1988.

13. A. Friedman, *Differential Games*, Wiley- Interscience, 1971.
14. X. Ge, W. Kohn, A. Nerode, and J.B. Remmel, "Algorithms for Chattering Approximations to Relaxed Optimal Control. MSI Tech. Report 95-1, Cornell University. (1995)
15. X. Ge, W. Kohn, A. Nerode, and J.B. Remmel, "Feedback Derivations: Near Optimal Controls for Hybrid Systems", *Hybrid Systems III*, Lecture Notes in Computer Science 1036, Springer-Verlag, (1995), 76-100.
16. R. Grossman, A. Nerode, H. Rischel, A. Ravn, eds., *Hybrid Systems*, Springer Lecture Notes in Computer Science 736, (1993).
17. Y.Gurevich and L. Harrington, Trees, Automata and Games, Proc. of the 14th Ann. ACM Symp. on Theory of Comp., pp. 60-65, 1982.
18. O. Hajek,*Pursuit Games*, Mathematics in Science and Engineering, vol. 120, Academic Press, New York, 1975.
19. J. Hilgert, K. H. Hofmann, and J. Lawson, *Lie Groups, Convex Cones, and Semigroups*, Oxford Clarendon Press, 1988.
20. R. Isaacs,*Differential Games*, SIAM Series in Applied Mathematics, John Wiley and Sons, Inc., 1965.
21. W. Kohn, Hierarchical Control Systems for Autonomous Space Robots, Proc. AIAA, 1988.
22. W. Kohn and A. Nerode, An Autonomous Control Theory: An Overview, Proc. IEEE CACSD92, Napa Valley, March, 1992.
23. W. Kohn and A. Nerode, Multiple Agent Autonomous Control Systems, Proc. 31st IEEE CDC Tucson, Ar., 2956-2966, 1993.
24. W. Kohn and A. Nerode, Models for Hybrid Systems: Automata, Topologies, Controllability, Observability, in [16], 1993.
25. W. Kohn and A. Nerode, Multiple Agent Autonomous Control, A Hybrid Systems Architecture, to appear in *Logical Methods: A Symposium in honor of Anil Nerode's 60th birthday*, Birkhauser, 1993.
26. W. Kohn, A. Nerode, and J.B. Remmel, " Hybrid Systems as Finsler Manifolds: Finite State Control as Approximation to Connections", In [2], (1995), 294-321
27. Kohn, W., Nerode, A. and Remmel, J.B., "Continualization: A Hybrid Systems Control Technique for Computing", Proceedings of CESA'96, (1996), 507-511.
28. Kohn, W., Nerode, A. and Remmel, J.B., "Feedback Derivations: Near Optimal Controls for Hybrid Systems", Proceedings of CESA'96, (1996), 517-521.
29. N.N. Krasovskii and A.I. Subbotin, *Game-Theoretical Control Problems*, Springer-Verlag, 1988.
30. Z. Manna and A. Pnueli, *The Temporal Logic of Reactive and Concurrent Systems*, Springer-Verlag, 1992.
31. E. B. Lee and L. Marcus. Foundations of optimal control theory, John Wiley & Sons, 1967.
32. K. Marzullo, F. Schneider, N. Budhiraja, Derivation of Sequential, Real-Time, Process-Control Programs, Technical Report 91- 1217, Department of Computer Science, Cornell University, Ithaca, NY 14853-7501.
33. R. McNaughton, Infinite Games Played on Finite Graphs, Annals of Pure and Appl. Logic, 65 (1993), 149-184.
34. A. Nerode and J.B. Remmel, A Model for Hybrid Systems, Hybrid System Workshop Notes, MSI, Cornell University, Ithaca, NY, June 1990.
35. A. Nerode, J.B. Remmel and A. Yakhnis, "McNaughton Games and Extracting Strategies for Concurrent Programs", to appear Annals of Pure and Applied Logic.

36. A. Nerode, A. Yakhnis, Modelling Hybrid Systems as Games, Proceedings of the Conference on Decision and Control, pp.2947-2952, 1992.

37. A. Nerode, A. Yakhnis, Hybrid Games and Hybrid Systems, Technical Report No. 93-77, October 1993, Mathematical Sciences Institute, Cornell University, 409 College Ave., Ithaca, NY 14850.

38. A. Nerode, A. Yakhnis, V. Yakhnis, Concurrent Programs as Strategies in Games, in *Logic from Computer Science*, (Y. Moschovakis, ed.), Springer-Verlag, 1992.

39. A. Nerode, A. Yakhnis, V. Yakhnis, Distributed Programs as Strategies in Games, in a volume honoring Anil Nerode 60th birthday, Birkheuser, 1994.

40. L.S. Pontryagin, On the Theory of Differential Games, Russian Mathematical Surveys 21 (No.4), pp. 193-246, 1966.

41. J. Slotine and W. Li, *Applied Nonlinear Control*, Prentice-Hall 1991.

42. E. D. Sontag, *Mathematical Control Theory*, Springer-Verlag, 1990.

43. V. I. Utkin, *Sliding Modes in Control Optimization*, Springer-Verlag, 1992.

44. J. Warga, *Optimal Control of Differential and Functional Equations*, Academic Press, 1972.

45. J. Warga, Some Selected Problems of Optimal Control, in Emilio O. Roxin (ed.), *Modern Optimal Control*, Marcel Dekker, Inc., 1989.

46. A. Yakhnis, Game-Theoretic Semantics for Concurrent Programs and Their Specifications, Ph. D. Diss., Cornell University, 1990.

47. A. Yakhnis, Hybrid Games, Technical Report 92-38, Mathematical Sciences Institute, Cornell University, October 1992.

48. A. Yakhnis, V. Yakhnis, Extension of Gurevich-Harrington's Restricted Memory Determinacy Theorem, Ann. Pure and App. Logic 48, 277-297, 1990.

49. A. Yakhnis, V. Yakhnis, Gurevich-Harrington's games defined by finite automata, Ann. Pure and App. Logic 62, 265-294, 1993.

Hybrid Control Design for a Three Vehicle Scenario Demonstration Using Overlapping Decompositions

Ümit Özgüner[1], Cem Hatipoğlu[1], Altuğ İftar[2] and Keith Redmill[1]

[1] The Ohio State University, Columbus, OH 43210-1272, USA
[2] Anadolu University, 26470 Eskişehir, Turkey

Abstract. Hybrid system models, representing both the dynamics of the continuous-time system and the set of distinct, discrete situations that can occur in a true "world", often tend to be large and unmanageable for controller design. Overlapping decomposition techniques are employed for controller design purposes which aim to regulate the continuous and the discrete states of such complex hybrid systems in a systematic way. In this paper, the hybrid system controller design for a string of three vehicles in a decentralized manner is studied for a scripted scenario. The considered scenario consists of three vehicles all of which will be equipped with on-board sensors and processors, and will be capable of performing advanced maneuvers on highways autonomously. A simulation model has been developed to study the performance of the proposed controller in a laboratory environment, and the control strategy will be tested on three cars by Summer 1997.

1 Introduction

Hybrid system models, representing both the dynamics of the continuous-time system and the set of distinct, discrete situations that can occur in a true "world", often tend to be large and unmanageable for controller design. In this paper, we employ overlapping decomposition techniques for controller design purposes to regulate the continuous and the discrete states of such complex hybrid systems in a systematic way.

Briefly, overlapping decomposition techniques build a framework for systematic decentralized controller design for large scale systems. Although the general sense opposes the idea of switching to a larger order space for controller design purposes, it is mostly the case that possible symmetry properties are exploited in the expanded system and a generic controller is designed for a single subsystem which is confined to a lower order subspace than the original. Then, if certain conditions are satisfied, a decentralized controller for the original system can be contracted out of the design in the expansion system. Moreover, stability of the subsystems in the expanded system has implications on the overall stability of the original system. It may turn out that stability analysis of an individual subsystem rather than the overall system is a relatively easier task. No need to say, this depends on the control objective, hybrid system configuration, complexity of the original system, coupling between units, and the symmetry embedded in the system. The answers to the listed issues above, in general, outline whether or not "overlapping decompositions" is feasible for an application. The extension of overlapping decompositions to hybrid systems is very recent [8]. In the present chapter we outline the basics of overlapping decompositions for hybrid systems, then provide full details of an example in the AHS area.

In the past decade, there has been extensive study in the field of Automated Highway Systems (AHS) regarding the theory and practice behind autonomous control of vehicles using vision and radar based sensors or magnetic readers. Such efforts are genuinely supported by the government and automobile companies for possible actuation in the near future. As a consequence of this collaborative research various theoretical results have been presented and some early proto-types of experimental setups have been developed. Some near future goals have been set to inform the general public about the improvements in this area and make them aware of what might be awaiting in the future regarding advanced control possibilities in ground vehicles.

Deployment seems to be the major issue to shape the future of these studies. One national demonstration has been scheduled by the National Automated Highway Systems Consortium (NAHSC) at San Diego on I-15 in August 1997. Some universities, automobile companies, research oriented institutions are scheduled to perform demonstrations to public for national exposure and possibly recognition. Center for Intelligent Transportation Research (CITR) of The Ohio State University (OSU), an associate member of NAHSC, will be among the demonstrators. Every participant has a scripted scenario which they have to prove to be safe both theoretically and experimentally prior to actual demonstration.

AHS is a complex, multi-agent controller design problem. Among the most commonly mentioned advantages of a possible AHS structure are the increased highway capacity and improved safety, which could be of conflicting nature. After all, as noted in [11] "the safest highway is an empty highway". Not surprisingly, the proponents of AHS face the situation to compromise between these trends. In the literature, the use of vehicle platoons turn out to be the most commonly emphasized AHS applications (led by PATH researchers) as "increased through-put of an existing highway" is assumed the relatively more crucial goal of the indicated two. Therefore, "safety" has to be reviewed such that hierarchical controllers could be designed mostly as a combination of discrete event (DE) and continuous system states yielding a hybrid structure, (see [11, 2]).

Putting more emphasis on "increasing the capacity of existing highways" while analyzing AHS case is the logical approach as many urban traffic sites are suffering from congestion, transportation delays and poor use of scarce resources. Building new highways to overcome these difficulties appear as the easy yet un-likely solution due to the excessive (short-term) construction and (long-term) maintenance costs. It is, hence, agreed that "efforts to increase the capacity of an existing highway by fully automating the longitudinal and lateral motions of vehicles operating on it" rest close to the top of the "goals" list in AHS implementation, especially when the industrial urban areas are considered. However, there are also numerous vehicles on US interstates which do not suffer much from this sort of congestion, yet AHS concept might serve their drivers for safer and more comfortable rides. The extent of its usefulness and feasibility are yet to be determined, however, one simple control application in automotive systems stands promising for future: Clearly, one of the earliest efforts to ease the driver's task has been the introduction of the "cruise control (CC) unit" on production line vehicles. CC is a very simple, yet useful option for us drivers, especially during long distance driving. It also represents the first step through the automation of the longitudinal motions of a vehicle. It is local, therefore decentralized, feasible and cheap (all very attractive from design and production point of views).

We intend to develop a more sophisticated decentralized multi level controller which will perform "intelligent cruise control" and "intelligent steering control" actions coordinated at a supervisory level, merely based on local sensors and regulated through steering, throttle and brake actuators. No sort of communication is assumed in the proposed structure. As it has been mentioned in various other papers such as [11], the abstraction of the goal and task allocation yield a DES which can be modeled using Petri-nets, finite state machines, Neural-nets and/or Fuzzy logic. This, together with the information flow from the decision layer to the actual physical system (and vice versa) constitute an interface layer for synchronous or asynchronous control of data flow from one side to the other. In general, updates of the continuous state system are done at a faster rate. Therefore, the decision layer and the continuous state system operate at different time scales (similar to [10]).

Briefly, we define the large scale goal for a vehicle as follows: Keep lane, maintain a safety distance between vehicles (relaxes the objective of "increased highway capacity"), perform lane change maneuvers to pass slower vehicles and to avoid obstacles during dangerous emergency situations (where pure longitudinal control is not sufficient). In this paper, we assume that the highway is a two lane road with only three vehicles operating on it (which is the case for our three vehicle scenario). Details about the employed low level (continuous state) controllers are not the concerns of this paper although it is an integral part of the overall closed loop system. The interested reader will be referred to the relevant papers, which contain detailed information on the mentioned subject, throughout the text. The prime objective of this paper is set to be decentralized controller design for a three vehicle demonstration scenario by making use of "overlapping decomposition" techniques which, we believe, is a relatively new, efficient tool for systematic hybrid controller design for large scale systems with inherent symmetry properties. We are using "divide, divide and conquer, combine" approach where the first "divide" stands for decomposing the overall hybrid system into smaller (overlapping) subsystems, the phrase "divide and conquer" describes continuous and discrete controller being designed independently and then combined by an interface which is specific to the problem, [10], and "combine" symbolizes controller contraction for the original system from the expansion system. Decomposition helps represent the behavior of the overall system in a smaller scale, in a simpler way.

Some of the most recent studies in hybrid system modeling and controller design for vehicle automation towards AHS have been performed by the researchers at University of California, Berkeley under PATH grants. Lygeros *et. al.* have studied designing continuous and discrete event controllers for vehicle automation on AHS where they have mainly focused on platoons of vehicles, but also allowed lane change maneuvers, joining and departing from platoons, [11]. They have also examined the interfacing between CSS and DSS in the overall hybrid structure for the mentioned design in detail, [10].

It is safe to state that, when developing controllers for discrete event systems, the designer possesses some significant degree of freedom to approach the problem. First of all, modeling, in terms of the selected discrete states, inputs and outputs is not unique. Secondly, the task is an integral part of the controller design which is generally there to be specified for a certain application. Continuous system modeling and controller design are relatively better defined and more systematic.

In this paper, we will focus on the controller design issues at the hybrid system level. There are various low level controllers -like a throttle controller, brake controller, speed controller, steering controller e.t.c.,- which have been studied, proved to be safe, stable and feasible in [21], [4] and [19]. When those low level controllers are embedded into the system, the continuous state model changes with inputs being the reference longitudinal velocity and the reference offset from the lane center. This eases the analysis and controller design at the supervisory level by simplifying the system model.

We make use of overlapping decomposition techniques for hybrid control design as the three vehicle scenario that is examined in this paper has nice symmetry properties and the choice of subsystems in the decomposition process results the controller be specific to this application only although extensions for a relatively more general case is relatively trivial. Decomposition method is not unique and will be discussed briefly in the Conclusions Section along with means of possible generalizations.

The organization of the paper is as follows: Section 2 overviews the concept of overlapping decomposition technique in hybrid systems. Further details about overlapping decompositions, expansions, contractions, and stability analysis in hybrid systems can be found in [8] coauthored by İftar and Özgüner. Section 3 presents the 1997 San Diego Demo Scenario, decomposition technique used, the generation of the decomposed system dynamics from those of the original system as well as controller design and contraction issues. Section 4 studies the developed simulation model and finally, Section 5 concludes the paper with some discussions.

2 Overlapping Decompositions - an Overview

2.1 Hybrid System Modeling

It is clear that a "model" is essential for system analysis and controller design purposes. Many intelligent systems that are autonomously controlled involve certain decision making procedures, therefore, their dynamic behavior can be more conveniently represented with the combination of some numeric models (like differential, difference equations) and some symbolic models (like Petri-nets, finite state machines, Neural nets, Fuzzy logic). The physical system behavior develops as the result of a continuous time system interacting with the operation of a discrete event system (DES).

The continuous system portion of the hybrid system is formally better defined and straight forward. Using classical modeling techniques, the physical system can be represented with some differential-difference type equations. Various different hybrid modeling approaches have been considered for the DES portion of the hybrid structure. Passino and Özgüner described DES using finite automaton and linked DES and CSS parts via some "interface", [14]. Peleties and Decarlo based their DES model on Petri nets, where they have attempted to create macro events from so-called elementary events, [15, 16].

In this paper, we specify the DES portion of the hybrid system to be a finite state machine (finite automaton) similar to studies in [14, 1]. Figure 2(a) shows the hybrid system model that has been considered in these cited papers. Note that, we are dealing with large scale hybrid systems where the individual "units" of this so-called multi-unit system are hybrid systems themselves. They interact with each other at the DES and CSS levels and the evolution of their states depend on the rest of the units (within the big picture) as well as their own. Overlapping decomposition techniques are generally well suited for such large scale hybrid systems as depicted on Figure 2(b).

Before going into details regarding the principles behind overlapping decompositions and controller design procedure using contractions, we would like to explain what we mean by "large-scale hybrid systems", "units" of a large scale system and "symmetry" embedded in a system on a simple example. Consider a platoon of N vehicles on an automated highway. A "vehicle platoon" corresponds to a string of vehicles that operate in the same lane with small inter vehicle separations. Let us assume that no departure from the platoon is allowed which further simplifies the case. Also assume that vehicles are equipped with relative velocity and relative distance measuring sensors. The physical units of this system are the vehicles (N of them, each being a single "unit") which have continuous dynamics. Consider an individual unit except for the leader of the platoon. This car interacts with its leader in the continuous state space and exhibits some behavior during its course of operation which can be described with some finite number of "symbolic words" like *Close and Fast, Close but Slow, Far but Fast, Far and Slow*. Hence, the considered vehicle, its leader and the sensors build a hybrid sub-structure with some finite automaton. For $N > 2$ there are more than one such hybrid sub-structures in the original system. Because that its building sub-structures are hybrid systems, the original system becomes a hybrid system at the macro state as well. "Symmetry", in this example, describes that sub-structures are identical in terms of modeling and task allocation. Decentralized controller design issues using overlapping decomposition techniques for platooning has been studied and the results are presented in [8]. Now we are in the position to summarize the overlapping decomposition techniques for systematic decentralized controller design in large scale hybrid systems.

Throughout the paper, $\mathbb{R}^k$ denotes the k–dimensional real vector space, calligraphic capital letters (like $\mathcal{X}$, $\mathcal{U}$, $\mathcal{Y}$, $\mathcal{Z}$) indicate discrete sets (finite or countable), $\mathbb{N}$ denotes the set of natural numbers, $\mathbb{R}^+$ denotes the set of non-negative real numbers, I denotes the identity operator, for $a \in \mathbb{R}^+$, $[a]$ denotes the integer part of a, for $x \in \mathbb{R}^n$, $\|x\|$ denotes a norm of x on $\mathbb{R}^n$ (any norm on $\mathbb{R}^n$ can be used), and $(\cdot)^T$ denotes the transpose of $(\cdot)$.

2.2 Inclusion Principle

Consider hybrid systems with discrete-state parts evolving deterministically at periodic instants of time t with period T. The assumption of periodicity helps for notational convenience only, the results in this paper can easily be extended to the non-periodic case. It is assumed that the discrete-state part and the continuous-state part interact at the same instants. It is also assumed that the continuous-state part evolves continuously in time and that this behavior can be described by ordinary differential equations. Note that similar results may be developed for the case when the continuous-state part evolves at discrete instants and its behavior can be described by difference equations. In summary, we consider hybrid systems described as follows:

$$\Sigma : \begin{aligned} X(k+1) &= F(X(k), z(kT), U(k)) \\ Y(k) &= G(X(k), z(kT), U(k)) \\ Z(k) &= H(X(k), U(k)) \\ \dot{x}(t) &= f(x(t), Z([t/T]), u(t)) \\ y(t) &= g(x(t), Z([t/T]), u(t)) \\ z(t) &= h(x(t), u(t)) \end{aligned} \qquad , \tilde{\Sigma} : \begin{aligned} \tilde{X}(k+1) &= \tilde{F}(\tilde{X}(k), \tilde{z}(kT), \tilde{U}(k)) \\ \tilde{Y}(k) &= \tilde{G}(\tilde{X}(k), \tilde{z}(kT), \tilde{U}(k)) \\ \tilde{Z}(k) &= \tilde{H}(\tilde{X}(k), \tilde{U}(k)) \\ \dot{\tilde{x}}(t) &= \tilde{f}(\tilde{x}(t), \tilde{Z}([t/T]), \tilde{u}(t)) \\ \tilde{y}(t) &= \tilde{g}(\tilde{x}(t), \tilde{Z}([t/T]), \tilde{u}(t)) \\ \tilde{z}(t) &= \tilde{h}(\tilde{x}(t), \tilde{u}(t)) \end{aligned}$$

$$(1)$$

Here $X \in \mathcal{X} = \mathcal{X}_1 \times \mathcal{X}_2 \times \cdots \times \mathcal{X}_N$, $U \in \mathcal{U} = \mathcal{U}_1 \times \mathcal{U}_2 \times \cdots \times \mathcal{U}_M$, $Y \in \mathcal{Y} = \mathcal{Y}_1 \times \mathcal{Y}_2 \times \cdots \times \mathcal{Y}_L$, are, respectively, state, input and output vectors of the discrete-state part of the system Σ and $x \in \mathbb{R}^n$, $u \in \mathbb{R}^m$, and $y \in \mathbb{R}^l$ are, respectively, state, input, and output vectors of the continuous-state part of the system Σ. Similarly, $\tilde{X} \in \tilde{\mathcal{X}} = \tilde{\mathcal{X}}_1 \times \tilde{\mathcal{X}}_2 \times \cdots \times \tilde{\mathcal{X}}_{\tilde{N}}$, $\tilde{U} \in \tilde{\mathcal{U}} = \tilde{\mathcal{U}}_1 \times \tilde{\mathcal{U}}_2 \times \cdots \times \tilde{\mathcal{U}}_{\tilde{M}}$, $\tilde{Y} \in \tilde{\mathcal{Y}} = \tilde{\mathcal{Y}}_1 \times \tilde{\mathcal{Y}}_2 \times \cdots \times \tilde{\mathcal{Y}}_{\tilde{L}}$ are, respectively, state, input and output vectors of the discrete-state part of the system $\tilde{\Sigma}$ and $\tilde{x} \in \mathbb{R}^{\tilde{n}}$, $\tilde{u} \in \mathbb{R}^{\tilde{m}}$, and $\tilde{y} \in \mathbb{R}^{\tilde{l}}$ are, respectively, state, input, and output vectors of the continuous-state part of the system $\tilde{\Sigma}$. Furthermore, $Z \in \mathcal{Z} = \mathcal{Z}_1 \times \mathcal{Z}_2 \times \cdots \times \mathcal{Z}_\Lambda$ and $\tilde{Z} \in \tilde{\mathcal{Z}} = \tilde{\mathcal{Z}}_1 \times \tilde{\mathcal{Z}}_2 \times \cdots \times \tilde{\mathcal{Z}}_{\tilde{\Lambda}}$ are the *internal output vectors* of the discrete-state part of the systems Σ and $\tilde{\Sigma}$ respectively and they represent the interconnections from the discrete-state part to the continuous-state part of the respective system. Similarly, $z \in \mathbb{R}^\lambda$ and $\tilde{z} \in \mathbb{R}^{\tilde{\lambda}}$ are the *internal output vectors* of the continuous-state part of the systems Σ and $\tilde{\Sigma}$ respectively and they represent the interconnections from the continuous-state part to the discrete-state part of the respective system. It is assumed that $f : \mathbb{R}^n \times \mathcal{Z} \times \mathbb{R}^m \rightarrow \mathbb{R}^n$ and $\tilde{f} : \mathbb{R}^{\tilde{n}} \times \tilde{\mathcal{Z}} \times \mathbb{R}^{\tilde{m}} \rightarrow \mathbb{R}^{\tilde{n}}$ are such that the fourth equations in 1 have continuous solutions respectively for $x(t)$ and $\tilde{x}(t)$ for all $Z(k) \in \mathcal{Z}$, $\tilde{Z}(k) \in \tilde{\mathcal{Z}}$, $u(t) \in \mathbb{R}^m$, $\tilde{u}(t) \in \mathbb{R}^{\tilde{m}}$, and for all initial conditions in $\mathbb{R}^n$ and $\mathbb{R}^{\tilde{n}}$ respectively. The outputs $Y, y, \tilde{Y}$, and $\tilde{y}$ are assumed to be measurable. It is also assumed that $\tilde{N} \geq N$, $\tilde{M} \geq M$, $\tilde{L} \geq L$, $\tilde{\Lambda} \geq \Lambda$, $\tilde{n} \geq n$, $\tilde{m} \geq m$, $\tilde{l} \geq l$, and $\tilde{\lambda} \geq \lambda$. In the sequel, the system Σ is referred to as the *original system* and $\tilde{\Sigma}$ is referred to as the *expanded system*.

Consider the injective transformations:

$$P : \mathcal{X} \rightarrow \tilde{\mathcal{X}} \quad , \quad Q : \mathcal{U} \rightarrow \tilde{\mathcal{U}} \quad , \tag{2-a}$$

$$R : \mathcal{Y} \rightarrow \tilde{\mathcal{Y}} \quad , \quad S : \mathcal{Z} \rightarrow \tilde{\mathcal{Z}} \quad , \tag{2-b}$$

$$p : \mathbb{R}^n \rightarrow \mathbb{R}^{\tilde{n}} \quad , \quad q : \mathbb{R}^m \rightarrow \mathbb{R}^{\tilde{m}} \quad , \tag{2-c}$$

$$r : \mathbb{R}^l \rightarrow \mathbb{R}^{\tilde{l}} \quad , \quad s : \mathbb{R}^\lambda \rightarrow \mathbb{R}^{\tilde{\lambda}} \quad . \tag{2-d}$$

Also consider the surjective transformations:

$$P^\# : \tilde{\mathcal{X}} \rightarrow \mathcal{X} \quad , \quad Q^\# : \tilde{\mathcal{U}} \rightarrow \mathcal{U} \quad , \tag{2-e}$$

$$R^\# : \tilde{\mathcal{Y}} \rightarrow \mathcal{Y} \quad , \quad S^\# : \tilde{\mathcal{Z}} \rightarrow \mathcal{Z} \quad , \tag{2-f}$$

$$p^\# : \mathbb{R}^{\tilde{n}} \rightarrow \mathbb{R}^n \quad , \quad q^\# : \mathbb{R}^{\tilde{m}} \rightarrow \mathbb{R}^m \quad , \tag{2-g}$$

$$r^\# : \mathbb{R}^{\tilde{l}} \rightarrow \mathbb{R}^l \quad , \quad s^\# : \mathbb{R}^{\tilde{\lambda}} \rightarrow \mathbb{R}^\lambda \quad , \tag{2-h}$$

where $p^\#$ is linear and $P^\# P = I$, $Q^\# Q = I$, $R^\# R = I$, $S^\# S = I$, $p^\# p = I$, $q^\# q = I$, $r^\# r = I$, and $s^\# s = I$. We can now define the inclusion for hybrid systems described as in 1.

Definition 1. The system $\tilde{\Sigma}$ *includes* the system Σ, and the system Σ is *included by* the system $\tilde{\Sigma}$, if there exist transformations as in 2-a–2-h such that for any initial state $\{X_0 \in \mathcal{X}, x_0 \in \mathbb{R}^n\}$ of the system Σ and for any input $\{U(k) \in \mathcal{U}, u(t) \in \mathbb{R}^m\}$ $(k \in \mathbb{N}, t \in \mathbb{R}^+)$ of the system Σ the choice

$$\tilde{X}_0 = P(X_0), \quad \tilde{x}_0 = p(x_0) \tag{3-a}$$

for the initial state of the system $\tilde{\Sigma}$ and

$$\tilde{U}(k) = Q(U(k)), \quad \forall k \geq 0 \tag{3-b}$$

$$\tilde{u}(t) = q(u(t)), \quad \forall t \geq 0 \tag{3-c}$$

for the input of the system $\tilde{\Sigma}$ implies that

$$X(k) = P^\#(\tilde{X}(k)), \quad \forall k \geq 0 \tag{4-a}$$

$$x(t) = p^\#(\tilde{x}(t)), \quad \forall t \geq 0 \tag{4-b}$$

$$Y(k) = R^\#(\tilde{Y}(k)), \quad \forall k \geq 0 \tag{4-c}$$

$$y(t) = r^\#(\tilde{y}(t)), \quad \forall t \geq 0 \tag{4-d}$$

The following theorem gives sufficient conditions for the inclusion.

Theorem 2. *The system $\tilde{\Sigma}$ includes the system Σ if there exist transformations as in 2-a–2-h such that*

$$F(P^{\#}(\tilde{X}), s^{\#}(\tilde{z}), U) = P^{\#}(\tilde{F}(\tilde{X}, \tilde{z}, Q(U))) \ , \ \forall \tilde{X} \in \tilde{\mathcal{X}}, \forall \tilde{z} \in \mathbb{R}^{\tilde{\lambda}}, \forall U \in \mathcal{U} \qquad (5\text{-a})$$

$$G(P^{\#}(\tilde{X}), s^{\#}(\tilde{z}), U) = R^{\#}(\tilde{G}(\tilde{X}, \tilde{z}, Q(U))) \ , \ \forall \tilde{X} \in \tilde{\mathcal{X}}, \forall \tilde{z} \in \mathbb{R}^{\tilde{\lambda}}, \forall U \in \mathcal{U} \qquad (5\text{-b})$$

$$H(P^{\#}(\tilde{X}), U) = S^{\#}(\tilde{H}(\tilde{X}, Q(U))) \ , \ \forall \tilde{X} \in \tilde{\mathcal{X}}, \forall U \in \mathcal{U} \qquad (5\text{-c})$$

$$f(p^{\#}(\tilde{x}), S^{\#}(\tilde{Z}), u) = p^{\#}(\tilde{f}(\tilde{x}, \tilde{Z}, q(u))) \ , \ \forall \tilde{x} \in \mathbb{R}^{\tilde{n}}, \forall \tilde{Z} \in \tilde{\mathcal{Z}}, \forall u \in \mathbb{R}^{m} \qquad (5\text{-d})$$

$$g(p^{\#}(\tilde{x}), S^{\#}(\tilde{Z}), u) = r^{\#}(\tilde{g}(\tilde{x}, \tilde{Z}, q(u))) \ , \ \forall \tilde{x} \in \mathbb{R}^{\tilde{n}}, \forall \tilde{Z} \in \tilde{\mathcal{Z}}, \forall u \in \mathbb{R}^{m} \qquad (5\text{-e})$$

$$h(p^{\#}(\tilde{x}), u) = s^{\#}(\tilde{h}(\tilde{x}, q(u))) \ , \ \forall \tilde{x} \in \mathbb{R}^{\tilde{n}}, \forall u \in \mathbb{R}^{m} \qquad (5\text{-f})$$

Remark: If the systems Σ and $\tilde{\Sigma}$ do not have a discrete-state part and the continuous-state part is linear, then the above conditions reduce to the conditions given in [9] for linear CSS, which are not only sufficient but necessary as well.

2.3 Extension Principle

For CSS, a number of special cases of inclusion, namely *aggregation, restriction* [9] and *extension* [7], have been considered in the literature. Among these cases, extension is especially important for controller design, since any controller designed for the expanded system, which is an extension of the original system, is guaranteed to be contractible to a controller which can be applied to the original system. This property may not hold if the expanded system is not an extension of the original system [9]. In this section we will define the extension principle for hybrid systems.

Again consider the systems Σ and $\tilde{\Sigma}$, described by 1.

Definition 3. The system $\tilde{\Sigma}$ is an *extension* of the system Σ, and Σ is a *disextension* of $\tilde{\Sigma}$, if there exist transformations as in 2-a–2-h such that for any initial state $\{X_0 \in \mathcal{X}, x_0 \in \mathbb{R}^n\}$ of the system Σ and for any input $\{\tilde{U}(k) \in \tilde{\mathcal{U}}, \tilde{u}(t) \in \mathbb{R}^{\tilde{m}}\}$ $(k \in \mathbb{N}, t \in \mathbb{R}^+)$ of the system $\tilde{\Sigma}$ the choice

$$\tilde{X}_0 = P(X_0), \quad \tilde{x}_0 = p(x_0) \qquad (6\text{-a})$$

for the initial state of the system $\tilde{\Sigma}$ and

$$U(k) = Q^{\#}(\tilde{U}(k)), \quad \forall k \geq 0 \qquad (6\text{-b})$$

$$u(t) = q^{\#}(\tilde{u}(t)), \quad \forall t \geq 0 \qquad (6\text{-c})$$

for the input of the system Σ implies that

$$\tilde{X}(k) = P(X(k)), \quad \forall k \geq 0 \qquad (7\text{-a})$$

$$\tilde{x}(t) = p(x(t)), \quad \forall t \geq 0 \qquad (7\text{-b})$$

$$\tilde{Y}(k) = R(Y(k)), \quad \forall k \geq 0 \qquad (7\text{-c})$$

$$\tilde{y}(t) = r(y(t)), \quad \forall t \geq 0 \qquad (7\text{-d})$$

Remark: If the systems Σ and $\tilde{\Sigma}$ do not have a discrete-state part, then the above definition reduces to the definition first given in [7] for CSS. If the systems Σ and $\tilde{\Sigma}$ do not have a continuous-state part, then the above definition reduces to a definition of extension for DSS, which to the authors' knowledge was not available before.

The following theorem gives sufficient conditions for the extension.

Theorem 4. *The system $\tilde{\Sigma}$ is an extension of the system Σ if there exist transformations as in 2-a–2-h such that*

$$\tilde{F}(P(X), s(z), \tilde{U}) = P(F(X, z, Q^{\#}(\tilde{U}))) , \quad \forall X \in \mathcal{X} , \; \forall z \in \mathbb{R}^{\lambda} , \; \forall \tilde{U} \in \tilde{\mathcal{U}} \quad \text{(8-a)}$$

$$\tilde{G}(P(X), s(z), \tilde{U}) = R(G(X, z, Q^{\#}(\tilde{U}))) , \quad \forall X \in \mathcal{X} , \; \forall z \in \mathbb{R}^{\lambda} , \; \forall \tilde{U} \in \tilde{\mathcal{U}} \quad \text{(8-b)}$$

$$\tilde{H}(P(X), \tilde{U}) = S(H(X, Q^{\#}(\tilde{U}))) , \quad \forall X \in \mathcal{X} , \; \forall \tilde{U} \in \tilde{\mathcal{U}} \quad \text{(8-c)}$$

$$\tilde{f}(p(x), S(Z), \tilde{u}) = p(f(x, Z, q^{\#}(\tilde{u}))) , \quad \forall x \in \mathbb{R}^{n} , \; \forall Z \in \mathcal{Z} , \; \forall \tilde{u} \in \mathbb{R}^{m} \quad \text{(8-d)}$$

$$\tilde{g}(p(x), S(Z), \tilde{u}) = r(g(x, Z, q^{\#}(\tilde{u}))) , \quad \forall x \in \mathbb{R}^{n} , \; \forall Z \in \mathcal{Z} , \; \forall \tilde{u} \in \mathbb{R}^{m} \quad \text{(8-e)}$$

$$\tilde{h}(p(x), \tilde{u}) = s(h(x, q^{\#}(\tilde{u}))) , \quad \forall x \in \mathbb{R}^{n} , \; \forall \tilde{u} \in \mathbb{R}^{m} \quad \text{(8-f)}$$

Remark: If the systems Σ and $\tilde{\Sigma}$ do not have a discrete-state part and the continuous-state part is linear, then the above conditions reduce to the conditions given in [7] for linear CSS, which are not only sufficient but necessary as well.

Before concluding this section we will formally state that extension is a special case of inclusion.

Theorem 5. *Let $\tilde{\Sigma}$ be an extension of Σ. Then $\tilde{\Sigma}$ includes Σ.*

2.4 Controller Design with Extension

In this section, controller design for hybrid systems using extension is discussed. For simplicity we restrict ourselves to the case of static controllers. A static controller for the system Σ can be described by:

$$\Gamma: \quad \begin{aligned} V(k) &= C(Y(k), y(kT)) \\ v(t) &= c(y(t), Y([t/T])) \end{aligned} \quad (9)$$

where $V \in \mathcal{U}$ and $v \in \mathbb{R}^{m}$ are the outputs of the controller which are to be applied respectively to the inputs U and u of the system Σ in order to control it; *i.e.*: $U(k) = V(k)$, $k \in \mathbb{N}$, and $u(t) = v(t)$, $t \in \mathbb{R}^{+}$. Similarly, a static controller for the system $\tilde{\Sigma}$ can be described by:

$$\tilde{\Gamma}: \quad \begin{aligned} \tilde{V}(k) &= \tilde{C}(\tilde{Y}(k), \tilde{y}(kT)) \\ \tilde{v}(t) &= \tilde{c}(\tilde{y}(t), \tilde{Y}([t/T])) \end{aligned} \quad (10)$$

where $\tilde{V} \in \tilde{\mathcal{U}}$ and $\tilde{v} \in \mathbb{R}^{m}$ are the outputs of the controller which are to be applied respectively to the inputs $\tilde{U}$ and $\tilde{u}$ of the system $\tilde{\Sigma}$ in order to control it; *i.e.*: $\tilde{U}(k) = \tilde{V}(k)$, $k \in \mathbb{N}$, and $\tilde{u}(t) = \tilde{v}(t)$, $t \in \mathbb{R}^{+}$.

We now introduce *contractibility* of controllers:

Definition 6. The controller 10 is *contractible* to the controller 9 if there exist transformations as in 2-a–2-h such that for any initial state $\{X_0 \in \mathcal{X}, x_0 \in \mathbb{R}^n\}$ of the system Σ, and for any input $\{\tilde{U}(k) \in \tilde{\mathcal{U}}, \tilde{u}(t) \in \mathbb{R}^{\tilde{m}}\}$ $(k \in \mathbb{N}, t \in \mathbb{R}^+)$ of the system $\tilde{\Sigma}$ the choice

$$\tilde{X}_0 = P(X_0), \quad \tilde{x}_0 = p(x_0) \tag{11-a}$$

for the initial state of the system $\tilde{\Sigma}$ and

$$U(k) = Q^\#(\tilde{U}(k)), \quad \forall k \geq 0 \tag{11-b}$$
$$u(t) = q^\#(\tilde{u}(t)), \quad \forall t \geq 0 \tag{11-c}$$

for the input of the system Σ implies that

$$V(k) = Q^\#(\tilde{V}(k)), \quad \forall k \geq 0 \tag{12-a}$$
$$v(t) = q^\#(\tilde{v}(t)), \quad \forall t \geq 0 \tag{12-b}$$

The following theorem gives sufficient conditions for contractibility in the case when the expanded system is an extension of the original system.

Theorem 7. Let $\tilde{\Sigma}$ be an extension of Σ. Then the controller 10 is contractible to the controller 9 if

$$C(Y, y) = Q^\#(\tilde{C}(R(Y), r(y))), \quad \forall Y \in \mathcal{Y}, \forall y \in \mathbb{R}^l \tag{13-a}$$
$$c(y, Y) = q^\#(\tilde{c}(r(y), R(Y))), \quad \forall y \in \mathbb{R}^l, \forall Y \in \mathcal{Y} \tag{13-b}$$

The above result immediately leads to the following result, which states that if the expanded system is an extension of the original system, then any controller designed for the expanded system can be contracted to a controller for the original system. The importance of this result comes from the fact that the controller is first to be designed for the expanded system and then will be contracted and applied to the original system.

Corollary 8. Let $\tilde{\Sigma}$ be an extension of Σ. Then any controller of the form 10 is contractible to a controller of the form 9, where

$$C(\cdot, \cdot) := Q^\#(\tilde{C}(R(\cdot), r(\cdot))) \tag{14-a}$$
$$c(\cdot, \cdot) := q^\#(\tilde{c}(r(\cdot), R(\cdot))) \tag{14-b}$$

Remark: If the expanded system is not an extension of the original system, then a controller designed for the expanded system may not be contractible (see [9] for the case of CSS).

As mentioned earlier, it is important to satisfy contractibility in order to preserve desired relations between the expanded and the original systems following the application of the appropriate controllers. The following result shows that, under the assumption that both closed-loop systems are well-posed, one such relation, namely extension, is preserved if the controller for the expanded system is contractible to the controller for the original system. This result actually leads to the preservation of many other properties - such as stability.

Theorem 9. *Let $\tilde{\Sigma}$ be an extension of Σ and let $\tilde{\Gamma}$ be contractible to Γ. Furthermore, assume that the* original closed-loop system, *obtained by applying Γ to Σ (i.e., letting $U(k) = V(k)$ and $u(t) = v(t)$), and the* expanded closed-loop system, *obtained by applying $\tilde{\Gamma}$ to $\tilde{\Sigma}$ (i.e., letting $\tilde{U}(k) = \tilde{V}(k)$ and $\tilde{u}(t) = \tilde{v}(t)$), are well-posed. Then the expanded closed-loop system is an extension of the original closed-loop system.*

2.5 Overlapping Decompositions

In this section decentralized controller design with overlapping decompositions is discussed within the framework of extension. For notational simplicity, only systems with two overlapping subsystems are considered. The generalization of the results to systems with more subsystems is straightforward. In fact, the next section will present an example with such a generalization.

Consider the system Σ given in 1. Suppose that the state, the input, the output, and the internal output vectors are partitioned as (see Figure 3(a)):

$$
X = \begin{bmatrix} X_1 \\ X_2 \\ X_3 \end{bmatrix}, \qquad x = \begin{bmatrix} x_1 \\ x_2 \\ x_3 \end{bmatrix}, \tag{15-a}
$$

where $X_1 \in \hat{\mathcal{X}}_1 := \mathcal{X}_1 \times \mathcal{X}_2 \times \cdots \times \mathcal{X}_{N_1}$, $X_2 \in \hat{\mathcal{X}}_2 := \mathcal{X}_{N_1+1} \times \mathcal{X}_{N_1+2} \times \cdots \times \mathcal{X}_{N_1+N_2}$, $X_3 \in \hat{\mathcal{X}}_3 := \mathcal{X}_{N_1+N_2+1} \times \mathcal{X}_{N_1+N_2+2} \times \cdots \times \mathcal{X}_N$, $x_1 \in \mathbb{R}^{n_1}$, $x_2 \in \mathbb{R}^{n_2}$, and $x_3 \in \mathbb{R}^{n_3}$,

$$
U = \begin{bmatrix} U_1 \\ U_2 \\ U_3 \end{bmatrix}, \qquad u = \begin{bmatrix} u_1 \\ u_2 \\ u_3 \end{bmatrix}, \tag{15-b}
$$

where $U_1 \in \hat{\mathcal{U}}_1 := \mathcal{U}_1 \times \mathcal{U}_2 \times \cdots \times \mathcal{U}_{M_1}$, $U_2 \in \hat{\mathcal{U}}_2 := \mathcal{U}_{M_1+1} \times \mathcal{U}_{M_1+2} \times \cdots \times \mathcal{U}_{M_1+M_2}$, $U_3 \in \hat{\mathcal{U}}_3 := \mathcal{U}_{M_1+M_2+1} \times \mathcal{U}_{M_1+M_2+2} \times \cdots \times \mathcal{U}_M$, $u_1 \in \mathbb{R}^{m_1}$, $u_2 \in \mathbb{R}^{m_2}$, and $u_3 \in \mathbb{R}^{m_3}$,

$$
Y = \begin{bmatrix} Y_1 \\ Y_2 \\ Y_3 \end{bmatrix}, \qquad y = \begin{bmatrix} y_1 \\ y_2 \\ y_3 \end{bmatrix}, \tag{15-c}
$$

where $Y_1 \in \hat{\mathcal{Y}}_1 := \mathcal{Y}_1 \times \mathcal{Y}_2 \times \cdots \times \mathcal{Y}_{L_1}$, $Y_2 \in \hat{\mathcal{Y}}_2 := \mathcal{Y}_{L_1+1} \times \mathcal{Y}_{L_1+2} \times \cdots \times \mathcal{Y}_{L_1+L_2}$, $Y_3 \in \hat{\mathcal{Y}}_3 := \mathcal{Y}_{L_1+L_2+1} \times \mathcal{Y}_{L_1+L_2+2} \times \cdots \times \mathcal{Y}_L$, $y_1 \in \mathbb{R}^{l_1}$, $y_2 \in \mathbb{R}^{l_2}$, and $y_3 \in \mathbb{R}^{l_3}$,

$$
Z = \begin{bmatrix} Z_1 \\ Z_2 \\ Z_3 \end{bmatrix}, \qquad z = \begin{bmatrix} z_1 \\ z_2 \\ z_3 \end{bmatrix}, \tag{15-d}
$$

where $Z_1 \in \hat{\mathcal{Z}}_1 := \mathcal{Z}_1 \times \mathcal{Z}_2 \times \cdots \times \mathcal{Z}_{A_1}$, $Z_2 \in \hat{\mathcal{Z}}_2 := \mathcal{Z}_{A_1+1} \times \mathcal{Z}_{A_1+2} \times \cdots \times \mathcal{Z}_{A_1+A_2}$, $Z_3 \in \hat{\mathcal{Z}}_3 := \mathcal{Z}_{A_1+A_2+1} \times \mathcal{Z}_{A_1+A_2+2} \times \cdots \times \mathcal{Z}_A$, $z_1 \in \mathbb{R}^{\lambda_1}$, $z_2 \in \mathbb{R}^{\lambda_2}$, and $z_3 \in \mathbb{R}^{\lambda_3}$. Here it is assumed that $X_2, x_2, U_2, u_2, Y_2, y_2, Z_2$, and z_2 correspond to the overlapping parts of the state, input, output, and internal output spaces respectively.

To obtain an extension of the given system, the transformations defined in 2-a–2-h can be chosen as:

$$P\left(\begin{bmatrix} X_1 \\ X_2 \\ X_3 \end{bmatrix}\right) = \begin{bmatrix} X_1 \\ X_2 \\ X_2 \\ X_3 \end{bmatrix}, \qquad p\left(\begin{bmatrix} x_1 \\ x_2 \\ x_3 \end{bmatrix}\right) = \begin{bmatrix} x_1 \\ x_2 \\ x_2 \\ x_3 \end{bmatrix}, \qquad \text{(16-a)}$$

$\forall X_1 \in \hat{\mathcal{X}}_1, \forall X_2 \in \hat{\mathcal{X}}_2, \forall X_3 \in \hat{\mathcal{X}}_3, \forall x_1 \in \mathbb{R}^{n_1}, \forall x_2 \in \mathbb{R}^{n_2}, \forall x_3 \in \mathbb{R}^{n_3},$

$$Q\left(\begin{bmatrix} U_1 \\ U_2 \\ U_3 \end{bmatrix}\right) = \begin{bmatrix} U_1 \\ U_2 \\ U_2 \\ U_3 \end{bmatrix}, \qquad q\left(\begin{bmatrix} u_1 \\ u_2 \\ u_3 \end{bmatrix}\right) = \begin{bmatrix} u_1 \\ u_2 \\ u_2 \\ u_3 \end{bmatrix}, \qquad \text{(16-b)}$$

$\forall U_1 \in \hat{\mathcal{U}}_1, \forall U_2 \in \hat{\mathcal{U}}_2, \forall U_3 \in \hat{\mathcal{U}}_3, \forall u_1 \in \mathbb{R}^{m_1}, \forall u_2 \in \mathbb{R}^{m_2}, \forall u_3 \in \mathbb{R}^{m_3},$

$$R\left(\begin{bmatrix} Y_1 \\ Y_2 \\ Y_3 \end{bmatrix}\right) = \begin{bmatrix} Y_1 \\ Y_2 \\ Y_2 \\ Y_3 \end{bmatrix}, \qquad r\left(\begin{bmatrix} y_1 \\ y_2 \\ y_3 \end{bmatrix}\right) = \begin{bmatrix} y_1 \\ y_2 \\ y_2 \\ y_3 \end{bmatrix}, \qquad \text{(16-c)}$$

$\forall Y_1 \in \hat{\mathcal{Y}}_1, \forall Y_2 \in \hat{\mathcal{Y}}_2, \forall Y_3 \in \hat{\mathcal{Y}}_3, \forall y_1 \in \mathbb{R}^{l_1}, \forall y_2 \in \mathbb{R}^{l_2}, \forall y_3 \in \mathbb{R}^{l_3},$

$$S\left(\begin{bmatrix} Z_1 \\ Z_2 \\ Z_3 \end{bmatrix}\right) = \begin{bmatrix} Z_1 \\ Z_2 \\ Z_2 \\ Z_3 \end{bmatrix}, \qquad s\left(\begin{bmatrix} z_1 \\ z_2 \\ z_3 \end{bmatrix}\right) = \begin{bmatrix} z_1 \\ z_2 \\ z_2 \\ z_3 \end{bmatrix}, \qquad \text{(16-d)}$$

$\forall Z_1 \in \hat{\mathcal{Z}}_1, \forall Z_2 \in \hat{\mathcal{Z}}_2, \forall Z_3 \in \hat{\mathcal{Z}}_3, \forall z_1 \in \mathbb{R}^{\lambda_1}, \forall z_2 \in \mathbb{R}^{\lambda_2}, \forall z_3 \in \mathbb{R}^{\lambda_3}.$ In order to define the transformations $P^\#$, $Q^\#$, $R^\#$, and $S^\#$, we first define an *addition* (denoted by +) on $\hat{\mathcal{X}}_2$, $\hat{\mathcal{U}}_2$, $\hat{\mathcal{Y}}_2$, and $\hat{\mathcal{Z}}_2$ such that $X + X = X, \forall X \in \hat{\mathcal{X}}_2$, $U + U = U, \forall U \in \hat{\mathcal{U}}_2, Y + Y = Y, \forall Y \in \hat{\mathcal{Y}}_2$, and $Z + Z = Z, \forall Z \in \hat{\mathcal{Z}}_2$. The rest of the transformations can now be defined as:

$$P^\#\left(\begin{bmatrix} X_1 \\ X_{2_1} \\ X_{2_2} \\ X_3 \end{bmatrix}\right) = \begin{bmatrix} X_1 \\ X_{2_1} + X_{2_2} \\ X_3 \end{bmatrix}, \qquad p^\#\left(\begin{bmatrix} x_1 \\ x_{2_1} \\ x_{2_2} \\ x_3 \end{bmatrix}\right) = \begin{bmatrix} x_1 \\ \frac{1}{2}(x_{2_1} + x_{2_2}) \\ x_3 \end{bmatrix}, \qquad \text{(16-e)}$$

$\forall X_1 \in \hat{\mathcal{X}}_1, \forall X_{2_1} \in \hat{\mathcal{X}}_2, \forall X_{2_2} \in \hat{\mathcal{X}}_2, \forall X_3 \in \hat{\mathcal{X}}_3, \forall x_1 \in \mathbb{R}^{n_1}, \forall x_{2_1} \in \mathbb{R}^{n_2},$
$\forall x_{2_2} \in \mathbb{R}^{n_2}, \forall x_3 \in \mathbb{R}^{n_3},$

$$Q^\#\left(\begin{bmatrix} U_1 \\ U_{2_1} \\ U_{2_2} \\ U_3 \end{bmatrix}\right) = \begin{bmatrix} U_1 \\ U_{2_1} + U_{2_2} \\ U_3 \end{bmatrix}, \qquad q^\#\left(\begin{bmatrix} u_1 \\ u_{2_1} \\ u_{2_2} \\ u_3 \end{bmatrix}\right) = \begin{bmatrix} u_1 \\ \frac{1}{2}(u_{2_1} + u_{2_2}) \\ u_3 \end{bmatrix}, \qquad \text{(16-f)}$$

$\forall U_1 \in \hat{\mathcal{U}}_1,\ \forall U_{2_1} \in \hat{\mathcal{U}}_2,\ \forall U_{2_2} \in \hat{\mathcal{U}}_2,\ \forall U_3 \in \hat{\mathcal{U}}_3,\ \forall u_1 \in \mathbb{R}^{m_1},\ \forall u_{2_1} \in \mathbb{R}^{m_2},\ \forall u_{2_2} \in \mathbb{R}^{m_2},\ \forall u_3 \in \mathbb{R}^{m_3},$

$$R^{\#}\left(\begin{bmatrix} Y_1 \\ Y_{2_1} \\ Y_{2_2} \\ Y_3 \end{bmatrix}\right) = \begin{bmatrix} Y_1 \\ Y_{2_1} + Y_{2_2} \\ Y_3 \end{bmatrix}, \qquad r^{\#}\left(\begin{bmatrix} y_1 \\ y_{2_1} \\ y_{2_2} \\ y_3 \end{bmatrix}\right) = \begin{bmatrix} y_1 \\ \frac{1}{2}(y_{2_1} + y_{2_2}) \\ y_3 \end{bmatrix}, \quad \text{(16-g)}$$

$\forall Y_1 \in \hat{\mathcal{Y}}_1,\ \forall Y_{2_1} \in \hat{\mathcal{Y}}_2,\ \forall Y_{2_2} \in \hat{\mathcal{Y}}_2,\ \forall Y_3 \in \hat{\mathcal{Y}}_3,\ \forall y_1 \in \mathbb{R}^{l_1},\ \forall y_{2_1} \in \mathbb{R}^{l_2},\ \forall y_{2_2} \in \mathbb{R}^{l_2},\ \forall y_3 \in \mathbb{R}^{l_3},$

$$S^{\#}\left(\begin{bmatrix} Z_1 \\ Z_{2_1} \\ Z_{2_2} \\ Z_3 \end{bmatrix}\right) = \begin{bmatrix} Z_1 \\ Z_{2_1} + Z_{2_2} \\ Z_3 \end{bmatrix}, \qquad s^{\#}\left(\begin{bmatrix} z_1 \\ z_{2_1} \\ z_{2_2} \\ z_3 \end{bmatrix}\right) = \begin{bmatrix} z_1 \\ \frac{1}{2}(z_{2_1} + z_{2_2}) \\ z_3 \end{bmatrix}, \quad \text{(16-h)}$$

$\forall Z_1 \in \hat{\mathcal{Z}}_1,\ \forall Z_{2_1} \in \hat{\mathcal{Z}}_2,\ \forall Z_{2_2} \in \hat{\mathcal{Z}}_2,\ \forall Z_3 \in \hat{\mathcal{Z}}_3,\ \forall z_1 \in \mathbb{R}^{\lambda_1},\ \forall z_{2_1} \in \mathbb{R}^{\lambda_2},\ \forall z_{2_2} \in \mathbb{R}^{\lambda_2},\ \forall z_3 \in \mathbb{R}^{\lambda_3}.$

Once these transformations are chosen as above, the functions of the expanded system $\tilde{\Sigma}$ must then be chosen to satisfy 8-a-8-f. The function $\tilde{F}$: $\tilde{\mathcal{X}} \times \mathbb{R}^{\tilde{\lambda}} \times \tilde{\mathcal{U}} \to \tilde{\mathcal{X}}$, for example, must be chosen such that:

$$\tilde{F}\left(\begin{bmatrix} X_1 \\ X_2 \\ X_2 \\ X_3 \end{bmatrix}, \begin{bmatrix} z_1 \\ z_2 \\ z_2 \\ z_3 \end{bmatrix}, \begin{bmatrix} U_1 \\ U_{2_1} \\ U_{2_2} \\ U_3 \end{bmatrix}\right) = \begin{bmatrix} F_1\left(\begin{bmatrix} X_1 \\ X_2 \\ X_3 \end{bmatrix}, \begin{bmatrix} z_1 \\ z_2 \\ z_3 \end{bmatrix}, \begin{bmatrix} U_1 \\ U_{2_1} + U_{2_2} \\ U_3 \end{bmatrix}\right) \\ F_2\left(\begin{bmatrix} X_1 \\ X_2 \\ X_3 \end{bmatrix}, \begin{bmatrix} z_1 \\ z_2 \\ z_3 \end{bmatrix}, \begin{bmatrix} U_1 \\ U_{2_1} + U_{2_2} \\ U_3 \end{bmatrix}\right) \\ F_2\left(\begin{bmatrix} X_1 \\ X_2 \\ X_3 \end{bmatrix}, \begin{bmatrix} z_1 \\ z_2 \\ z_3 \end{bmatrix}, \begin{bmatrix} U_1 \\ U_{2_1} + U_{2_2} \\ U_3 \end{bmatrix}\right) \\ F_3\left(\begin{bmatrix} X_1 \\ X_2 \\ X_3 \end{bmatrix}, \begin{bmatrix} z_1 \\ z_2 \\ z_3 \end{bmatrix}, \begin{bmatrix} U_1 \\ U_{2_1} + U_{2_2} \\ U_3 \end{bmatrix}\right) \end{bmatrix} \quad (17)$$

$\forall X_1 \in \hat{\mathcal{X}}_1,\ \forall X_2 \in \hat{\mathcal{X}}_2,\ \forall X_3 \in \hat{\mathcal{X}}_3,\ \forall z_1 \in \mathbb{R}^{\lambda_1},\ \forall z_2 \in \mathbb{R}^{\lambda_2},\ \forall z_3 \in \mathbb{R}^{\lambda_3},\ \forall U_1 \in \hat{\mathcal{U}}_1,$ $\forall U_{2_1} \in \hat{\mathcal{U}}_2,\ \forall U_{2_2} \in \hat{\mathcal{U}}_2,\ \text{and}\ \forall U_3 \in \hat{\mathcal{U}}_3,\ \text{where}\ F_1 : \mathcal{X} \times \mathbb{R}^{\lambda} \times \mathcal{U} \to \hat{\mathcal{X}}_1,\ F_2 :$ $\mathcal{X} \times \mathbb{R}^{\lambda} \times \mathcal{U} \to \hat{\mathcal{X}}_2,\ \text{and}\ F_3 : \mathcal{X} \times \mathbb{R}^{\lambda} \times \mathcal{U} \to \hat{\mathcal{X}}_3$ indicate the appropriate rows of $F : \mathcal{X} \times \mathbb{R}^{\lambda} \times \mathcal{U} \to \mathcal{X}$.

The expanded system now appears as an interconnected system of two subsystems (see Figure 3(b)). The discrete state-space of the first subsystem is $\hat{\mathcal{X}}_1 \times \hat{\mathcal{X}}_2 := \mathcal{X}_1 \times \mathcal{X}_2 \times \cdots \times \mathcal{X}_{N_1+N_2}$, the continuous state-space of it is $\mathbb{R}^{n_1+n_2}$, the discrete input space of it is $\hat{\mathcal{U}}_1 \times \hat{\mathcal{U}}_2 := \mathcal{U}_1 \times \mathcal{U}_2 \times \cdots \times \mathcal{U}_{M_1+M_2}$, the continuous input space of it is $\mathbb{R}^{m_1+m_2}$, the discrete output space of it is

$\hat{\mathcal{Y}}_1 \times \hat{\mathcal{Y}}_2 := \mathcal{Y}_1 \times \mathcal{Y}_2 \times \cdots \times \mathcal{Y}_{L_1+L_2}$, the continuous output space of it is $\mathbb{R}^{l_1+l_2}$, the discrete internal output space of it is $\hat{\mathcal{Z}}_1 \times \hat{\mathcal{Z}}_2 := \mathcal{Z}_1 \times \mathcal{Z}_2 \times \cdots \times \mathcal{Z}_{\Lambda_1+\Lambda_2}$, and the continuous internal output space of it is $\mathbb{R}^{\lambda_1+\lambda_2}$. On the other hand, the discrete state-space of the second subsystem is $\hat{\mathcal{X}}_2 \times \hat{\mathcal{X}}_3 := \mathcal{X}_{N_1+1} \times \mathcal{X}_{N_1+2} \times \cdots \times \mathcal{X}_N$, the continuous state-space of it is $\mathbb{R}^{n_2+n_3}$, the discrete input space of it is $\hat{\mathcal{U}}_2 \times \hat{\mathcal{U}}_3 := \mathcal{U}_{M_1+1} \times \mathcal{U}_{M_1+2} \times \cdots \times \mathcal{U}_M$, the continuous input space of it is $\mathbb{R}^{m_2+m_3}$, the discrete output space of it is $\hat{\mathcal{Y}}_2 \times \hat{\mathcal{Y}}_3 := \mathcal{Y}_{L_1+1} \times \mathcal{Y}_{L_1+2} \times \cdots \times \mathcal{Y}_L$, the continuous output space of it is $\mathbb{R}^{l_2+l_3}$, the discrete internal output space of it is $\hat{\mathcal{Z}}_2 \times \hat{\mathcal{Z}}_3 := \mathcal{Z}_{\Lambda_1+1} \times \mathcal{Z}_{\Lambda_1+2} \times \cdots \times \mathcal{Z}_\Lambda$, and the continuous internal output space of it is $\mathbb{R}^{\lambda_2+\lambda_3}$.

A decentralized controller for the expanded system can now be designed. Such a controller may be described by 10, where

$$
\tilde{C}(\tilde{Y}(k), \tilde{y}(kT)) = \begin{bmatrix} \tilde{C}_1\left(\begin{bmatrix} Y_1(k) \\ Y_{2_1}(k) \end{bmatrix}, \begin{bmatrix} y_1(kT) \\ y_{2_1}(kT) \end{bmatrix}\right) \\ \tilde{C}_2\left(\begin{bmatrix} Y_{2_2}(k) \\ Y_3(k) \end{bmatrix}, \begin{bmatrix} y_{2_2}(kT) \\ y_3(kT) \end{bmatrix}\right) \end{bmatrix} \tag{18-a}
$$

$$
\tilde{c}(\tilde{y}(t), \tilde{Y}([t/T])) = \begin{bmatrix} \tilde{c}_1\left(\begin{bmatrix} y_1(t) \\ y_{2_1}(t) \end{bmatrix}, \begin{bmatrix} Y_1([t/T]) \\ Y_{2_1}([t/T]) \end{bmatrix}\right) \\ \tilde{c}_2\left(\begin{bmatrix} y_{2_2}(t) \\ y_3(t) \end{bmatrix}, \begin{bmatrix} Y_{2_2}([t/T]) \\ Y_3([t/T]) \end{bmatrix}\right) \end{bmatrix} \tag{18-b}
$$

where $\tilde{C}_1 : \hat{\mathcal{Y}}_1 \times \hat{\mathcal{Y}}_2 \times \mathbb{R}^{l_1+l_2} \to \hat{\mathcal{U}}_1 \times \hat{\mathcal{U}}_2$ and $\tilde{c}_1 : \mathbb{R}^{l_1+l_2} \times \hat{\mathcal{Y}}_1 \times \hat{\mathcal{Y}}_2 \to \mathbb{R}^{m_1+m_2}$ are designed for the first subsystem (possibly considering or perhaps ignoring the interactions with the rest of the system) and $\tilde{C}_2 : \hat{\mathcal{Y}}_2 \times \hat{\mathcal{Y}}_3 \times \mathbb{R}^{l_2+l_3} \to \hat{\mathcal{U}}_2 \times \hat{\mathcal{U}}_3$ and $\tilde{c}_2 : \mathbb{R}^{l_2+l_3} \times \hat{\mathcal{Y}}_2 \times \hat{\mathcal{Y}}_3 \to \mathbb{R}^{m_2+m_3}$ are designed for the second subsystem (possibly considering or perhaps ignoring the interactions with the rest of the system).

This decentralized controller can now be contracted by using 14-a–14-b. The contracted controller, which can be applied to the original system, is of the form 9, where

$$
C(Y(k), y(kT)) =
$$

$$
\begin{bmatrix} \tilde{C}_{1_1}\left(\begin{bmatrix} Y_1(k) \\ Y_2(k) \end{bmatrix}, \begin{bmatrix} y_1(kT) \\ y_2(kT) \end{bmatrix}\right) \\ \tilde{C}_{1_2}\left(\begin{bmatrix} Y_1(k) \\ Y_2(k) \end{bmatrix}, \begin{bmatrix} y_1(kT) \\ y_2(kT) \end{bmatrix}\right) + \tilde{C}_{2_1}\left(\begin{bmatrix} Y_2(k) \\ Y_3(k) \end{bmatrix}, \begin{bmatrix} y_2(kT) \\ y_3(kT) \end{bmatrix}\right) \\ \tilde{C}_{2_2}\left(\begin{bmatrix} Y_2(k) \\ Y_3(k) \end{bmatrix}, \begin{bmatrix} y_2(kT) \\ y_3(kT) \end{bmatrix}\right) \end{bmatrix} \tag{19-a}
$$

where $\tilde{C}_{1_1} : \hat{\mathcal{Y}}_1 \times \hat{\mathcal{Y}}_2 \times \mathbb{R}^{l_1+l_2} \to \hat{\mathcal{U}}_1$ and $\tilde{C}_{1_2} : \hat{\mathcal{Y}}_1 \times \hat{\mathcal{Y}}_2 \times \mathbb{R}^{l_1+l_2} \to \hat{\mathcal{U}}_2$ indicate the appropriate rows of $\tilde{C}_1 : \hat{\mathcal{Y}}_1 \times \hat{\mathcal{Y}}_2 \times \mathbb{R}^{l_1+l_2} \to \hat{\mathcal{U}}_1 \times \hat{\mathcal{U}}_2$ and $\tilde{C}_{2_1} : \hat{\mathcal{Y}}_1 \times \hat{\mathcal{Y}}_2 \times$

$\mathbb{R}^{l_2+l_3} \to \hat{\mathcal{U}}_2$ and $\tilde{C}_{2_2} : \hat{\mathcal{Y}}_1 \times \hat{\mathcal{Y}}_2 \times \mathbb{R}^{l_2+l_3} \to \hat{\mathcal{U}}_3$ indicate the appropriate rows of $\tilde{C}_2 : \hat{\mathcal{Y}}_1 \times \hat{\mathcal{Y}}_2 \times \mathbb{R}^{l_2+l_3} \to \hat{\mathcal{U}}_2 \times \hat{\mathcal{U}}_3$ and

$$c(y(t), Y([t/T])) =$$

$$
\begin{bmatrix}
\tilde{c}_{1_1}\left(\begin{bmatrix} y_1(t) \\ y_2(t) \end{bmatrix}, \begin{bmatrix} Y_1([t/T]) \\ Y_2([t/T]) \end{bmatrix} \right) \\
\frac{1}{2}\left(\tilde{c}_{1_2}\left(\begin{bmatrix} y_1(t) \\ y_2(t) \end{bmatrix}, \begin{bmatrix} Y_1([t/T]) \\ Y_2([t/T]) \end{bmatrix} \right) + \tilde{c}_{2_1}\left(\begin{bmatrix} y_2(t) \\ y_3(t) \end{bmatrix}, \begin{bmatrix} Y_2([t/T]) \\ Y_3([t/T]) \end{bmatrix} \right) \right) \\
\tilde{c}_{2_2}\left(\begin{bmatrix} y_2(t) \\ y_3(t) \end{bmatrix}, \begin{bmatrix} Y_2([t/T]) \\ Y_3([t/T]) \end{bmatrix} \right)
\end{bmatrix}
\qquad \text{(19-b)}
$$

where $\tilde{c}_{1_1} : \mathbb{R}^{l_1+l_2} \times \hat{\mathcal{Y}}_1 \times \hat{\mathcal{Y}}_2 \to \mathbb{R}^{m_1}$ and $\tilde{c}_{1_2} : \mathbb{R}^{l_1+l_2} \times \hat{\mathcal{Y}}_1 \times \hat{\mathcal{Y}}_2 \to \mathbb{R}^{m_2}$ indicate the appropriate rows of $\tilde{c}_1 : \mathbb{R}^{l_1+l_2} \times \hat{\mathcal{Y}}_1 \times \hat{\mathcal{Y}}_2 \to \mathbb{R}^{m_1+m_2}$ and $\tilde{c}_{2_1} : \mathbb{R}^{l_2+l_3} \times \hat{\mathcal{Y}}_2 \times \hat{\mathcal{Y}}_3 \to \mathbb{R}^{m_2}$ and $\tilde{c}_{2_2} : \mathbb{R}^{l_2+l_3} \times \hat{\mathcal{Y}}_2 \times \hat{\mathcal{Y}}_3 \to \mathbb{R}^{m_3}$ indicate the appropriate rows of $\tilde{c}_2 : \mathbb{R}^{l_2+l_3} \times \hat{\mathcal{Y}}_2 \times \hat{\mathcal{Y}}_3 \to \mathbb{R}^{m_2+m_3}$.

The resulting controller, which can be implemented on the original system as shown in Figure 4, has an *overlapping decentralized structure*. Note that p, given in 16-a is a continuous transformation. Suppose that both the expanded closed-loop system and the original closed-loop system are well-posed. Then, if the controller 18-a–18-b is designed to stabilize, asymptotically stabilize (with region of attraction $\tilde{\omega} \subset \mathbb{R}^{\tilde{n}}$, where $\tilde{\omega}$ is such that $p(p^{\#}(\tilde{\omega})) \subset \tilde{\omega}$), or globally asymptotically stabilize the continuous-state of the system $\tilde{\Sigma}$ with equilibrium continuous-state $\tilde{x}_e \in p(\mathbb{R}^n)$), then the contracted controller 19-a–19-b (shown in Figure 4) respectively stabilizes, asymptotically stabilizes (with region of attraction $p^{\#}(\tilde{\omega})$), or globally asymptotically stabilizes the continuous-state of the system Σ (with equilibrium continuous-state $p^{\#}(\tilde{x}_e)$). If, on the other hand, the controller 18-a–18-b is designed to stabilize, asymptotically stabilize (with region of attraction $\{\tilde{\Omega} \subset \tilde{\mathcal{X}}, \tilde{\omega} \subset \mathbb{R}^{\tilde{n}}\}$, where $\tilde{\Omega}$ and $\tilde{\omega}$ are such that $P(P^{\#}(\tilde{\Omega})) \subset \tilde{\Omega}$ and $p(p^{\#}(\tilde{\omega})) \subset \tilde{\omega}$), or globally asymptotically stabilizes the system $\tilde{\Sigma}$ with equilibrium set $\{\tilde{\mathcal{X}}_e \subset P(\mathcal{X}), \tilde{x}_e \in p(\mathbb{R}^n)\}$, then the contracted controller 19-a–19-b (shown in Figure 4) respectively stabilizes, asymptotically stabilizes (with region of attraction $\{P^{\#}(\tilde{\Omega}), p^{\#}(\tilde{\omega})\}$), or globally asymptotically stabilizes the system Σ (with equilibrium set $\{P^{\#}(\tilde{\mathcal{X}}_e), p^{\#}(\tilde{x}_e)\}$). For formal definitions of the mentioned stabilities, proofs of the above statements refer to [8].

If the extension principle is used then any controller designed in the expanded spaces is contractible to the original spaces for implementation. Formal stability definitions for hybrid systems have been omitted in this paper, but we hereby note that we follow the exact same definitions as provided in [8]. If a system, which includes another system is stable, then the included system is also stable. Furthermore, if a controller designed for the expanded system achieves stability then the contracted controller also achieves stability for the original system.

Decentralized controller design with overlapping decompositions has been discussed within the framework of extension. An overlappingly decomposed hybrid system can be expanded such that the subsystems appear as disjoint and such that the expanded system is an extension of the original system. Decentralized controllers for the expanded system, which appears as an interconnected system, can then be designed. These controllers can be contracted to overlappingly decentralized controllers for implementation on the original system.

It may be easier to design a controller for the expanded system, since it appears as an interconnected system of disjoint subsystems. Many methods and software packages are available to design decentralized controllers for such systems at least in the case of CSS. There have also been some preliminary results on designing decentralized controllers for DSS. (e.g., [17]).

Next, we will apply the method of hybrid system controller design using overlapping decomposition techniques to a three vehicle demonstration scenario.

3 OSU Three Vehicle Demo Scenario

In this section, we consider a three vehicle demonstration example for which we will use overlapping decompositions and contraction methods for systematic hybrid controller design. The demonstration scenario is visually summarized on Figure 5. Referring to Figure 5, the scenario can be outlined as follows:

Initially, all three vehicles are driving in the same (right-most) lane of a two-lane highway. Again initially, every follower, in this three vehicle string, travels faster than its leader with more than "safe" inter-vehicle separation between subsequent vehicles. Eventually the 2nd car (we like to refer it as a Teenager driven car, or the *Teenager* in short) closes up to the 1st car (*Grandma*), as the 3rd car (*Jack*) closes up to the *Teenager*. Later, the *Teenager* runs out of patience, changes lane, resumes its original (set) speed, passes *Grandma* and soon completes its vehicle passing maneuver returning to its original lane. In the meanwhile, *Jack* closes the gap between itself and the *Grandma* upon *Teenager*'s departure.

On Figure 5, *Grandma* has been selected as the reference vehicle and the motions of the *Teenager* and *Jack* are depicted with respect to the *Grandma* (constant velocity) driven vehicle. The driving habits of a given person are characterized by the set speed, acceleration/deceleration rates, and the patience level. For example, *Grandma* in this context, prefers to drive relatively slow (without loss of generality we may assume slower than the speed limit of the highway), avoids jerky behavior in both the lateral and longitudinal controls of the vehicle, starts taking action when the relative distance between her car and the one in her field of vision is large. She has great patience and preferably remains at her initial lane. We define *patience* as the amount of time one spends at following a vehicle which travels slower than the preferred set speed. It is generally a function of personality and the difference between the desired and the traveling speeds. There are some other factors at determining the patience: For example, if the driver is about to take an exit on the right, s/he becomes more patient at staying in the right-most lane. It may be time varying based on some extra objective specifications, however, there exists a patience factor -the duration of time one follows a slower vehicle before initiating lane change maneuver for passing purposes that is- associated with every driver. The objective of this control design study is to come up with a single modular decentralized controller which will work for each vehicle and the decision making rules will depend only on the characterization of the driver, namely the patience level, set speed and acceleration/deceleration preferences.

Note that, this scenario involves much more sophisticated vehicle to vehicle interactions than the previously mentioned "platooning" example. First of all, vehicles have more degrees of freedom as lane changing and vehicle passing are allowed. Secondly, units which interact with each other are not fixed unlike it was in the platooning case. Finally, the interface between the DES and the CSS becomes more complicated and requires more detailed study.

3.1 The Hybrid System

We model the three vehicles operating on a two lane highway as a multi-agent hybrid control problem. Individual vehicles are treated as the "units", and the three vehicles constitute a 3-unit large scale hybrid system which are linked to each other via laser range finder and the side looking radar sensors. Figure 6(a) depicts the overall hybrid structure. The states, inputs, outputs associated with the DSS and CSS are denoted by upper and lower case letters respectively. We will first consider the CSS model of the system.

Continuous State Dynamics The continuous state dynamics of the overall system is composed of the differential equations that describe the motions of all three vehicles in the continuous state space. The complexity of a vehicle model can vary from a two state bicycle model to a highly sophisticated full car model with the engine dynamics (which may have more than forty states per car). Depending on the application, it is generally the case that, the simplest valid model is picked for designing a controller. Sometimes, a low level controller is incorporated into the system which decouples some other modes of operation. In this study, we assume that a master speed controller (MSpC) and a master steering controller (MStC) have already been developed and wrapped around the CSS. Details about MSpC and MStC will be omitted here which have been presented in [19, 20, 4, 18] and [21, 12, 3, 5] respectively. MSpC and MStC assume inputs from the local continuous state system only, therefore can be treated as an integral part of the CSS if kept in the loop once and for all times during the autonomous operation.

The resulting CSS system can be simply described as follows:

$$\dot{\nu}_i = -\alpha_i \nu_i + \nu_{ref_i} \tag{20-a}$$

$$\dot{y}_i = -\beta_i y_i + y_{ref_i} \tag{20-b}$$

$$\dot{d}_{ij} = -\nu_i + \nu_j \tag{20-c}$$

($\forall \{i, j\} \subset \{1, 2, 3\}$), where ν_i denotes the longitudinal velocity of the vehicle i, d_{ij} denotes the relative distance between vehicles i and j; $\alpha_i, \beta_i > 0$ are the drag coefficients for the longitudinal and lateral dynamics respectively, ν_{ref_i} denotes the reference longitudinal velocity to the ith vehicle, and y_{ref_i} is the commanded deviation from the original lane center. We assume that ν_i, d_{ij}, and $\dot{d}_{ij}$ are the only local measurements. Based on the indicated differential equations the continuous system states x_i, inputs u_i and outputs y_i are given as: $x_i = [\nu_i, y_i, d_{ij}]^T$, $u_i = [\nu_{ref_i}, y_{ref_i}]^T$, $y_i = [\nu_i, d_{ij}, \dot{d}_{ij}]^T$, $\forall \{i, j\} \subset \{1, 2, 3\}$.

Discrete Event System Model The interface that represents communications and interactions between the DES and the continuous time system will be examined following this section. Here, we develop the finite state machine for the scripted scenario. The occurrence of certain events in the continuous state system which is passed to the DES side via the interface describe the DES state transition function. Let the set of low level events be denoted by the set $\mathcal{E}_c$. In fact, $\mathcal{E}_c = [\mathcal{E}_{c_1}, \mathcal{E}_{c_2}, \mathcal{E}_{c_3}, \mathcal{E}_{c_4}]^T$ where the event sets $\mathcal{E}_{c_1}, \mathcal{E}_{c_2}, \mathcal{E}_{c_3}$ and $\mathcal{E}_{c_4}$ are given by $\mathcal{E}_{c_1} = \{e_1^1, e_1^2\}$, $\mathcal{E}_{c_2} = \{e_2^1, e_2^2, e_2^3\}$, $\mathcal{E}_{c_3} = \{e_3^1, e_3^2, e_3^3\}$ and $\mathcal{E}_{c_4} = \{e_4^1, e_4^2, e_4^3\}$ which describe the events as summarized in Table 1. Those events are interpreted at the interface layer and passed to the DES side, which will be discussed in the next section.

Table 1. The list of low level events.

e_1^1 : Vehicle is manually operated;
e_1^2 : Vehicle is automaticly operated;
e_2^1 : Keeping the right lane;
e_2^2 : Keeping the left lane;
e_2^3 : Lane changing;
e_3^1 : Vehicle is speeding up;
e_3^2 : Vehicle is slowing down;
e_3^3 : Vehicle is maintaining its current speed;
e_4^1 : No vehicle is detected ahead;
e_4^2 : A vehicle is detected ahead & speed and distance are matched;
e_4^3 : A vehicle is detected ahead & speed and distance are NOT matched.

There is one discrete state variable $X_i \in \mathcal{D}_1$ where $\mathcal{D}_1 = \{ACCinR, ACCinL, CRUinR, CRUinL, DECinR, DECinL, FOLinR, FOLinL, LLC, RLC, MAN\}$ (see Table 2 for full descriptions),

The discrete system state transition function $F(\cdot, \cdot)$ is defined as,

$$X_i(k+1) = F\{X_i(k), \phi(z(kT))\} \qquad (21)$$

where $\phi(z(kT)) \in \mathcal{E}_c$ denotes the low level events passed on to the DES side, the function $F : \mathcal{D}_1 \times \mathcal{E}_c \rightarrow \mathcal{D}_1$ is given on Table 3.

Table 2. The discrete states' descriptions.

$ACCinR$	: **ACC**elerate in **R**ight Lane,
$ACCinL$	: **ACC**elerate in **L**eft Lane,
$CRUinR$	: **CRU**ise in **R**ight Lane,
$CRUinL$	: **CRU**ise in **L**eft Lane,
$DECinR$	: **DEC**elerate in **R**ight Lane,
$DECinL$	: **DEC**elerate in **L**eft Lane,
$FOLinR$	: **FOL**low in **R**ight Lane,
$FOLinL$	: **FOL**low in **L**eft Lane,
LLC	: **L**eft **L**ane **C**hange,
RLC	: **R**ight **L**ane **C**hange,
MAN	: **Man**ual.

Table 3. Discrete Event System Transitions.

X_i	e_1^k	e_2^l	e_3^m	e_4^n	$F\{X_i(k), \phi(z(kT))\}$
any	e_1^1	any	any	any	MAN
any	e_1^1	e_2^1	e_3^1	e_4^1, e_4^3	$ACCinR$
				e_4^2	$FOLinR$
			e_3^2	e_4^1, e_4^3	$DECinR$
				e_4^2	$FOLinR$
			e_3^3	e_4^1, e_4^3	$CRUinR$
				e_4^2	$FOLinR$
		e_2^2	e_3^1	e_4^1, e_4^3	$ACCinL$
				e_4^2	$FOLinL$
			e_3^2	e_4^1, e_4^3	$DECinL$
				e_4^2	$FOLinL$
			e_3^3	e_4^1, e_4^3	$CRUinL$
				e_4^2	$FOLinL$
$\{any\}inR$ OR LLC	e_1^2	e_2^3	any	any	LLC
$\{any\}inL$ OR RLC	e_1^2	e_2^3	any	any	RLC

3.2 Interface between Continuous and Discrete State Systems

Recall that the objective of the controller design is to develop a DES supervisor to regulate the system dynamics to the desired trajectories. The interface layer has the major task of building the bridge between the continuous state system and the discrete state system (within the hybrid model) as shown on Figure 1. The information exchange between the DSS and the CSS is inevitable for high-level supervisor design. In general, the DSS is a discretized version of the CSS. The local orientation sensing devices on the vehicle provide information regarding the vehicle's position with respect to the "World", where *World* is defined as the combination of the road and the other vehicles traveling on the highway in this AHS example. The sensors equipped on the car, and the information they provide to the supervisory controller can be summarized as follows:

- A *Longitudinal Velocity Sensor* provides the speed of the vehicle,
- A *Look-Ahead Radar* detects the offset from the lane center at a look-ahead point when there exists frequency selective stripe (FSS) in the middle of the reference lane. It also measures the relative longitudinal distance to the near-most vehicle ahead,
- *Laser Range Finder* is capable of providing the relative distance Δd_i, relative velocity Δv_i and the relative angle to the target $\Delta \gamma_i$. It also tracks multiple vehicles (identified with subscript i) at a time. In some sense, look-ahead radar and laser range finder have overlapping redundancy,
- A *CCD Camera* processes the picture frames to detect the markers on either side of the lane and outputs a similar (to the look-ahead radar output) offset signal from the lane center,
- A *Timer* is used to measure how long the controlled vehicle stays at an operational mode (DES state),
- *Side-Looking Radars* on 4 sides of the vehicle are located such that there are no dead-zones. They provide the information whether or not there exists another vehicle in the adjacent (possibly passing) lane. The information is ON/OFF type, so it is of discrete state nature. The field of range is adjusted such that if a vehicle is not detected, initiating a lane change maneuver is marginally safe.
- A *Yaw Rate Sensor* is used mainly in the low level controllers within the CSS system, however, it also provides redundant information regarding the vehicle orientation which is passed to the DES side.

Note that, although some of the raw data is used directly, most of the measurements are processed for immunity against noise (with the aid of observers). A DES supervisor will command some CSS inputs through the interface unit (D/A converters) and the controller design procedure will be discussed shortly. When the CSS and DSS were presented in the previous sections, it has been indicated that there needs to be a two-way information flow through the interface. We define the interface from the continuous time system to the DSS by (the partial function),

$$\phi : \mathbb{R}^n \times \mathbb{R}^m \to \mathcal{E}_c \tag{22}$$

so that $\phi(x(t), u(t)) = e_p^s(t)$ represents a low level event in $\mathcal{E}_c$ that occurs at the time instant t, where n and m are the orders of the continuous state and input spaces respectively. Note that $u(t)$ denotes the control generated by the CSS, which refers to the low level controller inputs like the throttle opening, brake pressure, steering signal.

Similarly the supervised control law generated by the DES supervisor is interpreted at the Interface layer, and passed to the continuous state system input generator. Based on the suggested control law, certain continuous input is selected from a finite set of all possible inputs to automate the longitudinal and lateral motions of the considered vehicle. The interface to the continuous time system, which specifies how, logical operations in the system can directly influence the continuous time system is given by (the partial function),

$$\psi : \mathcal{P}(\mathcal{E}) \times \mathcal{X} \to \mathbb{R}^l \tag{23}$$

where $\mathcal{P}(\mathcal{E})$ denotes the power set of the events set, X is the set of DES states and l is the order of the continuous inputs generated through the DES supervisor. Now that we have presented the individual CSS, DES systems, and the interface that lies between those two, we can apply decomposition techniques and design the DES supervisor.

3.3 Overlappingly Decomposed System

Decompose the system into three overlapping subsystems each of which contains two of the three cars, i.e, subsystem 1 contains *Grandma* and the *Teenager*, Subsystem 2 has the *Teenager* and *Jack*, and finally, Subsystem 3 consists of the *Grandma* and *Jack*. See Figure 6(b).

Let $\tilde{X}_i$, $\tilde{U}_i$, $\tilde{Y}_i$, $\tilde{x}_i$, $\tilde{u}_i$, $\tilde{y}_i$ respectively denote the discrete states, discrete state inputs, discrete state outputs, continuous states, continuous state inputs and continuous state outputs of the ith subsystem after decomposition. Then, the continuous and the DES dynamics for each and every subsystem can be described (compactly) as in the following sections.

3.4 Expanded System Discrete State Dynamics

The dynamics of the discrete state part of the expanded system can be described as follows:

$$X_{i_{a,b}}(k+1) = F\{X_{i_{a,b}}(k), \phi(z_{i_{a,b}}(kT))\} \tag{24-a}$$
$$X_{j_{a,b}}(k+1) = F\{X_{j_{a,b}}(k), \phi(z_{j_{a,b}}(kT))\} \tag{24-b}$$

$\forall \{i,j\} \subset \{1,2,3\}$ and where a and b are notational conveniences to refer to the subsystem that is being considered.

3.5 Expanded System Continuous State Dynamics

The dynamics of the continuous state part, on the other hand, are described by the following equations,

$$\dot{\nu}_{i_{a,b}} = -\alpha_i \nu_{i_{a,b}} + \nu_{ref_i} \tag{25-a}$$
$$\dot{y}_{i_{a,b}} = -\beta_i y_{i_{a,b}} + y_{ref_i} \tag{25-b}$$
$$\dot{\nu}_{j_{a,b}} = -\alpha_j \nu_{j_{a,b}} + \nu_{ref_j} \tag{25-c}$$
$$\dot{y}_{j_{a,b}} = -\beta_j y_{j_{a,b}} + y_{ref_j} \tag{25-d}$$
$$\dot{d}_{ij} = -\nu_{i_{a,b}} + \nu_{j_{a,b}} \tag{25-e}$$

$\forall \{i,j\} \subset \{1,2,3\}$ (two element subsets), where the subscript a,b denotes which subsystem (after decomposition) the states belong to (as before). Recall that every vehicle appears in exactly two of the three subsystems. It can be shown that the expanded system, with the discrete and continuous system dynamics as given in the previous subsections, is an extension of the original system.

3.6 Controller Design for the Expanded System

Now, consider a single subsystem of the expanded system (Also see Figure 6(b)). Note that this subsystem contains only two vehicles. Denote the discrete state of this subsystem by $[\,X_p\,X_s\,]^T$. For the second subsystem, for example, X_p and X_s respectively correspond to X_{2_b} and X_{3_a}. Both vehicles are equipped with on-board sensors and actuators since decentralized control is essential. The control laws are described based on the conditions (in terms of boolean variables) as listed on Table 5. Refer to this table while interpreting the controllers' logic. Note also that, given the subsystem with p and s, the DES supervisor (yet to be designed) and the resulting CSS control actions are identical for both cars due to the inherent symmetry properties. The subsystem behavior mentioned is characterized by two (and only two) vehicles traveling on a two-lane highway. These vehicles proceed at their set speeds as long as they do not "interact". Vehicle *interaction* we define as: At least one of them being detected by the other via the on-board sensors. Assuming that they have different set speeds, depending on the initial orientation, the two vehicles might never interact (e.g., if the leading vehicle in the original setting has a faster set speed), might interact for infinitely long duration of time (e.g., The preceding car may follow the leader within its sensor range) or they may interact for a finite duration of time (e.g.,if the leading vehicle has a slower set speed, and the vehicles are on an infinitely long road with finite sensor range, then the follower vehicle will eventually approach such that the slower vehicle will appear in its sensor range, later it might pass it, resume its original set speed, and soon disappear from the sensors of the slower vehicle cutting the interaction). Although one way of defining "interaction" might be independent of sensors (i.e. by setting a separate "domain of interaction") we have chosen the subjective approach of relying on the sensors here.

The objective of the controller design in the hybrid systems context is to automate the longitudinal and lateral motions of a vehicle in a possible AHS framework such that it becomes capable of regulating its speed and lateral motion by emulating the behavior of humans during driving. Overlapping decompositions help model the overall (relatively more complex) system as weakly interacting smaller order (relatively simpler) subsystems. Once overlappingly decomposed, controllers can be designed for the smaller order subsystems as long as the decomposed system is an extension of the original system and a controller for the original system is contractible in the end.

Considering the "(only) two vehicles on a two lane highway" case, the desired closed loop transitions are as given on Figure 7, and the DES Supervisor that yield this desired behavior are described next.

3.7 Discrete Event System Supervisor

The inputs to the DES supervisor are $\phi(z(kT))$ and the conditions denoted by the set $\mathcal{C}$. These conditions which are in the form of some boolean variables are listed on Table 5. DES supervisory controller interprets the situation outlined by the current operational mode and the current conditions and generates a control input $U_p \in \mathcal{D}_2$ to the CSS via the interfacing unit. $\mathcal{D}_2 = \{SU, SUgrsd,$ $SUwol, MS, MSgrsd, MSwol, SD, SLL, RRL, STA, MM\}$ is the set of all DES commands which are explained on Table 4.

Table 4. The discrete commands' descriptions.

STA	: STart Automatic Mode,
MM	: Switch to Manual Mode,
MS	: Maintain Speed,
$MSgrsd$	: Maintain Speed but get ready to slow down,
$MSwol$	: Maintain Speed but watch the other lane,
SU	: Speed Up,
$SUgrsd$	: Speed Up but get ready to slow down,
$SUwol$	: Speed Up but watch the other lane,
SD	: Slow Down,
SM	: Switch to Manual,
SLL	: Switch to Left Lane,
RRL	: Return Right Lane,
ELC	: Emergency Lane Change.

The resulting supervised DES operation can be summarized as follows:

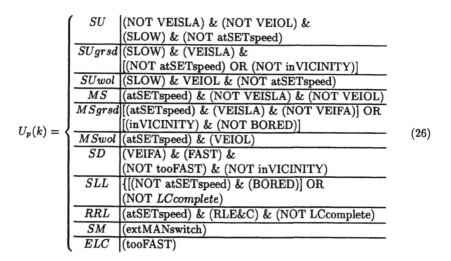

$$U_p(k) = \begin{cases} SU & \text{(NOT VEISLA) \& (NOT VEIOL) \&} \\ & \text{(SLOW) \& (NOT atSETspeed)} \\ SUgrsd & \text{(SLOW) \& (VEISLA) \&} \\ & \text{[(NOT atSETspeed) OR (NOT inVICINITY)]} \\ SUwol & \text{(SLOW) \& VEIOL \& (NOT atSETspeed)} \\ MS & \text{(atSETspeed) \& (NOT VEISLA) \& (NOT VEIOL)} \\ MSgrsd & \text{[(atSETspeed) \& (VEISLA) \& (NOT VEIFA)] OR} \\ & \text{[(inVICINITY) \& (NOT BORED)]} \\ MSwol & \text{(atSETspeed) \& (VEIOL)} \\ SD & \text{(VEIFA) \& (FAST) \&} \\ & \text{(NOT tooFAST) \& (NOT inVICINITY)} \\ SLL & \text{\{[(NOT atSETspeed) \& (BORED)] OR} \\ & \text{(NOT } LCcomplete)\text{)} \\ RRL & \text{(atSETspeed) \& (RLE\&C) \& (NOT LCcomplete)} \\ SM & \text{(extMANswitch)} \\ ELC & \text{(tooFAST)} \end{cases} \qquad (26)$$

3.8 Continuous State Input Generator

The supervised command is converted to the CSS signal through the "Interface". As described earlier, $\psi(U(k))$ is input to the CSS input generator. This unit has the task to simultaneously generate the reference longitudinal velocity and reference offset signals. Let $\nu_{ref} = \Gamma(U(k))$, and $y_{ref} = \Lambda(U(k))$. Note that, if no fault is assumed in the system (i.e. the continuous state system behaves as the supervisor commands), the supervisor regulates the state transitions of the finite state machine. The functions $\Gamma(\cdot)$ and $\Lambda(\cdot)$ are given as follows:

$$
a_{ref} = \begin{cases} \max\left(-|\mathcal{D}_{max}|, \frac{-(\Delta\nu)^2}{\Delta d - d_{safe}}\right) & U(k) = SD, ELC \\ \min\left(|\mathcal{A}_{max}|, \frac{-(\Delta\nu)^2}{\Delta d - d_{safe}}\right) & U(k) = \begin{cases} SU, SUgrsd, \\ SUwol \end{cases} \\ \begin{array}{c|c} 0 & X(k) \neq D, F \\ \hline \begin{array}{c} -\beta_1(\Delta d - d_{safe}) \\ -\beta_2\Delta\nu \end{array} & X(k) = D, F \end{array} & U(k) = MSgrsd \\ 0 & U(k) = \begin{cases} MS, MSwol, \\ SLL, RRL \end{cases} \\ \mathcal{A}_{max} & U(k) = STA \end{cases}
\tag{27}
$$

where $\nu_{ref} = \Gamma(U(k)) = \int_0^t a_{ref}(\tau)d\tau$, and $\mathcal{D}_{max}$ and $\mathcal{A}_{max}$ denote the maximum deceleration and acceleration rates respectively, and β_1 and β_2 are state feedback gains to ensure stability in the linear region.

$$
y_{ref} = \Lambda(U(k)) = \begin{cases} 0 & \begin{array}{l} U(k) = STA, MS, MSgrsd, MSwol, \\ SU, SUgrsd, SUwol, SD, MM \end{array} \\ Y_{ref} & \begin{array}{l} (U(k) = SLL) \\ OR \\ [(U(k) = ELC) \& (LLE\&C)] \end{array} \\ -Y_{ref} & \begin{array}{l} (U(k) = RRL) \\ OR \\ [(U(k) = ELC) \& (RLE\&C)] \end{array} \end{cases}
\tag{28}
$$

where Y_{ref} is generated by the reference lateral jerk signal passed through a prefilter which basicly identifies the inverse characteristics of the vehicle dynamics involving the lateral motion. Lateral jerk signal is picked as a sum of step functions such that strict bounds on both the lateral jerk and lateral acceleration specifications are met. Further details on the generation of this reference signal is available upon request.

Note that the described controller is a dynamic controller since it involves integration to yield ν_{ref_i}. Recall that only static controllers have been considered in the overview of overlapping decomposition techniques, however, it has also been remarked that dynamic extensions are relatively straight forward.

4   Simulation Model Development

The motivation behind this study is to develop a model for the closed loop system such that the performance of the proposed controller can be tested effectively in a laboratory environment. This model has to describe the lateral and longitudinal dynamics of a vehicle, the relevant actuator dynamics, sensors and the road structure. To emulate the closed loop system, the exact same information will be made available for each and every vehicle in the loop. A master steering controller (MStC) and a master longitudinal controller (MSpC) are assumed incorporated into the system during the controller design phase to avoid dealing with complicated system dynamics, yet they are modeled as suggested in [21] and [19] in the simulation model. ©MATLAB *Simulink* has been used extensively for modeling purposes.

Consider a single car in the three vehicle string. This car is characterized by three parameters at the hybrid level: the patience level, initial set velocity and the preferred maximum acceleration and deceleration rates. It has two continuous state inputs that are regulated by the DES supervisor: the reference longitudinal velocity and the reference offset from the lane center. At the CSS alone, velocity is regulated to the reference longitudinal speed via the throttle, brake and master speed controllers with feedbacks from the throttle plate, brake pressure and vehicle speed. Also, the relative distance and the relative velocity information between the controlled vehicle and the vehicle ahead is available to the supervisory controllers.

The simulation model is modular in the sense that road structure, number of vehicles on the road with any possible initial orientation, number of lanes available on the road and the vehicle characteristics can be changed easily and even more complicated scenarios can be demonstrated. However, we have extensively focused on the 1997 San Diego demo example within this paper and have set the number of vehicles on the road to three, characterized them as *Grandma* (with low set speed, slow acceleration/deceleration preferences, and high patience), *Teenager* (with high set speed, fast acc/dec preferences, and low patience), and *Jack* (with medium set speed, medium acc/dec preferences and medium patience). It should be noted that it is possible to make those parameters time and/or state varying without any extensive effort at all, at least in simulations. Also, number of lanes have been fixed at two.

The top level block describes the *World* which collects data from all possible vehicles, identifies the road structure and generates the appropriate sensor information to each and every vehicle based on the configuration and the sensor characteristics. In general, it provides the information that comes from the laser range finder and the radar sensor to individual cars. Every vehicle has a *Longitudinal Decision* and a *Lateral Decision* subblock which, based on continuous states, both identifies the discrete state modes and generates the discrete state control inputs which in return control the continuous states. Longitudinal decision laws are studied in [4], [19] and [6] in detail. It is our intention not to go into further details regarding the simulation model in this paper, however, extra information may be available upon request. We simply would like to state that the closed loop system performs as desired in the simulations starting from different initial conditions.

5 Conclusions

In this paper we have overviewed a relatively new and systematic hybrid system control method, namely the overlapping decompositions and controller design with contractions. We have particularly focused on a three vehicle demonstration scenario as an application example. The discussion in the Introduction section of this paper lists various reasons to justify the extensive work being done in the field of highway automation. However, it is also pointed out that AHS is a very difficult control problem: Safety, feasibility, realizability, stability, cost, efficiency, sensor fusion, redundancy, e.t.c. are a few of the many issues that have not been "convincingly" answered yet.

An AHS is a multi-lane world with many vehicles operating on it. It can be modeled as a multi-agent, large-scale hybrid system with the control objectives being specified accordingly in a decentralized manner. In this paper, we have dealt with a relatively easier case which involves three vehicles operating on a two lane highway. Applications of the overlapping decompositions have helped further simplify the problem. There are less number of possible scenarios involving two cars compared to a three-vehicle case. However, we should note that, the original system itself is not very complicated, hence, the advantages of using overlapping decompositions may not be best demonstrated in this example. On the other hand, the studied three vehicle scenario is considered as a step towards a more generalized case where (arbitrarily) many vehicles exist on a highway with (arbitrarily) many lanes. Let us refer to this as a "generalized AHS". Considering the "simplified AHS" we have examined in this paper, and comparing it to the "generalized AHS", we immediately observe the need for a different sort of decomposition, because (i) Lane change maneuvers are no longer one dimensional (in general) and (ii) More than 2 external vehicles might effect the supervised decision. From the controlled vehicle's point of view, the dominant units are the closest vehicles in the same lane ahead and the ones on the two adjacent lanes. Clearly, there will be more number of states in the finite-state machine as there are more low-level events coming from the continuous state system. However, the results of this paper's work can be modified relatively easily to fit the structure and needs of the so-called "generalized AHS". Some modeling and modification studies have been already performed controller design procedure but in this paper we specifically focus on OSU 1997 Demo scenario.

Stability issues regarding the hybrid systems and the safety concept within the AHS context are still uncertain. Unfortunately, there is no consensus hybrid stability definition in the literature. "Safety" on the other hand is a marginal concept, and has to be "relaxed" for any possible automation application. Since AHS involves "humans" (as passengers), safety and stability definitions turn out to be even more "delicate". Fault detection and obstacle avoidance, therefore, become more and more important. In our design, we have included an emergency lane change maneuver which is activated when the vehicle processor concludes that a collision is inevitable without steering and the adjacent lane is clear to accomplish a lane change maneuver. If it is not available, the controller (possibly) outputs (audible) emergency messages and switches to manual mode immediately. This is a very generic case but does not cover all possible "faults". A more involved analysis regarding fault detection and a "safer ride" is under comprehensive study and the results will be presented in another paper. Interested reader is referred to some previous works related with this topic presented in [12, 3, 18, 21, 13, 5, 4, 19, 20, 6, 8].

References

1. M. Doğruel and Ü. Özgüner, "Modeling and stability Issues in Hybrid Systems", *Hybrid Systems and Autonomous Control, Lecture Notes in computer Science*, Springer Verlag, pp 148-165, 1995.
2. D.N. Godbole, J. Lygeros and S. Sastry, "Hierarchical Hybrid Control: a Case Study", Proceedings of the 1994 Control and Decision Conference, Lake Buena Vista, FL, pp 1592-1597, 1994.
3. C. Hatipoğlu, *Lateral Control of Vehicles for Highway Automation*, Master's Thesis, The Ohio State University, Department of Electrical Engineering, 1995.
4. C. Hatipoğlu, Ü. Özgüner and M. Sommerville "Longitudinal Headway Control of Vehicles on Automated Highways", Proceedings of the 1996 IEEE International Conference on Control Applications, Dearborn, MI, pp 721-726, 1996.
5. C. Hatipoğlu, Ü. Özgüner, and K.A. Ünyelioğlu, "On Optimal Design of a Lane Change Controller", Proceedings of the Intelligent Vehicles '95 Symposium, pp 436-441, Detroit, MI, 1995.
6. C. Hatipoğlu and M. Sommerville, "Design of a Computationally Efficient Time-Domain Engine Model", CITR Technical Report, 96-02, February 1996.
7. A. İftar, "Decentralized Estimation and Control with Overlapping Input, State and Output Decomposition", *Automatica*, vol. 29, pp 511-516, 1993.
8. A. İftar and Ü. Özgüner, "Overlapping Decompositions, Expansions, Contractions, and Stability of Hybrid Systems", to appear in *IEEE Transactions in Automatic Control*, also CITR-OSU Technical Report 96-08, 1996.
9. M.Ikeda and D.D.Šiljak, "Overlapping decentralized control with input, state, and output inclusion," *Control Theory and Advanced Technology*, vol. 2, pp. 155–172, 1986.
10. J. Lygeros and D.N. Godbole, "An Interface between Continuous & Discrete-Event Controllers for Vehicle Automation", Proceedings of the 1994 Control and Decision Conference, Lake Buena Vista, FL, pp 801-805, 1994.
11. J. Lygeros, D.N. Godbole and S. Sastry, "A Verified Hybrid Controller for Automated Vehicles", Proceedings of the 1996 Conference on Control and Decision, Kobe, Japan, pp 2289-2294 , 1996.
12. Ü. Özgüner, K.A. Ünyelioğlu, C. Hatipoğlu, F. Kautz "Design of a Lateral Controller for Cooperative Vehicle Systems", *SAE Paper* 950474, also (SP-1076), pp 27-34.
13. Ü. Özgüner, K.A. Ünyelioğlu, and C. Hatipoğlu, "An Analytical Study of Vehicle Steering Control", Proceedings of the 1995 IEEE Conference on Control Applications, Albany, NY, pp 125-130, 1995.
14. K. Passino and Ü. Özgüner, "Modeling and Analysis of Hybrid Systems: Examples", Proceedings of the 1991 IEEE International Symposium on Intelligent Control, Arlington, VA, pp 251-256, 1991.

15. P. Peleties and R. DeCarlo, "Modeling of Interacting Continuous Time and Discrete event Systems: An Example", Proceedings of the 26th Allerton Conference on Communication, Control and Computing, pp 1150-1159, Oct 1988.

16. P. Peleties and R. DeCarlo, "A Modeling Strategy with Event Structures for Hybrid Systems", Proceedings of the 28th Conference on Decision and Control, pp 1308-1313, Tampa, FL, 1989.

17. K. Rudie and J.C. Willems, "Decentralized Discrete Event Systems and Computational Complexity", *Discrete Event Systems, Manufacturing Systems and Communication Networks*, P.R.Kumar and P.P. Varaiya (Eds.), pp 225-241, New York: Springer Verlag, 1995.

18. M. Sommerville, *Implementation of a Longitudinal Controller for use on an Automated Highway System*, Master's Thesis, The Ohio State University, Department of Electrical Engineering, 1996.

19. M. Sommerville, C. Hatipoğlu and Ü. Özgüner, "On the Variable Structure Control of a Throttle Actuator for Speed Control Applications", Proceedings of 1996 IEEE International Workshop on Variable Structure Systems, Kobe Japan, pp 187-192 1996.

20. M. Sommerville, K. Redmill and Ü. Özgüner, "A Multi-Level Automotive Speed Controller", SAE Paper 961011, Detroit, MI, 1996.

21. K.A. Ünyelioğlu, C. Hatipoğlu, Ü. Özgüner, "Design and Stability Analysis of a Lane Following Controller", *IEEE Transactions on Control Systems Technology*, Vol 5, pp 127-134, Jan 1997.

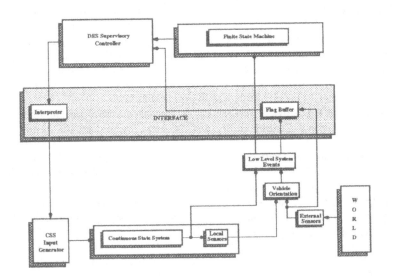

Fig. 1. DES, CSS and Interface Scheme.

Table 5. List of boolean variables that are used in the discrete and continuous state controllers.

LLE&C	Left Lane Exists w.r.t. the current lane and is clear; Availability of a left lane is sensed by the vision system by tracking the dashed lines, or by providing initial orientation, number of existing lanes info and keeping track of vehicle lateral transitions.
RLE&C	Right Lane Exists and is clear; Conditions are similar to LLE. In general, (LLE) $\neq$ (NOT RLE).
VEISLA	Vehicle Exists In the Same Lane Ahead; There is a vehicle detected in the same lane by the look-ahead radar or laser range finder. The condition that the detected vehicle is indeed in the same lane is checked with the angle info provided by the laser range finder.
VEIFA	Vehicle Exists in the Field of Action; VEISLA is automatically TRUE, moreover, the target is closer to the controlled vehicle such that slowing down is required. Helps insure that sensors did not pick noise but a real target.
VEIOL	Vehicle exists in the Other Lane; The side looking sensors have detected a vehicle in the sensor range, therefore lane change maneuvers can not be performed.
inVICINITY	In the vicinity of the aim point, i.e. ($\|d - d_{safe}\| \leq \zeta$) & ($\|\Delta\nu\| \leq \xi$)
BORED	Stayed inVICINITY for the last $\Delta t_{patience}$ amount of time, which is a characteristics of the driver and a measure of $\frac{his}{her}$ patience.
CROSSover	While accomplishing a lane change maneuver, the lane sensing system measurement changes sign after crossing over the lane marker between adjacent lanes. When this happens a crossover is assumed detected.
LCcomplete	Lane Change maneuver is completed; LCcomplete is reset with either of the ILC, RRL commands, and becomes true after the following sequence occurs: Δy becomes greater than ϵ_y, a crossover is detected, and Δ_y becomes less than ϵ_y again where Δ_y is the vehicle center of gravity deviation from the lane center and ϵ_y is a threshold value.
SLOW/ FAST	SLOW if ($\nu < \nu_{set}$) & {[(VEIFA) & (VISL) & ($\Delta\nu <$ (μ + [SLOW/$\overline{FAST}$]$\Delta\mu)\Delta d$)] OR (NOT VISL) OR (NOT VEIFSR)} where μ is a design parameter, $\Delta\mu$ is the designed hysteresis to avoid high frequency switchings, u is the speed, Δd is $d_{actual} - d_{safe}$, ν_{set} is the initial set speed.
atSETspeed	Vehicle is traveling at or near set speed, i.e., $\|\nu - \nu_{set}\| \leq \epsilon$.
tooFAST	Emergency is detected; ($\Delta d \geq \frac{1}{2|\mathcal{D}_{max}|}\Delta\nu^2 - d_{safe}$), i.e. the vehicle may not avoid collision even if decelerated at maximum rate, $\mathcal{D}$, without steering.
extMANsw	External boolean checks the steering clutch and throttle plate.

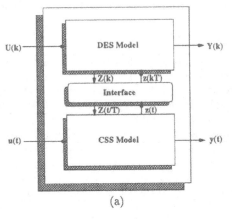

(a)

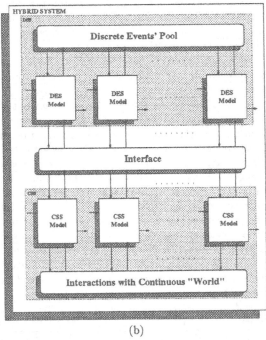

(b)

Fig. 2. (a) A hybrid system model; (b) A large scale hybrid system model.

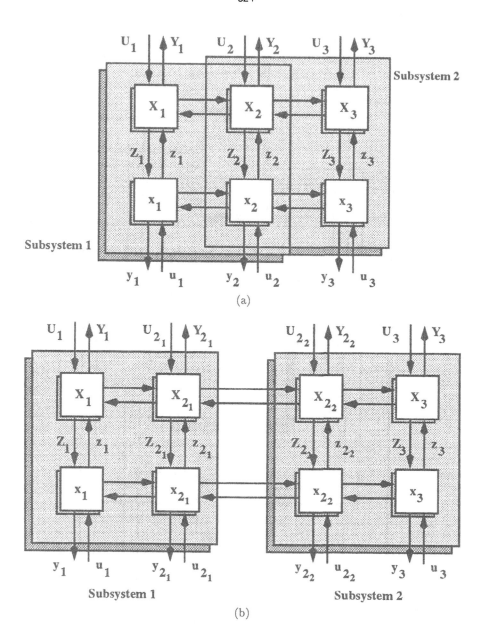

Fig. 3. (a)Overlappingly decomposed hybrid system. (b)Expanded hybrid system.

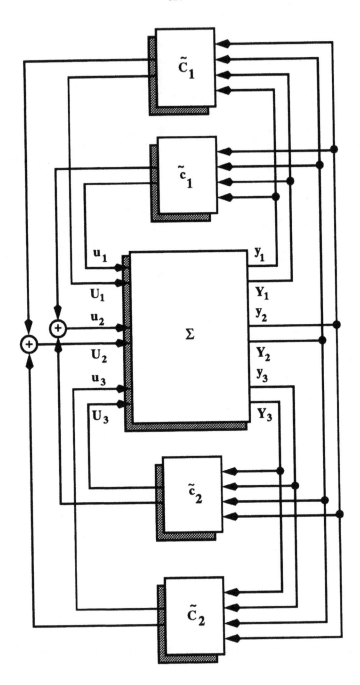

Fig. 4. Implementation of contracted controllers.

326

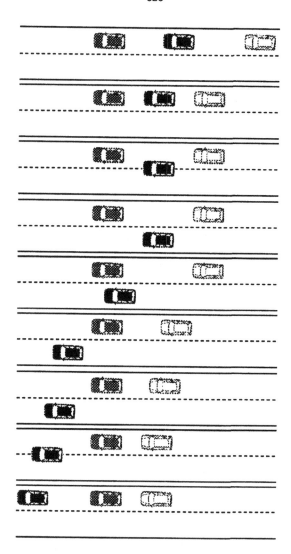

Fig. 5. Demonstration Scenario: The 9 snapshots in this figure aim to illustrate the '97 OSU demo. All pictures are depicted with respect to *Grandma* (Gray). The *Teenager* (Black) performs two consecutive lane change maneuvers to pass Grandma. Jack (White) maintains safety distance between itself and the leading car in the meanwhile.

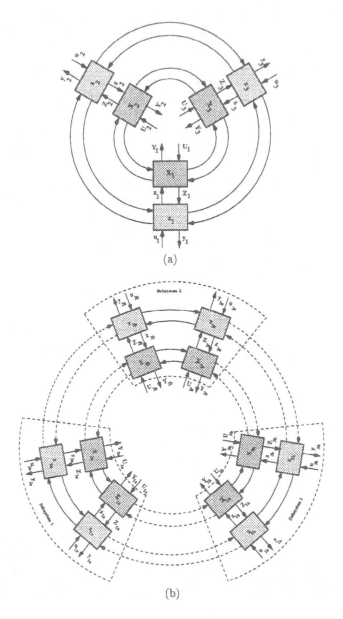

Fig. 6. (a) Three vehicle demo hybrid model; (b) Decomposed system.

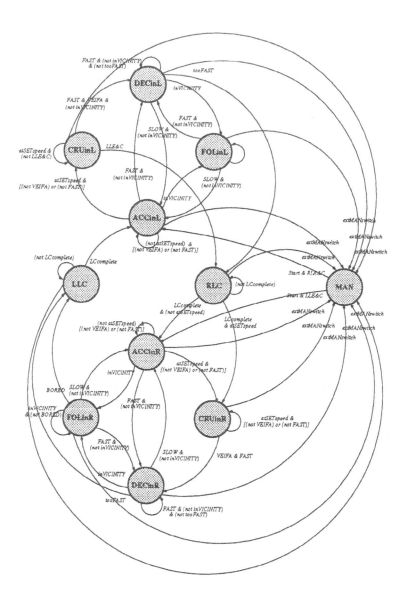

Fig. 7. Finite State Machine Model of the Discrete Desired State Transition for a Single Decomposed Subsystem.

Towards Continuous Abstractions of Dynamical and Control Systems*

George J. Pappas and Shankar Sastry

Department of Electrical Engineering and Computer Sciences
University of California at Berkeley
Berkeley, CA 94720
{gpappas,sastry}@eecs.berkeley.edu

Abstract. The analysis and design of large scale systems is usually an extremely complex process. In order to reduce the complexity of the analysis, simplified models of the original system, called *abstractions*, which capture the system behavior of interest are obtained and analyzed. If the abstraction of system can be shown to satisfy certain properties of interest then so does the original complex plant. In hybrid systems, discrete or hybrid abstractions of continuous systems are of great interest. In this paper, the notion of abstractions of continuous systems is formalized.

1   Introduction

Large scale systems such as intelligent highway systems [1] and air traffic control systems [2] result in systems of very high complexity. The design process for large scale systems consists of imposing an overall system architecture as well as designing communication and control algorithms for achieving a desired overall system performance. The merging of discrete communication protocols and continuous control laws results in *hybrid systems* ([3, 4, 5]). The analysis process for complex, hybrid systems consists of proving or verifying that the designed system indeed meets certain specifications. However, both the design and the analysis may be formidable due to the complexity and magnitude of the system.

In the design process, complexity is reduced by imposing a hierarchical structure ([6]) on the system architecture. By imposing this structure, systems of higher functionality reside at higher levels of the hierarchy and are therefore unaware of unecessary details regarding the lower levels of the hierarchy. This structure clearly reduces complexity since every level of the hierarchy is required to know only the necessary infomation in order to successfully complete its function. This may also increase efficiency and performance of the overall system since each level of the hierarchy can focus on its specific function which will be of minimal complexity.

From an analysis perspective, complexity reduction is performed by focusing on the dynamics of interest. For example, aircraft are usually modeled by

---

* Research supported by the Army Research Office under grants DAAH 04-95-1-0588 and DAAH 04-96-1-0341.

detailed differential equations which describe the behavior of engine dynamics, aerodynamics etc. A desired specification may be that any two aircraft reach their destinations and do not collide with each other. Proving that the system indeed meets the specification may be prohibitingly complex due to the detailed modeled dynamics as well as the large scale of the system.

However, in the above example, it is clear that the specification is not interested in the details of aircraft operation, but only in the relative position of the aircraft. We can therefore reduce the complexity of the analysis by by ignoring certain aspects of system behavior in a manner which is consistent with the behavior of the original system. This is essentially the idea behind system abstraction. Once a system abstraction has been obtained, standard analysis methods are utilized on the abstracted models. For example, verification algorithms of hybrid systems are based on abstracting continuous dynamics by rectangular differential inclusions [7, 8].

Webster's dictionary defines the word abstraction as *"the act or process of separating the inherent qualities or properties of something from the actual physical object or concept to which they belong"*. In system theory, the objects are usually dynamical or control systems, the properties are usually the behaviors of certain variables of interest and the act of separation is essentially the act of capturing all interesting behaviors. In summary, Webster's definition can be applied to define the *abstraction of a system to be another system which captures all system behavior of interest*. Behaviors of interest are captured by an *abstracting map* denoted by α. Abstracting maps are provided by the user depending on what information is of interest.

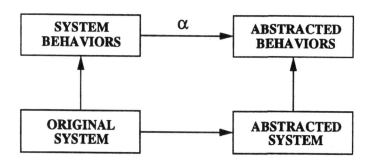

Fig. 1. System Abstractions

Figure 1 displays graphically the broad definition of a system abstraction. The original system may be modeled by ordinary or partial differential equations, discrete event systems or hybrid systems. The original system generates certain behaviors which are simply the system trajectories. The abstracting map α then selects the system behaviors which are of interest. The abstracted system must then be able to reproduce the same set of abstracted behaviors. The abstracted system must reproduce the system behaviors either *exactly* or *approximately*, resulting in exact or approximate abstractions respectively. Classical model reduction techniques can thus be thought of as approximate abstractions in this framework. The abstracted and original system do not have to be similar from a modeling point of view. For example, the original model may be an ordinary differential equation but the abstracted system may be a discrete event system. The main problem then is the following: *Given an original system and an abstracting map, find an abstracted system which generates the abstracted behaviors either exactly or approximately.*

In this paper, we consider the above problem for exact abstractions of dynamical and control systems. The notion of system abstraction is formalized and we consider the problem of abstracting continuous systems (differential equations and inclusions) by continuous systems. Necessary and sufficient geometric conditions under which one system is an exact abstraction of another with respect to a given abstracting map are derived. Although abstractions of systems may capture all behaviors of interest, they might also allow evolutions which are not feasible by the original system. This results in *overapproximating* the abstracted behaviors. This is due to the information reduction which naturally occurs during the abstraction process and it is the price one has to pay in order to reduce complexity. System abstractions can therefore be ordered based on the "size" of redundant allowable system evolutions leading to a notion of *best abstraction*. Furthermore, we show that certain properties of interest, such as controllability, propagate from the original system to the abstracted system.

The structure of this paper is as follows: In Section 2 we review some facts from differential geometry which will be used throughout the paper. In Section 3 abstracting maps are introduced in order to define system behaviors of interest. A notion of an abstraction of a dynamical system is defined in Section 4 and we discuss when one vector field is an abstraction of another. Section 5 generalizes these notions for control systems. Finally, Section 6 discusses issues of further research.

2   Mathematical Background

We first review some basic facts from differential geometry. The reader may wish to consult numerous books on the subject such as [9, 10, 11].

Let M be a differentiable manifold. The set of all tangent vectors at $p \in M$ is called the tangent space of M at p and is denoted by T_pM. The collection of all tangent spaces of the manifold,

$$TM = \bigcup_{p \in M} T_pM$$

is called the tangent bundle. The tangent bundle has a naturally associated projection map $\pi : TM \longrightarrow M$ taking a tangent vector $X_p \in T_pM \subset TM$ to the point $p \in M$. The tangent space T_pM can then be thought of as $\pi^{-1}(p)$.

The tangent space can be thought of as a special case of a more general mathematical object called a fiber bundle. Loosely speaking, a fiber bundle can be thought of as gluing sets at each point of the manifold in a smooth way.

Definition 1 (Fiber Bundles [12]). A *fiber bundle* is a five-tuple $(B, M, \pi, U, \{O_i\}_{i \in I})$ where B, M, U are smooth manifolds called the *total space*, the *base space* and the *standard fiber* respectively. The map $\pi : B \longrightarrow M$ is a surjective submersion and $\{O_i\}_{i \in I}$ is an open cover of M such that for every $i \in I$ there exists a diffeomorphism $\Phi_i : \pi^{-1}(O_i) \longrightarrow O_i \times U$ satisfying

$$\pi_o \circ \Phi = \pi$$

where π_o is the projection from $O_i \times U$ to O_i. The submanifold $\pi^{-1}(p)$ is called the *fiber* at $p \in M$. If all the fibers are vector spaces of constant dimension, then the fiber bundle is called a *vector bundle*.

Now let M and N be smooth manifolds and $f : M \longrightarrow N$ be a smooth map. Let $p \in M$ and let $q = f(p) \in N$. We push forward tangent vectors from T_pM to T_qN using the induced push forward map $f_* : T_pM \longrightarrow T_qN$. If $f : M \longrightarrow N$ and $g : N \longrightarrow K$ then

$$(g \circ f)_* = g_* \circ f_*$$

which is essentially the chain rule. A vector field or dynamical system on a manifold M is a continuous map F which places at each point p of M a tangent vector from T_pM. Let $I \subseteq \Re$ be an open interval containing the origin. An integral curve of a vector field is a curve $c : I \longrightarrow M$ whose tangent at each point is identically equal to the vector field at that point. Therefore an integral curve satisfies for all $t \in I$,

$$c' = c_*(1) = X(c)$$

Finally, we have the following definition.

Definition 2 (f-related Vector Fields). Let X and Y be vector fields on manifolds M and N respectively and $f : M \longrightarrow N$ be a smooth map. Then X and Y are *f-related* iff $f_* \circ X = Y \circ f$.

3 Abstracting Maps

Let M be the state space of a system. In abstracting system dynamics, information about the state of the system which is not useful in the analysis process is usually ignored in order to produce a simplified model of reduced complexity. The state $p \in M$ is thus mapped to an abstracted state $q \in N$. It is clear that *complexity reduction requires that the dimension of N should be lower than the dimension of M*.

For example, each state could be mapped to part of the state or to certain outputs of interest. What state information is relevant usually depends on the properties which need to be satisfied. The desired specification, however, could be quite different even for the same system since the functionality of the system may be different in various modes of system operation. It is therefore clear that it is very difficult to intrinsically obtain a system abstraction without any knowledge of the particular system functionality. System functionality determines what state information is of interest for analysis purposes. Given the functionality of the system, a notion of equivalent states is obtained by defining an equivalence relation on the state space. For example, given a dynamic model of some mechanical system one may be interested only in the configuration of the system. In this case, two states are equivalent if the corresponding configurations are the same.

Once a specific equivalence has been chosen, then the quotient space $M/\sim$ is the state space of the abstracted system. In order for the quotient space to have a manifold structure, the equivalence relation must be regular [10]. The surjective map $\alpha : M \longrightarrow M/\sim$ which sends each state $p \in M$ to its equivalence class $[p] \in M/\sim$ is called the quotient map and is the map which sends each state to its abstracted state. In general, we have the following definition.

Definition 3 (Abstracting Maps). Let M and N be given manifolds with $dim(N) \leq dim(M)$. A surjective map $\alpha : M \longrightarrow N$ from the state space M to the abstracted state space N is called an *abstracting map*.

The quotient map is an example of an abstracting map. Other typical abstracting maps could be projection maps, output maps as well as the identity map. Since in this paper we are interested with continuous systems, we will assume that M and N are manifolds and the abstracting maps to be smooth submersions.

4 Abstractions of Dynamical Systems

Once an abstracting map α has been given, then given a vector field X which governs the state evolution on M, then one is interested in obtaining the evolution of the abstracted dynamics. The evolution of a dynamical system is characterized by its integral curves. Let c be any integral curve of X. Then if we push forward the curve c by the abstracting map α we obtain that $\alpha \circ c$ describes the evolution of the abstracted dynamics on N. If we therefore want to abstract the vector field X on M by a vector field Y on N, then $\alpha \circ c$ should be an integral curve of Y. This motivates the following definition.

Definition 4 (Abstractions of Dynamical Systems). Let X and Y be vector fields on M and N respectively and let $\alpha : M \longrightarrow N$ be a smooth abstracting map. Then vector field Y is *an abstraction of vector field X with respect to α* iff for every integral curve c of X, $\alpha \circ c$ is an integral curve of Y.

Therefore if the curve c satisfies

$$c' = c_*(1) = X(c)$$

then it must also be true that

$$(\alpha \circ c)' = (\alpha \circ c)_*(1) = Y(\alpha \circ c)$$

From Definition 4 it is clear that a vector field Y may be an abstraction of some vector field X for some abstracting map α_1, but may not be for another abstracting map α_2.

In building hierarchical models of large scale systems, the system may be modeled at many levels of abstraction. The following proposition shows that abstracting dynamical systems is transitive.

Proposition 5 (Transitivity of Abstractions). *Let X_1, X_2, X_3 be vector fields on manifolds M_1, M_2 and M_3 respectively. If X_2 is an abstraction of X_1 with respect to the abstracting map $\alpha_1 : M_1 \to M_2$ and X_3 is an abstraction of X_2 with respect to abstracting map $\alpha_2 : M_2 \to M_3$ then X_3 is an abstraction of X_1 with respect to abstracting map $\alpha_2 \circ \alpha_1$.*

Proof: Let c be any integral curve of X_1. Since X_2 is an abstraction of X_1, then by definition $\alpha_1(c)$ is an integral curve of X_2. But since X_3 is an abstraction of X_2, $\alpha_2(\alpha_1(c)) = (\alpha_2 \circ \alpha_1)(c)$ is an integral curve of X_3. Thus for any integral curve c of X_1, $(\alpha_2 \circ \alpha_1)(c)$ is an integral curve of X_3. Thus X_3 is an abstraction of X_1 with respect to abstracting map $\alpha_2 \circ \alpha_1$. $\square$

The following theorem shows that Definition 4 is equivalent to saying that the two vector fields are α-related.

Theorem 6. *Vector field Y on N is an abstraction of vector field X on M with respect to the map α if and only if X and Y are α-related.*

Proof: Let vector field Y on N be an abstraction with respect to α of vector field X on M. Then by Definition 4, for any integral curve c of X, $\alpha \circ c$ is an integral curve of Y. Thus

$$(\alpha \circ c)' = (\alpha \circ c)_*(1) = Y(\alpha \circ c) \Rightarrow$$
$$\alpha_* \circ c_*(1) = Y \circ \alpha \circ c \Rightarrow$$
$$\alpha_* \circ X(c) = Y \circ \alpha \circ c \Rightarrow$$
$$\alpha_* \circ X \circ c = Y \circ \alpha \circ c \Rightarrow$$
$$\alpha_* \circ X = Y \circ \alpha$$

But then, by Definition 2, X and Y are α-related. Conversely, let X and Y be α related. Then for any integral curve c of X,

$$\alpha_* \circ X = Y \circ \alpha \Rightarrow$$
$$\alpha_* \circ X \circ c = Y \circ \alpha \circ c \Rightarrow$$
$$\alpha_* \circ X(c) = Y(\alpha \circ c) \Rightarrow$$
$$\alpha_* \circ c_*(1) = Y(\alpha \circ c) \Rightarrow$$
$$(\alpha \circ c)_*(1) = Y(\alpha \circ c)$$

and thus $\alpha \circ c$ is an integral curve of Y. Therefore Y is an abstraction of vector field X with respect to α. $\square$

Theorem 6 is important because it allows to check a condition on the vector fields rather than explicitly computing integral curves and verifying Definition 4. However, α-relatedness of two vector fields is a very restrictive condition which limits the cases where one dynamical system is an exact abstraction of another. This forces us to examine approximate abstractions of dynamical systems in our future work.

5 Abstractions of Control Systems

The notions of Section 4 for dynamical systems will be extended to control systems. Control systems can also be thought of as differential inclusions depending on whether one has a design or analysis perspective. We first need to introduce some facts about control systems.

Definition 7 (Control Systems [13]). A *control system* $S = (B, F)$ consists of a fiber bundle $\pi : B \longrightarrow M$ called the control bundle and a smooth map $F : B \longrightarrow TM$ which is fiber preserving and hence satisfies

$$\pi' \circ F = \pi$$

where $\pi' : TM \longrightarrow M$ is the tangent bundle projection.

Essentially, the base manifold M of the control bundle is the state space and the fibers $\pi^{-1}(p)$ are the state dependent control spaces. In a local coordinate chart (V, x), the map F can be expressed as $\dot{x} = F(x, u)$ with $u \in U(x) = \pi^{-1}(x)$.

Definition 8 (Integral Curves of Control Systems). A curve $c : I \longrightarrow M$ is called *an integral curve of the control system* $S = (B, F)$ if there exists a curve $c^B : I \longrightarrow B$ satisfying

$$\pi \circ c^B = c$$
$$c' = c_*(1) = F(c^B)$$

Again in local coordinates, the above definition simply says that $x(t)$ is a solution to a control system if there exists an input $u \in U(x) = \pi^{-1}(x)$ satisfying $\dot{x} = F(x, u)$. We now define abstractions of control systems in a manner similar to dynamical systems.

Definition 9 (Abstractions of Control Systems). Let $S_M = (B_M, F_M)$ with $\pi_M : B_M \longrightarrow M$ and $S_N = (B_N, F_N)$ with $\pi_N : B_N \longrightarrow N$ be two control systems. Let $\alpha : M \longrightarrow N$ be an abstracting map. Then control system S_N is *an abstraction of S_M with respect to abstracting map α* iff for every integral curve c_M of S_M, $\alpha \circ c_M$ is an integral curve of S_N.

From Definition 9 it is clear that a control system S_N may be an abstraction of S_M for some abstracting map α_1 but may not be for another abstracting map α_2. It can be easily shown that Definition 9 is transitive. Since the definition of an abstraction is at the level of integral curves, it is clearly difficult to conclude that one control system is an abstraction of another system by directly using Definition 9 since this would require integration of the system. One is therefore interested in easily checkable conditions under which one system is an abstraction of another. The following theorem, provides necessary and sufficient geometric conditions under which one control system is an abstraction of another system with respect to some abstracting map.

Theorem 10 (Conditions for Control System Abstractions). *Let $S_N = (B_N, F_N)$ and $S_M = (B_M, F_M)$ be two control systems and $\alpha : M \longrightarrow N$ be an abstracting map. Then S_N is an abstraction of S_M with respect to abstracting map α if and only if*

$$\alpha_* \circ F_M \circ \pi_M^{-1}(p) \subseteq F_N \circ \pi_N^{-1} \circ \alpha(p) \tag{1}$$

at every $p \in M$.

Proof: Before we proceed with the proof, we remark that condition (1) can be visualized using the following diagram,

$$
\begin{array}{ccc}
M & \xrightarrow{\alpha} & N \\
\pi_M^{-1} \downarrow & & \downarrow \pi_N^{-1} \\
B_M & & B_N \\
F_M \downarrow & & \downarrow F_N \\
TM & \xrightarrow{\alpha_*} & TN
\end{array}
\tag{2}
$$

Then condition (1) states that in the above diagram the set of tangent vectors produced in the direction $(M \xrightarrow{\pi_M^{-1}} B_M \xrightarrow{F_M} TM \xrightarrow{\alpha_*} TN)$ is a subset of the tangent vectors produced in the direction $(M \xrightarrow{\alpha} N \xrightarrow{\pi_N^{-1}} B_N \xrightarrow{F_N} TN)$.

We begin the proof, by first showing that if $\alpha_* \circ F_M \circ \pi_M^{-1} \subseteq F_N \circ \pi_N^{-1} \circ \alpha$ at every point $p \in M$ then F_N is an abstraction of F_M. We will prove the contrapositive. Assume that F_N is not an abstraction of F_M. Then there exists an integral curve c_M of F_M such that $\alpha \circ c_M$ is not an integral curve of F_N. Therefore for all curves $c_N^B : I \longrightarrow B_N$ such that $\pi_N \circ c_N^B = \alpha \circ c_M$ we have that at some point $t^* \in I$

$$(\alpha \circ c_M)'(t^*) \neq F_N(c_N^B(t^*))$$

But since this is true for all curves c_N^B satisfying $\pi_N \circ c_N^B(t^*) = \alpha \circ c_M(t^*)$ and since π_N is a surjection we have

$$
\begin{aligned}
(\alpha \circ c_M)'(t^*) &\notin F_N(\pi_N^{-1}(\alpha \circ c_M(t^*))) \Rightarrow \\
(\alpha \circ c_M)'(t^*) &\notin F_N \circ \pi_N^{-1} \circ \alpha \circ c_M(t^*) \Rightarrow \\
\alpha_* \circ c_{M*}(t^*)(1) &\notin F_N \circ \pi_N^{-1} \circ \alpha \circ c_M(t^*) \Rightarrow \\
\alpha_* \circ F_M \circ c_M^B(t^*) &\notin F_N \circ \pi_N^{-1} \circ \alpha \circ c_M(t^*)
\end{aligned}
\tag{3}
$$

for some curve $c_M^B : I \longrightarrow B_M$ such that $\pi_M \circ c_M^B = c_M$. But then $c_M^B(t^*) \in \pi_M^{-1}(c_M(t^*)) = \pi_M^{-1} \circ c_M(t^*)$. Therefore, there exists a tangent vector $Y_{\alpha(c_M(t^*))} \in T_{\alpha(c_M(t^*))}N$, namely

$$Y_{\alpha(c_M(t^*))} = \alpha_* \circ F_M \circ c_M^B(t^*)$$

such that

$$Y_{\alpha(c_M(t^*))} \in \alpha_* \circ F_M \circ \pi_M^{-1} \circ c_M(t^*)$$

since $c_M^B(t^*) \in \pi_M^{-1} \circ c_M(t^*)$ but

$$Y_{\alpha(c_M(t^*))} \notin F_N \circ \pi_N^{-1} \circ \alpha \circ c_M(t^*)$$

by condition (3). But then we have that at $c_M(t^*) \in M$,

$$\alpha_* \circ F_M \circ \pi_M^{-1}(c_M(t^*)) \nsubseteq F_N \circ \pi_N^{-1} \circ \alpha(c_M(t^*)) \tag{4}$$

Conversely, we now prove that if F_N is an abstraction of F_M then $\alpha_* \circ F_M \circ \pi_M^{-1} \subseteq F_N \circ \pi_N^{-1} \circ \alpha$. We will use contradiction. Assume that F_N is an abstraction of F_M but at some point $p \in M$ we have $\alpha_* \circ F_M \circ \pi_M^{-1}(p) \nsubseteq F_N \circ \pi_N^{-1} \circ \alpha(p)$. Then there exists tangent vector $Y_{\alpha(p)} \in T_{\alpha(p)}N$ such that

$$Y_{\alpha(p)} \in \alpha_* \circ F_M \circ \pi_M^{-1}(p) \tag{5}$$
$$Y_{\alpha(p)} \notin F_N \circ \pi_N^{-1} \circ \alpha(p) \tag{6}$$

Since $Y_{\alpha(p)} \in \alpha_* \circ F_M \circ \pi_M^{-1}(p)$, we can write $Y_{\alpha(p)} = \alpha_*(X_p)$ for some (not necessarily unique) tangent vector $X_p \in F_M \circ \pi_M^{-1}(p)$. But since $X_p \in F_M \circ \pi_M^{-1}(p)$ then there exists an integral curve $c_M : I \longrightarrow M$ such that at some $t^* \in I$ we have

$$c_M(t^*) = p \tag{7}$$
$$c_M'(t^*) = X_p \tag{8}$$

To see that such a curve exists assume that such an integral curve does not exist. But then for all curves c_M satisfying (7,8) and for all curves $c_M^B : I \longrightarrow B_M$ such that $\pi_M \circ c_M^B = c_M$ we have that

$$c_M'(t^*) \neq F_M(c_M^B) \Rightarrow X_p \neq F_M(c_M^B) \tag{9}$$

But since this is true for all such c_M^B we obtain

$$X_p \notin F_M(\pi_M^{-1}(c_M(t^*)))$$

which is clearly a contradiction. Therefore, an integral curve satisfying (7,8) always exists.

We know that F_N is an abstraction of F_M. Therefore by definition, for every integral curve c_M of F_M, $\alpha \circ c_M$ must be an integral curve of F_N. Let c_M be the integral curve satisfying (7,8). Then it must be true that

$$(\alpha \circ c_M)' = F_N(c_N^B)$$

for some $c_N^B : I \longrightarrow B_N$ such that $\pi_N \circ c_N^B = \alpha \circ c_M$. But at $t^* \in I$ we have that

$$(\alpha \circ c_M)'(t^*) = \alpha_* \circ c_{M*}(t^*)(1) = \alpha_*(X_p) = Y_{\alpha(p)}$$

But by condition (6), $Y_{\alpha(p)} \notin F_N \circ \pi_N^{-1} \circ \alpha(p)$ and therefore for all curves c_N^B satisfying $\pi_N \circ c_N^B = \alpha \circ c_M$ we get

$$(\alpha \circ c_M)'(t^*) = Y_{\alpha(p)} \notin F_N(c_N^B(t^*))$$

But then $\alpha \circ c_M$ is not an integral curve of F_N which is a contradiction since we assumed that F_N is an abstraction of F_M with respect to the abstracting map α. Therefore, at all points $p \in M$ we must have $\alpha_* \circ F_M \circ \pi_M^{-1} \subseteq F_N \circ \pi_N^{-1} \circ \alpha$. This completes the proof. $\square$

Theorem 10 is the analogue of Theorem 6 for control systems. However, unlike Theorem 6 which required the α-relatedness of two vector fields, Theorem 10 does not require the commutativity of diagram 2. This is actually quite fortunate since, as the following corollaries of Theorem 10 show, *every* control and dynamical system is abstractable by another control system.

Corollary 11 (Abstractable Control Systems). *Every control system $S_M = (B_M, F_M)$ is abstractable by a control system S_N with respect to any abstracting map $\alpha : M \longrightarrow N$.*

Proof: Simply let $B_N = TN$ and $F_N : TN \longrightarrow TN$ equal the identity. Then condition (1) is trivially satisfied. Thus $S_N = (B_N, F_N)$ is an abstraction of S_M. $\square$

As a subcollorary of Corollary 11 we have.

Corollary 12 (Abstractable Dynamical Systems). *Every dynamical system on M is abstractable by a control system with respect to any abstracting map $\alpha : M \longrightarrow N$.*

Proof: Every vector field X can be thought of a trivial control system $S_M = (B_M, F_M)$ where $B_M = M \times \{0\}$ and F_M is equal to $X \circ \pi$. Then Corollary 11 applies. $\square$

Corollary 12 states the fact that *any dynamical system can be exactly abstracted at the cost of nondeterminism.* In local coordinates, Corollaries 11 and 12 simply state the fact that the behavior of any system can be abstracted by a differential inclusion $\dot{x} \in \Re^n$ where x are the local coordinates of interest and n is the dimension of manifold N. However, such an abstraction may not be useful in proving properties. Therefore, it is clear that there is a notion of order among abstractions of a given system.

If one considers fiber subbundles Δ of the tangent bundle TN where at each $q \in N$,

$$\Delta(q) = F_N \circ \pi_N^{-1}(q) \subseteq T_q N \tag{10}$$

for a control system $S_N = (B_N, F_N)$ then Theorem 10 essentially allows us to think of abstractions of a given system $S_M = (B_M, F_M)$ as subbundles $\Delta \subseteq TN$ that satisfy at each point $p \in M$,

$$\alpha_* \circ F_M \circ \pi_M^{-1}(p) \subseteq \Delta(\alpha(p)) \tag{11}$$

and therefore capture all possible tangent directions in which the abstracted dynamics may evolve. Note that Δ is not needed to be a distribution or to have any vector space structure.

It is clear from (10,11) that if Δ is an abstraction of a control system S_M then so is any superset of Δ, say $\bar{\Delta}$ and thus $\bar{\Delta}$ is also an abstraction. But if $\Delta \subset \bar{\Delta}$ then a straightforward application of Theorem 1 shows that $\bar{\Delta}$ is an abstraction of Δ with respect to the identity map $i : N \longrightarrow N$. Therefore, any integral curve of Δ is also an integral curve of $\bar{\Delta}$ but not vice versa. But since Δ has captured all evolutions of S_M which are of interest, $\bar{\Delta}$ can only contain more redundant evolutions which are not feasible by S_M. It is therefore clear that Δ is a more desirable abstraction than $\bar{\Delta}$. This raises a notion of order among abstractions.

Let $S_M = (B_M, F_M)$ be a control system and an abstracting map $\alpha : M \longrightarrow N$ be given. Let control systems $S_{N_1} = (B_{N_1}, F_{N_1})$ and $S_{N_2} = (B_{N_2}, F_{N_2})$ be abstractions of S_M with respect to α. Define at each $q \in N$,

$$\Delta_1(q) = F_{N_1} \circ \pi_{N_1}^{-1}(q) \subseteq T_q N$$
$$\Delta_2(q) = F_{N_2} \circ \pi_{N_2}^{-1}(q) \subseteq T_q N$$

Then we say that S_{N_1} is a better abstraction than S_{N_2}, denoted $S_{N_1} \preceq S_{N_2}$ iff at each point $p \in M$ we have

$$\Delta_1(\alpha(p)) \subseteq \Delta_2(\alpha(p)) \tag{12}$$

It is clear that $\preceq$ is a partial order among abstractions since the order is essentially set inclusion at each fiber. The following Theorem shows that the resulting lattice has a diamond-like structure since there is a unique minimal and maximal element.

Theorem 13 (Structure of Abstractions). *The partial order $\preceq$ has a unique maximal and minimal element.*

Proof: It is easy to see that the unique maximal abstraction is given by $\bar{S} = (TN, i)$ where i is the identity map from TN to TN.

From condition (11) it is clear that it is clear that if

$$\Delta_1(q) = F_{N_1} \circ \pi_{N_1}^{-1}(q) \subseteq T_q N$$
$$\Delta_2(q) = F_{N_2} \circ \pi_{N_2}^{-1}(q) \subseteq T_q N$$

are abstractions of a control system S_M with respect to α then so is the control system $\Delta = \Delta_1 \cap \Delta_2$ where the intersection of the two bundles is defined at each fiber. It is therefore clear that the unique minimal element of $\preceq$ is given by the intersection of all abstractions of S_M. But the intersection of all abstractions can be seen from condition (11) to be the subbundle that satisfies

$$\Delta(\alpha(p)) = \alpha_* \circ F_M \circ \pi_M^{-1}(p) \tag{13}$$

for every $p \in M$. $\square$

Therefore the best abstraction results in diagram (2) being commutative.

Once a system abstraction has been obtained, it is useful to propagate properties of interest from the original system to the abstracted system. For control systems, one of those properties is controllability.

Definition 14 (Controllability). Let $S = (B, F)$ be a control system. Then S is called controllable iff given any two points $p_1, p_2 \in M$, there exists an integral curve c such that for some $t_1, t_2 \in I$ we have $c(t_1) = p_1$ and $c(t_2) = p_2$.

Theorem 15 (Controllable Abstractions). *Let control system $S_N = (B_N, F_N)$ be an abstraction of $S_M = (B_M, F_M)$ with respect to some abstracting map α. If S_M is controllable then S_N is controllable.*

Proof: Let q_1 and q_2 be any two points on N. Then let $p_1 \in \alpha^{-1}(q_1)$ and $p_2 \in \alpha^{-1}(q_2)$ be any two points on M. Since F_M on B_M is controllable then there exists an integral curve c_M such that $c_M(t_1) = p_1$ and $c_M(t_2) = p_2$. The curve $\alpha \circ c_M$ satisfies $\alpha \circ c_M(t_1) = q_1$ and $\alpha \circ c_M(t_2) = q_2$. But since F_N is an abstraction of F_M, then $\alpha \circ c_M$ is an integral curve of F_N on B_N. Therefore, the abstracted system is controllable. $\square$

Other properties, such as local accesibility, also propagate. Stability, however, does not propagate since the abstracted system allows redundant evolutions which could be unstable.

6 Conclusions - Issues for Further Research

In this paper, preliminary results on abstracting dynamical and control systems have been presented. A notion of system abstraction has been defined and necessary and sufficient conditions under which one system is an exact abstraction of another have been obtained. Furthermore, a notion of order among abstractions was introduced by ordering the conservativeness of the given abstractions. Finally, desirable system properties were found to propagate from original models to abstracted models.

Issues for further research include, on the theoretical front, extending these results to approximate, discrete and hybrid abstractions. Approximate abstractions approximate integral curves of a given system with some guaranteed margin of error. Discrete abstractions are generated when the codomain of the abstracting map is a finite set. In that case the abstracted behaviors are timed sequences of events and we seek an automaton reproducing these sequences. However, there are many problems in obtaining vector field conditions similar to those of Theorem 10. Some of these issues are topological and have been addressed in the literature [14, 15]. Furthermore, a more challenging problem is the following: *Given an original system and a property of interest, find an abstracting map which preserves this property.* Then checking the property at the abstracted system ensures us that original system has the property as well. This is very important for analysis purposes. For example, given a stable system the abstracting map could be a Lyapunov function. Then checking some properties on the Lyapunov function ensures that the original system is stable.

Finally, the developments presented in this paper will be applied to various applications of interest. Particular applications of interest include aircraft and automobile models.

References

1. Pravin Varaiya. Smart cars on smart roads: problems of control. *IEEE Transactions on Automatic Control*, AC-38(2):195–207, 1993.
2. S. Sastry, G. Meyer, C. Tomlin, J. Lygeros, D. Godbole, and G. Pappas. Hybrid control in air traffic management systems. In *Proceedings of the 1995 IEEE Conference in Decision and Control*, pages 1478–1483, New Orleans, LA, December 1995.
3. Robert L. Grossman, Anil Nerode, Anders P. Ravn, and Hans Rischel, editors. *Hybrid Systems*. Lecture Notes in Computer Science. Springer-Verlag, 1993.
4. Panos Antsaklis, Wolf Kohn, Anil Nerode, and Shankar Sastry, editors. *Hybrid Systems II*. Lecture Notes in Computer Science. Springer-Verlag, 1995.
5. R. Alur, T.A. Henzinger, and E.D. Sontag, editors. *Hybrid Systems III*. Lecture Notes in Computer Science 1066. Springer-Verlag, 1996.
6. Peter Caines and Y.J. Wei. The hierarchical lattices of a finite state machine. *Systems and Control Letters*, 25:257–263, 1995.
7. Anuj Puri and Pravin Varaiya. Decidability of hybrid systems with rectangular differential inclusions. In *Computer Aided Verification*, pages 95–104, 1994.
8. T.A. Henzinger and H. Wong-Toi. Linear phase-portrait approximations for nonlinear hybrid systems. In R. Alur, T.A. Henzinger, and E.D. Sontag, editors, *Hybrid Systems III*, Lecture Notes in Computer Science 1066, pages 377–388. Springer-Verlag, 1996.
9. Michael Spivak. *A Comprehensive Introduction to Differential Geometry.* Publish or Perish, 1979.
10. Abraham R., Marsden J., and Ratiu T. *Manifolds, Tensor Analysis and Applications.* Applied Mathematical Sciences. Springer-Verlag, 1988.
11. James R. Munkres. *Analysis on Manifolds.* Addison-Wesley, 1991.
12. Nijmeijer H. and van der Schaft A.J. *Nonlinear Dynamical Control Systems.* Springer-Verlag, 1990.
13. Roger Brockett. Global descriptions of nonlinear control problems; vector bundles and nonlinear control theory. manuscript, 1980.
14. A. Nerode and W. Kohn. Models for hybrid systems: Automata, topologies, controllability, observability. In Robert L. Grossman, Anil Nerode, Anders P. Ravn, and Hans Rischel, editors, *Hybrid System*, pages 317–356. Springer Verlag, New York, 1993.
15. Michael Branicky. Topology of hybrid systems. In *Proceedings of the 32nd IEEE Conference in Decision and Control*, pages 2309–2314, San Antonio, TX, December 1993.

A Totally Ordered Set of Discrete Abstractions for a given Hybrid or Continuous System

Jörg Raisch[1] * and Siu O'Young[2] **

[1] Institut für Systemdynamik und Regelungstechnik
Universität Stuttgart
Pfaffenwaldring 9
D-70550 Stuttgart, FR Germany
email: raisch@isr.uni-stuttgart.de
[2] Department of Electrical and Computer Engineering
University of Toronto
Toronto, Ontario, Canada, M5S 1A4
email: oyoung@control.utoronto.ca

Abstract. This contribution proposes a hierarchy of discrete abstractions for a given hybrid or continuous system with quantized measurements and symbolic control inputs. The continuous (or hybrid) base system and its discrete abstractions form a totally ordered set of models; ordering is in the sense of set inclusion of model behaviours or, equivalently, in terms of approximation accuracy. The ordering is shown to be invariant under feedback; this provides theoretical justification for designing feedback control for the underlying hybrid system on the basis of a discrete abstraction. Also, within this ordered set, the notion of a "least accurate" (and therefore least complex) model which allows a given set of specifications to be met makes sense. The discrete abstractions are realized as nondeterministic automata; they are in observer-canonical form and hence, by construction, observable. Non-reachable states are also "weeded out" by construction, leaving a minimal state set for each approximating automaton.

1 Introduction

The motivation for the work presented here stems from a "standard approach" in hybrid control systems design which was pioneered by *Antsaklis, Lemmon,* and *Stiver* (e.g. [18, 2]), and by *J. Lunze* (e.g. [8, 9, 10]). They address the following problem: the plant is a continuous system, i.e. its state evolves in $\mathbb{R}^n$, whereas measurements and control inputs are discrete-valued, or symbolic; both

---

* Support from Deutsche Forschungsgemeinschaft under Grant Ra 516/2-2 and through "Sonderforschungsbereich" SFB 412 is gratefully acknowledged. Part of this work was done while the author visited the Systems Control Group at the University of Toronto.

** Research supported by the Information Technology Research Centre and Condata Technologies Ltd., both of Ontario, Canada.

the set of measurement symbols, Y_d, and the set of control symbols, U_d, are assumed to be finite[3]. One is then concerned with finding an appropriate feedback structure mapping symbolic measurement signals into (sets of) symbolic control inputs. This is done by "building" a discrete approximation[4] for the continuous plant, hence converting the hybrid control problem into a purely discrete problem, which can subsequently be solved using tools from DES (Discrete Event Systems) theory (e.g. [17]) . In the original contributions pursuing this line of thought (e.g. [18, 2, 8, 9]), the achievable accuracy of the discrete approximation is completely determined by the measurement map $q_y : \mathbb{R}^n \to Y_d$ – the function q_y partitions the plant state space, and the "cells" induced by this partition can be interpreted as states of a discrete substitute model; abstraction, or approximation, is therefore simply the process of "lumping" all continuous states which are mapped to the same measurement symbol. Hence, the number of states in the discrete approximation is given by the number of measurement symbols. If the resulting model is "too coarse" to allow design specifications to be met, one has "run out of luck" (unless one can change the measurement map). This motivated the authors of the present paper to come up with a modified approximation scheme [13, 14, 15, 16], which is characterized by the fact that the degree of accuracy is *not* completely determined by the coarseness of measurement quantization, but can be adjusted to suit various specifications. This is achieved by identifying subsets of $\mathbb{R}^n$ which are compatible with *strings* of measurement and control symbols.

The purpose of this contribution is to provide theoretical justification for that approach. It will be shown that the continuous "base" system and the discrete abstractions proposed in [14, 15, 16] form a totally ordered set, where the order is in the sense of set inclusion of the associated behaviours or, equivalently, in the sense of approximation accuracy. Furthermore, we will show that this order is invariant if the models in the set are subject to interaction with a given discrete system. In particular, it is invariant under (supervisory) feedback control. There are two major consequences: 1) if the plant itself is a hybrid system, it suffices to find discrete abstractions for its continuous part. The abstractions of the hybrid plant (consisting of an abstraction of the continuous part interacting with the discrete plant component) are ordered in the same way as the discrete approximations for the continuous part. 2) If a discrete abstraction under feedback satisfies a given set of design specifications, all more accurate members of the model set (in particular the continuous or hybrid "base" system) also satisfy the design requirements when subject to the same feedback law. In other words: design of (supervisory) feedback control for hybrid plants can be based on discrete abstractions.

---

[3] This paper is set in a discrete-time framework, i.e. the domain of all signals is $\{t_0, t_1, \ldots\}$, with $t_i - t_{i-1}$ being constant. This understood, the adjectives "discrete" and "continuous" will in the sequel only be used to refer to the *codomain* of signals: the codomain of a discrete, or discrete-valued, signal is a set of symbols; the codomain of a continuous, or continuous-valued, signal are the real numbers.

[4] The expressions "(discrete) abstraction" and "(discrete) approximation (of a given continuous or hybrid system)" are used synonymously throughout the paper.

Although the emphasis of this paper is on (input/output) behaviours of discrete abstractions, we will also discuss details of their realization: discrete abstractions will be realized as nondeterministic automata in observer-canonical form. Observability is therefore guaranteed by construction. As non-reachable states are also eliminated when computing the approximating automata, state sets are guaranteed to be minimal.

Beside the references given above, the following papers deal with closely related topics: *Pappas* and *Sastry* [11] consider the (mathematically much more intricate) problem of finding *continuous* abstractions of continuous dynamical systems. Interesting work on discrete abstractions of continuous systems has been published by *Caines* and *Wei* [4, 5]: they consider the lattice of dynamically consistent partition machines associated with a given continuous system. Of related interest is also the work by *Niinomi*, *Krogh*, and *Cury* [12]: they design supervisory control on the basis of approximating automata. In contrast to our work, their discrete approximations are purely logical, i.e. timing information (apart from the temporal order of events) is *not* retained in the approximation.

Finally, it goes without saying that the way we interpret our results is almost entirely in terms of *J. C. Willems'* "behavioural systems theory" ([19] and the references therein). Behaviours (in *Willems'* sense) are a compact and illustrative way of thinking about a variety of dynamical systems and their abstractions.

The paper is organized as follows: in Section 2, the hybrid plant is introduced. Section 3 describes how to build discrete abstractions for the continuous part of the hybrid system. It is shown that the state equations of these discrete approximations are in canonical form and minimal by construction. Furthermore, it is pointed out that the discrete abstractions can be interpreted as observers for the continuous part of the "base" system. Section 4 contains a brief review of the concept of behaviours of dynamical systems; it states – in terms of behaviours – the main requirement that any abstraction has to meet. In Section 5, the main results on ordering are given: the continuous part of the "base" system and the discrete abstractions proposed in Section 3 form a totally ordered set. The ordering is shown to be invariant if the elements in the model set interact with a given discrete system; in particular, the ordering is invariant under feedback.

Our notation may seem a bit involved, but really is completely straightforward: we distinguish discrete-valued, or symbolic, signals from continuous-valued signals by using the subscript "d". Signals are represented by lower case letters, their codomains by the corresponding upper case letters. For example, $u_d : \{t_0, t_1, \dots\} \to U_d$ is the (discrete-valued) input signal, which is defined on the sampling grid $\{t_0, t_1, \dots\}$ and "lives" (takes values) in the (discrete) set U_d. The signal $w : \{t_0, t_1, \dots\} \to W$ is continuous-valued, its codomain W a dense subset of Euclidean space. The codomains of all discrete-valued signals are assumed to be finite, their elements (the possible values the signal can take at each sampling instant) are characterized by superscripts: the i-the element in the set U_d, for example, is denoted by $u_d^{(i)}$.

2 The Hybrid Plant Model

The "base" model of the plant consists of a continuous and a discrete part. The former is described by

$$x(t_{k+1}) = f(x(t_k), w(t_k), u_d(t_k)), \tag{1}$$
$$z_d(t_k) = q_z(x(t_k)), \tag{2}$$
$$y_d(t_k) = q_y(x(t_k)), \tag{3}$$

where $k \in \{0, 1, 2, \dots\}$ is the time index, $x(t_k) \in \mathbb{R}^n$ the state of the continuous component at time t_k, and $w(t_k) \in \mathbb{R}^r$ an unknown but bounded disturbance:

$$w(t_k) \in W := \{w \,|\, w \in \mathbb{R}^r, \|w\|_\infty \le 1\}, \tag{4}$$

with $\|w\|_\infty := \max_i |w_i|$. $u_d(t_k) \in U_d$, $z_d(t_k) \in Z_d$, and $y_d(t_k) \in Y_d$ are input, output, and measurement symbols, respectively. The input $u_d(t_k)$ is assumed to be measurable – in case of a purely continuous plant (the discrete part described below is non-existent), it takes the role of a control input. The output z_d is introduced to capture design specifications which cannot be expressed in terms of inputs or measurement symbols – this is standard practice, for example, in H_∞-control theory. In H_∞-theory, this additional output usually depends directly on the (control) input to allow penalizing unrealistic input signals. In our case, this is not necessary, as, by definition, u_d can only "live" on a restricted set U_d. Clearly, the choice of the outputs is part of the design process. For example, if safety is our only concern, the codomain of the output map q_z is $Z_d = \{\texttt{forbidden}, \texttt{legal}\}$. The sets U_d, Z_d, and Y_d are always assumed to be finite:

$$U_d = \{u_d^{(1)}, \dots, u_d^{(\alpha)}\},$$
$$Z_d = \{z_d^{(1)}, \dots, z_d^{(\beta)}\},$$
$$Y_d = \{y_d^{(1)}, \dots, y_d^{(\gamma)}\}.$$

The only requirement on $f : \mathbb{R}^n \times \mathbb{R}^r \times U_d \to \mathbb{R}^n$ is that its restriction to $\mathbb{R}^n$ be invertible. Therefore, (1) can be solved for the first argument on the right hand side, and the solution is denoted by $x(t_k) = \tilde{f}^{-1}(x(t_{k+1}), w(t_k), u_d(t_k))$. Both output and measurement map, $q_z : \mathbb{R}^n \to Z_d$ and $q_y : \mathbb{R}^n \to Y_d$, are assumed to be onto.

The discrete part of the plant is modelled as a Moore automaton with transition function δ and output function q_u:

$$\xi_d(t_{k+1}) = \delta(\xi_d(t_k), y_d(t_k), \tilde{u}_d(t_k)), \tag{5}$$
$$u_d(t_k) = q_u(\xi_d(t_k)), \tag{6}$$

where $\xi_d(t_k) \in \Xi_d$ is the state of the discrete component at time t_k, and its state set Ξ_d is assumed to be finite. The output of the discrete part (u_d) serves as input to the continuous component, and the measured output of the continuous part (y_d) as (internal) input for the automaton. The external input $\tilde{u}_d(t_k) \in \tilde{U}_d$ is the control input for the overall hybrid system (Fig. 1).

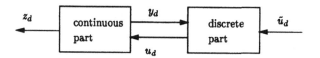

Fig. 1. "Base" model for the hybrid plant.

3 Nondeterministic Automata as Discrete Abstractions for Continuous Systems

In this section, it will be shown how to generate a set of nondeterministic automata as abstractions for the continuous part of the plant. First of all, choose a non-negative integer v – this will parametrize our set of discrete abstractions. Then, define the state of our discrete abstraction at time t_k as

$$x_d(t_k) := \begin{cases} ([y_d(t_k), \dots, y_d(t_0)], [u_d(t_{k-1}), \dots, u_d(t_0)]), & \text{if } k = 0, 1, \dots, v-1, \\ ([y_d(t_k), \dots, y_d(t_{k-v})], [u_d(t_{k-1}), \dots, u_d(t_{k-v})]), & \text{if } k \geq v. \end{cases} \tag{7}$$

Hence, the current state of the abstraction is defined to be the string of measurements and (measurable) input symbols reaching back over a certain interval $\min(k, v)$. This choice is reminiscent of observer canonical realizations in (continuous) control theory (e.g. [7]) – the state is made up of known quantities, and hence is trivially observable. As both U_d, the set of input symbols, and Y_d, the set of measurement symbols, are finite, the state set X_d of the discrete abstraction is finite. An upper bound for the number of elements of X_d is

$$\bar{N}_v = \sum_{i=0}^{v} \gamma^{i+1} \alpha^i$$

– this is the number of different strings (7) one gets by exhaustive permutation of measurement and input symbols.

It is obvious, however, that the continuous system (1), (3) cannot generate *all* these strings. In the next step, one therefore eliminates all strings which are not compatible with the continuous model (1), (3) and the disturbance assumptions: let $0 \leq \rho \leq v$ and denote $\tilde{f}^{-1}(x, w, u_d^{(k)})$ by $\tilde{f}_k^{-1}(x, w)$. Then, $\left(\left[y_d^{(i_0)}, \dots, y_d^{(i_\rho)} \right], \left[u_d^{(k_1)}, \dots, u_d^{(k_\rho)} \right] \right)$ is an element in the state set of the discrete abstractions if and only if

$$y_d^{(i_0)} = q_y(x) \tag{8}$$

$$y_d^{(i_1)} = q_y \left(\tilde{f}_{k_1}^{-1}(x, w_{j_1}) \right) \tag{9}$$

$$y_d^{(i_2)} = q_y \left(\tilde{f}_{k_2}^{-1} \left(\tilde{f}_{k_1}^{-1}(x, w_{j_1}), w_{j_2} \right) \right) \tag{10}$$

$$\vdots$$

$$y_d^{(i_\rho)} = q_y \left(\tilde{f}_{k_\rho}^{-1} \cdots \left(\tilde{f}_{k_1}^{-1}(x, w_{j_1}), \ldots, w_{j_\rho} \right) \right) \tag{11}$$

subject to

$$\|w_{j_l}\|_\infty \leq 1, \quad l = 1, \ldots \rho, \tag{12}$$

has a non-empty solution set for $[x', w'_{j_1}, \ldots, w'_{j_\rho}]'$. Of course, it is a bit ambitious to try checking a general nonlinear set of equations for the existence of solutions. For an important special case, however, this reduces to a numerically straightforward procedure – checking whether a set of *linear inequalities* possesses a non-empty solution set. This special case is characterized by the fact that the right hand side of (1) is affine in the state $x(t_k)$ and the unknown disturbance vector $w(t_k)$, and the measurement map has the form $q_y = Q_y \circ C_y$ (where $C_y : \mathbb{R}^n \to \mathbb{R}^p$ is a linear map, and the "quantizer" $Q_y : \mathbb{R}^p \to Y_d$ partitions $\mathbb{R}^p$ into finitely many rectangular boxes with edges parallel to the coordinate axes). Details can be found in [15, 16]. For completeness, the computational procedure is repeated in Appendix A.

This second step boils down to "weeding out" non-reachable states; the remaining state structure is therefore guaranteed to be minimal. The number of elements in this minimal state set X_d is denoted by N_v:

$$X_d := \{x_d^{(1)}, \ldots, x_d^{(N_v)}\}. \tag{13}$$

$x_d^{(i)}$ belongs to the set of possible initial states X_{d0}, if it contains exactly one measurement symbol (and no input symbols), i.e. $X_{d0} = Y_d$. This reflects the fact that we do not assume any a-priori knowledge on the continuous system state: at time t_0 (when we "start looking at the system"), it could be anywhere in $\mathbb{R}^n$, and any measurement symbol in Y_d is therefore possible at time t_0.

Denote the strings of input and measurement symbols associated with a particular $x_d^{(i)}$ by $u^*(x_d^{(i)})$ and $y^*(x_d^{(i)})$, respectively, and introduce a "forgetting operator" $\mathcal{F}$ which deletes the "oldest" symbol from strings $y_d^*(x_d(t_k))$ and $u_d^*(x_d(t_k))$, if $k \geq v$:

$$\mathcal{F}(y_d^*(x_d(t_k))) := \begin{cases} [y_d(t_k), \ldots, y_d(t_0)], & \text{if } k = 0, 1, \ldots, v-1 \\ [y_d(t_k), \ldots, y_d(t_{k-v+1})], & \text{if } k \geq v, \end{cases}$$

$$\mathcal{F}(u_d^*(x_d(t_k))) := \begin{cases} [u_d(t_{k-1}), \ldots, u_d(t_0)], & \text{if } k = 0, 1, \ldots, v-1 \\ [u_d(t_{k-1}), \ldots, u_d(t_{k-v+1})], & \text{if } k \geq v. \end{cases}$$

Now, writing down the transition structure of the discrete abstraction is trivial: $(x_d^{(i)}, u_d^{(j)}, x_d^{(k)})$ is a transition iff there exists a $y_d^{(l)} \in Y_d$ such that

$$y_d^*(x_d^{(k)}) = \left[y_d^{(l)}, \mathcal{F}(y_d^*(x_d^{(i)})) \right],$$

$$u_d^*(x_d^{(k)}) = \left[u_d^{(j)}, \mathcal{F}(u_d^*(x_d^{(i)})) \right].$$

$x_d^{(i)}$ and $x_d^{(k)}$ are called the exit state and the entrance state of the transition; the input symbol $u_d^{(j)}$ is its transition label. Each state $x_d^{(i)}$ has an associated unique (measured) output, which is simply the leftmost symbol in $y^*(x_d^{(i)})$. Hence, for each nonnegative integer v, we get a finite Moore automaton as a discrete abstraction for the continuous part of the plant. It is clear that in most cases the resulting automata will be nondeterministic: several transitions exiting from a state may carry the same label. This is further explained in Section 3.1 and illustrated in the example below. It is understood that the discrete abstractions evolve on the same sampling grid as the underlying continuous system: the time needed for a transition is the sampling interval $t_{i+1} - t_i$. In case one wants to avoid this implicit notion of time and prefers to introduce explicit time, the transition structure of the automaton can be augmented by a simple clock process. It introduces a `tick` event (representing the passage of one sampling interval), which "separates" the occurrence of any two input symbols. In this case, instead of the state transitions of the Moore-automaton, the `tick` event is synchronized with an external clock. The overall (explicitly timed) discrete approximation is then simply the synchronous composition of the automaton and the clock.

Example 1. Suppose, we are dealing with a system with two measurement symbols ($\gamma = 2$) and two input symbols ($\alpha = 2$). Let $v = 1$. Then, we have $\bar{N}_v = 2 + 2^2 2 = 10$ as upper bound for the number of states in the approximating automaton. Suppose furthermore that only $N_v = 8$ of them turn out to be compatible with the underlying continuous model and its disturbance assumptions. This is characterized by the fact that 8 out of 10 different systems (8) – (12) have a non-empty set of solutions. Hence, the discrete approximation has a minimal realization with 8 states, which, in this example, are assumed to be:

$$x_d^{(1)} := [y_d^{(1)}]$$
$$x_d^{(2)} := [y_d^{(2)}]$$
$$x_d^{(3)} := [[y_d^{(1)}, y_d^{(1)}], u_d^{(1)}]$$
$$x_d^{(4)} := [[y_d^{(1)}, y_d^{(1)}], u_d^{(2)}]$$
$$x_d^{(5)} := [[y_d^{(1)}, y_d^{(2)}], u_d^{(2)}]$$
$$x_d^{(6)} := [[y_d^{(2)}, y_d^{(1)}], u_d^{(1)}]$$
$$x_d^{(7)} := [[y_d^{(2)}, y_d^{(2)}], u_d^{(1)}]$$
$$x_d^{(8)} := [[y_d^{(2)}, y_d^{(2)}], u_d^{(2)}]$$

Then, the (Moore) transition structure follows by inspection. It is shown in the left part of Fig. 2. Initial states are shaded; states which produce a $y_d^{(1)}$-output are shown as squares, states generating a $y_d^{(2)}$-symbol as circles. $u_d^{(1)}$-transitions are drawn as solid lines, $u_d^{(2)}$-transitions as dashed lines. The same conventions are used for the clock in the right part of Fig. 2: the initial state is shaded; $u_d^{(1)}$-

and $u_d^{(2)}$-transitions are represented by a solid and a dashed line, respectively, and the `tick` event by a dotted line.

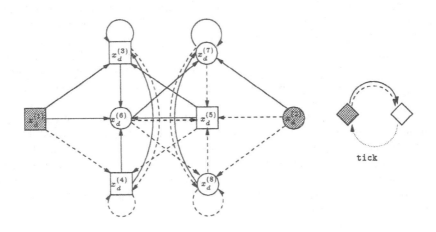

Fig. 2. Moore transition structure (left) and clock (right).

3.1 Discrete Abstractions as Observers for the Continuous Plant State

By construction, X_d, the state set of the discrete abstraction, contains only elements (i.e. strings of input and measurement symbols) which are compatible with (1), (3) and the assumptions on the unknown disturbance signal w. In other words, $x_d^{(j)}$ is an element in X_d if and only if there exists a $x(t_{\max(k-v,0)}) \in \mathbb{R}^n$ and $w(t_i) \in \mathbb{R}^r$, $\|w(t_i)\|_\infty \leq 1$, $i = \max(k-v,0), \ldots, k-1$, such that applying the input sequence $u_d^*(x_d^{(j)})$ produces the string $y_d^*(x_d^{(j)})$ of measurement symbols. This implies that the set of continuous states $x(t_k) \in \mathbb{R}^n$ which are compatible with the continuous plant equations, the disturbance assumptions and the strings of input and measurement symbols embodied in $x_d^{(j)}$ is non-empty. Such a (non-empty) set will be denoted by $X(x_d^{(j)})$, $j = 1, \ldots, N_v$, and it can be interpreted as a set-valued estimate of the underlying continuous plant state based on the (observed) input and measurement strings collected in $x_d^{(j)}$. In fact, the set $X(x_d^{(j)})$ is just the projection of the solution set $[x', w'_{j_1}, \ldots, w'_{j_\rho}]'$ of (8) – (12) onto its first n components. For the special case described in Appendix A, these sets are polyhedra in $\mathbb{R}^n$.

Hence, if we want a discrete abstraction to act as an observer for the continuous part of the plant, we run both systems in parallel (Fig. 3); the continuous part of the plant is fed with a string of input symbols and responds with a string of measurement symbols. Both $u_d(t_k)$ and $y_d(t_k)$ are provided as inputs for the discrete abstraction; these signals uniquely determine its current state $x_d(t_k) \in X_d$, and hence the set $X(x_d(t_k))$ – the estimate for $x(t_k)$.

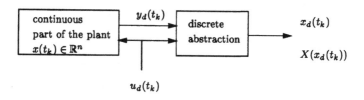

$$u_d(t_k)$$

Fig. 3. Discrete abstraction acting as observer for the continuous part of the plant.

Clearly, $\bigcup_{j=1}^{N_v} X(x_d^{(j)}) = \mathbb{R}^n$, and, in general, $X(x_d^{(i)}) \cap X(x_d^{(j)}) \neq \emptyset$. Hence, the sets $X(x_d^{(j)})$ form a *cover* of the continuous plant state set. Intuitively, the smaller the sets $X(x_d^{(j)})$, the more accurate the discrete approximation (the notion of accuracy will be made precise in the next sections). Obviously, a state set $X(x_d^{(j)})$ never increases (and, in general, decreases) in "size", if the input and measurement strings embodied in $x_d^{(j)}$ are extended further into the past – this is an immediate consequence of the "triangular" structure of (8) – (12). Increasing v, the maximum length of strings, is therefore equivalent to generating a finer "granularity" for the finite cover of $\mathbb{R}^n$ – the nonnegative integer v can be seen as a design parameter, which may be used to improve the accuracy of the discrete model. This of course implies that the number of states, and hence the complexity of the discrete model, also increases.

This mental picture is also helpful for understanding the intrinsic nondeterminism of discrete abstractions: if there were no unknown disturbances, a (known) input $u_d(t_k)$ would drive the state of the continuous part of the plant from $x(t_k)$ into a unique successor state $x(t_{k+1})$. A state $x_d(t_k) = x_d^{(i)}$ of the discrete abstraction, however, corresponds to a *set* $X(x_d^{(i)}) \subset \mathbb{R}^n$. An input $u_d(t_k) = u_d^{(j)}$ then maps this set onto another set. Only for very special continuous models[5] (1), (3), will the latter be contained in exactly one $X(x_d^{(k)})$ and not intersect any $X(x_d^{(l)})$, $l \neq k$, i.e. only in exceptional cases will the discrete state $x_d(t_k) = x_d^{(i)}$ have a unique successor state $x_d(t_{k+1}) = x_d^{(k)}$ under input $u_d^{(j)}$. Existence of unknown disturbances in the "base" model merely increases the "level of nondeterminism" in its discrete abstraction.

---

[5] Necessary and sufficient conditions in the autonomous, linear and time-invariant case $x(t_{k+1}) = Ax(t_k)$, $y(t_k) = x(t_k)$, $v = 0$, have been given in [9]. They imply that the matrix A has to be diagonal (up to permutation) and impose severe restrictions on its eigenvalues.

3.2 Discrete Abstractions with Measurement and Output Symbols

Up to now, our discrete abstractions do not reflect one important aspect of the continuous "base system": the latter is equipped with a symbolic "external" output z_d, which is used to express design specifications. Clearly, if controller synthesis is to be based on discrete abstractions instead of the continuous "base model", we also have to provide them with z_d-outputs. But this is easy: recall that each state $x_d^{(i)}$ in a discrete abstraction corresponds to a set $X(x_d^{(i)})$ of continuous states, and simply define a symbol $z_d^{(j)}$ to be an output of state $x_d^{(i)}$, if $X(x_d^{(i)})$ intersects the "z_d-cell" $\{\zeta \in \mathbb{R}^n \mid z_d^{(j)} = q_z(\zeta)\}$. Note that $X(x_d^{(i)})$ can intersect several "z_d-cells", hence a state $x_d^{(i)}$ can be associated with a (non-empty) set of possible output symbols $z_d^{(j)}$; the interpretation is that the automaton, when in state $x_d^{(i)}$, will generate an output symbol from the appropriate subset of Z_d, but we don't know which one. Therefore, an approximating automaton is equipped with a measurement map from X_d onto Y_d (generating a unique measurement symbol $y_d^{(k)}$ for each state) and an output map from X_d into 2^{Z_d} (the power set of Z_d). To decide whether an output symbol $z_d^{(j)}$ should be attached to a particular state $x_d^{(i)}$, simply add

$$z_d^{(j)} = q_z(x) \tag{14}$$

to (8) – (12): if a string of input and measurement symbols has passed the test for being an element in X_d, i.e. if there exists a non-empty set of solutions $[x', w'_{j_1}, \ldots, w'_{j_\rho}]'$ to (8) – (12), one checks whether at least one of these solutions also satisfies (14) (i.e. whether the extended system (8) – (12),(14) also has a solution). If so, we attach the output symbol $z_d^{(j)}$ to the discrete state corresponding to the considered strings of input and measurement symbols.

4 Behaviours

Let $T \subset \mathbb{R}$ be the chosen sampling grid, i.e. $T = \{t_0, t_1, \ldots\}$. Denote the set of all functions from T into $(Y_d \times U_d \times Z_d)$ by $(Y_d \times U_d \times Z_d)^T$. The continuous "base" model is denoted by M, the discrete abstraction corresponding to parameter v by A_v (recall that the nonnegative integer v parametrizes the set of abstractions obtained in the previous section). Then, the behaviours $\mathcal{B}(M) \subseteq (Y_d \times U_d \times Z_d)^T$ and $\mathcal{B}(A_v) \subseteq (Y_d \times U_d \times Z_d)^T$ are the sets of input/output/measurement signals which are compatible with the the continuous model (1) – (3) and its discrete abstraction A_v. For a survey on "behavioural" systems theory see [19].

Clearly, a *conditio sine qua non* for any discrete abstraction is that its behaviour $\mathcal{B}(A_v)$ must contain the discrete-time behaviour $\mathcal{B}(M)$ of the underlying continuous model: $\mathcal{B}(M) \subseteq \mathcal{B}(A_v)$ implies that every sequence of input/output/measurement symbols that the continuous part of the plant model can generate, can also be produced by the discrete approximation. If this condition were violated, the continuous system could respond to a given input signal with an unacceptable output or measurement signal which would not be predictable by the discrete approximation. Hence, this unacceptable phenomenon could not be suppressed by a control strategy based on the discrete approximation – the approximation would be useless for the purposes of control systems design. Hence, we have to show that, for the abstraction scheme proposed in the previous section, the inclusion $B(M) \subseteq B(A_v)$ holds for all non-negative integers v, i.e. for all models in the abstraction set. This will we be done in the next section.

If $B(M) \subseteq B(A_v)$ holds, the "size" of the difference $B(A_v) \setminus B(M)$ is an indicator for the accuracy of the discrete approximation: the "smaller" $B(A_v) \setminus B(M)$, the smaller the loss in "prediction power" when replacing the continuous model by its discrete abstraction. Equality of the two sets $B(M)$, $B(A_v)$ would imply that the discrete abstraction (which, by construction, is always finite-state) and the underlying continuous model (by definition infinite-state) exhibit exactly the same behaviour on the chosen sampling grid. In other words, the continuous model could be reduced to a discrete one without any loss of accuracy.

5 Ordering and Approximation Accuracy

The issue of approximation accuracy will now be formalized and investigated in terms of model behaviours. Recall that $B(M)$ has been defined as the behaviour of the continuous part of the plant model, and $B(A_v)$ as the behaviour of the discrete abstraction A_v, $v = 0, 1, \dots$. Abstraction A_{v_i} is called "at least as accurate" (or, in *Willems'* terminology, "at least as powerful") as abstraction A_{v_j} if $B(A_{v_i}) \subseteq B(A_{v_j})$ – it predicts the future behaviour at least as precisely. Although not very surprising, the following property (illustrated in Fig. 4) is important:

Property 1 *In terms of accuracy, the continuous "base" model M and its discrete abstractions A_v, $v = 0, 1, \dots$, form a totally ordered set:*

$$B(M) \subseteq B(A_{v_i}) \subseteq B(A_{v_j}); \quad v_i, v_j = 0, 1, \dots; \quad v_i \geq v_j.$$

Proof. We need the following additional notation:

$$T_k := \{t_0, \dots, t_k\},$$
$$T_{k+} := \{t_{k+1}, t_{k+2}, \dots, \},$$
$$B_k(M) := \{b_k \in (U_d \times Y_d \times Z_d)^{T_k} \mid \exists b_{k+} \in (U_d \times Y_d \times Z_d)^{T_{k+1}} \text{ such that }$$
$$[b_k, b_{k+}] \in B(M)\} ,$$
$$B_k(A_v) := \{b_k \in (U_d \times Y_d \times Z_d)^{T_k} \mid \exists b_{k+} \in (U_d \times Y_d \times Z_d)^{T_{k+1}} \text{ such that }$$
$$[b_k, b_{k+}] \in B(A_v)\} .$$

The proof is by induction:

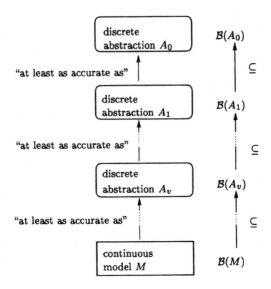

Fig. 4. Continuous "base" model and discrete abstractions form a totally ordered set.

1. The induction basis

$$\mathcal{B}_0(M) \subseteq \mathcal{B}_0(A_{v_i}) \subseteq \mathcal{B}_0(A_{v_j}); \quad v_i, v_j = 0, 1, \dots ; \; v_i \geq v_j, \qquad (15)$$

is trivially true: there are no restrictions regarding the initial state of the continuous model M; hence, at time t_0, M can generate any measurement symbol in Y_d and any output symbol in Z_d. The set of possible initial states for all abstractions A_{v_i}, A_{v_j} is Y_d (see Section 3); therefore these models can also generate any $y_d^{(j)} \in Y_d$ at time t_0. The sets of continuous states compatible with an initial state $y_d^{(j)}$ of an abstraction are the "y_d-cells" $\{\zeta \in \mathbb{R}^n \mid y_d^{(j)} = q_y(\zeta)\}$. As their union is all of $\mathbb{R}^n$, any z_d-cell is intersected by at least one of the y_d-cells; hence any of the abstractions A_{v_i}, A_{v_j} can generate any output symbol z_d at time t_0. Finally, u_d is an input for both the continuous model and its discrete abstractions, therefore the same input symbols $u_d^{(k)} \in U_d$ can occur at time t_0 for all the models under consideration. This shows that $\mathcal{B}_0(M) = \mathcal{B}_0(A_{v_i}) = \mathcal{B}_0(A_{v_i})$; hence (15) holds.

2. Assume

$$\mathcal{B}_{k-1}(M) \subseteq \mathcal{B}_{k-1}(A_{v_i}) \subseteq \mathcal{B}_{k-1}(A_{v_j}), \quad v_i, v_j = 0, 1, \dots, \quad v_i \geq v_j.$$

Pick any element $b_{k-1} \in \mathcal{B}_{k-1}(M)$. Then we need to show that for any such b_{k-1} and any "extension" $(u_d(t_k), y_d(t_k), z_d(t_k)) \in (U_d \times Y_d \times Z_d)$, the following implications hold:

$$[b_{k-1}, (u_d(t_k), y_d(t_k), z_d(t_k))] \in \mathcal{B}_k(M)$$
$$\Rightarrow [b_{k-1}, (u_d(t_k), y_d(t_k), z_d(t_k))] \in \mathcal{B}_k(A_{v_i}) \tag{16}$$
$$\Rightarrow [b_{k-1}, (u_d(t_k), y_d(t_k), z_d(t_k))] \in \mathcal{B}_k(A_{v_j}), \quad v_i \geq v_j. \tag{17}$$

By definition, the same input signal can be applied to all the models. Therefore, extension of b_{k-1} by $u_d(t_k) \in U_d$ does not jeopardize either of the implications, and (16) and (17) need only be shown with respect to the measurement symbol $y_d(t_k)$ and the output symbol $z_d(t_k)$. Recall that the three statements in (16) and (17) are equivalent to saying that

$$z_d(t_k) = q_z(x)$$
$$y_d(t_k) = q_y(x)$$
$$y_d(t_{k-1}) = q_y\left(\tilde{f}_{k-1}^{-1}(x, w_{k-1})\right)$$
$$\vdots$$
$$y_d(t_\rho) = q_y\left(\tilde{f}_\rho^{-1} \ldots \left(\tilde{f}_{k-1}^{-1}(x, w_{k-1}), \ldots \right.\right.$$
$$\left.\left. \ldots, w_\rho)\right)\right)$$

subject to

$$\|w_l\|_\infty \leq 1, \quad l = \rho \ldots k-1.$$

has a nonempty solution set for $[x', w'_{k-1}, \ldots, w'_\rho]'$, where either
- $\rho = 0$ for the statement on the left hand side of (16) – all symbols going back to time t_0 have to be compatible with the continuous model,
- $\rho = \max(k - v_i, 0)$ for the statement on the right hand side of (16) – all symbols going back to time $t_{\max(k-v_i,0)}$ have to be compatible with the continuous model, or
- $\rho = \max(k - v_j, 0)$ for the statement on the right hand side of (17) – all symbols going back to time $t_{\max(k-v_j,0)}$ have to be compatible with the continuous model.

Clearly, $0 \leq \max(k - v_i, 0) \leq \max(k - v_j, 0)$ for $v_i \geq v_j$. Because of the "triangular" structure in the above set of equations and inequalities, increasing ρ is equivalent to omitting a number of restraints. Hence, if the solution set is non-empty for $\rho = 0$, it will also be non-empty for $\rho = \max(k - v_i, 0)$. If it is non-empty for $\rho = \max(k - v_i, 0)$, it is also non-empty for $\rho = \max(k - v_j, 0)$. This shows that (16) and (17) hold and concludes the proof. $\square$

5.1 Interaction with a Discrete System

Up to now, we have only investigated how to find discrete approximations A_v, $v = 0, 1, \ldots$, for the continuous part of the plant model, M. Now, we want to show that the automata A_v, $v = 0, 1, \ldots$, when connected to the discrete part of the plant model, D, form a totally ordered set of discrete abstractions for the hybrid "base system" (1) – (6). In other words, we want to show that the order in Property 1 remains invariant when the continuous model part M and its abstractions A_v are connected to the discrete system D. The "base system" (D interacting with M) is denoted by DM, its abstractions (D interacting with A_v) by DA_v, $v = 0, 1, \ldots$.

On the level of behaviours, connecting two systems essentially means intersecting their behaviour sets [19]. There is a (minor) complication, when the systems under consideration don't "live" on the same signal set. Then, an inverse projection has to be introduced to provide suitable extension of system behaviours. In our case, M and its abstractions "live" on $(U_d \times Y_d \times Z_d)^T$, whereas the discrete plant component "lives" on $(\tilde{U}_d \times Y_d \times U_d)^T$ (see Fig. 1). Define

$$\mathrm{Proj}_{\tilde{U}_d}^{-1}(\mathcal{B}(M)) := \{(u_d, y_d, z_d, \tilde{u}_d) \mid (u_d, y_d, z_d) \in \mathcal{B}(M)\},$$

$$\mathrm{Proj}_{\tilde{U}_d}^{-1}(\mathcal{B}(A_v)) := \{(u_d, y_d, z_d, \tilde{u}_d) \mid (u_d, y_d, z_d) \in \mathcal{B}(A_v)\},$$

$$\mathrm{Proj}_{Z_d}^{-1}(\mathcal{B}(D)) := \{(u_d, y_d, z_d, \tilde{u}_d) \mid (\tilde{u}_d, y_d, u_d) \in \mathcal{B}(D)\}.$$

Then,

$$\mathcal{B}(DM) := \mathrm{Proj}_{\tilde{U}_d}^{-1}(\mathcal{B}(M)) \cap \mathrm{Proj}_{Z_d}^{-1}(\mathcal{B}(D)), \tag{18}$$

$$\mathcal{B}(DA_v) := \mathrm{Proj}_{\tilde{U}_d}^{-1}(\mathcal{B}(A_v)) \cap \mathrm{Proj}_{Z_d}^{-1}(\mathcal{B}(D)). \tag{19}$$

It is obvious that neither inverse projection ($\mathrm{Proj}_{\tilde{U}_d}^{-1}$) nor intersection with another set ($\mathrm{Proj}_{Z_d}^{-1}(\mathcal{B}(D))$) affects the order in Property 1. Hence, we have the following:

Property 2 *The order $\subseteq$ in Property 1 is invariant under interaction with a discrete dynamical system D:*

$$\mathcal{B}(DM) \subseteq \mathcal{B}(DA_{v_i}) \subseteq \mathcal{B}(DA_{v_j}); \ v_i, v_j = 0, 1, \ldots; \ v_i \geq v_j. \tag{20}$$

5.2 Ordering under Feedback

Suppose we have come up with a (family of) discrete abstraction(s) for the continuous part of the plant, and by implication, with a (totally ordered set of) discrete approximation(s) for the hybrid plant (1) - (6). Then, we design feedback control on the basis of such an approximation. In the present context, it does not matter whether control is interpreted in the "traditional" sense (i.e. the control mechanism uniquely determines the next value of the control input $\tilde{u}_d(t_k)$), or in the sense of "supervisory control"[6]. If the design is any good, the supervised

---

[6] The term "supervisory control" is from DES (discrete event systems) control theory. It refers to the situation where feedback does *not* uniquely define the next control input, but merely narrows the choice to a subset of $\tilde{U}_d$. Hence, it is more general than the traditional notion of feedback: past and present measurement information are not mapped into $\tilde{U}_d$, but the power set of $\tilde{U}_d$. See the standard reference [17] for more details.

abstraction satisfies the specifications, i.e. it is guaranteed to exhibit a certain "desired" behaviour and to avoid certain "forbidden" patterns. In terms of its behaviour, $\mathcal{B}(DA_vS)$ (the "S" indicates that the model DA_v is under supervision), this can be written as: $\mathcal{B}(DA_vS) \subseteq \mathcal{B}_{\text{desired}}$ and $\mathcal{B}(DA_vS) \cap \mathcal{B}_{\text{forbidden}} = \emptyset$. Does the hybrid "base" system, when subjected to the *same* control law, also satisfy the specifications, i.e. does $\mathcal{B}(DMS) \subseteq \mathcal{B}_{\text{desired}}$ and $\mathcal{B}(DMS) \cap \mathcal{B}_{\text{forbidden}} = \emptyset$ hold? Or, in other words, does it make sense to base the design of symbolic feedback controllers for continuous or hybrid systems on a discrete approximation? As feedback is just a special case of interaction with another system, the answer is obvious: Property 3 (illustrated in Fig. 5) follows immediately from Property 2:

Property 3 *Suppose both the hybrid system DM (1) - (6) and its discrete abstractions DA_v are subject to the same feedback law. Then, their supervised behaviours are ordered in the following sense:*

$$\mathcal{B}(DMS) \subseteq \mathcal{B}(DA_{v_i}S) \subseteq \mathcal{B}(DA_{v_j}S), \ v_i, v_j = 0, 1, \ldots, \ v_i \geq v_j.$$

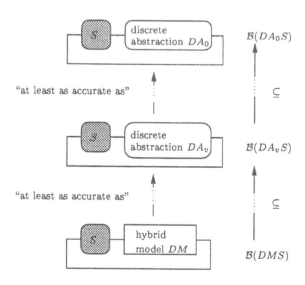

Fig. 5. Ordering is invariant under feedback.

6 Conclusions

In this contribution, a hierarchy of discrete abstractions for a continuous system has been proposed. It has been shown that the continuous "base" system and its discrete abstractions form a totally ordered set of models, where ordering is in the sense of set inclusion of model behaviours or, equivalently, in the sense of model accuracy. The ordering has been shown to be invariant under interaction with a given discrete dynamical system. This implies that abstractions of a hybrid system (consisting of abstractions of the continuous part interacting with the discrete system component) are ordered in the same way as abstractions of the continuous part. Another implication is that the ordering is invariant under feedback. Hence, any feedback law that forces *any* model in the proposed set of abstractions to obey a given set of specifications, will also guarantee that the hybrid "base" system meets the specifications. In other words: the design of a discrete (supervisory) feedback structure for a hybrid system can be based on a discrete approximation. Obviously, within the proposed set of discrete models, there exists a uniquely defined "coarsest", or least accurate (and therefore least complex), model which still allows a given set of specifications to be met. This, of course, is the most "economical" model for controller design. An interesting open question is whether this can be found without searching the hierarchy from "the top".

References

1. R. Alur, T. A. Henzinger, and E. D. Sontag, editors. *Hybrid Systems III*, Lecture Notes in Computer Science, Vol. 1066. Springer-Verlag, 1996.
2. P. J. Antsaklis, J. A. Stiver, and M. Lemmon. Hybrid system modelling and autonomous control systems. In [6], pages 366-392.
3. P. Antsaklis, W. Kohn, A. Nerode, and S. Sastry, editors. *Hybrid Systems II*, Lecture Notes in Computer Science, Vol. 999. Springer-Verlag, 1995.
4. P. E. Caines and Y.-J. Wei. On dynamically consistent hybrid systems. In [3].
5. P. E. Caines and Y.-J. Wei. Hierarchical hybrid control systems: a lattice theoretic formulation. 1996. Submitted for publication.
6. R. L. Grossman, A. Nerode, A. P. Ravn, and H. Rischel, editors, *Hybrid Systems*, Lecture Notes in Computer Science, Vol. 736. Springer-Verlag, 1993.
7. T. Kailath, *Linear Systems*. Prentice-Hall, 1980.
8. J. Lunze. Ein Ansatz zur qualitativen Modellierung und Regelung dynamischer Systeme. *at – Automatisierungstechnik*, 41:451–460, 1993.
9. J. Lunze. Qualitative modelling of linear dynamical systems with quantized state measurements. *Automatica*, 30:417–431, 1994.
10. J. Lunze. Stabilization of nonlinear systems by qualitative feedback controllers. *International Journal of Control*, 62:109–128, 1995.
11. G.J. Pappas and S. Sastry. Towards continuous abstractions of dynamical and control systems. Technical Report UCB/ERL M96/53, University of California at Berkeley, October 1996.
12. T. Niinomi, B. H. Krogh, and J. E. R. Cury. Synthesis of Supervisory Controllers for Hybrid Systems Based on Approximating Automata. In *Proc. 34th IEEE Conference on Decision and Control*, 1995.
13. J. Raisch and S. D. O'Young. A DES approach to control of hybrid dynamical systems. In [1], pages 563–574.

14. J. Raisch and S. D. O'Young. Time-driven supervisory control of hybrid dynamical systems. Proc. 5th International Conference on CONTROL'96, IEE, Exeter, UK. 1996, pages 716-721.

15. J. Raisch and S. D. O'Young. Discrete approximation and supervisory control of continuous systems. Report 96-5, Institut für Systemdynamik und Regelungstechnik, Universität Stuttgart, 1996. Submitted for publication.

16. J. Raisch. Nondeterministic automata as approximations for continuous systems – an approach with an adjustable degree of accuracy. Proc. 2nd MATHMOD (International Symposium on Mathematical Modelling), pp. 195–202. IMACS, Vienna, Austria. February 1997.

17. P. J. Ramadge and W. M. Wonham. Supervisory control of a class of discrete event systems. *SIAM J. Control and Optimization*, 25:206–230 1987.

18. J. A. Stiver and P. Antsaklis. Modeling and analysis of hybrid control systems. In *Proc. 31st IEEE Conference on Decision and Control*, 1992.

19. J. C. Willems. Paradigms and puzzles in the theory of dynamical systems. *IEEE Transactions on Automatic Control*, 36:259–294, 1991.

A How to Eliminate Non-reachable States in the State Set of a Discrete Abstraction – Computational Procedure for a Special Case

For the following special case the removal of non-reachable states can be done in a numerically straightforward and reliable way. It is characterized by the fact that the right hand side of (1) is affine in the state $x(t_k)$ and the unknown disturbance vector $w(t_k)$, and the measurement map has the form $q_y = Q_y \circ C_y$, where $C_y : \mathbb{R}^n \to \mathbb{R}^p$ is a linear map, and the "quantizer" $Q_y : \mathbb{R}^p \to Y_d$ partitions $\mathbb{R}^p$ into finitely many rectangular boxes with edges parallel to the coordinate axes:

$$x(t_{k+1}) = a(y_d(t_k), u_d(t_k))x(t_k) + g(y_d(t_k), u_d(t_k)) +$$
$$h(y_d(t_k), u_d(t_k))w(t_k) , \qquad (21)$$
$$y_d(t_k) = Q_y(C_y x(t_k)) . \qquad (22)$$

(21) – (22) is said to be in (nonlinear) observer form[7]: as both $y_d(t_k)$ and $u_d(t_k)$ are known (observed) variables, the quantities $a(y_d(t_k), u_d(t_k))$, $g(y_d(t_k), u_d(t_k))$, and $h(y_d(t_k), u_d(t_k))$ are also known (but time-variant).

Consider the quantization box corresponding to a certain measurement symbol $y_d^{(i)}$. Denote the vectors of its upper and lower bounds by $\hat{y}^{(i)}$ and $\check{y}^{(i)}$, respectively:

$$\check{y}^{(i)} < \{\zeta | Q_y(\zeta) = y_d^{(i)}\} \leq \hat{y}^{(i)},$$

where the "<" and "≤"-signs are understood to be elementwise. Elements of $\hat{y}^{(i)}$ can be $+\infty$; elements of $\check{y}^{(i)}$ may be $-\infty$. In this special case, and for $\rho = 0$, the

---

[7] Not to be confused with observer *canonical* form.

solution of (8) – (12) is trivial. For $\rho \geq 1$, define

$$
\hat{y}_P := \begin{bmatrix} \hat{y}^{(i_1)} \\ \vdots \\ \hat{y}^{(i_\rho)} \end{bmatrix}, \quad
\check{y}_P := \begin{bmatrix} \check{y}^{(i_1)} \\ \vdots \\ \check{y}^{(i_\rho)} \end{bmatrix},
$$

$$
g_P := \begin{bmatrix} g_1 \\ \vdots \\ g_\rho \end{bmatrix}, \quad
w_P := \begin{bmatrix} w_{j_1} \\ \vdots \\ w_{j_\rho} \end{bmatrix},
$$

i.e. collect the "forcing terms" $g_1 := g(y_d^{(i_1)}, u_d^{(k_1)}), \ldots, g_\rho := g(y_d^{(i_\rho)}, u_d^{(k_\rho)})$ in g_P and the (unknown) disturbance inputs $w_{j_1}, \ldots, w_{j_\rho}$ in w_P. 1_r and I_r denote a column vector with ρr "ones" and the (ρr)-dimensional identity matrix. Then, the string of input and measurement symbols, $([y_d^{(i_0)}, \ldots, y_d^{(i_\rho)}], [u_d^{(k_1)}, \ldots, u_d^{(k_\rho)}])$, $1 \leq \rho \leq v$, is compatible with (21) – (22) and the disturbance assumptions (4) (and hence an element in the (minimal) state set of abstraction A_v) if and only if the set of solutions $[x' \ w_P']'$ for the following *linear* inequality is nonempty:

$$
\begin{bmatrix} \check{y}^{(i_0)} \\ \check{y}_P \\ -1_r \end{bmatrix} + \begin{bmatrix} 0 \\ \Phi_{PU} \\ 0 \end{bmatrix} g_P <
\begin{bmatrix} \begin{bmatrix} C_y \\ C_y a_1^{-1} \\ \vdots \\ C_y \prod_{i=1}^{\rho} a_i^{-1} \\ 0 \end{bmatrix} & \begin{matrix} 0 \\ \\ \Phi_{PW} \\ \\ I_r \end{matrix} \end{bmatrix}
\begin{bmatrix} x \\ w_P \end{bmatrix}
$$

$$
\leq \begin{bmatrix} \hat{y}^{(i_0)} \\ \hat{y}_P \\ 1_r \end{bmatrix} + \begin{bmatrix} 0 \\ \Phi_{PU} \\ 0 \end{bmatrix} g_P \tag{23}
$$

where

$$
\Phi_{PU} := \begin{bmatrix}
C_y a_1^{-1} & 0 & \cdots & 0 \\
C_y a_2^{-1} a_1^{-1} & C_y a_2^{-1} & \cdots & 0 \\
\vdots & & \ddots & \vdots \\
C_y \prod_{i=1}^{\rho} a_i^{-1} & \cdots & \cdots & C_y a_\rho^{-1}
\end{bmatrix},
$$

$$
\Phi_{PW} := -\Phi_{PU} \begin{bmatrix}
h_1 & 0 & \cdots & 0 \\
0 & h_2 & \cdots & 0 \\
\vdots & & \ddots & \vdots \\
0 & \cdots & \cdots & h_\rho
\end{bmatrix},
$$

$$
a_l := a(y_d^{(i_l)}, u_d^{(k_l)}), \quad h_l := h(y_d^{(i_l)}, u_d^{(k_l)}), \quad l = 1, \ldots \rho,
$$

and $\prod$ means "left product" (i.e.: $\prod_{i=1}^{\rho} a_i^{-1} = a_\rho^{-1} \ldots a_1^{-1}$). Existence of a solution for this set of inequalities can be checked using the "feasibility part" of any linear programming algorithm.

If a string of input and measurement symbols fails this test, it corresponds to a non-reachable state of the discrete abstraction, and is immediately discarded.

This procedure is repeated for all possible combinations of measurement and input symbols. Hence, this procedure eliminates all non-reachable states and guarantees a minimal state set for the discrete abstraction (it is observable by construction).

Comparing Timed and Hybrid Automata
as Approximations of Continuous Systems

**Olaf Stursberg, Stefan Kowalewski, Ingo Hoffmann
and Jörg Preußig**

Process Control Group (CT-AST), Department of Chemical Engineering,
University of Dortmund, D-44221 Germany
e-mail: {olaf | stefan | ingo | joerg}@ast.chemietechnik.uni-dortmund.de

Abstract. We describe two approaches to derive Timed and Linear
Hybrid Automata from continuous models given as systems of ordinary
differential equations. A semiquantitative modeling method is applied
which yields a qualitative description of the system dynamics and quantitative bounds for the residence times in the discrete states or the state
variable derivatives. We discuss the problem of spurious trajectories and
illustrate the two aproaches by means of a simple process engineering example. Results of a reachability analysis obtained with the tool HyTech
are presented.

1 Introduction

This paper deals with the problem of approximating continuous systems by discrete models which retain some information about the quantitative dynamics
from the original model. In particular, we describe two approximation procedures using Timed or Hybrid Automata, respectively, as the target modeling
framework and compare how these approaches treat a simple process engineering example. The paper is focussed on the application results for this example
and does not present a general theory for the discretization of continuous systems.

The background of this contribution is the problem of formal verification of discrete controllers for technical systems, in particular for plants in the chemical
process industry. Common approaches to this problem are based on a finite state

model of the uncontrolled plant behavior and a compatible model of the given controller, with reachability analysis being applied to the composition of both models [11], [6]. Usually, the modeling framework is untimed (like SMV in [11]). This is sufficient if the continuous dynamics of the plant can be neglected or approximated by purely discrete models and if there are no timers used in the control program. Especially in the case of process control systems this situation is rarely encountered. Instead, often the plant's continuous dynamics determines whether a discrete controller matches the specification or not: E. g., if the emergency cooling of an exothermal chemical reaction is switched on by a discrete controller at a certain temperature, the intrinsic continuous dynamics of the reaction are most important to verify whether this control law will prevent overheating of the reactor. In principle, a description of the controlled plant is *hybrid*, since it combines the continuous dynamics of the plant with the discrete controller. In order to synthesize or to verify a controller, one needs a discrete approximation of the continuous parts of the hybrid system (see Fig. 1). The discrete approximation of the hybrid model should contain precise quantitative and timing information about the possible plant behaviors. On the other hand, the timed discrete model must still be analyzable, in particular, reachability analysis has to be feasible. Therefore, Timed Automata [2] or other decidable subclasses of linear hybrid systems [1] are natural candidates for this application.

Fig. 1. Abstraction from hybrid to timed discrete models

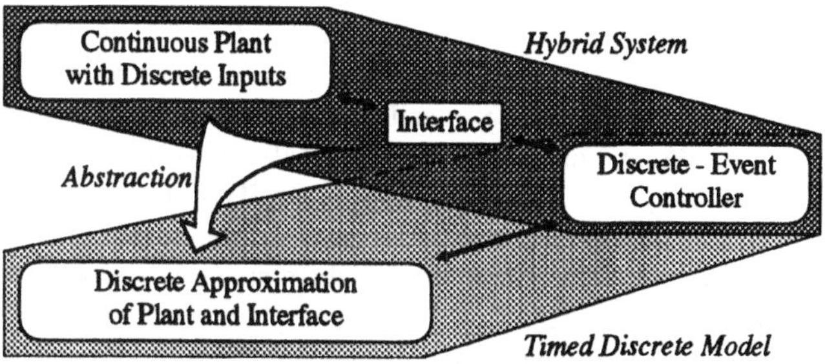

As simulation and model-based optimization are increasingly used in modern process systems' design, continuous models very often already exist when discrete controllers for a process are designed. It is therefore desirable to *derive* discrete models from continuous descriptions instead of creating them from scratch. We will discuss two different approaches to this problem. In both cases, the starting point is a system of first order ordinary, possibly nonlinear differential equations which constitutes the continuous model. We describe a simple approximation method which leads to a so-called *semiquantitative* substitution of the continuous system. The expression *semiquantitative* is chosen to denote that the discrete model represents the system's behavior qualitatively and contains quantitative timing information. The semiquantitative model can be converted into usual types of timed transition systems, as Timed Automata [2], timed condition/event systems [8] and timed Petri nets [16]. For the last paradigm and for the more general model of Linear Hybrid Automata [1], we present a transformation procedure and investigate the quality of the discrete approximations. For this purpose, the real physical behavior of the example plant is compared to the transitions which exist in the discrete models. The amount of physically impossible trajectories contained in the automaton, the so-called *spurious solutions*, are used as an indicator of the inaccuracy of the approximation.

The idea of deriving a discrete model from a continuous one algorithmically is not new. The whole field of *Qualitative Modeling and Simulation* [9] is concerned with the question of how a discrete (= qualitative) description of a physical system can be obtained systematically. However, only rarely quantitative timing information is included in the discrete model. For example, the approaches of Preisig [14], Raisch [15] and Krogh et al [13], or Lunze's derivation of stochastic automata [10] omit quantitative timing information. Antsaklis, Stiver and Lemmon convert continuous behaviors into sequences of discrete symbols by partitioning the continuous state space into common–flow regions and assigning specific symbols to each region [17]. Kokar succeeded in deriving spurious–solution–free discrete models by the so–called Q^2-*Symbolic Reasoning*, where the continuous state space is discretized by the introduction of *hypersurfaces* [7]. The abstraction–procedure presented in this paper differs from these approaches in two regards: First, we retain quantitative information for the residence in the discrete states. Secondly, we consider a box partition of the continuous state space which is given from technical requirements (i. e. sensor positions). Further related work is the one by Henzinger and Wong-Toi [5] who approximate continuous systems given as so-called *Nonlinear* Hybrid Automata by Linear Hybrid Automata (where the the terms *linear* and *nonlinear* do not refer to the differential equations but their solutions). To achieve this, the continuous state space is partitioned into areas with linear borders and limited flow directions. The main difference to the approach presented in this paper is that in the general case a suitable partition has to be found by intuition, whereas our method starts from a basic discretization and yields the approximative dynamics automatically.

The remainder of the paper is organized as follows. In the next section an example taken from the field of chemical engineering, a *two-tank-system*, is described which will be used to illustrate our approach. The principle of modeling continuous systems semiquantitatively is described in Section 3. The following two parts explain the transformation to Timed and Hybrid Automata and give some analysis results obtained with the symbolic model–checking tool HYTECH. Section 6 contains a discussion and an outlook on future research.

2 Example: A Two–Tank System

Our example is a simple two–tank system which is used in a laboratory course for chemical engineering students at the University of Dortmund. Although the process is quite simple, it shows interesting dynamics and has been used as research object for control algorithms before [3]. The plant consists of two tanks which are connected to build a system of two communicating tubes as illustrated in Fig. 2. For the purpose of this example, we choose both tanks to be identical in their geometrical properties. The first tank is fed by an inflow characterized by the parameter k_1 and the inlet stream of the second tank is the outflow of the first one. The stream from tank 1 to tank 2 depends on the difference between the tanks' liquid levels, the geometric properties of the connecting pipe (characterized by parameter k_2) and its height k_3 above the ground of tank 2. The liquid level in this tank and the dimensions of its outlet pipe (characterized by constant k_4) determines the flow out of tank 2. Applying Toricelli's law yields our underlying continuous model:

$$
\begin{pmatrix} \dot{x}_1 \\ \dot{x}_2 \end{pmatrix} = \begin{cases} \begin{pmatrix} k_1 - k_2\sqrt{x_1 - x_2 + k_3} \\ k_2\sqrt{x_1 - x_2 + k_3} - k_4\sqrt{x_2} \end{pmatrix} & \text{if } x_2 > k_3 \\ \begin{pmatrix} k_1 - k_2\sqrt{x_1} \\ k_2\sqrt{x_1} - k_4\sqrt{x_2} \end{pmatrix} & \text{if } x_2 \leq k_3 \end{cases}, \qquad (1)
$$

where $\mathbf{x} = (x_1, x_2)$ denotes the both liquid levels, the states of the model. Equation (1) defines a flow $\dot{\mathbf{x}} = \mathbf{f}(\mathbf{x}, k_1, ..., k_4)$ that moves the system to the equilibrium point $\mathbf{x_s}$ for all $k_i > 0$ and $x_i > 0$. The continuous model changes its structure when the liquid level in the second tank is equal to the height of the connecting pipe. For the sake of simplicity, we omit units (metres for x_1 and x_2, seconds as time unit) in the sequel and choose the parameters $k_2 = k_4 = 1, k_3 = 0.5$ and $k_1 = 0.75$, from which the gradient field shown in Fig. 3 results.

Fig. 2. Scheme of the plant

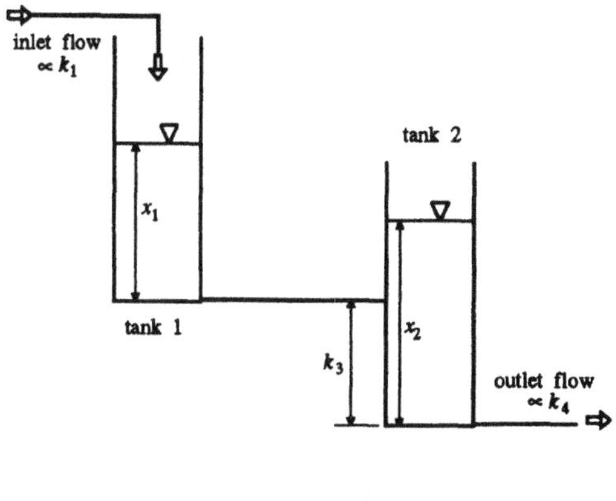

It is usual practice in designing control equipment for such parts in chemical plants, to consider only a few discrete intervals of the process variables. For example, the liquid level within a reactor can be partitioned into the states *low*, *normal*, *high* and *critical* and only the information about transitions between these states is obtained from discrete level sensors and delivered to the controller. In continuous operation, an appropriate control target could be to avoid that the liquid levels will ever reach the states *low* or *critical*. Following this philosophy and restricting the analysis to the sector of the continuous state space which is depicted in Fig. 3, we divide the ranges of the both process variables (x_1, x_2) in four and three states, respectively:

$$x_1 : \quad \{[0.45, 0.55[, [0.55, 0.6[, [0.6, 0.7[, [0.7, 0.8]\} \tag{2}$$
$$x_2 : \quad \{[0.45, 0.5[, [0.5, 0.6[, [0.6, 0.65]\},$$

Obviously, the introduction of discrete intervals for each state variable results in a *hyperbox* partition of the state space [7]. It is important for the procedure described in the sequel that one box boundary corresponds to the x_2-value at which the structural change in Eq. (1) occurs. Although, the system constitutes a simple autonomous dynamical system when the parameter k_1 is constant (it depends on the position of the input valve), it is sufficient to demonstrate the principle of our modeling method.

Fig. 3. Gradient field for the chosen parametrization

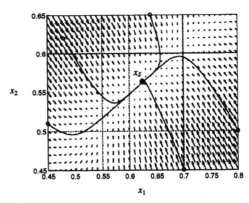

The dynamic behavior of the tank system can be understood from the vector field respectively the trajectories ending in the steady state $x_s = (0.625, 0.563)$. The inserted mesh corresponds to the state space partition determined by sensor positions.

3   Semiquantitative modeling of continuous physical systems

In deriving discrete from continuous models, a crucial step is to decide which level of abstraction is chosen, i. e. how much of the information contained in the continuous system is included in the discrete analogon. The starting point of our considerations is a state space representation of the continuous system in terms of a set of ordinary differential equations (in minimal realization):

$$\dot{\mathbf{x}}(t) = \frac{d\mathbf{x}(t)}{dt} = \mathbf{f}\left(\mathbf{x}(t), \mathbf{u}(t)\right), \quad x \in \mathbf{X}, \quad \dim(\mathbf{X}) = n \in \mathbb{N} \tag{3}$$

where $\mathbf{x}$ and $\mathbf{u}$ denote the state vector and the vector of inputs. The derivative $\mathbf{f}(\bullet)$ is continuously defined in (a subspace of) the n–dimensional state space $\mathbf{X}$. We restrict the following considerations to the case of a constant input vector $\mathbf{u}$. An approach on a low level of abstraction is to generate a discrete model by integrating Eq. (3) and to combine continuous trajectories with similar characteristics to sequences of discrete states (see e. g. [17]). Here, we describe a method on a higher abstraction level: The system's behavior is approximated by investigating the gradient field given by Eq. (3). Inside boxlike sectors of the state space, intervals for the flow $\dot{\mathbf{x}}$ are determined. Doing so, we abstract from the exact description and adopt a more qualitative point of view, this is why we call it a semiquantitative model.

As pointed out in Sec. (2) for the two-tank example, an initial partition of the continuous state space is often determined by the process itself, the instrumentation or the control specification. To formalize this partition, we introduce an ordered set of landmarks for each state variable: $L_j = \{l_{j,0}, \ldots, l_{j,p_j}\}, \forall j = \{1, \ldots, n\}$, where the j-th component p_j of $\mathbf{p}$ denotes the number of landmarks for x_j. A landmark $l_{j,r}, r \in \{1, \ldots, p_j\}$ represents the boundary between adjacent intervals which correspond to the technically relevant states (*low, normal,* ...) of x_j. We define a mapping $\mathrm{D} : \mathbf{X} \to \{1, \ldots, p_1\} \times \ldots \times \{1, \ldots, p_n\}$ that divides the continuous state space into a set of $\pi = p_1 \cdot \ldots \cdot p_n$ partition elements. It generates an index vector $\mathbf{d} = \{d_1, \ldots, d_n\}$ which specifies an element of the partition by containing the number of the corresponding interval of x_j:

$$d_j = \mathrm{D}(\mathbf{x}_j) = \begin{cases} k & \text{if } x_j \in [l_{k-1}, l_k[, k \in \{1, \ldots, l_{p_j-1}\} \\ p_j & \text{if } x_j \in [l_{p_j-1}, l_{p_j}] \end{cases} . \tag{4}$$

The index vector is the label of a cell of the state space $\mathbf{X}$. Denoting such a cell by $^{\mathrm{D}}\mathbf{x}$, we obtain a partitioned state space with hyberbox structure:

$$^{\mathrm{D}}\mathbf{X} = \{^{\mathrm{D}}\mathbf{x}_1, \ldots, {}^{\mathrm{D}}\mathbf{x}_\pi\}. \tag{5}$$

When substituting the continuous state vector $\mathbf{x}$ by a discretized version $^{\mathrm{D}}\mathbf{x}$, Eq. (3) has to be replaced by an interval–arithmetical expression of the form:

$$^{\mathrm{D}}\dot{\mathbf{x}} = \Psi\left(^{\mathrm{D}}\mathbf{x}\right) = \left(\psi_1\left(^{\mathrm{D}}\mathbf{x}\right), \ldots, \psi_n\left(^{\mathrm{D}}\mathbf{x}\right)\right), \tag{6}$$

in the case of an autonomous system. In this formula, $^D\dot{\mathbf{x}}$ does not define a partition of the gradient field but denotes the range of $\dot{\mathbf{x}}$ in the boxes. It is necessary to insert landmarks $l_{j,r}$ in $\mathbf{X}$ at values of x_j at which structural changes of $\mathbf{f}$ occur, i. e. at $x_2 = 0.5$ for the two-tank example. (We omit here the investigation of structural changes depending on more than one state variable and of jumps between non-connected subspaces of $\mathbf{X}$.)

We will use the elements of $^D\mathbf{X}$ as the states of a discrete transition system (see below). Hence, the next step is to determine which transitions between two discrete states $\mathbf{d}_a$ and $\mathbf{d}_b, a, b \in \{1, \ldots \pi\}$ are possible. These states are called *adjacent*, if their index vectors differ in only one component: $\exists_1 k \in \{1, \ldots, n\}$: $d_{b,k} = d_{a,k} \pm 1, \forall l \in \{1, \ldots, n\} \neq k : d_{b,l} = d_{a,l}$. We call single transitions starting in $\mathbf{d}_a$ *elementary transitions* since these represent the elements from which trajectories in the discrete model are composed. Two types of transitions can be distinguished: An elementary transition $\phi_{\mathbf{d}_a \to \mathbf{d}_b}$ describing an actual transition between two adjacent cells $^D\mathbf{x}_a, ^D\mathbf{x}_b \in ^D\mathbf{X}$, denoted by their index vectors $\mathbf{d}_a$ and $\mathbf{d}_b$, exists if:

$$\exists \mathbf{x} \in \partial_{\mathbf{d}_a, \mathbf{d}_b} : {}^D\dot{x}_k(\mathbf{x}) \gtrless 0, \quad d_b(k) = d_a(k) \pm 1 \quad k = \{1, \ldots, n\}, \tag{7}$$

where $\partial_{\mathbf{d}_a, \mathbf{d}_b}$ denotes the boundary separating $^D\mathbf{x}_a$ and $^D\mathbf{x}_b$. Note that from the definition of adjacent cells, transitions can only occur in the direction of one coordinate, i. e. diagonal transitions are not possible. Such transitions are represented as sequences of $1, \ldots, n$ elementary transitions.

An elementary transition $\phi_{\mathbf{d}_a \to \mathbf{d}_a}$ which describes that the state remains inside cell $^D\mathbf{x}_a$ (*self-loop transition*) exists if in the continuous model, the trajectory does not leave the cell for a constant $\mathbf{u}$ after reaching it. This occurs if either a steady state ($\dot{\mathbf{x}} = 0$) or an attractor lies inside of $^D\mathbf{x}_a$. To illustrate the determination of elementary transitions, Fig. 4 shows the procedure for the cell $^D\mathbf{x}_9$, which corresponds to $\mathbf{d} = (1, 3)$, of the two–tank example: Since a flow out of $^D\mathbf{x}_9$ exists across the right and across the lower border, the transitions $\phi_{(1,3)\to(2,3)}$ and $\phi_{(1,3)\to(1,2)}$ are inserted into Φ as elementary transitions from this state.

Technically, the procedure is realized by introducing a subgrid in the partitioned state space with a meshsize chosen sufficiently fine to allow the detection of characteristic changes of the gradient field. In our example, we chose at least 5 gridpoints on all boundaries of each cell. For each of these gridpoints, the sign of the $^D\dot{\mathbf{x}}$–component with orthogonal orientation to the state boundary is evaluated. If a transition out of the cell $^D\mathbf{x}_a$ is possible, the elementary transition $\phi_{\mathbf{d}_a \to \mathbf{d}_b}$ is inserted into the set Φ.

To generate *timed* discrete models, we calculate lower and upper bounds for the *residence time* in the cell $^D\mathbf{x}_a$. Since the distance to $\partial_{\mathbf{d}_a, \mathbf{d}_b}$ and the components of the gradient are intervals, we define a *residence time interval* $\Delta t_{\phi_{\mathbf{d}_a \to \mathbf{d}_b}}$ as

Fig. 4. Elementary transitions for the state denoted by $d = (1,3)$

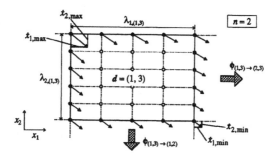

conservative estimation of the time the systems needs to leave $^D\mathbf{x}_a$. Its lower bound is always zero because the corresponding continuous trajectory within $^D\mathbf{x}_a$ may start infinitesimally close to $\partial_{\mathbf{d}_a,\mathbf{d}_b}$. The upper bound follows from dividing the length $\lambda_{\mathbf{d}_a,k}$ in direction k of the elementary transition $\phi_{\mathbf{d}_a \to \mathbf{d}_b}$ by the minimum value of the gradient in this direction $^D\dot{\mathbf{x}}_{a,min}$. For a self-loop elementary transition $\phi_{\mathbf{d}_a \to \mathbf{d}_a}$, the residence time is arbitrary unless $\mathbf{u}$ changes:

$$\Delta t_{\phi_{\mathbf{d}_a \to \mathbf{d}_b},min} = 0, \quad \Delta t_{\phi_{\mathbf{d}_a \to \mathbf{d}_b},max} = \frac{\lambda_{\mathbf{d}_a,k}}{^D\dot{\mathbf{x}}_{a,min}}, \tag{8}$$

$$\Delta t_{\phi_{\mathbf{d}_a \to \mathbf{d}_a}} = [0, \infty[. \tag{9}$$

For an implementation of the calculation of $\Delta t_{\phi_{\mathbf{d}_a \to \mathbf{d}_b}}$, $^D\dot{\mathbf{x}}_{a,min}$ is evaluated for all gridpoints within the box $^D\mathbf{x}_{\mathbf{d}_a}$. A procedure to determine elementary transitions including residence times has been implemented for one– and two–dimensional systems using the Tool MATLAB.

By modeling a given continuous system using the described semiquantitative method, we generate a *timed transition system*, where the partitioned state space $^D\mathbf{X}$ is the set of states S, the elementary transitions $\phi_{\mathbf{d}_a \to \mathbf{d}_b}$, $\phi_{\mathbf{d}_a \to \mathbf{d}_a}$ are the edges of the transition system, the residence times $\Delta t_{\phi_{\mathbf{d}_a \to \mathbf{d}_b}}$ are introduced as timing constraints for the edges, and trajectories (*runs*) of the transition system are built as timed sequences of elementary transitions:

$$\rho_{\mathbf{d}_1 \to \mathbf{d}_k} = \left(\phi_{\mathbf{d}_1 \to \mathbf{d}_2}, \Delta t_{\mathbf{d}_1 \to \mathbf{d}_2}\right), \dots, \left(\phi_{\mathbf{d}_{(k-1)} \to \mathbf{d}_k}, \Delta t_{\mathbf{d}_{(k-1)} \to \mathbf{d}_k}\right). \tag{10}$$

Thus, the semiquantitative model can be represented as a timed transition system and is easily transformed into other discrete frameworks as Timed Automata [2], timed Petri nets [16], or timed condition/event systems [8].

4 Analysis based on a Timed Automaton Model

In this section, we show the transformation of the semiquantitative model into Timed Automata for the two–tank example and analyse the resulting model using the symbolic model checking tool HyTech. According to the definition in [2], a *Timed Automata* (TA) is a 6-tuple $\{\Sigma, S, S_0, C, E, F\}$ with a finite alphabet Σ, a finite set of states S and initial states $S_0 \subseteq S$, a finite set of clocks C and a set of transitions $E \subseteq S \times S \times \Sigma \times 2^C \times \Psi(C)$ with a set $\Psi(C)$ of clock constraints. A transition between two states $s_1, s_2 \in S$ at reading an input symbol $a \in \Sigma$ is denoted by $\langle s_1, s_2, a, \lambda, \delta \rangle$, where $\lambda \subseteq C$ is the set of clocks reset to zero with the transition and δ is a clock constraint over C. F denotes an acceptance criterion, i. e. the subset of S consisting of states which are visited infinitely often throughout a run of the system [2]. In some versions of TA *invariants* are used to enforce transitions [12].

The idea is now to translate the timed transition system obtained from semiquantitative modeling into a TA with *clock costraints* reflecting the maximal residence times calculated via Eq. (11). This is achieved by the following translation procedure:

1. One state $s \in S$ of the automaton is assigned to each discrete cell $^D x_i \in {}^D X$. A subset $^D X_0 \in {}^D X$ represents the set of start states.

2. For systems with variable input vectors $\mathbf{u}$ (not considered in this paper) the discretized input space $^D \mathbf{u} \in {}^D \mathbf{U}$ corresponds to the input alphabet Σ of the TA.

3. One clock t_k is introduced for each component x_k of $\mathbf{x}$ and t_k is reset whenever a state boundary in the corresponding direction is crossed. Additionally, a clock t_{total} measures the overall time of a run. Hence we have $C = \{t_1, t_2, \ldots, t_n, t_{total}\}$.

4. A transition $e \in E$ is assigned to each elementary transition $\phi_{d_a \to d_b} \in \Phi$ and the corresponding timing constraint δ over C is $t_k \leq \Delta t_{\phi_{d_a \to d_b}}$. This defines a period in which a transition must occur.

5. An invariant is attached to each state $s \in S$ which is a conjunction of the constraints δ of all transitions from the state s.

Following this scheme, the translation of the semiquantitative model into a Timed Automaton for the example results as shown in Fig. 5: For each of the twelve states the invariants and the edges refering to elementary transitions including the clocks to be reset are shown. The timing constraints for the edges are redundant and therefore omitted in the figure. The time scale has been multiplied by a factor of 100. To investigate the properties of this model, we carried out a reachability analysis using the symbolic model checking tool HyTech [4]. Choosing the discrete state denoted by $\mathbf{d} = (4, 1)$ as the initial state, HyTech produces the following output ($t_{total} \equiv \mathbf{tt}$):

```
==========================================================================
Number of locations in product: 12
Reachability Analysis:
Number of iterations required for reachability: 7
Location: 1_43
   t2 >= t1  & t1 >= 0  & tt >= t2  & tt <= t2 + 407
|
   tt = t1  & t2 >= 0  & t1 >= t2  & t1 <= t2 + 407
Location: 1_42
   tt = t1  & t1 >= t2  & t2 >= 0  & t1 <= t2 + 39  & t1 <= 407
Location: 1_41
   tt = t1  & t2 = t1  & t1 >= 0  & t1 <= 39
Location: 1_33
   t2 >= t1  & t1 >= 0  & tt >= t2  & tt <= t2 + 407
Location: 1_32
   tt >= t2  & t2 >= t1  & t1 >= 0
|
   t2 >= t1  & t1 >= 0  & tt >= t2  & tt <= t2 + 145
|
   t1 >= t2  & tt >= t1  & t2 >= 0
|
   t2 >= 0  & t1 >= t2  & tt >= t1  & tt <= t2 + 74  & tt <= t1 + 39
|
   t1 >= 0  & t2 >= t1  & tt >= t2  & tt <= t1 + 407  & tt <= t2 + 39
Location: 1_31
   tt = t2  & t2 >= t1  & t1 >= 0  & t2 <= t1 + 39  & t2 <= 74
Location: 1_22
   tt >= t2  & t2 >= t1  & t1 >= 0
|
   t2 >= 0  & t1 >= t2  & tt >= t1  & tt <= t2 + 145  & tt <= t1 + 74
|
   t2 >= t1  & t1 >= 0  & tt >= t2  & tt <= t2 + 74
Location: 1_21
   tt = t2  & t2 >= t1  & t1 >= 0  & t2 <= t1 + 74  & t2 <= 145
==========================================================================
```

For each reachable state the timing conditions over the clocks t_1, t_2 and t_{total} required for residence in this state are computed. From these inequalities, we can extract lower and upper boundaries for the residence times in reachable states.

In Fig. 6 the reachability set determined by HyTech for the discrete model (starting in state $\mathbf{d} = (4,1)$) is compared with the real physical behavior of the system. Trajectories starting from the edges of the cell (4,1) show that the set of the actually reachable states is $R_c = \{(3,1),(3,2),(4,1),(4,2)\}$. In contrast, the set of reachable states $R_{d_{\text{TA}}} = \{(2,1),(2,2),(3,1),(3,2),(3,3),(4,1),(4,2), (4,3)\}$ generated by HyTech consists of states marked by squares in the left part of Fig. 6. Hence, the set $R_s = R_{d_{\text{TA}}} \backslash R_c$, marked by bold squares in Fig. 6, denotes solutions of the discrete model which do not have a counterpart in the underlying physical system. Following [10], we call these solutions *spurious trajectories*. It is

Fig. 5. Two–tank system modeled as Timed Automaton

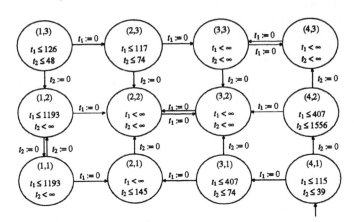

a well-known fact, (see e. g. [10]) that spurious solutions are an inherent problem of abstraction methods, in which the exact quantitative description is replaced by a set of interval–based relations. Particularly in our derivation method of TA from continuous models, one reason for spurious solutions is the independent consideration of transitions in different directions. In the following section, we describe the translation of the semiquantitative model to a Hybrid Automaton where the gradient values in all directions are compared such that the number of spurious solutions is reduced.

5   Analysis based on a Hybrid Automaton Model

In the preceding section we showed that the TA–approximation derived from the semiquantitative model contain a considerable number of spurious solutions. This number can be reduced by translating the model into another paradigm, the *Hybrid Automaton* (HA) according to the definition of Alur et al. [1]. A HA is a 6–tuple $H = (Loc, Var, Lab, Edg, Act, Inv)$, where Loc denotes the set of locations, Var the set of variables, Lab the set of synchronization labels, Edg the set of transitions, Act the set of activities, and $Inv(l)$ the invariants for the residence in the actual location $l \in Loc$. In this formulation, HA can be seen as a generalization of TA because the derivatives of real–valued variables (the *activities*) can be specified with values different from 1 (the rate of the clocks in the TA paradigm). We restrict our considerations to the class of *Linear Hybrid Automata* (LHA), in which the activities are of the form $\dot{x}_k = c_{x_k}, c_{x_k} \in \mathbf{Q}$ and the invariants are linear formulas as well.

The basic idea is to translate the semiquantitative transition system derived in Sec. 3 into an LHA with activities which reflect the extremal values of the components of the derivatives $[^D\dot{x}_k]$ within each state. In detail, the following

Fig. 6. Reachability Analysis for the Timed Automaton

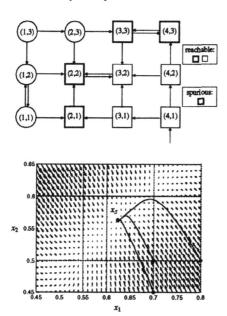

The upper figure shows the set of reachable states obtained with HyTech for the example modeled as TA. The behavior of the continuous system (lower figure) shows that the states marked with bold type squares are spurious solutions.

translation procedure is used:

1. A location $l \in Loc$ of the LHA is assigned to each cell $^{D}\mathbf{x}_i \in {^{D}\mathbf{X}}$.

2. A variable $x_k \in Var$ is introduced for each component of the continuous state vector $\mathbf{x} \in \mathbf{X}$.

3. An invariant $\mu \subseteq Inv$ is attached to each location $l \in Loc$, which denotes that x_k is within the boundaries of the discrete cell specified by $\mathbf{d}_i$: $x_k \in [l_{k,r}, l_{k,r+1}]_i$, $r \in \{1, \ldots, p_k\}$.

4. An edge $e = \langle l_1, a, l_2, \mu \rangle$ of the LHA (where $l_1, l_2 \in Loc$, $a \in A$ an input symbol and $\mu \subseteq Inv$ a transition relation), corresponds to an elementary transition $\phi_{\mathbf{d}_a \to \mathbf{d}_b} \in \Phi$ between two cells $^{D}\mathbf{x}_a$, $^{D}\mathbf{x}_b$.

5. The activity of each location specifies that the derivative of each state vector component is between its extremal values for each cell: $\dot{x}_k \in \left[^{D}\dot{x}_{k,\min}, {^{D}\dot{x}_{k,\max}} \right]_i$.

For the two-tank-system, this translation scheme yields the H A which is shown in Fig. 7: The invariants for residence in the twelve locations are given at the right and at the lower margin of the figure. They are the same for each row (x_2)

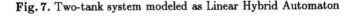

Fig. 7. Two-tank system modeled as Linear Hybrid Automaton

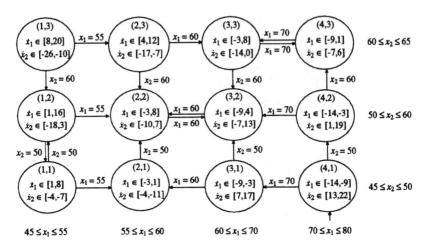

respectively column (x_1). The constraints attached to the edges correspond to the landmark value that is crossed when the corresponding transition occurs. Additionally, the derivatives of the x–components are shown as activities within each state. As for the TA model, we carried out a reachability analysis for the LHA implementation of the system by use of HyTech. Starting again in the state denoted by $d = (4, 1)$ the following output is generated:

```
================================================================
Number of locations in product: 12
Reachability Analysis:
Number of iterations required for reachability: 5
Location: 1_43
    x2 >= 60   & 19x1 <= 1520   & x2 <= 65   & 19x1 >= 1330
|
    x1 >= 70   & x2 <= 65   & x2 >= 60   & x1 <= 80
Location: 1_42
    x1 >= 70   & 3x2 >= 150   & 19x1 + 3x2 <= 1670   & 3x2 <= 180
Location: 1_41
    x1 <= 80   & x2 <= 50   & x2 >= 45   & x1 >= 70
Location: 1_33
    x1 <= 70   & x2 >= 60   & x2 <= 65   & x1 >= 60
Location: 1_32
    x1 <= 70   & x2 <= 60   & x2 >= 50   & x1 >= 60
|
    x1 >= 60   & 63x2 >= 3150   & x1 <= 70   & 63x2 <= 3780
|
    x1 >= 60   & x2 >= 50   & x2 <= 60   & x1 <= 70
|
    x1 >= 60   & x2 <= 60   & x2 >= 50   & x1 <= 70
```

```
Location: 1_31
    7x1 + 9x2 >= 895    & x1 <= 70    & x2 <= 50
Location: 1_22
    x1 <= 60    & x2 <= 60    & x2 >= 50    & x1 >= 55
==================================================================
```

Fig. 8. Reachability result for the LHA obtained with HyTech

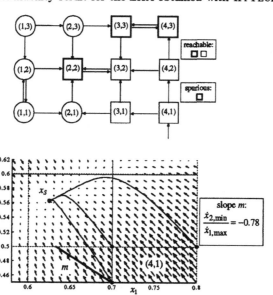

For state $^D x_{(3,1)}$ the straight line with slope m divides the cell in a reachable right upper and an unreachable left lower section. Hence, state $(2,1)$ is not reachable in the LHA model.

Whereas no timing information can be extracted from this output explicitly it gives more exact information about reachables parts of the continuous state space than the equivalent result for the TA: For each reachable location the section being reachable is represented by a set of inequalities for the state variables. While in most of the reachable states the whole area is reachable, the inequalities for location $(3,1)$ indicate that the system can only move into the upper right section of the corresponding cell. Figure 8 shows the reachable locations of the LHA model. Comparing this to $R_{d_{TA}}$, the set of reachable states using the LHA implementation is obviously reduced by the state $(2,1)$, a spurious solution of the TA model. The reason for $(2,1) \notin R_{d_{LHA}}$ is the inequality for state $(3,1)$:

$$7 \cdot x_1 + 9 \cdot x_2 \geq 895. \tag{11}$$

In the lower part of Fig. 8, the straight line with slope $\dot{x}_{2,min}/\dot{x}_{1,max} = 7/9 \approx 0.78$ divides the cell into a reachable and a non–reachable section corresponding to Eq. (11). Since the left border of (3,1) is not reachable, the elementary transition $\phi_{(3,1)\rightarrow(2,1)}$ can not occur. However, Fig. 8 reveals that although the number of spurious transitions is reduced a considerable amount of spurious solutions still remains in the LHA model of the system (marked by bold squares). It should be pointed out that the occurence of spurious solutions does not mean that the discrete model is unsuited as a basis for controller synthesis and verification but that the controller possibly must be more restrictive than necessary for the real system.

6   Conclusion and Outlook

We sketched a method to derive semiquantitative transition systems from conti-nuous models with a box–like partition of the state space. Then the translation of this transition system into two existing paradigms of real–time automata was described. We showed that the TA approximation may contain physically im-possible trajectories even for rather simple vector fields inside the cells. By using HA, some of the spurious trajectories could be eliminated.

The semiquantitative modeling approach described here gives a conservative estimation of the residence times. If a cell is crossed in one coordinate directi-on, i. e. the index vectors $\{d_1, d_2, d_3\}$ of two subsequent elementary transitions $\phi_{d_1\rightarrow d_2}, \phi_{d_2\rightarrow d_3}$ differ in the same component, the accuracy of the lower time boundary can be improved by using [18]:

$$\Delta t_{\phi_{d_a \rightarrow d_b},min} = \frac{\lambda_{d_a,k}}{D\dot{x}_{a,max}}. \tag{12}$$

For our example, the value of $\Delta t_{\phi_{(4,2)\rightarrow(4,3)},min}$ is 533 time units if the preceding transition was $\phi_{(4,1)\rightarrow(4,2)}$. The reason for omitting this extension in the semi-quantitative approach in Sec. 3 is that the $\Delta t_{\phi_{i\rightarrow j},min}$–value and the correspon-ding constraint in the TA model then depends on the initial state ($s_0 \equiv (4,2)$ implies $\Delta t_{\phi_{(4,2)\rightarrow(4,3)},min} = 0$). This dependency cannot be represented in the usual definitions of real–time automata.

Our current research aims at a further reduction of the number of spurious so-lutions. One possibility is to abandon the idea of introducing one state for each discrete cell of $^D\mathbf{X}$. Instead, discrete states can be introduced for parts of the boundaries of the cells with the same sign of the component of the derivative or-thogonal to the border, and for each steady state (see Fig. 9). The transitions can be determined together with an interval for the residence times by integrating the continuous model for the grid points on the relevant part of the boundary. By this approach, further elimination of the spurious solutions is possible. Sub-sequently, this finer and more accurate state graph has to be mapped back into the original state space partition $^D\mathbf{X}$.

Fig. 9. Transitions for a subpartitioned system

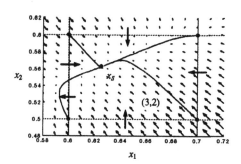

A further topic of research is the incorporation of switched inputs. Here, the basic idea is to derive discrete models for each value of $^D\mathbf{u}$ and to introduce transitions between these models to adjacent states on the other level only. This is equivalent to the assumption that switching of the input only occurs at the instance when the system state $\mathbf{x}(t)$ crosses a partition boundary.

Acknowledgements

We thank Prof. S. Engell for helpful and inspiring discussions. The work was supported in part by the German Research Council (DFG) in the temporary graduate school ("Graduiertenkolleg") *Modeling and Model-based Design of Complex Technological Systems* (first and third author) and in the special program *KONDISK – Analysis and Design of Technical Systems with Continuous Discrete Dynamics* (grant En 152/19, fourth author).

References

1. R. Alur, C. Courcoubetis, N. Halbwachs, T. A. Henzinger, P.– H. Ho, X. Nicollin, A. Olivero, J. Sifakis and S. Yovine, "The Algorithmic Analysis of Hybrid Systems", *Theoretical Computer Science*, Vol. 138, pp. 3-34, 1995.

2. R. Alur and D. L. Dill, "A Theory of Timed Automata", *Theoretical Computer Science*, Vol. 126, pp. 183-235, 1994.

3. T. Heckenthaler and S. Engell, "Approximately Time–Optimal Fuzzy Control of a Two–Tank System", *IEEE Control Systems*, Vol. 14, No. 3, pp. 24-30, 1994.

4. T. A. Henzinger and P.– H. Ho, "HYTECH: The Cornell HYbrid TECHnology Tool", *Basic Research in Computer Science*, Proc. Workshop on Tools and Algorithms for the Construction and Analysis of Systems, Aarhus, Denmark, May 1995.

5. T. A. Henzinger and H. Wong-Toi, "Linear Phase-portrait Approximations for Nonlinear Hybrid Systems", *Hybrid Systems III: Verification and Control, LNCS* 1066, Springer, pp. 377-388, 1996.

6. S. Kowalewski, R. Gesthuisen and V. Roßmann "Model-based Verification of Batch Process Control Software", *Proc. IEEE Conf. on Systems, Man and Cybernetics*, San Antonio, USA, pp. 331-336, 1994.

7. M. M. Kokar, "On Consistent Symbolic Representations of General Dynamic Systems", *IEEE Trans. Systems, Man, and Cybernetics*, Vol. 25, No. 8, August 1995.

8. S. Kowalewski and J. Preußig, "Timed Condition/Event Sytems: A Framework for Modular Discrete Models of Chemical Plants and Verification of Their Real-Time Discrete Control", in *Tools and Algorithms for the Construction and Analysis of Systems, LNCS* 1055, Springer, 1996.

9. B. Kuipers, "Qualitative Simulation", *Artificial Intelligence*, Vol. 29, pp. 289-338, 1986.

10. J. Lunze, "Qualitative Modelling of Linear Dynamical Systems with Quantized State Measurements", *Automatica*, Vol. 30, No. 3, pp. 417-431, 1994.

11. I. Moon, G. J. Powers, J. R. Burch and E. M. Clarke, "Automatic Verification of Sequential Control Systems Using Temporal Logic", *AICHE Journal*, Vol. 38, No. 1, pp. 67-75, 1992.

12. X. Nicollin, J. Sifakis and S. Yovine, "Compiling Real-Time Specifications into Extended Automata", *IEEE Trans. on Software Eng.*, 18 (9), pp. 794-804, 1992.

13. T. Niinomi, B. H. Krogh and J. E. R. Cury, "Synthesis of Supervisory Controllers for Hybrid Systems based on Approximating Automata", *Conf. on Decision and Control*, New Orleans, 1995.

14. H. A. Preisig and J. Renz, "Synthesis of a Supervisory Controller from First Principles", Annual *AICHE* Meeting, Miami, November 1992.

15. J. Raisch and S. O'Young, "A DES Approach to Control of Hybrid Dynamical Systems", Workshop on *Analysis and Design of Event-driven Operations in Process-Systems (ADEDOPS)*, London, 1995.

16. J. Sifakis, "Use of Petri nets for performance evaluation", In H. Beilner and E. Gelenebe (editors), *Measuring, modelling and evaluating computer systems*, pp. 75-93. North-Holland, 1977.

17. J. A. Stiver and P. J. Antsaklis, "State Space Partitioning for Hybrid Control Systems", *Proc. of the American Control Conference*, San Francisco, California, pp. 2303-2304, June 1993.

18. O. Stursberg, S. Kowalewski and S. Engell, "Generating Timed Discrete Models of Continuous Systems", *2nd IMACS Symposium on Mathematical Modelling (MATHMOD'97)*, Vienna, Austria, Feb. 5-7th, 1997.

Hybrid Control Models of Next Generation Air Traffic Management *

C. Tomlin, G. Pappas, J. Lygeros, D. Godbole, and S. Sastry

Department of Electrical Engineering and Computer Sciences
University of California at Berkeley
Berkeley, CA 94720

Abstract. The study of hierarchical, hybrid control systems in the framework of air traffic management (ATM) is presented. The need for a new ATM arises from the overcrowding of large urban airports and the need to more efficiently handle larger numbers of aircraft, without building new runways. Recent technological advances, such as the availability of relatively inexpensive and fast real time computers both on board the aircraft and in the control tower, make a more advanced air traffic control system possible. The benefits from these technological advances are limited by today's Air Traffic Control (ATC), a ground-based system which routes aircraft along predefined jet ways in the sky, allowing the aircraft very little autonomy in choosing their own routes. In this paper we propose a *decentralized* ATM framework, meaning that much of the current ATC functionality is moved on board each aircraft. Within this framework, we describe our work in on-board conflict resolution strategies between aircraft, and in deriving the flight mode switching logic in the flight vehicle management systems of each aircraft.

1 Introduction

For decades, commercial air travel has played an indispensable role in our economy and society. The increasing demand for air travel has so far been met by building larger and more modern airports. Little has been done however to improve the efficiency of air traffic management. Most of the effort in this area has been centered on simplifying the job of the air traffic controllers by providing them with advisory systems, better displays, etc. The use of automatic control has mostly been restricted to on-board autopilots with relatively small degrees of autonomy. The research presented here aims at improving air travel conditions by introducing automation to air traffic management.

Many of the current air traffic control (ATC) practices are dictated by the absolute desire to maintain safety and the consequent need to keep the task of the human controllers simple. For example, aircraft are currently routed along prespecified paths to avoid having to deal with the complications of "free flight".

* Research supported by NASA under grant NAG 2-1039 and AATT grant NAS 2-14291 (as a subcontract through Honeywell Technology Center), and by ARO under grants DAAH 04-95-1-0588 and DAAH 04-96-1-0341.

In addition, because of heavy workload, air traffic controllers are primarily concerned with maintaining safe spacing between aircraft, ignoring considerations such as fuel consumption, travel times, etc. We believe that the introduction of automation can lead to great savings in terms of travel times, unplanned delays, and fuel consumption, and can possibly increase the number of aircraft handled. An additional benefit will be an increase in the safety of the flights (reduced number of aborted landings, near collisions, etc.). The improvement is likely to be more dramatic in the case of degraded conditions of operation, such as aircraft malfunctions, ATC malfunctions (e.g. power failure), shifting winds (that cause changes in approach patterns), bad weather, switching from manual to instrumented landings, etc. It should be noted that conditions like these occur regularly in practice and can cause severe degradation in the system performance. These topics are discussed in greater detail in Section 2.

The air traffic management (ATM) we envision will be automated[2] and will involve the harmonious union between on-board air traffic control and flight vehicle management systems. This system uses advances in Communication, Navigation and Surveillance (CNS) both on board aircraft and on the ground, along with advances in avionics on board aircraft. Our models are inspired by our research on the control of *hierarchical hybrid systems*. Because air traffic management requires coordination and control of a large number of semi-autonomous agents (aircraft), the number of control decisions that have to be made and the complexity of the resulting decision process dictates a hierarchical, decentralized solution. Complexity management is achieved in a hierarchy by moving from detailed, decentralized models at the lower levels to abstract, centralized models at the higher. For reasons of economic and reliable information transfer among the agents and the centralized controller, coordination among the agents is usually in the form of communication protocols which are modeled by discrete event systems. Since the dynamics of individual agents is modeled by differential equations, we are left with a combination of interacting discrete event dynamical systems and differential equations. An important issue in the area of hybrid systems is the design and analysis of protocols for communication between the agents, continuous control laws for each agent and interfaces between the two.

One of the most important conceptual issues to be addressed in the architecture of these control systems is their degree of decentralization. For example, current air traffic control practice is completely centralized with the regional centers, airport control towers and gate controllers providing all of the instructions, while current roadway driving practice is completely decentralized with individual drivers (usually adopting "greedy strategies") setting their driving control laws. There are clear drawbacks to each: the completely decentralized solution is *inefficient and leads to conflict*, while the completely centralized one is *not tolerant of faults in the central controller, computationally and conceptually complicated and slow to respond to emergencies*. The focus of our research has been to strike a compromise in the form of partially decentralized control

---

[2] Parts of our work can also be used to produce advisories for ATC and pilots in a semi-automated ATM.

laws for guaranteeing *reliable, safe control of the individual agents* while providing *some measure of unblocked, fair, and optimum utilization of the scarce resource. In our design paradigm, agents have control laws to maintain their safe operation, and try to optimize their own performance measures. They also coordinate with neighboring agents and a centralized controller to resolve conflicts as they arise and maintain efficient operation.*

Hybrid systems also arise in the operation of a single aircraft. In the trajectory and regulation levels discrete changes are observed because of *flight mode switching.* The use of discrete modes to describe phases of the aircraft operation is a common practice for pilots and autopilots and is dictated partly by the aircraft dynamics themselves. The modes may reflect, for example, changes in the outputs that the controller is asked to regulate: depending on the situation, the controller may try to achieve a certain airspeed, climb rate, angle of attack, etc. or combinations of those. The modes may also be dictated by input constraints: saturated inputs can no longer be used effectively, certain controls (e.g. the flaps) may not be used in certain situations (e.g. high airspeeds), etc.

In this paper we present an overview of our research effort in the area of ATM. To motivate the problem, we first give a brief overview of current ATC practice, in Section 2. In Section 3 we present the proposed hierarchical ATM structure that we believe can alleviate some of the problems experienced by the current system. A discussion on issues of centralization versus decentralization is first given followed by an overview of the functionality of the on-board flight vehicle management system. In Sections 4 and 5 we present results on two of the research directions pursued within this framework: in Section 4 we present the algorithms proposed for coordination among aircraft for the purpose of conflict resolution, while in Section 5 we discuss flight mode switching. Due to space limitations only brief discussions are given for certain areas of our research while certain others are only mentioned. We provide references where more details can be found throughout the text.

2 Current ATC Practice

Air Traffic Control (ATC) in the United States is currently organized hierarchically with a single *Air Traffic Control System Command Center (ATCSCC)* supervising the overall traffic flow management (TFM). This is supported by 20 *Air Traffic Control System Command Centers (ARTCCs)* organized by geographical area. Coastal ARTCCs have jurisdiction over oceanic waters. For example, the Fremont (California) ARTCC has jurisdiction from roughly Eureka to Santa Barbara and from Japan in the West to the Sierra Nevada mountains in the East. In addition, around large urban airports there are *Terminal Radar Approach Control facilities (TRACONs)* numbering over 150. For instance, the Bay Area TRACON includes the San Francisco, Oakland and San Jose airports along with smaller airfields at Moffett Field, San Carlos, Fremont, etc. The TRACONs are supported by control towers at more than 400 airports. There are roughly 17,000 landing facilities in the United States serving nearly 220,000 aircraft. Of these the commercial aircraft number about 6,000 and the number of commercially used airstrips is roughly the 400 that have control towers. The overall system is referred to as *National Airspace System (NAS)*.

The main goal of both the ARTCCs and the TRACONs is to maintain safe separation between aircraft while guiding them to their destinations. Due to their heavy workloads, minimizing flight delays and fuel spent en route are not prime considerations of controllers when they determine trajectories for the aircraft to follow, even though the airline flight dispatch offices and the cockpits do negotiate with the ATC to achieve these objectives. Inefficiencies cause unplanned delays in average flight times, and thus deviations from pre-negotiated airline schedules, forcing air traffic controllers and flight dispatch offices to manually schedule and reschedule aircraft landings according to when the aircraft enters the TRACON region. In addition, there is minimal communication between the ARTCCs and TRACON ATCs which makes forecasting delays almost impossible. Studies conducted by ATC researchers at NASA Ames have illustrated that, when presented with tables of flight data (position, air velocity, ground velocity, wind speed, etc.) of two aircraft in the TRACON region, a human controller does not have the ability to quickly predict the future motion of the two aircraft. Controllers therefore guide the aircraft along predetermined jet ways both in the TRACON and in the en route airspace. In the TRACON, this results in some aircraft left in holding patterns at the edge of the TRACON while others are performing their final approach for landing.

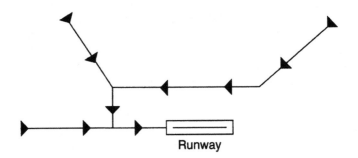

Fig. 1. Typical route pattern for arriving aircraft

Figure 1 depicts the horizontal projection of a typical route inside the TRACON. Because aircraft must land into the wind with as low a cross-wind as possible to maintain lift at low ground speed, the runway configuration in large airports is such that, frequently, only one set of two parallel runways is used at any given time. The aircraft are sequenced manually as they enter the TRACON, and they maintain this sequence along the illustrated route. Where the routes converge, ATC decides which aircraft is allowed to go first and what the ensuing sequence will be. If an aircraft enters the TRACON in an emergency state and must land as quickly as possible, ATC manually reroutes and reschedules the other TRACON aircraft so that priority can be given to the troubled aircraft.

In the regions outside airport TRACONs, the ARTCCs perform the routing and scheduling tasks for each aircraft. These tasks are considerably less intensive and the workload is much lighter than for TRACON controllers. The ARTCC also uses predefined air routes or jet ways (flight maps describing these routes are published each year) and one of their main tasks is to predict and avoid conflicts. If ATC predicts that the separation between two aircraft will become less than the regulatory separation, it either slows down one of the aircraft or puts it into a delay loop. Other current ATC practices are listed below.

- ATC uses only discrete levels of altitude when routing aircraft between TRA-CONs (for example, westbound aircraft fly at even thousand feet altitude while eastbound fly at odd thousand feet);
- if the optimal route of an aircraft takes it to an altitude of less than 11,000 feet above an en route TRACON, ATC directs the aircraft *around* the intermediate airport so that the TRACON-ATC's workload is not increased;
- shifting winds and inclement weather at airports cause problems in scheduling, since the airport must be reconfigured to use different runways, and as a result, aircraft are delayed;
- due to the fixed routes between TRACONs, delays at destination airports are communicated back to origin airports, and aircraft at origins up to 4 hours away from the destinations may be delayed.

ATM efficiency is a complex quantity to define, but includes the following features:

Airport and Airspace Capacity. Airport capacity is defined as the maximum number of aircraft takeoffs and landings that can be supported by the airfield under given climatic conditions when there is a continuous demand for service. Airport capacity is a function of the runway-taxiway configurations, aircraft mix, weather conditions, and landing aids. Airspace capacity is the maximum number of operations that can be processed per unit time in a certain volume of the airspace given a continuous demand. In this definition a distinction is made between different modes of operation, such as *level flight at fixed heading, climbing, descending,* and *changes in heading.* Airspace capacity is a function of aircraft count, activity mix, and protocols for conflict detection and resolution, as well as Federal Aviation Authority (FAA) regulations. It is our contention in this paper that it is this latter capacity that can be increased by better protocols which do not compromise safety.

Delays caused by ATC. Ground holds that are imposed by the FAA on departing aircraft in anticipation of congestion due to forecast bad weather at the destination are examples of delays caused by ATC. This practice may be inefficient since the inclement weather may fail to materialize (resulting in starvation of arrivals at the destination airport) or because it may be acceptable to have a few aircraft in holding patterns while a TRACON is reconfigured to account for changes in weather conditions.

Operating Costs. Operating costs are incurred because of procedures which could be more flexible. For example, frequently the so-called "user preferred routes" (shorter or low fuel consumption routes that take advantage of tailwind) are disallowed because of the requirement to use prescribed jet ways or the need to go from point to point along jagged paths over ground based "fixes". Airlines claim that very large savings can be effected (for the U.S. estimates mentioned range from 1 to 3 billion annually) by using advances in avionics and automated ATC capacity both on board the aircraft and on the ground to detect and resolve conflicts. This procedure is referred to as *free flight*.

A summary of the efficiency issues of the current ATM and a description of ATM technologies that will become available in the near future is presented in [1]. In order to improve efficiency, researchers at NASA Ames are developing a system which automates some parts of ATC. The system is called the Center-TRACON Automation System (CTAS), and is described in [2]. CTAS is a program which generates *advisories*, or suggested trajectories, runway assignments, landing sequences, and schedules, which the controller may use in managing air traffic.

3 A Distributed Decentralized ATM

The tradeoff between centralized and decentralized decision making raises a fundamental issue that has to be addressed by any proposed ATM. The above discussion indicates that the current ATC system is primarily centralized; all safety critical decisions are taken centrally (at the ATC centers) and distributed to the local agents (aircraft) for execution. Because of the complexity of the problem and the limited computational power (provided primarily by the human operators in the current system) this practice may lead, as we have seen, to inefficient operation. Recent technological advances, such as Global Positioning Systems (GPS), better communication and navigation equipment and more powerful on board computers make it possible to distribute part of the decision making responsibility to the local agents. It is hoped that this will lead to improved system performance.

A number of issues should be considered when deciding on the appropriate level of centralization. An obvious one is the *optimality* of the resulting design. Even though optimality criteria may be difficult to define for the air traffic problem (refer to the discussion in Section 2) it seems that, in principle, the higher the level of centralization the closer one can get to the globally optimal solution[3]. However, the complexity of the problem also increases in the process; to implement a centralized design one has to solve a small number of more complex problems as opposed to large number of simpler ones. As a consequence

---

[3] Any decentralized solution can also be implemented centrally.

the implementation of a centralized solution requires a greater effort on the part of the designer to produce control algorithms and greater computational power to execute them. One would ideally like to reach a compromise that leads to acceptable efficiency while keeping the problem tractable.

Another issue that needs to be considered is *reliability* and *scalability*. The greater the responsibility assigned to a central controller the more dramatic are likely to be the consequences if this controller fails[4]. In this respect there seems to be a clear advantage in implementing a decentralized design: if a single aircraft's computer system fails, most of the ATM system is still intact and the affected aircraft may be guided by voice to the nearest airport. Similarly, a distributed system is better suited to handling increasing number of aircraft, since each new aircraft can easily be added to the system, its own computer contributing to the overall computational power. A centralized system on the other hand would require regular upgrades of the ATC computers. This may be an important feature given the current rate of increase of the demand for air travel.

Finally, the issue of *flexibility* should also be taken into account. A decentralized system will be more flexible from the point of view of the agents, in this case the pilots and airlines. This may be advantageous for example in avoiding turbulence or taking advantage of favorable winds, as the aircraft will not have to wait for clearance from ATC to change course in response to such transient or local phenomena. Improvements in performance may also be obtained by allowing aircraft to individually fine tune their trajectories making use of the detailed dynamical models contained in the autopilot. Finally, greater flexibility may be preferable to the airlines as it allows them to utilize their resources in the best way they see fit.

The above discussion indicates that determining an appropriate mix of centralized and decentralized decision making is a delicate process. It seems, however, that given the current demand and technological limitations the system could benefit by distributing more decision making responsibility to the aircraft. In the next section we propose a control architecture that implements what we believe is a reasonable balance between complete centralization and complete decentralization.

3.1 Proposed ATM Structure

In our proposed ATM structure, each aircraft is equipped with a hierarchical planning and control algorithm, and an algorithm to resolve potential collision conflicts with other aircraft. Each aircraft follows a nominal path from source airport to destination airport. This nominal path is calculated off-line in consultation with ATC and is designed to be time-optimal and conflict-free. However,

---

[4] Indeed, in August 1995, the central computer in the FAA control center at Fremont, California, experienced a 65 minute power failure, leaving close to 70 aircraft with no communication to ATC. Separations between aircraft were maintained (just) by communication between the pilots, a natural process of decentralized decision making.

once the aircraft are airborne and outside the TRACON, bad weather, high winds, or delays may cause conflicts with other aircraft and force the aircraft to deviate from this nominal route. In the current system, these deviations are calculated by the central ATC and each aircraft must obtain a *clearance* from ATC before altering its course. In our proposed system, the aircraft may plan its own deviation trajectories without consulting ATC. This semi-autonomy is enabled by on-board conflict resolution algorithms, which allow the aircraft to coordinate among each other. Inside the airport TRACONs, the aircraft trajectories would continue to be strictly regulated by ATC.

A block diagram of the proposed ATM structure is presented in Figure 2. The levels of architecture below ATC reside on the individual aircraft and comprise what is known as the aircraft's *Flight Vehicle Management System*, or FVMS. The FVMS consists of four layers, the strategic, tactical, and trajectory planners, and the regulation layer. Each layer of this architecture is described in the following sections. We begin with a discussion of the airspace structure.

Airspace Structure. Nominal trajectories through the airspace are defined in terms of *waypoints*, which are fixed points in the airspace defined by VOR (Visual Omni Range) points on the ground. Aircraft flying in the range of the waypoint's radio transmission (shown as an inverse cone in Figure 3) obtain *fixes* as to their position and orientation relative to the waypoint. The waypoints are a necessary navigation tool for aircraft which are not equipped with the more sophisticated GPS. Figure 3 also illustrates the approach routes into the San Francisco airport in terms of these waypoints.

We assume for our architecture that the waypoint structure of the airspace is intact, so that trajectories are defined at the coarsest level in terms of sequences of these waypoints. These are the trajectories that are communicated between each aircraft and ATC: the FVMS of each aircraft refines the waypoints into full state and input trajectories.

Air Traffic Control. ATC has more control over aircraft in the TRACON than over aircraft outside the TRACON airspace, referred to as the enroute airspace. In both regions, ATC passes a sequence of waypoints to the strategic planner on board the aircraft, defining a nominal trajectory. These waypoints are a discretization of a trajectory, accessed from a database of stored trajectories, which have been calculated off-line for different combinations of aircraft kinematics, wind magnitude and direction, and runway configurations. These pre-computed trajectories have been optimized to provide a minimum-time path for the given aircraft kinematics. The waypoints from ATC are time-stamped to provide a suggested arrival schedule at the destination airport, which is designed to meet the announced arrival times and reflects compromises between airline schedules. Once these waypoints have been negotiated they are passed to the strategic planner, and all of the planning and control tasks are taken over by the FVMS on board the individual aircraft.

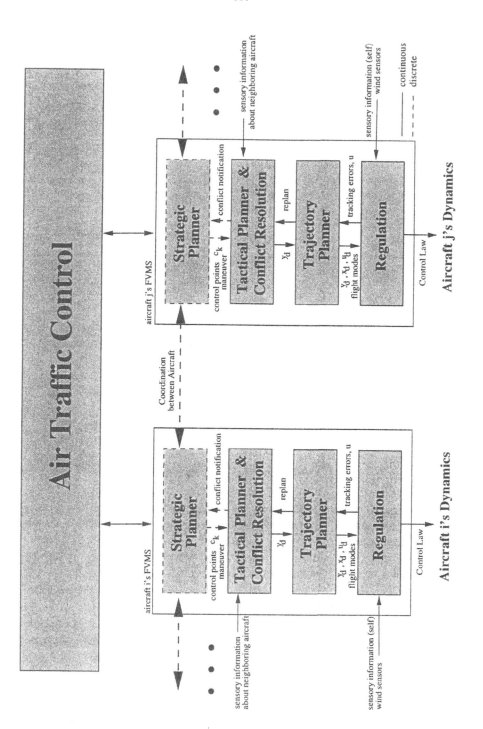

Fig. 2. Proposed ATM Structure

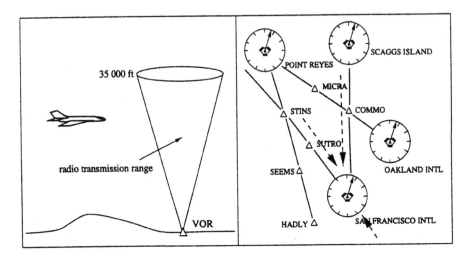

Fig. 3. Airspace Structure

Outside the TRACON region, the FVMS is allowed to alter its nominal trajectory by changing the waypoints and coordinating with the FVMSs of other aircraft. For these deviations, the tactical planner takes over the role of calculating an initial kinematic trajectory for the aircraft. The role of the ATC is limited to keeping track of these changes and providing the aircraft with global information about enroute traffic and weather conditions.

Strategic Planner. The main objectives of the strategic planner are to design a coarse trajectory for the aircraft in the form of a sequence of control points, c_k, which interpolate the waypoints from ATC, and to resolve conflicts between aircraft.

If the tactical planner on board the aircraft predicts that a conflict will occur between it and another aircraft, it notifies the strategic planner. The strategic planners of all aircraft involved in the potential conflict determine a sequence of maneuvers which will result in conflict-free trajectories, either using communication with each other through satellite datalink, or by calculating safe trajectories assuming the worst possible actions of the other aircraft. Each strategic planner then commands its own tactical planner to follow these maneuvers.

Tactical Planner. The tactical planner refines the strategic plan by interpolating the control points with a smooth output trajectory, denoted by y_d in Figure 2. The tactical planner is also responsible for predicting conflicts.

The tactical planner uses a simple kinematic model of the aircraft for all trajectory calculations. For conflict prediction, it uses information about the positions and velocities of neighboring aircraft (available through radar) and kinematic models to predict their movement. If more information, such as neighboring aircraft type and capabilities, is available through communication, the models can be refined. Simple models are used at this stage since very detailed models may unnecessarily complicate the calculations, which are assumed to be approximate and have large safety margins. The assumptions made in extrapolating aircraft trajectories plays a crucial role in conflict prediction. If we assume no a-priori knowledge of the other aircrafts' intentions we can assume that they will maintain the same velocity over the horizon of prediction. A more conservative approach is to assume that the other aircraft will do their best to cause conflict. Predicting the trajectories under this assumption involves solving a dynamic game in which the cost function encodes the spacing between the aircraft in question and its neighbors (that the neighbors seek to minimize). Clearly this approach will predict more conflicts than the constant velocity extrapolation. The aircraft may also be able to communicate with each other at the strategic level to resolve the conflict. In this case, the maneuvers and resulting commands are accessed from a database of precomputed solutions to possible conflicts. Examples of conflict resolution maneuvers are presented in the next section, and in more detail in [3].

When the tactical planner predicts that a conflict will occur, it sends a discrete signal to the strategic planner. After conflict resolution, a new tactical plan needs to be established and new conflicts predicted. Verification is needed to guarantee that this process eventually leads to an acceptable, conflict-free trajectory. Because of the relative simplicity of the kinematic models we hope to be able to carry out this verification using finite state and timed automata techniques.

Trajectory Planner. The trajectory planner uses a detailed dynamic model of the aircraft, sensory data about the wind magnitude and direction, and the tactical plan consisting of an output trajectory, to design full state and input trajectories for the aircraft, and a sequence of *flight modes* necessary to execute the dynamic plan. The flight modes represent different modes of operation of the aircraft and correspond to controlling different variables in the aircraft dynamics. A derivation of the flight mode logic necessary for safe operation of a CTOL (Conventional Take Off and Landing) aircraft is presented in Section 5, and in more detail, in [4].

The resulting trajectory, denoted y_d, x_d, and u_d in Figure 2, is given to the regulation layer which directly controls the aircraft. The task of the trajectory planner is complicated by the presence of non-minimum phase dynamics [5], [6] and actuator saturation [7].

Regulation Layer. Once a feasible dynamic trajectory has been determined, the regulation layer is asked to track it. Assuming that the aircraft dynamic model used by the trajectory planner is a good approximation of the true dynamics of the aircraft, tracking should be nearly perfect. In the presence of large external disturbances (such as wind shear or malfunctions), however, tracking can severely deteriorate. The regulation layer has access to sensory information about the actual state of the aircraft dynamics, and can calculate tracking errors. These errors are passed back to the trajectory planner, to facilitate replanning if necessary. Clearly verification is needed to show that the scheme eventually converges to an acceptable trajectory. Due to the increased complexity of the models it is unlikely that timed automata techniques will be adequate in this setting. More elaborate (possibly hybrid) techniques, such as those in [4] may be useful here.

4 Conflict Resolution

The operation of the proposed ATM involves the interaction of continuous and discrete dynamics. Such *hybrid* phenomena arise, for example, from the coordination between aircraft at the strategic level. The conflict resolution maneuvers are implemented in the form of discrete communication protocols. These maneuvers appear to the (primarily continuous) tactical planner as discrete resets of the desired waypoints. One would like to determine the effect of these discrete changes on the continuous dynamics (and vice versa) and ultimately obtain guarantees on the minimum aircraft separation possible under the proposed control scheme.

In this section, we describe an algorithm for resolving possible collision conflicts between aircraft. This algorithm is presented in greater depth in [3]. Research in the area of conflict detection and resolution for air traffic has been centered on predicting conflict and deriving maneuvers assuming that the intent of each aircraft is known to all other aircraft involved in the conflict, for both deterministic [8], [9] and probabilistic [10],[11] models. For example, the current emergency collision avoidance algorithm on-board aircraft, called Traffic Alert and Collision Avoidance System (TCAS) [12] assumes the other aircraft involved in the conflict will not change its trajectory.

In our research, we stipulate that any conflict resolution scheme should work not only when the aircraft have the ability to communicate with each other, but also when this communication breaks down, when the distances between the aircraft are too large, for example, or because one or more of the aircraft involved in the conflict is a general aviation aircraft not equipped with the sensing and communication technology of the larger commercial aircraft. We therefore differentiate between two types of conflict resolution: *noncooperative* and *cooperative* (Figure 4). The algorithms described in this section fit into the FVMS as shown in the detail in Figure 5.

4.1 Noncooperative Conflict Resolution

If an aircraft detects that a conflict may occur between itself and another aircraft, and it is not able to communicate with this aircraft to determine its intentions

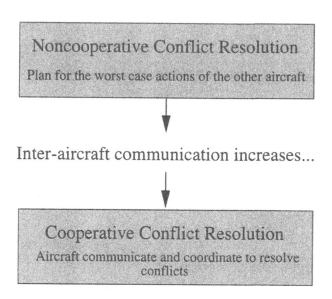

Fig. 4. Noncooperative and cooperative Conflict Resolution

or to resolve the conflict, then the safest action that this aircraft can take is to choose a strategy which resolves the conflict for the *worst possible action of the other aircraft*. We therefore formulate the noncooperative conflict resolution strategy as a zero sum dynamical game of the pursuit-evasion style [13], [14]. The aircraft are treated as players in this game. Each player is aware only of the possible actions of the other agents. These actions are modeled as disturbances, assumed to lie within a known set but with their particular values unknown. Each aircraft solves the game for the worst possible disturbance. The performance index over which the aircraft compete is the relative distance between the aircraft, required to be above a certain threshold (the Federal Aviation Administration requires a 5 mile horizontal separation). Assuming that a saddle solution to the game exists, the saddle solution is *safe* if the performance index evaluated at the saddle solution is above the required threshold. The sets of *safe states* and *safe control actions* for each aircraft may be calculated: the saddle solution defines the boundaries of these sets. The aircraft may choose any trajectory in its set of safe states, and a control policy from its set of safe control actions; coordination with the other aircraft is unnecessary. If the saddle solution to the game is unsafe, it may be because the disturbance sets are too large. Partial or full coordination between the aircraft is then necessary in order to reduce the disturbance sets.

For kinematic aircraft models in two dimensions, it is straightforward to work out the noncooperative conflict resolution strategy. Consider two aircraft with

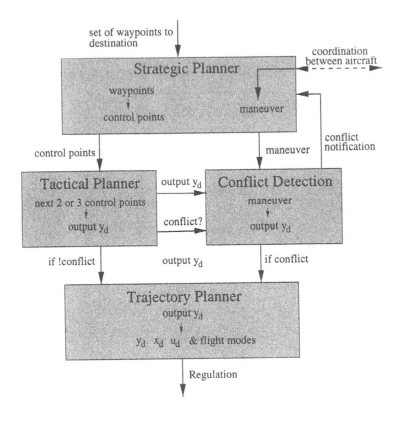

Fig. 5. Conflict Resolution

kinematic models in the Lie group $SE(2)$

$$\dot{g}_1 = g_1 X_1$$
$$\dot{g}_2 = g_2 X_2 \tag{1}$$

where $g_1, g_2 \in SE(2)$ and $X_1, X_2 \in se(2)$, the Lie algebra associated with $SE(2)$. The relative configuration of aircraft 2 with respect to aircraft 1 is denoted $g_r = g_1^{-1} g_2$. The resulting model is

$$\dot{x}_r = -v_1 + v_2 \cos \theta_r + \omega_1 y_r$$
$$\dot{y}_r = v_2 \sin \theta_r - \omega_1 x_r \tag{2}$$
$$\dot{\theta}_r = \omega_2 - \omega_1$$

where $X = (x_r, y_r, \theta_r)$ represents the relative position and orientation, and ω_i, v_i represent the angular and linear velocities of each aircraft. We consider this system in the framework of a pursuit-evasion game, in which aircraft 1, at the origin of the relative axis frame, is the *evader*, and aircraft 2 is the *pursuer*. The control inputs are the actions of the evader, and the disturbances are the actions of the pursuer:

$$u = [v_1, \ \omega_1]^T \in \mathbb{R}^2$$
$$d = [v_2, \ \omega_2]^T \in \mathbb{R}^2$$

The cost function in the game is the relative distance between the two aircraft:

$$J_s(X_0, u, d) = \inf_{t \geq 0} \sqrt{x_r(t)^2 + y_r(t)^2} \tag{3}$$

with a threshold of 5 miles.

Consider the case in which the aircraft do not deviate from their original paths, but only change their linear velocities to resolve the conflict. In this case, ω_1 and ω_2 are set to zero, and equations (2) may be solved analytically. The control and disturbance variables are restricted to lie in intervals of the positive real line:

$$u \in [\underline{v_1}, \ \overline{v_1}] \in \mathbb{R}^+$$
$$d \in [\underline{v_2}, \ \overline{v_2}] \in \mathbb{R}^+$$

The saddle solution for the game, which describes the *best* control strategy for the *worst* disturbance, is summarized in Figure 6. The saddle solution may be described in words as: if the pursuer is in front of the evader, the evader should fly as slowly as possible, otherwise, the evader should fly as fast as possible; if the pursuer is heading towards the evader, the pursuer should fly as fast as possible, otherwise, the pursuer should fly as slowly as possible. Having calculated the saddle solution, we can calculate the unsafe sets of initial states for the pursuer. These are illustrated in Figure 7 for various relative orientations of the two aircraft. The arrows indicate the relative orientations of the evader (at the center of the protected zone) and the pursuer.

4.2 Cooperative Conflict Resolution

In cooperative conflict resolution, safety is ensured by full coordination among the aircraft. The aircraft follow predefined maneuvers which are proven to be safe. The class of maneuvers constructed to resolve conflicts must be rich enough to cover all possible conflict scenarios.

Protocol for Two Aircraft A general conflict scenario is depicted in Figure 8. Aircraft 2 with speed v_2 and initial heading θ_r has desired *relative* trajectory $(x_r^d(t), y_r^d(t))$, which is the straight line path joining point A and point C a distance d away from the origin (seen as the dotted line in Figure 8). To simplify the analysis, the protected zone of aircraft 2 is translated to aircraft 1, to make the protected zone around aircraft 1 twice its original radius. If aircraft 2 were to continue along its original desired path, it would cut through this protected zone, and come into conflict with aircraft 1. To avoid the protected zone, the proposed deviation for aircraft 2 is the triangular path ABC tangent to the protected zone at two places and parameterized by the deviation angle θ (represented by the dashed line in Figure 8).

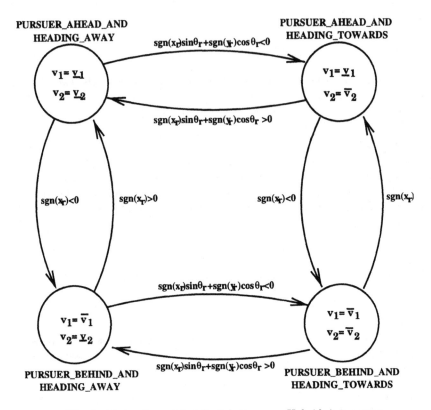

Fig. 6. Abstraction of Saddle Solution as a Hybrid Automaton

Aircraft 2 follows the specified path ABC if the component of its relative velocity normal to this path is zero. Since straight line paths are considered, the relative velocity of aircraft 2 is described by the model (2). The angle θ is calculated to minimize the time it takes for aircraft 1 to travel along the path ABC. Its optimal value is obtained by minimizing with respect to θ the length of ABC divided by the speed of the aircraft along this path. As the ratio v_2/v_1 gets large, the optimal value for θ approaches 45° [3].

This *Overtake* maneuver is a special case of the general class of triangular conflict resolution maneuvers. In each aircraft's FVMS, a routine exists which computes θ for the different parameters r, d, θ_r, and v_2/v_1:

$$\theta = Overtake(r, d, \theta_r, v_2/v_1) \tag{4}$$

It is assumed in this architecture that the aircraft with the greater speed must perform the maneuver; the other aircraft remains on its original course.

Consider now a *HeadOn* conflict, in which aircraft 1 is heading towards aircraft 2 ($\theta_r = 180°$) along the x_r axis ($d = 0$). A potential conflict exists regardless of the speeds of aircraft 2 and aircraft 1. Although the conflict may be resolved using the general maneuver discussed above, the issue of *fairness* arises.

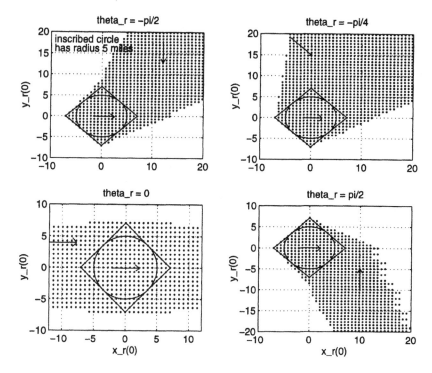

Fig. 7. Unsafe sets $(x_r(0), y_r(0))$ for $[\underline{v}_1, \bar{v}_1] = [2, 4]$, $[\underline{v}_2, \bar{v}_2] = [1, 5]$ and $\theta_r = -\pi/2$, $-\pi/4$, 0, and $\pi/2$.

If $v_1 \approx v_2$, it is not clear how to choose which aircraft deviates from its original trajectory. A natural solution is to define a maneuver in which both aircraft deviate from their original trajectories:

$$(\theta_1, \theta_2) = HeadOn(r, d, \theta_r, v_2/v_1) \tag{5}$$

Inspired by the Overtake maneuver, θ_1 and θ_2 are set to 45° and −45°, respectively, when $d = 0$ and $\theta_r = 180°$. The Overtake maneuver is *safe by design*, since the construction of the deviation path explicitly avoids the protected zone of one of the aircraft. In order to ensure that the HeadOn conflict is safe by design, both aircraft must deviate a horizontal distance of 5 miles (the minimum aircraft separation) away from their original paths. Figure 9 illustrates why, in the absolute frame of the two aircraft. As with the Overtake maneuver, the HeadOn maneuver in its general form may be used for relative headings θ_r other than 180°.

Protocol for Three Aircraft For three aircraft coming into potential conflict, there are many more possibilities for types of conflict. For example, two aircraft could have intersecting trajectories, and then conflict resolution between these

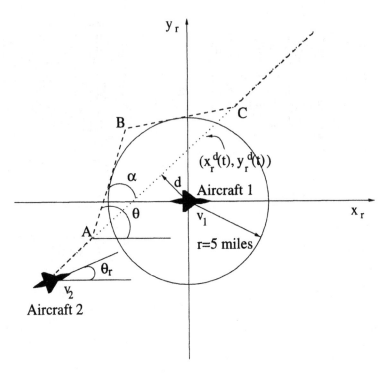

Fig. 8. Showing the triangular path deviation (dashed line), at optimal angle θ, to be used in pairwise conflict avoidance

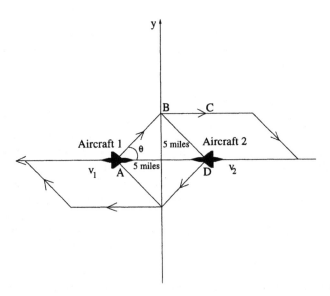

Fig. 9. Showing the HeadOn conflict and subsequent conflict resolution maneuver

two could result in a new conflict with a third aircraft. Pairwise conflict resolution may not work in cases such as these: it is worthwhile to design a maneuver which works for three aircraft, with the possibility to extend it to more than three aircraft. A maneuver which is inspired by the potential field algorithms of the robotics literature [15] is the *Roundabout* maneuver, illustrated in Figure 10 for the case of three aircraft with two initial points of conflict. For this maneuver,

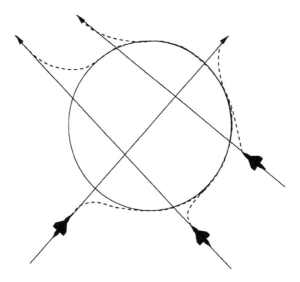

Fig. 10. Conflict Resolution for three aircraft: the Roundabout maneuver

a circular path is defined around the conflict points of all three trajectories as shown. The aircraft are restricted to fly along the circular path segments with a given speed, as not to overtake the other aircraft already involved in the maneuver. An aircraft may not enter the Roundabout until the other aircraft are outside its protected zone; in extreme cases this may force an aircraft to enter a holding pattern to delay its entry.

5 Flight Mode Switching

We present in this section a simplified example of hybrid dynamics that arise on a single flight vehicle management system (FVMS). This example was originally presented as part of a research program to develop models of hybrid systems [16], [4]. In the example, the goal of the FVMS is to keep the state of the aircraft in a given subset of the state space dictated in principle by stall constraints. The task is complicated by input saturation which also dictates the flight mode switching. The example is based on the dynamic aircraft equations and the design specification of [17]. The equations model the speed and the flight path angle dynamics of a commercial aircraft in still air. The control inputs to the equations are the thrust T, accessed through the engine throttle, and the pitch angle θ, accessed through the elevators. The outputs we wish to control are the speed V and the flight path angle γ. There are three primary modes of operation:

1. **Mode 1:** The thrust T is between its specified operating limits ($T_{min} < T < T_{max}$), the control inputs are T and θ, and both V and γ are controlled outputs.
2. **Mode 2:** The thrust saturates ($T = T_{min} \vee T = T_{max}$) and thus it is no longer available as a control input; the only input is θ, and the only controlled output is V.
3. **Mode 3:** The thrust saturates ($T = T_{min} \vee T = T_{max}$); the input is again θ, and the controlled output is γ.

Within Modes 2 and 3 there are two submodes depending on whether $T = T_{min}$ (idle thrust) or $T = T_{max}$ (maximum thrust).

Safety regulations for the aircraft dictate that V and γ must remain within specified limits: for ease of presentation we simplify this *safety envelope*, S, of [17] to

$$S = \{(V, \gamma) | (V_{min} \le V \le V_{max}) \cap (\gamma_{min} \le \gamma \le \gamma_{max})\}$$

where $V_{min}, V_{max}, \gamma_{min}, \gamma_{max}$ are constant values.

The specification is to design a control scheme, an FVMS, which will cause the aircraft to reach a target operating point $(V, \gamma)_{target}$ in S from any initial operating point in S. The resulting trajectory $(V(t), \gamma(t))$ must satisfy acceleration constraints imposed for passenger comfort, and must not exit the envelope at any time. Here we describe the minimally restrictive set of controllers which guarantees safe operation of the aircraft, by classifying all of the control inputs that keep the $(V(t), \gamma(t))$ trajectory within the safety envelope and establishing the mode switching logic required for safety. A secondary requirement for passenger comfort is then optimized within the class of safe controls.

5.1 System Model

The flight path angle dynamics of the aircraft can be summarized using two state variables, $x = [V \ \gamma]^T \in \mathbb{R} \times S^1$, where V (m/s) is the airspeed and γ (rad) is the flight path angle. The dynamics of the system are given by:

$$\dot{V} = \frac{T - D}{m} - g \sin \gamma, \quad \dot{\gamma} = \frac{L}{mV} - \frac{g \cos \gamma}{V} \tag{6}$$

where T (N) is the thrust, m (kg) is the mass of the aircraft, g (m/s^2) is gravitational acceleration and L and D are the aerodynamic lift and drag forces. The aerodynamic forces can be modeled by:

$$L = a_L V^2 (1 + c(\theta - \gamma)), \quad D = a_D V^2 (1 + b(1 + c(\theta - \gamma))^2) \tag{7}$$

where a_L and a_D are the lift and drag coefficients, b and c are small positive constants, and θ is the aircraft pitch angle. We assume that the pilot has direct control over the thrust T and the pitch angle θ, thus $u = [T, \theta]$. Substituting the lift and drag equations into the dynamic equations, and assuming that b is small enough to neglect the quadratic term in the drag, the system dynamics are:

$$
\begin{bmatrix} \dot{x}_1 \\ \dot{x}_2 \end{bmatrix} = f(x, u) = \begin{bmatrix} -\frac{a_D x_1^2}{m} - g \sin x_2 + \frac{1}{m} u_1 \\ \frac{a_L x_1 (1 - c x_2)}{m} - \frac{g \cos x_2}{x_1} + \frac{a_L c x_1}{m} u_2 \end{bmatrix} \tag{8}
$$

For these equations to be meaningful we need to assume that $x_1 > 0$ and $-\pi/2 \leq x_2 \leq \pi/2$, i.e. $X \subset (0, \infty) \times [-\pi/2, \pi/2]$. Clearly this will be the case for realistic aircraft. Moreover, physical considerations also impose constraints on the inputs, $U = [T_{min}, T_{max}] \times [\theta_{min}, \theta_{max}]$.

To guarantee safety we need to ensure that $x(t) \in S$ for all t. Let ∂S denote the boundary of S. Safety is maintained by operating within the largest subset V_1 of S which can be rendered invariant by using a control input $u \in \mathcal{U}$. Let ∂V_1 denote the boundary of V_1. We calculate the set V_1 by solving an optimal control problem over a time interval $[t, t_f]$. In this problem, we are not interested in a running cost: we are interested only in whether or not the state leaves S. Thus, we define t_f as

$$
t_f = \inf\{\tau \in \mathbb{R} | x(\tau) \notin S\} \tag{9}
$$

and we let t be free. If $t_f = \infty$ for all u, then for all possible control actions the trajectory never leaves S and $V_1 = S$. If on the other hand t_f is finite, we set $t_f = 0$ and consider negative initial times t (without loss of generality, as the dynamics are time invariant).

The cost $J_1(x, t, u(\cdot))$ is a function only of the state at the terminal time:

$$
J_1(x, t, u(\cdot)) = l(x(0)) \tag{10}
$$

where $l(x)$ is defined to be zero on the boundary ∂S, is positive inside S and is negative outside S. We can now formally define V_1 and the corresponding safe set of control inputs $\mathcal{U}_1$ as

$$
V_1 = \{x \in S | \exists u \in \mathcal{U}, J_1(x, t, u(\cdot)) \geq 0\} \tag{11}
$$
$$
\mathcal{U}_1(x) = \{u \in \mathcal{U} | J_1(x, t, u(\cdot)) \geq 0\} \tag{12}
$$

It is clear that the optimal control input $u^* \in \mathcal{U}$ is the one which maximizes $J_1(x, t, u(\cdot))$:

$$
u^* = \arg\max_{u \in \mathcal{U}} J_1(x, t, u(\cdot)), \quad J_1^*(x, t) = \max_{u \in \mathcal{U}} J_1(x, t, u(\cdot)) \tag{13}
$$

and at any instant t, the set $\{x \in S | J_1^*(x, t) \geq 0\}$ defines the safe set of states starting from time t. We would like to calculate the "steady state" safe set, or the safe set of states for all $t \in [-\infty, 0]$. We construct the Hamilton-Jacobi equation for this system and attempt to calculate its steady state solution. Define the Hamiltonian $H(x, p, u(\cdot)) = p^T f(x, u(\cdot))$ where $p \in T^* \mathbb{R}^2$ is the costate. The optimal Hamiltonian is given by

$$
H^*(x, p) = \max_{u \in \mathcal{U}} H(x, p, u(\cdot)) = H(x, p, u^*) \tag{14}
$$

If $J_1^*(x,t)$ is a smooth function of x and t, then $J_1^*(x,t)$ satisfies the Hamilton-Jacobi equation:

$$\frac{\partial J_1^*(x,t)}{\partial t} = -H^*(x, \frac{\partial J_1^*(x,t)}{\partial x}) \tag{15}$$

with boundary condition $J_1^*(x,0) = l(x(0))$. Our goal is to compute the safe set $\{x \in S | J_1^*(x,-\infty) \geq 0\}$ where $J_1^*(x,-\infty)$ is the steady state solution of (15). However, it is difficult to guarantee that the PDE (15) have solutions $\forall t \leq 0$, due to the occurrence of "shocks". In what follows, we assume that there are no shocks in the solution of (15), and compute $J_1^*(x,-\infty)$ by setting the left hand side of the Hamilton-Jacobi equation to zero, thus $H^*(x, \frac{\partial J_1^*(x,-\infty)}{\partial x}) = 0$ which implies that $\frac{\partial J_1^*(x,-\infty)}{\partial x}$ is normal to the vector field $f(x,u^*)$.

Cost functions involving the linear and angular accelerations can be used to encode the requirement for passenger comfort:

$$J_2(x,u(\cdot)) = \max_{t \geq 0} |\dot{x}_1(t)|, \quad J_2'(x,u(\cdot)) = \max_{t \geq 0} |x_1(t)\dot{x}_2(t)| \tag{16}$$

The requirement that the linear and angular acceleration remain within the limits determined for comfortable travel are encoded by thresholds:

$$J_2(x,u(\cdot)) \leq 0.1g, \quad J_2'(x,u(\cdot)) \leq 0.1g \tag{17}$$

5.2 The Least Restrictive Safe Control Scheme

We construct the safe set of states V_1 by considering each side of the boundary ∂S separately. Define $l_1(x) = x_1 - V_{min}$, $l_2(x) = -x_2 + \gamma_{max}$, $l_3(x) = -x_1 + V_{max}$ and $l_4(x) = x_2 - \gamma_{min}$. with $x \in S$.

We describe the construction of the safe set starting from the left boundary $\{x \in S | l_1(x) = 0\}$. The inward pointing normal to $l_1(x) = 0$ is $p = [1,0]^T$, so that along this boundary, $u_1^* = T_{max}$ but u_2 is indeterminate. Because of the loss of dependency on u_2 of the optimal Hamiltonian, the points in $\{x \in S | l_1(x) = 0\}$ are called *abnormal extremals*. Define $(V_{min}, \gamma_a) = \{x \in S | l_1(x) = 0 \cap H^*(x) = 0\}$ and calculate γ_a by:

$$\gamma_a = \sin^{-1}(\frac{T_{max}}{mg} - \frac{a_D V_{min}^2}{mg}) \tag{18}$$

Integrate the system dynamics

$$\dot{x} = f(x,u^*), \quad x(0) = (V_{min}, \gamma_a) \tag{19}$$

backwards from $t = 0$ to $t = -T$, where T is chosen to be large enough so that the solution to (19) intersects $l_2(x) = 0$. The optimal control u_2^* is required for this calculation. At the abnormal extremal (V_{min}, γ_a), any $u_2 \in [\theta_{min}, \theta_{max}]$ may be used. However, if we perturb the system slightly along the system dynamics, we leave the abnormal extremal regardless of the choice of u_2 instantaneously, and u_2^* can be uniquely determined: for all $u_2 \in [\theta_{min}, \theta_{max}]$, for all $\delta \in \mathbb{R}^+$, the inward pointing normal to $f(x(-\delta), [u_1^* \ u_2]^T)$ is such that p_2 is negative. Thus,

$u_2^* = \theta_{min}$. Denote the point of intersection of the solution of (19) with $l_2(x) = 0$ as (V_a, γ_{max}), and the solution to (19) between (V_{min}, γ_a) and (V_a, γ_{max}) as ∂V_1^a, as shown in Figure 11. In this example, the abnormal extremal was not complicated enough as to cause difficulties in construction: we will resolve this situation in general in [18].

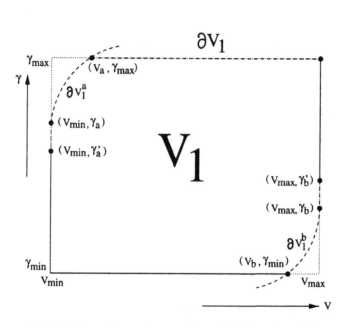

Fig. 11. The safe set of states, V_1, and its boundary ∂V_1

Repeat this calculation for the remaining three boundaries. Only $\{x \in S | l_3(x) = 0\}$ contains a point at which $H^*(x)$ vanishes. We denote this point as (V_{max}, γ_b) where

$$\gamma_b = \sin^{-1}\left(\frac{T_{min}}{mg} - \frac{a_D V_{max}^2}{mg}\right) \tag{20}$$

and similarly calculate ∂V_1^b and V_b, as shown in Figure 11.

Lemma 1 *The boundary ∂V_1 of the safe set of states V_1 is given by*

$$
\begin{aligned}
\partial V_1 = \{(V, \gamma)| \ & (V = V_{min}) \wedge (\gamma_{min} \le \gamma \le \gamma_a) \quad \vee \\
& \partial V_1^a \qquad\qquad\qquad\qquad\qquad\qquad \vee \\
& (\gamma = \gamma_{max}) \wedge (V_a \le V \le V_{max}) \quad \vee \\
& (V = V_{max}) \wedge (\gamma_b \le \gamma \le \gamma_{max}) \quad \vee \\
& \partial V_1^b \qquad\qquad\qquad\qquad\qquad\qquad \vee \\
& (\gamma = \gamma_{min}) \wedge (V_{min} \le V \le V_b)\}
\end{aligned}
\tag{21}
$$

Proof: See [4].

The safe set of control inputs U_1 can be characterized as a set-valued feedback map $U_1 : S \rightarrow 2^U$, in which $U_1(x)$ is the subset of U which guarantees that the requirement on J_1 is satisfied at x. Consider the left side of ∂S, $\{x \in S | l_1(x) = 0\}$. Clearly, for the points $x = (V_{min}, \gamma)$ with $\gamma > \gamma_a$, $U_1(x)$ maps to the empty set. It is perhaps less clear that for some (V_{min}, γ) with $\gamma < \gamma_a$, U_1 is restricted to map to a subset of U. For each x in $\{x \in S | l_1(x) = 0\}$, denote by $(T_a(\gamma), \theta_a(\gamma))$ the values of (T, θ) for which the vector field $f(x, [T, \theta]^T)$ becomes tangent to $l_1(x) = 0$ (i.e. $\dot{V} = 0$). Setting $\dot{V} = 0$ leads to:

$$T_a(\gamma) = a_D V_{min}^2 + mg \sin \gamma \qquad (22)$$

for all $\theta_a(\gamma) \in [\theta_{min}, \theta_{max}]$. Therefore, the safe set of inputs along $\{x \in S | l_1(x) = 0\}$ are all $T \in [T_{min}, T_{max}]$ with $T(\gamma) \geq T_a(\gamma)$ and all $\theta \in [\theta_{min}, \theta_{max}]$. At the point (V_{min}, γ_a'), where $\gamma_a' = \{\gamma | T_a(\gamma) = T_{min}\}$ the cone of vector fields $f([V_{min}, \gamma_a'], U)$ points completely inside S. At $\gamma_a = \{\gamma | T_a(\gamma) = T_{max}\}$ the cone of vector fields points completely outside S, and T_{max} is the unique thrust which keeps the system trajectory tangent to S. These calculations may be repeated for the remaining three sides of ∂S.

In Figure 11, the portions of ∂V_1 for which all control inputs are safe ($U_1(x) = U(x)$) are indicated with solid lines; those for which only a subset are safe ($U_1(x) \subset U(x)$) are indicated with dashed lines. The map defines the *least restrictive safe control scheme* and determines the mode switching logic. On ∂V_1^a and ∂V_1^b, the system must be in **Mode 2** or **Mode 3**. Anywhere else in V_1, any of the three modes is valid as long as the input constraints are satisfied. In the regions $S \backslash V_1$ (the upper left and lower right corners of S), no control inputs are safe.

5.3 Additional Constraints for Passenger Comfort

Within the class of safe controls, a control scheme which addresses the passenger comfort (efficiency) requirement can be constructed. To do this, we solve the optimal control problem:

$$\begin{aligned}
J_2^*(x) &= \min_{u \in \mathcal{U}_1} J_2(x, u(\cdot)), & u^*(x) &= \arg\min_{u \in \mathcal{U}_1} J_2(x, u(\cdot)) \\
J_2'^*(x) &= \min_{u \in \mathcal{U}_1} J_2'(x, u(\cdot)), & u'^*(x) &= \arg\min_{u \in \mathcal{U}_1} J_2'(x, u(\cdot))
\end{aligned} \qquad (23)$$

for $x \in V_1$.

From this calculation, we determine the set of "comfortable" states and controls:

$$V_2 = \{x \in V_1 | J_2^*(x) \leq 0.1g \wedge J_2'^*(x) \leq 0.1g\} \qquad (24)$$

$$\mathcal{U}_2(x) = \{u \in \mathcal{U}_1 | J_2(x, u(\cdot)) \leq 0.1g \wedge J_2'(x, u(\cdot)) \leq 0.1g\} \qquad (25)$$

These sets may be easily calculated by substituting the bounds on the accelerations into equation (8) to get

$$\begin{aligned}
-0.1mg + a_D V^2 + mg \sin \gamma &\leq T \leq 0.1mg + a_D V^2 + mg \sin \gamma \\
-\frac{0.1mg}{a_L V^2 c} - \frac{1 - c\gamma}{c} + \frac{mg \cos \gamma}{a_L V^2 c} &\leq \theta \leq \frac{0.1mg}{a_L V^2 c} - \frac{1 - c\gamma}{c} + \frac{mg \cos \gamma}{a_L V^2 c}
\end{aligned} \qquad (26)$$

These constraints provide lower and upper bounds on the thrust and the pitch angle which may be applied at any point (V, γ) in V_2. Figure 12 illustrates these lower and upper bounds for the thrust input (diagonal planes) intersected with T_{min} and T_{max} (horizontal planes). The resulting set V_2 is also shown.

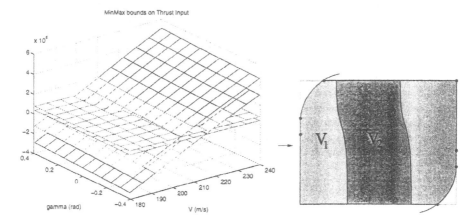

Fig. 12. Showing comfort constraint on thrust intersected with existing bounds, and the Safe and Comfortable Sets of States: V_1 and V_2

6 Conclusions

The technological advances that make free flight feasible include on-board GPS, satellite datalinks, and powerful on-board computation such as the Traffic Collision and Avoidance System (TCAS), currently certified by the FAA to provide warnings of ground, traffic, and weather proximity. Navigation systems use GPS which provides each aircraft with its four dimensional coordinates with extreme precision. For conflict detection, current radar systems are adequate. Conflict prediction and resolution, however, require information regarding the position, velocity and intent of other aircraft in the vicinity. This will be accomplished by satellite datalinks which will provide this information to sophisticated algorithms, such as the ones presented in this paper. These advances will be economically feasible only for commercial aviation aircraft: how to merge the proposed architecture with general aviation aircraft (considered disturbances in the system in this paper) is a critical issue. Furthermore, the transition from the current to the proposed system must be smooth and gradual. Above all, the algorithms must be verified for correctness and safety before the implementation stage. This is one of the main challenges facing the systems and verification community.

References

1. S. Kahne and I. Frolow, "Air traffic management: Evolution with technology," *IEEE Control Systems Magazine*, vol. 16, no. 4, pp. 12–21, 1996.
2. H. Erzberger, T. J. Davis, and S. Green, "Design of center-tracon automation system," in *Proceedings of the AGARD Guidance and Control Syposium on Machine Intelligence in Air Traffic Management*, pp. 11.1–11.12, 1993.
3. C. Tomlin, G. Pappas, and S. Sastry, "Conflict resolution for air traffic management: A case study in multi-agent hybrid systems," tech. rep., UCB/ERL M96/38, Electronics Research Laboratory, University of California, Berkeley, 1996.
4. J. Lygeros, C. Tomlin, and S. Sastry, "Multiobjective hybrid controller synthesis," in *Springer-Verlag Proceedings of the International Workshop on Hybrid and Real-Time Systems*, (Grenoble), pp. 109–123, 1997.
5. C. Tomlin, J. Lygeros, L. Benvenuti, and S. Sastry, "Output tracking for a nonminimum phase dynamic CTOL aircraft model," in *Proceedings of IEEE Conference on Decision and Control*, (New Orleans, LA), pp. 1867–1872, 1995.
6. C. Tomlin and S. Sastry, "Bounded tracking for nonminimum phase nonlinear systems with fast zero dynamics," tech. rep., UCB-ERL Memo M96/46, Electronics Research Laboratory, UC Berkeley, CA 94720, 1996. To appear in the International Journal of Control.
7. G. J. Pappas, J. Lygeros, and D. N. Godbole, "Stabilization and tracking of feedback linearizable systems under input constraints," in *Proceedings of IEEE Conference on Decision and Control*, 1995.
8. Y.-B. Chen and A. Inselberg, "Conflict resolution for air traffic control," tech. rep., USC-CS-93-543, Computer Science Department, University of Southern California, 1993.
9. J. Krozel, T. Mueller, and G. Hunter, "Free flight conflict detection and resolution analysis," in *Proceedings of the American Institute of Aeronautics and Astronautics Guidance Navigation and Control Conference, AIAA-96-3763*, 1996.
10. J. K. Kuchar, *A Unified Methodology for the Evaluation of Hazard Alerting Systems*. PhD thesis, Massachussets Institute of Technology, 1995.
11. R. A. Paielli and H. Erzberger, "Conflict probability and estimation for free flight," in *Proceedings of the 35th Meeting of the American Institute of Aeronautics and Astronautics, AIAA-97-0001*, (Reno), 1997.
12. Radio Technical Commission for Aeronautics, "Minimum operational performance standards for traffic alert and collision avoidance system (TCAS) airborn equipment," Tech. Rep. RTCA/DO-185, RTCA, September 1990. Consolidated Edition.
13. T. Başar and G. J. Olsder, *Dynamic Non-cooperative Game Theory*. Academic Press, second ed., 1995.
14. J. Lewin, *Differential Games*. Springer-Verlag, 1994.
15. J. Košecká, C. Tomlin, G. Pappas, and S. Sastry, "Generation of conflict resolution maneuvers for air traffic management," in *International Conference on Intelligent Robots and Systems (IROS)*, (Grenoble), 1997.
16. J. Lygeros, D. Godbole, and S. Sastry, "A game theoretic approach to hybrid system design," tech. rep., UCB-ERL Memo M95/77, Electronics Research Laboratory, University of California, Berkeley, CA 94720, 1995.

17. C. Hynes and L. Sherry, "Synthesis from design requirements of a hybrid system for transport aircraft longitudinal control." preprint, NASA Ames Research Center, Honeywell Air Transport Division, 1996.

18. C. Tomlin, S. Sastry, and R. Montgomery, "Computing safe sets using the Hamilton-Jacobi equation." (to be published), 1997.

Index

Arehart 1
Bett 235
Branicky 18, 31
Brayman 57
Broucke 77
Cofer 93
Deshpande 113
Dolginova 18
Godbole 378
Göllü 113
Hatipoğlu 294
Heymann 134
Hoffmann 361
İftar 294
Knight 160
Kohn 174
Kolen 215
Kourjanski 228
Kowalewski 361
Lemmon 235
Lin 134
Luense 160
Lygeros 378
Lynch 18
Mattsson 31
Meyer 134
Nerode 174, 248
O'Young 342
Özgüner 294
Pappas 329, 378
Preußig 361
Raisch 342
Redmill 294
Remmel 174, 248
Sastry 329, 378
Stursberg 361
Tomlin 378
Vagners 57
Varaiya 77, 113, 228
Wolovich 1
Yakhnis 248
Zhao 215

Springer
and the
environment

At Springer we firmly believe that an international science publisher has a special obligation to the environment, and our corporate policies consistently reflect this conviction.

We also expect our business partners – paper mills, printers, packaging manufacturers, etc. – to commit themselves to using materials and production processes that do not harm the environment. The paper in this book is made from low- or no-chlorine pulp and is acid free, in conformance with international standards for paper permanency.

 Springer

Lecture Notes in Computer Science

For information about Vols. 1–1210

please contact your bookseller or Springer-Verlag

Vol. 1211: E. Keravnou, C. Garbay, R. Baud, J. Wyatt (Eds.), Artificial Intelligence in Medicine. Proceedings, 1997. XIII, 526 pages. 1997. (Subseries LNAI).

Vol. 1212: J. P. Bowen, M.G. Hinchey, D. Till (Eds.), ZUM '97: The Z Formal Specification Notation. Proceedings, 1997. X, 435 pages. 1997.

Vol. 1213: P. J. Angeline, R. G. Reynolds, J. R. McDonnell, R. Eberhart (Eds.), Evolutionary Programming VI. Proceedings, 1997. X, 457 pages. 1997.

Vol. 1214: M. Bidoit, M. Dauchet (Eds.), TAPSOFT '97: Theory and Practice of Software Development. Proceedings, 1997. XV, 884 pages. 1997.

Vol. 1215: J. M. L. M. Palma, J. Dongarra (Eds.), Vector and Parallel Processing – VECPAR'96. Proceedings, 1996. XI, 471 pages. 1997.

Vol. 1216: J. Dix, L. Moniz Pereira, T.C. Przymusinski (Eds.), Non-Monotonic Extensions of Logic Programming. Proceedings, 1996. XI, 224 pages. 1997. (Subseries LNAI).

Vol. 1217: E. Brinksma (Ed.), Tools and Algorithms for the Construction and Analysis of Systems. Proceedings, 1997. X, 433 pages. 1997.

Vol. 1218: G. Păun, A. Salomaa (Eds.), New Trends in Formal Languages. IX, 465 pages. 1997.

Vol. 1219: K. Rothermel, R. Popescu-Zeletin (Eds.), Mobile Agents. Proceedings, 1997. VIII, 223 pages. 1997.

Vol. 1220: P. Brezany, Input/Output Intensive Massively Parallel Computing. XIV, 288 pages. 1997.

Vol. 1221: G. Weiß (Ed.), Distributed Artificial Intelligence Meets Machine Learning. Proceedings, 1996. X, 294 pages. 1997. (Subseries LNAI).

Vol. 1222: J. Vitek, C. Tschudin (Eds.), Mobile Object Systems. Proceedings, 1996. X, 319 pages. 1997.

Vol. 1223: M. Pelillo, E.R. Hancock (Eds.), Energy Minimization Methods in Computer Vision and Pattern Recognition. Proceedings, 1997. XII, 549 pages. 1997.

Vol. 1224: M. van Someren, G. Widmer (Eds.), Machine Learning: ECML-97. Proceedings, 1997. XI, 361 pages. 1997. (Subseries LNAI).

Vol. 1225: B. Hertzberger, P. Sloot (Eds.), High-Performance Computing and Networking. Proceedings, 1997. XXI, 1066 pages. 1997.

Vol. 1226: B. Reusch (Ed.), Computational Intelligence. Proceedings, 1997. XIII, 609 pages. 1997.

Vol. 1227: D. Galmiche (Ed.), Automated Reasoning with Analytic Tableaux and Related Methods. Proceedings, 1997. XI, 373 pages. 1997. (Subseries LNAI).

Vol. 1228: S.-H. Nienhuys-Cheng, R. de Wolf, Foundations of Inductive Logic Programming. XVII, 404 pages. 1997. (Subseries LNAI).

Vol. 1230: J. Duncan, G. Gindi (Eds.), Information Processing in Medical Imaging. Proceedings, 1997. XVI, 557 pages. 1997.

Vol. 1231: M. Bertran, T. Rus (Eds.), Transformation-Based Reactive Systems Development. Proceedings, 1997. XI, 431 pages. 1997.

Vol. 1232: H. Comon (Ed.), Rewriting Techniques and Applications. Proceedings, 1997. XI, 339 pages. 1997.

Vol. 1233: W. Fumy (Ed.), Advances in Cryptology — EUROCRYPT '97. Proceedings, 1997. XI, 509 pages. 1997.

Vol 1234: S. Adian, A. Nerode (Eds.), Logical Foundations of Computer Science. Proceedings, 1997. IX, 431 pages. 1997.

Vol. 1235: R. Conradi (Ed.), Software Configuration Management. Proceedings, 1997. VIII, 234 pages. 1997.

Vol. 1236: E. Maier, M. Mast, S. LuperFoy (Eds.), Dialogue Processing in Spoken Language Systems. Proceedings, 1996. VIII, 220 pages. 1997. (Subseries LNAI).

Vol. 1238: A. Mullery, M. Besson, M. Campolargo, R. Gobbi, R. Reed (Eds.), Intelligence in Services and Networks: Technology for Cooperative Competition. Proceedings, 1997. XII, 480 pages. 1997.

Vol. 1239: D. Sehr, U. Banerjee, D. Gelernter, A. Nicolau, D. Padua (Eds.), Languages and Compilers for Parallel Computing. Proceedings, 1996. XIII, 612 pages. 1997.

Vol. 1240: J. Mira, R. Moreno-Díaz, J. Cabestany (Eds.), Biological and Artificial Computation: From Neuroscience to Technology. Proceedings, 1997. XXI, 1401 pages. 1997.

Vol. 1241: M. Akşit, S. Matsuoka (Eds.), ECOOP'97 – Object-Oriented Programming. Proceedings, 1997. XI, 531 pages. 1997.

Vol. 1242: S. Fdida, M. Morganti (Eds.), Multimedia Applications, Services and Techniques – ECMAST '97. Proceedings, 1997. XIV, 772 pages. 1997.

Vol. 1243: A. Mazurkiewicz, J. Winkowski (Eds.), CONCUR'97: Concurrency Theory. Proceedings, 1997. VIII, 421 pages. 1997.

Vol. 1244: D. M. Gabbay, R. Kruse, A. Nonnengart, H.J. Ohlbach (Eds.), Qualitative and Quantitative Practical Reasoning. Proceedings, 1997. X, 621 pages. 1997. (Subseries LNAI).

Vol. 1245: M. Calzarossa, R. Marie, B. Plateau, G. Rubino (Eds.), Computer Performance Evaluation. Proceedings, 1997. VIII, 231 pages. 1997.

Vol. 1246: S. Tucker Taft, R. A. Duff (Eds.), Ada 95 Reference Manual. XXII, 526 pages. 1997.

Vol. 1247: J. Barnes (Ed.), Ada 95 Rationale. XVI, 458 pages. 1997.

Vol. 1248: P. Azéma, G. Balbo (Eds.), Application and Theory of Petri Nets 1997. Proceedings, 1997. VIII, 467 pages. 1997.

Vol. 1249: W. McCune (Ed.), Automated Deduction – CADE-14. Proceedings, 1997. XIV, 462 pages. 1997. (Subseries LNAI).

Vol. 1250: A. Olivé, J.A. Pastor (Eds.), Advanced Information Systems Engineering. Proceedings, 1997. XI, 451 pages. 1997.

Vol. 1251: K. Hardy, J. Briggs (Eds.), Reliable Software Technologies – Ada-Europe '97. Proceedings, 1997. VIII, 293 pages. 1997.

Vol. 1252: B. ter Haar Romeny, L. Florack, J. Koenderink, M. Viergever (Eds.), Scale-Space Theory in Computer Vision. Proceedings, 1997. IX, 365 pages. 1997.

Vol. 1253: G. Bilardi, A. Ferreira, R. Lüling, J. Rolim (Eds.), Solving Irregularly Structured Problems in Parallel. Proceedings, 1997. X, 287 pages. 1997.

Vol. 1254: O. Grumberg (Ed.), Computer Aided Verification. Proceedings, 1997. XI, 486 pages. 1997.

Vol. 1255: T. Mora, H. Mattson (Eds.), Applied Algebra, Algebraic Algorithms and Error-Correcting Codes. Proceedings, 1997. X, 353 pages. 1997.

Vol. 1256: P. Degano, R. Gorrieri, A. Marchetti-Spaccamela (Eds.), Automata, Languages and Programming. Proceedings, 1997. XVI, 862 pages. 1997.

Vol. 1258: D. van Dalen, M. Bezem (Eds.), Computer Science Logic. Proceedings, 1996. VIII, 473 pages. 1997.

Vol. 1259: T. Higuchi, M. Iwata, W. Liu (Eds.), Evolvable Systems: From Biology to Hardware. Proceedings, 1996. XI, 484 pages. 1997.

Vol. 1260: D. Raymond, D. Wood, S. Yu (Eds.), Automata Implementation. Proceedings, 1996. VIII, 189 pages. 1997.

Vol. 1261: J. Mycielski, G. Rozenberg, A. Salomaa (Eds.), Structures in Logic and Computer Science. X, 371 pages. 1997.

Vol. 1262: M. Scholl, A. Voisard (Eds.), Advances in Spatial Databases. Proceedings, 1997. XI, 379 pages. 1997.

Vol. 1263: J. Komorowski, J. Zytkow (Eds.), Principles of Data Mining and Knowledge Discovery. Proceedings, 1997. IX, 397 pages. 1997. (Subseries LNAI).

Vol. 1264: A. Apostolico, J. Hein (Eds.), Combinatorial Pattern Matching. Proceedings, 1997. VIII, 277 pages. 1997.

Vol. 1265: J. Dix, U. Furbach, A. Nerode (Eds.), Logic Programming and Nonmonotonic Reasoning. Proceedings, 1997. X, 453 pages. 1997. (Subseries LNAI).

Vol. 1266: D.B. Leake, E. Plaza (Eds.), Case-Based Reasoning Research and Development. Proceedings, 1997. XIII, 648 pages. 1997 (Subseries LNAI).

Vol. 1267: E. Biham (Ed.), Fast Software Encryption. Proceedings, 1997. VIII, 289 pages. 1997.

Vol. 1268: W. Kluge (Ed.), Implementation of Functional Languages. Proceedings, 1996. XI, 284 pages. 1997.

Vol. 1269: J. Rolim (Ed.), Randomization and Approximation Techniques in Computer Science. Proceedings, 1997. VIII, 227 pages. 1997.

Vol. 1270: V. Varadharajan, J. Pieprzyk, Y. Mu (Eds.), Information Security and Privacy. Proceedings, 1997. XI, 337 pages. 1997.

Vol. 1271: C. Small, P. Douglas, R. Johnson, P. King, N. Martin (Eds.), Advances in Databases. Proceedings, 1997. XI, 233 pages. 1997.

Vol. 1272: F. Dehne, A. Rau-Chaplin, J.-R. Sack, R. Tamassia (Eds.), Algorithms and Data Structures. Proceedings, 1997. X, 476 pages. 1997.

Vol. 1273: P. Antsaklis, W. Kohn, A. Nerode, S. Sastry (Eds.), Hybrid Systems IV. X, 405 pages. 1997.

Vol. 1274: T. Masuda, Y. Masunaga, M. Tsukamoto (Eds.), Worldwide Computing and Its Applications. Proceedings, 1997. XVI, 443 pages. 1997.

Vol. 1275: E.L. Gunter, A. Felty (Eds.), Theorem Proving in Higher Order Logics. Proceedings, 1997. VIII, 339 pages. 1997.

Vol. 1276: T. Jiang, D.T. Lee (Eds.), Computing and Combinatorics. Proceedings, 1997. XI, 522 pages. 1997.

Vol. 1277: V. Malyshkin (Ed.), Parallel Computing Technologies. Proceedings, 1997. XII, 455 pages. 1997.

Vol. 1278: R. Hofestädt, T. Lengauer, M. Löffler, D. Schomburg (Eds.), Bioinformatics. Proceedings, 1996. XI, 222 pages. 1997.

Vol. 1279: B. S. Chlebus, L. Czaja (Eds.), Fundamentals of Computation Theory. Proceedings, 1997. XI, 475 pages. 1997.

Vol. 1280: X. Liu, P. Cohen, M. Berthold (Eds.), Advances in Intelligent Data Analysis. Proceedings, 1997. XII, 621 pages. 1997.

Vol. 1281: M. Abadi, T. Ito (Eds.), Theoretical Aspects of Computer Software. Proceedings, 1997. XI, 639 pages. 1997.

Vol. 1282: D. Garlan, D. Le Métayer (Eds.), Coordination Languages and Models. Proceedings, 1997. X, 435 pages. 1997.

Vol. 1283: M. Müller-Olm, Modular Compiler Verification. XV, 250 pages. 1997.

Vol. 1284: R. Burkard, G. Woeginger (Eds.), Algorithms — ESA '97. Proceedings, 1997. XI, 515 pages. 1997.

Vol. 1285: X. Jao, J.-H. Kim, T. Furuhashi (Eds.), Simulated Evolution and Learning. Proceedings, 1996. VIII, 231 pages. 1997. (Subseries LNAI).

Vol. 1286: C. Zhang, D. Lukose (Eds.), Multi-Agent Systems. Proceedings, 1996. VII, 195 pages. 1997. (Subseries LNAI).

Vol. 1289: G. Gottlob, A. Leitsch, D. Mundici (Eds.), Computational Logic and Proof Theory. Proceedings, 1997. VIII, 348 pages. 1997.

Vol. 1292: H. Glaser, P. Hartel, H. Kuchen (Eds.), Programming Languages: Implementations, Logigs, and Programs. Proceedings, 1997. XI, 425 pages. 1997.

Vol. 1294: B. Kaliski (Ed.), Advances in Cryptology — CRYPTO '97. Proceedings, 1997. XII, 539 pages. 1997.

Vol. 1299: M.T. Pazienza (Ed.), Information Extraction. Proceedings, 1997. IX, 213 pages. 1997. (Subseries LNAI).

Vol. 1300: C. Lengauer, M. Griebl, S. Gorlatch (Eds.), Euro-Par'97 Parallel Processing. Proceedings, 1997. XXX, 1379 pages. 1997.